# DERIVATIVES, CURRENCY MANAGEMENT, AND FIXED INCOME

CFA® Program Curriculum
2023 • LEVEL III • VOLUME 2

WILEY

© 2022, 2021, 2020, 2019, 2018, 2017, 2016, 2015, 2014, 2013, 2012, 2011, 2010, 2009, 2008, 2007, 2006 by CFA Institute. All rights reserved.

This copyright covers material written expressly for this volume by the editor/s as well as the compilation itself. It does not cover the individual selections herein that first appeared elsewhere. Permission to reprint these has been obtained by CFA Institute for this edition only. Further reproductions by any means, electronic or mechanical, including photocopying and recording, or by any information storage or retrieval systems, must be arranged with the individual copyright holders noted.

CFA®, Chartered Financial Analyst®, AIMR-PPS®, and GIPS® are just a few of the trademarks owned by CFA Institute. To view a list of CFA Institute trademarks and the Guide for Use of CFA Institute Marks, please visit our website at www.cfainstitute.org.

This publication is designed to provide accurate and authoritative information in regard to the subject matter covered. It is sold with the understanding that the publisher is not engaged in rendering legal, accounting, or other professional service. If legal advice or other expert assistance is required, the services of a competent professional should be sought.

All trademarks, service marks, registered trademarks, and registered service marks are the property of their respective owners and are used herein for identification purposes only.

ISBN 978-1-953337-12-2 (paper)
ISBN 978-1-953337-36-8 (ebk)

10 9 8 7 6 5 4 3 2 1

Please visit our website at www.WileyGlobalFinance.com.

# CONTENTS

**How to Use the CFA Program Curriculum**     ix
    Background on the CBOK     ix
    Organization of the Curriculum     x
    Features of the Curriculum     x
    Designing Your Personal Study Program     xi
    CFA Institute Learning Ecosystem (LES)     xii
    Prep Providers     xiii
    Feedback     xiv

## Portfolio Management

**Study Session 4**     **Derivatives and Currency Management**     3

**Reading 8**     **Options Strategies**     5
    Introduction     6
    Position Equivalencies     6
        Synthetic Forward Position     7
        Synthetic Put and Call     9
    Covered Calls and Protective Puts     11
        Investment Objectives of Covered Calls     12
    Investment Objectives of Protective Puts     20
        Loss Protection/Upside Preservation     20
        Profit and Loss at Expiration     22
    Equivalence to Long Asset/Short Forward Position     24
        Writing Puts     25
    Risk Reduction Using Covered Calls and Protective Puts     28
        Covered Calls     28
        Protective Puts     28
        Buying Calls and Writing Puts on a Short Position     29
    Spreads and Combinations     32
        Bull Spreads and Bear Spreads     32
    Straddle     40
        Collars     43
        Calendar Spread     46
    Implied Volatility and Volatility Skew     48
    Investment Objectives and Strategy Selection     52
        The Necessity of Setting an Objective     52
        Criteria for Identifying Appropriate Option Strategies     53
    Uses of Options in Portfolio Management     55
        Covered Call Writing     55
        Put Writing     57
        Long Straddle     58
        Collar     61
        Calendar Spread     61

◙ indicates an optional segment

| | | |
|---|---|---|
| | Hedging an Expected Increase in Equity Market Volatility | 63 |
| | Establishing or Modifying Equity Risk Exposure | 65 |
| | *Summary* | 68 |
| | *Practice Problems* | 71 |
| | *Solutions* | 78 |
| **Reading 9** | **Swaps, Forwards, and Futures Strategies** | **83** |
| | Managing Interest Rate Risk with Swaps | 83 |
| | Changing Risk Exposures with Swaps, Futures, and Forwards | 84 |
| | Managing Interest Rate Risk with Forwards, Futures and Fixed-Income Futures | 88 |
| | Fixed-Income Futures | 90 |
| | Managing Currency Exposure | 95 |
| | Currency Swaps | 95 |
| | Currency Forwards and Futures | 98 |
| | Managing Equity Risk | 99 |
| | Equity Swaps | 100 |
| | Equity Forwards and Futures | 102 |
| | Cash Equitization | 105 |
| | Volatility Derivatives: Futures and Options | 106 |
| | Volatility Futures and Options | 106 |
| | Volatility Derivatives: Variance Swaps | 108 |
| | Using Derivatives to Manage Equity Exposure and Tracking Error | 112 |
| | Solution: | 112 |
| | Cash Equitization | 112 |
| | Using Derivatives in Asset Allocation | 113 |
| | Changing Allocations between Asset Classes Using Futures | 113 |
| | Rebalancing an Asset Allocation Using Futures | 116 |
| | Changing Allocations between Asset Classes Using Swaps | 117 |
| | Using Derivatives to Infer Market Expectations | 119 |
| | Using Fed Funds Futures to Infer the Expected Average Federal Funds Rate | 120 |
| | Inferring Market Expectations | 121 |
| | *Summary* | 122 |
| | *Practice Problems* | 124 |
| | *Solutions:* | 131 |
| **Reading 10** | **Currency Management: An Introduction** | **139** |
| | Introduction | 139 |
| | Review of Foreign Exchange Concepts | 140 |
| | Spot Markets | 141 |
| | Forward Markets | 143 |
| | FX Swap Markets | 145 |
| | Currency Options | 146 |
| | Currency Risk and Portfolio Risk and Return | 147 |
| | Return Decomposition | 147 |
| | Volatility Decomposition | 149 |
| | Strategic Decisions in Currency Management: Overview | 152 |
| | The Investment Policy Statement | 153 |

◉ indicates an optional segment

# Contents

| | | |
|---|---|---|
| | The Portfolio Optimization Problem | 153 |
| | Choice of Currency Exposures | 155 |
| Strategic Decisions in Currency Management: Spectrum of Currency Risk Management Strategies | | 158 |
| | Passive Hedging | 158 |
| | Discretionary Hedging | 158 |
| | Active Currency Management | 159 |
| | Currency Overlay | 159 |
| Strategic Decisions in Currency Management: Formulating a Currency Management Program | | 162 |
| Active Currency Management: Based on Economic Fundamentals, Technical Analysis and the Carry Trade | | 164 |
| | Active Currency Management Based on Economic Fundamentals | 164 |
| | Active Currency Management Based on Technical Analysis | 166 |
| | Active Currency Management Based on the Carry Trade | 168 |
| Active Currency Management: Based on Volatility Trading | | 170 |
| Currency Management Tools: Forward Contracts, FX Swaps and Currency Options | | 175 |
| | Forward Contracts | 176 |
| | Currency Options | 182 |
| Currency Management Strategies | | 185 |
| | Over-/Under-Hedging Using Forward Contracts | 186 |
| | Protective Put Using OTM Options | 186 |
| | Risk Reversal (or Collar) | 187 |
| | Put Spread | 187 |
| | Seagull Spread | 188 |
| | Exotic Options | 189 |
| | Section Summary | 190 |
| Hedging Multiple Foreign Currencies | | 192 |
| | Cross Hedges and Macro Hedges | 193 |
| | Minimum-Variance Hedge Ratio | 195 |
| | Basis Risk | 196 |
| Currency Management Tools and Strategies: A Summary | | 198 |
| Currency Management for Emerging Market Currencies | | 203 |
| | Special Considerations in Managing Emerging Market Currency Exposures | 203 |
| | Non-Deliverable Forwards | 205 |
| *Summary* | | 206 |
| *Practice Problems* | | 209 |
| *Solutions* | | 221 |

| | | |
|---|---|---|
| **Study Session 5** | **Fixed-Income Portfolio Management (1)** | **235** |
| **Reading 11** | **Overview of Fixed-Income Portfolio Management** | **237** |
| | Introduction | 237 |
| | Roles of Fixed-Income Securities in Portfolios | 238 |
| | Diversification Benefits | 238 |
| | Benefits of Regular Cash Flows | 240 |
| | Inflation-Hedging Potential | 241 |

◙ indicates an optional segment

|  |  |
|---|---|
| Classifying Fixed-Income Mandates | **242** |
| Liability-Based Mandates | 243 |
| Total Return Mandates | 243 |
| Fixed-Income Mandates with ESG Considerations | 244 |
| Fixed-Income Portfolio Measures | **246** |
| Portfolio Measures of Risk and Return | 249 |
| Correlations between Fixed-Income Sectors | 250 |
| Use of Measures of Risk and Return in Portfolio Management | 250 |
| Bond Market Liquidity | **252** |
| Liquidity among Bond Market Sub-Sectors | 253 |
| The Effects of Liquidity on Fixed-Income Portfolio Management | 253 |
| A Model for Fixed-Income Returns | **257** |
| Decomposing Expected Returns | 257 |
| Estimation of the Inputs | 261 |
| Limitations of the Expected Return Decomposition | 262 |
| Leverage | **263** |
| Using Leverage | 263 |
| Methods for Leveraging Fixed-Income Portfolios | 264 |
| Risks of Leverage | 266 |
| Fixed-Income Portfolio Taxation | **268** |
| Principles of Fixed-Income Taxation | 268 |
| Investment Vehicles and Taxes | 269 |
| *Summary* | 271 |
| *Practice Problems* | 274 |
| *Solutions* | 279 |

## Reading 12   Liability-Driven and Index-Based Strategies — **283**

|  |  |
|---|---|
| Introduction | 283 |
| Liability-Driven Investing | **284** |
| Liability-Driven Investing vs. Asset-Driven Liabilities | 285 |
| Types of Liabilities | 285 |
| Interest Rate Immunization: Managing the Interest Rate Risk of a Single Liability | **287** |
| A Numerical Example of Immunization | 288 |
| Interest Rate Immunization: Managing the Interest Rate Risk of Multiple Liabilities | **299** |
| Cash Flow Matching | 300 |
| Laddered Portfolios | 303 |
| Duration Matching | 306 |
| Derivatives Overlay | 312 |
| Contingent Immunization | 316 |
| Liability-Driven Investing: An Example of a Defined Benefit Pension Plan | **318** |
| Model Assumptions | 318 |
| Model Inputs | 319 |
| Calculating Durations | 320 |
| Addressing the Duration Gap | 321 |
| Risks in Liability-Driven Investing | **330** |
| Model Risk in Liability-Driven Investing | 330 |
| Spread Risk in Liability-Driven Investing | 331 |

*indicates an optional segment*

| | |
|---|---:|
| Counterparty Credit Risk | 332 |
| Asset Liquidity Risk | 332 |
| Bond Indexes and the Challenges of Matching a Fixed-Income Portfolio to an Index | 334 |
| Size and Breadth of the Fixed-Income Universe | 335 |
| Array of Characteristics | 336 |
| Unique Issuance and Trading Patterns | 336 |
| Primary Risk Factors | 337 |
| Alternative Methods for Establishing Passive Bond Market Exposure | 340 |
| Full Replication | 340 |
| Enhanced Indexing | 341 |
| Alternatives to Investing Directly in Fixed-Income Securities | 344 |
| Benchmark Selection | 344 |
| *Summary* | 347 |
| *Practice Problems* | 352 |
| *Solutions* | 361 |

**Glossary** — G-1

◘ indicates an optional segment

# How to Use the CFA Program Curriculum

Congratulations on your decision to enter the Chartered Financial Analyst (CFA®) Program. This exciting and rewarding program of study reflects your desire to become a serious investment professional. You are embarking on a program noted for its high ethical standards and the breadth of knowledge, skills, and abilities (competencies) it develops. Your commitment should be educationally and professionally rewarding.

The credential you seek is respected around the world as a mark of accomplishment and dedication. Each level of the program represents a distinct achievement in professional development. Successful completion of the program is rewarded with membership in a prestigious global community of investment professionals. CFA charterholders are dedicated to life-long learning and maintaining currency with the ever-changing dynamics of a challenging profession. CFA Program enrollment represents the first step toward a career-long commitment to professional education.

The CFA exam measures your mastery of the core knowledge, skills, and abilities required to succeed as an investment professional. These core competencies are the basis for the Candidate Body of Knowledge (CBOK™). The CBOK consists of four components:

- A broad outline that lists the major CFA Program topic areas (www.cfainstitute.org/programs/cfa/curriculum/cbok);
- Topic area weights that indicate the relative exam weightings of the top-level topic areas (www.cfainstitute.org/programs/cfa/curriculum);
- Learning outcome statements (LOS) that advise candidates about the specific knowledge, skills, and abilities they should acquire from readings covering a topic area (LOS are provided in candidate study sessions and at the beginning of each reading); and
- CFA Program curriculum that candidates receive upon exam registration.

Therefore, the key to your success on the CFA exams is studying and understanding the CBOK. The following sections provide background on the CBOK, the organization of the curriculum, features of the curriculum, and tips for designing an effective personal study program.

## BACKGROUND ON THE CBOK

CFA Program is grounded in the practice of the investment profession. CFA Institute performs a continuous practice analysis with investment professionals around the world to determine the competencies that are relevant to the profession, beginning with the Global Body of Investment Knowledge (GBIK®). Regional expert panels and targeted surveys are conducted annually to verify and reinforce the continuous feedback about the GBIK. The practice analysis process ultimately defines the CBOK. The CBOK reflects the competencies that are generally accepted and applied by investment professionals. These competencies are used in practice in a generalist context and are expected to be demonstrated by a recently qualified CFA charterholder.

© 2021 CFA Institute. All rights reserved.

The CFA Institute staff—in conjunction with the Education Advisory Committee and Curriculum Level Advisors, who consist of practicing CFA charterholders—designs the CFA Program curriculum in order to deliver the CBOK to candidates. The exams, also written by CFA charterholders, are designed to allow you to demonstrate your mastery of the CBOK as set forth in the CFA Program curriculum. As you structure your personal study program, you should emphasize mastery of the CBOK and the practical application of that knowledge. For more information on the practice analysis, CBOK, and development of the CFA Program curriculum, please visit www.cfainstitute.org.

## ORGANIZATION OF THE CURRICULUM

The Level III CFA Program curriculum is organized into six topic areas. Each topic area begins with a brief statement of the material and the depth of knowledge expected. It is then divided into one or more study sessions. These study sessions should form the basic structure of your reading and preparation. Each study session includes a statement of its structure and objective and is further divided into assigned readings. An outline illustrating the organization of these study sessions can be found at the front of each volume of the curriculum.

The readings are commissioned by CFA Institute and written by content experts, including investment professionals and university professors. Each reading includes LOS and the core material to be studied, often a combination of text, exhibits, and in-text examples and questions. End of Reading Questions (EORQs) followed by solutions help you understand and master the material. The LOS indicate what you should be able to accomplish after studying the material. The LOS, the core material, and the EORQs are dependent on each other, with the core material and EORQs providing context for understanding the scope of the LOS and enabling you to apply a principle or concept in a variety of scenarios.

*The entire readings, including the EORQs, are the basis for all exam questions and are selected or developed specifically to teach the knowledge, skills, and abilities reflected in the CBOK.*

You should use the LOS to guide and focus your study because each exam question is based on one or more LOS and the core material and practice problems associated with the LOS. As a candidate, you are responsible for the entirety of the required material in a study session.

We encourage you to review the information about the LOS on our website (www.cfainstitute.org/programs/cfa/curriculum/study-sessions), including the descriptions of LOS "command words" on the candidate resources page at www.cfainstitute.org.

## FEATURES OF THE CURRICULUM

**End of Reading Questions/Solutions**  All End of Reading Questions (EORQs) as well as their solutions are part of the curriculum and are required material for the exam. In addition to the in-text examples and questions, these EORQs help demonstrate practical applications and reinforce your understanding of the concepts presented. Some of these EORQs are adapted from past CFA exams and/or may serve as a basis for exam questions.

**Glossary**   For your convenience, each volume includes a comprehensive Glossary. Throughout the curriculum, a **bolded** word in a reading denotes a term defined in the Glossary.

Note that the digital curriculum that is included in your exam registration fee is searchable for key words, including Glossary terms.

**LOS Self-Check**   We have inserted checkboxes next to each LOS that you can use to track your progress in mastering the concepts in each reading.

**Source Material**   The CFA Institute curriculum cites textbooks, journal articles, and other publications that provide additional context or information about topics covered in the readings. As a candidate, you are not responsible for familiarity with the original source materials cited in the curriculum.

Note that some readings may contain a web address or URL. The referenced sites were live at the time the reading was written or updated but may have been deactivated since then.

> Some readings in the curriculum cite articles published in the *Financial Analysts Journal®*, which is the flagship publication of CFA Institute. Since its launch in 1945, the *Financial Analysts Journal* has established itself as the leading practitioner-oriented journal in the investment management community. Over the years, it has advanced the knowledge and understanding of the practice of investment management through the publication of peer-reviewed practitioner-relevant research from leading academics and practitioners. It has also featured thought-provoking opinion pieces that advance the common level of discourse within the investment management profession. Some of the most influential research in the area of investment management has appeared in the pages of the *Financial Analysts Journal*, and several Nobel laureates have contributed articles.
>
> Candidates are not responsible for familiarity with *Financial Analysts Journal* articles that are cited in the curriculum. But, as your time and studies allow, we strongly encourage you to begin supplementing your understanding of key investment management issues by reading this, and other, CFA Institute practice-oriented publications through the Research & Analysis webpage (www.cfainstitute.org/en/research).

**Errata**   The curriculum development process is rigorous and includes multiple rounds of reviews by content experts. Despite our efforts to produce a curriculum that is free of errors, there are times when we must make corrections. Curriculum errata are periodically updated and posted by exam level and test date online (www.cfainstitute.org/en/programs/submit-errata). If you believe you have found an error in the curriculum, you can submit your concerns through our curriculum errata reporting process found at the bottom of the Curriculum Errata webpage.

## DESIGNING YOUR PERSONAL STUDY PROGRAM

**Create a Schedule**   An orderly, systematic approach to exam preparation is critical. You should dedicate a consistent block of time every week to reading and studying. Complete all assigned readings and the associated problems and solutions in each study session. Review the LOS both before and after you study each reading to ensure that you have mastered the applicable content and can demonstrate the knowledge, skills, and abilities described by the LOS and the assigned reading. Use the LOS self-check to track your progress and highlight areas of weakness for later review.

Successful candidates report an average of more than 300 hours preparing for each exam. Your preparation time will vary based on your prior education and experience, and you will probably spend more time on some study sessions than on others.

You should allow ample time for both in-depth study of all topic areas and additional concentration on those topic areas for which you feel the least prepared.

# CFA INSTITUTE LEARNING ECOSYSTEM (LES)

As you prepare for your exam, we will email you important exam updates, testing policies, and study tips. Be sure to read these carefully.

Your exam registration fee includes access to the CFA Program Learning Ecosystem (LES). This digital learning platform provides access, even offline, to all of the readings and End of Reading Questions found in the print curriculum organized as a series of shorter online lessons with associated EORQs. This tool is your one-stop location for all study materials, including practice questions and mock exams.

The LES provides the following supplemental study tools:

**Structured and Adaptive Study Plans** The LES offers two ways to plan your study through the curriculum. The first is a structured plan that allows you to move through the material in the way that you feel best suits your learning. The second is an adaptive study plan based on the results of an assessment test that uses actual practice questions.

Regardless of your chosen study path, the LES tracks your level of proficiency in each topic area and presents you with a dashboard of where you stand in terms of proficiency so that you can allocate your study time efficiently.

**Flashcards and Game Center** The LES offers all the Glossary terms as Flashcards and tracks correct and incorrect answers. Flashcards can be filtered both by curriculum topic area and by action taken—for example, answered correctly, unanswered, and so on. These Flashcards provide a flexible way to study Glossary item definitions.

The Game Center provides several engaging ways to interact with the Flashcards in a game context. Each game tests your knowledge of the Glossary terms a in different way. Your results are scored and presented, along with a summary of candidates with high scores on the game, on your Dashboard.

**Discussion Board** The Discussion Board within the LES provides a way for you to interact with other candidates as you pursue your study plan. Discussions can happen at the level of individual lessons to raise questions about material in those lessons that you or other candidates can clarify or comment on. Discussions can also be posted at the level of topics or in the initial Welcome section to connect with other candidates in your area.

**Practice Question Bank** The LES offers access to a question bank of hundreds of practice questions that are in addition to the End of Reading Questions. These practice questions, only available on the LES, are intended to help you assess your mastery of individual topic areas as you progress through your studies. After each practice question, you will receive immediate feedback noting the correct response and indicating the relevant assigned reading so you can identify areas of weakness for further study.

**Mock Exams** The LES also includes access to three-hour Mock Exams that simulate the morning and afternoon sessions of the actual CFA exam. These Mock Exams are intended to be taken after you complete your study of the full curriculum and take practice questions so you can test your understanding of the curriculum and your readiness for the exam. If you take these Mock Exams within the LES, you will receive feedback afterward that notes the correct responses and indicates the relevant assigned readings so you can assess areas of weakness for further study. We recommend that you take Mock Exams during the final stages of your preparation for the actual CFA exam. For more information on the Mock Exams, please visit www.cfainstitute.org.

## PREP PROVIDERS

You may choose to seek study support outside CFA Institute in the form of exam prep providers. After your CFA Program enrollment, you may receive numerous solicitations for exam prep courses and review materials. When considering a prep course, make sure the provider is committed to following the CFA Institute guidelines and high standards in its offerings.

Remember, however, that there are no shortcuts to success on the CFA exams; reading and studying the CFA Program curriculum *is* the key to success on the exam. The CFA Program exams reference only the CFA Institute assigned curriculum; no prep course or review course materials are consulted or referenced.

### SUMMARY

Every question on the CFA exam is based on the content contained in the required readings and on one or more LOS. Frequently, an exam question is based on a specific example highlighted within a reading or on a specific practice problem and its solution. To make effective use of the CFA Program curriculum, please remember these key points:

1 All pages of the curriculum are required reading for the exam.

2 All questions, problems, and their solutions are part of the curriculum and are required study material for the exam. These questions are found at the end of the readings in the print versions of the curriculum. In the LES, these questions appear directly after the lesson with which they are associated. The LES provides immediate feedback on your answers and tracks your performance on these questions throughout your study.

3 We strongly encourage you to use the CFA Program Learning Ecosystem. In addition to providing access to all the curriculum material, including EORQs, in the form of shorter, focused lessons, the LES offers structured and adaptive study planning, a Discussion Board to communicate with other candidates, Flashcards, a Game Center for study activities, a test bank of practice questions, and online Mock Exams. Other supplemental study tools, such as eBook and PDF versions of the print curriculum, and additional candidate resources are available at www.cfainstitute.org.

4 Using the study planner, create a schedule and commit sufficient study time to cover the study sessions. You should also plan to review the materials, answer practice questions, and take Mock Exams.

5 Some of the concepts in the study sessions may be superseded by updated rulings and/or pronouncements issued after a reading was published. Candidates are expected to be familiar with the overall analytical framework contained in the assigned readings. Candidates are not responsible for changes that occur after the material was written.

## FEEDBACK

At CFA Institute, we are committed to delivering a comprehensive and rigorous curriculum for the development of competent, ethically grounded investment professionals. We rely on candidate and investment professional comments and feedback as we work to improve the curriculum, supplemental study tools, and candidate resources.

Please send any comments or feedback to info@cfainstitute.org. You can be assured that we will review your suggestions carefully. Ongoing improvements in the curriculum will help you prepare for success on the upcoming exams and for a lifetime of learning as a serious investment professional.

# Portfolio Management

## STUDY SESSIONS

| | |
|---|---|
| **Study Session 1** | Behavioral Finance |
| **Study Session 2** | Capital Market Expectations |
| **Study Session 3** | Asset Allocation and Related Decisions in Portfolio Management |
| **Study Session 4** | Derivatives and Currency Management |
| **Study Session 5** | Fixed-Income Portfolio Management (1) |
| **Study Session 6** | Fixed-Income Portfolio Management (2) |
| **Study Session 7** | Equity Portfolio Management (1) |
| **Study Session 8** | Equity Portfolio Management (2) |
| **Study Session 9** | Alternative Investments Portfolio Management |
| **Study Session 10** | Private Wealth Management (1) |
| **Study Session 11** | Private Wealth Management (2) |
| **Study Session 12** | Portfolio Management for Institutional Investors |
| **Study Session 13** | Trading, Performance Evaluation, and Manager Selection |
| **Study Session 14** | Cases in Portfolio Management and Risk Management |

This volume includes Study Sessions 4 and 5.

© 2021 CFA Institute. All rights reserved.

## TOPIC LEVEL LEARNING OUTCOME

The candidate should be able to prepare an appropriate investment policy statement and asset allocation; formulate strategies for managing, monitoring, and rebalancing investment portfolios; and evaluate portfolio performance.

# PORTFOLIO MANAGEMENT
## STUDY SESSION

# 4

# Derivatives and Currency Management

The purpose of this study session is to illustrate ways in which derivatives might be used in typical investment situations. Few asset managers or individual investors will ever use all of the strategies described here. However, an informed investment professional should still be aware of these important strategies and understand the associated risk–return trade-offs.

The first reading examines widely used options strategies, including covered calls, protective puts and select spread and combination option strategies. Derivatives strategy selection is discussed and demonstrated in a series of applications.

The second reading shows how swaps, forwards, and futures can be used to change the risk exposure of an existing position. There are many ways in which investment managers and investors can use swaps, forwards, futures, and volatility derivatives. The typical applications of these derivatives involve modifying investment positions for hedging purposes or for taking directional bets, creating or replicating desired payoffs, implementing asset allocation and portfolio rebalancing decisions, and even inferring current market expectations.

When the strategic asset allocation includes exposure to global markets, non-domestic currencies create additional sources of portfolio volatility and potential returns. The final reading in this study session explores how currency exposures can be managed to reflect a client's investment objectives and constraints.

© 2021 CFA Institute. All rights reserved.

## READING ASSIGNMENTS

**Reading 8** Option Strategies
by Adam Schwartz, PhD, CFA, and Barbara Valbuzzi, CFA

**Reading 9** Swaps, Forwards, and Futures Strategies
by Barbara Valbuzzi, CFA

**Reading 10** Currency Management: An Introduction
by William A. Barker, PhD, CFA

# READING
# 8

## Options Strategies

by Adam Schwartz, PhD, CFA, and Barbara Valbuzzi, CFA

*Adam Schwartz, PhD, CFA, is at Bucknell University (USA). Barbara Valbuzzi, CFA (Italy).*

| LEARNING OUTCOMES | |
|---|---|
| Mastery | The candidate should be able to: |
| ☐ | a. demonstrate how an asset's returns may be replicated by using options; |
| ☐ | b. discuss the investment objective(s), structure, payoff, risk(s), value at expiration, profit, maximum profit, maximum loss, and breakeven underlying price at expiration of a covered call position; |
| ☐ | c. discuss the investment objective(s), structure, payoff, risk(s), value at expiration, profit, maximum profit, maximum loss, and breakeven underlying price at expiration of a protective put position; |
| ☐ | d. compare the delta of covered call and protective put positions with the position of being long an asset and short a forward on the underlying asset; |
| ☐ | e. compare the effect of buying a call on a short underlying position with the effect of selling a put on a short underlying position; |
| ☐ | f. discuss the investment objective(s), structure, payoffs, risk(s), value at expiration, profit, maximum profit, maximum loss, and breakeven underlying price at expiration of the following option strategies: bull spread, bear spread, straddle, and collar; |
| ☐ | g. describe uses of calendar spreads; |
| ☐ | h. discuss volatility skew and smile; |
| ☐ | i. identify and evaluate appropriate option strategies consistent with given investment objectives; |
| ☐ | j. demonstrate the use of options to achieve targeted equity risk exposures. |

CFA Institute would like to thank Robert Strong, PhD, CFA, and Russell Rhoads, CFA, for their work on previous versions of this reading.

© 2019 CFA Institute. All rights reserved.

# 1 INTRODUCTION

Derivatives are financial instruments through which counterparties agree to exchange economic cash flows based on the movement of underlying securities, indexes, currencies, or other instruments or factors. A derivative's value is thus *derived* from the economic performance of the underlying. Derivatives may be created directly by counterparties or may be facilitated through established, regulated market exchanges. Direct creation between counterparties has the benefit of tailoring to the counterparties' specific needs but also the disadvantage of potentially low liquidity. Exchange-traded derivatives often do not match counterparties' specific needs but do facilitate early termination of the position, and, importantly, mitigate counterparty risk. Derivatives facilitate the exchange of economic risks and benefits where trades in the underlying securities might be less advantageous because of poor liquidity, transaction costs, regulatory impediments, tax or accounting considerations, or other factors.

Options are an important type of contingent-claim derivative that provide their owner with the right but not an obligation to a payoff determined by the future price of the underlying asset. Unlike other types of derivatives (i.e., swaps, forwards, and futures), options have nonlinear payoffs that enable their owners to benefit from movements in the underlying in one direction without being hurt by movements in the opposite direction. The cost of this opportunity, however, is the upfront cash payment required to enter the options position.

Options can be combined with the underlying and with other options in a variety of different ways to modify investment positions, to implement investment strategies, or even to infer market expectations. Therefore, investment managers routinely use option strategies for hedging risk exposures, for seeking to profit from anticipated market moves, and for implementing desired risk exposures in a cost-effective manner.

The main purpose of this reading is to illustrate how options strategies are used in typical investment situations and to show the risk–return trade-offs associated with their use. Importantly, an informed investment professional should have such a basic understanding of options strategies to competently serve his investment clients.

Section 2 of this reading shows how certain combinations of securities (i.e., options, underlying) are equivalent to others. Sections 3–6 discuss two of the most widely used options strategies, covered calls and protective puts. In Sections 7 and 8, we look at popular spread and combination option strategies used by investors. The focus of Section 9 is implied volatility embedded in option prices and related volatility skew and surface. Section 10 discusses option strategy selection. Sections 11 and 12 demonstrate a series of applications showing ways in which an investment manager might solve an investment problem with options. The reading concludes with a summary.

# 2 POSITION EQUIVALENCIES

a   demonstrate how an asset's returns may be replicated by using options;

It is useful to think of derivatives as building blocks that can be combined to create a specific payoff with the desired risk exposure. A synthetic position can be created for any option or stock strategy. Most of the time, market participants use synthetic positions to transform the payoff profile of their positions when their market views change. We cover a few of these relationships in the following pages. First, a brief recap of put–call parity and put–call–forward parity will help readers to understand such synthetic positions.

# Position Equivalencies

As you may remember, put–call parity shows the equivalence (or parity) of a portfolio of a call and a risk-free bond with a portfolio of a put and the underlying, which leads to the relationship between put and call prices. Put–call parity can be expressed in the following formula, where $S_0$ is the price of the underlying; $p_0$ and $c_0$ are the prices (i.e., premiums) of the put and call options, respectively; and $X/(1 + r)^T$ is the present value of the risk-free bond: $S_0 + p_0 = c_0 + X/(1 + r)^T$.

A closely related concept is put–call–forward parity, which identifies the equivalence between buying a fiduciary call, given by the purchase of a call and the risk-free bond, and a synthetic protective put. The latter involves the purchase of a put option and a forward contract on the underlying that expires at the same time as the put option. In the put–call–forward parity formula, $S_0$ is replaced with a forward contract to buy the underlying, where the forward price is given by $F_0(T) = S_0(1 + r)^T$. Therefore, put–call–forward parity is: $F_0(T)/(1 + r)^T + p_0 = c_0 + X/(1 + r)^T$.

## 2.1 Synthetic Forward Position

The combination of a long call and a short put with identical strike price and expiration, traded at the same time on the same underlying, is equivalent to a **synthetic long forward position**. In fact, the long call creates the upside and the short put creates the downside on the underlying.

Consider an investor who buys an at-the-money (ATM) call and simultaneously sells a put with the same strike and the same expiration date. Whatever the stock price at expiration, one of the two options will be in the money. If the contract has a physical settlement, the investor will buy the underlying stock by paying the strike price. In fact, on the expiration date, the investor will exercise the call she owns if the stock price is above the strike price. Otherwise, if the underlying price is below the strike price, the put owner will exercise his right to deliver the stock and the investor (who sold the put) must buy it for the strike price. Exhibit 1 shows the values of the two options and the combined position at expiration, compared with the value of the stock purchase at that same time. The stock in this case does not pay dividends.

| Exhibit 1  Synthetic Long Forward Position at Expiration | | | |
|---|---|---|---|
| Stock price at expiration: | 40 | 50 | 60 |
| **Alternative 1:** | | | |
| Long 50-strike call payoff | 0 | 0 | 10 |
| Short 50-strike put payoff | −10 | 0 | 0 |
| Total value | −10 | 0 | 10 |
| **Alternative 2:** | | | |
| Long stock at 50 | −10 | 0 | 10 |
| Total value | −10 | 0 | 10 |

We now compare the same option strategy with the payoff of a forward or futures contract in Exhibit 2. The motivation to create a synthetic long forward position could be to exploit an arbitrage opportunity presented by the actual forward price or the need for an alternative to the outright purchase of a long forward position. Frequently, a forward contract is used instead of futures to acquire a stock position because it allows for contract customization.

### Exhibit 2  Synthetic Long Forward Position vs. Long Forward/Futures

| Stock price at expiration: | 40 | 50 | 60 |
|---|---|---|---|
| **Alternative 1:** | | | |
| Long 50-strike call payoff | 0 | 0 | 10 |
| Short 50-strike put payoff | −10 | 0 | 0 |
| Total value | −10 | 0 | 10 |
| **Alternative 3:** | | | |
| Long forward/futures at 50 | | | |
| Value | −10 | 0 | 10 |

### EXAMPLE 1

## Synthetic Long Forward Position vs. Long Forward/Futures

A market maker has sold a three-month forward contract on Vodafone that allows the client (counterparty) to buy 10,000 shares at 200.35 pence (100p = £1) at expiration. The current stock price ($S_0$) is 200p, and the stock does not pay dividends until after the contract matures. The annualized interest rate is 0.70%. The cost (i.e., premium) of puts and calls on Vodafone is identical.

1. Discuss (a) how the market maker can hedge her short forward position upon the sale of the forward contract and (b) the market maker's position upon expiration of the forward contract.
2. Discuss how the market maker can hedge her short forward contract position using a synthetic long forward position, and explain what happens at expiry if the Vodafone share price is above or below 200.35p.

### Solution 1:

**a** To offset the short forward contract position, the market maker can borrow £20,000 (= 10,000 × $S_0$/100) and buy 10,000 Vodafone shares at 200p. There is no upfront cost because the stock purchase is 100% financed.

**b** At the expiry of the forward contract, the market maker delivers the 10,000 Vodafone shares she owns to the client that is long the forward, and then the market maker repays her loan. The net outflow for the market maker is zero because the following two transactions offset each other:

Amount received for the delivery of shares: 10,000 × 200.35p = £20,035

Repayment of loan: 10,000 × 200p [1 + 0.700% × (90/360)] = £20,035

### Solution 2:

To hedge her short forward position, the market maker creates a synthetic long forward position. She purchases a call and sells a put, both with a strike price of 200.35p and expiring in three months.

# Position Equivalencies

> At the expiry of the forward contract, if the stock price is above 200.35p, the market maker exercises her call, pays £20,035 (=10,000 × 200.35p), and receives 10,000 Vodafone shares. She then delivers these shares to the client and receives £20,035.
>
> At the expiry of the forward contract, if the stock price is below 200.35p, the owner of the long put will exercise his option, and the market maker receives the 10,000 Vodafone shares for £20,035. She then delivers these shares to the client and receives £20,035.

Consider now a trader who wants to short a stock over a specified period. He needs to borrow the stock from the market and then sell the borrowed shares. Instead, the trader can create a **synthetic short forward position** by selling a call and buying a put at the same strike price and maturity. When using options to replicate a short stock position, it is important to be aware of early assignment risk that could arise with American-style options. As Exhibit 3 shows, the payoff is the exact opposite of the synthetic long forward position.

The same outcome can be achieved be selling forwards or futures contracts (as seen in Exhibit 3). These instruments are also commonly used to eliminate future price risk. Consider an investor who owns a stock and wants to lock in a future sales price. The investor might enter into a forward or futures contract (as seller) requiring her to deliver the shares at a future date in exchange for a cash amount determined today. Because the initial and final stock prices are known, this investment should pay the risk-free rate. For a dividend-paying stock, the dividends expected to be paid on the stock during the term of the contract will decrease the price of the forward or futures.

### Exhibit 3   Synthetic Short Forward Position

| Stock price at expiration: | 40 | 50 | 60 |
|---|---|---|---|
| **Alternative 1:** | | | |
| Short 50-strike call payoff | 0 | 0 | −10 |
| Long 50-strike put payoff | 10 | 0 | 0 |
| Total value | 10 | 0 | −10 |
| **Alternative 2:** | | | |
| Short stock at 50 | 10 | 0 | −10 |
| Value | 10 | 0 | −10 |
| **Alternative 3:** | | | |
| Short forward/futures at 50 | 10 | 0 | −10 |
| Value | 10 | 0 | −10 |

Synthetic forwards on stocks and equity indexes are often used by market makers that have sold a forward contract to customers—to hedge the risk, the market-maker would implement a synthetic long forward position—or by investment banks wishing to hedge forward exposure arising from structured products.

## 2.2 Synthetic Put and Call

As already described, market participants can use synthetic positions to transform the payoff and risk profile of their positions. The symmetrical payoffs of long and short stock, forward, and futures positions can be altered by implementing synthetic options positions. For example, the symmetric payoff of a short stock position can become asymmetrical if the investor transforms it into a synthetic long put position by buying a call.

Exhibit 4 shows the payoffs of a synthetic long put position that consists of short stock at 50 and a long call with an exercise price of 50. It can be seen that the payoffs from this synthetic put position at various stock prices at option expiration are identical to those of a long put with a 50-strike price. Of course, all positions are assumed to expire at the same time. Note that the same transformation of payoff and risk profile for a position of short forwards or futures can also be accomplished using long call options.

| Exhibit 4 Synthetic Long Put | | | |
|---|---|---|---|
| **Stock price at expiration:** | **40** | **50** | **60** |
| **Alternative 1:** | | | |
| Short stock at 50 | 10 | 0 | −10 |
| Long 50-strike call payoff | 0 | 0 | +10 |
| Total value | 10 | 0 | 0 |
| **Alternative 2** | | | |
| Long 50-strike put payoff | 10 | 0 | 0 |
| Value | 10 | 0 | 0 |

### EXAMPLE 2

### Synthetic Long Put

Three months ago, Wing Tan, a hedge fund manager, entered into a short forward contract that requires him to deliver 50,000 Generali shares, which the fund does not currently own, at €18/share in one month from now. The stock price is currently €16/share. The hedge fund's research analyst, Gisele Rossi, has a non-consensus expectation that the company will report an earnings "beat" next month. The stock does not pay dividends.

1. Under the assumption that Tan maintains the payoff profile of his current short forward position, discuss the conditions for profit or loss at contract expiration.

2. After discussing with Rossi her earnings outlook, Tan remains bearish on Generali. He decides to hedge his risk, however, in case the stock does report a positive earnings surprise. Discuss how Tan can modify his existing position to produce an asymmetrical, risk-reducing payoff.

### Solution 1:

If Tan decides to keep the current payoff profile of his position, at the expiry date, given a stock price of $S_T$, the profit or loss on the short forward will be 50,000 × (€18 − $S_T$). The position will be profitable only if $S_T$ is below €18; otherwise the manager will incur in a loss.

**Solution 2:**

Tan decides to modify the payoff profile on his short forward position so that, at expiration, it will benefit from any stock price decrease below €16 while avoiding losses if the stock rises above that price. He purchases a call option with a strike price €16 and one month to maturity at a cost (premium) of €0.50. At expiration, the payoffs are as follows:

- On the short forward contract: $50{,}000 \times (€18 - S_T)$
- On the long call: $50{,}000 \times \{\text{Max}[0,(S_T - €16)] - €0.50\}$
- On the combined position: $50{,}000 \times \{(€18 - S_T) + [\text{Max}[0,(S_T - €16)] - €0.50]\}$

If $S_T \leq €16$, the call will expire worthless and the profit will amount to $50{,}000 \times (€18 - S_T + 0 - €0.50)$.

If $S_T > €16$, the call is exercised and the Generali shares delivered for a maximum profit of $50{,}000 \times (€18 - €16 - €0.50) = €75{,}000$.

In similar fashion, an investor with a long stock position can change his payoff and risk profile into that of a long call by purchasing a put ("protective put" strategy). The long put eliminates the downside risk, whereas the long stock leaves the profit potential unlimited. As shown in Exhibit 5, the strategy has a payoff profile resembling that of a long call. Again, all positions are assumed to expire at the same time. We will have much more to say about the protective put strategy later in this reading. Finally, the payoff profile of a long call can also be achieved by adding a long put to a long forward or futures position, all with the same expiration dates and the same strike and forward (or futures) prices.

**Exhibit 5   Synthetic Long Call**

| Stock price at expiration: | 40 | 50 | 60 |
|---|---|---|---|
| **Alternative 1:** | | | |
| Long stock at 50 | –10 | 0 | 10 |
| Long 50-strike put payoff | 10 | 0 | 0 |
| Total value | 0 | 0 | 10 |
| **Alternative 2** | | | |
| Long 50-strike call payoff | 0 | 0 | 10 |
| Value | 0 | 0 | 10 |

# COVERED CALLS AND PROTECTIVE PUTS

**b** discuss the investment objective(s), structure, payoff, risk(s), value at expiration, profit, maximum profit, maximum loss, and breakeven underlying price at expiration of a covered call position;

Writing a **covered call** is a very common option strategy used by both individual and institutional investors. In this strategy, a party that already owns shares sells a call option, giving another party the right to buy their shares at the exercise price.[1] The investor owns the shares and has taken on the potential obligation to deliver the shares to the call option buyer and accept the exercise price as the price at which she sells the shares. For her willingness to do this, the investor receives the premium on the option.

When someone simultaneously holds a long position in an asset and a long position in a put option on that asset, the put is often called a **protective put**. The name comes from the fact that the put protects against losses in the value of the underlying asset.

The examples that follow use the convention of identifying an option by the underlying asset, expiration, exercise price, and option type. For example, in Exhibit 6, the PBR October 16 call option sells for 1.42. The underlying asset is Petróleo Brasileiro (PBR) common stock, the expiration is October, the exercise price is 16, the option is a call, and the call premium is 1.42. It is important to note that even though we will refer to this as the October 16 option, it does not expire on 16 October. Rather, 16 reflects the price at which the call owner has the right to buy, otherwise known as the exercise price or strike.

| Petróleo Brasileiro (PBR) | October | 16 | Call |
|---|---|---|---|
| *Underlying asset* | *Expiration* | *Exercise price* | *Option type* |

On some exchanges, certain options may have weekly expirations in addition to a monthly expiration, which means investors need to be careful in specifying the option of interest. For a given underlying asset and exercise price, there may be several weekly and one monthly option expiring in October. The examples that follow all assume a single monthly expiration.

## 3.1 Investment Objectives of Covered Calls

Consider the option data in Exhibit 6. Suppose there is one month until the September expiration. By convention, option listings show data for a single call or put, but in practice, the most common trading unit for an exchange-traded option is one contract covering 100 shares. Besides call and put premiums for various strike (i.e., exercise) prices and monthly expirations, the option data also shows implied volatilities as well as the "Greeks" (variables so named because most of the common ones are denoted by Greek letters). Implied volatility is the value of the unobservable volatility variable that equates the result of an option pricing model—such as the Black–Scholes–Merton (BSM) model—to the market price of an option, using all other required (and observable) input variables, including the option's strike price, the price of the underlying, the time to option expiration, and the risk-free interest. Before proceeding further, we provide a brief review of the Greeks because they will be an integral part of the discussion of the various option strategies to be presented.

- **Delta** ($\Delta$) is the change in an option's price in response to a change in price of the underlying, all else equal. Delta provides a good approximation of how an option's price will change for a small change in the underlying's price. Delta for long calls is always positive; delta for long puts is always negative. *Delta ($\Delta$) ≈ Change in value of option/Change in value of underlying.*
- **Gamma** ($\Gamma$) is the change in an option's delta for a change in price of the underlying, all else equal. Gamma is a measure of the curvature in the option price in relationship to the underlying price. Gamma for long calls and long puts is always positive. *Gamma ($\Gamma$) ≈ Change in delta/Change in value of underlying.*

---

[1] When someone creates (writes) a call without owning the underlying asset, it is known as a "naked" call.

## Covered Calls and Protective Puts

- **Vega (v)** is the change in an option's price for a change in volatility of the underlying, all else equal. Vega measures the sensitivity of the underlying to volatility. Vega for long calls and long puts is always positive. *Vega (v) ≈ Change in value of option/Change in volatility of underlying.*
- **Theta (Θ)** is the daily change in an option's price, all else equal. Theta measures the sensitivity of the option's price to the passage of time, known as time decay. Theta for long calls and long puts is generally negative.

Assume the current PBR share price is 15.84 and the risk-free rate is 4%. Now let us consider three different market participants who might logically use covered calls.

### Exhibit 6  PBR Option Prices, Implied Volatilities, and Greeks

| Call Prices | | | Exercise Price | Put Prices | | |
|---|---|---|---|---|---|---|
| SEP | OCT | NOV | | SEP | OCT | NOV |
| 1.64 | 1.95 | 2.44 | 15 | 0.65 | 0.99 | 1.46 |
| 0.97 | 1.42 | 1.90 | 16 | 1.14 | 1.48 | 1.96 |
| 0.51 | 1.02 | 1.44 | 17 | 1.76 | 2.09 | 2.59 |

| Call Implied Volatility | | | | Put Implied Volatility | | |
|---|---|---|---|---|---|---|
| SEP | OCT | NOV | | SEP | OCT | NOV |
| 64.42% | 57.33% | 62.50% | 15 | 58.44% | 56.48% | 62.81% |
| 55.92% | 56.11% | 60.37% | 16 | 59.40% | 56.35% | 62.27% |
| 51.07% | 55.87% | 58.36% | 17 | 59.59% | 56.77% | 63.40% |

**Delta: change in option price per change of +1 in stock price, all else equal**

| Call Deltas | | | | Put Deltas | | |
|---|---|---|---|---|---|---|
| SEP | OCT | NOV | | SEP | OCT | NOV |
| 0.657 | 0.647 | 0.642 | 15 | −0.335 | −0.352 | −0.359 |
| 0.516 | 0.540 | 0.560 | 16 | −0.481 | −0.460 | −0.438 |
| 0.351 | 0.434 | 0.475 | 17 | −0.620 | −0.564 | −0.513 |

**Gamma: change in delta per change of +1 in stock price, all else equal**

| Call Gammas | | | | Put Gammas | | |
|---|---|---|---|---|---|---|
| SEP | OCT | NOV | | SEP | OCT | NOV |
| 0.125 | 0.100 | 0.075 | 15 | 0.136 | 0.102 | 0.075 |
| 0.156 | 0.109 | 0.082 | 16 | 0.147 | 0.109 | 0.080 |
| 0.159 | 0.109 | 0.086 | 17 | 0.140 | 0.107 | 0.079 |

**Theta: daily change in option price, all else equal**

| Call Thetas (daily) | | | | Put Thetas (daily) | | |
|---|---|---|---|---|---|---|
| SEP | OCT | NOV | | SEP | OCT | NOV |
| −0.019 | −0.012 | −0.011 | 15 | −0.015 | −0.010 | −0.009 |
| −0.018 | −0.013 | −0.011 | 16 | −0.017 | −0.011 | −0.010 |
| −0.015 | −0.012 | −0.011 | 17 | −0.016 | −0.011 | −0.010 |

*(continued)*

### Exhibit 6 (Continued)

**Vega: change in option price per 1% increase in volatility, all else equal**

| Call Vegas (per %) | | | | Put Vegas (per %) | | |
|---|---|---|---|---|---|---|
| SEP | OCT | NOV | | SEP | OCT | NOV |
| 0.017 | 0.024 | 0.030 | 15 | 0.017 | 0.024 | 0.030 |
| 0.018 | 0.026 | 0.031 | 16 | 0.018 | 0.026 | 0.031 |
| 0.017 | 0.025 | 0.032 | 17 | 0.017 | 0.025 | 0.032 |

#### 3.1.1 Market Participant #1: Yield Enhancement

The most common motivation for writing covered calls is cash generation in anticipation of limited upside moves in the underlying. The call option writer keeps the premium regardless of what happens in the future. Some covered call writers view the premium they receive as an additional source of income in the same way they view cash dividends. For a covered call, a long position in 100 shares of the underlying is required for each short call contract. No additional cash margin is needed if the long position in the underlying is maintained. If the stock price exceeds the strike price at expiry, the underlying shares will be "called away" from the covered call writer and then delivered to satisfy the option holder's right to buy shares at the strike price. It is important to recognize, however, that when someone writes a call option, he is essentially giving up the returns above the strike price to the call holder.

Consider an individual investor who owns PBR and believes the stock price is likely to remain relatively flat over the next few months. With the stock currently trading at just under 16, the investor might think it unlikely that the stock will rise above 17. Exhibit 6 shows that the premium for a call option expiring in September with an exercise price of 17, referred to as the SEP 17 call, is 0.51. She could write that call and receive this premium. Alternatively, she could write a different call, say the NOV 17 call, and receive 1.44. There is a clear trade-off between the size of the option premium and the likelihood of option exercise. The option writer would get more cash from writing the longer-term option (because of a larger time premium), but there is a greater chance that the option would move in the money, resulting in the option being exercised by the buyer and, therefore, the stock being called away from the writer. The view of the covered call writer can be understood in terms of the call option's implied volatility. Essentially, writing the call expresses the view that the volatility of the underlying asset will be lower than the pricing of the option suggests. As shown in Exhibit 6, the implied volatility of the NOV 17 options is 58.36%. By writing the NOV 17 call for 1.44, the covered call investor believes that the volatility of the underlying asset will be less than the option's implied volatility of 58.36%. The call buyer believes the stock will move far enough above the strike price of 17 to provide a payoff greater than the 1.44 cost of the call.

Although it may be acceptable to think of the option premium as income, it is important to remember that the call writer has given up an important benefit of stock ownership: capital gains above the strike price. This dynamic can be seen in Exhibit 7. Consider an investor with a long position in PBR stock (with delta of +1) and a short position in a PBR NOV 17 call. The investor enjoys the benefit of the call premium of 1.44. This cushions the value of the position (Stock – Call, or S – C) as the PBR share price drops. If the PBR stock price drops to 5, the call option will drop to essentially 0. The portfolio will be worth about 6.44, as shown in Exhibit 7. As the stock price increases, however, the short call position begins to limit portfolio gains. If the price of PBR shares rises to 30, the call option delta approaches 1, so the delta of the portfolio (S – C) approaches 0. The portfolio gains from the long PBR stock position will be reduced by losses on the short call position. As the in-the-money option expires, the maximum value of the portfolio will approach 18.44, the exercise price of 17 plus the 1.44 premium, as in Exhibit 7.

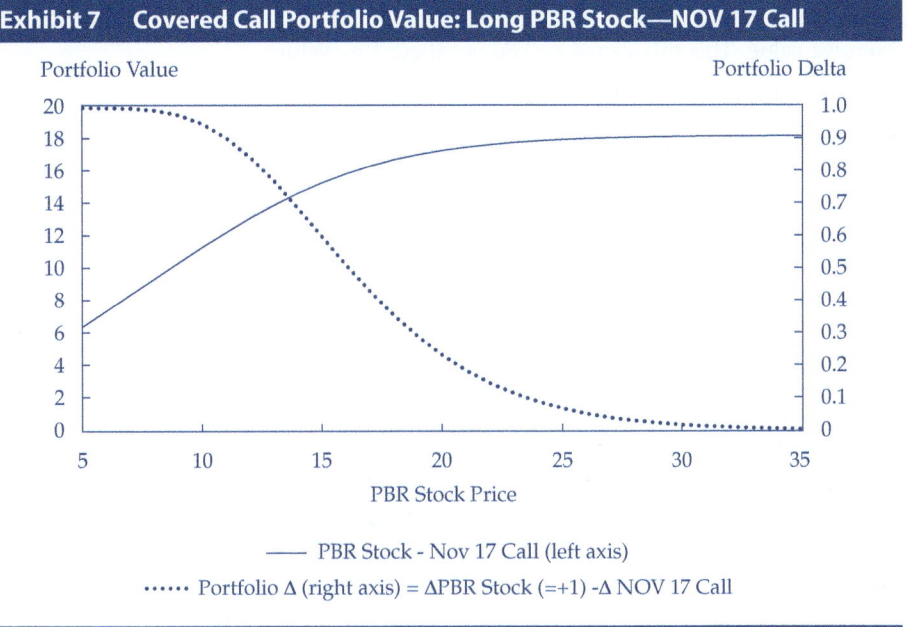

Exhibit 7   Covered Call Portfolio Value: Long PBR Stock—NOV 17 Call

### 3.1.2 Market Participant #2: Reducing a Position at a Favorable Price

Next, consider Sofia Porto, a retail portfolio manager with a portfolio that has become overweighted in energy companies. She wants to reduce this imbalance. Porto holds 5,000 shares of PBR, an energy company, and she expects the price of this stock to remain relatively stable over the next month. She may decide to sell 1,000 shares for 15.84 each. As an alternative, Porto might decide to write 10 exchange-traded PBR SEP 15 call contracts. This means she is creating 10 option contracts, each of which covers 100 shares. In exchange for this contingent claim, she receives the option premium of 1.64/call × 100 calls/contract × 10 contracts = 1,640. Because the current PBR stock price (15.84) is above the exercise price of 15, the options she writes are in the money. Given her expectation that the stock price will be stable over the next month, it is likely that the option will be exercised. Because Porto wants to reduce the overweighting in energy stocks, this outcome is desirable. If the option is exercised, she has effectively sold the stock at 16.64. She receives 1.64 when she writes the option, and she receives 15 when the option is exercised. Porto could have simply sold the shares at their original price of 15.84, but in this specific situation, the option strategy resulted in a price improvement of 0.80 ([15 + 1.64] − 15.84) per share, or 5.05% (0.80/15.84), in a month's time.[2] By maintaining the stock position and selling a 15 call, she still risks the possibility of a stock price decline during the coming month resulting in a realized price lower than the current market price of 15.84. For example, if the PBR share price declined to 10 over the next month, Porto would realize only 10 + 1.64 = 11.64 on her covered call position.

---

[2] Porto's effective selling price of 16.64 is 0.80 higher than the original price of 15.84: 0.80/15.84 = 5.05%.

An American option premium can be viewed as having two parts: exercise value (also called intrinsic value) and time value.[3]

Call Premium = Time Value + Intrinsic Value = Time Value + Max(0,$S - X$)

In this case, the right to buy at 15 when the stock price is 15.84 has an exercise (or intrinsic) value of 0.84. The option premium is 1.64, which is 0.80 more than the exercise value. This difference of 0.80 is called time value.

1.64 = Time Value + (15.84 − 15)

Someone who writes covered calls to improve on the market is capturing the time value, which augments the stock selling price. Remember, though, that giving up part of the return distribution would result in an opportunity loss if the underlying goes up.

### 3.1.3 Market Participant #3: Target Price Realization

A third popular use of options is really a hybrid of the first two objectives. This strategy involves writing calls with an exercise price near the target price for the stock. Suppose a bank trust department holds PBR in many of its accounts and that its research team believes the stock would be properly priced at 16 per share, which is only slightly higher than its current price. In those accounts for which the investment policy statement permits option activity, the manager might choose to write near-term calls with an exercise price near the target price, 16 in this case. Suppose an account holds 500 shares of PBR. Writing 5 SEP 16 call contracts at 0.97 brings in 485 in cash. If the stock is above 16 in a month, the stock will be called away at the strike price (target price), with the option premium adding an additional 6% positive return to the account.[4] If PBR fails to rise to 16, the manager might write a new OCT expiration call with the same objective in mind.

Although this strategy is popular, the investor should not view it as a source of free money. The stock is currently very close to the target price, and the manager could simply sell it and be satisfied. Although the covered call writing program potentially adds to the return, there is also the chance that the stock could experience bad news or the overall market might pull back, resulting in an opportunity loss relative to the outright sale of the stock. The investor also would have an opportunity loss if the stock rose sharply above the exercise price and it was called away at a lower-than-market price.

The exposure from the short position in the PBR SEP 16 call can be understood in terms of the Greeks in Exhibit 6. Delta measures how the option price changes as the underlying asset price changes, and gamma measures the rate of change in delta.[5] A PBR SEP 16 call has a delta = 0.516 and a gamma of 0.156. A short call will reduce the delta of the portfolio (S − C) from +1 to +0.484 (= +1[Share] − 0.516[Short Call]). The lower portfolio delta will reduce the upside opportunity. A share price increase of 1 will result in a portfolio gain of approximately 0.484.[6] The delta of the portfolio is not constant. By selling the PBR 16 call, the portfolio is now "short gamma". Remember, gamma is the rate of change of delta. Although the underlying PBR share has a gamma of 0, the short call will make the gamma of the portfolio −0.156. As the price of PBR

---

[3] In addition to exercise value, some use the term "economic value" for intrinsic value because it is the value of the option if the investor were to exercise it at this very moment and trade out of the stock position.
[4] Relative to a stock price of 16, the option premium of 0.97 is 0.97/16 = 6.06%.
[5] Delta is the calculus first derivative of the option price with respect to the underlying asset price. Gamma is the second derivative of the option price with respect to the underlying asset price.
[6] The delta approximates the portfolio price change for very small changes in the underlying price. The delta itself is changing at a rate of gamma. For a change as large as 1%, the actual portfolio value will increase at a rate of less than 0.484 because it is short gamma.

shares increases above 16, the delta of the PBR call position will change, at a rate of gamma. Gamma is greatest for a near-the-money option and becomes progressively smaller as the option moves either into or out of the money (as seen in Exhibit 8).

Gamma of an ATM option can increase dramatically as the time to expiration approaches or volatility increases. Traders with large gamma exposure (especially large negative gamma) should be aware of the speed with which the position values can change. The change in portfolio delta and gamma for a PBR SEP 16 covered call as a function of share price can be seen in Exhibit 8. As the price of PBR shares increase, the portfolio delta changes at a rate of gamma. As the share price moves above the exercise price of 16, the portfolio (S – C) delta drops at a rate gamma towards its eventual limit of 0, effectively eliminating any remaining upside in the position.

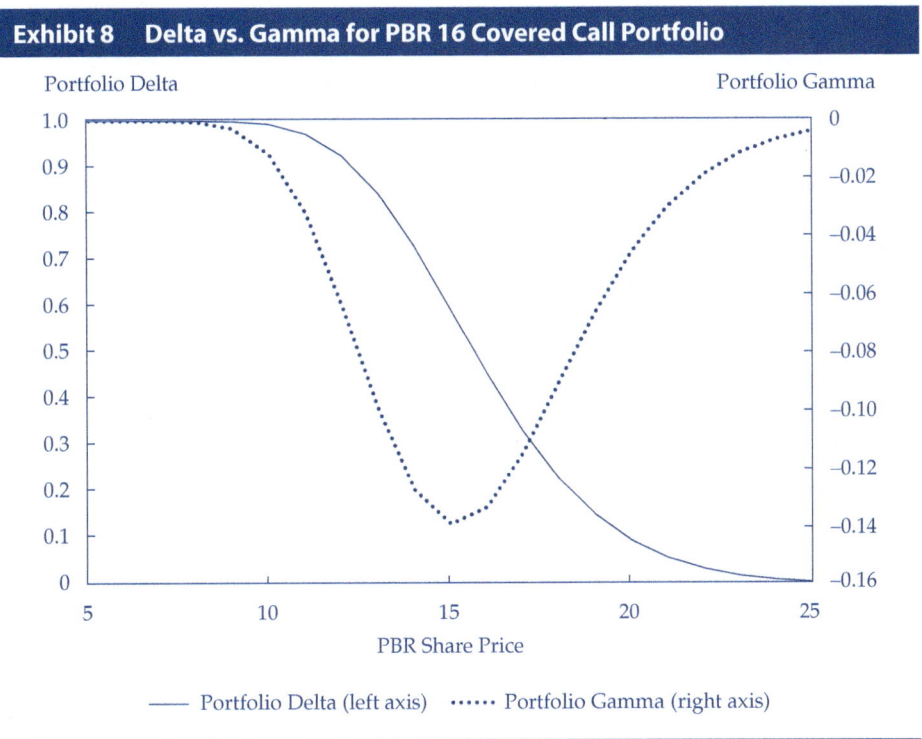

**Exhibit 8   Delta vs. Gamma for PBR 16 Covered Call Portfolio**

### 3.1.4 *Profit and Loss at Expiration*

In the process of learning option strategies, it is always helpful to look at a graphical display of the profit and loss possibilities at the option expiration. Suppose an investor owns PBR, currently trading at 15.84. The investor believes gains may be limited above a price of 17 and decides to write a call against the long share position. The 17 strike calls will have no intrinsic value because the share price is currently 15.84. The investor must now consider the available option maturities (SEP, OCT, and NOV) as shown in Exhibit 6. In deciding which option to write, the investor may consider the option premiums and implied volatilities. Based on the investor's view that volatility will remain low over the next three months, the investor chooses to write the NOV call. At 58.36%, the NOV 17 call has highest implied volatility of the available 17 strike options, so it would be the most overvalued assuming low volatility. The option premium of 1.44 is completely explained by the time value of the NOV option, because the NOV 17 option has no exercise value (Option premium = Time value + Intrinsic value; 1.44 = Time value + Max[0,15.84 – 17]). If the stock is above 17 at expiration, the option holder will exercise the call option and the investor will deliver the shares in exchange for the exercise price of 17. The maximum gain with a covered call is the appreciation to the exercise price plus the option premium.[7]

Some symbols will be helpful in learning these relationships:

$S_0$ = Stock price when option position opened
$S_T$ = Stock price at option expiration
$X$ = Option exercise price
$c_0$ = Call premium received or paid

The maximum gain is $(X - S_0) + c_0$. With a starting price of 15.84, a sale price of 17 results in 1.16 of price appreciation. The option writer would keep the option premium of 1.44 for a total gain of 1.16 + 1.44 = 2.60. This is the maximum gain from this strategy because all price appreciation above 17 belongs to the call holder. The call writer keeps the option premium regardless of what the stock does, so if it were to drop, the overall loss is reduced by the option premium received. Exhibit 9 shows the situation. The breakeven price for a covered call is the stock price minus the premium, or $S_0 - c_0$. In other words, the breakeven point occurs when the stock falls by the premium received—in this example, 15.84 − 1.44 = 14.40. The maximum loss would occur if the stock became worthless; it equals the original stock price minus the option premium received, or $S_0 - c_0$.[8] In this single unlikely scenario, the investor would lose 15.84 on the stock position but still keep the premium of 1.44, for a total loss of 14.40.

At option expiration, the *value* of the covered call position is the stock price minus the exercise value of the call. Any appreciation beyond the exercise price belongs to the option buyer, so the covered call writer does not earn any gains beyond that point. Symbolically,

$$\text{Covered Call Expiration Value} = S_T - \text{Max}[(S_T - X), 0]. \qquad (1)$$

The *profit* at option expiration is the covered call value plus the option premium received minus the original price of the stock:

$$\text{Covered Call Profit at Expiration} = S_T - \text{Max}[(S_T - X), 0] + c_0 - S_0. \qquad (2)$$

In summary:

$$\text{Maximum gain} = (X - S_0) + c_0$$
$$\text{Maximum loss} = S_0 - c_0$$
$$\text{Breakeven price} = S_0 - c_0$$
$$\text{Expiration value} = S_T - \text{Max}[(S_T - X), 0]$$
$$\text{Profit at expiration} = S_T - \text{Max}[(S_T - X), 0] + c_0 - S_0$$

---

[7] If someone writes an in-the-money covered call, there is "depreciation" to the exercise price, so the difference would be subtracted. For instance, if the stock price is 50 and a 45 call sells for 7, the maximum gain is −(50 − 45) + 7 = 2.
[8] Note that with a covered call, the breakeven price and the maximum loss are the same value.

### Exhibit 9  Covered Call P&L Diagram: Stock at 15.84, Write 17 Call at 1.44

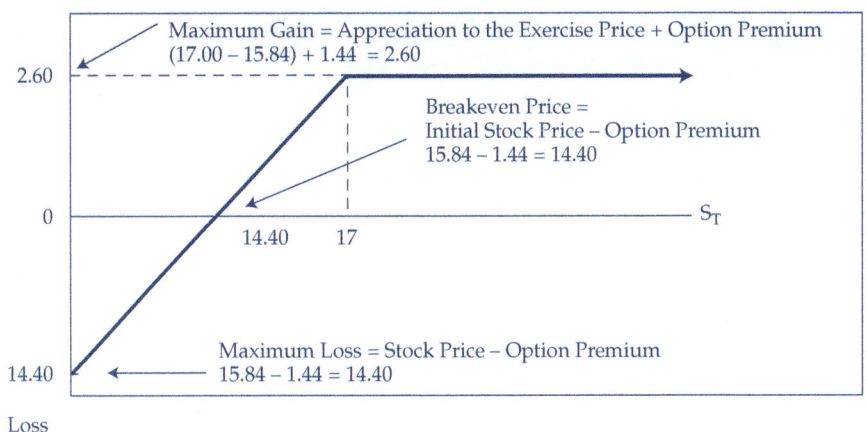

It is important to remember that these profit and loss diagrams depict the situation only at the end of the option's life.[9] Most equity covered call writing occurs with exchange-traded options, so the call writer always has the ability to buy back the option before expiration. If, for instance, the PBR stock price were to decline by 1 shortly after writing the covered call, the call value would most likely also decline. If this investor correctly believed the decline was temporary, he might buy the call back at the new lower option premium, making a profit on that trade, and then write the option again after the share price recovered.

### EXAMPLE 3

### Characteristics of Covered Calls

$S_0$ = Stock price when option position opened = 25.00
$X$ = Option exercise price = 30.00
$S_T$ = Stock price at option expiration = 31.33
$c_0$ = Call premium received = 1.55

1. Which of the following correctly calculates the maximum gain from writing a covered call?

   A  $(S_T - X) + c_0 = 31.33 - 30.00 + 1.55 = 2.88$
   B  $(S_T - S_0) - c_0 = 31.33 - 25.00 - 1.55 = 4.78$
   C  $(X - S_0) + c_0 = 30.00 - 25.00 + 1.55 = 6.55$

2. Which of the following correctly calculates the breakeven stock price from writing a covered call?

   A  $S_0 - c_0 = 25.00 - 1.55 = 23.45$
   B  $S_T - c_0 = 31.33 - 1.55 = 29.78$
   C  $X + c_0 = 30.00 + 1.55 = 31.55$

---

[9] It is also important to note that the general shape of the profit and loss diagram for a covered call is the same as that of writing a put. Covered call writing is the most common use of options by individual investors, whereas writing puts is the least common.

3 Which of the following correctly calculates the maximum loss from writing a covered call?
   A  $S_0 - c_0 = 25.00 - 1.55 = 23.45$
   B  $S_T - c_0 = 31.33 - 1.55 = 29.78$
   C  $S_T - X + c_0 = 31.33 - 30.00 + 1.55 = 2.88$

### Solution to 1:

C is correct. The covered call writer participates in gains up to the exercise price, after which further appreciation is lost to the call buyer. That is, $X - S_0 = 30.00 - 25.00 = 5.00$. The call writer also keeps $c_0$, the option premium, which is 1.55. So, the total maximum gain is $5.00 + 1.55 = 6.55$.

### Solution to 2:

A is correct. The call premium of 1.55 offsets a decline in the stock price by the amount of the premium received: $25.00 - 1.55 = 23.45$.

### Solution to 3:

A is correct. The stock price can fall to zero, causing a loss of the entire investment, but the option writer still keeps the option premium received: $25.00 - 1.55 = 23.45$

## 4  INVESTMENT OBJECTIVES OF PROTECTIVE PUTS

c  discuss the investment objective(s), structure, payoff, risk(s), value at expiration, profit, maximum profit, maximum loss, and breakeven underlying price at expiration of a protective put position;

The protective put is often viewed as a classic example of buying insurance. The investor holds a risky asset and wants protection against a loss in value. He then buys insurance in the form of the put, paying a premium to the seller of the insurance, the put writer. The exercise price of the put is similar to the coverage amount for an insurance policy. The insurance policy deductible is similar to the difference between the current asset price and the strike price of the put. A protective put with a low exercise price is like an insurance policy with a high deductible. Although less expensive, a low strike put involves greater price exposure before the payoff function goes into the money. For an insurance policy, a higher deductible is less expensive and reflects the increased risk borne by the insured party. For a protective put, a lower exercise price is less costly and has a greater risk of loss in the position.

Like traditional term insurance, this form of insurance provides coverage for a period of time. At the end of the period, the insurance expires and either pays off or not. The buyer of the insurance may or may not choose to renew the insurance by buying another put. A protective put can appear to be a great transaction with no drawbacks, because it provides downside protection with upside potential, but let us take a closer look.

### 4.1  Loss Protection/Upside Preservation

Suppose a portfolio manager has a client with a 50,000 share position in PBR. Her research suggests there may be a negative shock to the stock price in the next four to six weeks, and he wants to guard against a price decline. Consider the put prices shown in Exhibit 6; the purchase of a protective put presents the manager with some choices. Puts represent a right to sell at the strike price, so higher-strike puts will be more expensive. For this reason, the put buyer may select the 15-strike PBR put. Longer-term American puts are more expensive than their equivalent (same strike price) shorter-maturity puts. The put buyer must be sure the put will not expire before the expected price shock has occurred. The portfolio manager could buy a one-month (SEP) 15-strike put for 0.65. This put insures against the portion of the underlying return distribution that is below 15, but it will not protect against a price shock occurring after the SEP expiration.

Alternatively, the portfolio manager could buy a two-month option, paying 0.99 for an OCT 15 put, or she could buy a three-month option, paying 1.46 for a NOV 15 put. Note that there is not a linear relationship between the put value and its time until expiration. A two-month option does not sell for twice the price of a one-month option, nor does a three-month option sell for three times the price of a one-month option. The portfolio manager can also reduce the cost of insurance by increasing the size of the deductible (i.e., the current stock price minus the put exercise price), perhaps by using a put option with a 14 exercise price. A put option with an exercise price of 14 would have a lower premium but would not protect against losses in the stock until it falls to 14.00 per share. The option price is cheaper, but on a 50,000 share position, the deductible would be 50,000 more than if the exercise price of 15 were selected.[10]

Because of the uncertainty about the timing of the "shock event" she anticipates, the manager might consider the characteristics of the available option maturities. Given our assumptions, three of the BSM model inputs for the available 15 strike options are the same (PBR stock price 15.84, the strike price 15 and the risk-free rate of interest 4%). The difference in the cost of the SEP, OCT, and NOV options will be explained by the differences in time and the term structure of volatility. The BSM model assumes option volatility does not change over time or with strike price. In practice, volatility can vary across time and strike prices. For the 15 puts, the implied volatility is slightly greater for the NOV option, perhaps reflecting other traders' concerns about a shock event before expiration. Because the PBR stock price is 15.84 and the put options are all 15 strike, all three maturities have no intrinsic value.

The cost of each PBR 15 strike option is entirely explained by the remaining time value. If the stock price does not fall below 15, the SEP, OCT, and NOV put option values will erode to 0 as they approach their expiration dates. The erosion of the options value with time is approximated by the theta. The daily thetas (Theta/365) for the PBR puts and calls are given in Exhibit 6. Notice, all the theta values in the table are negative. These values approximate the daily losses on the option positions as time passes, all else equal. The NOV 15 put (90 days) has a theta of –0.009 and the SEP 15 put (30 days) has a theta of –0.015. If the NOV 15 option is held for one day, and the price and volatility of the underlying do not change, the put value will decline by approximately 0.009 to approximately 1.45 (= 1.46 – 0.009).

The graph of the BSM theta function for the PBR NOV 15 option as it approaches maturity is shown in Exhibit 10. Notice how the rate of decline changes as maturity approaches. If the PBR price does not drop below 15, the NOV 15 put will expire out-of-the-money and the option price will gradually fall to 0. All else equal, the sum of the daily losses approximated by theta will explain the entire loss of 1.46 in option value over that time. The complex shape of the theta graph in Exhibit 10 results from the nature of the BSM theta formula, which includes terms to reflect the probability that the stock price will fall below the strike price during the remaining time. Note that if the price of PBR remains at 15.84 for the last 10 days to maturity,

---

[10] The deductible is 50,000 × (15.84 – 15.00) with a strike price of 15. With a strike price of 14, the deductible would be 50,000 × (15.84 – 14.00), or 50,000 more.

the BSM put option value will erode to 0 at varying rates averaging about −0.03/day. Assumptions of the BSM model explain the negative peak in theta around three days prior to maturity as the remaining time value rapidly decays to 0. Theta values might help the investor decide which maturity to choose. If he were to buy the cheaper SEP put, the daily erosion of value (−0.015) would be greater than for the more expensive NOV put (−0.009).

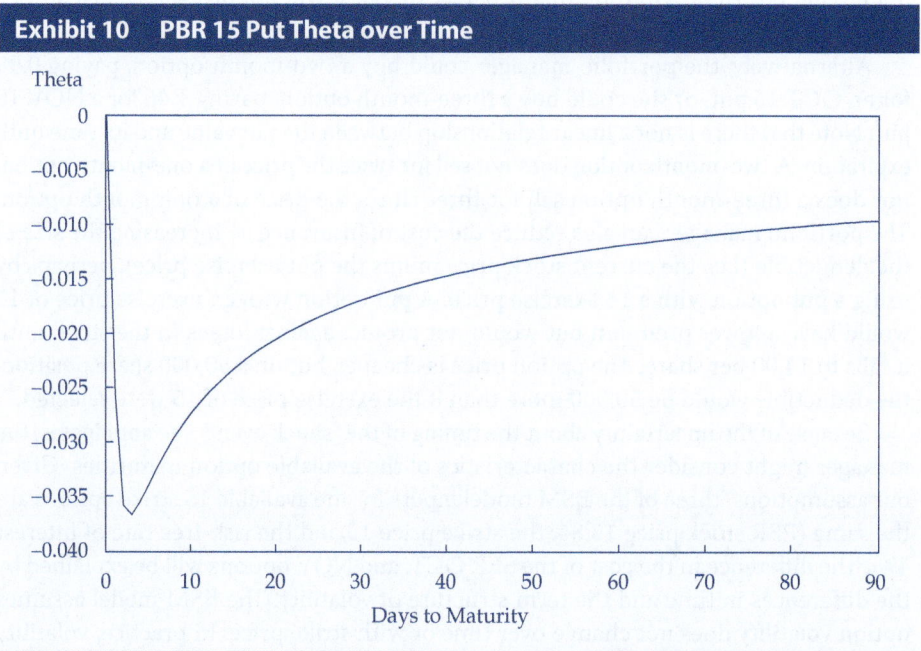

**Exhibit 10    PBR 15 Put Theta over Time**

Given the four- to six-week time horizon for the shock event anticipated by the portfolio manager, the OCT put seems appropriate, but there is still the potential to lose the premium without realizing any benefit. With a 0.99 premium for the OCT 15 put and 50,000 shares to protect, the cost to the account would be almost 50,000. One advantage of the NOV option is that although it is more expensive, it has the smallest daily loss of value, as captured by theta. This option also has a greater likelihood of not having expired before the news hits. Also, although the portfolio manager could hold onto the put position until its expiration, she might find it preferable to close out the option prior to maturity and recover some of the premium paid.[11]

## 4.2  Profit and Loss at Expiration

Exhibit 11 shows the profit and loss diagram for the protective put.[12] The stock can rise to any level, and the position would benefit fully from the appreciation; the maximum gain is unlimited. On the downside, losses are "cut off" once the stock price falls to the exercise price. With a protective put, the maximum loss is the depreciation to the exercise price plus the premium paid, or $S_0 - X + p_0$. At the option expiration,

---

[11] A price shock to the underlying asset might increase the market's expectations of future volatility, thereby likely increasing the put premium. By selling the option early, the investor would capture this increase. Also, once the adverse event occurred, there may be no reason to continue to hold the insurance. If the investor no longer needs it, he should cancel it and get part of the purchase price back. In other words, he should sell the put and recapture some of its cost.

[12] Note that the profit and loss diagram for a protective put has a shape similar to a long call position, which is the result of put–call parity. Long the asset and long the put is equivalent to long a call plus long a risk-free bond.

# Investment Objectives of Protective Puts

the value of the protective put is the greater of the stock price or the exercise price. The reason is because the stock can rise to any level but has a floor value of the put exercise price. In symbols,

Value of Protective Put at Expiration = $S_T + \text{Max}[(X - S_T), 0]$. (3)

The profit or loss at expiration is the ending value minus the beginning value. The initial value of the protective put is the starting stock price minus the put premium. In symbols,

Profit of Protective Put at Expiration = $S_T + \text{Max}[(X - S_T), 0] - S_0 - p_0$. (4)

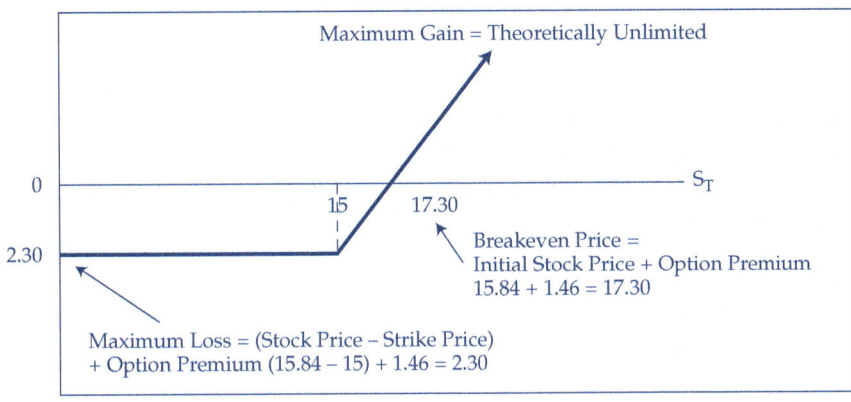

**Exhibit 11  Protective Put P&L Diagram: Stock at 15.84, Buy 15 Put at 1.46**

To break even, the underlying asset must rise by enough to offset the price of the put that was purchased. The breakeven point is the initial stock price plus the option premium. In symbols, Breakeven Price = $S_0 + p_0$.

In summary:

Maximum gain = $S_T - S_0 - p_0$ = Unlimited
Maximum loss = $S_0 - X + p_0$
Breakeven price = $S_0 + p_0$
Expiration value = $S_T + \text{Max}[(X - S_T), 0]$
Profit at expiration = $S_T + \text{Max}[(X - S_T), 0] - S_0 - p_0$

## EXAMPLE 4

### Characteristics of Protective Puts

$S_0$ = Stock price when option position opened = 25.00
$X$ = Option exercise price = 20.00
$S_T$ = Stock price at option expiration = 31.33
$p_0$ = Put premium paid = 1.15

1 Which of the following correctly calculates the gain with the protective put?

A  $S_T - S_0 - p_0 = 31.33 - 25.00 - 1.15 = 5.18$

**B** $S_T - S_0 + p_0 = 31.33 - 25.00 + 1.15 = 7.48$

**C** $S_T - X - p_0 = 31.33 - 20.00 - 1.15 = 10.18$

2 Which of the following correctly calculates the breakeven stock price with the protective put?

**A** $S_0 - p_0 = 25.00 - 1.15 = 23.85$

**B** $S_0 + p_0 = 25.00 + 1.15 = 26.15$

**C** $S_T + p_0 = 31.33 + 1.15 = 32.48$

3 Which of the following correctly calculates the maximum loss with the protective put?

**A** $S_0 - X + p_0 = 25.00 - 20.00 + 1.15 = 6.15$

**B** $S_T - X - p_0 = 31.33 - 20.00 - 1.15 = 10.18$

**C** $S_0 - p_0 = 25.00 - 1.15 = 23.85$

### Solution to 1:

A is correct. If the stock price is above the put exercise price at expiration, the put will expire worthless. The profit is the gain on the stock ($S_T - S_0$) minus the cost of the put. Note that the maximum profit with a protective put is theoretically unlimited, because the stock can rise to any level and the entire profit is earned by the stockholder.

### Solution to 2:

B is correct. Because the option buyer pays the put premium, she does not begin to make money until the stock rises by enough to recover the premium paid.

### Solution to 3:

A is correct. Once the stock falls to the put exercise price, further losses are eliminated. The investor paid the option premium, so the total loss is the "deductible" plus the cost of the insurance.

## 5. EQUIVALENCE TO LONG ASSET/SHORT FORWARD POSITION

**d** compare the delta of covered call and protective put positions with the position of being long an asset and short a forward on the underlying asset;

All investors who consider option strategies should understand that some options are more sensitive to changes in the underlying asset than others. As we have seen, this relationship is measured by delta, an indispensable tool to an options user. Because a long call increases in value and a long put decreases in value as the underlying asset increases in price, call deltas range from 0 to 1 and put deltas range from 0 to –1. (Naturally, the signs are reversed for short positions in these options.) A long position in the underlying asset has a delta of 1.0, whereas a short position has a delta of –1.0. When the share price is close to the strike price, a rough approximation is that a long ATM option will have a delta that is approximately 0.5 (for a call) or –0.5 (for a put). Exhibit 12 shows the delta for the PBR SEP 16 put and call versus share price. As the stock price moves toward 16 (the strike price), the call option delta is approximately 0.52 and the put delta is –0.48. In general, Call Delta – Put Delta = 1 for options on the same underlying with the same BSM model inputs.

## Equivalence to Long Asset/Short Forward Position

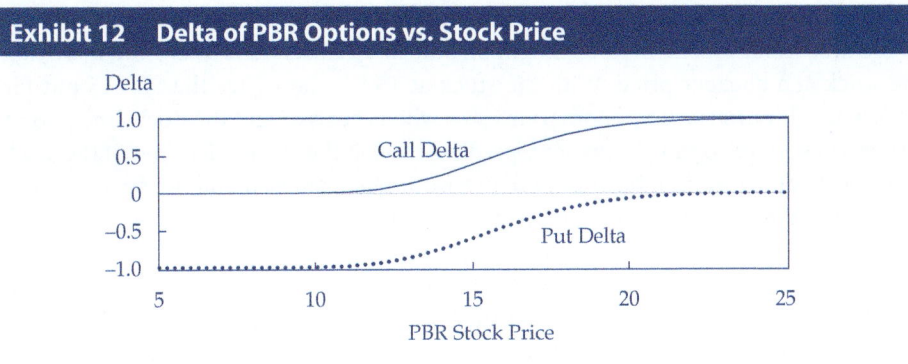

**Exhibit 12  Delta of PBR Options vs. Stock Price**

Delta can be applied to a portfolio as well. Suppose on the Tokyo Stock Exchange, Honda Motor Company stock sells for ¥3,500. A portfolio contains 100 shares, and the manager writes one exchange-traded covered call contract with a ¥3,500 strike. The delta of the 100-share position will be 100 × +1 = +100. Because the call is at the money, meaning that the stock price and exercise price are equal, it will have a delta of approximately 0.5. The portfolio, however, is short one call contract. From the perspective of the portfolio, the delta of the short call contract is −0.5 × 100 = −50. A short call *loses* money as the underlying price rises. So, this covered call has a **position delta** (which is an overall or portfolio delta) of 50, consisting of +100 points for the stock and −50 points for the short call. Compare this call with a protective put, in which someone buys 100 shares of stock and one contract of an ATM put. Its position delta would also be 50: +100 points for the stock and −50 points for the long put.

Finally, consider a long stock position of 100 shares and a short forward position of 50 shares. Because futures and forwards on non-dividend-paying stocks are essentially proxies for the stock, their deltas are also 1.0 for a long position and −1.0 for a short position. In this example, the short forward position "cancels" half the long stock position, so the position delta is also 50. These examples show three different positions: an ATM covered call, an ATM protective put, and a long stock/short forward position that all have the same delta. For small movements in the price of the underlying asset, these positions will show very similar gains and losses.

## 5.1 Writing Puts

If someone writes a put option and simultaneously deposits an amount of money equal to the exercise price into a designated account, it is called writing a **cash-secured put**.[13] This strategy is appropriate for someone who is bullish on a stock or who wants to acquire shares at a particular price. The fact that the option exercise price is escrowed provides assurance that the put writer will be able to purchase the stock if the option holder chooses to exercise. Think of the cash in a cash-secured put as being similar to the stock part of a covered call. When an investor sells a covered call, she takes on the obligation to sell a stock, and this obligation is covered by ownership in the shares. When a put option is sold to create a new position, the obligation that accompanies this position is to purchase shares. In order to cover the obligation to purchase shares, the portfolio should have enough cash in the account to make good on this obligation. The short put position is covered or secured by cash in the account.

---

**13** This strategy is also called a *fiduciary put*. Note that for a European option, the amount deposited would equal the present value of the exercise price. When someone writes a put but does not escrow the exercise price, it is sometimes called a *naked put*. Note that this is a slightly different use of the adjective "naked" than with a naked call. When writing a naked call, the call writer does not have the underlying *asset* to deliver if the call is exercised. When an investor writes a naked put, he has not set aside the *cash* necessary to buy the asset if the put is exercised.

Now consider two slightly different scenarios using the price data from Exhibit 6. In the first scenario, one investor might be bullish on PBR and is interested in buying the stock at a cheaper price. With the stock at 15.84, she writes the SEP 15 put for 0.65, which is purchased by another investor who is bearish on PBR stock. The option writer will keep the option premium regardless of what the stock price does. If the stock is below 15 at expiration, however, the put would be exercised and the option writer would be obliged to purchase shares from the option holder at the exercise price of 15.

Possible small (and independent) changes to the variables from Exhibit 6 are simulated in Exhibit 13 for the *long* PBR SEP 15 put position. The long put is illustrated here for simplicity—these statistics for the long put position should also help the put writer to understand the risks and returns for her position, because a short position is simply the mirror image of the long position. The initial values are 15.84 for the stock and 0.65 for the put, and the put buyer has acquired a delta of −0.335 and a gamma of 0.136.[14]

As demonstrated in change #1, if the stock price rises by 0.10 from 15.84 to 15.94, the long (short) put will lose (gain) approximately −0.335 × 0.10 = −0.0335 (+0.0335), as the put value drops from 0.65 to approximately 0.617 (≈ 0.6165 = 0.65 − 0.0335). Remember, this approximation is good for only a small change in the underlying share price. As the stock price rises, the long put's initial delta, −0.335, will change at a rate of gamma, 0.136, so the delta then becomes −0.321.

**Exhibit 13  Long PBR SEP 15 PUT, Greeks and Put Price Changes for Small, Independent Changes in Inputs**

|  | Stock Price (S) | Delta (Δ) | Gamma (Γ) | Option Price (p) |
|---|---|---|---|---|
| Initial Values | 15.84 | −0.335 | 0.136 | 0.65 |
| **Change #1: Stock Price Increases by 0.10, from 15.84 to 15.94** | | | | |
| ΔS = +0.10<br>Δt = 0<br>ΔVol = 0 | 15.94 | Δ changes at rate of Γ, so:<br>$\Delta_1 \approx \Delta_0 + (\Gamma \times \Delta S)$<br>−0.321 ≈<br>−0.335 + (0.136 × 0.10) | Γ changes slightly to 0.133 | $p_1 \approx p_0 + (\Delta_0 \times \Delta S)$<br>*0.617* ≈<br>0.65 + (−0.335 × 0.10) |
| **Change #2: Time to Expiration Changes by 1 Day, from 30 to 29 Days** | | | | |
| ΔS = 0<br>Δt = 1 day (to 29 Days)<br>ΔVol = 0 | 15.84 | −0.335 | 0.136 | $p_1 \approx p_0 + (\Theta \times \Delta t)$<br>*0.635* ≈<br>0.65 + (−0.015 × 1) |
| **Change #3: Implied Volatility Increases by 1 Percentage Point, from 58.44% to 59.44%** | | | | |
| ΔS = 0<br>Δt = 0<br>ΔVol = +1% (to 59.44%) | 15.84 | −0.335 | 0.136 | $p_1 \approx p_0 + (\nu \times \Delta Vol)$<br>*0.667* ≈<br>0.65 + (0.017 × 1) |

The long SEP 15 put position also has a theta of −0.015 and a vega of +0.017.[15] As time decays, the long (short) put option will lose (gain) value at a rate of theta, so the value of long (short) position will decrease (increase) by approximately 0.015/per day. As demonstrated in change #2 (which is separate and independent from change

---

[14] The put writer (short position) will have a delta of −(−0.335) = +0.335.
[15] All else equal, a long put loses time value as it approaches expiration (negative theta). All else equal, a long put increases in value as the volatility is increased (positive vega). In the case of a short put, the signs are reversed.

#1), all else equal, the long put value would drop from about 0.65 to 0.635 as the put moves one day closer to expiration (from 30 to 29 days). If the implied volatility of the SEP 15 put were to increase by 1% (from 58.44% to 59.44%), all else equal, the option price would increase by 0.017 to approximately 0.667, as demonstrated in change #3. The increase in volatility would benefit the put holder at the expense of the writer, because the short put position would lose 0.017.

If the stock is above 15 at expiration, the put option will expire unexercised. At the expiration date, the put writer will either keep the premium or have PBR shares put to her at 15. Because the put writer was bullish on PBR and wanted to purchase it at a cheaper price, she may be happy with this result. Netting out the option premium received by the put writer would make her effective purchase price 15.00 − 0.65 = 14.35.

In another scenario, an institutional investor might be interested in purchasing PBR. Suppose the investor wrote the SEP 17 put for 1.76. This strategy will have slightly different values for the Greeks compared with the previous strategy. The delta of the SEP 17 short put position will be +0.62, gamma will be −0.140, and theta will equal +0.016. This position will be more sensitive to changes in the stock price than the SEP 15 put. If the PBR share price increases 0.10 from 15.84 to 15.94, the put writer will now profit by approximately +0.62 × 0.10 = 0.062. The higher strike price makes the short SEP 17 put a more bullish position than the SEP 15 put. This dynamic is reflected in the larger delta for the short SEP 17 put at +0.620 (versus +0.335 for the short SEP 15 put).

If the stock is below 17 at expiration, the SEP 17 puts will be exercised and the investor (i.e., put writer) will pay 17 for the shares, resulting in a net price of 17.00 − 1.76 = 15.24. Anytime someone writes an option, the maximum gain is the option premium received, so in this case, the maximum gain is 1.76. The maximum loss when writing a put occurs when the stock falls to zero. The option writer pays the exercise price for worthless stock but still keeps the premium. In this example, the maximum loss would be 17.00 − 1.76 = 15.24. Exhibit 14 shows the corresponding profit and loss diagram.

**Exhibit 14    Short Put P&L Diagram: Write SEP 17 Put at 1.76**

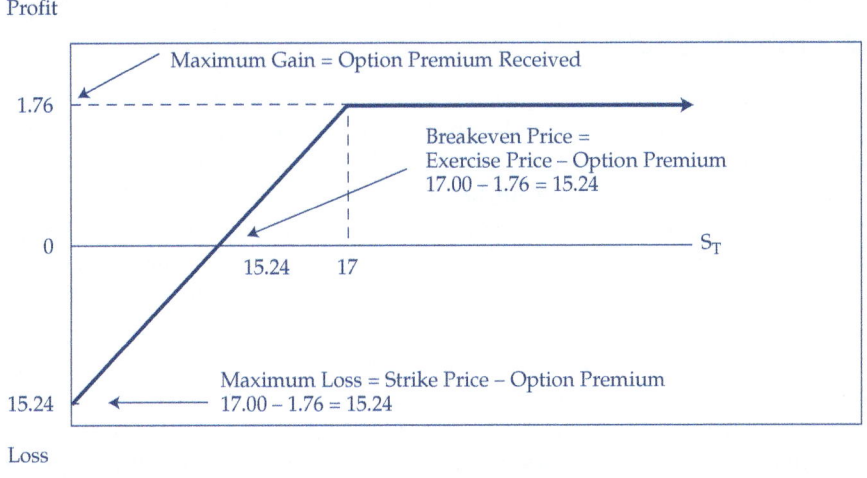

Note the similar shape of the covered call position in Exhibit 9 and the short put in Exhibit 14. Writing a covered call and writing a put are very similar with regard to their risk and reward characteristics.[16]

## 6. RISK REDUCTION USING COVERED CALLS AND PROTECTIVE PUTS

e  compare the effect of buying a call on a short underlying position with the effect of selling a put on a short underlying position;

Covered calls and protective puts may both be viewed as risk-reducing or hedging strategies. In the case of a covered call, some price uncertainty is eliminated for price increases. For a protective put, the price uncertainty is eliminated for price decreases. The risk reduction can be understood by considering hedge statistics.

### 6.1 Covered Calls

Consider the individual who owns 100 shares of a PBR stock at 15.84. The long position has a delta of +100. Suppose the investor now writes a NOV 17 call contract against this entire position. These options have a delta of 0.475. This covered call position has a position delta of $(100 \times +1.0) - (100 \times 0.475) = +52.5$. A position delta of 52.5 is equivalent (for small changes) to owning 52.5 shares of the underlying asset. An investor can lose more money on a 100-share position than on a 52.5-share position. Even if the stock declines to nearly zero, the loss is reduced only by the amount of the option premium received. Viewed this way, the covered call position is less risky than the underlying asset held alone. The lower position delta will work against the investor if the share price increases. A PBR share price above 17 would result in the shares getting called away, and portfolio gains per share are limited to $2.60 = (X - S_0) + c_0 = (17 - 15.84) + 1.44$.

### 6.2 Protective Puts

Similar logic applies to the use of protective puts. An investor who buys a put is essentially buying insurance on the stock. An investor owning PBR stock could purchase a NOV 15 put with an option delta of –0.359. The position delta from 100 shares of PBR stock and one NOV 15 put contract would be $+100 + (-0.359 \times 100) = +64.1$ For small changes in price, the protective put portfolio reduces the risk of the 100-share PBR position to the equivalent of a 64.1 share position. This insurance lasts only until NOV. One buys insurance to protect against a risk, and the policyholder should not feel bad if the risk event does not materialize and he does not get to use the insurance. Stated another way, a homeowner should be happy if the fire insurance on his house goes unused. Still, we do not want to buy insurance we do not need, especially if it is expensive. Continually purchasing puts to protect against a possible stock price decline will result in lower volatility in the overall portfolio, but the trade-off between premium cost and risk reduction must be carefully considered. Such continuous purchasing of puts to protect against a possible stock price decline is an expensive strategy that

---

16 The two strategies are very similar due to put–call parity. Recall that P = C – S + PV of X, implying that –P ≈ –C + S (ignoring PV of X), thus showing that a short put payoff profile is similar to that of a covered call.

would wipe out most of the long-term gain on an otherwise good investment. The occasional purchase of a protective put to manage a temporary situation, however, can be a sensible risk-reducing activity.

## 6.3 Buying Calls and Writing Puts on a Short Position

The discussion on protective puts (Stock + Put) and covered calls (Stock − Call) describes risk-reduction strategies for investors with long positions in the underlying asset. How can investors reduce risk when they are short the underlying asset? The short investor is worried the underlying stock will go up and profits if the underlying stock goes down. To offset the risks of a short position, an investor may purchase a call. The new portfolio will be (Call − Stock). The long call will offset portfolio losses when the share price increases.

To generate income from option premiums, the investor may also sell a put. As the stock drops in value, the investor profits from the short stock position, but the portfolio (− Put − Stock) gains will be reduced by the short put. When the share price increases, the short position loses money. The put expires worthless, meaning the investor will keep the put premium. The loss on the short position can still be substantial but is somewhat reduced by the put option premium.

Let us consider these two scenarios using the price data from Exhibit 6. In both cases, the investor is bearish on PBR and shorts the stock at 15.84. In the first case, she purchases the SEP 16 call for 0.97. As the share price increases above 16, the payoff from the call will act to offset losses in the short position. Exhibit 15 illustrates this dynamic. As the share price increases, portfolio losses never exceed 1.13. The profit on the short stock position plus the profit from the in-the-money call equals $(15.84 − S) + [(S − 16) − 0.97] = −1.13$. If the share price decreases, the investor profits from the short but loses the call premium of 0.97. The delta from the short PBR shares is −1. The SEP 16 call delta is 0.516. The overall portfolio delta is still negative at −0.484, making this a bearish strategy. The investor is also long vega from purchasing the call, 0.018, and the position is exposed to time decay, because theta is −0.018 per day. So, she is hoping to profit from increased downside volatility from the short PBR shares while the long call cushions losses from increased upside volatility.

**Exhibit 15. P&L of Long PBR SEP 16 Call and Short PBR Stock**

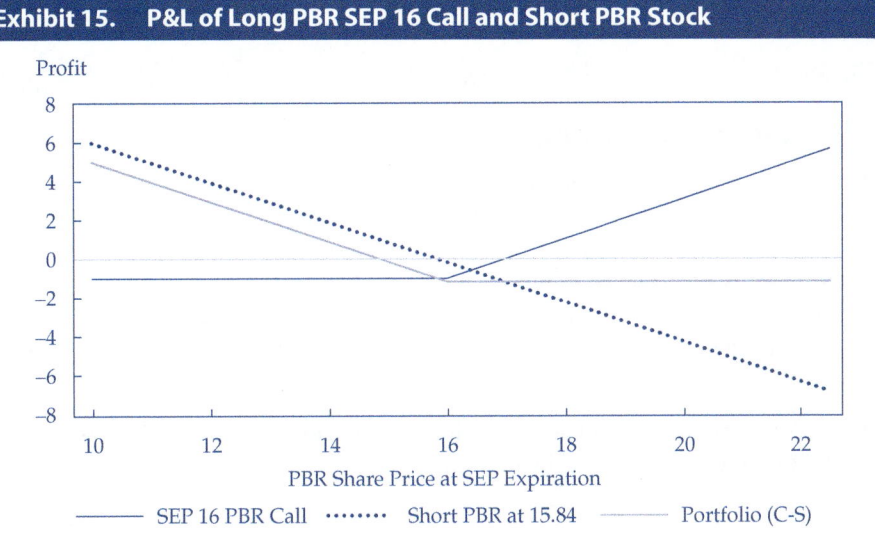

In the second scenario, the investor writes the SEP 15 put for 0.65 and collects the put premium. The upside protection from the long call in the first scenario is not provided by writing a put. The short stock position can have potentially unlimited losses. As shown in Exhibit 16, the potential gain from a falling PBR price now belongs to the put owner. The maximum gain from this strategy is given by the profit on the short stock position plus the profit from the out-of-the-money short put, which equals $(15.84 - S) - [(15 - S) - 0.65] = 1.49$. Losses from the short stock position will be cushioned only by the 0.65 premium collected from writing the put. The delta of the short PBR shares is −1, and the delta of the short put is − (−0.335), so the position delta is −1 + 0.335 = −0.665. The investor is bearish and hoping to profit from a downward price move. She is also short vega from writing the put, (−0.017), and benefits from time decay, as theta of the short put is +0.015 (= − [−0.015]). So, she is hoping for reduced volatility to give her an opportunity to collect the put premium without losing from the short on PBR shares.

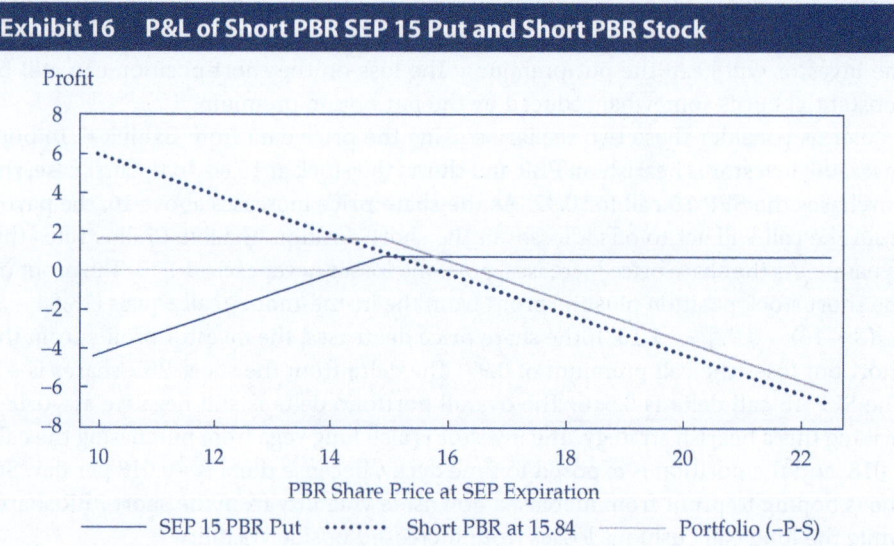

Exhibit 16  P&L of Short PBR SEP 15 Put and Short PBR Stock

### EXAMPLE 5

### Risk-Reduction Strategies

Janet Reiter is a US-based investor who holds a limited partnership investment in a French private equity firm. She has received notice from the firm's general partner of an upcoming capital call. Reiter plans to purchase €1,000,000 in three months to meet the capital call due at that time. The current exchange rate is US$1.20/€1, but Reiter is concerned the euro will strengthen against the US dollar. She considers the following instruments to reduce the risk of the planned purchase:

- A three-month USD/EUR call option (to buy euros) with a strike rate $X$ = US$1.25/€1 and costing US$0.02/€1

- A three-month EUR/USD put option (to sell dollars) with a strike rate $X = $ €0.8080/US\$1 priced at €0.0134/US\$1
- A three-month USD/EUR futures contract (to buy euros) with $f_0 = $ US\$1.2052/€1

1 Discuss the position required in each instrument to reduce the risk of the planned purchase.

2 Reiter purchases call options for US\$20,000, and the exchange rate increases to US\$1.29/€1 (EUR currency strengthens) over the next three months. The effective price Reiter pays for her 1,000,000 EUR purchase is closest to:

   A  US\$1,270,000.
   B  US\$1,290,000.
   C  US\$1,310,000.

3 Calculate the price Reiter will pay for the EUR using the three instruments if the exchange rate in three months falls to US\$1.10/€1 (EUR currency weakens).

### Solution to 1:

Reiter could purchase a €1,000,000 call option struck at US\$1.25/€1 for US\$20,000. If the EUR price were to increase above US\$1.25, she would exercise her right to buy EUR for US\$1.25. She would also benefit from being able to purchase EUR at a cheaper price should the exchange rate weaken. A call on the euro is like a put on the US dollar. So, a put to sell dollars struck at an exchange rate of $X = $ €0.8000/US\$1 can be viewed as a call to buy Euro at an exchange rate of US\$1/€0.8000 = US\$1.25/€1. Reiter could also buy a put option on USD struck at $X = $ €0.8080/US\$1 which would allow her to sell US\$1,237,624 (= €1,000,000/[€0.8080/\$1]) to receive the €1,000,000 should the dollar weaken below that level. This would cost her €0.0134/US\$1 × US\$1,237,624 = €16,584 or US\$19,901 upfront. If USD appreciated against the EUR, Reiter would still be able to benefit from the lower cost to purchase the EUR. She could instead enter a long position in a three-month futures contract at US\$1.2052. Reiter would have the obligation to purchase €1,000,000 at US\$1.2052 regardless of the exchange rate in three months. The futures position requires a margin deposit, but no premium is paid.

### Solution to 2:

A is correct. At an exchange rate of US\$1.29/€1, the call with strike of $X = $ US\$1.25/€1 will be exercised. Including the call premium (US\$0.02/€1), the price effectively paid for the euros is US\$1.27/€1 × €1,000,000 = US\$1,270,000.

### Solution to 3:

Both the call and the put options will expire unexercised and Reiter benefits from the lower rate by purchasing €1,000,000 for US\$1,100,000. However, she will lose the premiums she paid for the options. For the futures contract, she pays US\$1.2052/€1 or US\$1,205,200 for €1,000,000 regardless of the more favorable rate.

## 7 SPREADS AND COMBINATIONS

**f** discuss the investment objective(s), structure, payoffs, risk(s), value at expiration, profit, maximum profit, maximum loss, and breakeven underlying price at expiration of the following option strategies: bull spread, bear spread, straddle, and collar;

Option spreads and combinations can be useful option strategies. We first consider money spreads, in which the two options differ only by exercise price. The investor buys an option with a given expiration and exercise price and sells an option with the same expiration but a different exercise price. Of course, the options are on the same underlying asset. The term *spread* is used here because the payoff is based on the difference, or spread, between option exercise prices. For a bull or bear spread, the investor buys one call and writes another call option with a different exercise price, or the investor buys one put and writes another put with a different exercise price.[17] Someone might, for instance, buy a NOV 16 call and simultaneously write a NOV 17 call, or one might buy a SEP 17 put and write a SEP 15 put. An option combination typically uses both puts and calls. The most important option combination is the straddle, on which we focus in this reading. We will investigate spreads first.

### 7.1 Bull Spreads and Bear Spreads

Spreads are classified in two ways: by market sentiment and by the direction of the initial cash flows. A spread that becomes more valuable when the price of the underlying asset rises is a **bull spread**; a spread that becomes more valuable when the price of the underlying asset declines is a **bear spread**. Because the investor buys one option and sells another, there is typically an initial net cash outflow or inflow. If establishing the spread requires a cash payment by the investor, it is referred to as a debit spread. Debit spreads are effectively long because the long option value exceeds the short option value. If the spread initially results in a cash inflow to the investor, it is referred to as a credit spread. Credit spreads[18] are effectively short because the short option value exceeds the long option value. Any of these strategies can be created with puts or calls. The motivation for a spread is usually to place a directional bet, giving up part of the profit potential in exchange for a lower cost of the position. Some examples will help make this clear.

#### 7.1.1 Bull Spread

Regardless of whether someone constructs a bull spread with puts or with calls, the strategy requires buying one option and writing another with a *higher* exercise price. Because the higher exercise price call is less expensive than the lower strike, a call bull spread involves an initial cash outflow (debit spread). A bull spread created from puts also requires the investor to write the higher-strike option and buy the lower-strike one. Because the higher-strike put is more expensive, a put bull spread involves an initial cash inflow (credit spread).

Let's consider a call bull spread. Suppose, for instance, an investor thought it likely that by the September option expiration, PBR would rise to around 17 from its current level of 15.84. Based on the price data in Exhibit 6, what option strategy would capitalize on this anticipated price movement? If he were to buy the SEP 15

---

[17] One important exception to the typical option spread is a *butterfly spread*, which is essentially two simultaneous spreads and can be done using only calls or only puts.
[18] The use of the term credit spread has a different interpretation than in fixed income investing. For bond investors, the credit spread is a measure of compensation for the bond's default risk.

## Spreads and Combinations

call for 1.64 and the stock rose to 17 at expiration, the call would be worth $S_T - X = 17 - 15 = 2$. If the price of the option was 1.64, the profit is 0.36. The maximum loss is the price paid for the option, or 1.64. If, instead, an investor bought the SEP 16 call for 0.97, at an expiration stock price of 17, the call would be worth 1.00 for a gain of 0.03. A spread could make more sense with the following option values. If he believes the stock will not rise above 17 by September expiration, it may make sense to "sell off" the part of the return distribution above that price. The investor would receive 0.51 for each SEP 17 call sold.

The value of the spread at expiration ($V_T$) depends on the stock price at expiration $S_T$. For a bull spread, the investor buys the low strike option (struck at $X_L$) and sells the high strike option (struck at $X_H$), so that:

$$V_T = \text{Max}(0, S_T - X_L) - \text{Max}(0, S_T - X_H). \tag{5}$$

Therefore, the value depends on the terminal stock price $S_T$:

$V_T = 0 - 0 = 0$ if $S_T \le X_L$
$V_T = S_T - X_L - 0 = S_T - X_L$ if $X_L < S_T < X_H$
$V_T = S_T - X_L - (S_T - X_H) = X_H - X_L$ if $S_T \ge X_H$

The profit is obtained by subtracting the initial outlay for the spread from the foregoing value of the spread at expiration. To determine the initial outlay, recall that a call option with a lower exercise price will be more expensive than a call option with a higher exercise price. Because we are buying the call with the lower exercise price (for $c_L$) and selling the call with the higher exercise price (for $c_H$), the call we buy will cost more than the call we sell ($c_L > c_H$). Hence, the spread will require a net outlay of funds. This net outlay is the initial value of the position, $V_0 = c_L - c_H$, which we call the net premium. The profit is:

$$\Pi = \text{Max}(0, S_T - X_L) - \text{Max}(0, S_T - X_H) - (c_L - c_H). \tag{6}$$

In this manner, we see that the profit is the profit from the long call, $\text{Max}(0, S_T - X_L) - c_L$, plus the profit from the short call, $-\text{Max}(0, S_T - X_H) + c_H$. Broken down into ranges, the profit is as follows:

$\Pi = -c_L + c_H$ if $S_T \le X_L$
$\Pi = S_T - X_L - c_L + c_H$ if $X_L < S_T < X_H$
$\Pi = X_H - X_L - c_L + c_H$ if $S_T \ge X_H$

If $S_T$ is below $X_L$, the strategy will lose a limited amount of money. When both options expire out of the money, the investor loses the net premium, $c_L - c_H$. The profit on the upside, if $S_T$ is at least $X_H$, is also limited to the difference in strike prices minus the net premium.

Consider two alternatives for the call purchase leg of the bull spread: 1) buy the SEP 15 call or 2) buy the SEP 16 call instead. Which is preferred? With Alternative 1, the SEP 15 call costs 1.64. Writing the SEP 17 call brings in 0.51, so the net cost is 1.64 − 0.51 = 1.13. Traders would refer to this position as a PBR SEP 15/17 bull call spread. The maximum profit would occur at or above the exercise price of 17 because all gains above this level belong to the owner of the PBR SEP 17 call. At an underlying price of 17 or higher, from the trader's perspective, the position is worth 2, which represents the price appreciation from 15 to 17 (i.e., the difference in strikes). The maximum profit is

$$\Pi = X_H - X_L - c_L + c_H = 17 - 15 - 1.64 + 0.51 = 0.87.$$

Another way to look at it is that at a price above 17, the trader exercises the long call, buying the stock at 15, and is forced to sell the stock at 17 to the holder of his short call.

With Alternative 2, the investor buys the SEP 16 call and pays 0.97 for it. Writing the SEP 17 call brings in 0.51, so the net cost would be 0.97 – 0.51 = 0.46. At an underlying price of 17 or higher, the spread would be worth 1.00, so the maximum profit is

$$\Pi = X_H - X_L - c_L + c_H = 17 - 16 - 0.97 + 0.51 = 0.54.$$

Exhibit 17 compares the profit and loss diagrams for these two alternatives.

To determine the breakeven price with a spread, find the underlying asset price that will cause the exercise value of the two options combined to equal the initial cost of the spread. A spread has two exercise prices. There are also two option premiums. Mathematically, the breakeven price for a call bull spread can be derived from $\Pi = S_T^* - X_L - c_L + c_H = 0$ and is

$$S_T^* = X_L + c_L - c_H,$$

which represents the lower exercise price plus the cost of the spread. In the examples here, Alternative 1 costs 1.13 (= 1.64 – 0.51). The breakeven $S_T^* = X_L + c_L - c_H = 15 + 1.64 - 0.51 = 16.13$. If at option expiration the stock is 16.13, the 15-strike option would be worth 1.13 and the 17-strike call would be worthless. The breakeven price $S_T^*$ is 15.00 + 1.13 = 16.13, as Exhibit 17 shows.

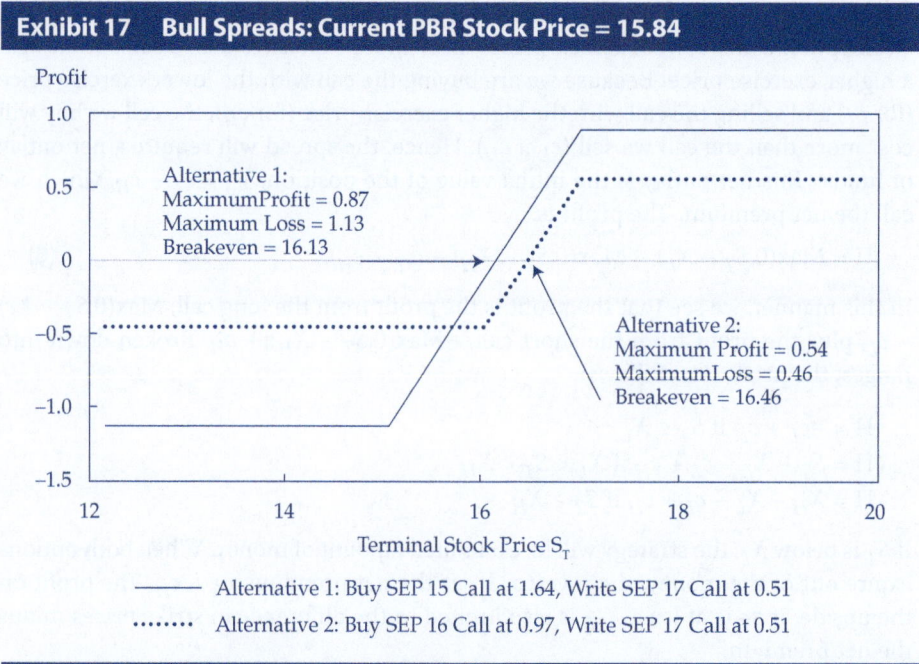

Which of the alternatives is preferable? There is no clear-cut answer. As Exhibit 17 shows, the maximum loss for alternative 1 is 1.64 – 0.51 = 1.13, compared with a maximum loss of 0.97 – 0.51 = 0.46 for Alternative 2. However, Alternative 1 is potentially more profitable for a move above 17 and has a lower breakeven price.

With Alternative 1, the breakeven point of 16.13 is less than 2% above the current level of 15.84, whereas with Alternative 2, reaching the breakeven point requires almost a 4% rise in the stock price. There is some additional information in Exhibit 6 the investor may wish to consider. The SEP 15/17 spread involves buying the SEP15 call with implied volatility of 64.42% and selling the SEP 17 call option with implied volatility of 51.07%. The investor may believe the SEP 15 call being purchased is relatively expensive compared with the SEP 17 call being sold. The PBR SEP 16/17 involves buying a SEP 16 call at a cost of 0.97 with an implied volatility of 55.92%. The investor may believe the SEP 16 call represents a better value than the SEP 15 call and so may choose the PBR SEP 16/17 spread.

# Spreads and Combinations

We can calculate the Greek values for the spread. For example, using Exhibit 6, we see the theta of the PBR SEP 15/17 spread is –0.004 = –0.019 – (–0.015), and the theta of the PBR SEP 16/17 is –0.003 = –0.018 – (–0.015). Therefore, the SEP 16/17 should experience slightly less erosion of value resulting from time decay. The investor may also consider the delta and gamma that each spread would add to her PBR position. The delta of the PBR SEP 15/17 spread is +0.306 = 0.657 – 0.351, and the delta of the PBR SEP 16/17 spread is +0.165 = 0.516 – 0.351. From the current PBR price of 15.84, the long position in the PBR 15 call will make the SEP 15/17 PBR spread slightly more sensitive to an increase in share price than the SEP 16/17 spread. For the SEP 15/17, we have gamma = –0.034 = 0.125 – 0.159 and for the SEP 16/17 gamma = –0.003 = 0.156 – 0.159. The more negative gamma value for the SEP 15/17 spread means that the position delta will decrease at a faster rate than the SEP 16/17 spread as the price of PBR shares increase. By carefully selecting the expiration and exercise prices for the options for the spread, an investor can choose the risk–return mix that most closely matches her investment outlook.

### 7.1.2 Bear Spread

With a bull spread, the investor buys the lower exercise price and writes the higher exercise price. It is the opposite with a bear spread: buy the higher exercise price and sell the lower. Because puts with higher exercise prices are (all else equal) more expensive, a put bear spread will result in an initial cash outflow (be a debit spread). For a call bear spread, the investor buys a higher exercise price call and sells the lower exercise price call. Because the higher exercise price call being purchased is less expensive than the lower strike being sold, a call bear spread will result in an initial cash inflow (credit spread).

If a trader believed PBR stock would be below 15 by the November expiration, one strategy would be to buy the PBR NOV 16 put at 1.96 and write the NOV 15 put at 1.46. This spread has a net cost of 0.50; this amount is the maximum loss, and it occurs at a PBR stock price of 16 or higher. The maximum gain is also 0.50, which occurs at a stock price of 15 or lower. (A useful way to see this result is to realize that reversing the signs of the trades leaves the horizontal axes in a diagram like Exhibit 17 intact, but it flips the profit/loss and cost lines vertically! A debit from buying a spread must be consistent with the seller of the same spread receiving a credit.) Finding the breakeven price uses the same logic as with a bull spread: find the underlying asset price at which the exercise value equals the initial cost. Let $p_L$ represent the lower-strike put premium and $p_H$ the higher-strike put premium. Mathematically, the value of this bear spread position at expiration is:

$$V_T = \text{Max}(0, X_H - S_T) - \text{Max}(0, X_L - S_T). \tag{7}$$

Broken down into ranges, we have the following relations:

$V_T = X_H - S_T - (X_L - S_T) = X_H - X_L$ if $S_T \leq X_L$
$V_T = X_H - S_T - 0 = X_H - S_T$ if $X_L < S_T < X_H$
$V_T = 0 - 0 = 0$ if $S_T \geq X_H$

To obtain the profit, we subtract the initial outlay. Because we are buying the put with the higher exercise price and selling the put with the lower exercise price, the put we are buying is more expensive than the put we are selling. The initial value of the bear spread is $V_0 = p_H - p_L$. The profit is, therefore, $V_T - V_0$, which is:

$$\Pi = \text{Max}(0, X_H - S_T) - \text{Max}(0, X_L - S_T) - (p_H - p_L). \tag{8}$$

We see that the profit is that on the long put, $\text{Max}(0, X_H - S_T) - p_H$, plus the profit from the short put, $-\text{Max}(0, X_L - S_T) + p_L$. Broken down into ranges, the profit is as follows:

$\Pi = X_H - X_L - p_H + p_L$ if $S_T \leq X_L$
$\Pi = X_H - S_T - p_H + p_L$ if $X_L < S_T < X_H$
$\Pi = -p_H + p_L$ if $S_T \geq X_H$

The breakeven point, $S_T^* = X_H - p_H + p_L$, sets the profit equal to zero between the strike prices. In this example, $16 - 1.96 + 1.46 = 15.50$. That is, at a stock price of 15.50 on the expiration day, the 16-strike put would be worth 0.50 and the 15-strike put would be worthless. Exhibit 18 shows the profit and loss for a NOV 15/16 bear spread.[19]

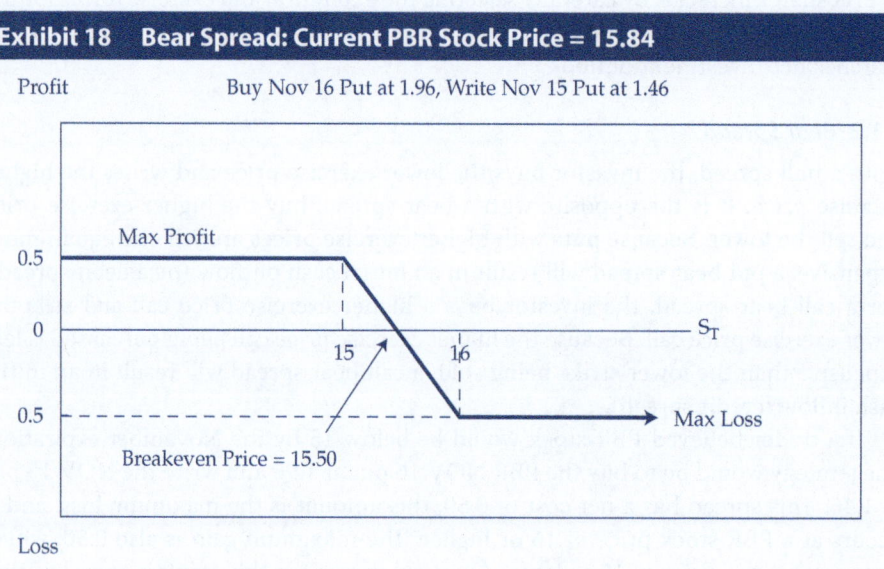

### 7.1.3 Refining Spreads

It is not necessary that both legs of a spread be established at the same time or maintained for the same period. Options are very versatile, and positions can typically be quickly adjusted as market conditions change. Here are a few examples of different tactical adjustments an option trader might consider.

#### 7.1.3.1 Adding a Short Leg to a Long Position
Consider Carlos Aguila, a trader who in September paid a premium of 1.50 for a NOV 40 call when the underlying stock was selling for 37. A month later, in October, the stock has risen to 48. He observes the following premiums for one-month call options.

---

[19] Bull spreads can also be created with puts, and bear spreads can also be created with calls. In both cases, the result is a credit spread with an initial cash inflow. Recall that American exercise–style options may be exercised at any time prior to expiration. Bull spreads with American puts have an additional risk, which is that the short put could be exercised early when the long put is not yet in the money. If the bull spread uses American calls and the short call is exercised, the long call is deeper in the money, which offsets that risk. A similar point can be applied to bear spreads using calls. Bear spreads with American calls have increased risk, because the short call may be exercised early when the long call may not yet be in the money. Thus, with American options, bull spreads with calls and bear spreads with puts are generally preferred but, of course, not required.

# Spreads and Combinations

| Strike | Premium |
|---|---|
| 40 | 8.30 |
| 45 | 4.42 |
| 50 | 1.91 |

This position has become very profitable. The call he bought is now worth 8.30. He paid 1.50, so his profit at this point is 8.30 − 1.50 = 6.80. He thinks the stock is likely to stabilize around its new level and doubts that it will go much higher. Aguila is considering writing a call option with an exercise price of either 45 or 50, thereby converting his long call position into a bull spread. Looking first at the NOV 50 call, he notes that the 1.91 premium would more than cover the initial cost of the NOV 40 call. If he were to write this call, the new profit and loss diagram would look like Exhibit 19. To review, consider the following points:

- At stock prices of 50 or higher, the exercise value of the spread is 10.00. The reason is because both options would be in the money, and a call with an exercise price of 40 would always be worth 10 more at exercise than a call with an exercise price of 50. The initial cost of the call with an exercise price of 40 was 1.50, and there would be a 1.91 cash inflow after writing the call with an exercise price of 50. The profit is 10.00 − 1.50 + 1.91 = 10.41.

- At stock prices of 40 or lower, the exercise value of the spread is zero; both options would be out of the money. The initial cost of the call with an exercise price of 40 was 1.50, and there would be a 1.91 cash inflow after writing the call with an exercise price of 50. The profit is 0 − 1.50 + 1.91 = 0.41.

- Between the two strike prices (40 and 50), the exercise value of the spread rises steadily as the stock price increases. For every unit increase up to the higher strike price, the exercise value of this spread increases by 1.0.

For instance, if the stock price remains unchanged at 48, the exercise value of the spread is 8.00. The reason is because the call with an exercise price of 40 would be worth 8.00 and the call with an exercise price of 50 would be worthless. The initial cost of the 40-strike call was 1.50, and there would be a 1.91 cash inflow when the 50-strike call was written. The profit is 8.00 − 1.50 + 1.91 = 8.41.

Now assume that he has written the NOV 50 call. Aguila needs to be careful how he views this new situation. No matter what happens to the stock price between now and expiration, the position is profitable, relative to his purchase price of the calls with an exercise price of 40. If the stock were to fall by any amount from its current level, however, he would have an opportunity loss. His profit would decrease progressively if the price trended back to 40. Aguila would be correct in saying that the bull spread will make a profit of at least 0.41. But, writing the NOV 50 call only partially hedges against a decline in the value of his new strategy. The position can still lose about 96% of its maximum profit, because only about 4% (0.41/10.41) has been hedged.

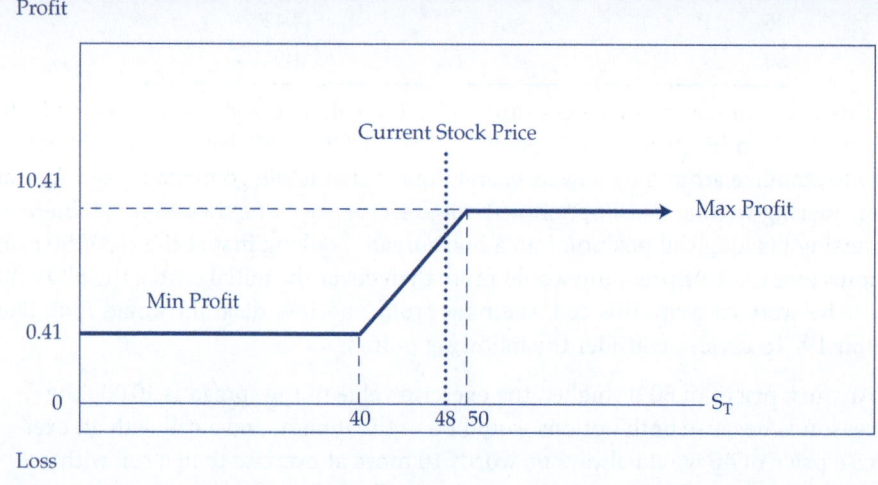

Exhibit 19  Spread Creation: Buy a Call with Exercise Price of 40 at 1.50; Write a Call Later with Exercise Price of 50 at 1.91

#### 7.1.3.2 Spreads and Delta
A spread strategy may be adapted to a changing market view. Suppose the market has been rising, and Lars Clive, an options trader, expects this trend to continue. Hypothetical company ZKQ currently sells for $44. Suppose Clive buys a NOV 45 call for 5.25. He computes the delta of this call as +0.55 and gamma as +0.028. Initially, Clive will profit at a rate of 0.55 for an increase of $1 in the price of ZKQ stock. For small changes, the delta of his position will increase at a rate of 0.028 for an increase of $1 in the price of ZKQ shares.

Three days later, the stock price has risen to $49, the value of the NOV 45 call has increased to 8.18, and the call delta has increased to +0.68. For the NOV 45 call, the option price increased by 2.93 (= 8.18 − 5.25) instead of by 2.75 (= 5 × 0.55, the stock price change multiplied by the initial delta value). Because delta is changing at a rate gamma, the approximation works best for small changes in share prices. With the stock at $49, a higher-strike NOV 50 call sells for 5.74 and has a delta of +0.55. Now Clive establishes a 45/50 bull call spread by writing the NOV 50 call. Clive is less bullish at the price of 49, and his 45/50 spread portfolio now has a delta of +0.13 = +0.68 − 0.55.

Now suppose another five days pass and the stock price falls to 45. The new option values would be 5.41 for the NOV 45 call and 3.55 for the NOV 50 call. Clive closes out the NOV 50 short call by buying it back. He sold the call for 5.74 and bought it back for 3.55, so he makes 5.74 − 3.55 = 2.19, or 2.19 per contract. He still holds the long position in the NOV 45 call, and his portfolio delta increases to +0.57.

Another four days pass, and ZKQ has risen to 48. The new price for the NOV 50 call is 4.71 with a delta of 0.51. Clive owns the NOV 45 with a price of 7.10 and a delta of 0.66. He then decides to write a NOV 50 call and lower his position delta to 0.15 (= 0.66 − 0.51).

At this point, Clive has had two cash outflows totaling 8.80: the initial 5.25 plus the 3.55 to buy back the NOV 50 call. He has two cash inflows totaling 10.45: the premium income of 5.74 and then 4.71 from the two instances of writing the NOV 50 calls. Exhibit 20 provides a summary of the results of Clive's trades. Because the inflows of 10.45 exceed the outflows of 8.80, he has a resulting profit and loss diagram similar to the plot in Exhibit 19 that we saw in the previous example. Clive's timing was excellent—in each case, he increased his portfolio delta prior to an increase in ZKQ stock and decreased delta before the share price decreased. The important point is that increasing portfolio delta will result in greater profits (losses) when the underlying asset value increases (decreases).

# Spreads and Combinations

### Exhibit 20  Spreads and Deltas: A Summary of Results of Clive's Trades

| Day | ZKQ Price | Activity | Portfolio Delta | Cash Out | Cash In |
|---|---|---|---|---|---|
| 1 | 44 | Buy NOV 45 call | 0.55 | 5.25 | — |
| 4 | 49 | Sell NOV 50 call | 0.13 (= 0.68 − 0.55) | — | 5.74 |
| 9 | 45 | Buy NOV 50 call | 0.57 | 3.55 | — |
| 13 | 48 | Sell NOV 50 call | 0.15 (= 0.66 − 0.51) | — | 4.71 |
| Total | | | | 8.80 | 10.45 |
| Net Inflow | | | | | 1.65 |

Spreads are primarily a directional play on the underlying asset's spot price (and also potentially on its volatility); still, spread traders can attempt to take advantage of changes in price, and it is easy to create a hypothetical example like this one. There obviously is no guarantee that any assumed price trend will continue. In fact, in actual practice, the excellent results shown in Exhibit 20 are exceedingly difficult to achieve. Still, the experienced option user knows to look for opportunistic plays that arise from price swings.

### EXAMPLE 6

## Spreads

Use the following information to answer questions 1 to 3 on spreads.

$S_0 = 44.50$

OCT 45 call = 2.55, OCT 45 put = 2.92

OCT 50 call = 1.45, OCT 50 put = 6.80

1 What is the maximum gain with an OCT 45/50 bull call spread?
   A  1.10
   B  3.05
   C  3.90

2 What is the maximum loss with an OCT 45/50 bear put spread?
   A  1.12
   B  3.88
   C  4.38

3 What is the breakeven price with an OCT 45/50 bull call spread?
   A  46.10
   B  47.50
   C  48.88

### Solution to 1:

C is correct. With a bull spread, the maximum gain occurs at the high exercise price. At an underlying price of 50 or higher, the spread is worth the difference in the strike prices, or 50 − 45 = 5. The cost of establishing the spread is the price paid for the lower-strike option minus the price received for the higher-strike option: 2.55 − 1.45 = 1.10. The maximum gain is 5.00 − 1.10 = 3.90.

> **Solution to 2:**
>
> B is correct. With a bear spread, an investor buys the higher exercise price and writes the lower exercise price. When this strategy is done with puts, the higher exercise price option costs more than the lower exercise price option. Thus, the investor has a debit spread with an initial cash outlay, which is the most he can lose. The initial cash outlay is the cost of the OCT 50 put minus the premium received from writing the OCT 45 put: 6.80 − 2.92 = 3.88.
>
> **Solution to 3:**
>
> A is correct. An investor buys the OCT 45 call for 2.55 and sells the OCT 50 call for 1.45, for a net cost of 1.10. She breaks even when the position is worth the price she paid. The long call is worth 1.10 at a stock price of 46.10, and the OCT 50 call will expire out of the money and thus be worthless. The breakeven price is the lower exercise price of 45 plus the 1.10 cost of the spread, or 46.10.

## 8. STRADDLE

**f** discuss the investment objective(s), structure, payoffs, risk(s), value at expiration, profit, maximum profit, maximum loss, and breakeven underlying price at expiration of the following option strategies: bull spread, bear spread, straddle, and collar;

**g** describe uses of calendar spreads;

A long **straddle** is an option combination in which one buys *both* puts and calls, with the same exercise price and same expiration date, on the same underlying asset.[20] If someone *writes* both options, it is a short straddle. Because a long call is bullish and a long put is bearish, this strategy may seem illogical. When the Greeks are considered, the trader's position becomes clearer. The classic example is in anticipation of some event in which the outcome is uncertain but likely to significantly affect the price of the underlying asset, regardless of how the event is resolved.

A straddle is an example of a directional play on the underlying volatility, expressing the view that volatility will either increase, for a long straddle, or decrease, for a short straddle, from its current level. A profitable outcome from a long straddle, however, usually requires a significant price movement in the underlying asset. The straddle buyer pays the premium for two options, so to make a profit, the underlying asset must move either above or below the option exercise price by at least the total amount spent on the straddle. As an example, suppose in the next few days there is a verdict expected in a liability lawsuit against an automobile manufacturer. An investor expects the stock to move sharply one way or the other once the verdict is revealed. When the exercise price is chosen close to the current stock price, the straddle is neither a bullish nor a bearish strategy—the delta of the straddle is close to zero. With any other exercise price, there may be a directional bias (non-zero delta) because one of the options will be in the money and one will be out of the money. If the price increases (decreases) significantly, the delta of the call will approach +1 (0), and the put delta will approach 0 (−1), making the delta of the position approximately +1 (−1).

Experienced option traders know that it is difficult to make money with a straddle. In the example, other people will also be watching the court proceedings. The market consensus will predict higher volatility once the verdict is announced, and option

---
[20] If someone buys puts and calls with different exercise prices, the position is called a *strangle*.

# Straddle

prices rise when volatility expectations rise. This increased volatility means that both the puts and the calls become expensive well before the verdict is revealed, and the long straddle requires the purchase of both options. To make money, the straddle buyer must be correct in his view that the "true" underlying volatility is higher than the market consensus. Essentially, the bet is that the straddle buyer is right and the other market participants, on average, are wrong by underestimating volatility.

Suppose the underlying stock sells for 50, and an investor selects 30-day options with an exercise price of 50. The call sells for 2.29 and the put for 2.28, for a total investment of 4.57. At prices above 50, the call is in the money. At prices below 50, the put is in the money. For the straddle to be profitable, one of these two options must be profitable enough to pay for the costs of both the put and call. To recover this cost, the underlying asset must either rise or fall by at least 4.57, as shown by the breakeven points in Exhibit 21.

**Exhibit 21  Long Straddle: Current Stock Price = 50; Buy 50-Strike Call at 2.29, Buy 50-Strike Put at 2.28**

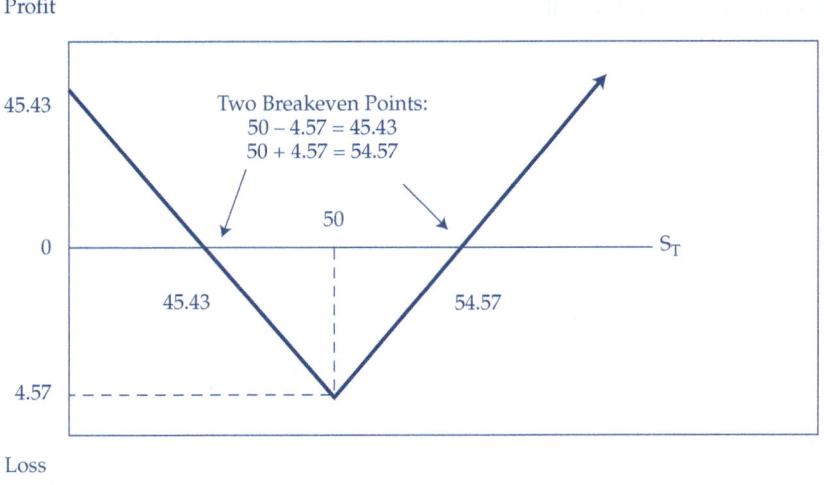

The straddle portfolio and Greeks are shown in Exhibit 22. The long straddle initially has a very low delta (+0.069 for this example) with a high gamma (0.139). The trader does not initially favor an increase or a decrease in the share price but knows the delta may quickly change. Once a direction (increase or decrease in the underlying price) asserts itself, the trader's position will take on a non-zero delta value. The trader's view can be better understood from a vega perspective. The long straddle will be profitable only if the stock price moves enough to recover both premiums. The short straddle writer collects the put and call premiums but will lose if the stock price moves more than 4.57 away from the strike price. The long (short) straddle trade is said to be long (short) volatility. The long straddle is a bet that increased volatility will move the stock price strongly above or below the strike price. The sensitivity of the straddle to changes in volatility is measured by vega. As shown in Exhibit 22, vega for our long straddle is +0.114, meaning the portfolio will profit by approximately 0.114 from increased volatility of 1% in the underlying. A stock price change large enough to cause the price of one option to exceed the cost of the combined premiums is needed to make the straddle trade profitable. A large increase in the underlying price will cause the delta of the call option to approach +1 and the delta of the put to approach 0. A large decrease in the underlying price will cause the delta of the call to drop to 0 and the put delta to approach −1.

### Exhibit 22  Long and Short Straddle Greeks

| | Call | Put | Long Straddle = Call + Put | Short Straddle = −Call + −Put |
|---|---|---|---|---|
| Cost | 2.29 | 2.28 | 4.570 | −4.570 |
| Delta | 0.534 | −0.465 | 0.069 | −0.069 |
| Gamma | 0.072 | 0.067 | 0.139 | −0.139 |
| Vega | 0.057 | 0.057 | 0.114 | −0.114 |
| Theta | −0.039 | −0.036 | −0.075 | 0.075 |
| Implied Volatility | 38% | 41% | — | — |

Theoretically, the stock can rise to any level, so the maximum profit with the long call is unlimited. If the stock declines, it can fall to no lower than zero. If that happens, the long put would be worth 50. Subtracting the 4.57 cost of the straddle gives a maximum profit of 45.43 from a stock drop. The value of a straddle at expiration is the combined value of the call and the put:

$$V_T = \text{Max}(0, S_T - X) + \text{Max}(0, X - S_T). \tag{9}$$

Broken down into ranges,

$$V_T = X - S_T \text{ if } S_T < X, \text{ and}$$
$$V_T = S_T - X \text{ if } S_T > X.$$

The profit is $V_T - V_0$, or $\Pi = \text{Max}(0, S_T - X) + \text{Max}(0, X - S_T) - c_0 - p_0.$ (10)

Broken down into ranges,

$$\Pi = X - S_T - c_0 - p_0 \text{ if } S_T < X, \text{ and}$$
$$\Pi = S_T - X - c_0 - p_0 \text{ if } S_T > X.$$

As can be seen in Exhibit 21, the straddle has two breakeven points. The lower breakeven for the straddle is $S_{TL}^* = X - c_0 - p_0$, and the upper breakeven is $S_{TH}^* = X + c_0 + p_0$.

For the straddle buyer, the worst outcome is if the stock closes exactly at 50, meaning both the put and the call would expire worthless. At any other price, one of the options will have a positive exercise value. Note that at expiration, the straddle is not profitable if the stock price is in the range 45.43 to 54.57. The long straddle shown in Exhibit 21 requires more than a 9% price move in one month to be profitable. A trader who believed such a move was unlikely might be inclined to *write* the straddle, in which case the profit and loss diagram in Exhibit 21 is reversed, with a maximum gain of 4.57 and a theoretically unlimited loss if prices rise. The risk of a long straddle is limited to the amount paid for the two option positions. The straddle can also be understood in terms of theta. As shown in Exhibit 22, theta of the long straddle is −0.075. All else equal, the long put and call positions will lose their time value as expiration approaches. The long straddle buyer is betting on a large price move in the underlying prior to expiration. If the stock price does not change significantly, the short straddle, which has a positive theta, will benefit from the erosion of time value of the short put and call positions.

## 8.1 Collars

A **collar** is an option position in which the investor is long shares of stock and then buys a put with an exercise price below the current stock price and writes a call with an exercise price above the current stock price.[21] Collars allow a shareholder to acquire downside protection through a protective put but reduce the cash outlay by writing a covered call. By carefully selecting the options, an investor can often offset most of the put premium paid by the call premium received. Using a collar, the profit and loss on the equity position is limited by the option positions.

For equity investors, the collar typically entails ownership of the underlying asset and the purchase of a put, which is financed with the sale of a call. In a typical investment or corporate finance setting, an interest rate collar may be used to hedge interest rate risk on floating-rate assets or liabilities. For example, a philanthropic foundation funds the grants it makes from income generated by its investment portfolio of floating-rate securities. The foundation's chief investment officer (CIO) wants to hedge interest rate risk (the risk of rates falling on its floating securities) by buying an interest rate floor (a portfolio of interest rate puts) and paying for it by writing a cap (a portfolio of interest rate calls). Should the rates on the portfolio fall, the long floor will provide a lower limit for the income generated by the portfolio. To finance the floor purchase, the foundation sells a cap. The cap will limit the income generated from the floating rate portfolio in the event the floating rate rises. The CIO is still holding a floating-rate securities portfolio but has restricted the returns using the collar. By setting both a minimum and a maximum portfolio return, the CIO may be better able to plan funding requests.

### 8.1.1 Collars on an Existing Holding

A zero-cost collar involves the purchase of a put and sale of a call with the same premium. In Exhibit 6, for instance, the NOV 15 put costs 1.46 and the NOV 17 call is 1.44, very nearly the same. A collar written in the over-the-counter market can be easily structured to provide a precise offset of the put premium with the call premium.[22]

The value of the collar at expiration is the sum of the value of the underlying asset, the value of the long put (struck at $X_1$), and the value of the short call (struck at $X_2$):

$$V_T = S_T + \text{Max}(0, X_1 - S_T) - \text{Max}(0, S_T - X_2), \text{ where } X_2 > X_1. \quad (11)$$

The profit is the profit on the underlying share plus the profit on the long put and the short call so that:

$$\Pi = S_T + \text{Max}(0, X_1 - S_T) - \text{Max}(0, S_T - X_2) - S_0 - p_0 + c_0. \quad (12)$$

Broken down into ranges, the total profit on the portfolio is as follows:

$$\Pi = X_1 - S_0 - p_0 + c_0 \text{ if } S_T \leq X_1$$
$$\Pi = S_T - S_0 - p_0 + c_0 \text{ if } X_1 < S_T < X_2$$
$$\Pi = X_2 - S_0 - p_0 + c_0 \text{ if } S_T \geq X_2$$

---

[21] A collar is also called a *fence* or a *hedge wrapper*.
[22] Most collars are structured so that the call and put premiums completely offset each other. If the investor starts with the put at a specific exercise price, he then sells a call that has the same premium. There is one specific call with the same premium, and it has a particular exercise price, which is above the exercise price of the put. An algorithm can be used to search for the exercise price on the call that has the same premium as that of the put, which is then the call that the investor should sell. Most collars are structured and transacted in the over-the-counter market because the exercise price on the call must be a specific one. Exchange-traded options have standardized exercise prices, whereas the exercise prices of over-the-counter options can be set at whatever the investor wants.

Consider the risk–return trade-off for a shareholder who previously bought PBR stock at 12 and now buys the NOV 15 put for 1.46 and simultaneously writes the NOV 17 covered call for 1.44. Exhibit 23 shows a profit and loss worksheet for the three positions. Exhibit 24 shows the profit and loss diagram.

**Exhibit 23  Collar P&L: Stock Purchased at 12, NOV 15 Put Purchased at 1.46, NOV 17 Call Written at 1.44**

| Stock price at expiration | 5 | 10 | 15 | 16 | 17 | 20 |
|---|---|---|---|---|---|---|
| Profit/loss from long stock | −7.00 | −2.00 | 3.00 | 4.00 | 5.00 | 8.00 |
| Profit/loss from long 15 put | 8.54 | 3.54 | −1.46 | −1.46 | −1.46 | −1.46 |
| Profit/loss from short 17 call | 1.44 | 1.44 | 1.44 | 1.44 | 1.44 | −1.56 |
| Total | 2.98 | 2.98 | 2.98 | 3.98 | 4.98 | 4.98 |

At or below the put exercise price of 15, the collar realizes a profit of $X_1 - S_0 - p_0 + c_0 = 15 - 12 - 1.46 + 1.44 = 2.98$. At or above the call exercise price of 17, the profit is constant at $X_2 - S_0 - p_0 + c_0 = 17 - 12 - 1.46 + 1.44 = 4.98$.

In this example, because the stock price had appreciated before establishing the collar, the position has a minimum gain of at least 2.98 as shown in Exhibit 24. Investors typically establish a collar on a position that is already outstanding.

**Exhibit 24  Collar P&L Diagram: Stock Purchased at 12, NOV 15 Put Purchased at 1.46, NOV 17 Call Written at 1.44**

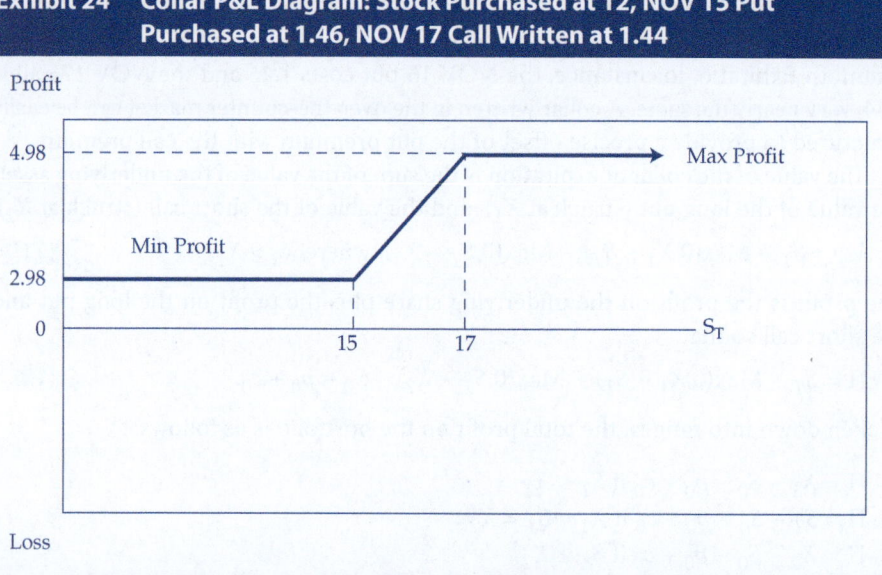

### 8.1.2 The Risk of a Collar

We have already discussed the risks of covered calls and protective puts. The collar is essentially the simultaneous holding of both of these positions. See Exhibit 25 for the return distribution of a collar. A collar sacrifices the positive part of the return distribution in exchange for the removal of the adverse portion. With the short call option, the option writer sold the right side of the return distribution, which includes the most desirable outcomes. With the long put, the investor is protected against the left side of the distribution and the associated losses. The option premium paid for the put is largely and, often precisely, offset by the option premium received from writing the call. The collar dramatically narrows the distribution of possible investment outcomes, which is risk reducing. In exchange for the risk reduction, the return potential is limited.

The risks of the collar can be understood in terms of the Greeks from Exhibit 6. For example, with a long share the delta of the portfolio = +1. With a collar, the portfolio delta is equal to the delta of the share plus the delta of the long NOV 15 put (−0.359) and short NOV 17 call (−0.475), so the portfolio delta = +1 + (−0.359) + (−0.475) = +0.166. Portfolio gamma, which equals put gamma minus call gamma, will be close to zero, −0.011 (= 0.075 − 0.086). By writing a call and buying a put, the investor reduces the portfolio's delta at a price of 15.84 from +1 to +0.166 and the gamma is very close to zero. If the stock price moves outside the range depicted in Exhibit 25, the delta of the position will approach zero over time. If the share price moves above 17, the NOV 17 call approaches a delta of +1, and the put will approach a delta of 0. The collar is short the call, so above 17 the portfolio delta (long stock with delta = +1 plus a short call with delta = −1) will approach zero. At prices below 15, the NOV 17 call will have a delta approaching 0, but the long put approaches a delta of −1, so the portfolio delta will again approach zero (long stock with delta = +1 plus the long put with delta = −1). The portfolio's sensitivity to changes in the stock price will be limited, as shown in Exhibit 25.

**Exhibit 25    Collars and Return Distribution: Stock at 15.84, Write NOV 17 Call and Buy NOV 15 Put**

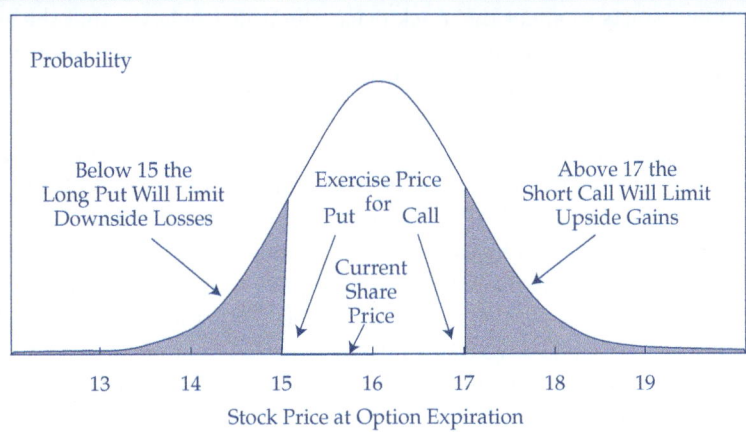

As the chosen put and call exercise prices move successively farther in opposite directions from the current price, the combined collar position begins to replicate the underlying gain/loss pattern of a long position in the underlying security. Conversely, as the chosen strike prices approach and meet each other, the expected returns and volatility become less and less equity-like and eventually converge on those of a risk-free, fixed income return to the time horizon. Thus, a collar position is, economically, intermediate between pure equity and fixed-income exposure.

### 8.1.3 The Risk of Spreads

Note that the shape of the profit and loss diagram for the bull spread in Exhibit 17 is similar to that of the collar in Exhibit 24. The upside return potential is limited, but so is the maximum loss. As with the risk–return tradeoff with the collar, an option spread takes the tails of the distribution out of play and leaves only price uncertainty between the option exercise prices. Looking at this scenario another way, if someone were to simply buy a long call, the maximum gain would be unlimited and the maximum loss would be the option premium paid. If someone decides to convert this to a spread, doing so limits the maximum gain while simultaneously reducing the total cost.

## 8.2 Calendar Spread

A strategy in which one sells an option and buys the same type of option but with different expiration dates, on the same underlying asset and with the same strike, is commonly referred to as a **calendar spread**. When the investor buys the more distant call and sells the near-term call, it is a long calendar spread. The investor could also buy a near-term call and sell a longer-dated one, known as a short calendar spread. Calendar spreads can also be done with puts; the investor would still buy a long-maturity put and sell a near-term put with the same strike and underlying to create a long calendar spread. As discussed previously, a portion of the option premium is time value. Time value decays over time and approaches zero as the option expiration date nears. Taking advantage of this time decay is a primary motivation behind a calendar spread. Time decay is more pronounced for a short-term option than for one with a long time until expiration. A calendar spread trade seeks to exploit this characteristic by purchasing a longer-term option and writing a shorter-term option.

Here is an example of how someone might use a calendar spread. Suppose XYZ stock is trading at 45 a share in August. XYZ has a new product to be introduced to the public early the following year. A trader believes this new product introduction will have a positive effect on the share price. Until the excitement associated with this announcement starts to affect the stock price, the trader believes that the stock will languish around the current level. See the option prices, deltas and thetas in Exhibit 26. Based on the bullish outlook for the stock going into January, the trader purchases the XYZ JAN 45 call with a theta (indicator of daily price erosion) of −0.014 for a price of 3.81. Noting that the near-term price forecast is neutral, the trader also decides to sell the XYZ SEP 45 call for 1.55. The theta for the XYZ SEP 45 Call is −0.029. The position costs 2.26 (= 3.81 − 1.55) to create and has an initial theta of +0.015 (= −0.014 − (−0.029)). If the stock price of XYZ remains constant over the next 30 days, the XYZ SEP 45 call will lose time value more rapidly than the JAN 45 call. The delta of calendar spread equals the delta of the JAN 45 call less the delta of the SEP 45 call and will be very low (Delta = +0.041 = 0.572 − 0.531).

Now move forward to the September expiration and assume that XYZ is trading at 45. The September option will now expire with no value, which is a good outcome for the calendar spread trader. The value of the position (now just the XYZ JAN 45 call) is 3.48, a gain of 1.22 over the position cost of 2.26. If the trader still believes that XYZ will stay around 45 into October before starting to move higher, the trader may continue to execute this strategy. An XYZ OCT 45 call might be sold for 1.55 with the hope that it also expires with no value.

**Exhibit 26  Calendar Spread Call Option Prices, Deltas, and Thetas**

*150 days until January option expiration. Underlying stock price = 45*

| Exercise Price | SEP | OCT | JAN |
| --- | --- | --- | --- |
| 40 | 5.15 | 5.47 | 6.63 |
| 45 | 1.55 | 2.19 | 3.81 |
| 50 | 0.22 | 0.62 | 1.99 |

## Straddle

**Exhibit 26  (Continued)**

|  | Delta | | |
|---|---|---|---|
| 40 | 0.975 | 0.902 | 0.800 |
| 45 | 0.531 | 0.545 | 0.572 |
| 50 | 0.121 | 0.217 | 0.363 |

|  | Theta (daily) | | |
|---|---|---|---|
| 40 | −0.007 | −0.011 | −0.011 |
| 45 | −0.029 | −0.020 | −0.014 |
| 50 | −0.014 | −0.014 | −0.013 |

*Just before September option expiration. Underlying stock price = 45*

| Exercise Price | SEP | OCT | JAN |
|---|---|---|---|
| 40 | 5.00 | 5.15 | 6.39 |
| 45 | 0 | 1.55 | 3.48 |
| 50 | 0 | 0.22 | 1.69 |

In this example, the calendar spread trader has a directional opinion on the stock but does not believe that the price movement is imminent. Rather, the trader sees an opportunity to capture time value in one or more shorter-lived options that are expected to expire worthless.

A short calendar spread is created by purchasing the near-term option and selling a longer-dated option. Thetas for in-the-money calls may provide motivation for a short calendar spread. Assume a trader purchases the XYZ SEP 40 call with a theta of −0.007 for a price of 5.15. The trader sells the OCT 40 call with a theta of −0.011 for 5.47 to offset the cost of the SEP 40 call. The position nets the trader a cash inflow of 0.32 (= 5.47 − 5.15), and the initial position theta is slightly positive −0.007 − (−0.011) = +0.004.

If the stock price of XYZ remains at 45 (above the strike of 40) at the SEP expiration, the XYZ OCT 40 call will lose time value more rapidly than the SEP 40 call. The trader may close the position at the SEP expiration and make a profit of 0.17 = 0.32 + (5 − 5.15). Note that the profit consists of the 0.32 initial inflow plus the net cost of selling the SEP 40 call (at 5.00) and buying the OCT 40 call (at 5.15). In the event of a larger move, the position values will vary. For a large down move, for example an extreme case in which XYZ loses all of its value (so $S = 0$ at expiration), the long and the short call positions will be approximately worthless and the profit on the spread will be around 0.32 (= 0.32 + [0 − 0])). For a smaller down move to the strike price ($S = 40$ at expiration), the short calendar spread may result in a loss. If the XYZ stock price were to fall to 40 at the SEP expiration, the long position in the SEP 40 call would expire worthless but the OCT 40 call would still have a BSM model value of about 1.00 (not shown in Exhibit 26). This scenario would result in a loss of 0.68 = 0.32 + (0 − 1) to close the position. The writer of a calendar spread would typically be looking for a large move away from the strike price in either direction.

In sum, a big move in the underlying market or a decrease in implied volatility will help a short calendar spread, whereas a stable market or an increase in implied volatility will help a long calendar spread. Thus, calendar spreads are sensitive to movement of the underlying but also sensitive to changes in implied volatility.

# 9. IMPLIED VOLATILITY AND VOLATILITY SKEW

**h** discuss volatility skew and smile;

An important factor in the current price of an option is the outlook for the future volatility of the underlying asset's returns, the **implied volatility**. Implied volatility is not observable per se, but it is derived from an option pricing model—such as the Black–Scholes–Merton (BSM) model—and it is value that equates the model price of an option to its market price. Note that all other input variables to the BSM model, including the option's strike price, the price of the underlying, the time to option expiration, and the risk-free interest rate, are observable. Implied volatilities incorporate investors' expectations about the future course of financial asset returns and the level of market uncertainty associated with them.

Implied volatilities for options on a specific asset may differ with strike price (i.e., moneyness), side (i.e., put or call), and time to expiration. In particular, out-of-the-money (OTM) puts typically command higher implied volatilities than ATM or OTM calls. This phenomenon is attributed to investors' reassessments of the probabilities of negative "fat-tailed" market events such as the 2007–2009 global financial crisis.

Implied volatility is often compared with **realized volatility** (i.e., historical volatility), which is the square root of the realized variance of returns and measures the range of past returns for the underlying asset. To calculate the historical volatility for the given option, stock, or equity index, a series of past prices is needed. For example, to calculate the volatility of the S&P 500 Index over the past month (i.e., 21 trading days), it is necessary to first calculate the daily percentage change for each day's index closing price. This is done using the following formula, where $P_t$ is the closing price and $P_{t-1}$ is the prior day's closing price: $(P_t - P_{t-1})/P_{t-1}$. The next step is to apply the standard deviation formula you learned in Level I Quantitative Methods to the daily percentage change data to calculate the standard deviation (i.e., volatility) of the S&P 500 for the selected period, which in this case is the past month.

The standard deviation over the past month is then annualized by multiplying by the square root of the number of periods in a year. Because we assume the average number of trading days in a year and in a month are 252 and 21 (excluding weekends and holidays), respectively, the formula is:

$$\sigma_{Annual}(\%) = \sigma_{Monthly}(\%) \sqrt{\frac{252}{21}} \tag{13}$$

Note that this example uses one month of daily return data, but the process is equally applicable to any other period.

Obviously, we cannot use the previous formula for realized volatility, which is based on past prices, to obtain implied volatility, which is the expected volatility of future returns of the underlying asset. Instead, the one-month annualized implied volatility can be derived from the current price of an option maturing in one month by using the BSM model. Once the one-month annualized implied volatility is obtained, it can then be converted into an estimate of the volatility expected on the underlying asset over the 21-day life of the option. This expected monthly volatility is given by the one-month annualized implied volatility divided by the square root of the number of 21-day periods in a 252-day trading year, as follows:

$$\sigma_{Monthly}(\%) = \sigma_{Annual}(\%) \Big/ \sqrt{\frac{252}{21}} \tag{14}$$

## Implied Volatility and Volatility Skew

When option prices are compared within or across asset classes or relative to their historical values, they are assessed by their implied volatility. Exhibit 27 shows a comparison of the one-month annualized (ATM) implied volatility at a given point in time for options across three European equity indexes (Euro Stoxx 50, FTSE MIB, and DAX). The DAX shows the lowest implied volatility among the three indexes.

**Exhibit 27   One-Month Annualized Implied Volatility**

| Underlying Index | Implied Volatility | Three-Year Low | Three-Year High |
|---|---|---|---|
| Euro Stoxx 50 | 9.56 | 9.0 | 17.9 |
| FTSE MIB | 14.22 | 11.0 | 21.7 |
| DAX | 9.29 | 7.3 | 13.9 |

Using the one-month annualized implied volatility for DAX index options of 9.29%, the volatility expected to materialize in the DAX index over the next month (21 trading days) can be calculated as follows:

$$\sigma_{Monthly}(\%) = 9.29\% \Big/ \sqrt{\frac{252}{21}} = 2.68\%$$

So, for example, if an investor buys an ATM one-month (21-day) straddle using puts and calls on the DAX, in order for the strategy to be profitable at expiration, the index must move up or down by at least 2.68%. The investor can compare this price movement needed to reach breakeven with the DAX's realized volatility over similar time horizons in the past. If such a price change is considered reasonable, then the investor can elect to implement the strategy.

The implied volatility of ATM options, calculated from the options' market prices using the BSM model, remains the simplest way to measure the prevailing volatility level. The BSM model assumes that volatility is constant, and notably, before the 1987 stock market crash, there was little volatility skew in equity index markets. Today, however, options prices on several asset classes display persistent volatility skew and, in some circumstances, volatility smile. The implied volatilities of options of a given expiration are thus dependent on their strike prices.

Exhibit 28 plots implied volatility (*y*-axis) against strike price (*x*-axis) for options on the same underlying, the FTSE MIB (trading at 19,000), with the same expiration. When the implied volatilities priced into both OTM puts and calls trade at a premium to implied volatilities of ATM options (those with strike price at 19,000), the curve is U-shaped and is called a **volatility smile**, because it resembles the shape of a smile. The more common shape of the implied volatility curve, however, is a **volatility skew**, where the implied volatility increases for OTM puts and decreases for OTM calls, as the strike price moves away from the current price. This shape persists across asset classes and over time because investors have generally less interest in OTM calls whereas OTM put options have found universal demand as portfolio insurance against a market sell-off.

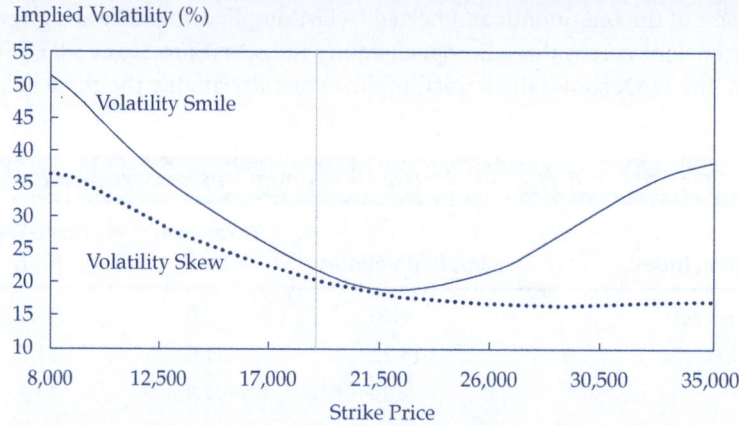

**Exhibit 28  Implied Volatility Curves for Three-Month Options on FTSE MIB**

The extent of the skew depends on several factors, including investor sentiment and the relative supply/demand for puts and calls, among others. Several theoretical models try to use these factors to forecast skew variation. However, these models do not lead to unique predictions. In general, we can say that when the implied volatility is significantly higher (relative to historical levels) for puts with strike prices below the underlying asset's price, it means that there is an imbalance in the supply and demand for options. In fact, when investors are looking to hedge the underlying asset, the demand for put options exceeds that for call options. Option traders, who meet this excess demand by selling puts, increase the relative price of these options, thereby raising the implied volatility. A sharp increase in the level of the skew, accompanied with a surge in the absolute level of implied volatility, is an indicator that market sentiment is turning bearish. In contrast, higher implied volatilities (relative to historical levels) for calls with strike prices above the underlying asset's price indicate that investors are bullish and the demand for OTM calls to take on upside exposure is strong.

To better understand how to measure the volatility skew, consider Exhibit 29, which shows the levels of implied volatility at different degrees of moneyness for options expiring in three months on equity indexes where liquid derivatives markets exist. The 90% moneyness option is a put with strike ($X$) equal to 90% of the current underlying price ($S$); thus $X/S = 90\%$. The 110% moneyness of the call is calculated similarly. Also shown is the skew, calculated as the difference between the implied volatilities of the 90% put and the 110% call.

**Exhibit 29  Implied Volatilities and Skew for Three-Month Options**

| | Implied Volatility by Moneyness | | | 90%–110% |
|---|---|---|---|---|
| Index | ATM | Put: 90% | Call: 110% | Volatility Skew |
| Nikkei 225 | 12.9 | 18.9 | 12.4 | 6.5 |
| S&P 500 | 10.3 | 17.7 | 9.4 | 8.3 |
| Euro Stoxx 50 | 12.3 | 17.8 | 9.3 | 8.5 |
| DAX | 14.5 | 20.0 | 11.0 | 9.0 |

## Implied Volatility and Volatility Skew

For most asset classes, the level of option skew varies over time. Exhibit 30 presents the skew on the S&P 500, measured as the difference between the implied volatilities of options with 90% (puts) and 110% (calls) moneyness, and with three months to expiration.

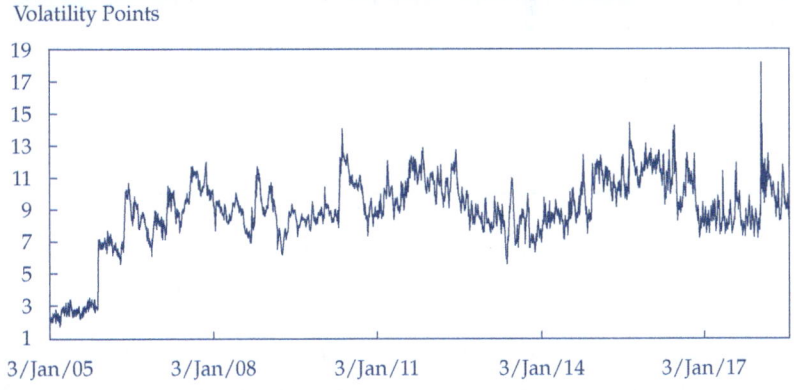

Exhibit 30  90% Put–110% Call Implied Volatility Skew for Three-Month Options on S&P 500

There are trading strategies that attempt to profit from the existence of an implied volatility skew and from changes in its shape over time. A common strategy is to take a long or short position in a **risk reversal**, which is then delta hedged. Using OTM options, a combination of long (short) calls and short (long) puts on the same underlying with the same expiration is a long (short) risk reversal. In particular, when a trader thinks that the put implied volatility is too high relative to the call implied volatility, she creates a long risk reversal, by selling the OTM put and buying the same expiration OTM call. The options position is then delta-hedged by selling the underlying asset. The trader is not aiming to profit from the movement in the overall level in implied volatility. In fact, depending on the strikes of the put and the call, the trade could be vega-neutral. For the trade to be profitable, the trader expects that the call will rise more (or decrease less) in implied volatility terms relative to the put.

Typically, implied volatility is not constant across different maturities, which means that options with the same strike price but with different maturities display different implied volatilities. This determines the **term structure of volatility**, which is often in contango, meaning that the implied volatilities for longer-term options are higher than for near-term ones. When markets are in stress and de-risking sentiment prevails, however, market participants demand short-term options, pushing up their prices and causing the term structure of volatility to invert. Exhibit 31 shows, for options on the S&P 500, a common indicator watched by market participants: the spread between the implied volatilities of 12-month and 3-month ATM options. Values below zero indicate that the term structure is inverted with 3-month options having a higher implied volatility than the 12-month options. In periods when equity markets experience large sell-offs, such as during the 2007–2009 global financial crisis, the term structure of implied volatility typically shows significant inversion. In such periods, the general level of equity volatility and skew also remain high.

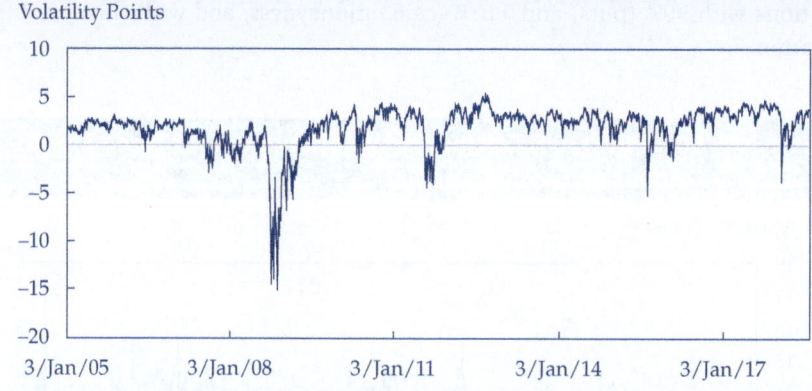

**Exhibit 31  12M–3M Implied Volatility Term Structure of S&P 500 Options**

The **implied volatility surface** can be thought of as a three-dimensional plot, for put and call options on the same underlying asset, of days to expiration (*x*-axis), option strike prices (*y*-axis), and implied volatilities (*z*-axis). It simultaneously shows the volatility skew (smile) and the term structure of implied volatility. Considering that implied volatility varies across different option maturities and displays skew, the implied volatility surface is typically not flat as the BSM model may suggest. By observing the implied volatility surface, one can infer changes in market expectations. Several studies have focused on ways to extract information embedded in option market prices. The skew can provide insight into market participants' perceptions about the price movement of the underlying asset over a specified horizon. The general interpretation is that the shape of the volatility skew reflects varying degrees of market participants' fear about future market stress.

# 10  INVESTMENT OBJECTIVES AND STRATEGY SELECTION

i. identify and evaluate appropriate option strategies consistent with given investment objectives;

## 10.1 The Necessity of Setting an Objective

Every trade is based on an outlook on the market. With stocks and most assets, one thinks about the direction of the market: Is it going up or down, or is it stable? When dealing with options, it is not enough to think about the market *direction*; it is also important to think about the Greeks beyond delta: gamma, theta, and vega. Where option valuation is concerned, what matters is not only the direction in which the asset underlying the derivative contract is headed but also the volatility of the underlying and even other investors' perception of that volatility. The investor's investment objective may not be achieved if one of these factors moves in an undesired direction. Gamma could lead to a faster loss or gain, depending on whether the investor is short or long the option, whereas theta could lead to a loss despite the underlying asset moving in the right direction. Vega could rise or fall if market expectations of implied volatility change, leading to a loss or profit for the options position. Furthermore, the option premium paid (if long) or received (if short) must be considered when calculating a

# Investment Objectives and Strategy Selection

position's total profit and loss at maturity. For example, in a simple call option purchase, the underlying asset must go up enough so that the call option reaches breakeven by overcoming the premium paid for the call.

Moreover, with the introduction of volatility-based derivatives, investors increasingly view these investments as a way to protect their portfolios against downside risk and also as a method to improve their portfolios' efficiency. When considering hedging strategies, it is important to differentiate between situations in which the investor's goal is to benefit from rising volatility (long volatility)—for example, in hedging a long stock position—and situations in which the investor wants to benefit from falling volatility (short volatility)—for example, by writing a short straddle position.

Derivatives are used by portfolio managers, traders, and corporations to adjust their risk exposures, to achieve a specific investment objective, or even to infer market expectations in the short term (for example, inferring market expectations for central banks' interest rate decisions). The main advantage of derivatives is that they allow two parties with differing needs and market views to adjust quickly without having to enter into potentially costly and difficult trades in the underlying. Another advantage of using derivatives instead of investing in the physical underlying securities is leverage. The fact that investors can take on a large exposure to the underlying asset by putting up only a fraction of the amount of risk capital is an important feature of derivatives. Liquidity is another key aspect favoring derivatives usage in many markets—for example, the ability to buy or sell credit protection using index credit derivatives (CDS) instead of trading the actual underlying, and likely less liquid, bonds provides a huge liquidity advantage to traders and investors. In sum, given an actual or anticipated portfolio of equities, bonds, rates, currencies, or other assets; a market outlook and a timeframe; and an understanding of the benefits and limitations of derivatives, it is important to set realistic investment objectives, be they for hedging, for taking direction bets, or for capturing arbitrage opportunities.

## 10.2 Criteria for Identifying Appropriate Option Strategies

Investors use derivatives to achieve a target exposure based on their outlook for the underlying asset. Exhibit 32 shows one way of looking at the interplay of direction and volatility. The strategies identified are most profitable given the expected change in implied volatility and the outlook for the direction of movement of the underlying asset.

**Exhibit 32  Choosing Options Strategies Based on Direction and Volatility of the Underlying Asset**

| | | Outlook on the Trend of Underlying Asset | | |
|---|---|---|---|---|
| | | Bearish | Trading Range/ Neutral View | Bullish |
| Expected Move in Implied Volatility | Decrease | Write calls | Write straddle | Write puts |
| | Remain Unchanged | Write calls and buy puts | Calendar spread | Buy calls and write puts |
| | Increase | Buy puts | Buy straddle | Buy calls |

Consider an investor who is bearish about a market. If he expects that implied volatility will increase as the market sells off, then he will buy a put to protect his investments. If instead he believes that volatilities are expected to fall, writing a call would likely be a profitable strategy. Investors need to keep in mind, however, that the two strategies have two different payoffs and risk management implications. As we have seen previously, a position in which the investor writes the call and buys the put is a collar, and it is often associated with holding a long position in the underlying asset. Investors use collars against a long stock position to hedge risk and smooth volatility. In fact, by selling a covered call while purchasing a protective put, the investor establishes a combined position with fixed downside protection while still providing some opportunity for profits.

Now consider an investor who has a bullish view. Buying calls is an option strategy that will allow the investor to benefit if her outlook is correct and implied volatility increases. When implied volatilities are expected to fall, writing a put represents an alternative strategy to take advantage of a bullish market view with declining volatility. If this happens, the position will likely be profitable, because as the stock rises and implied volatility decreases, the short put moves farther out of the money and its price will decrease. The combined position in which the investor is long calls and short puts (i.e., a long risk reversal) is used to implement a bullish view (the investor buys the calls) while lowering the cost (the investor sells the puts) of the long position in the underlying asset that will be established upon exercising the options.

Investors can also decide to sell puts when they want to buy a stock only if the price declines below a determined target price (the strike price of the puts will be the same as this target price). In this case, by selling the put options when implied volatilities are elevated (and the puts are expensive), the investor can realize an effective stock purchase price that is less than the target (strike) price by the size of the premium received.

The purchase of call or put spreads tends to be most appropriate when the investor has a bullish view (call bull spread) or a bearish view (put bear spread) but the underlying market is not clearly trending upward or downward. Furthermore, such spreads are a way to reduce the total cost, given that the spread is normally constructed by buying one option and writing another. Importantly, if the implied volatility curve is skewed, with the implied volatility of OTM puts relatively higher than for nearer-to-the-money options, the cost of a bearish spread is even lower. This is because in the put bear spread, the lower exercise price, more OTM (but relatively more expensive) put is sold and the higher exercise price, nearer-to-the-money (but relatively less expensive) put is purchased.

Now suppose that the market is expected to trade in range. Again, the investor should consider volatility. Suppose he believes the current consensus estimate of volatility implied in option prices is too low and the rate of the change in underlying prices will increase—that is, vega will increase. If the investor is neutral on market direction, the appropriate strategy will be a long straddle, because this strategy takes advantage of an increase in the long call or long put option prices in response to realization of the expected surge in volatility, vega, and gamma. At expiry, the long straddle will be profitable if the price of the call (put) is greater (less) than the upper (lower) breakeven price. In contrast, an investor who expects the market to trade in range and volatility to fall may want to write the straddle instead.

We now consider a strategy that combines a longer-term bullish/bearish outlook on the underlying asset with a near-term neutral outlook. This approach is the calendar spread (or time spread), a strategy using two options of the same type (puts or calls) and same strike price but with different maturity dates. Typically, a long calendar spread—wherein the shorter-maturity option is sold and the longer-maturity option is purchased—is a long volatility trading strategy because the longer-term option has a higher vega than the shorter-term option. The maximum profit is obtained when the short-term option expires worthless, then implied volatility surges, increasing the price of the remaining long-term option. Although the delta for a calendar spread is approximately zero, gamma is not, so the main risk for the calendar strategy is that the underlying stock price moves too fast and too far from the strike prices. For this reason, the calendar spread is typically implemented in option markets characterized by low implied volatility when the underlying stock is expected to remain in a trading range, but only until the maturity of the short-term option.

# USES OF OPTIONS IN PORTFOLIO MANAGEMENT

## 11

j   demonstrate the use of options to achieve targeted equity risk exposures.

This section uses "mini cases" to illustrate some of the ways in which different market participants use derivative products to solve a problem or to alter a risk exposure. Note that with the wide variety of derivatives available, there are almost always multiple ways in which derivatives might logically be used in a particular situation. These mini cases cover only a few of them.

### 11.1 Covered Call Writing

Carlos Rivera is a portfolio manager in a small asset management firm focusing on high-net-worth clients. In mid-April, he is preparing for an upcoming meeting with Parker, a client whose daughter is about to marry. Parker and her husband have just decided to pay for their daughter's honeymoon and need to raise $30,000 relatively quickly. The client's portfolio is 70% invested in equities and 30% in fixed income and is by policy slightly aggressive. Currently the Parkers are "asset rich and cash poor," having largely depleted their cash reserves prior to the wedding expenses. The recently revised investment policy statement permits most option activity except the writing of naked calls.

Parker's account contains 5,000 shares of Manzana (MNZA) stock, a stock that she is considering selling in the near future. Rivera's firm has a bearish market outlook for MNZA shares over the next six months. Rivera reviews information on the 44-day exchange-listed options, which expire in May (shown in Exhibit 33). He is considering writing MNZA calls, which will accomplish two objectives. First, the sale of calls will generate the required cash for his client. Secondly, the sale will reduce the delta of Parker's account in line with his firm's bearish short-term outlook for MNZA shares. The current delta of Parker's MNZA position is 5,000(+1) or +5,000. Exhibit 33 contains call and put price information for May MNZA options with strike prices close to the current market price of MNZA shares ($S_0$ = $169).

| Exhibit 33 | Manzana Inc. May Options With 44 Days to Expiration, MNZA Stock = $169 | | | | |
|---|---|---|---|---|---|
| Call Premium | Call Delta | Exercise Price | Put Premium | Put Delta | Put or Call Vega |
| 12.55 | 0.721 | 160 | 3.75 | −0.289 | 0.199 |
| 9.10 | 0.620 | 165 | 5.30 | −0.384 | 0.224 |
| 6.45 | 0.504 | 170 | 7.69 | −0.494 | 0.234 |
| 4.03 | 0.381 | 175 | 10.58 | −0.604 | 0.225 |
| 2.50 | 0.271 | 180 | 14.10 | −0.702 | 0.199 |

Discuss the factors that Rivera should consider and the strategy he should recommend to Parker.

*Solution:*

To generate cash, Rivera will want to write options. The account permits the writing of covered calls. Manzana options trade on an organized exchange with a standard contract size of 100 shares per contract. With 5,000 shares in the account, 50 call contracts would be covered.

If Rivera were to write the MAY 180 calls, doing so would not generate the required cash, $2.50 × 100 × 50 = $12,500. Writing the MAY 165 calls would generate more than enough income: $9.10 × 100 × 50 = $45,500. However, the May 165 call is in the money. Although the firm's outlook is bearish for the shares, Rivera feels there is a high likelihood of Parker's MNZA shares being called away at expiration. Writing the May 175 call would generate only $4.03 × 100 × 50 = $20,150. Although Rivera believes the 175 call would not be exercised, the cash generated would be only about two-thirds of the client's projected need. The May 170 call would generate $6.45 × 100 × 50 = $32,250, which looks good from a cash-generation perspective. The current price of MNZA shares is 169, so there is a considerable risk that MNZA shares will sell above that level at expiration. If MNZA stock trades above the strike price at the May expiration, then Parker would be exposed to having her shares called at 170. Given the firm's bearish outlook for MNZA shares and, as stated previously, "Parker is considering selling the stock in the near future," this risk might be acceptable. Using the May 170 call option data from Exhibit 33, the delta of Parker's MNZA position would be reduced from +5,000 to 5,000 × (+1 − 0.504) = +2,480.[23] The profit graph for the recommended sale of 50 May 170 call contracts against Parker's 5,000 share long position at 169 is shown in Exhibit 34.

**Exhibit 34    Profit and Loss for MNZA May 170 Covered Call ($S_0 = 169$, $c_0 = 6.45$)**

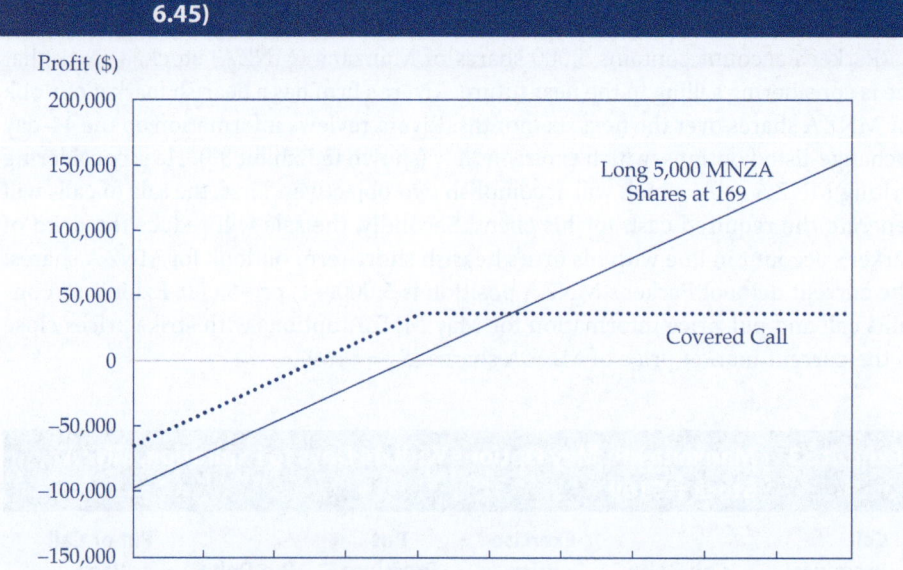

---

[23] Delta for the short calls will approach −1 if the stock price moves strongly above 170 close to maturity. The likelihood of the shares being called away in that scenario would push the position delta to 0 (= +5000 from the shares, −5000 for the short ITM calls).

The $32,250 generated by the call option sales is Parker's to keep. There are two risks, however, that Rivera should point out to Parker using Exhibit 34. The first risk is that his outlook for MNZA shares might be incorrect. The reduced delta may cost his client a potential gain on the long position. If MNZA shares increase above 170, the profits will go to the call owner. Parker's MNZA shares may be called away at 170, limiting her profit to the option premium of $32,250 plus the $5,000 from selling her MNZA shares at a profit of $1 (= $170 − $169) as shown in Exhibit 34.[24] The second risk is that to write the covered call, Parker must continue to hold 5,000 MNZA shares. If the firm's bearish outlook is correct, the shares may drop in value during the next month, resulting in a loss on the long stock position. The loss would be cushioned somewhat by the 6.45 call premium, but a drop of more than 3.8% (below 162.55 = 169 − 6.45; 6.45/169 = 3.8%) results in an overall loss on the position. After Rivera explains the risks to Parker, she elects to write the MNZA 170 calls.

## 11.2 Put Writing

Oscar Quintera is the chief financial officer for Tres Jotas, a private investment firm in Buenos Aires. He wants to purchase 50,000 MNZA shares for the firm, but at the current price he considers MNZA shares to be a bit expensive. The current share price is $169, and Quintera is willing to buy the stock at a price not higher than $165. Quintera decides to write out-of-the-money puts on MNZA shares.

Discuss the outcome of the transaction, a short position in MNZA May 165 puts, assuming two scenarios:

- Scenario A: MNZA is $163 per share on the option expiration day.
- Scenario B: MNZA is $177 per share on the option expiration day.

*Solution:*

Quintera can write OTM puts to effectively "get paid" to buy the stock. He sells puts and the firm keeps the cash regardless of what happens in the future. If the stock is above the exercise price at expiration, the put options will not be exercised. Otherwise, the option is exercised, Quintera purchases the stock and, as desired, Tres Jotas becomes an owner of the stock. Exhibit 33 shows the options information for 44-day MAY put options. Because his target price is 165, Quintera writes 500 May MNZA 165 put contracts and receives premium income of 500 × 100 × $5.30 = $265,000. The company keeps these funds regardless of future stock price movements. But, the firm is obligated to buy stock at $165 if the put holder chooses to exercise. By writing the puts, Quintera has established a bullish position in MNZA stock. The delta of this MNZA position is −500 × 100 × −0.384 = +19,200, the equivalent of a long position in 19,200 MNZA shares. The portfolio profit on the short put is shown in Exhibit 35.

---

[24] Note that if the shares are called away at 170, there may also be tax consequences for Parker.

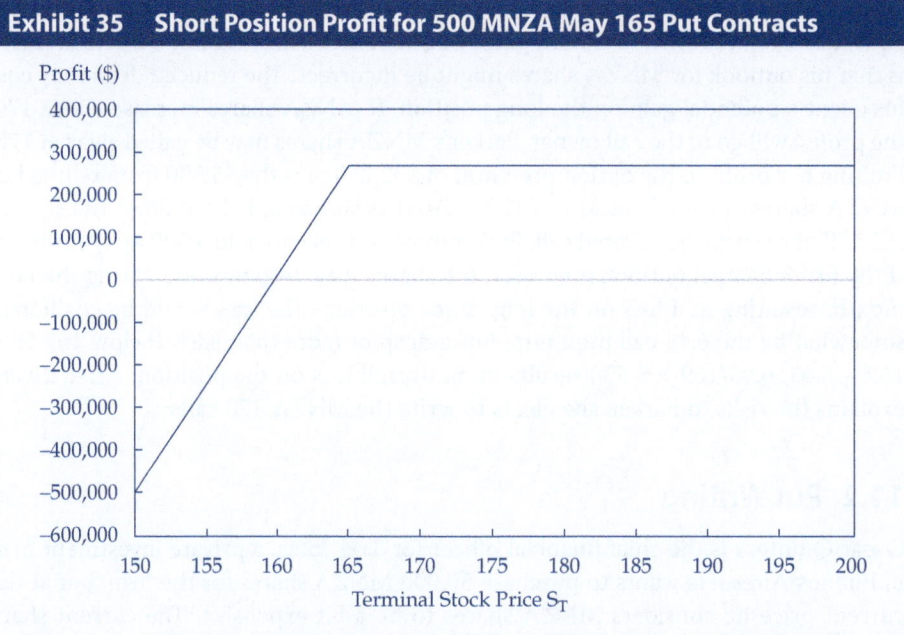

**Exhibit 35    Short Position Profit for 500 MNZA May 165 Put Contracts**

**Scenario A:**   The stock is $163 per share on the option expiration day. With an exercise price of 165, the put is in the money and will be exercised. Quintera will be assigned to buy 50,000 shares at the exercise price of 165. The cost is 50,000 × $165 = $8,250,000. Quintera is satisfied with the outcome, because the firm keeps the premium income of $265,000, so the net cost of purchase is $8,250,000 − $265,000 = $7,985,000. On 50,000 shares, this means the *effective purchase price* is $7,985,000/50,000 = $159.70, which is below the maximum $165 price Quintera was willing to pay. If the price of MNZA shares drops below 165, the effective purchase price will always be $X - p =$ 165 − 5.30 = $159.70. This is the breakeven point for the short put position. At prices below the breakeven amount, Quintera would have been better off not writing the put and just buying MNZA shares outright. For example, if the MNZA price fell to $150, Quintera would have been obligated to buy shares at 165, $15 more than the market price. When the $5.30 premium is considered, the $15 difference would amount to a loss of $9.70 per share or $485,000 which can be seen in Exhibit 35.

**Scenario B:**   The stock price is $177 on the option expiration day. With an exercise price of 165.00, the MNZA puts are out of the money and would not be exercised. Tres Jotas keeps the $265,000 premium received from writing the option. This approach adds to the company's profitability, but Tres Jotas did not acquire the MNZA shares and experienced an opportunity cost relative to an outright purchase of the stock at $169. Any price above 165, will result in earning the premium of $265,000, as can be seen in Exhibit 35.

### 11.3  Long Straddle

Katrina Hamlet has been following Manzana stock for the past year. She anticipates the announcement of a major new product soon, but she is not sure how the critics will react to it. If the new product is praised, she believes the stock price will increase dramatically. If the product does not impress, she believes the share price will fall substantially. Hamlet has been considering trading around the event with a straddle.

## Uses of Options in Portfolio Management

The stock is currently priced at $169.00, and she is focused on close-to-the-money (170) calls and puts selling for 6.45 and 7.69, respectively. Her initial strategy is presented as Exhibit 36.

Hamlet expects that the stock will move at least 10% either way once the product announcement is made, making the straddle strategy potentially appropriate. The vega of her position would be 0.234 + 0.234 = +0.468, meaning a 1% move in the options' volatility would result in a gain of about $0.468 in the value of the straddle. The straddle's delta would be approximately zero, at +0.01 (Call Delta + Put Delta = (0.504 + [−0.494]). This strategy is long volatility. After the market close, Hamlet hears a news story indicating that the product will be unveiled at a trade show in two weeks. The following morning after the market opens, she goes to place her trade and finds that although the stock price remains at $169.00, the option prices have adjusted upward to $10.20 for the call and $10.89 for the put.

Discuss whether the new option premiums have any implications for Hamlet's intended straddle strategy.

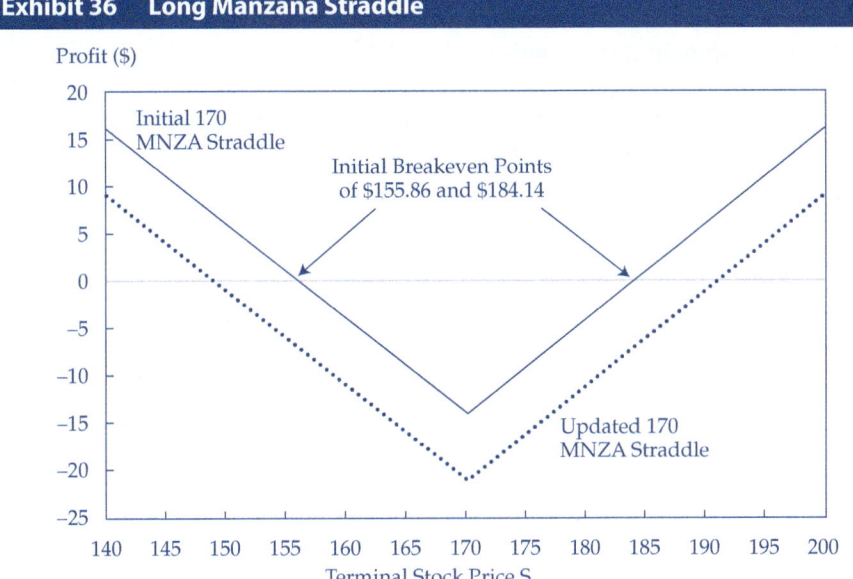

**Exhibit 36   Long Manzana Straddle**

### Solution:

Hamlet is betting on a substantial price movement in the underlying MNZA shares to make money with this trade. That price movement, up or down, must be large enough to recover the two premiums paid. In her earlier planning, that total was $6.45 + $7.69 = $14.14. She expects at least a 10% price movement, which on a stock selling for $169.00 would be an increase of $16.90. This price movement would be sufficient to recover the $14.14 cost of the straddle and make her strategy profitable. The breakeven points were $155.86 and $184.14, as shown in Exhibit 36.

The news report about the imminent product unveiling, however, has increased the implied volatility in the options, from about 30% to about 45%, raising their prices and making it more difficult to achieve the new breakeven points. After the news report, Hamlet finds the MAY 170 call now costs $10.20 and the MAY 170 put is trading for $10.89, so the MAY 170 straddle costs $21.09 ($10.20 + $10.89) to implement. Relating back to the vega she calculated the day before, Hamlet computed an initial vega (pre-announcement) of +0.468 for the straddle. Now she sees the approximate

15 percentage point rise in implied volatility (to 45%) in both the put and call. According to her initial vega calculation, she would expect an increase of 15 × 0.468 = $7.02 in her straddle value after the announcement. The announcement increased the price of the straddle by $6.95 (= 21.09 − 14.14), which is very close to the $7.02 increase predicted by the vega calculation. To reach the new breakeven points (170 ± 21.09), she now needs the stock to move by more than 12%, a larger move than 10% from the current level of 169. Given that Hamlet expects only a 10% price movement, she decides against executing this straddle trade.

> **EXAMPLE 7**
>
> ### Straddle Analytics
>
> Use the following information to answer Questions 1 to 3 on straddles.
>
> XYZ stock price = 100.00
>
> 100-strike call premium = 8.00
>
> 100-strike put premium = 7.50
>
> Options expire in three months
>
> 1. If Yelena Strelnikov, a portfolio manager, buys a straddle on XYZ stock, she is *best* described as expecting a:
>    - A higher volatility market.
>    - B lower volatility market.
>    - C stable volatility market.
> 2. This strategy will break even at expiration stock prices of:
>    - A 92.50 and 108.50.
>    - B 92.00 and 108.00.
>    - C 84.50 and 115.50.
> 3. Reaching an upside breakeven point implies an annualized rate of return on XYZ stock *closest* to:
>    - A 16%.
>    - B 31%.
>    - C 62%.
>
> **Solution to 1:**
>
> A is correct. A straddle is directionally neutral in terms of price; it is neither bullish nor bearish. The straddle buyer wants higher volatility and wants it quickly but does not care in which direction the price of the underlying moves. The worst outcome is for the underlying asset to remain stable.
>
> **Solution to 2:**
>
> C is correct. To break even, the stock price must move enough to recover the cost of both the put and the call. These premiums total to $15.50, so the stock must move up at least to $115.50 or down to $84.50.

> **Solution to 3:**
>
> C is correct. The price change to a breakeven point is 15.50 points, or 15.5% on a 100 stock. This is for three months. Ignoring compounding, this outcome is equivalent to an annualized rate of 62% on XYZ stock, found by multiplying by 12/3 (15.5% × 4 = 62%).

## 11.4 Collar

Bernhard Steinbacher has a client with a holding of 100,000 shares in Tundra Corporation, currently trading for €14 per share. The client has owned the shares for many years and thus has a very low tax basis on this stock. Steinbacher wants to safeguard the position's value because the client does not want to sell the shares. He does not find exchange-traded options on the stock. Steinbacher wants to present a way in which the client could protect the investment portfolio from a decline in Tundra's stock price.

Discuss an option strategy that Steinbacher might recommend to his client.

*Solution:*

In the over-the-counter market, Steinbacher might buy a put and then write an out-of-the money call. This strategy is a collar. The put provides downside protection below the put exercise price, and the call generates income to help offset the cost of the put. The investor decides the strike prices of the put and the call to achieve a specific level of downside protection, while still keeping some benefit from an increase in the stock price. When the strike of the call is set so that the call premium (to be received) exactly offsets the put premium (to be paid), then the position is called a "zero-cost collar." Recalling Exhibit 25 and the underlying return distribution, this strategy effectively sells the right tail of the distribution, which represents potential large gains, in exchange for eliminating the left tail, which represents potential large losses.

## 11.5 Calendar Spread

Ivanka Dubois is a professional advisor to high-net-worth investors. She expects little price movement in the Euro Stoxx 50 in the next three months but has a bearish long-term outlook. The consensus sentiment favoring a flat market shows no signs of changing over the next few months, and the Euro Stoxx 50 is currently trading at 3500. Exhibit 37 shows prices for two put options with strike price of 3500 that are available on the index. Both options have the same implied volatility.

**Exhibit 37  3,500 Strike Put Options on Euro Stoxx 50**

|  | Option A | Option B |
|---|---|---|
| Current Price | €119 | €173 |
| Time to Maturity | 3 months | 6 months |

1. Discuss how can Dubois take advantage of her out-of-consensus view.
2. Analyze four scenarios that Dubois might likely face for the Stoxx 50 index at the expiry of the three-month option (these scenarios are provided at the beginning of the Solution to 2).

*Solution to 1:*

Dubois's view is best implemented with a long position in a calendar spread that combines a longer-term bearish outlook on the underlying asset with a near-term neutral outlook. She is bearish long-term and so would buy a calendar put spread. A long calendar spread is a long volatility trading strategy whereby the maximum profit is obtained when the short-term at the money option expires worthless with the underlying almost unchanged.

Dubois can implement a put calendar spread trade by selling the three-month put option (A) for €119 and buying the six-month same strike put option (B) at the price for €173. Therefore, the cost of establishing this strategy is a net debit of €54 per contract (given by €173 − €119). Remember, Dubois has a bearish long-term outlook. If the put calendar spread is not profitable at the expiry of the three-month put, the short option expires worthless and then she owns the longer-term option free and clear. Thus, Dubois has managed to lower the cost of purchasing a longer-term put option, which could be kept for hedging her portfolio's downside risk.

*Solution to 2:*

If the put calendar spread position is held until the expiry of the three-month put, then Dubois might likely face one of the four following scenarios for the Euro Stoxx 50. In the first three scenarios, the implied volatility is assumed to remain constant:

- Scenario 1: The index is still trading at 3500 as expected.
- Scenario 2: The index has increased and is trading at 4200.
- Scenario 3: The index has decreased and is trading at 3000.
- Scenario 4: The index has decreased and is trading at 3000, but the implied volatility has significantly increased.

**Scenario 1:** The Euro Stoxx 50 is still trading at 3500 as expected. The three-month put option expires worthless, and the original longer-term six-month option, which now has three months remaining to expiration, is worth €119 (because the implied volatility has remained constant). The total cost of the calendar spread was €54, and Dubois can sell the remaining put to a dealer for a profit of €65 (given by €119 − €54). As can be seen in Exhibit 38, which shows the profit and loss diagram for the calendar spread at the time of the expiration of the three-month put, this corresponds to the level of maximum payoff for this strategy.

**Exhibit 38  P&L for 3,500 Strike Calendar Spread at Expiration of Three-Month Put**

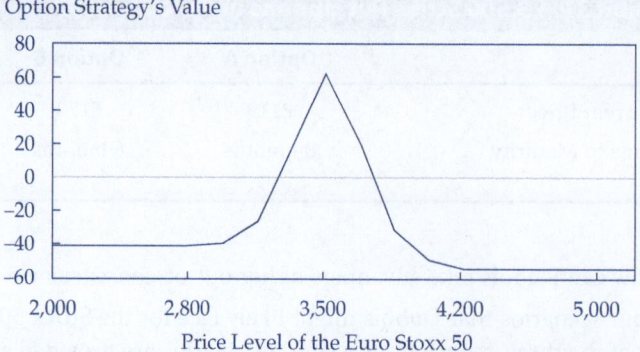

**Scenario 2:** The Euro Stoxx 50 has increased and is trading at 4200. The three-month put option expires worthless. Also, the value of the six-month put is near zero, and if Dubois unwinds her (long) put option position she will lose all €54 (given by €173 – €119), the cost of the put calendar spread.

**Scenario 3:** The Euro Stoxx 50 index has decreased and is trading at 3000. Dubois must pay €500 (€3,500 – €3,000) to settle the (short) three-month put option at expiration. The (long) put option with three months remaining to expiration is deep in the money and, assuming volatility is still unchanged, it is worth €515 (given by Intrinsic Value of €500 + €15 of Time Value). If Dubois sells this put to a dealer, she will lose €39 (= €515 – €500 – €54) on the put calendar spread.

**Scenario 4:** The Euro Stoxx 50 has decreased and is trading at 3000, and the implied volatility has significantly increased. Dubois must pay €500 (€3,500 – €3,000) to settle the (short) three-month put option at expiration. The (long) put option with three months remaining to expiration is deep in the money and, assuming volatility has increased, it is worth €530 (given by Intrinsic Value of €500 + €30 of Time Value). If Dubois sells this put to a dealer, she will realize a loss of €24 (= €530 – €500 – €54) on the put calendar spread. Exhibit 39 adds the profit and loss diagram for the calendar spread at the time of the expiration of the three-month put, assuming that implied volatility of the six-month put has significantly increased.

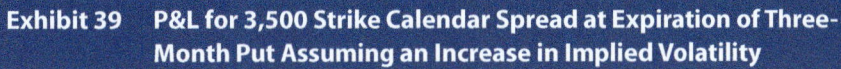

**Exhibit 39  P&L for 3,500 Strike Calendar Spread at Expiration of Three-Month Put Assuming an Increase in Implied Volatility**

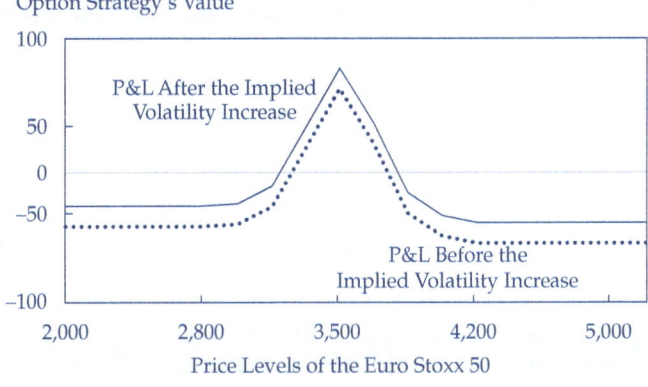

# HEDGING AN EXPECTED INCREASE IN EQUITY MARKET VOLATILITY

**j** demonstrate the use of options to achieve targeted equity risk exposures.

Jack Wu is a fund manager who oversees a stock portfolio valued at US$50 million that is benchmarked to the S&P 500. He expects an imminent significant correction in the US stock market and wants to profit from an anticipated jump in short-term volatility to hedge his portfolio's tail risk.

The VIX Index is currently at 14.87, and the front-month VIX futures trades at 15.60. Wu observes the quotes shown in Exhibit 40 for options on the VIX (these options have same implied volatility). It is important to note that VIX option prices reflect the VIX futures prices. Given that the VIX futures trade at 15.60 while the spot VIX is 14.87, the call is at the money while the put is out of the money by 5.45% (= [14.75 − 15.60]/15.60).

At maturity, the options' payoffs will depend on the settlement price of the relevant VIX futures contracts. The options will expire one month from now, and the contract size is 100.

### Exhibit 40  Options on VIX Index

|  | Call Option | Put Option |
| --- | --- | --- |
| Option Strike | 15.60 | 14.75 |
| Option Price | 2.00 | 1.55 |

Discuss the following:

1 A strategy Wu can implement to hedge tail risk in his equity portfolio, by taking advantage of his expected increase in volatility while lowering his hedging cost
2 Profit and loss on the strategy at options expiration
3 Relevant issues and advantages of this strategy

*Solution to 1:*

Wu decides to purchase the 15.60 call on the VIX and, to partially finance the purchase, he sells an equal number of the 14.75 VIX puts. The total cost of the options strategy is 0.45 (= 2.00 − 1.55) per contract.

*Solution to 2:*

At maturity, the options' payoffs will depend on the settlement price of the relevant VIX futures. Exhibit 41 shows the profit and loss diagram for the option strategy at the time of the options' expiration. In particular, the horizontal axis shows the values corresponding to the relevant VIX futures contracts.

### Exhibit 41  Profit and Loss of the VIX Options Strategy

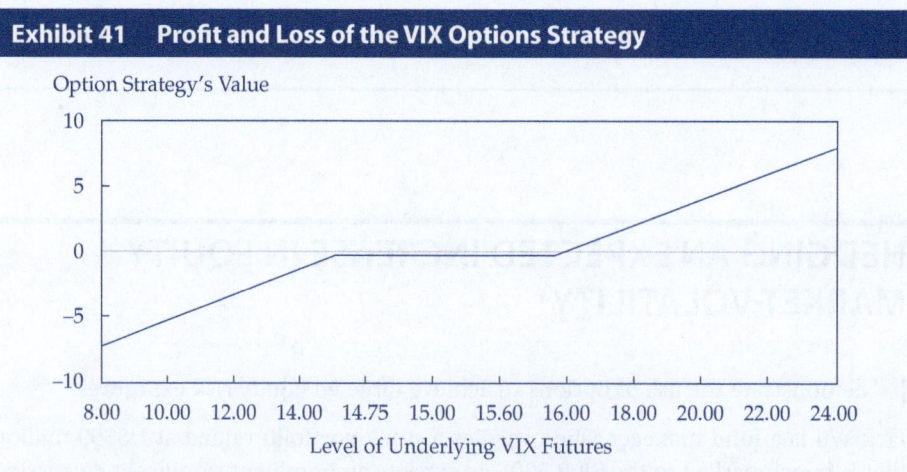

In this case, at the expiry the strategy will be profitable if volatility spikes up (as anticipated) and the VIX futures increase above 16.05. This is calculated as the call strike of 15.60 plus the net cost of the options (15.60 + 0.45). Above this level, the

# Hedging an Expected Increase in Equity Market Volatility

strategy will gain proportionally. In contrast, Wu's option strategy will lose proportionally to its exposure to the short puts if the VIX futures' settlement price is below 14.75 (put strike).

***Solution to 3:***

The hedge ratio that determines the number of calls to buy could be determined based on regression and scenario analysis on the portfolio's profit and loss versus rates of increase in implied volatility during significant stock market sell-offs in the past. Of course, a risk is that past correlations may not be indicative of future correlations. Importantly, the relative advantage of implementing this long volatility hedging strategy by purchasing calls on the VIX over buying VIX futures depends on the difference in leverage available, the difference in payoff profiles (asymmetrical for options and symmetrical for futures), and the shape of the volatility futures term structure, as well as the cost of the options compared with the cost of the index futures.

## 12.1 Establishing or Modifying Equity Risk Exposure

In this section, we examine some examples in which investors use derivatives for establishing an equity risk exposure, for risk management, or for implementing tactical asset allocation decisions. The choice of derivative that will satisfy the investment goal depends on the outlook for the underlying asset, the investment horizon, and expectations for implied volatility over that horizon.

### 12.1.1 Long Call

Armando Sanchez is a private wealth advisor working in London. He expects the shares of Markle Co. Ltd. will move from the current price of £60 a share to £70 a share over the next three months, thanks to an increase of positive news flows regarding the company's new fintech services. He also expects that the implied volatilities of options on Markle's stock will stay almost unchanged over the same period. Prices for three-month call options on the stock are shown in Exhibit 42 (note that each call contract represents one share). For his high-net-worth clients whose investment policy statements allow the use of derivatives, Sanchez plans to recommend that they purchase the call option that, based on the budget they intend to spend for implementing the strategy, would maximize profits if the stock price increases to £70 a share or more over the next three months.

**Exhibit 42  Three-Month Call Options on Markle Co. Ltd.**

|        | Option A | Option B | Option C |
|--------|---------|---------|---------|
| Strike | £58.00  | £60.00  | £70.00  |
| Price  | £4.00   | £3.00   | £0.40   |
| Delta  | 0.6295  | 0.5227  | 0.1184  |
| Gamma  | 0.0304  | 0.0322  | 0.0160  |

Discuss the option strategy that Sanchez should recommend to his clients.

**Solution:** Sanchez has a bullish view because he anticipates a nearly 17% price increase in Markle shares over the next three months, from the current price of £60. He expects that implied volatilities of the options on Markle shares will stay unchanged, making the purchase of options a profitable strategy if his outlook materializes within the given timeframe.

The best strategy would be a long position in the £60 strike calls (option B). The breakeven price of the position is £63 (£60 + £3), so at option expiry, the overall position would profitable at any stock price above £63. In contrast, the breakeven price of the 58-strike call (option A) is £62 (£58 + £4) and for the 70-strike call (option C) the breakeven is £70.40 (£70 + £0.40). Therefore, Sanchez would not use option C to implement his strategy because the breakeven price is above his target price of £70/share.

Given the £60 strike call has a lower price (premium) than the £58 strike call, Sanchez's clients can purchase more of these lower-priced options for a given investment size. Moreover, the 60-strike call offers the largest profit potential per unit of premium paid if the stock price increases to £70 (as expected).

Call strike £58: (£70 − £62)/£4 = 2.0

Call strike £60: (£70 − £63)/£3 = 2.3

Purchasing the £60 strike call (option B) is the most profitable strategy given that Sanchez's expectations are realized. A position in the £60 strike call has a lower delta (= 0.5227) compared with the £58 strike call (delta = 0.6295), so at current prices of the underlying, the change in value of the £60 strike call is lower. If Markle's stock reaches £70 per share during the life of the option, however, the £60 strike call will benefit from having a larger gamma (= 0.0322) compared with the £58 strike call (gamma = 0.0304).

**12.1.2** *Risk Management: Protective Put Position*

Investors use protective puts, collars, and equity swaps against a long stock position to hedge market risk. Here we turn to a practical application of protective puts.

Eliot McLaire manages a Glasgow-based hedge fund that holds 100,000 shares of Relais Corporation, currently trading at €42.00.

**Situation A: Before Relais Corporation's quarterly earnings release:** Relais has a quarterly earnings announcement scheduled in one week. Although McLaire expects an earnings increase, he believes the company will miss the consensus earnings estimate, in which case he expects that the maximum drawdown from the current price of €42.00 would be 10%. He would like to protect the fund's position in the company for several days around the earnings announcement while keeping the cost of the protection to a minimum. Exhibit 43 provides information on options prices for Relais Corporation. Note that each put contract represents one share.

| Exhibit 43 | One-Month Put Options on Relais Corporation | | |
|---|---|---|---|
| | Option A | Option B | Option C |
| Strike | €40.00 | €42.50 | €45.00 |
| Price | €1.45 | €1.72 | €3.46 |
| Delta | −0.4838 | −0.5385 | −0.7762 |
| Gamma | 0.0462 | 0.0460 | 0.0346 |

1 Discuss an options strategy that McLaire can implement to hedge his fund's portfolio against a short-term decline in the share price of Relais Corp.

*Solution to 1:* McLaire can purchase a protective put with the intent of selling it soon after the earnings announcement. He expects that the maximum drawdown from the current price of €42.00 will be 10%, to €37.80. This expectation narrows the choice of put options based on the following breakeven prices:

Put strike 40.0 (option A): €40.00 − €1.45 = €38.55

Put strike 42.5 (option B): €42.50 − €1.72 = €40.78

Put strike 45.0 (option C): €45.00 − €3.46 = €41.54

The put with strike price of 42.50 (option B) best fits the objective of keeping the cost of adequate protection to a minimum. This is because the 40-strike put (option A) offers limited protection because it is profitable only below €38.55, offering a profit of just €0.75 if the stock falls to €37.80. Furthermore, the 42.50-strike put offers a larger profit per unit of premium paid than the 45.00-strike put if the stock price decreases to €37.80.

Put strike 42.5: (€40.78 − €37.80)/€1.72 = 1.73

Put strike 45.0: (€41.54 − €37.80)/€3.46 = 1.08

The 42.50 strike put has a lower delta (= −0.5385) in absolute value terms than the 45.0 strike put (delta = −0.7762), but it has more gamma. If Relais Corporation's stock falls to €37.80 per share during the life of the option, a position in the 42.50 strike put will benefit from having a larger gamma (= 0.0460) compared with the 45.0 strike put (gamma = 0.0346).

Therefore, McLaire purchases 100,000 of the 42.50-strike puts at €1.72 for a total cost of €172,000.

If Relais Corporation's soon-to-be announced earnings miss the market's expectations, the stock is likely to fall, thereby increasing the long put value and partially offsetting the loss on the stock. If the earnings meet market expectations, then the put may be sold at a price near its purchase price. If the earnings are better than expected and the stock price rises, then the put will decline in value. McLaire would no longer need the "insurance," and he would sell the put position, thereby recovering part of the purchase price.

**Situation B: One week later, just after Relais Corporation's earnings release:** McLaire holds the 100,000 puts with the exercise price of €42.50. Seven days have passed since the options' purchase; Relais has just released its earnings, and they turn out to be surprisingly good. Earnings beat the consensus estimate, and immediately after the announcement the stock price rises by 5% to €44.10. Exhibit 44 shows the options' prices on the day of the announcement, after the stock price has increased to €44.10 (the implied volatility remains unchanged).

**Exhibit 44    23-Day Put Options on Relais**

|  | Option A | Option B | Option C |
|---|---|---|---|
| **Strike** | €40.00 | €42.50 | €45.00 |
| **Price** | €0.15 | €0.66 | €1.85 |
| **Delta** | −0.0923 | −0.3000 | −0.5916 |
| **Gamma** | 0.0218 | 0.0460 | 0.0514 |

*(continued)*

| Exhibit 44 (Continued) | | | |
|---|---|---|---|
|  | Option A | Option B | Option C |
| Price Change | −90% | −62% | −47% |
| Loss on 100,000 Puts from Price Change | €130,000 | €106,000 | €161,000 |

2. Discuss how the strategy fared and how McLaire should proceed, assuming earnings beat the consensus estimate and Relais's stock price rises by 5% to €44.10.

*Solution to 2:* The 42.50-strike put held by McLaire has 23 days to expiration. The price has declined from €1.72 to €0.66 (−62%), for a total loss of €106,000 (= [€1.72 − €0.66] × 100,000). This is less than the loss McLaire would have incurred if he had purchased the other options. At the same time the value of the 100,000 Relais shares held by the fund has increased by €210,000 (= ($44.10 − $42.00) × 100,000). Now that the earnings announcement has been made, McLaire no longer needs the protection from the put options, so he should sell them and recover €66,000 from the original €172,000 put purchase price.

# SUMMARY

This reading on options strategies shows a number of ways in which market participants might use options to enhance returns or to reduce risk to better meet portfolio objectives. The following are the key points.

- Buying a call and writing a put on the same underlying with the same strike price and expiration creates a synthetic long position (i.e., a synthetic long forward position).
- Writing a call and buying a put on the same underlying with the same strike price and expiration creates a synthetic short position (i.e., a synthetic short forward position).
- A synthetic long put position consists of a short stock and long call position in which the call strike price equals the price at which the stock is shorted.
- A synthetic long call position consists of a long stock and long put position in which the put strike price equals the price at which the stock is purchased.
- Delta is the change in an option's price for a change in price of the underlying, all else equal.
- Gamma is the change in an option's delta for a change in price of the underlying, all else equal.
- Vega is the change in an option's price for a change in volatility of the underlying, all else equal.
- Theta is the daily change in an option's price, all else equal.
- A covered call, in which the holder of a stock writes a call giving someone the right to buy the shares, is one of the most common uses of options by individual investors.

# Summary

- Covered calls can be used to change an investment's risk–reward profile by effectively enhancing yield or reducing/exiting a position when the shares hit a target price.
- A covered call position has a limited maximum return because of the transfer of the right tail of the return distribution to the option buyer.
- The maximum loss of a covered call position is less than the maximum loss of the underlying shares alone, but the covered call carries the potential for an opportunity loss if the underlying shares rise sharply.
- A protective put is the simultaneous holding of a long stock position and a long put on the same asset. The put provides protection or insurance against a price decline.
- The continuous purchase of protective puts maintains the upside potential of the portfolio, while limiting downside volatility. The cost of the puts must be carefully considered, however, because this activity may be expensive. Conversely, the occasional purchase of a protective put to deal with a bearish short-term outlook can be a reasonable risk-reducing strategy.
- The maximum loss with a protective put is limited because the downside risk is transferred to the option writer in exchange for the payment of the option premium.
- With an option spread, an investor buys one option and writes another of the same type. This approach reduces the position cost but caps the maximum payoff.
- A bull spread expresses a bullish view on the underlying and is normally constructed by buying a call option and writing another call option with a higher exercise price (both options have same underlying and same expiry).
- A bear spread expresses a bearish view on the underlying and is normally constructed by buying a put option and writing another put option with a lower exercise price (both options have same underlying and same expiry).
- With either a bull spread or a bear spread, both the maximum gain and the maximum loss are known and limited.
- A long (short) straddle is an option combination in which the investor buys (sells) puts and calls with the same exercise price and expiration date. The long (short) straddle investor expects increased (stable/decreased) volatility and typically requires a large (small/no) price movement in the underlying asset in order to make a profit.
- A collar is an option position in which the investor is long shares of stock and simultaneously writes a call with an exercise price above the current stock price and buys a put with an exercise price below the current stock price. A collar limits the range of investment outcomes by sacrificing upside gain in exchange for providing downside protection.
- A long (short) calendar spread involves buying (selling) a long-dated option and writing (buying) a shorter-dated option of the same type with the same exercise price. A long (short) calendar spread is used when the investment outlook is flat (volatile) in the near term but greater (lesser) return movements are expected in the future.
- Implied volatility is the expected volatility an underlying asset's return and is derived from an option pricing model (i.e., the Black–Scholes–Merton model) as the value that equates the model price of an option to its market price.

- When implied volatilities of OTM options exceed those of ATM options, the implied volatility curve is a volatility smile. The more common shape is a volatility skew, in which implied volatility increases for OTM puts and decreases for OTM calls, as the strike price moves away from the current price.
- The implied volatility surface is a 3-D plot, for put and call options on the same underlying, showing expiration time ($x$-axis), strike prices ($y$-axis), and implied volatilities ($z$-axis). It simultaneously displays volatility skew and the term structure of implied volatility.
- Options, like all derivatives, should always be used in connection with a well-defined investment objective. When using options strategies, it is important to have a view on the expected change in implied volatility and the direction of movement of the underlying asset.

# PRACTICE PROBLEMS

## The following information relates to Questions 1–10

Aline Nuñes, a junior analyst, works in the derivatives research division of an international securities firm. Nuñes's supervisor, Cátia Pereira, asks her to conduct an analysis of various option trading strategies relating to shares of three companies: IZD, QWY, and XDF. On 1 February, Nuñes gathers selected option premium data on the companies, presented in Exhibit 1.

| Exhibit 1 | Share Price and Option Premiums as of 1 February (share prices and option premiums in €) | | | |
|---|---|---|---|---|
| Company | Share Price | Call Premium | Option Date/Strike | Put Premium |
| IZD | 93.93 | 9.45 | April/87.50 | 1.67 |
|  |  | 2.67 | April/95.00 | 4.49 |
|  |  | 1.68 | April/97.50 | 5.78 |
| QWY | 28.49 | 4.77 | April/24.00 | 0.35 |
|  |  | 3.96 | April/25.00 | 0.50 |
|  |  | 0.32 | April/31.00 | 3.00 |
| XDF | 74.98 | 0.23 | February/80.00 | 5.52 |
|  |  | 2.54 | April/75.00 | 3.22 |
|  |  | 2.47 | December/80.00 | 9.73 |

Nuñes considers the following option strategies relating to IZD:

**Strategy 1:** Constructing a synthetic long put position in IZD

**Strategy 2:** Buying 100 shares of IZD and writing the April €95.00 strike call option on IZD

**Strategy 3:** Implementing a covered call position in IZD using the April €97.50 strike option

Nuñes next reviews the following option strategies relating to QWY:

**Strategy 4:** Implementing a protective put position in QWY using the April €25.00 strike option

**Strategy 5:** Buying 100 shares of QWY, buying the April €24.00 strike put option, and writing the April €31.00 strike call option

**Strategy 6:** Implementing a bear spread in QWY using the April €25.00 and April €31.00 strike options

Finally, Nuñes considers two option strategies relating to XDF:

**Strategy 7:** Writing both the April €75.00 strike call option and the April €75.00 strike put option on XDF

**Strategy 8:** Writing the February €80.00 strike call option and buying the December €80.00 strike call option on XDF

1. Strategy 1 would require Nuñes to buy:
   A  shares of IZD.
   B  a put option on IZD.
   C  a call option on IZD.

2. Based on Exhibit 1, Nuñes should expect Strategy 2 to be *least* profitable if the share price of IZD at option expiration is:
   A  less than €91.26.
   B  between €91.26 and €95.00.
   C  more than €95.00.

3. Based on Exhibit 1, the breakeven share price of Strategy 3 is *closest* to:
   A  €92.25.
   B  €95.61.
   C  €95.82.

4. Based on Exhibit 1, the maximum loss per share that would be incurred by implementing Strategy 4 is:
   A  €2.99.
   B  €3.99.
   C  unlimited.

5. Strategy 5 is *best* described as a:
   A  collar.
   B  straddle.
   C  bear spread.

6. Based on Exhibit 1, Strategy 5 offers:
   A  unlimited upside.
   B  a maximum profit of €2.48 per share.
   C  protection against losses if QWY's share price falls below €28.14.

7. Based on Exhibit 1, the breakeven share price for Strategy 6 is *closest* to:
   A  €22.50.
   B  €28.50.
   C  €33.50.

8. Based on Exhibit 1, the maximum gain per share that could be earned if Strategy 7 is implemented is:
   A  €5.74.
   B  €5.76.
   C  unlimited.

9. Based on Exhibit 1, the *best* explanation for Nuñes to implement Strategy 8 would be that, between the February and December expiration dates, she expects the share price of XDF to:
   A  decrease.
   B  remain unchanged.

**C** increase.

10 Over the past few months, Nuñes and Pereira have followed news reports on a proposed merger between XDF and one of its competitors. A government antitrust committee is currently reviewing the potential merger. Pereira expects the share price to move sharply upward or downward depending on whether the committee decides to approve or reject the merger next week. Pereira asks Nuñes to recommend an option trade that might allow the firm to benefit from a significant move in the XDF share price regardless of the direction of the move.

The option trade that Nuñes should recommend relating to the government committee's decision is a:

**A** collar.

**B** bull spread.

**C** long straddle.

# The following information relates to Questions 11–16

Stanley Kumar Singh, CFA, is the risk manager at SKS Asset Management. He works with individual clients to manage their investment portfolios. One client, Sherman Hopewell, is worried about how short-term market fluctuations over the next three months might impact his equity position in Walnut Corporation. Although Hopewell is concerned about short-term downside price movements, he wants to remain invested in Walnut shares because he remains positive about its long-term performance. Hopewell has asked Singh to recommend an option strategy that will keep him invested in Walnut shares while protecting against a short-term price decline. Singh gathers the information in Exhibit 1 to explore various strategies to address Hopewell's concerns.

Another client, Nigel French, is a trader who does not currently own shares of Walnut Corporation. French has told Singh that he believes that Walnut shares will experience a large move in price after the upcoming quarterly earnings release in two weeks. French also tells Singh, however, that he is unsure which direction the stock will move. French asks Singh to recommend an option strategy that would allow him to profit should the share price move in either direction.

A third client, Wanda Tills, does not currently own Walnut shares and has asked Singh to explain the profit potential of three strategies using options in Walnut: a long straddle, a bull call spread, and a bear put spread. In addition, Tills asks Singh to explain the gamma of a call option. In response, Singh prepares a memo to be shared with Tills that provides a discussion of gamma and presents his analysis on three option strategies:

**Strategy 1:** A long straddle position at the $67.50 strike option

**Strategy 2:** A bull call spread using the $65 and $70 strike options

**Strategy 3:** A bear put spread using the $65 and $70 strike options

### Exhibit 1  Walnut Corporation Current Stock Price: $67.79
### Walnut Corporation European Options

| Exercise Price | Market Call Price | Call Delta | Market Put Price | Put Delta |
|---|---|---|---|---|
| $55.00 | $12.83 | 1.00 | $0.24 | −0.05 |
| $65.00 | $3.65 | 0.91 | $1.34 | −0.29 |
| $67.50 | $1.99 | 0.63 | $2.26 | −0.42 |
| $70.00 | $0.91 | 0.37 | $3.70 | −0.55 |
| $80.00 | $0.03 | 0.02 | $12.95 | −0.76 |

*Note*: Each option has 106 days remaining until expiration.

**11** The option strategy Singh is *most likely* to recommend to Hopewell is a:
  **A** collar.
  **B** covered call.
  **C** protective put.

**12** The option strategy that Singh is *most likely* to recommend to French is a:
  **A** straddle.
  **B** bull spread.
  **C** collar.

**13** Based on Exhibit 1, Strategy 1 is profitable when the share price at expiration is *closest* to:
  **A** $63.00.
  **B** $65.24.
  **C** $69.49.

**14** Based on Exhibit 1, the maximum profit, on a per share basis, from investing in Strategy 2, is *closest* to:
  **A** $2.26.
  **B** $2.74.
  **C** $5.00.

**15** Based on Exhibit 1, and assuming the market price of Walnut's shares at expiration is $66, the profit or loss, on a per share basis, from investing in Strategy 3, is *closest* to:
  **A** $2.36.
  **B** $1.64.
  **C** $2.64.

**16** Based on the data in Exhibit 1, Singh would advise Tills that the call option with the *largest* gamma would have a strike price *closest* to:
  **A** $ 55.00.
  **B** $ 67.50.
  **C** $ 80.00.

## Practice Problems

# The following information relates to Questions 17–23

Anneke Ngoc is an analyst who works for an international bank, where she advises high-net-worth clients on option strategies. Ngoc prepares for a meeting with a US-based client, Mani Ahlim.

Ngoc notes that Ahlim recently inherited an account containing a large Brazilian real (BRL) cash balance. Ahlim intends to use the inherited funds to purchase a vacation home in the United States with an expected purchase price of US$750,000 in six months. Ahlim is concerned that the Brazilian real will weaken against the US dollar over the next six months. Ngoc considers potential hedge strategies to reduce the risk of a possible adverse currency movement over this time period.

Ahlim holds shares of Pselftarô Ltd. (PSÔL), which has a current share price of $37.41. Ahlim is bullish on PSÔL in the long term. He would like to add to his long position but is concerned about a moderate price decline after the quarterly earnings announcement next month, in April. Ngoc recommends a protective put position with a strike price of $35 using May options and a $40/$50 bull call spread using December options. Ngoc gathers selected PSÔL option prices for May and December, which are presented in Exhibit 1.

### Exhibit 1  Selected PSÔL Option Prices (all prices in US dollars)

| Exercise Price | Expiration Month | Call Price | Put Price |
|---|---|---|---|
| 35 | May | 3.00 | 1.81 |
| 40 | December | 6.50 | 10.25 |
| 50 | December | 4.25 | 20.50 |

Ahlim also expresses interest in trading options on India's NIFTY 50 (National Stock Exchange Fifty) Index. Ngoc gathers selected one-month option prices and implied volatility data, which are presented in Exhibit 2. India's NIFTY 50 Index is currently trading at a level of 11,610.

### Exhibit 2  Selected One-Month Option Prices and Implied Volatility Data: NIFTY 50 Index (all prices in Indian rupees)

| Exercise Price | Market Call Price | Market Put Price | Implied Call Volatility | Implied Put Volatility |
|---|---|---|---|---|
| 11,200 | 526.00 | 61.90 | 5.87 | 17.72 |
| 11,400 | 365.45 | 102.60 | 10.80 | 17.01 |
| 11,600 | 240.00 | 165.80 | 12.26 | 16.44 |
| 11,800 | 135.00 | 213.00 | 12.14 | 16.39 |
| 12,000 | 65.80 | 370.00 | 11.98 | 16.56 |

Ngoc reviews a research report that includes a one-month forecast of the NIFTY 50 Index. The report's conclusions are presented in Exhibit 3.

## Exhibit 3   Research Report Conclusions: NIFTY 50 Index

**One-month forecast:**

- We have a neutral view on the direction of the index's move over the next month.
- The rate of the change in underlying prices (vega) is expected to increase.
- The implied volatility of index options is expected to be above the consensus forecast.

Based on these conclusions, Ngoc considers various NIFTY 50 Index option strategies for Ahlim.

17 Which of the following positions would best mitigate Ahlim's concern regarding the purchase of his vacation home in six months?

   A  Sell an at-the-money six-month BRL/USD call option.
   B  Purchase an at-the-money six-month USD/BRL put option.
   C  Take a short position in a six-month BRL/USD futures contract.

18 Based on Exhibit 1, the maximum loss per share of Ngoc's recommended PSÔL protective put position is:

   A  $0.60.
   B  $2.41.
   C  $4.22.

19 Based on Exhibit 1, the breakeven price per share of Ngoc's recommended PSÔL protective put position is:

   A  $35.60.
   B  $36.81.
   C  $39.22.

20 Based on Exhibit 1, the maximum profit per share of Ngoc's recommended PSÔL bull call spread is:

   A  $2.25.
   B  $7.75.
   C  $12.25.

21 Based on Exhibit 1, the breakeven price per share of Ngoc's recommended PSÔL bull call spread is:

   A  $42.25.
   B  $47.75.
   C  $52.25.

22 Based on Exhibit 2, the NIFTY 50 Index implied volatility data *most likely* indicate a:

   A  risk reversal.
   B  volatility skew.
   C  volatility smile.

23 Based on Exhibit 3, which of the following NIFTY 50 Index option strategies should Ngoc recommend to Ahlim?

   A  Buy a straddle.

**Practice Problems**

**B** Buy a call option.
**C** Buy a calendar spread.

# SOLUTIONS

1. C is correct. To construct a synthetic long put position, Nuñes would buy a call option on IZD. Of course, she would also need to sell (short) IZD shares to complete the synthetic long put position.

2. A is correct. Strategy 2 is a covered call, which is a combination of a long position in shares and a short call option. The breakeven point of Strategy 2 is €91.26, which represents the price per share of €93.93 minus the call premium received of €2.67 per share ($S_0 - c_0$). So, at any share price less than €91.26 at option expiration, Strategy 2 incurs a loss. If the share price of IZD at option expiration is greater than €91.26, Strategy 2 generates a gain.

3. A is correct. Strategy 3 is a covered call strategy, which is a combination of a long position in shares and a short call option. The breakeven share price for a covered call is the share price minus the call premium received, or $S_0 - c_0$. The current share price of IZD is €93.93, and the IZD April €97.50 call premium is €1.68. Thus, the breakeven underlying share price for Strategy 3 is $S_0 - c_0$ = €93.93 − €1.68 = €92.25.

4. B is correct. Strategy 4 is a protective put position, which is a combination of a long position in shares and a long put option. By purchasing the €25.00 strike put option, Nuñes would be protected from losses at QWY share prices of €25.00 or lower. Thus, the maximum loss per share from Strategy 4 would be the loss of share value from €28.49 to €25.00 (or €3.49) plus the put premium paid for the put option of €0.50: $S_0 - X + p_0$ = €28.49 − €25.00 + €0.50 = €3.99.

5. A is correct. Strategy 5 describes a collar, which is a combination of a long position in shares, a long put option with an exercise price below the current stock price, and a short call option with an exercise price above the current stock price.

6. B is correct. Strategy 5 describes a collar, which is a combination of a long position in shares, a long put option, and a short call option. Strategy 5 would require Nuñes to buy 100 QWY shares at the current market price of €28.49 per share. In addition, she would purchase a QWY April €24.00 strike put option contract for €0.35 per share and collect €0.32 per share from writing a QWY April €31.00 strike call option. The collar offers protection against losses on the shares below the put strike price of €24.00 per share, but it also limits upside to the call strike price of €31.00 per share. Thus, the maximum gain on the trade, which occurs at prices of €31.00 per share or higher, is calculated as $(X_2 - S_0) - p_0 + c_0$, or (€31.00 − €28.49) − €0.35 + €0.32 = €2.48 per share.

7. B is correct. Strategy 6 is a bear spread, which is a combination of a long put option and a short put option on the same underlying, where the long put has a higher strike price than the short put. In the case of Strategy 6, the April €31.00 put option would be purchased and the April €25.00 put option would be sold. The long put premium is €3.00 and the short put premium is €0.50, for a net cost of €2.50. The breakeven share price is €28.50, calculated as $X_H - (p_H - p_L)$ = €31.00 − (€3.00 − €0.50) = €28.50.

8. B is correct. Strategy 7 describes a short straddle, which is a combination of a short put option and a short call option, both with the same strike price. The maximum gain is €5.76 per share, which represents the sum of the two option premiums, or $c_0 + p_0$ = €2.54 + €3.22 = €5.76. The maximum gain per share is realized if both options expire worthless, which would happen if the share price of XDF at expiration is €75.00.

# Solutions

**9** C is correct. Nuñes would implement Strategy 8, which is a long calendar spread, if she expects the XDF share price to increase between the February and December expiration dates. This strategy provides a benefit from the February short call premium to partially offset the cost of the December long call option. Nuñes likely expects the XDF share price to remain relatively flat between the current price €74.98 and €80 until the February call option expires, after which time she expects the share price to increase above €80. If such expectations come to fruition, the February call would expire worthless and Nuñes would realize gains on the December call option.

**10** C is correct. Nuñes should recommend a long straddle, which is a combination of a long call option and a long put option, both with the same strike price. The committee's announcement is expected to cause a significant move in XDF's share price. A long straddle is appropriate because the share price is expected to move sharply up or down depending on the committee's decision. If the merger is approved, the share price will likely increase, leading to a gain in the long call option. If the merger is rejected, then the share price will likely decrease, leading to a gain in the long put option.

**11** C is correct. A protective put accomplishes Hopewell's goal of short-term price protection. A protective put provides downside protection while retaining the upside potential. Although Hopewell is concerned about the downside in the short term, he wants to remain invested in Walnut shares because he is positive on the stock in the long term.

**12** A is correct. The long straddle strategy is based on expectations of volatility in the underlying stock being higher than the market consensus. The straddle strategy consists of simultaneously buying a call option and a put option at the same strike price. Singh could recommend that French buy a straddle using near at-the-money options ($67.50 strike). This allows French to profit should the Walnut stock price experience a large move in either direction after the earnings release.

**13** A is correct. The straddle strategy consists of simultaneously buying a call option and buying a put option at the same strike price. The market price for the $67.50 call option is $1.99, and the market price for the $67.50 put option is $2.26, for an initial net cost of $4.25 per share. Thus, this straddle position requires a move greater than $4.25 in either direction from the strike price of $67.50 to become profitable. So, the straddle becomes profitable at $67.50 – $4.26 = $63.24 or lower, or $67.50 + $4.26 = $71.76 or higher. At $63.00, the profit on the straddle is positive.

**14** A is correct. The bull call strategy consists of buying the lower-strike option and selling the higher-strike option. The purchase of the $65 strike call option costs $3.65 per share, and selling the $70 strike call option generates an inflow of $0.91 per share, for an initial net cost of $2.74 per share. At expiration, the maximum profit occurs when the stock price is $70 or higher, which yields a $5.00 per share payoff ($70 – $65) on the long call position. After deduction of the $2.74 per share cost required to initiate the bull call spread, the profit is $2.26 ($5.00 – $2.74).

**15** B is correct. The bear put spread consists of buying a put option with a high strike price ($70) and selling another put option with a lower strike price ($65). The market price for the $70 strike put option is $3.70, and the market price for the $65 strike put option is $1.34 per share. Thus, the initial net cost of the bear spread position is $3.70 – $1.34 = $2.36 per share. If Walnut shares are $66 at expiration, the $70 strike put option is in the money by $4.00, and the short position in the $65 strike put expires worthless. After deducting the cost of $2.36 to initiate the bear spread position, the net profit is $1.64 per contract.

**16** B is correct. The $67.50 call option is approximately at the money because the Walnut share price is currently $67.79. Gamma measures the sensitivity of an option's delta to a change in the underlying. The largest gamma occurs when options are trading at the money or near expiration, when the deltas of such options move quickly toward 1.0 or 0.0. Under these conditions, the gammas tend to be largest and delta hedges are hardest to maintain.

**17** B is correct. Ahlim could mitigate the risk of the Brazilian real weakening against the US dollar over the next six months by (1) purchasing an at-the-money six-month BRL/USD call option (to buy US dollars), (2) purchasing an at-the-money six-month USD/BRL put option (to sell Brazilian reals), or (3) taking a long position in a six-month BRL/USD futures contract (to buy US dollars).

Purchasing an at-the-money six-month USD/BRL put option (to sell Brazilian reals) would mitigate the risk of a weakening Brazilian real. If the Brazilian real should weaken against the US dollar over the next six months, Ahlim could exercise the put option and sell his Brazilian reals at the contract's strike rate (which would have been the prevailing market exchange rate at the time of purchase, since the option is at the money).

A is incorrect because purchasing (not selling) an at-the-money six-month BRL/USD call option (to buy US dollars) would mitigate the risk of the Brazilian real weakening against the US dollar over the next six months. The long call position would give Ahlim the right to buy US dollars (and sell Brazilian reals). A call on US dollars is similar to a put on Brazilian reals. So, a put to sell Brazilian reals at a given strike rate can be viewed as a call to buy US dollars.

C is incorrect because going long (not short) a six-month BRL/USD futures contract (to buy US dollars) would mitigate the risk of the Brazilian real weakening against the US dollar over the next six months. A long futures position would obligate Ahlim to buy US dollars (and sell Brazilian reals) at the futures contract rate.

**18** C is correct. Ngoc recommends a protective put position with a strike price of $35 using May options. The maximum loss per share on the protective put is calculated as

Maximum loss per share of protective put = $S_0 - X + p_0$.
Maximum loss per share of protective put = $37.41 - $35.00 + $1.81 = $4.22.

In summary, with the protective put in place, Ahlim is protected against losses below $35.00. Thus, taking into account the put option purchase price of $1.81, Ahlim's maximum loss occurs at the share price of $33.19, resulting in a maximum loss of $4.22 per share (= $37.41 − $33.19).

A is incorrect because $0.60 reflects incorrectly subtracting (rather than adding) the put premium in the calculation of the maximum loss of protective put (i.e., $37.41 − $35.00 − $1.81 = $0.60).

B is incorrect because $2.41 does not include the put premium in the calculation but only reflects the difference between the current share price ($37.41) and the put exercise price ($35.00).

## Solutions

**19** C is correct. Ngoc recommends a protective put position with a strike price of $35 using May options. The breakeven price per share on the protective put is calculated as

Breakeven price per share of protective put = $S_0 + p_0$.
Breakeven price per share of protective put = $37.41 + $1.81 = $39.22.

In summary, Ahlim would need PSÔL's share price to rise by the price of the put option ($1.81) from the current price of $37.41 to reach the breakeven share price—the price at which the gain from the increase in the value of the stock offsets the purchase price of the put option.

A is incorrect because $35.60 represents incorrectly subtracting (rather than adding) the put premium in the calculation of the protective put breakeven price: $37.41 − $1.81 = $35.60.

B is incorrect because $36.81 represents incorrectly adding the put premium to the strike price (not the current share price): $35.00 + $1.81 = $36.81.

**20** B is correct. Ngoc recommends a $40/$50 bull call spread using December options. To construct this spread, Ahlim would buy the $40 call, paying the $6.50 premium, and simultaneously sell the $50 call, receiving a premium of $4.25. The maximum gain or profit of a bull call spread occurs when the stock price reaches the high exercise price ($50) or higher at expiration. Thus, the maximum profit per share of a bull call spread is the spread difference between the strike prices less the net premium paid, calculated as

Maximum profit per share of bull call spread = $(X_H − X_L) − (c_L − c_H)$.
Maximum profit per share of bull call spread = ($50 − $40) − ($6.50 − $4.25).
Maximum profit per share of bull call spread = $7.75.

A is incorrect because $2.25 represents only the net premium and does not include the spread difference.

C is incorrect because $12.25 represents the net premium being incorrectly added (rather than subtracted) from the spread difference.

**21** A is correct. Ngoc recommends a $40/$50 bull call spread using December options. To construct this spread, Ahlim would buy the $40 call, paying a $6.50 premium, and simultaneously sell the $50 call, receiving a $4.25 premium. The breakeven price per share of a bull call spread is calculated as

Breakeven price per share of bull call spread = $X_L + (c_L − c_H)$.
Breakeven price per share of bull call spread = $40 + ($6.50 − $4.25).
Breakeven price per share of bull call spread = $42.25.

In summary, in order to break even, the PSÔL stock price must rise above $40 by the amount of the net premium paid of $2.25 to enter into the bull call spread. At the price of $42.25, the lower $40 call option would have an exercise value of $2.25, exactly offsetting the $2.25 cost of entering the trade.

B is incorrect because $47.75 represents the net premium being incorrectly subtracted from the high exercise price (rather than being added to the low exercise price): $50 − ($6.50 − $4.25) = $47.75.

C is incorrect because $52.25 represents the net premium being added to the high exercise price (rather than the low exercise price): $50 + ($6.50 − $4.25) = $52.25.

22 B is correct. When the implied volatility decreases for OTM (out-of-the-money) calls relative to ATM (at-the-money) calls and increases for OTM puts relative to ATM puts, a volatility skew exists. Put volatility is higher, rising from 16.44 ATM to 17.72 OTM, likely because of the higher demand for puts to hedge positions in the index against downside risk. Call volatility decreases from 12.26 for ATM calls to 11.98 for OTM calls since calls do not offer this valuable portfolio insurance.

A is incorrect because a risk reversal is a delta-hedged trading strategy seeking to profit from a change in the relative volatility of calls and puts.

C is incorrect because a volatility smile exists when both call and put volatilities, not just put volatilities, are higher OTM than ATM.

23 A is correct. The research report concludes that the consensus forecast of the implied volatility of index options is too low and anticipates greater-than-expected volatility over the next month. Given the neutral market direction forecast, Ngoc should recommend a long straddle, which entails buying a one-month 11,600 call and buying a one-month put with the same exercise price. If the future NIFTY 50 Index level rises above its current level plus the combined cost of the call and put premiums, Ahlim would exercise the call option and realize a profit. Similarly, if the index level falls below the current index level minus the combined cost of the call and put premiums, Ahlim would exercise the put option and realize a profit. Thus, Ahlim profits if the index moves either up or down enough to pay for the call and put premiums.

B is incorrect because the strategy to buy a call option would be reasonable given an increase in expected implied volatility with a bullish NIFTY 50 Index forecast, not a neutral trading range.

C is incorrect because a long calendar spread is based on the expectation that implied volatility will remain unchanged, not increase, until the expiry of the shorter-term option.

# READING
# 9

# Swaps, Forwards, and Futures Strategies

by Barbara Valbuzzi, CFA

*Barbara Valbuzzi, CFA (Italy).*

| LEARNING OUTCOMES | |
|---|---|
| Mastery | The candidate should be able to: |
| ☐ | a. demonstrate how interest rate swaps, forwards, and futures can be used to modify a portfolio's risk and return; |
| ☐ | b. demonstrate how currency swaps, forwards, and futures can be used to modify a portfolio's risk and return; |
| ☐ | c. demonstrate how equity swaps, forwards, and futures can be used to modify a portfolio's risk and return; |
| ☐ | d. demonstrate the use of volatility derivatives and variance swaps; |
| ☐ | e. demonstrate the use of derivatives to achieve targeted equity and interest rate risk exposures; |
| ☐ | f. demonstrate the use of derivatives in asset allocation, rebalancing, and inferring market expectations. |

## 1. MANAGING INTEREST RATE RISK WITH SWAPS

a   demonstrate how interest rate swaps, forwards, and futures can be used to modify a portfolio's risk and return;

There are many ways in which investment managers and investors can use swaps, forwards, futures, and volatility derivatives. The typical applications of these derivatives involve modifying investment positions for hedging purposes or for taking directional bets, creating or replicating desired payoffs, implementing asset allocation and portfolio rebalancing decisions, and even inferring current market expectations. The following table shows some common uses of these derivatives in portfolio management and the types of derivatives used by investors and portfolio managers.

© 2019 CFA Institute. All rights reserved.

| Common Uses of Swaps, Forwards, and Futures | Typical Derivatives Used |
|---|---|
| Modifying Portfolio Returns and Risk Exposures (Hedging and Directional Bets) | Interest Rate, Currency, and Equity Swaps and Futures; Fixed-Income Futures; Variance Swaps |
| Creating Desired Payoffs | Forwards, Futures, Total Return Swaps |
| Performing Asset Allocation and Portfolio Rebalancing | Equity Index Futures, Government Bond Futures, Index Swaps |
| Inferring Market Expectations for Interest Rates, Inflation, and Volatility | Fed Funds Futures, Inflation Swaps, VIX Futures |

It is important for an informed investment professional to understand how swaps, forwards, futures, and volatility derivatives can be used and their associated risk–return trade-offs. Therefore, the purpose of this reading is to illustrate ways in which these derivatives might be used in typical investment situations. Sections 2–4 of this reading show how swaps, forwards, and futures can be used to modify the risk exposure of an existing position. Sections 5–6 provide a discussion on derivatives on volatility. Sections 7–9 demonstrate a series of applications showing ways in which a portfolio manager might solve an investment problem with these derivatives. The reading concludes with a summary.

## 1.1 Changing Risk Exposures with Swaps, Futures, and Forwards

Financial managers can use swaps, forwards, and futures markets to quickly and efficiently alter the underlying risk exposure of their asset portfolios or anticipated investment transactions. This section covers a variety of common examples that use swaps, futures, and forwards.

### 1.1.1 Managing Interest Rate Risk

**1.1.1.1 Interest Rate Swaps** An interest rate swap is an over-the-counter (OTC) contract between two parties that agree to exchange cash flows on specified payment dates—one based on a *variable* (floating) interest rate and the other based on a *fixed* rate (the "swap rate")—determined at the time the swap is initiated. The swap tenor is when the swap is agreed to expire. Both interest rates are applied to the swap's notional value to determine the size of each payment. Normally, the resulting two payments (one fixed, one floating) are in the same currency but will not be equal, so they are typically netted, with the party owing the greater amount paying the difference to the other party. In this manner, a party that currently has a fixed (floating) risk or other obligation can effectively convert it into a floating (fixed) one.

Interest rate swaps are among the most widely used instruments to manage interest rate risk. In particular, they are designed to manage the risk on cash flows arising from investors' assets and liabilities. Interest rate swaps and futures can also be used to modify the risk and return profile of a portfolio. This is associated with managing a portfolio of bonds that generally involves controlling the portfolio's duration. Although futures are commonly used to make duration changes, swaps can also be used, and we shall see how in this reading. Finally, interest rate swaps are used by financial institutions to hedge the interest rate risk exposure deriving from the issuance of financial instruments sold to clients. Example 1 shows how an interest rate swap is used to convert floating-rate securities into fixed-rate securities. Here the firm initially expects continuing low interest rates, so it issues floating-rate bonds. But after concluding that rates are likely to increase, the firm seeks to convert its interest rate risk to a fixed obligation, even though doing so means making higher payments up front.

## EXAMPLE 1

### Using an Interest Rate Swap to Convert Floating-Rate Securities into Fixed-Rate Securities

An investment firm has sold £20 million of three-year floating-rate bonds that pay a semiannual coupon equal to the six-month market reference rate plus 50 bps. A few days later, the firm's outlook changes substantially, and it now expects higher rates in the future. The firm enters into an interest rate swap with a tenor of approximately three years and semiannual payments, where the firm pays a fixed par swap rate of 1.25% and receives the six-month reference rate. The swap settlement dates are the same as the coupon payment dates on the floating-rate bonds. At the first swap settlement date, the six-month reference rate is 0.75%.

### Analysis:

At the first coupon payment and swap settlement date, the six-month reference rate is 0.75% (annualized). This means that on the swap the investment firm will make a net payment of £50,000 as follows:

- Receive based on the reference rate: 0.75% × £20 million × (180/360) = £75,000.
- Pay based on the fixed rate: 1.25% × £20 million × (180/360) = £125,000.
- Net payment *made* by the firm to swap dealer: £125,000 − £75,000 = £50,000.

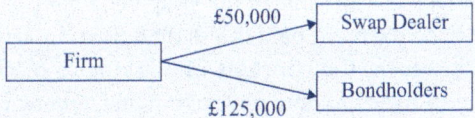

At the same time, the first semiannual coupon payment on the securities will be (0.75% + 0.50%) × £20 million × (180/360) = £125,000.

The total payment made by the investment firm on the securities and the swap is £175,000 (= £125,000 + £50,000).

Now assume that as we move forward to the second coupon payment and swap settlement date, interest rates have increased and the six-month reference rate is 1.50%.

On the swap, the investment firm will receive a net payment of £25,000 as follows:

- Receive based on the new reference rate: 1.50% × £20 million × (180/360) = £150,000.
- Pay based on the fixed rate: 1.25% × £20 million × (180/360) = £125,000.
- Net payment *received* by the firm: £150,000 − £125,000 = £25,000.

The coupon payment on the securities will be (1.50% + 0.50%) × £20 million × (180/360) = £200,000.

The total payment made by the investment firm on the securities and the swap is again £175,000 (= £200,000 − £25,000).

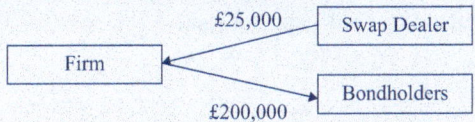

> The investment firm has effectively fixed its all-in borrowing costs. Since this fixed cost is synthesized by a combination of the underlying debt position and the derivative contract, it can be described as a synthetic fixed security.

Why should the investment firm decide to pay a fixed rate of 1.25%, on a semi-annual basis, for the remaining life of the securities when the reference rate is only 0.75% today? The reason is that the firm's outlook is now for higher rates in the future, as expressed by market participants in the upward-sloping yield curve. An upward-sloping yield curve reflects that investors require higher risk premium compensation for holding longer-term securities.

The agreed-on fixed rate on the swap is based on the term structure of rates at the time the deal is initiated. If the term structure changes, the new fixed rate agreed on by the counterparties on a swap with the same residual time to maturity as the original one will be different from the original rate. This means that the market value of the swap will become positive or negative. In particular, the investment firm in Example 1 has managed to fix the interest rate on future payments but has given away the opportunity to benefit from possible lower interest rates in the future. If the term structure of interest rates has a parallel shift downward, meaning that all rates across tenors decrease, the value of the swap will become negative from the perspective of the fixed-rate payer, depending on the new swap market fixed rate. The investment firm has managed to achieve the desired fixed profile of future cash flows, but it might incur a loss if the firm wants to unwind the interest rate swap before maturity. Alternatively, if rates rise, as now expected, the swap can be unwound at a profit by the same reasoning in reverse: The value of the swap becomes positive from the fixed-rate payer's view; fixed-rate payment paid is less than floating-rate payment received.

This explanation introduces the concepts of marking to market of the swap and how swaps can be used in fixed-income portfolio management with the objective to hedge the changes in value of a portfolio with fixed cash flows.

When a bond portfolio is fully hedged, its value is immunized with respect to changes in yields. This can be stated as $\Delta P = (N_s)(\Delta S)$, where $\Delta P$ is the change in the value of the bond portfolio and $\Delta S$ is the change in the value of the swap for a given change in interest rates. The notional principal of the swap $(N_s)$ will be determined as $N_s = \Delta P/\Delta S$. To reduce changes in value of a fixed-rate portfolio, the manager will want to lower the overall duration by exchanging part of this fixed-rate income stream for a floating-rate stream. This can be done by entering an interest rate swap where the portfolio manager will pay the fixed rate and receive the floating rate.

It is important to keep in mind that most of the time, the hedging instrument and the asset or portfolio to be hedged are imperfect substitutes. The result is a market risk, called *basis risk* or *spread risk*—the difference between the market performance of the asset and the derivative instrument used to hedge it. When using an interest rate swap to hedge, it is possible that the changes in the underlying rate of the derivative contract, and thus in the value of the swap, do not perfectly mirror changes in the value of the bond portfolio.

Furthermore, the composition of the bond portfolio could bear additional market risks other than interest rate risk. For instance, suppose a portfolio of corporate bonds is hedged with an interest rate swap. In this case, even if interest rate risk is hedged, the investor is still exposed to credit spread risk.

# Managing Interest Rate Risk with Swaps

The main underlying assumptions we will use are that the change in value of the bond portfolio can be approximated by using the concept of modified duration,[1] the yield curve is flat, and it is affected only by parallel shifts. Furthermore, we assume here that the portfolio and the derivative contract used to hedge are perfect substitutes.

A measure for the change in the value of the bond portfolio ($\Delta P$) for a change in interest rates is given by the portfolio's modified duration, $MDUR_P$. The same measure calculated for the interest rate swap, $MDUR_S$, is used to determine the change in the value of the swap, $\Delta S$. The target modified duration for the combined portfolio is $MDUR_T$, and $MV_P$ is the market value of the bond portfolio.

By properly choosing the notional value and the tenor of the swap, the portfolio manager can achieve a combination of the existing portfolio and the interest rate swap that sets the overall portfolio duration to the target duration: $(MV_P)(MDUR_P) + (N_S)(MDUR_S) = (MV_P)(MDUR_T)$.

The equivalence $\Delta P = (N_S)(\Delta S)$ becomes $(MV_P)(MDUR_T - MDUR_P) = (N_S)(MDUR_S)$. To find the swap notional principal, $N_S$, we need to solve for the following formula:

$$N_S = \left(\frac{MDUR_T - MDUR_P}{MDUR_S}\right)(MV_P) \qquad (1)$$

The modified duration of a swap ($MDUR_S$) is the net of the modified durations of the equivalent positions in fixed- and floating-rate bonds. Thus, the position of the pay-fixed party in a pay-fixed, receive-floating swap has the modified duration of a floating-rate bond minus the modified duration of a fixed-rate bond, where the floating- and fixed-rate bonds have cash flows equivalent to the corresponding cash flows of the swap. A pay-fixed, receive-floating swap has a negative (positive) duration from the perspective of a fixed-rate payer (receiver), because the duration of a fixed-rate bond is positive and larger than the duration of a floating-rate bond, which is near zero. Moreover, the negative duration of this position to the fixed-rate payer/floating-rate receiver makes sense in that the position would be expected to benefit from rising interest rates.

### EXAMPLE 2

## Using an Interest Rate Swap to Achieve a Target Duration

Consider a portfolio manager with an investment portfolio of €50 million of fixed-rate German bonds with an average modified duration of 5.5. Because he fears that interest rates will rise, he wants to reduce the modified duration of the portfolio to 4.5, but he does not want to sell any of the securities. One way to do this would be to add a negative-duration position by entering into an interest rate swap where he pays the fixed rate and receives the floating rate. A two-year interest rate swap has an estimated modified duration of −2.00 from the perspective of the fixed-rate payer.

Demonstrate how the manager can use this interest rate swap to achieve the target modified duration.

---

1 Although there are various duration measures, we are concerned here with modified duration, which is an approximate measure of how a bond price changes given a small change in the level of interest rates.

> **Solution:**
>
> The portfolio manager's goal is for the bonds and the swap to combine to create a portfolio with a market value of €50 million and a target modified duration of 4.5. This relationship can be expressed as follows:
>
> €50,000,000(5.50) + $(N_S)(MDUR_S)$ = €50,000,000(4.50),
>
> where
>
> $N_S$ = Interest rate swap's notional principal
> $MDUR_S$ = Interest rate swap's modified duration, set equal to –2.00
>
> So, the notional principal of this interest rate swap that the manager should use is determined using Equation 1, as follows:
>
> $N_S$ = [(4.50 – 5.50)/(–2.00)] × €50,000,000 = €25,000,000.

## 2. MANAGING INTEREST RATE RISK WITH FORWARDS, FUTURES AND FIXED-INCOME FUTURES

a demonstrate how interest rate swaps, forwards, and futures can be used to modify a portfolio's risk and return;

The market in short-term interest rate derivatives is large and liquid, and the instruments involved are forward rate agreements (FRAs) and interest rate futures. A forward rate agreement is an OTC derivative instrument that is used mainly to hedge a loan expected to be taken out in the near future or to hedge against changes in the level of interest rates in the future. In fact, with advanced settled at maturity, an FRA will settle only the discounted difference between the interest rate agreed on in the contract and the actual rate prevailing at the time of settlement, applied on the notional amount of the contract. In general, managing short-term interest rate risk with an interest rate forward contract can also be done with an interest rate futures contract. Forwards, like swaps, are OTC instruments and are especially useful because they can be customized, but they do have counterparty risk. In contrast, exchange-traded interest rate futures contracts are standardized and guaranteed by a clearinghouse, so counterparty risk is virtually zero.[2]

Forward rate agreements and interest rate futures are widely used to hedge the risk associated with interest rates changing from the time a loan or a deposit is anticipated until it is actually implemented. Example 3 demonstrates how interest rate futures are used to lock in an interest rate.

---

[2] Regulatory changes in global markets are moving both over-the-counter swaps and forward contracts toward a clearing process as well. The clearing process reduces the risk that one counterparty will default on its obligations (by requiring collateral for trades and by daily marking to market of open positions), and for this reason, the counterparty risk associated with each single trade is virtually zero. However, there is still the risk that a major counterparty will fail to carry out its obligations (e.g., Lehman Brothers), causing operational risks for investors.

> **EXAMPLE 3**
>
> ### Using Interest Rate Futures to Lock in an Interest Rate
>
> Amanda Wright, the chief investment officer (CIO) of a US-based philanthropic foundation is expecting a donation of $30 million in two months' time from a member of the foundation's founding family. This significant donation will then be invested for three months and subsequently will be divided into smaller grants to be made to medical and educational institutions supported by the foundation. The current (i.e., spot) three-month reference rate is 2.40% (annualized). The CIO expects interest rates to fall, and she decides to hedge the rate on the deposit with Eurodollar futures.
>
> To provide background information, Eurodollar futures are cash settled on the basis of the market reference rate for an offshore deposit having a principal value of $1 million and a three-month maturity. These contracts are quoted in terms of the "IMM index"[3] that is equal to 100 less the annualized yield on the security. A 1 bp (0.01% or 0.0001) change in the value of the futures contract equates to a $25.00 movement in the contract value. Thus, the basis point value (BPV) of a $1 million face value, 90-day money market instrument is given by
>
> $$BPV = \text{Face value} \times \left(\frac{\text{Days}}{360}\right) \times 0.01\% = \$1,000,000 \times \left(\frac{90}{360}\right) \times 0.01\% = \$25$$
>
> **Analysis:**
>
> Wright buys 30 of the Eurodollar futures contracts at 97.60, locking in a forward rate of 2.40%. After two months, the donation is received and the CIO initiates the deposit at the then-lower spot rate of 2.10%. She unwinds the hedge at a futures price of 97.90, which is 30 bps higher than where the position was initiated.
>
> The foundation will receive $180,000 from the deposit plus the hedge, as follows:
>
> 1. Interest obtained on the deposit: 2.10% × $30 million × (90/360) = $157,500.
> 2. Profit on the hedge is 30 bps (30 × $25 = $750), which for 30 contracts corresponds to $22,500 (= $750 × 30).
>
> This corresponds to the return on an investment at the initial three-month reference rate of 2.40%, or 2.40% × $30 million × (90/360) = $180,000. This calculation demonstrates that by buying the Eurodollar futures, Wright did indeed lock in a forward rate of 2.40%.

Institutional investors and bond traders can decide to use interest rate futures or fixed-income futures (also referred to as "bond futures") contracts, which are longer dated, to hedge interest rate risk exposure. The choice will depend on the maturity of the bond or portfolio to be hedged. Since they are listed, interest rate futures have a limited number of maturities. Furthermore, the nearest months' contracts have higher liquidity than the longer tenors. For these reasons, interest rate futures (e.g., Eurodollar futures) are commonly used to hedge short-term bonds, with up to two to three years remaining to maturity. When using interest rate futures to hedge a short-term bond, an effective and widely adopted technique to construct the hedge is to use a strip of

---

[3] The IMM, or International Monetary Market, was established as a division of CME many years ago. The distinction is seldom made today because CME operates as a unified entity, but references to IMM persist today.

futures contracts. Having measured the responsiveness of the bond to an interest rate change, it is now necessary to measure the sensitivity of each cash flow to changes in the relevant forward rate. Then, one can calculate the number of futures contracts needed to hedge the interest rate exposure for each cash flow. Fixed-income futures contracts remain, however, the preferred instrument to hedge bond positions, given that their liquidity is very high. This is especially true for US Treasury bond futures.

## 2.1 Fixed-Income Futures

Portfolio managers that want to hedge the duration risk of their bond portfolios usually use fixed-income futures. They are standardized forward contracts listed on an exchange that have as underlying a basket of deliverable bonds with remaining maturities within a predefined range. The most liquid contracts include T-note and T-bond futures listed on the Chicago Board of Trade or the Chicago Mercantile Exchange. Contracts expire in March, June, September, and December, and the underlying assets include Treasury bills, notes, and bonds. In Europe, the most liquid and most heavily traded fixed-income futures are traded on the Eurex, and these are the Euro-Bund (FGBL), Euro-Bobl (FGBM), and Euro-Schatz (FCBS).[4] These futures contracts have German federal government–issued bonds with different maturities as underlying. The Schatz is also known as the short bund futures contract because the maturities of the underlying bonds range from 21 to 27 months. In contrast, maturities of underlying bonds range from 4.5 years to 5.5 years for the Bobl futures contract and are even longer (between 10 years and 30 years) for the Bund futures contract.

Bond futures are used by hedgers to protect an existing bond portfolio against adverse interest rate movements and by arbitrageurs to gain from price differences in equivalent instruments.

A fixed-income futures contract has as its underlying reference assets a basket of deliverable bonds with a range of different coupon levels and maturity dates. Most futures contracts are closed before delivery or rolled into the next contract month. However, in the case of delivery, the futures contract seller has the obligation to deliver and the right to choose which security to deliver. For this reason, the duration of a futures contract is usually consistent with the forward behavior of the cheapest underlying deliverable bond. This is called the cheapest-to-deliver (CTD) bond, the eligible bond that the seller will most likely choose to deliver under the futures contract if he decides to deliver (rather than close out the futures position). The price sensitivity of the bond futures will, therefore, reflect the duration of the CTD bond.

Within the underlying basket of bonds, the seller will deliver the CTD bond, the one that presents the greatest profit or smallest loss at delivery. To provide a guide for choosing the CTD bond, the concept of the conversion factor (CF) has been introduced. Given that the short side has the option of delivering any eligible security, a conversion factor invoicing system that allows for a less biased comparison in choosing among deliverable bonds has been established. In fact, the amount the futures contract seller receives at delivery will depend on the conversion factor that, when multiplied by the futures settlement price, will generate a price at which the deliverable bond would

---

[4] "Bobl" comes from the German term "Bundesobligation," which corresponds to a federal government bond. "Schatz" is the English word for "Bundesschatzanweisungen," or "Schätze," which is two-year debt issued by the German federal government, whereas "Bunds" represent long-term obligations.

# Managing Interest Rate Risk with Forwards, Futures and Fixed-Income Futures

trade if its coupon were the notional coupon of the futures contract specification (e.g., 6% coupon and 20 years to maturity). The principal invoice amount at maturity is given in the following equation:[5]

Principal invoice amount =
(Futures settlement price/100) × $CF$ × Contract size.  (2)

The cheapest-to-deliver bond is determined on the basis of duration, relative bond prices, and yield levels. In particular, a bond with a low (high) coupon rate, a long (short) maturity, and thus a long (short) duration will most likely be the CTD bond if the market yield is above (below) the notional yield of the fixed-income futures contract. The notional yield is usually in line with the prevailing interest rate.

The pricing discrepancy between the price of the cash security and that of the fixed-income futures is the basis. It is determined by the spot cash price less the futures price multiplied by the conversion factor. The possibility of physical delivery of the underlying asset guarantees convergence of futures and spot prices on the delivery date. In fact, the no-arbitrage condition requires the basis to be zero on the delivery date; otherwise, substantial arbitrage profits can be made. However, basis traders look for arbitrage opportunities by capitalizing on relatively small pricing differences. If the basis is negative, a trader would make a profit by "buying the basis"—that is, purchasing the bond and shorting the futures. In contrast, the trader would make a profit by "selling the basis" when the basis is positive; in this case, she would sell the bond and buy the futures. Example 4 demonstrates how to determine the CTD bond for delivery under a Treasury bond futures contract.

### EXAMPLE 4

### Delivery on a Fixed-Income Futures Contract

A trader has sold 10-year US Treasury bond futures contracts expiring in June and now has the obligation to deliver and the right to choose which security to deliver (the CTD bond). The futures contract reference security is a US Treasury bond with 20 years to maturity and a coupon of 6%. The T-bond futures contract size is $100,000. The futures contract settlement price is $143.47. The trader now needs to determine which of the two bonds in the following table is cheapest to deliver.

|  | Bond A | Bond B |
|---|---|---|
| Cash Bond | T 4½ 02/15/36 | T 5 05/15/37 |
| Cash Dirty Price | $120.75 | $128.50 |
| Bond Purchase Value | $120,750 | $128,500 |
| Futures Settlement Price | 143.47 | 143.47 |
| Conversion Factor | 0.8388 | 0.8883 |
| Contract Size | $100,000 | $100,000 |
| Principal Invoice Amount | $120,342.64 | $127,444.40 |
| Delivery Gain/Loss | −$407.36 = $120,342.64 − $120,750 | −$1,055.60 = $127,444.40 − $128,500 |

---

[5] If there is accrued interest due on the CTD bond, the futures contract seller will receive the following at delivery: Total invoice amount = Principal invoice amount + Accrued interest.

**Analysis:**

The trader will try to maximize the difference between the amount received upon delivery, given by the futures contract settlement price (divided by 100) times the conversion factor times $100,000, and the cost of acquiring the bond for delivery, given by its market price plus any accrued interest (i.e., the dirty price). Note that this example assumes no accrued interest.

The conversion factors for both bonds are less than 1 since both bonds have a coupon lower than 6%, the coupon for the futures contract standard. Bond A can be purchased for $120,750 and Bond B for $128,500, both per $100,000 face value. These purchase prices are compared with the amounts received upon delivery. Principal invoice amounts are calculated using Equation 2, as follows:

Principal invoice amount = (Futures settlement price/100) × CF × $100,000.

Bond A: 143.47/100 × 0.8388 × $100,000 = $120,342.64.

Bond B: 143.47/100 × 0.8883 × $100,000 = $127,444.40.

The cheapest to deliver is Bond A, the 4½% T-bond with a maturity date of 02/15/36, since the loss on delivering Bond A ($407.36) is less than the loss on delivering Bond B ($1,055.60).

Continuing with the previous analysis where we hedged a portfolio of fixed-rate securities, we now determine the hedge ratio (HR) expressed as the number of fixed-income futures contracts to be sold or purchased. The relation $\Delta P = (HR)(\Delta F)$ is still valid; note that we saw it previously in the context of swaps as $\Delta P = (N_s)(\Delta S)$, where $\Delta P$ is the change in the value of the bond portfolio and $\Delta F$ is the change in the value of the fixed-income futures. The "ideal" hedge balances any change in value in the cash securities with an equal and opposite-sign change in the futures' value.

With futures, however, we have to consider the cheapest-to-deliver bond price and the conversion factor. Because the basis of the CTD bond is generally closest to zero, any change in the futures price level ($\Delta F$) will be a reflection of the change in the value of the CTD bond adjusted by its conversion factor. By considering the relative price movement of the bond futures contract to the cheapest-to-deliver bond, we have $\Delta F = \Delta CTD/CF$. By substituting into the equation $\Delta P = (HR)(\Delta F)$, the hedge ratio becomes

$$HR = \frac{\Delta P}{\Delta CTD}(CF) \qquad (3)$$

In the case where the bond to hedge is the CTD, then a hedge ratio based on the conversion factor is likely to be quite effective (given that the price of a fixed-income futures contract tends to track closely with that of the cheapest-to-deliver bond).

However, for other securities with different coupons and maturities, the number of bond futures that are used to hedge against price changes of a fixed-rate bond is calculated on the basis of a duration-based hedge ratio. Moreover, the relationship between the bond's price and its yield can also be stated in terms of basis point value and the portfolio's target modified duration, $MDUR_T$, such that the portfolio's target basis point value ($BPV_T$) is

$$BPV_T = MDUR_T \times 0.01\% \times MV_P \qquad (4)$$

In the special case where the objective is to completely hedge the portfolio, $BPV_T = 0$. The effect of the basis point value hedge ratio ($BPVHR$) is then conceptualized as $BPV_P + BPVHR \times BPV_F = 0$. Thus, $BPVHR = -BPV_P/BPV_F$, which uses the basis point value of the portfolio to be hedged ($BPV_P$) and that of the futures contract ($BPV_F$), where

$$BPV_P = MDUR_P \times 0.01\% \times MV_P \qquad (5)$$

and

$$BPV_F = BPV_{CTD}/CF \qquad (6)$$

In Equation 6, the numerator is $BPV_{CTD}$, the basis point value of the cheapest-to-deliver bond under the futures contract, and the denominator is $CF$, its conversion factor. The basis point value of the cheapest-to-deliver bond is determined, in a manner analogous to Equations 4 and 5, as

$$BPV_{CTD} = MDUR_{CTD} \times 0.01\% \times MV_{CTD} \qquad (7)$$

where $MV_{CTD}$ = (CTD price/100) × Futures contract size.

Finally, for small changes in yield, by substituting into the equation $BPVHR = -BPV_P/BPV_F$, where $BPV_F$ becomes $BPV_{CTD}/CF$, in the special case of complete hedging, $BPVHR$ in terms of number of futures contracts is

$$BPVHR = \frac{-BPV_P}{BPV_{CTD}} \times \text{Conversion factor} \qquad (8)$$

### EXAMPLE 5

#### Hedging Bond Holdings with Fixed-Income Futures

A portfolio manager is holding €50 million (principal) in German bunds (DBRs) and wants to fully hedge the value of the bond investment against a rise in interest rates. The portfolio has a modified duration of 9.50 and a market value of €49,531,000. Moreover, the manager wishes to fully hedge the bond portfolio (so, $BPV_T = 0$) with a short position in Euro-Bund futures with a price of 158.33. The cheapest-to-deliver bond is the DBR 0.25% 02/15/27 that has a price of 98.14, modified duration of 8.623, and conversion factor of 0.619489. The size of the futures contract is €100,000.

Determine the following:

1. The $BPV_P$ of the portfolio to be hedged
2. The $BPV_{CTD}$ of the futures contract hedging instrument
3. The number of Euro-Bund futures contracts to sell to fully hedge the portfolio

#### Solution to 1:

The basis point value of the portfolio ($BPV_P$), stated in terms of the change in value for a 1 bp (0.01%) change in yield, is calculated using Equation 5, as follows:

$BPV_P = MDUR_P \times 0.01\% \times MV_P$

| | |
|---|---|
| Portfolio Principal | €50,000,000 |
| Portfolio Market Value | €49,531,000 |
| Modified Duration | 9.50 |

$BPV_P$ = 9.50 × 0.0001 × €49,531,000 = €47,054.45.

Thus, the portfolio to be hedged has a $BPV_P$ of €47,054.45 per €50 million notional.

#### Solution to 2:

The basis point value of the CTD bond underlying the futures contract ($BPV_{CTD}$) is calculated using Equation 7, as follows:

$BPV_{CTD} = MDUR_{CTD} \times 0.01\% \times MV_{CTD}$

| Futures Hedge | |
|---|---|
| Euro-Bund Futures Price | 158.33 |
| Contract Size | €100,000 |

| Cheapest-To-Deliver Bond | |
|---|---|
| DBR 0¼ 02/15/27 Gov't. | |
| Modified Duration | 8.623 |
| Bond Price | 98.14 |
| Conversion Factor | 0.619489 |

$BPV_{CTD} = 8.623 \times 0.0001 \times [(98.14/100) \times €100,000] = €84.63$.

So, the BPV of the CTD bond ($BPV_{CTD}$) is €84.63.

**Solution to 3:**

Using Equation 8 and the Solutions to 1 and 2, we have:

$$BPVHR = \frac{-BPV_P}{BPV_{CTD}} \times CF = \frac{-€47,054.45}{€84.63} \times 0.619489 = -344.437 \approx -344$$

Therefore, the number of Euro-Bund futures to *sell* to fully hedge the portfolio is 344 contracts.

In the real world, however, the hedging results are imperfect because (1) the hedge is done with the cheapest-to-deliver bond, and since the CTD bond can change over the holding period, the duration of the futures contract can also change; (2) the relationship between interest rates and bond prices is not linear, owing to convexity; and (3) the term structure of interest rates often changes via non-parallel moves.

Reconsidering Example 2 from before, in which the manager whose portfolio has a modified duration of 5.5 years wants to lower the duration to 4.5 years, the general principle is the same. What needs to be determined is the number of futures contracts that are required to reduce the portfolio's modified duration to the target level. In this more general case, where $MDUR_T$ (and $BPV_T$) is non-zero, stated in terms of basis point value and BPVHR, we have $BPV_P + BPVHR \times BPV_F = BPV_T$.

Solving for BPVHR and substituting for $BPV_F$, we have the more general version of Equation 8:

$$\begin{aligned}BPVHR &= \left(\frac{BPV_T - BPV_P}{BPV_F}\right) \\ &= \left(\frac{BPV_T - BPV_P}{BPV_{CTD}/CF}\right) \\ &= \left(\frac{BPV_T - BPV_P}{BPV_{CTD}}\right) \times CF\end{aligned} \qquad (9)$$

### EXAMPLE 6

### Decreasing Portfolio Duration with Futures

Consider the portfolio manager from Example 5 who now decides to decrease the portfolio's modified duration from 9.50 to 8.50. The yield curve is flat. Additionally, we have already demonstrated that given the portfolio's market value of €49,531,000, the $BPV_P$ is €47,054.50. Finally, assume the CTD bond underlying the Euro-Bund futures is the same as before, DBR 0.25% 02/15/27, with a $BPV_{CTD}$ of €84.63 and a conversion factor of 0.619489.

Determine the following:

1 The $BPV_T$ of the portfolio to be hedged
2 The number of Euro-Bund futures contracts to sell to reduce the portfolio's modified duration to 8.50

**Solution to 1:**

Using Equation 4 with a $MDUR_T$ of 8.50, the portfolio's target basis point value ($BPV_T$) will be

$$BPV_T = 8.50 \times 0.0001 \times €49,531,000 = €42,101.35.$$

**Solution to 2:**

To achieve the target modified duration of 8.50, the portfolio manager must implement a short position in Euro-Bund futures. Using the same cheapest-to-deliver bond with a $BPV_{CTD}$ of €84.63 and a conversion factor of 0.619489, the number of Euro-Bund futures to sell to decrease the portfolio's duration is calculated using Equation 9:

$$BPVHR = \left(\frac{€42,101.35 - €47,054.50}{€84.63}\right) \times 0.619489$$

$$= -36.26 \approx -36 \text{ futures contracts}$$

Therefore, the number of Euro-Bund futures to *sell* to achieve the target portfolio duration of 8.50 is 36 contracts.

# MANAGING CURRENCY EXPOSURE

**3**

**b** demonstrate how currency swaps, forwards, and futures can be used to modify a portfolio's risk and return;

Currency swaps, forwards, and futures can be used to effectively alter currency risk exposures. Currency risk is the risk that the value of a current or future asset (liability) in a foreign currency will decrease (increase) when converted into the domestic currency.

## 3.1 Currency Swaps

A currency swap is similar to an interest rate swap, but it is different in two ways: (1) The interest rates are associated with different currencies, and (2) the notional principal amounts may or may not be exchanged at the beginning and end of the swap's life.[6]

Currency swaps help the parties in the swap to hedge against the risk of exchange rate fluctuations and to achieve better rate outcomes. In particular, a **cross-currency basis swap** exchanges notional principals because the goal of the transaction is to issue at a more favorable funding rate and swap the amount back to the currency of

---

[6] Although an exchange of notional principals often occurs, the parties may agree not to do this. Some types of hedge transactions are designed to hedge only foreign interest cash flows and not principal payments, so a principal exchange on a currency swap would not be necessary.

choice. Firms that need foreign-denominated cash can obtain the funding in their local currency and then swap the local currency for the required foreign currency using a cross-currency basis swap. The swap periodically sets interest rate payments, mostly floating for floating, separately in two different currencies. The net effect is to use a loan in a local currency to take out a loan in a foreign currency while avoiding any foreign exchange risk. In fact, the exchange rate is fixed, as illustrated in Example 7.

> **EXAMPLE 7**
>
> ### Cross-Currency Basis Swap
>
> Consider a Canadian private equity (PE) firm that is executing a leveraged buyout (LBO) of a small, struggling US-based electronics manufacturer. The goal is to turn around the company by implementing new robotics technology for making servers and infrastructure devices for "bitcoin mining." Exit from the LBO via initial public offering is expected in three years. To execute the LBO and provide working capital for US operations, the PE firm needs USD40 million. The rate on a US dollar loan is the semiannual US dollar reference floating rate plus 100 bps. The PE firm discovers that it can borrow more cheaply in the local Canadian market and decides to fund the LBO in Canadian dollars (CAD) by borrowing CAD50 million for three years at the semiannual Canadian dollar reference floating rate plus 65 bps. Then it contacts a New York–based dealer and requests a quote for a three-year cross-currency basis swap with semiannual interest payments to exchange the CAD50 million into US dollars. The three-year CAD–USD cross-currency basis swap is quoted at –15 bps at a rate of USD/CAD 0.8000 (expressed as US dollars per 1 Canadian dollar). The swap agreement provides that both parties pay the semiannual reference floating rate, but the Canadian dollar rate also includes a "basis." Here the basis is the difference between interest rates in the cross-currency basis swap and those used to determine the forward exchange rates. If covered interest rate parity holds, a forward exchange rate is determined by the spot exchange rate and the interest rate differential between foreign and domestic currencies over the term of the forward rate. However, usually covered interest rate parity does not hold and thus gives rise to the basis.
>
> The basis is quoted on the non-USD leg of the swap. "Paying" the basis would mean borrowing the other currency versus lending US dollars, whereas "receiving" the basis implies lending the other currency versus borrowing US dollars. The three-year CAD–USD cross-currency swap in this case is quoted at –15 bps. This means that the Canadian PE firm, the "lender" of the Canadian dollars in the swap, will receive the Canadian dollar reference rate, assumed to be 1.95%, minus 15 bps every six months in exchange for paying the US dollar reference rate for the US dollars it has "borrowed." Given that the PE firm pays the Canadian dollar floating rate plus 65 bps on its bank loan, the effective spread paid becomes 80 bps (= 65bps + 15 bps). This compares with a spread of 100 bps if instead it borrowed in US dollars.
>
> **Analysis:**
>
> We now examine the cash flows in the cross-currency basis swap, where $N$ is the notional principal of the Canadian dollar leg of the swap and $S_0$, agreed at the start, is the spot exchange rate for all payments (at inception, on interest payment dates, and at maturity). For the Canadian PE firm, this means that
>
> $N$ = CAD50 million and $S_0$ = USD/CAD 0.8000.

*Flows at the inception of the swap.*

At inception, the Canadian PE firm delivers Canadian dollars ($N$) in exchange for US dollars (at a rate of $N \times S_0$).

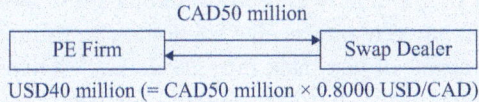
CAD50 million
USD40 million (= CAD50 million × 0.8000 USD/CAD)

At each payment date, the PE firm makes a floating-rate payment in US dollars and receives a floating-rate payment in Canadian dollars that is passed on to the local Canadian lender. At maturity, the PE firm returns the USD40 million to the dealer and in return receives the CAD50 million, which it uses to pay off its lender.

*Periodic payments.*

At each swap payment date, the Canadian PE firm receives interest on Canadian dollars ($N$) in exchange for paying interest on US dollars ($N \times S_0$). Importantly, the "basis" component (of –15 bps) will be included along with the semiannual Canadian dollar reference floating rate.

Suppose that on the first settlement date the semiannual reference floating rate in Canadian dollars is 1.95% and the basis is –15 bps. Therefore, the Canadian dollar rate on the swap is 1.80% (= 1.95% – 15 bps), and we assume the US dollar rate is 2.50% (the semiannual reference floating rate). For the PE firm, the first of a sequence of periodic cash flows resulting from the swap amounts to:

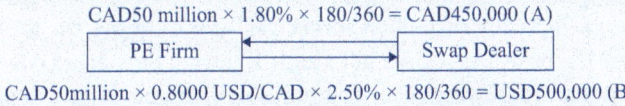
CAD50 million × 1.80% × 180/360 = CAD450,000 (A)
CAD50million × 0.8000 USD/CAD × 2.50% × 180/360 = USD500,000 (B)

The interest rate payment on the PE firm's loan is CAD50 million × (1.95% + 0.65%) × (180/360) = CAD650,000. Considering the CAD450,000 received on the swap (A), the PE firm's net payment is CAD200,000.

At USD/CAD 0.8000, this net payment of CAD200,000 corresponds to a payment of USD160,000, which when added to the USD500,000 paid on the swap (B) totals USD660,000. Importantly, note that had the Canadian PE firm taken out the US loan instead, it would have paid periodically USD700,000 (= USD40 million × [2.50% + 1.0%] × [180/360]).

*Flows at maturity.*

At the maturity of the swap (and after a successful exit from the LBO via a US IPO), the Canadian PE firm swaps back US dollars in exchange for Canadian dollars (USD × $1/S_0$).

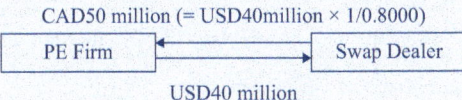
CAD50 million (= USD40million × 1/0.8000)
USD40 million

In this specific example, it is worth noting that the exchange rate was assumed not to change.

---

A common use of currency swaps by investors is in transactions meant to earn extra yield by investing in a foreign bond market and swapping the proceeds into the domestic currency. Given that the investment is hedged against the risk of exchange rate fluctuations, this corresponds to a synthetic domestic yield, but the repackaging allows the investor to earn a higher yield compared with the yield from direct purchase of the domestic asset, because of the level of the basis on the cross-currency swap. For example, during periods when demand for US dollars is strong relative to demand for Japanese yen (JPY), the US–Japan interest rate differential implied by the currency markets may be significantly wider than the actual interest rate differential. During such a period, a US investor might choose among the following two options: (1) Invest in short-term US Treasury bonds, or (2) use a cross-currency swap to lend an equivalent amount of US dollars and buy yen; buy short-term Japanese government debt; each period pay yen and receive US dollars on the swap; and at maturity swap an equivalent amount of yen back into US dollars. When the basis is largely negative, due to relatively weak (strong) demand for yen (US dollars) from swap market participants, the borrowing costs in yen (US dollars) are low (high), making the return from lending US dollars via a cross-currency swap particularly attractive. By choosing Option 2, the investor can earn more than he could from the investment in short-term US Treasury debt.

The rates on the cross-currency basis swaps will depend on the demand for US dollar funding, because when the US dollar reference floating rate is elevated, the counterparty receiving US dollars at initiation of the swap will be willing to receive a lower interest rate on the non-dollar currency periodic payments. Exhibit 1 shows the levels of the basis for one-year cross-currency swaps from May 2016 to April 2018 in the Australian dollar (AUD), the Canadian dollar (CAD), the euro (EUR), and the British pound (GBP) versus USD Libor (quoted as six-month USD Libor versus six-month AUD bank bills, six-month CAD Libor, six-month Euribor, and six-month GBP Libor, respectively). Cross-currency basis spreads vary over time and are driven by credit and liquidity factors, and supply and demand for cross-currency financing. As noted previously, relatively strong demand for US dollar financing against the foreign currency would require the US dollar "borrower" in the swap to accept a lower rate on the periodic foreign currency cash flows it receives—for example, the foreign periodic reference rate less the basis. As shown in Exhibit 1, during the period covered this was the case for US dollar borrowers receiving periodic swap payments in all currencies shown except the Australian dollar.

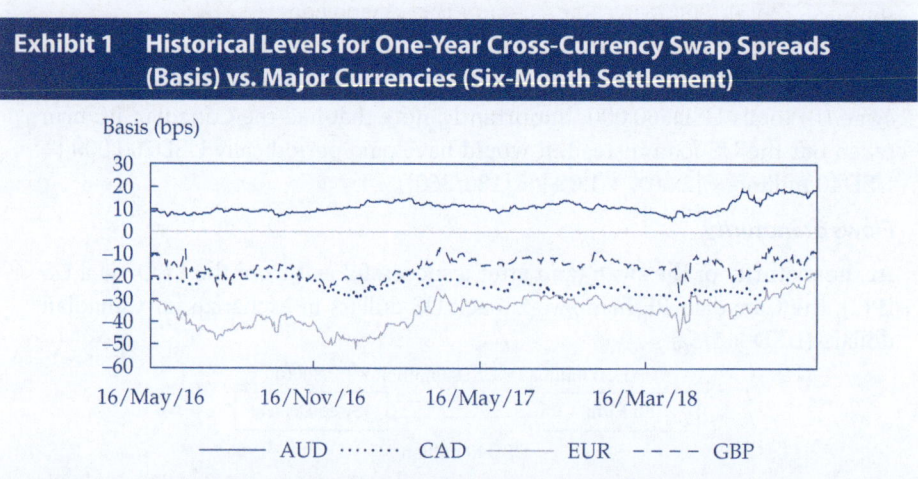

**Exhibit 1  Historical Levels for One-Year Cross-Currency Swap Spreads (Basis) vs. Major Currencies (Six-Month Settlement)**

## 3.2 Currency Forwards and Futures

Currency forwards and futures are actively used to manage currency risk. These two financial instruments are used to hedge against undesired moves in the exchange rate by buying or selling a specified amount of foreign currency, at a defined time in the future and at an agreed-on price at contract initiation. Futures contracts are standardized and best meet dealers' and investors' needs to manage their portfolios' currency risk. Corporations often use customized forward contracts to manage the risk of cash flows in foreign currencies because they can be customized according to their needs.

For example, consider the general partner of a US-based venture capital (VC) firm that is calling down capital commitments for investment in "fintech" startups in Silicon Valley. It will receive in 30 days a payment of CAD50 million from a limited partner residing in Vancouver, British Columbia, and will immediately transfer the funds to its US dollar account. If the Canadian dollar were to depreciate versus the US dollar before the payment date, the US VC firm will receive fewer US dollars in exchange for the CAD50 million. To eliminate the foreign exchange risk associated with receiving this capital commitment, the firm can fix the price of the US dollars now via a forward contract in which it promises to sell CAD50 million for an agreed-on number of US dollars, based on the forward exchange rate, in 30 days.

### EXAMPLE 8

### Hedging Currency Risk with Futures

Consider the same US-based VC firm that is calling down capital commitments and will receive CAD50 million in 30 days. The general partner now decides to sell futures contracts to lock in the current USD/CAD rate. The hedge ratio is assumed to be equal to 1. The firm hedges its risk by selling Canadian dollar futures contracts with the closest expiry to the future Canadian dollar inflow.

Given a price for the Canadian dollar futures contract of USD/CAD 0.7838 (number of US dollars for 1 Canadian dollar) and a contract size of CAD100,000, determine how many Canadian dollar futures contracts the VC firm must sell to hedge its risk.

### Solution:

To hedge the risk of the Canadian dollar depreciating against the US dollar, the VC firm must sell 500 futures contracts:

$$\frac{\text{CAD}50{,}000{,}000}{\text{CAD}100{,}000} = 500 \text{ contracts}$$

When the futures contracts expire, the VC firm will receive (pay) any depreciation (appreciation) in the Canadian dollar versus the US dollar compared with the futures contract price of USD0.7838/CAD.[7] If the changes in futures and spot prices are equal during the life of the futures contract, the hedge will be fully effective. A basis risk arises when the differential given by Futures price$_t$ − Spot price$_t$ is either positive or negative. In the absence of arbitrage, between the time when a hedging position is initiated and the time when it is liquidated, this spread may either widen or narrow to zero.

## MANAGING EQUITY RISK

4

c demonstrate how equity swaps, forwards, and futures can be used to modify a portfolio's risk and return;

---

[7] Remember that, assuming covered interest rate parity holds, the forward rate $(F_{f/d})$—expressed as units of foreign currency (f) for 1 unit of domestic currency (d)—is calculated from the exchange spot rate $(S_{f/d})$ and the differential between the foreign $(i_f)$ and domestic $(i_d)$ interest rates. The forward rate is calculated on the basis of the following formula: $F_{f/d} = S_{f/d} \times \left[(1 + i_f \times ACT/360)/(1 + i_d \times ACT/360)\right]$.

Investors can achieve or modify their equity risk exposures using equity swaps and equity forwards and futures. The asset underlying these financial instruments could be an equity index, a single stock, or a basket of stocks.

## 4.1 Equity Swaps

An equity swap is a derivative contract in which two parties agree to exchange a series of cash flows whereby one party pays a variable series that will be determined by a single stock, a basket of stocks, or an equity index and the other party pays either (1) a variable series determined by a different equity or rate or (2) a fixed series. An equity swap is used to convert the returns from an equity investment into another series of returns, which either can be derived from another equity series or can be a fixed rate. There are three main types of equity swaps:

- receive-equity return, pay-fixed;
- receive-equity return, pay-floating; and
- receive-equity return, pay-another equity return.

Because they are an OTC derivative instrument, each counterparty in the equity swap bears credit risk exposure to the other. For this reason, equity swaps are usually collateralized in order to reduce the credit risk exposure. At the same time, as equity swaps are created in the OTC market, they can be customized as desired by the counterparties.

A total return swap is a slightly modified equity swap; it also includes in the performance any dividends paid by the underlying stocks or index during the period until the swap maturity. The swap has a fixed tenor and may provide for one single payment at the end of the swap's life, although more typically a series of periodic payments would be arranged instead. In another variation, at the time of each periodic payment, the notional amount could be reset or remain unchanged.

Equity swaps provide synthetic exposure to physical stocks. They are preferred by some investors over ownership of shares when access to a specific market is limited, when taxes are levied for owning physical stocks (e.g., stamp duty) but are not levied on swaps, the custodian fees are high, or the cost of monitoring the stock position is elevated (e.g., because of corporate actions). However, it is important to note that equity swaps require putting up collateral, are relatively illiquid contracts, and do not confer voting rights.

Example 9 shows how an equity swap might be used by an institutional investor with a portfolio indexed to the performance of the S&P 500 Index. He believes the stock market will decline over the next six months and would like to temporarily hedge part of the market exposure of his portfolio. He can do this by entering into a six-month equity swap with one payment at termination, exchanging the total return on the S&P 500 for a floating rate. We will consider two scenarios: In the first scenario, in six months the underlying portfolio is up 5%; in the second, it is down 5%.

> **EXAMPLE 9**
>
> ### Six-Month Equity Swap
>
> An institutional investor holds a $100 million portfolio of US stocks indexed to the S&P 500. He expects the index will fall in the next six months and wants to reduce his market exposure by 30%. He enters into an equity swap with notional principal of $30 million whereby he agrees to pay the return on the index and to receive the floating reference interest rate, assumed to be 2.25%, minus 25 bps—so, 2.00% per annum.

# Managing Equity Risk

### Scenario 1:

In the first scenario, the stock market has increased by 5%. Thus, at swap settlement the institutional investor has an obligation to pay 5% × $30 million, or $1.5 million, and would receive 2% × 180/360 × $30 million, or $300,000. The two parties would net the payments and provide for a single payment of $1.2 million, which the institutional investor would pay. Because the portfolio has gained $5 million in this scenario, the profit and loss (P&L) on the combined position (including the original portfolio and the swap) is positive and equal to $3.8 million.

**Scenario 1 Equity Portfolio Rises 5%**

| | |
|---|---|
| US equity portfolio: $100 million × 5% = | +$5,000,000 |
| P&L on the stock portfolio: | +$5,000,000 |
| | |
| *Swap settlement:* | |
| Pay: $30 million × 5% = | –$1,500,000 |
| Receive: $30 million × 2% × 180/360 = | +$300,000 |
| Net payment on the swap: | –$1,200,000 |
| P&L on the net position (70% of original exposure and 30% hedged): | |
| $5,000,000 – $1,200,000 = | +$3,800,000 |

### Scenario 2:

In the second scenario, the stock market has decreased by 5%. So, it is slightly more complicated because the equity return that the institutional investor must pay is *negative*, which means he will receive money. He would receive $1.5 million because the S&P 500 had a negative performance in addition to receiving the $300,000. Because the portfolio has lost $5 million in this case, the P&L on the combined position is –$3.2 million. When the swap ends, the institutional investor returns to the same position in which he started, with the equity portfolio fully invested, and it is thereafter subject to full market risk once again.

**Scenario 2 Equity Portfolio Declines 5%**

| | |
|---|---|
| US equity portfolio: $100 million × –5% = | –$5,000,000 |
| P&L on the stock portfolio: | –$5,000,000 |
| | |
| *Swap settlement:* | +$1,500,000 |
| *Receive (Pay negative return): $30 million × 5% =* | |
| Receive: $30 million × 2% × 180/360 = | +$300,000 |
| Net payment on the swap: | +$1,800,000 |
| P&L on the net position (70% of original exposure and 30% hedged): | |
| –$5,000,000 + $1,800,000 = | –$3,200,000 |

> To test the reasonableness of the result, a portfolio comprising 70% equities and 30% money market instruments assumed to earn 2% (1% over the six months) would achieve a return of 3.8% (= 0.7 × 5% + 0.3 × [2%/2]) or $3.8 million on $100 million in the bullish scenario (Scenario 1). In the bearish scenario (Scenario 2), the return would be −3.2% (= 0.7 × −5% + 0.3 × [2%/2]) or −$3.2 million on the initial $100 million portfolio. The total return swap effectively removes the risk associated with 30% of the equity portfolio allocation and converts it into money market equivalent returns.

Consider now a private high-net-worth investor who holds a large, concentrated position in a particular company's stock that pays dividends on a regular basis. She expects that in the next six months the total return from the stock, including the dividends received, will be negative, so she wants to temporarily neutralize her long exposure. At the same time, she does not wish to lose ownership and her voting rights by selling the stock on an exchange.

This investor can enter into a total return swap requiring her to transfer the total performance of the stock (i.e., total return) to the counterparty of the swap, at prespecified dates for an agreed-on fee. Under the terms of the swap, she will pay to the counterparty the share price appreciation plus the dividends received over the life of the contract. If the stock price decreases, she will receive the share price depreciation but net of the dividends. At the same prespecified dates, the investor will receive in exchange from the counterparty an agreed-on floating-rate interest payment based on the swap notional.

Equity swaps that have a single stock as underlying can be cash settled or physically settled. If the swap is cash settled, on the termination date of the contract the equity swap receiver will receive (pay) the equity appreciation (depreciation) in cash. If the swap is physically settled, on the termination date the equity swap receiver will receive the quantity of single stock specified in the contract and pay the notional amount. Let us assume for example that a portfolio manager is the receiver in a six-month equity swap with notional principal of €4.5 million and no interim cash flows that requires physical settlement, at maturity, of 300,000 shares of the Italian insurer Generali. At maturity of the swap, the portfolio manager will receive 300,000 shares of Generali and will pay €4.5 million, which corresponds to a purchase price per share of €15 (= €4.5 million/300,000). He will also pay the interest on the swap based on the agreed-on rate. Now let us also assume that at the swap's maturity the price of Generali is €16. This price implies a gain of €300,000 (= [€16 − €15] × 300,000) for the portfolio manager, assuming he sells the shares received in the swap at €16. If the same swap had cash settlement, instead of physical settlement, at maturity the portfolio manager would have received €300,000—given by €16 (the swap settlement price) less €15 (the agreed price on the swap) and multiplied by 300,000—against the payment of the interest on the swap.

## 4.2 Equity Forwards and Futures

Equity index futures are an indispensable tool for many investment managers: They are a low-cost instrument to implement tactical allocation decisions, achieve portfolio diversification, and attain international exposure. They are standardized contracts listed on an exchange, and when the underlying is a stock index, only cash settlement is available at contract expiration.

Single stock futures are also available to investors to acquire the desired exposure to a specific stock. This exposure is also achievable with equity forwards, which are OTC contracts that are used when the counterparties need a customized agreement.

The underlying of a single stock futures contract is one specified stock, and the investor can receive or pay its performance. At expiration, the contract could require cash settlement or physical settlement using the stock.

In Example 9, rather than using an equity swap, the institutional investor could temporarily remove part of the market risk by selling S&P 500 Index futures. In the practical implementation of a stock index futures trade, we need to remember that the actual futures contract price is the quoted futures price times a designated multiplier. In determining the hedge ratio, the stock index futures price should be quoted on the same order of magnitude as the stock index.

For example, assume that a one-month futures contract on the S&P 500 is quoted at 2,700. Given the multiplier of $250, the actual futures price is equal to $675,000 (= 2,700 × $250). We also assume that the portfolio to be hedged carries average market risk, meaning a beta of 1.0.[8] To hedge 30% of the $100 million portfolio, the portfolio manager would want to sell 44 S&P 500 futures contracts, determined as follows:

$$\frac{\$30 \text{ million}}{2{,}700(\$250)} = 44.444 \approx 44 \text{ contracts}$$

Suppose the institutional investor sold the 44 futures at 2,700 and at expiration the S&P 500 *rises* by 0.5%. The cash settlement of the contract is at 2,713.5. Because the futures position is short and the index rose, there is a "loss" of 13.5 index points—each point being worth $250—on 44 contracts, for a total cash outflow, paid by the institutional investor, of $148,500:

−13.5 points per contract × $250 per point × 44 contracts = −$148,500 (a loss).

If the S&P 500 Index rose by 0.5%, the 30% of the portfolio that has been hedged would also be expected to rise by the same amount, but there is a small difference due to rounding the number of futures contracts used for the hedge:

$30,000,000 × 0.5% = $150,000.

If instead the S&P 500 *fell* by 0.5%, the numbers would be the same, but the signs would change. The institutional investor would receive the "gain" because he had a short stock index futures position when the index fell, which would offset the loss on the hedged portion of his stock portfolio. In sum, the equity market risk is hedged away.

In the previous example, the beta of the portfolio was the same as the beta of the equity index futures. This situation usually does not occur, and in most hedging strategies, it is necessary to determine the exact "hedge ratio" in terms of the number of futures contracts. Consider that the investment manager wishes to change the beta of the equity portfolio, $\beta_S$, to a target beta of $\beta_T$. Because the value of the futures contract begins each day at zero, the dollar beta of the combination of stocks and futures, assuming the target beta is achieved, is $\beta_T S$, where $S$ is the market value of the stock portfolio.[9] The number of futures contracts we shall use is $N_f$, which can be determined by setting the target dollar beta equal to the dollar beta of the stock portfolio ($\beta_S S$) and the dollar beta of $N_f$ futures ($N_f \beta_f F$), where $\beta_f$ is the beta of the futures and $F$ is the value per futures contract:

$$\beta_T S = \beta_S S + N_f \beta_f F$$

---

**8** If the portfolio carried above-market risk—say, with a beta of 1.10—the number of contracts needed to hedge would increase by this factor. Similarly, a lower-risk portfolio would require proportionately fewer contracts.

**9** Recall that the market value of the portfolio will still be the same as the market value of the stock, because the value of the futures is zero. The futures value becomes zero whenever it is marked to market, which takes place at the end of each day. In other words, the target beta does not appear to be applied to the value of the futures in the preceding analysis because the value of the futures is zero.

We then solve for $N_f$ and obtain

$$N_f = \left(\frac{\beta_T - \beta_S}{\beta_f}\right)\left(\frac{S}{F}\right) \quad (10)$$

Note that if the investor wants to increase the portfolio's beta, $\beta_T$ will exceed $\beta_S$ and the sign of $N_f$ will be positive, which means that she must buy futures. If she wants to decrease the beta, $\beta_T$ will be less than $\beta_S$, the sign of $N_f$ will be negative, and she must sell futures. This relationship should make sense: Selling futures will offset some of the risk of holding the stock, whereas buying futures will add risk.

In the special case in which the goal is to eliminate market risk, $\beta_T$ would be set to zero and the formula would reduce to

$$N_f = -\left(\frac{\beta_S}{\beta_f}\right)\left(\frac{S}{F}\right)$$

In this case, the sign of $N_f$ will always be negative, which makes sense, because in order to hedge away all the market risk, futures must be sold.

### EXAMPLE 10

### Increasing the Beta of a Portfolio with Futures

Paulo Bianchi is the manager of a fund that invests in UK defensive stocks, such as consumer staples producers and utilities. His firm's market outlook for the next quarter has become more positive, so Bianchi decides to increase the beta on the £40 million portfolio he manages from its current level of $\beta_S = 0.85$ to $\beta_T = 1.10$ for the next three months. He will execute this increase in equity market risk exposure using futures on the FTSE 100 Index. The futures contract price is currently £7,300, the contract's multiplier is £10 per index point (so each futures contract is worth £73,000), and its beta, $\beta_f$, is 1.00.

At the end of the three-month period, the UK stock market has increased by 2%. The stock portfolio has increased in value to £40,680,000, calculated as £40,000,000 × [1 + (0.02 × 0.85)]. The FTSE 100 futures contract has risen to £74,460.

1. Determine the appropriate number of FTSE 100 Index futures Bianchi should buy to increase the portfolio's beta to 1.10.

2. Demonstrate how the effective beta of the portfolio of stocks and the FTSE 100 Index futures matched Bianchi's target beta of 1.10.

### Solution to 1:

Using Equation 10 and the preceding data, the appropriate number of futures contracts to buy to increase the portfolio's beta to 1.10 would be 137.

$$N_f = \left(\frac{\beta_T - \beta_S}{\beta_f}\right)\left(\frac{S}{F}\right) = \left(\frac{1.10 - 0.85}{1.00}\right)\left(\frac{£40,000,000}{£73,000}\right) = 136.99 \text{ (rounded to 137)}$$

# Managing Equity Risk

> **Solution to 2:**
>
> The profit on the futures contracts is 137 × (£74,460 − £73,000) = £200,020. Adding the profit from the futures to the value of the stock portfolio gives a total market value of £40,680,000 + £200,020 = £40,880,020. The rate of return for the combined position is
>
> $$\frac{£40,880,020}{£40,000,000} - 1 = 0.0220, \text{ or } 2.2\%$$
>
> Because the market went up by 2% and the overall gain was 2.2%, the effective beta of the portfolio was
>
> $$\frac{0.0220}{0.020} = 1.10$$
>
> Thus, the effective beta matched the target beta of 1.10.

## 4.3 Cash Equitization

Cash securitization (also known as "cash equitization" or "cash overlay") is a strategy designed to boost returns by finding ways to "equitize" unintended cash holdings. By purchasing futures contracts, fund managers attempt to replicate the performance of the underlying market in which the cash would have been invested. Given the liquidity of the futures market, doing so would be relatively easy. An alternative solution could be to purchase calls and sell puts on the underlying asset with the same exercise price and expiry date.

In this case, we have a cash holding, implying $\beta_S = 0$, so the number of futures (with beta of $\beta_f$) that would need to be purchased in a cash equitization transaction is given by

$$N_f = \left(\frac{\beta_T}{\beta_f}\right)\left(\frac{S}{F}\right) \tag{11}$$

> **EXAMPLE 11**
>
> ### Cash Equitization
>
> Akari Fujiwara manages a large equity fund denominated in Japanese yen that is indexed to the Nikkei 225 stock index. She determines that the current level of excess cash that has built up in the portfolio amounts to JPY140 million. She decides to purchase futures contracts to replicate the return on her fund's target index. Nikkei 225 index futures currently trade at a price of JPY23,000 per contract, the contract multiplier is JPY1,000 per index point (so each futures contract is worth JPY23 million), and the beta, $\beta_f$, is 1.00.
>
> Determine the appropriate number of futures Fujiwara must buy to equitize her portfolio's excess cash position.
>
> **Solution:**
>
> Using Equation 11, which assumes $\beta_S = 0$, the answer is found as follows:
>
> $$N_f = \left(\frac{\beta_T}{\beta_f}\right)\left(\frac{S}{F}\right) = \left(\frac{1.00}{1.00}\right)\left(\frac{\text{JPY}140,000,000}{\text{JPY}23,000,000}\right) = 6.087 \text{ (rounded to 6)}$$
>
> The appropriate number of futures to buy to equitize the portfolio's excess cash position, based on the data provided, would be six contracts.

## 5 VOLATILITY DERIVATIVES: FUTURES AND OPTIONS

**d** demonstrate the use of volatility derivatives and variance swaps;

With the introduction of volatility futures and variance swaps, many investors now consider volatility an asset class in itself. In particular, long volatility exposure can be an effective hedge against a sell-off in a long equity portfolio, notably during periods of extreme market movements. Empirical studies have identified a negative correlation between volatility and stock index returns that becomes pronounced during stock market downturns. Importantly, variance swaps, which will be discussed in this section, have a valuable convexity feature—as realized volatility increases (decreases), the positive (negative) swap payoffs increase (decrease)—that makes them particularly attractive for hedging long equity portfolios. For example, some investors use strategies that systematically allocate to volatility futures or variance swaps to hedge the "tail" risk of their portfolios. Naturally, the counterparties are selling a kind of insurance; they expect such return tails will not materialize. The effectiveness of such hedges should be compared against more traditional "long volatility" hedging methods, such as implementing a rolling series of out-of-the-money put options or futures. The roll aspect affects portfolio returns, so the term structure should be carefully considered. For example, if futures prices are in backwardation (contango), then overall returns to an investor with a long position in the futures would be enhanced (diminished) owing to positive (negative) roll return. The results are necessarily reversed for the holder of the short futures position. In sum, all these derivatives strategies should be assessed on the basis of their ability to reduce portfolio risk and improve returns. In contrast, a common investment strategy implemented by opportunistic investors involves being systematically short volatility, thereby attempting to capture the risk premium embedded in option prices. This strategy is most profitable under stable market conditions, but it can lead to large losses if market volatility rises unexpectedly.

### 5.1 Volatility Futures and Options

The CBOE Volatility Index, known as the VIX or the "fear index," is a measure of investors' expectations of volatility in the S&P 500 over the next 30 days. It is calculated and published by the Chicago Board Options Exchange (CBOE) and is based on the prices of S&P 500 Index options. The CBOE began publishing real-time VIX data in 1993, and in 2004, VIX futures were introduced. Investors cannot invest directly in the VIX but instead must use VIX futures contracts that offer investors a pure play on the level of expected stock market volatility, regardless of the direction of the S&P 500. Volatility futures allow investors to implement their views depending on their expectations about the timing and magnitude of a change in implied volatility. For example, in order for a long VIX futures position to protect an equity portfolio during a downturn, the stock market's implied volatility, as derived from S&P 500 Index options, must increase by more than the consensus expectation of implied volatility prior to the sell-off.

A family of volatility indexes has also been introduced for European equity markets, and they are designed to reflect market expectations of near-term to long-term volatility. The most well known of these is the VSTOXX index, based on real-time option prices on the EURO STOXX 50 index. The family of volatility indexes also includes the VDAX-NEW Index, based on DAX stock index options.

Next, we discuss various shapes of the VIX futures term structure. The CBOE Futures Exchange (CFE) lists nine standard (monthly) VIX index futures contracts and six weekly expirations in VIX futures. Each weekly and monthly contract settles 30 calendar days prior to the subsequent standard S&P 500 Index option's expiration.

# Volatility Derivatives: Futures and Options

The weekly futures have lower volumes and open interest than the monthly futures contracts have. Exhibit 2 presents the first six monthly VIX futures contracts at three different fixed points in time for all expires; these are not consecutive days but, rather, are at intervals of about two months apart.

### Exhibit 2  VIX Futures Contracts

| CBOE VIX Futures Expiry | Day 1 | Day 60 | Day 120 |
| --- | --- | --- | --- |
| April | 16.68 | 33.46 | 9.77 |
| May | 17.00 | 19.85 | 14.05 |
| June | 17.00 | 19.10 | 14.55 |
| July | 17.35 | 18.50 | 15.25 |
| August | 17.51 | 18.75 | 15.60 |
| September | 17.80 | 18.90 | 16.10 |

Exhibit 3 shows the shape of the VIX futures term structure corresponding to the data in Exhibit 2. The vertical axis shows the futures prices, and the horizontal scale indicates the month of expiration.

### Exhibit 3  Shapes of the VIX Futures Term Structure

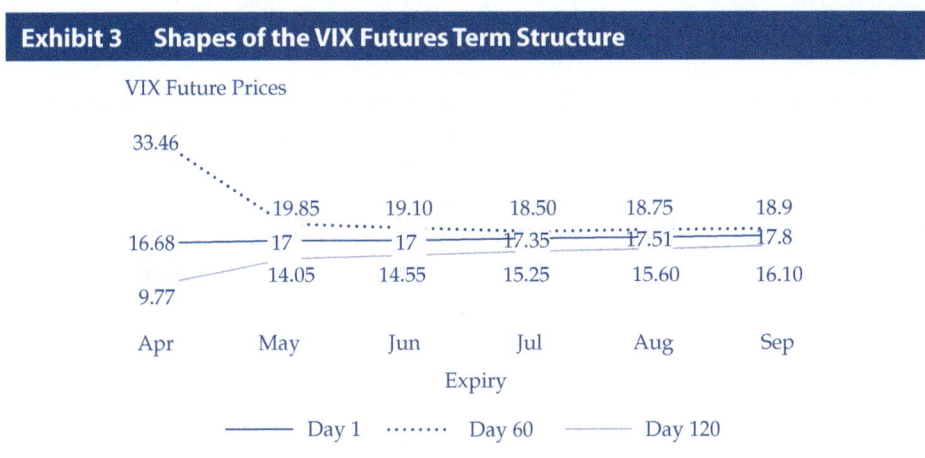

The shape of the VIX futures curve is always changing, reflecting the current volatility environment, investors' expectations regarding the future level of volatility, and the buying and selling activity in VIX futures contracts by market participants. Depending on the mix of these factors, the VIX futures term structure can change from being positively sloped to flat or inverted in just a few months' time.

Day 1 illustrates what happens when volatility is expected to remain stable over the near to long term: The term structure of VIX futures is flat. Day 60 shows the VIX futures in backwardation. This situation typically is a signal that investors expect more volatility in the short term and thus require higher prices for shorter-term contracts than for longer-term ones. In contrast, Day 120 is an example of the VIX futures being in contango. The curve is upward sloped, and it is steep for VIX buyers, with nearly 4.3 volatility points between the April and May expires. Higher longer-term VIX futures prices are interpreted as an expectation that the VIX will rise because of increasing long-term volatility.

The VIX futures converge to the spot VIX as expiration approaches, so the two must be equal at expiration. When the VIX futures curve is in contango (backwardation) and assuming volatility expectations remain unchanged, the VIX futures price will get "pulled" closer to the VIX spot price, and they will decrease (increase) in price as they approach expiration. Traders calculate the daily roll as the difference between the front-month VIX futures price and the VIX spot price, divided by the number of business days until the VIX futures contract settles. Assuming that the basis declines linearly until settlement, when the term structure is in contango (backwardation), the trader who is long in back-month VIX futures would realize roll-down losses (profits).

Importantly, VIX futures may not reflect the index, especially when the VIX experiences large spikes, because longer-maturity futures contracts are less sensitive to short-term VIX movements. Furthermore, establishing long positions in VIX futures can be very expensive over time. When the short end of the VIX futures curve is much steeper than the long end of the curve, the carrying costs created from the contract roll down are elevated.

This phenomenon is particularly evident for investors who cannot invest directly in futures but must invest in volatility funds that attempt to track the VIX. These funds have attracted interest and substantial money flows because they are easily accessed in the form of exchange-traded products (ETPs) and, in particular, exchange-traded notes (ETNs) that provide exposure to short- and medium-term VIX futures. Some of these products also provide leveraged exposure. When using these investment products to hedge against a rise in the VIX, the VIX futures term structure should be taken into in consideration because volatility ETPs typically hold a mix of VIX futures that is adjusted daily to keep the average time to expiration of the portfolio constant. The daily rebalancing requires shorter-term futures to be sold and longer-dated futures to be purchased. When the VIX futures are in contango, the cost of rolling over hedges (i.e., negative carry) increases, thereby reducing profits and causing the ETP to underperform relative to the movement in the VIX. In contrast, "inverse" VIX ETPs offer investors the opportunity to profit from decreases in S&P 500 volatility. However, the purchase of these funds implies a directional positioning on volatility, and investors must accept the risk of large losses when volatility increases sharply.

In 2006, VIX options were introduced, providing an asymmetrical exposure to potential increases or decreases in anticipated volatility. VIX options are European style, and their prices depend on the prices of VIX futures with similar expirations because the market makers of VIX options typically hedge the risk of their option positions using VIX futures. To understand the use of VIX calls and puts, it is very important to recognize that the increases in the VIX (and VIX futures) are negatively correlated with the prices of equity assets. In particular, a trader or investor would purchase VIX call options when he expects that volatility will increase owing to a significant sell-off in the equity market. In contrast, VIX put options would be bought to profit from an expectation that volatility will decrease because of stable equity market conditions. Options on the VSTOXX index also exist, but they have lower volumes and open interest than those on the VIX.

## 6. VOLATILITY DERIVATIVES: VARIANCE SWAPS

**d** demonstrate the use of volatility derivatives and variance swaps;

Variance swaps are instruments used by investors for taking directional bets on implied versus realized volatility for speculative or hedging purposes. The term "variance swap" refers to the fact that these instruments have a payoff analogous to that of a swap. In a variance swap, the buyer of the contract will pay the difference between the fixed *variance strike* agreed on in the contract and the *realized variance* (annualized) on the underlying over the period specified and applied to a variance notional. In variance swaps, there is no exchange of cash at the contract inception or during the life of the swap. The payoff at expiration of a long variance position will be positive (negative) when realized variance is greater (less) than the swap's variance strike. If the payment amount is positive (negative), the swap seller (buyer) pays the swap buyer (seller). The payoff at settlement is found as follows:

$$\text{Settlement amount}_T = (\text{Variance notional})(\text{Realized variance} - \text{Variance strike}) \quad (12)$$

The realized variance is calculated as follows, where $R_i = \ln(P_{i+1}/P_i)$ and $N$ is the number of days observed:

$$\text{Realized variance} = 252 \times \left[\sum_{i=1}^{N-1} R_i^2 \bigg/ (N-1)\right] \quad (13)$$

Since most market participants are accustomed to thinking in terms of volatility, variance swap traders typically agree on the following two things: (1) a variance swap trade size expressed in **vega notional**, $N_{Vega}$ (not in variance notional), and (2) the strike ($X$), which represents the expected future variance of the underlying, expressed as volatility (not variance). This approach is intuitive because the vega notional represents the average profit and loss of the variance swap for a 1% change in volatility from the strike. For example, when the vega notional is $50,000, the profit and loss for one volatility point of difference between the realized volatility and the strike will be close to $50,000.

We must bear in mind that this is an approximation because the variance swap payoff is convex and the profit and loss is not linear for changes in the realized volatility. Specifically, to calculate the exact payoff, the variance strike is the strike squared and the **variance notional**, $N_{variance}$, is defined and calculated as

$$\text{Variance notional} = \frac{\text{Vega notional}}{2 \times \text{Strike price}} \quad (14)$$

Thus, given the realized volatility ($\sigma$), we have the following equivalence:

$$\text{Settlement amount}_T = N_{Vega}\left(\frac{\sigma^2 - X^2}{2 \times \text{Strike price}}\right) = N_{variance}(\sigma^2 - X^2) \quad (15)$$

The strike on a variance swap is calculated on the basis of the implied volatility skew for a specific expiration, derived from calls and puts quoted in the market. As discussed previously, volatility skew is a plot of the differences in implied volatilities of a basket of options with the same maturity and underlying asset but with different strikes (and thus moneyness). As a rule of thumb, the strike of a variance swap typically corresponds to the implied volatility of the put that has 90% moneyness (calculated as the option's strike divided by the current level of the underlying).

The mark-to-market valuation of a variance swap at time $t$ (VarSwap$_t$) will depend on realized volatility from the swap's initiation to $t$, RealizedVol$(0,t)$, and implied volatility at $t$, ImpliedVol$(t,T)$, over the remaining life of the swap $(T - t)$. $PV_t(T)$ is the present value at time $t$ of \$1 received at maturity $T$. The value of a variance swap at time $t$ is given by the following formula:[10]

$$\text{VarSwap}_t = \text{Variance notional} \times PV_t(T) \times$$
$$\left\{ \frac{t}{T} \times \left[\text{RealizedVol}(0,t)\right]^2 + \frac{T-t}{T} \times \left[\text{ImpliedVol}(t,T)\right]^2 - \text{Strike}^2 \right\} \quad (16)$$

Importantly, the sensitivity of a variance swap to changes in implied volatility diminishes over time.

A feature of variance swaps that makes them particularly interesting to investors is that their payoffs are convex in volatility, as seen Exhibit 4. This convexity occurs because being long a variance swap is equivalent to be long a basket of options and short the underlying asset (typically by selling a futures contract). A long position in a variance swap is thus long gamma and has a convex payoff. This characteristic allows volatility sellers to sell variance swaps at a higher price than at-the-money options because the swap's convex payoff profile is attractive to investors who desire a long volatility position as a tail risk hedge.

**Exhibit 4  The Payoff of a Variance Swap Is Convex in Volatility**

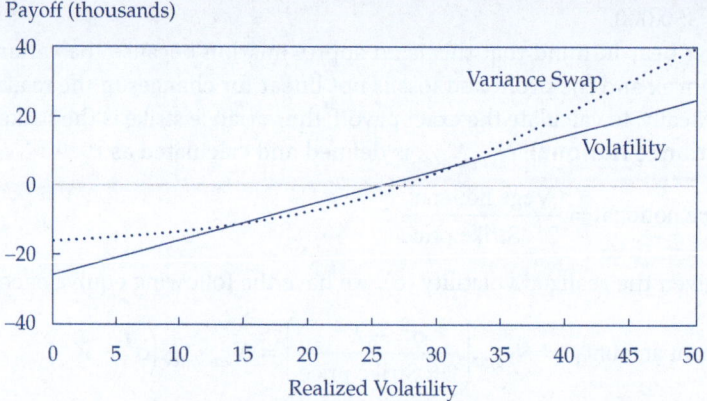

### EXAMPLE 12

## Variance Swap Valuation and Settlement

Olivia Santos trades strategies that systematically sell volatility on the S&P 500 Index. She sells \$50,000 vega notional of a one-year variance swap on the S&P 500 at a strike of 20% (quoted as annual volatility).

Now six months have passed, and the S&P 500 has experienced a realized volatility of 16% (annualized). On the same day, the fair strike of a new six-month variance swap on the S&P 500 is 19%.

---

**10** Note that the terms in the braces—RealizedVol, ImpliedVol, and Strike—are all expressed in volatility units. They are squared so that they are expressed in variance units for determining the value of a variance swap.

Determine the following:

1. The current value of the variance swap sold by Santos (note that the annual interest rate is 2.5%)
2. The settlement amount at expiration of the swap if the one-year realized volatility is 18%

**Solution to 1:**

Santos sold $50,000 vega notional of a one-year variance swap on the S&P 500 with a strike (in volatility terms) of 20%. The value of the variance swap sold by Santos is found using Equation 16:

$$\text{VarSwap}_t = \text{Variance notional} \times PV_t(T) \times \left\{ \frac{t}{T} \times \left[\text{RealizedVol}(0,t)\right]^2 + \frac{T-t}{T} \times \left[\text{ImpliedVol}(t,T)\right]^2 - \text{Strike}^2 \right\}$$

Values for the inputs are as follows:

Volatility strike on existing swap = 20.

Variance strike on existing swap = $20^2$ = 400.

From Equation 14, Variance notional = $\dfrac{\text{Vega notional}}{2 \times \text{Strike}} = \dfrac{\$50,000}{2 \times 20} = 1,250$.

RealizedVol$(0,t)^2 = 16^2 = 256$.
ImpliedVol$(t,T)^2 = 19^2 = 361$.
$t$ = 6 months.
$T$ = 12 months.
$PV_t(T) = 1/[1 + (2.5\% \times 6/12)] = 0.987654$ (= Present Value Interest Factor for six months, where the annual rate is 2.5%).

The current value of the swap is

$\text{VarSwap}_t = 1,250 \times (0.987654) \times [(6/12) \times 256 + (6/12) \times 361 - 400]$
$= -\$112,962.9263$.

Given that Santos is short the variance swap, the mark-to-market value is positive for her, and it equals $112,963.

**Solution to 2:**

The settlement amount is calculated using Equation 12 as follows:

$\text{Settlement}_T$ = Variance notional × (Realized variance − Variance strike) =
$1,250 \times (18^2 - 20^2)$
$= -\$95,000$

If the payment amount is positive (negative), the swap seller (buyer) pays the swap buyer (seller). So, in this case, Santos would receive $95,000 from the swap buyer.

## 7 USING DERIVATIVES TO MANAGE EQUITY EXPOSURE AND TRACKING ERROR

e  demonstrate the use of derivatives to achieve targeted equity and interest rate risk exposures;

Bernhard Steinbacher has a client with a holding of 100,000 shares in Tundra Corporation, currently trading for €14 per share. The client has owned the shares for many years and thus has a very low tax basis on this stock. Steinbacher wants to safeguard the value of the position since the client does not want to sell the shares. He cannot find exchange-traded options on the stock. Steinbacher wants to present a way in which the client could protect the investment portfolio from a decline in Tundra's stock price.

Discuss a swap strategy that Steinbacher might recommend to his client.

### Solution:

A possible solution is to enter into an equity swap trading the Tundra stock return for the floating reference interest rate. Given Tundra's current share price of €14, the position is worth €1.4 million. Steinbacher can agree to exchange the *total return* on the shares (which includes the price performance and the dividends received) for the reference rate return on this sum of money. Now he needs to determine the time over which the protection is needed and must match the swap tenor to this period. After consulting with his client, Steinbacher decides on six months. The floating reference rate is 0.34%, expressed as an annual rate.

*Scenario A:*

Over the six months, Tundra pays a €0.10 dividend and the share price rises 1%.

The total return on the stock is $\frac{(14 \times 1.01) - 14 + 0.10}{14} = 1.71\%$. For a six-month period, the reference rate return would be half the annual rate, or 0.17%. Tundra's total return *exceeds* the six-month reference rate return: (1.71% − 0.17%) × €1.4 million = €21,620, which is a positive amount, so Steinbacher's client would need to *pay* the swap counterparty.

*Scenario B:*

Over the six months, Tundra pays a €0.10 dividend and the share price falls 1%.

The total return on the stock is $\frac{(14 \times 0.99) - 14 + 0.10}{14} = -0.29\%$. Tundra's total return is less than the six-month reference rate return: (−0.29% − 0.17%) × €1.4 million = −€6,380, which is a negative amount, so Steinbacher's client would *receive* the negative return and the reference rate return from the swap counterparty (meaning the client will receive a positive cash inflow of €6,380).

### 7.1 Cash Equitization

Georgia McMillian manages a fund invested in UK stocks that is indexed to the FTSE 100 Index. The fund has £250 million of total assets under management, including £20 million of cash reserves invested at the three-month British pound floating rate of 0.63% (annualized). McMillian does not have an expectation on the direction of UK stocks over the next quarter. However, she is keen to minimize tracking error risk, so she implements a cash equitization strategy attempting to replicate the performance of the FTSE 100 on the cash reserves. Futures on the FTSE 100 settling in three months currently trade at a price of £7,900, the contract's value is £10 per index point (so each futures contract is worth £79,000), and its beta, $\beta_f$, is 1.0.

McMillian engages in a synthetic index strategy to gain exposure on a notional amount of £20 million to the FTSE 100 by purchasing equity index futures. The number of futures she must purchase is given by the following:

$$N_f = \left(\frac{\beta_T}{\beta_f}\right)\left(\frac{S}{F}\right) = \left(\frac{1.0}{1.0}\right)\left(\frac{20,000,000}{79,000}\right) = 253.16 \approx 253$$

where the beta of the futures contract, $\beta_f$, and the target beta, $\beta_T$, are both equal to 1.0.

*Scenario: Three months later, the FTSE 100 Index has increased by 5%.*

Three months later, the FTSE 100 has increased by 5%, and the original value of £230 million invested in UK stocks has increased to £241.5 million. The price of the FTSE 100 Index futures contract has increased to £8,282.5. Interest on the cash invested at the three-month floating rate amounts to £31,500 (£20,000,000 × 0.63% × 90/360). McMillian bought the futures at £7,900, and the cash settlement of the contract at is £8,282.5. So, there is a "gain" of 382.5 index points, each point being worth £10, on 253 contracts for a total cash inflow of £967,725 (382.5 points per contract × £10 per point × 253 contracts). Adding to the portfolio the profit from the futures and the cash reserves plus the interest earned on the cash gives a total market value for McMillian's portfolio of £262,499,225 (= £241,500,000 + £20,000,000 + £967,725 + £31,500). The rate of return for the combined position is:

$$\frac{£262,499,225}{£250,000,000} - 1 = 0.05, \text{ or } 5\%$$

Importantly, without implementing this strategy, McMillian's return would have been slightly over 4.6%, calculated as (£230 million/£250 million) × 5.0% + (£20 million/£250 million) × 0.63% × (90/360). So, she accomplished her goal of minimizing tracking error by following this strategy.

## USING DERIVATIVES IN ASSET ALLOCATION    8

f   demonstrate the use of derivatives in asset allocation, rebalancing, and inferring market expectations.

### 8.1 Changing Allocations between Asset Classes Using Futures

Mario Rossi manages a €500 million portfolio that is allocated 70% to stocks and 30% to bonds. Over the next three-month horizon, he is bearish on eurozone stocks, except for German shares, and is bullish on Italian bonds. So, Rossi wants to reduce the overall allocation to stocks by 10%, to 60%, and achieve the same weight (30%) in Italian stocks (which have a beta of 1.1 with respect to the FTSE MIB Index) and German stocks (which have a beta of 0.9 with respect to the DAX index). He also wants to increase the overall allocation to Italian government bonds (BTPs) by 10%, to 40%. The bond portion of his portfolio has a modified duration of 6.45. In summary, as shown in Exhibit 5, Rossi needs to remove €100 million of exposure to Italian stocks, add €50 million of exposure to German stocks, and add €50 million of exposure to Italian bonds in his portfolio.

## Exhibit 5  Summary of Rossi's Original and New Asset Allocation

| Stock Index | Original (€350 Million, 70%) | New (€300 Million, 60%) | Transaction |
|---|---|---|---|
| FTSE MIB | €250 million (50%) | €150 million (30%) | Sell €100 million |
| DAX | €100 million (20%) | €150 million (30%) | Buy €50 million |

| Bonds | Original (€150 Million, 30%) | New (€200 Million, 40%) | Transaction |
|---|---|---|---|
| Italian BTPs | €150 million (30%) | €200 million (40%) | Buy €50 million |

Rossi uses stock index futures and bond futures to achieve this objective. Once the notional values to be traded are known, Rossi determines how many futures contracts should be purchased or sold to achieve the desired asset allocation. The FTSE MIB Index futures contract has a price of 23,100 and a multiplier of €5, for a value of €115,500. The DAX index futures contract has a price of 13,000 and a multiplier of €25, for a value of €325,000. Both futures contracts have a beta of 1. The BTP futures contract has a price of 132.50 and a contract size of €100,000. The cheapest-to-deliver bond has a price of €121; a modified duration of 8.19; a $BPV_{CTD}$ (from Equation 7) of €99.10, calculated as 8.19 × 0.0001 × [(121/100) × €100,000)]; and a conversion factor of 0.913292.

1. Determine how many stock index and bond futures contracts Rossi should use to implement the desired asset allocation and whether he should go long or short.

2. At the horizon date (three months later), the value of the Italian stock portfolio has fallen 5% whereas that of the German stock portfolio has increased 1%. The FTSE MIB futures price is 22,000, and the DAX futures price is 13,100. Determine the change in market value of the equity portfolio assuming the futures transactions specified in Part 1 have been carried out (note that you can ignore transaction costs).

3. At the horizon date, the Italian bond yield curve has a parallel shift downward of 25 bps. Determine the change in market value of the bond portfolio assuming the transactions specified in Part 1 have been carried out (note that you can ignore transactions costs).

### Solution to 1:

The market value of the Italian stocks is 0.50(€500,000,000) = €250,000,000, and Rossi wants to reduce the exposure to this market by 0.20(€500,000,000) = €100,000,000. The market value of the German stocks is 0.20(€500,000,000) = €100,000,000, and he wants to increase the exposure to this market by 0.10(€500,000,000) = €50,000,000. He decides to sell enough futures contracts on the FTSE MIB to reduce the exposure to Italian stocks by €100 million and to purchase enough futures on the DAX index to increase the exposure to German stocks by €50 million.

The number of stock index futures, $N_f$, is

$$N_f = \left(\frac{\beta_T - \beta_S}{\beta_f}\right)\left(\frac{S}{F}\right)$$

# Using Derivatives in Asset Allocation

where $\beta_T$ is the target beta of zero, $\beta_S$ is the stock beta of 1.1, $\beta_f$ is the futures beta of 1.0, $S$ is the market value of the stocks involved in the transaction, and $F$ is the value of the futures contract.

To achieve the desired reduction in exposure to Italian stocks, the market value of the stocks involved in the transaction will be $S = €100,000,000$. The Italian stocks' beta ($\beta_S$) is 1.1, and the target beta is $\beta_T = 0$. The FTSE MIB Index futures have a contract value of €115,500 and a beta ($\beta_f$) of 1.0:

$$N_f = \left(\frac{\beta_T - \beta_S}{\beta_f}\right)\left(\frac{S}{F}\right) = \left(\frac{0.0 - 1.1}{1.0}\right)\left(\frac{€100,000,000}{€115,500}\right) = -952.38$$

Rossi sells 952 futures contracts (after rounding).

To achieve the desired exposure to German stocks (which have a beta of 0.9), the market value of the stocks involved in the transaction will be $S = €50,000,000$. In this case, $\beta_S = 0.0$ because Rossi is starting with a notional "cash" position from the reduction in Italian stock exposure, and the target beta is now $\beta_T = 0.9$. Given the value of the DAX index futures contract of €325,000 and a beta ($\beta_f$) of 1.0, we obtain

$$N_f = \left(\frac{\beta_T - \beta_S}{\beta_f}\right)\left(\frac{S}{F}\right) = \left(\frac{0.9 - 0.0}{1.0}\right)\left(\frac{€50,000,000}{€325,000}\right) = 138.46$$

Rossi buys 138 futures contracts (after rounding).

The market value of the Italian bonds is 0.30(€500,000,000) = €150,000,000, and Rossi wants to increase the exposure to this market by 0.10(€500,000,000) = €50,000,000. He decides to purchase enough Euro-BTP futures so that €50 million exposure in Italian bonds is added to the portfolio. The target basis point value exposure ($BPV_T$) is determined using Equation 4:

$BPV_T = MDUR_T \times 0.01\% \times MV_P = 6.45 \times 0.0001 \times €50,000,000 = €32,250$

The cheapest-to-deliver bond is the BTP 4¾ 09/01/28, which has a conversion factor of 0.913292 and $BPV_{CTD}$ of €99.10. The number of Euro-BTP futures to buy to convert the €50 million in notional cash ($BPV_P = 0$) to the desired exposure in Italian bonds is found using Equation 9:

$$BPVHR = \left(\frac{BPV_T - BPV_P}{BPV_{CTD}}\right) \times CF = \left[(€32,250 - 0)/€99.10\right] \times 0.913292 = 297.21$$

Rossi buys 297 Euro-BTP futures contracts (after rounding).

### Solution to 2:

The value of the Italian stock portfolio decreases by €7,264,000. This outcome is the net effect of the following:

- The original Italian stock portfolio decreases by €12,500,000 (= €250 million × −5%).
- The short position in 952 FTSE MIB futures gains €5,236,000, calculated as

  − (22,000 − 23,100) × 952 × €5.

The value of the German stock portfolio increases by €1,345,000. This outcome is the net effect of the following:

- The original German stock portfolio increases by €1,000,000 (= €100 million × 1%).
- The long position in 138 DAX futures gains €345,000, calculated as (13,100 − 13,000) × 138 × €25.

The total value of the stock position has decreased by €5,919,000 or −1.691% (= −5,919,000/350,000,000).

Had Rossi sold the Italian stocks and then converted the proceeds into German stocks, the equity portfolio would have decreased by €6,000,000 or −1.71% (= −6,000,000/350,000,000). This outcome would have been the net effect of the following:

- A decrease in the new Italian stock portfolio of €7,500,000 (= €150 million × −5%)

- An increase in the new German stock portfolio of €1,500,000 (= €150 million × 1%)

*Solution to 3:*

The Italian bond yield curve had a parallel shift downward of 25 bps. The value of the Italian bond portfolio increases by €3,224,426. This outcome is the net effect of the following:

- The €150 million portfolio's $BPV_P$, per Equation 5, is €96,750 (= 6.45 × 0.0001 × €150,000,000). Thus, for a 25 bp decrease in rates, the portfolio value increases by €2,418,750 (= €96,750 × 25).

- The long position in 297 BTP futures has a $BPV_{CTD}$ of €99.10, and the $CF$ is 0.913292. So, using Equation 6, $BPV_F$ is €108.51 (= €99.10/0.913292). Thus, for a 25 bp decrease in rates, the futures position increases in value by €805,676, calculated as follows: $BPV_F$ × Change in yield × Number of futures contracts = €108.51 × 25 × 297.

Had Rossi bought the Italian bonds, the new €200 million bond portfolio would have increased by €3,225,000. The portfolio has a $BPV_P$ of 6.45 × 0.0001 × €200,000,000 = €129,000. Thus, for a 25 bp decrease in rates, the portfolio value increases by €3,225,000 (= €129,000 × 25).

## 8.2 Rebalancing an Asset Allocation Using Futures

Yolanda Grant manages a portfolio with a target allocation of 40% in stocks and 60% in bonds. Over the last month, the value of the portfolio has increased from €100 million to €106 million, and Grant wants to rebalance it back to the target allocation (40% stocks/60% bonds). As shown in Exhibit 6, the current portfolio has €46 million (43.4%) in European stocks (with beta of 1.2 with respect to the EURO STOXX 50 index) and €60 million (56.6%) in German bunds. The bonds have a modified duration of 9.5.

| Exhibit 6 | Summary of Grant's Current and Rebalanced Allocation | | |
|---|---|---|---|
| **Stocks** | **Current** | **Rebalanced** | **Transaction** |
| European stocks | €46 million (43.4%) | €42.4 million (40%) | Sell €3.6 million |
| **Bonds** | **Current** | **Rebalanced** | **Transaction** |
| German bunds | €60 million (56.6%) | €63.6 million (60%) | Buy €3.6 million |

Grant will use stock index futures and bond futures to achieve this objective. Once the notional values to be traded are known, she determines how many futures contracts should be purchased or sold to achieve the desired asset allocation.

# Using Derivatives in Asset Allocation

The EURO STOXX 50 index futures contract has a price of 3,500 and a multiplier of €10, for a value of €35,000. The Euro-Bund futures contract has a contract size of €100,000. The cheapest-to-deliver bond has a modified duration of 8.623 and a price of 98.14, so (per Equation 7) its $BPV_{CTD}$ is €84.63, calculated as 8.623 × 0.0001 × [(98.14/100) × €100,000)]. Its conversion factor is 0.619489.

Determine how many stock index and bond futures contracts Grant should use to implement the desired asset allocation and whether she should go long or short.

*Solution:*

The market value of the European stocks is €46,000,000, and Grant wants to reduce the exposure to this market to 40% or 0.40(€106,000,000) = €42,400,000. She decides to sell enough futures contracts on the EURO STOXX 50 to reduce the allocation to European stocks by 0.034(€106,000,000) = €3,604,000.

To achieve the desired reduction in exposure to European stocks, the market value of the stocks involved in the transaction (S) will be €3,604,000. The European stocks' beta ($\beta_S$) is 1.2, and the target beta is $\beta_T = 0$. The EURO STOXX 50 index futures have a contract value (F) of €35,000, with a beta ($\beta_f$) of 1.0, so

$$N_f = \left(\frac{\beta_T - \beta_S}{\beta_f}\right)\left(\frac{S}{F}\right) = \left(\frac{0.0 - 1.2}{1.0}\right)\left(\frac{€3,604,000}{€35,000}\right) = -123.57$$

Grant sells 124 futures contracts (after rounding).

The market value of the German bunds is €60,000,000, and Grant wants to increase the exposure to this market to 0.60(€106,000,000) = €63,600,000. She decides to purchase enough Euro-Bund futures so that €3,604,000 (= 0.034 × €106,000,000) of exposure to German bonds is added to the portfolio. The target basis point value ($BPV_T$) is given by Equation 4, as follows:

$BPV_T = MDUR_T \times 0.01\% \times MV_P = 9.5 \times 0.0001 \times €3,604,000 = €3,424$

The cheapest-to-deliver bond has a $BPV_{CTD}$ of €84.63 and a conversion factor of 0.619489. The number of Euro-Bund futures to buy to convert the €3.6 million in notional cash ($BPV_P = 0$) to the desired exposure in German bonds is found using Equation 9:

$$BPVHR = \left(\frac{BPV_T - BPV_P}{BPV_{CTD}}\right) \times CF$$
$$= \left[(€3,424 - 0)/€84.63\right] \times 0.619489 = 25.06 \approx 25 \text{ contracts}$$

So, Grant should buy 25 Euro-Bund futures contracts.

## 8.3 Changing Allocations between Asset Classes Using Swaps

Tactical Money Management Inc. (TMM) is interested in changing the asset allocation on a $200 million segment of its portfolio. This money is invested 75% in US stocks and 25% in US bonds. Within the stock allocation, the funds are invested 60% in large cap, 30% in mid-cap, and 10% percent in small cap. Within the bond sector, the funds are invested 80% in US government bonds and 20% in investment-grade corporate bonds.

Given that it is bullish on equities, especially large-cap stocks, over the next year, TMM would like to change the overall allocation to 90% stocks and 10% bonds. Specifically, TMM would like to split the stock allocation into 65% large cap, 25% mid-cap, and 10% small cap. It also wants to change the bond allocation to 75% US government and 25% investment-grade corporate. The current position, the desired new position, and the necessary transactions to get from the current position to the new position are shown in Exhibit 7.

**Exhibit 7  Summary of TMM's Current and New Asset Allocation**

| Stock | Current ($150 Million, 75%) | New ($180 Million, 90%) | Transaction |
|---|---|---|---|
| Large cap | $90 million (60%) | $117 million (65%) | Buy $27 million |
| Mid-cap | $45 million (30%) | $45 million (25%) | None |
| Small cap | $15 million (10%) | $18 million (10%) | Buy $3 million |

| Bonds | Current ($50 Million, 25%) | New ($20 Million, 10%) | Transaction |
|---|---|---|---|
| Government | $40 million (80%) | $15 million (75%) | Sell $25 million |
| Corporate | $10 million (20%) | $5 million (25%) | Sell $5 million |

TMM knows these changes would entail a considerable amount of trading in stocks and bonds. So, TMM decides to execute a series of swaps that would enable it to change its position temporarily but more easily and less expensively than by executing the physical transactions. TMM engages Dynamic Dealers Inc. to perform the swaps.

TMM decides to increase the allocation in the large-cap sector by investing in the S&P 500 Index and to increase that in the small-cap sector by investing in the S&P SmallCap 600 Index (SPSC). To reduce the allocation in the overall fixed-income sector, TMM decides to replicate the performance of the Bloomberg Barclays US Treasury Index (BBT) for the government bond sector and the BofA Merrill Lynch US Corporate Index (BAMLC) for the corporate bond sector.

Discuss how TMM can use a combination of equity and fixed-income swaps to synthetically implement its desired asset allocation.

*Solution:*

To achieve the desired asset allocation, TMM takes the following exposures:

- A long position of $27 million in the S&P 500
- A long position of $3 million in the SPSC
- A short position of $25 million in the BBT
- A short position of $5 million in the BAMLC

The mid-cap exposure of $45 million does not change, so TMM does not need to incorporate a mid-cap index into the swap. TMM uses a combination of equity and fixed-income swaps to achieve its target allocation and structures the swap to have all payments occur on the same dates six months apart. TMM also decides that the swap should mature in one year. If it wishes to extend this period, TMM would need to renegotiate the swap at expiration. Likewise, TMM could decide to unwind the position before one year elapses, which it could do by executing a new swap with opposite payments for the remainder of the life of the original swap.

Every six months and at maturity, each of the equity swaps involves the settlement of the following cash flows:

- *Equity swap 1:* TMM receives the total return of the S&P 500 and makes a floating payment tied to the market reference rate (MRR) minus the agreed-on spread, both on a notional principal of $27 million.
- *Equity swap 2:* TMM receives the total return of the SPSC and makes a floating payment tied to the MRR minus the agreed-on spread, both on a notional principal of $3 million.

The fixed-income swaps will require the following cash flow settlements every six months and at maturity:

- *Fixed-income swap 1:* TMM pays the total return of the BBT and receives floating payments tied to the MRR minus the agreed-on spread, both on notional principal of $25 million.
- *Fixed-income swap 2:* TMM pays the total return of the BAMLC and receives floating payments tied to the MRR minus the agreed-on spread, both on a notional principal of $5 million.

It is important to recognize that this transaction will not perfectly replicate the performance of TMM's equity and fixed-income portfolios, unless they are indexed to the indexes selected as underlying of the swaps. In addition, TMM could encounter a cash flow problem if its fixed-income payments exceed its equity receipts and its portfolio does not generate enough cash to fund its net obligation. The stock and bond portfolio will generate cash only from dividends and interest. Capital gains will not be received in cash unless a portion of the portfolio is sold. But avoiding selling a portion of the portfolio is the very reason why TMM wants to use swaps.

# USING DERIVATIVES TO INFER MARKET EXPECTATIONS

f demonstrate the use of derivatives in asset allocation, rebalancing, and inferring market expectations.

As mentioned at the beginning of this reading, an important use of derivatives by market participants is for inferring market expectations. These expectations can be for changes in interest rates; for changes in prices for the whole economy (i.e., inflation), individual stocks, or other assets; or even for changes in key factors, such as implied volatility. Exhibit 8 provides a brief list of some of the myriad applications by which information embedded in derivatives prices is used to infer current market expectations. It is important to emphasize that these inferences relate to *current expectations* of future events—they do not foretell what will actually happen—which can change with the arrival of new information.

**Exhibit 8  Some Typical Applications of Derivatives for Inferring Market Expectations**

| Use Cases/Applications | Derivative Type |
| --- | --- |
| 1. Inferring expectations for FOMC moves | Fed funds futures |
| 2. Inferring expectations for inflation rates | CPI (inflation) swaps |
| 3. Inferring expectations for market volatility | VIX futures |

The first application in Exhibit 8, using fed funds futures to infer expectations of federal funds rate changes by the Federal Open Market Committee (FOMC), is likely the most common and well-publicized use of derivatives for inferring market expectations, so it is the focus of the following discussion.

## 9.1 Using Fed Funds Futures to Infer the Expected Average Federal Funds Rate

Market participants are interested in knowing the probabilities of various interest rate level outcomes, deriving from central banks' future decisions, as implied by the pricing of financial instruments. This provides them with an indication about the extent to which markets are "pricing in" future monetary policy changes. Note that such implied probabilities represent the market's view and may diverge from the guidance provided by central banks in their regular communications about the likely future course of monetary policy actions. Furthermore, especially for the longer-term horizon, these inferred probabilities usually do not have strong predictive power. Most information providers and the business media report current implied probability data for selected interest rates and historical analysis charts that show how the implied probabilities of policy rate settings have changed over time.

A commonly followed metric is the probability of a change in the federal funds rate at upcoming FOMC meetings that is implied by the prices of fed funds futures contracts. When the US central bank began its rate hiking cycle in 2015, it declared an intention to maintain a 25 bp "target range" (lower and upper bounds) for the federal funds rate. The Fed regularly communicates its "forward guidance" along with the so-called dot plot, which shows where each FOMC meeting participant believes the federal funds rate should be at the end of the year, for the next few years, and in the longer run.

To derive probabilities of potential upcoming Fed interest rate actions, market participants look at the pricing of fed funds futures, which are tied to the **effective federal funds (FFE) rate**—the rate actually transacted between depository institutions—not the Fed's target federal funds rate. The underlying assumption is that the implied futures market rates are predicting the value of the monthly average effective federal funds rate. As shown in Exhibit 9, where the dots represent forecasts of the federal funds rate by each FOMC member, implied market expectations (dotted line) can diverge significantly from the Fed's forward guidance (solid line, the median of the dots).

**Exhibit 9   Hypothetical Example of Market's Implied Forecast vs. FOMC Forecast of Federal Funds Rate**

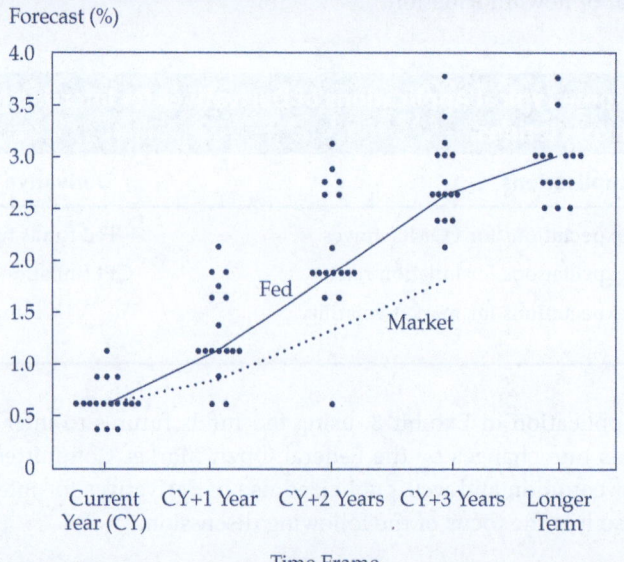

Fed funds futures are traded on the Chicago Board of Trade, and the contract price is quoted as 100 minus the market's expectation for the FFE rate, as follows:

Fed funds futures contract price = 100 − Expected FFE rate.  (17)

At expiration, the contract is cash settled to the simple average (overnight) effective federal funds rate for the delivery month. The overnight rate is calculated and reported daily by the Federal Reserve Bank of New York.

To determine the probability of a change in the federal funds rate, the following formula is used, where the current federal funds rate is the midpoint of the current target range:

$$\frac{\text{Effective federal funds rate implied by futures contract} - \text{Current federal funds rate}}{\text{Federal funds rate assuming a rate hike} - \text{Current federal funds rate}} \quad (18)$$

## 9.2 Inferring Market Expectations

Andrew Okyung manages a portfolio of short-term floating-rate corporate debt, and he is interested in understanding current market expectations for any Fed rate actions at the upcoming FOMC meeting. He observes that the current price for the fed funds futures contract expiring after the next FOMC meeting is 97.90. The current federal funds rate target range is set between 1.75% and 2.00%.

Demonstrate how Okyung can use the information provided to determine the following:

1  The expected average FFE rate
2  The probability of a 25 bp interest rate hike at the next FOMC meeting

### Solution to 1:

The FFE rate implied by the futures contract price is 2.10% (= 100 − 97.90). Okyung understands that this is the rate that market participants expect to be the average federal funds rate for that month.

### Solution to 2:

Okyung knows that given that the FFE rate embedded in the fed funds futures price is 2.10%, there is a high probability that the FOMC will increase rates by 25 bps from its current target range of 1.75%–2.00% to the new target range of 2.00%–2.25%. Given the Fed's declared incremental move size of 25 bps, he calculates the probability of a rate hike as

$$\frac{2.100\% - 1.875\%}{2.125\% - 1.875\%} = 0.90, \text{ or } 90\%$$

where 1.875% is the midpoint of the current target range (1.75%–2.00%) and 2.125% is the midpoint of the new target range (2.00%–2.25%) assuming a rate hike.

Exhibit 10 displays, as a hypothetical example, the trends in implied probabilities (y-axis) derived from fed funds futures prices of an FOMC rate action—either a 25 bp rate hike, a 25 bp rate cut, or no change—at the next FOMC meeting date. Note that the probability of a rate hike or cut is represented as the probability of a move from the current target range at the specified meeting date, and of course, the probabilities of all three actions at a particular meeting date sum to 1.

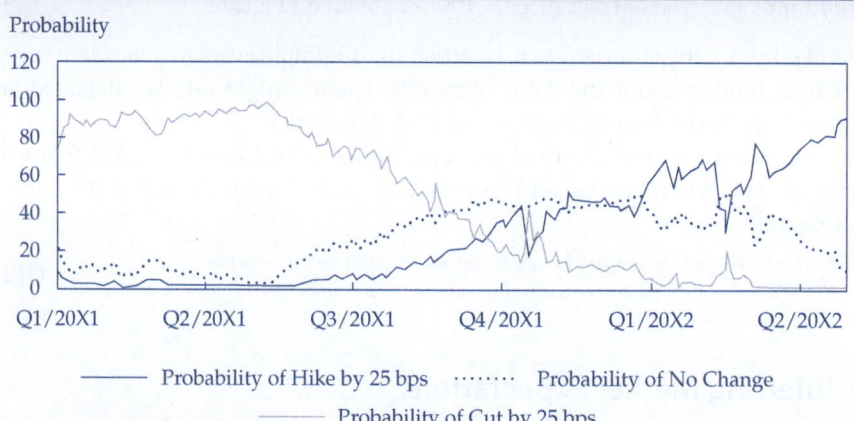

**Exhibit 10  Hypothetical Example of Trends of Probabilities for Federal Funds Rate Actions by the FOMC**

Importantly, typical end-of-month (EOM) activity by large financial and banking institutions often induces "dips" in the FFE rate that create bias issues when using the rate as the basis for probability calculations of potential FOMC rate moves. For example, if such activity increased the price for the relevant fed funds futures contract to 98.05, then the FFE rate would decline to 1.95% (= 100 − 98.05). In this case, using the same equation as before, the probability of an FOMC rate hike decreases from 90% to just 30%:

$$\frac{1.950 - 1.875}{0.25} = 0.30, \text{ or } 30\%$$

To overcome this end-of-month bias, data providers have implemented various methods of "smoothing" the EOM dips. One prominent data provider uses a method that builds a forward rate structure based on where the market believes interest rates will settle in non-FOMC meeting months and then uses these forward rates to make appropriate adjustments. For each FOMC meeting month, it is assumed that an effective rate prevails until the meeting date, and then some rate prevails after the meeting, with the average effective rate over the month being implied by the futures price.

# SUMMARY

This reading on swap, forward, and futures strategies shows a number of ways in which market participants might use these derivatives to enhance returns or to reduce risk to better meet portfolio objectives. Following are the key points.

- Interest rate, currency, and equity swaps, forwards, and futures can be used to modify risk and return by altering the characteristics of the cash flows of an investment portfolio.

- An interest rate swap is an OTC contract in which two parties agree to exchange cash flows on specified dates, one based on a floating interest rate and the other based on a fixed rate (swap rate), determined at swap initiation. Both rates are applied to the swap's notional value to determine the size of the payments, which are typically netted. Interest rate swaps enable a party with a fixed (floating) risk or obligation to effectively convert it into a floating (fixed) one.

# Summary

- Investors can use short-dated interest rate futures and forward rate agreements or longer-dated fixed-income (bond) futures contracts to modify their portfolios' interest rate risk exposure.

- When hedging interest rate risk with bond futures, one must determine the basis point value of the portfolio to be hedged, the target basis point value, and the basis point value of the futures, which itself is determined by the basis point value of the cheapest-to-deliver bond and its conversion factor. The number of bond futures to buy or sell to reach the target basis point value is then determined by the basis point value hedge ratio: $BPVHR = \left(\dfrac{BPV_T - BPV_P}{BPV_{CTD}}\right) \times CF$.

- Cross-currency basis swaps help parties in the swap to hedge against the risk of exchange rate fluctuations and to achieve better rate outcomes. Firms that need foreign-denominated cash can obtain funding in their local currency (likely at a more favorable rate) and then swap the local currency for the required foreign currency using a cross-currency basis swap.

- Equity risk in a portfolio can be managed using equity swaps and total return swaps. There are three main types of equity swap: (1) receive-equity return, pay-fixed; (2) receive-equity return, pay-floating; and (3) receive-equity return, pay-another equity return. A total return swap is a modified equity swap; it also includes in the performance any dividends paid by the underlying stocks or index during the period until the swap maturity.

- Equity risk in a portfolio can also be managed using equity futures and forwards. Equity futures are standardized, exchange-listed contracts, and when the underlying is a stock index, only cash settlement is available at contract expiration. The number of equity futures contracts to buy or sell is determined by $N_f = \left(\dfrac{\beta_T - \beta_S}{\beta_f}\right)\left(\dfrac{S}{F}\right)$.

- Cash equitization is a strategy designed to boost returns by finding ways to "equitize" unintended cash holdings. It is typically done using stock index futures and interest rate futures.

- Derivatives on volatility include VIX futures and options and variance swaps. Importantly, VIX option prices are determined from VIX futures, and both instruments allow an investor to implement a view depending on her expectations about the timing and magnitude of a change in implied volatility.

- In a variance swap, the buyer of the contract will pay the difference between the fixed variance strike specified in the contract and the realized variance (annualized) on the underlying over the period specified and applied to a variance notional. Thus, variance swaps allow directional bets on implied versus realized volatility.

- Derivatives can be used to infer market participants' current expectations for changes over the short term in inflation (e.g., CPI swaps) and market volatility (e.g., VIX futures). Another common application is using fed funds futures prices to derive the probability of a central bank move in the federal funds rate target at the FOMC's next meeting.

# PRACTICE PROBLEMS

1. A US bond portfolio manager wants to hedge a long position in a 10-year Treasury bond against a potential rise in domestic interest rates. He would *most likely*:
   - A  sell fixed-income (bond) futures.
   - B  enter a receive-fixed 10-year interest rate swap.
   - C  sell a strip of 90-day Eurodollar futures contracts.

2. A European bond portfolio manager wants to increase the modified duration of his €30 million portfolio from 3 to 5. She would *most likely* enter a receive-fixed interest rate swap that has principal notional of €20 million and:
   - A  a modified duration of 2.
   - B  a modified duration of 3.
   - C  a modified duration of 4.

3. The CIO of a Canadian private equity company wants to lock in the interest on a three-month "bridge" loan his firm will take out in six months to complete an LBO deal. He sells the relevant interest rate futures contracts at 98.05. In six-months' time, he initiates the loan at 2.70% and unwinds the hedge at 97.30. The effective interest rate on the loan is:
   - A  0.75%.
   - B  1.95%.
   - C  2.70%.

4. A US institutional investor in search of yield decides to buy Italian government bonds for her portfolio but wants to hedge against the risk of exchange rate fluctuations. She enters a cross-currency basis swap, with the same payment dates as the bonds, where at inception she delivers US dollars in exchange for euros for use in purchasing the Italian bonds. The notional principals on the swap are *most likely* exchanged:
   - A  at inception only.
   - B  at maturity only.
   - C  both at inception and at maturity.

5. Continuing from the previous question, assume demand for US dollars is strong relative to demand for euros, so there is a positive basis for "lending" US dollars. By hedging the position in Italian government bonds with the currency basis swap, the US investor will *most likely* increase the periodic net interest payments received from the swap counterparty in:
   - A  euros only.
   - B  US dollars only.
   - C  both euros and US dollars.

6. An equity portfolio manager is invested 100% in US large-cap stocks, but he wants to reduce the current allocation by 20%, to 80%, and allocate 20% to US small caps. He decides not to sell the stocks because of the high transaction costs. Rather, he will use S&P 500 Index futures and Russell 2000 Index futures for achieving the desired exposure in, respectively, US large caps and small caps. To achieve the new allocation, he will for an equivalent of 20% of the portfolio value:

**Practice Problems**

    **A**  purchase Russell 2000 futures only.

    **B**  purchase Russell 2000 futures and sell S&P 500 futures.

    **C**  sell Russell 2000 futures and purchase S&P 500 futures.

**7**  A volatility trader observes that the VIX term structure is upward sloping. In particular, the VIX is at 13.50, the front-month futures contract trades at 14.10, and the second-month futures contract trades at 15.40. Assuming the shape of the VIX term structure will remain constant over the next three-month period, the trader decides to implement a trade that would profit from the VIX carry roll down. She will *most likely* purchase the:

    **A**  VIX and sell the VIX second-month futures.

    **B**  VIX and sell the VIX front-month futures.

    **C**  VIX front-month futures and sell the VIX second-month futures.

**8**  The CEO of a corporation owns 100 million shares of his company's stock, which is currently priced at €30 a share. Given the huge exposure of his personal wealth to this one company, he has decided to sell 10% of his position and invest the funds in a floating interest rate instrument. A derivatives dealer suggests that he do so using an equity swap.

Explain how to structure such a swap.

**9**  A $30 million investment account of a bank trust fund is allocated one-third to stocks and two-thirds to bonds. The portfolio manager wants to change the overall allocation to 50% stock and 50% bonds and the allocation within the stock fund from 70% domestic stock and 30% foreign stock to 60% domestic and 40% foreign. The bond allocation will remain entirely invested in domestic corporate issues.

Explain how swaps can be used to implement this adjustment. The market reference rate is assumed to be flat for all swaps, and you do not need to refer to specific stock and bond indexes.

**10**  Sarah Ko, a private wealth adviser in Singapore, is developing a short-term interest rate forecast for her private wealth clients who have holdings in the US fixed-income markets. Ko needs to understand current market expectations for possible upcoming central bank (i.e., US Federal Reserve Board) rate actions. The current price for the fed funds futures contract expiring after the next FOMC meeting is 97.175. The current federal funds rate target range is set between 2.50% and 2.75%.

Explain how Ko can use this information to understand potential movements in the current federal funds rate.

# The following information relates to Questions 11–17

Global Mega (Global) is a diversified financial services firm. Yasuko Regan, senior trader, and Marcus Whitacre, junior trader, both work on the firm's derivatives desk. Regan and Whitacre assist in structuring and implementing trades for clients in the financial services industry that have limited derivatives expertise. Regan and Whitacre are currently assisting one of Global's clients—Monatize, an asset management firm—with two of its portfolios: Portfolio A and Portfolio B.

Portfolio A is a bond portfolio composed solely of US Treasury bonds. Monatize has asked Global to quote the number of Treasury futures contracts necessary to fully hedge this bond portfolio against a rise in interest rates. Exhibit 1 presents selected data on Portfolio A, the relevant Treasury futures contract, and the cheapest-to-deliver (CTD) bond.

**Exhibit 1  Selected Data on Portfolio A, the Treasury Futures Contract, and the CTD Bond**

| | Portfolio A | | Futures Contract and CTD Bond |
|---|---|---|---|
| Market value | $143,234,000 | Price | 145.20 |
| Modified duration | 9.10 | Modified duration | 8.75 |
| Basis point value | $130,342.94 | Basis point value | $127.05 |
| | | Conversion factor | 0.72382 |
| | | Contract size | $100,000 |

After an internal discussion, Monatize elects to not hedge Portfolio A but rather decrease the portfolio's modified duration to 3.10. Regan asks Whitacre to compute the number of Treasury futures contracts to sell in order to achieve this objective. Regan tells Whitacre to assume the yield curve is flat.

Portfolio B is a $100,000,000 equity portfolio indexed to the S&P 500 Index, with excess cash of $4,800,000. Monatize is required to equitize its excess cash to be fully invested, and the firm directs Global to purchase futures contracts to do so. To replicate the return of Portfolio B's target index, Whitacre purchases S&P 500 futures contracts, at a price of 3,300 per contract, that have a multiplier of $250 per index point and a beta of 1.00.

Monatize's CFO and Regan discuss two potential hedging strategies for Portfolio B to protect against a hypothetical extreme sell-off in equities. Regan first suggests that Monatize could enter into a total return equity swap, whereby Monatize agrees to pay the return on the S&P 500 and receive a fixed interest rate at pre-specified dates in exchange for a fee.

Regan next suggests that Monatize could alternatively hedge Portfolio B using variance swaps. Monatize's CFO asks Regan to calculate what the gain would be in five months on a purchase of $1,000,000 vega notional of a one-year variance swap on the S&P 500 at a strike of 15% (quoted as annual volatility), assuming the following:

- Over the next five months, the S&P 500 experiences a realized volatility of 20%;
- At the end of the five-month period, the fair strike of a new seven-month variance swap on the S&P 500 will be 18%; and
- The annual interest rate is 1.50%.

Regan and Whitacre discuss the use of federal funds futures contracts to infer probabilities of future monetary policy changes. Whitacre makes the following three statements about fed funds futures contracts:

Statement 1  Typical end-of-month activity by large financial and banking institutions often induces "dips" in the effective fed funds rate.

Statement 2  Especially for the longer-term horizon, the probabilities inferred from the pricing of fed funds futures usually have strong predictive power.

# Practice Problems

Statement 3   To derive probabilities of Federal Reserve interest rate actions, market participants look at the pricing of fed funds futures, which are tied to the Federal Reserve's target fed funds rate.

Whitacre then proposes to Regan that Global explore opportunities in bond futures arbitrage. Whitacre makes the following two statements:

Statement 4   If the basis is positive, a trader would make a profit by "selling the basis."

Statement 5   If the basis is negative, a trader would make a profit by selling the bond and buying the futures.

11  Based on Exhibit 1, the number of Treasury futures contracts Whitacre should sell to fully hedge Portfolio A is *closest* to:
   A   650.
   B   743.
   C   1,026.

12  Based on Exhibit 1, the number of Treasury futures contracts Whitacre should sell to achieve Monetize's objective with respect to Portfolio A is *closest* to:
   A   490.
   B   518.
   C   676.

13  The number of S&P 500 futures contracts that Whitacre should buy to equitize Portfolio B's excess cash position is *closest* to:
   A   6.
   B   121.
   C   1,455.

14  The derivative product first suggested by Regan as a potential hedge strategy for Portfolio B:
   A   is a relatively liquid contract.
   B   eliminates counterparty credit risk.
   C   allows Monatize to keep voting rights on its equity portfolio.

15  Based on the CFO's set of assumptions, the gain on the purchase of the variance swap on the S&P 500 in five months would be *closest* to:
   A   $4,317,775.
   B   $4,355,556.
   C   $4,736,334.

16  Which of Whitacre's three statements about fed funds futures is correct?
   A   Statement 1
   B   Statement 2
   C   Statement 3

17  Which of Whitacre's two statements regarding bond futures arbitrage is correct?
   A   Only Statement 4
   B   Only Statement 5
   C   Both Statement 4 and Statement 5

# The following information relates to Questions 18–20

Nisqually Uff is the portfolio manager for the Chehalis Fund (the Fund), which holds equities and bonds in its portfolio. Uff focuses on tactical portfolio strategies and uses derivatives to implement his strategies.

Uff has a positive short-term outlook for equities relative to bonds and decides to temporarily increase the beta of the portfolio's equity allocation from 0.9 to 1.2. He will use three-month equity index futures contracts to adjust the beta. Exhibit 1 displays selected data for the Fund's current equity allocation and the relevant futures contract.

**Exhibit 1  Selected Data for the Fund's Current Equity Allocation and Futures Contract**

| | |
|---|---|
| Current value of the Fund's equity allocation | €168,300,000 |
| Current portfolio beta | 0.9 |
| Target portfolio beta | 1.2 |
| Index futures contract value | €45,000 |
| Beta of futures contract | 1.0 |

18  Determine the appropriate number of equity index futures contracts that Uff should use to achieve the target portfolio beta. Identify whether the equity index futures contracts should be bought or sold.

One month later, Uff expects interest rates to rise. He decides to reduce the modified duration of the bond allocation of the Fund's portfolio without selling any of its existing bonds. To do so, Uff adds a negative-duration position by entering into an interest rate swap in which he pays the fixed rate and receives the floating rate. Exhibit 2 presents selected data for the Fund's bond allocation and the relevant swap contract.

**Exhibit 2  Selected Data for the Fund's Bond Allocation and Swap Contract**

| | |
|---|---|
| Current value of the Fund's bond allocation | €90,100,000 |
| Current portfolio average modified duration | 7.8000 |
| Target portfolio modified duration | 5.0000 |
| Swap modified duration for fixed-rate payer | −2.4848 |

19  Determine the required notional principal for the interest rate swap in order to achieve the target modified duration for the portfolio.

Six months later, Uff has since closed out both the equity index futures contract position and the interest rate swap position. In response to market movements, he now wants to implement a tactical rebalancing of the Fund's portfolio. Exhibit 3 presents the current and target asset allocations for the Fund's portfolio.

# Practice Problems

### Exhibit 3: Current and Target Asset Allocations for the Fund's Portfolio

| Asset Class | Current | Target |
|---|---|---|
| Equities | €201,384,000 (69.56%) | €188,181,500 (65.0%) |
| Bonds | €88,126,000 (30.44%) | €101,328,500 (35.0%) |
| Total | €289,510,000 | €289,510,000 |

Uff decides to use equity index and bond futures contracts to rebalance the portfolio. Exhibit 4 shows selected data on the Fund's portfolio and the relevant futures contracts.

### Exhibit 4: Selected Data on Fund's Portfolio and Relevant Futures Contracts

| | |
|---|---|
| Beta of the Fund's equities relative to index | 1.28 |
| Modified duration of the Fund's bonds | 4.59 |
| Equity index futures contract value | €35,000 |
| Beta of equity index futures contract | 1.00 |
| Basis point value of cheapest-to-deliver (CTD) bond | €91.26 |
| Conversion factor (CF) for CTD bond | 0.733194 |

20. Determine how many equity index and bond futures contracts Uff should use to rebalance the Fund's portfolio to the target allocation. Identify whether the futures contracts should be bought or sold.

## The following information relates to Questions 21–22

Canawacta Tioga is the CFO for Wyalusing Corporation, a multinational manufacturing company based in Canada. One year ago, Wyalusing issued fixed-rate coupon bonds in Canada. Tioga now expects Canadian interest rates to fall and remain low for three years. During this three-year period, Tioga wants to use a par interest rate swap to effectively convert the fixed-rate bond coupon payments into floating-rate payments.

21. Explain how to construct the swap that Tioga wants to use with regard to the swap:

    i. tenor
    ii. cash flows
    iii. notional value
    iv. settlement dates

Wyalusing will soon be building a new manufacturing plant in the United States. To fund construction of the plant, the company will borrow in its home currency of CAD because of favorable interest rates. Tioga plans to use a cross-currency basis swap so that Wyalusing will borrow in CAD but make interest payments in USD.

**22** Describe how the swap will function, from the perspective of Wyalusing, in terms of the:

   **i.** cash flows at inception.

   **ii.** periodic cash flows.

   **iii.** cash flows at maturity.

## The following information relates to Questions 23–24

Southern Sloth Sanctuary (Sanctuary) is a charitable organization that cares for orphaned and injured sloths from the rain forest in the country of Lushland. The organization is supported by both domestic and international contributions. The Sanctuary's CFO typically invests any funds that are not immediately needed for short-term operational expenses into a domestic index fund that tracks the Lushland 100 stock index, which is denominated in Lushland dollars (LLD).

The Sanctuary just received a large contribution from a local benefactor in the amount of LLD1,000,000. These funds are not needed for short-term operational expenses. The CFO intends to equitize this excess cash position using futures contracts to replicate the return on the Lushland 100 stock index. Exhibit 1 shows selected data for the Lushland 100 Index futures contract.

| Exhibit 1 | Selected Data for Lushland 100 Index Futures Contract |
|---|---|
| Quoted price of futures contract | 1,247 |
| Contract multiplier | LLD 200 |
| Contract beta | 1.00 |

**23** Determine the appropriate number of futures contracts that the CFO should buy to equitize the excess cash position.

A Japanese benefactor recently donated a plot of land in Japan to the Sanctuary. Ownership of the land has been transferred to the Sanctuary, which has a binding contract to sell the property for JPY500,000,000. The property sale will be completed in 30 days. The Sanctuary's CFO wants to hedge the risk of JPY depreciation using futures contracts. The CFO assumes a hedge ratio of 1.

**24** Describe a strategy to implement the CFO's desired hedge.

# SOLUTIONS

1. A is correct. The portfolio manager would *most likely* use a longer-dated fixed-income (bond) futures contract to hedge his interest rate risk exposure. The choice of the hedging instrument, in fact, will depend on the maturity of the bond being hedged. Interest rate futures, like 90-day Eurodollar futures, have a limited number of maturities and can be used to hedge short-term bonds. The mark-to-market value of a receive-fixed 10-year interest rate swap will become negative if interest rates rises, and thus the swap cannot be used as a hedge in this case.

2. B is correct. The portfolio manager's goal is to use the receive-fixed, pay-floating swap such that the €30 million of bonds, with modified duration of 3, and the €20 million swap will combine to make up a portfolio with a market value of €30 million and modified duration of 5. This relationship can be expressed as follows:

    €30,000,000(3) + ($N_S \times MDUR_S$) = €30,000,000(5).

    Given the swap's notional ($N_S$) of €20,000,000, its required modified duration can be obtained as:

    $MDUR_S$ = [(5 − 3)€30,000,000]/€20,000,000 = 3.

3. B is correct. The CIO sells the relevant interest rate future contracts at 98.05. After six months, the CIO initiates the bridge loan at a rate of 2.70%, but he unwinds the hedge at the lower futures price of 97.30, thus gaining 75 bps (= 98.05 − 97.30). The effective interest rate on the loan is 1.95% (= 2.70% − 0.75%).

4. C is correct. In a cross-currency basis swap, the goals of the transaction are to achieve favorable funding and exchange rates and to swap the foreign currency amounts back to the currency of choice—in this case, the US dollar—at maturity. There is one exchange rate specified in the swap that is used to determine the notional principals in the two currencies, exchanged at inception and at maturity.

5. B is correct. By hedging the position in Italian government bonds with the cross-currency basis swap, the US investor will most likely increase the periodic net interest she receives in US dollars. The reason is that the periodic net interest payments made by the swap counterparty to the investor will include the positive basis resulting from the relatively strong demand for US dollars versus euros.

6. B is correct. To reduce the current allocation by 20%, to 80%, in US large-cap stocks, the portfolio manager will sell S&P 500 futures. At the same time, to allocate this 20% to US small caps, he will purchase Russell 2000 futures for the same notional amount.

7. C is correct. VIX futures converge to the spot VIX as expiration approaches, and the two must be equal at expiration. When the VIX futures curve is in contango and assuming volatility remains stable, the VIX futures will get "pulled" closer to the spot VIX, and they will decrease in price as they approach expiration. Traders calculate the difference between the front-month VIX futures price and the VIX as 0.60, and the spread between the front-month and the second-month futures is 1.30. Assuming that the spread declines linearly until settlement, the trader would realize roll-down gains as the spread decreases from 1.30 to 0.60 as the front-month futures approaches its expiration. At

expiration, VIX futures are equal to the VIX, and the spread with the old second-month (and now the front-month) futures contract will be 0.60. Finally, since one cannot directly invest in the VIX, trades focusing on the VIX term structure must be implemented using either VIX futures or VIX options, so Answers A and B are not feasible.

8  The swap is structured such that the executive pays the return on 10 million shares of the company's stock, which is 10% of his holdings, and he receives the return based on a floating interest rate, such as the market reference rate, on a notional principal of €300 million (= €30/share × 10 million shares).

9  Currently the allocation is $10 million in stocks and $20 million in bonds. Within the stock category, the current allocation is $7 million domestic and $3 million foreign. The desired allocation is $15 million in stocks and $15 million in bonds. Thus, the allocation must change by moving $5 million into stocks and out of bonds. The desired stock allocation is $9 million domestic and $6 million foreign. The desired bond allocation is $15 million, all domestic corporate.

To make the changes with swaps, the manager must enter into swaps against the market reference rate, which is assumed to be flat for all swaps in this example. Using the swaps, the bank trust fund portfolio manager needs to (1) receive the returns on $2 million based on a domestic equity index and on $3 million based on a foreign equity index and (2) pay the return on $5 million based on a domestic corporate bond index. The market reference rate outflows from the swaps in (1) and the inflows from the swap in (2) will cancel out through summation.

10  First, Ko knows that the FFE rate implied by the futures contract price of 97.175 is 2.825% (= 100 − 97.175). This is the rate that market participants expect to be the average federal funds rate for that month.

Second, Ko should determine the probability of a rate change. She knows the 2.825% FFE rate implied by the futures signals a fairly high chance that the FOMC will increase rates by 25 bps from its current target range of 2.50%–2.75% to the new target range of 2.75%–3.00%. She calculates the probability of a rate hike as follows:

$$\frac{2.825\% - 2.625\%}{2.875\% - 2.625\%} = 0.80, \text{ or } 80\%$$

Ko can now incorporate this probability of a Fed rate hike into her forecast of short-term US interest rates.

11  B is correct. The basis point value of Portfolio A ($BPV_P$) is $130,342.94, and the basis point value of the cheapest-to-deliver bond ($BPV_{CTD}$) is $127.05 with a conversion factor of 0.72382. The basis point value hedge ratio ($BPVHR$), in the special case of complete hedging, provides the number of futures contracts needed, calculated as follows:

$$BPVHR = \frac{-BPV_P}{BPV_{CTD}} \times CF = \frac{-\$130,342.94}{\$127.05} \times 0.72382 = -742.58$$

Therefore, Whitacre should sell 743 Treasury bond futures to fully hedge Portfolio A.

## Solutions:

A is incorrect because it incorrectly uses the price of the cheapest-to-deliver bond (rather than its basis point value, $BPV_{CTD}$) in the denominator of the BPVHR calculation:

$$BPVHR = \frac{-BPV_P}{CTD\ Bond\ Price} \times CF = \frac{-\$130,342.94}{\$145.20} \times 0.72382 = -649.76$$

C is incorrect because it does not include the conversion factor for the cheapest-to-deliver bond when calculating BPVHR:

$$BPVHR = \frac{-BPV_P}{BPV_{CTD}} = \frac{-\$130,342.94}{\$127.05} = -1,025.92$$

**12** A is correct. Monetize wants to reduce Portfolio A's modified duration to a target of 3.10. $BPV_T$ is calculated as follows:

$$BPV_T = MDUR_T \times 0.01\% \times MV_P$$

$$BPV_T = (3.10) \times 0.0001 \times \$143,234,000 = \$44,402.54$$

The basis point value of Portfolio A ($BPV_P$) is $130,342.94, and the basis point value of the cheapest-to-deliver bond ($BPV_{CTD}$) is $127.05 with a conversion factor of 0.72382. The basis point value hedge ratio (BPVHR), which provides the number of futures contracts needed, is then calculated as follows:

$$BPVHR = \frac{BPV_T - BPV_P}{BPV_{CTD}} \times CF$$

$$BPVHR = \frac{\$44,402.54 - \$130,342.94}{\$127.05} \times 0.72382 = -489.6134$$

Thus, to decrease the modified duration of Portfolio A to 3.10, Whitacre should sell 490 Treasury bond futures contracts.

B is incorrect because it incorrectly subtracts 6.00 from the modified duration (equal to 9.10 − 3.10, or the change in the modified duration for Portfolio A) of the cheapest-to-deliver bond, rather than from the modified duration of the bond portfolio, in computing $BPV_T$.

$$BPV_T = (8.75 - 6.00) \times 0.0001 \times \$143,234,000 = \$39,389.35$$

This error results in an incorrect calculation of BPVHR:

$$BPVHR = \frac{\$39,389.35 - \$130,342.94}{\$127.05} \times 0.72382 = -518.1741$$

C is incorrect because it does not include the conversion factor for the cheapest-to-deliver bond when calculating BPVHR:

$$BPVHR = \frac{\$44,402.54 - \$130,342.94}{\$127.05} = -676.4298$$

**13** A is correct. The number of equity index futures contracts to purchase in order to equitize Monatize's excess cash position is calculated as follows:

$$N_f = \left(\frac{\beta_T}{\beta_f}\right)\left(\frac{S}{F}\right) = \left(\frac{1.00}{1.00}\right)\left(\frac{\$4,800,000}{\$825,000}\right) = 5.82,\ or\ 6\ contracts$$

The actual futures contract purchase value of $825,000 is the product of the quoted S&P 500 futures price of 3,300 and the designated multiplier of $250 per index point.

B is incorrect because $100,000,000, the total value of Portfolio B, is incorrectly used as the market value of the stock portfolio to equitize (S), instead of Portfolio B's excess cash position:

$$N_f = \left(\frac{\beta_T}{\beta_f}\right)\left(\frac{S}{F}\right) = \left(\frac{1.00}{1.00}\right)\left(\frac{\$100,000,000}{\$825,000}\right) = 121.21, \text{ or } 121 \text{ contracts}$$

C is incorrect because 3,300, the quoted S&P 500 futures price, is incorrectly used as the actual futures contract price, instead of calculating the actual futures contract price of $825,000:

$$N_f = \left(\frac{\beta_T}{\beta_f}\right)\left(\frac{S}{F}\right) = \left(\frac{1.00}{1.00}\right)\left(\frac{\$4,800,000}{\$3,300}\right) = 1,454.54, \text{ or } 1,455 \text{ contracts}$$

14  C is correct. The first hedging strategy suggested by Regan is entering into a total return equity swap in exchange for a fee. Equity swaps, which are relatively illiquid contracts and are OTC derivative instruments in which each party bears counterparty risk, do not confer voting rights to the counterparty receiving the performance of the underlying. Under the terms of the total return equity swap, at pre-specified dates, the counterparties will net the index total return (increase/decrease plus dividends) against the fixed interest payment. If the index total return exceeds the fixed interest payment, Monatize will pay the counterparty the net payment. If the index total return is less than the fixed interest payment, then Monatize will receive the net payment from the counterparty.

A is incorrect because equity swaps are relatively illiquid contracts.

B is incorrect because equity swaps are OTC derivative instruments, and each counterparty in the equity swap bears the risk exposure to the other counterparty. For this reason, equity swaps are usually collateralized in order to reduce credit risk exposure.

15  A is correct. The gain on the variance swap is calculated as:

$$VarSwap_t = Variance\ Notional \times PV_t(T)$$
$$\times \left\{\frac{t}{T} \times \left[RealizedVol(0,t)\right]^2 + \frac{T-t}{T} \times \left[ImpliedVol(t,T)\right]^2 - Strike^2\right\}$$

Values for the inputs are as follows:
Volatility strike on existing swap = 15
Variance strike on existing swap = $15^2$ = 225

$$Variance\ Notional = \frac{Vega\ Notional}{2 \times Strike} = \frac{\$1,000,000}{2 \times 15} = \$33,333.33$$

RealizedVol$(0,t)^2 = 20^2 = 400$
ImpliedVol$(t,T)^2 = 18^2 = 324$
$t = 5$
$T = 12$

## Solutions:

$$PV_t(T) = \frac{1}{1 + \left[1.50\%\left(\frac{7}{12}\right)\right]} = 0.991326,$$ which is the present value interest factor after five months (i.e., discounting for seven remaining months, from $t$ to $T$), where the annual interest rate is 1.50%.

Thus, the value of the swap in five months is calculated as follows:

$$VarSwap_t = \$33{,}333.33 \times 0.991326 \times \left\{\frac{5}{12} \times 400 + \frac{12-5}{12} \times 324 - 225\right\} = \$4{,}317{,}774.59$$

Given that Monatize would be long the swap, the mark-to-market value would be positive (i.e., a gain) for Monatize, equal to $4,317,775.

B is incorrect because the value of the variance swap in five months incorrectly omits the present value interest factor of 0.991326.

The value of the swap in five months, incorrectly omitting the present value interest factor, is calculated as follows:

$$VarSwap_t = \$33{,}333.33 \times \left\{\frac{5}{12} \times 400 + \frac{12-5}{12} \times 324 - 225\right\} = \$4{,}355{,}555.56$$

C is incorrect because the values of $[RealizedVol(0,t)]^2$ and $[ImpliedVol(t,T)]^2$ are incorrectly switched.

The value of the swap in five months, incorrectly switching the values of $[RealizedVol(0,t)]^2$ and $[ImpliedVol(t,T)]^2$, is calculated as follows:

$$VarSwap_t = \$33{,}333.33 \times 0.991326 \times \left(\frac{5}{12} \times 324 + \frac{12-5}{12} \times 400 - 225\right) = \$4{,}736{,}334.37$$

16. A is correct. Typical end-of-month (EOM) activity by large financial and banking institutions often induces "dips" in the effective federal funds (FFE) rate that create bias issues when using the rate as the basis for probability calculations of potential Federal Open Market Committee rate moves. If EOM activity increases the price for the relevant fed funds contract, the FFE rate would decline. A decline in the FFE rate would decrease the probability of a change in the fed funds rate. To overcome this EOM bias, data providers have implemented various methods of "smoothing" EOM dips.

Statement 2 is incorrect because the probabilities inferred from the pricing of fed funds futures usually do not have strong predictive power, especially for the longer-term horizon.

Statement 3 is incorrect because, to derive probabilities of Fed interest rate actions, market participants look at the pricing of fed funds futures, which are tied to the FFE rate—that is, the rate used in actual transactions between depository institutions, not the Fed's target fed funds rate.

B is incorrect because the probabilities inferred from the pricing of fed funds futures usually do not have strong predictive power, especially for the longer-term horizon.

C is incorrect because, to derive probabilities of Fed interest rate actions, market participants look at the pricing of fed funds futures, which are tied to the FFE rate—that is, the rate that depository institutions actually use for lending to each other, not the Fed's target federal funds rate. The underlying assumption is that the implied futures market rates are predicting the value of the monthly average FFE rate.

**17** A is correct. If the basis is positive, a trader would make a profit by "selling the basis"—that is, selling the bond and buying the futures. In contrast, when the basis is negative, the trader would make a profit by "buying the basis," in which the trader would purchase the bond and short the futures.

B is incorrect because Statement 5 is incorrect. If the basis is negative, a trader would make a profit by "buying the basis"—that is, purchasing (not selling) the bond and shorting (not buying) the futures.

C is incorrect because Statement 5 is incorrect. If the basis is negative, a trader would make a profit by "buying the basis"—that is, purchasing (not selling) the bond and shorting (not buying) the futures.

**18** The number of equity index futures contracts required to achieve the target portfolio beta of 1.2 is calculated as follows:

$$N_f = \left(\frac{\beta_T - \beta_S}{\beta_f}\right)\left(\frac{S}{F}\right)$$

$$N_f = \left(\frac{1.2 - 0.9}{1.0}\right)\left(\frac{€168,300,000}{€45,000}\right)$$

$$N_f = 1,122$$

Because the number of futures contracts ($N_f$) is positive, Uff should buy 1,122 equity index futures contracts.

**19** The swap notional principal required to achieve the target portfolio modified duration is calculated as follows:

$$N_S = \left(\frac{MDUR_T - MDUR_P}{MDUR_S}\right)(MV_P)$$

$$N_S = \left(\frac{5.0000 - 7.8000}{-2.4848}\right)(€90,100,000)$$

$$N_S = €101,529,298.13$$

Therefore, Uff should enter into the selected three-year par pay-fixed, receive-floating interest rate swap with a notional principal of approximately €101,529,298.

**20** Uff needs to reduce the equity allocation by €13,202,500 (= €201,384,000 − €188,181,500).

The number of equity index futures contracts required to rebalance the Fund's portfolio to the target allocation is calculated as follows:

$$N_f = \left(\frac{\beta_T - \beta_S}{\beta_f}\right)\left(\frac{S}{F}\right)$$

Uff needs to move to a notional "cash" position ($\beta_T = 0$) to reduce equity exposure, and the portfolio beta is $\beta_S = 1.28$. The beta of the equity index futures contract ($\beta_f$) is 1.00, so the number of equity index futures contracts required is calculated as follows:

$$N_f = \left(\frac{0.00 - 1.28}{1.00}\right)\left(\frac{€13,202,500}{€35,000}\right)$$

$$N_f = -482.83$$

Because the number of futures contracts ($N_f$) is negative, Uff should sell 483 equity index futures contracts (after rounding).

## Solutions:

Uff needs to increase the bond allocation by €13,202,500 (= €101,328,500 − €88,126,000).

The number of bond futures contracts required to rebalance the Fund's portfolio to the target allocation is calculated as follows:

$$BPVHR = \left(\frac{BPV_T - BPV_P}{BPV_{CTD}}\right) \times CF,$$

where

$BPV_T = MDUR_T \times 0.01\% \times MV_P$
$BPV_T = 4.59 \times 0.0001 \times €13,202,500$
$BPV_T = €6,059.95$

Now, starting with a notional "cash" position ($BPV_P = 0$) provided by the reduction in equity exposure above, and noting that $BPV_{CTD}$ = €91.26 and $CF$ = 0.733194, the number of bond futures contracts is calculated as follows:

$$BPVHR = \left(\frac{€6,059.95 - €0.00}{€91.26}\right) \times 0.733194$$

$BPVHR = 48.69$

Because the BPVHR is positive, Uff should buy 49 bond futures contracts (after rounding).

21 Explain how to construct the swap that Tioga wants to use with regard to the swap:

  i. The swap tenor will be three years, consistent with the length of time for which Tioga expects interest rates to remain low.

  ii. Tioga will establish an interest rate swap in which Wyalusing will make payments based on a floating reference rate and will receive payments based on a fixed rate. The source of the reference rate and the value of the fixed rate will be set at the time of the swap's inception. The net effect for Wyalusing of the combination of making fixed payments on its coupon bond, receiving fixed payments on the swap, and making floating payments on the swap is to convert the fixed obligations of its bond coupon payments into floating-rate-based obligations. This scenario will allow Wyalusing to benefit if Tioga's expectation of low interest rates is realized.

  iii. The notional value of the swap should be set such that the fixed payments that Wyalusing receives will equal the fixed coupon payments that Wyalusing must make on its fixed-rate bond obligations.

  iv. Swap settlement dates should be set on the same days as the fixed-rate bond's coupon payment dates.

22 Describe how the swap will function, from the perspective of Wyalusing, in terms of the:

  i. At inception, Wyalusing will pay the notional principal of CAD and will receive an amount of USD according to the USD/CAD exchange rate, agreed to at inception.

  ii. At each swap payment date, Wyalusing will receive interest in CAD and will pay interest in USD. Both payments are based on floating reference rates for their respective currencies. The CAD rate will also include a basis rate that is quoted separately. On each settlement date, Wyalusing will receive an amount of CAD based on the CAD floating rate minus the basis rate applied to the swap notional value, and it will pay an amount of USD based on the USD floating rate and the USD/CAD exchange rate that was set at inception.

iii. At maturity, Wyalusing will receive the notional principal of CAD and will pay an amount of USD according to the USD/CAD exchange rate that was set at inception, applied to the CAD notional principal. The cash flows at maturity are the inverses of the cash flows at inception.

23 The Lushland 100 Index futures contract value is calculated as the quoted futures price multiplied by the designated contract multiplier:

$$F = 1,247 \times LLD200$$
$$F = LLD249,400$$

The target beta is the index beta, which equals 1.00. The number of Lushland 100 Index futures contracts that the Sanctuary must buy to equitize its excess cash position is calculated as follows:

$$N_f = \left(\frac{\beta_T}{\beta_f}\right)\left(\frac{S}{F}\right)$$

$$N_f = \left(\frac{1}{1}\right)\left(\frac{LLD1,000,000}{LLD249,400}\right)$$

$$N_f = 4.01 \text{ (rounded to 4)}$$

Therefore, the CFO should buy four Lushland 100 Index futures contracts to equitize the excess cash position.

24 The Sanctuary's CFO can use currency futures contracts to lock in the current LLD/JPY exchange rate. The CFO can hedge the Sanctuary's exchange rate risk by selling JPY futures contracts with the closest expiry to the expected future JPY inflow. When the futures contracts expire, the Sanctuary will receive (pay) any depreciation (appreciation) in JPY relative to LLD (when compared with the original LLD/JPY futures contract price). The CFO can determine the number of contracts needed by dividing the property's sale price of JPY500,000,000 by the JPY futures contract value. Because the hedge ratio is assumed to equal 1, the changes in futures and spot prices will be equal during the life of the futures contract, and so the hedge will be fully effective.

# READING 10

# Currency Management: An Introduction

by William A. Barker, PhD, CFA

*William A. Barker, PhD, CFA (Canada).*

| LEARNING OUTCOMES | |
|---|---|
| Mastery | The candidate should be able to: |
| ☐ | a. analyze the effects of currency movements on portfolio risk and return; |
| ☐ | b. discuss strategic choices in currency management; |
| ☐ | c. formulate an appropriate currency management program given financial market conditions and portfolio objectives and constraints; |
| ☐ | d. compare active currency trading strategies based on economic fundamentals, technical analysis, carry-trade, and volatility trading; |
| ☐ | e. describe how changes in factors underlying active trading strategies affect tactical trading decisions; |
| ☐ | f. describe how forward contracts and FX (foreign exchange) swaps are used to adjust hedge ratios; |
| ☐ | g. describe trading strategies used to reduce hedging costs and modify the risk–return characteristics of a foreign-currency portfolio; |
| ☐ | h. describe the use of cross-hedges, macro-hedges, and minimum-variance-hedge ratios in portfolios exposed to multiple foreign currencies; |
| ☐ | i. discuss challenges for managing emerging market currency exposures. |

# 1. INTRODUCTION

Globalization has been one of the most persistent themes in recent history, and this theme applies equally to the world of finance. New investment products, deregulation, worldwide financial system integration, and better communication and information

© 2019 CFA Institute. All rights reserved.

networks have opened new global investment opportunities. At the same time, investors have increasingly shed their "home bias" and sought investment alternatives beyond their own borders.

The benefits of this trend for portfolio managers have been clear, both in terms of the broader availability of higher-expected-return investments as well as portfolio diversification opportunities. Nonetheless, investments denominated in foreign currencies also bring a unique set of challenges: measuring and managing foreign exchange risk. Buying foreign-currency denominated assets means bringing currency risk into the portfolio. Exchange rates are volatile and, at least in the short to medium term, can have a marked impact on investment returns and risks—*currency matters*. The key to the superior performance of global portfolios is the effective management of this currency risk.

This reading explores basic concepts and tools of currency management. Section 2 reviews some of the basic concepts of foreign exchange (FX) markets. The material in subsequent sections presumes an understanding of these concepts. Section 3 examines some of the basic mathematics involved in measuring the effects of foreign-currency investments on portfolio return and risk. Sections 4–6 discuss the *strategic* decisions portfolio managers face in setting the target currency exposures of the portfolio. The currency exposures that the portfolio can accept range from a fully hedged position to active management of currency risk. Sections 7–8 discuss some of the *tactical* considerations involving active currency management if the investment policy statement (IPS) extends some latitude for active currency management. A requisite to any active currency management is having a market view; so these sections includes various methodologies by which a manager can form directional views on future exchange rate movements and volatility. Sections 9–12 cover a variety of trading tools available to implement both hedging and active currency management strategies. Although the generic types of FX derivatives tools are relatively limited—spot, forward, option, and swap contracts—the number of variations within each and the number of combinations in which they can be used is vast. Section 13 examines some of the issues involved in managing the currency exposures of emerging market currencies—that is, those that are less liquid than the major currencies.

## 2. REVIEW OF FOREIGN EXCHANGE CONCEPTS

We begin with a review of the basic trading tools of the foreign exchange market: spot, forward, FX swap, and currency option transactions. The concepts introduced in this section will be used extensively in our discussion of currency management techniques in subsequent sections.

Most people think only of spot transactions when they think of the foreign exchange market, but in fact the spot market accounts for less than 40% of the average daily turnover in currencies.[1] Although cross-border *business* may be transacted in the spot market (making and receiving foreign currency payments), the *risk management* of these flows takes place in FX derivatives markets (i.e., using forwards, FX swaps, and currency options). So does the hedging of foreign currency assets and liabilities. It is unusual for market participants to engage in any foreign currency transactions without also managing the currency risk they create. Spot transactions typically generate derivative transactions. As a result, understanding these FX derivatives markets, and their relation to the spot market, is critical for understanding the currency risk management issues examined in this reading.

---

[1] 2013 Triennial Survey, Bank for International Settlements (2013).

## 2.1 Spot Markets

In professional FX markets, exchange rate quotes are described in terms of the three-letter currency codes used to identify individual currencies. Exhibit 1 shows a list of some of the more common currency codes.

| Exhibit 1 | Currency Codes |
|---|---|
| USD | US dollar |
| EUR | Euro |
| GBP | British pound |
| JPY | Japanese yen |
| MXN | Mexican peso |
| CHF | Swiss franc |
| CAD | Canadian dollar |
| SEK | Swedish krona |
| AUD | Australian dollar |
| KRW | Korean won |
| NZD | New Zealand dollar |
| BRL | Brazilian real |
| RUB | Russian ruble |
| CNY | Chinese yuan |
| INR | Indian rupee |
| ZAR | South African rand |

An exchange rate is the number of units of one currency (called the *price currency*) that one unit of another currency (called the *base currency*) will buy. For example, in the notation we will use a USD/EUR rate of 1.3650 which means that one euro buys $1.3650; equivalently, the price of one euro is 1.3650 US dollars. Thus, the euro here is the base currency and the US dollar is the price currency. The exact notation used to represent exchange rates can vary widely between sources, and occasionally the same exchange rate notation will be used by different sources to mean completely different things. The reader should be aware that the notation used here may not be the same as that encountered elsewhere. To avoid confusion, this reading will identify exchange rates using the convention of "P/B," which refers to the price of one unit of the base currency "B" expressed in terms of the price currency "P."

How the professional FX market quotes exchange rates—which is the base currency, and which is the price currency, in any currency pair—is not arbitrary but follows conventions that are broadly agreed on throughout the market. Generally, there is a hierarchy as to which currency will be quoted as the base currency in any given P/B currency pair:

1. Currency pairs involving the EUR will use the EUR as the base currency (for example, GBP/EUR).
2. Currency pairs involving the GBP, other than those involving the EUR, will use the GBP as the base currency (for example, CHF/GBP).

**3** Currency pairs involving either the AUD or NZD, other than those involving either the EUR or GBP, will use these currencies as the base currency (for example, USD/AUD and NZD/AUD). The market convention between these two currencies is for a NZD/AUD quote.

**4** All other currency quotes involving the USD will use USD as the base currency (for example, MXN/USD).

Readers are encouraged to familiarize themselves with the quoting conventions used in the professional FX market because they are the currency quotes that will be experienced in practice. Exhibit 2 lists some of the most commonly traded currency pairs in global FX markets and their market-standard quoting conventions. These market-standard conventions will be used for the balance of this reading.

**Exhibit 2  Select Market-Standard Currency Pair Quotes**

| Quote convention | Market name |
| --- | --- |
| USD/EUR | Euro-dollar |
| GBP/EUR | Euro-sterling |
| USD/GBP | Sterling-dollar |
| JPY/USD | Dollar-yen |
| USD/AUD | Aussie-dollar |
| CHF/USD | Dollar-Swiss |
| CAD/USD | Dollar-Canada |
| JPY/EUR | Euro-yen |
| CHF/EUR | Euro-Swiss |
| JPY/GBP | Sterling-yen |

Another convention used in professional FX markets is that most spot currency quotes are priced out to four decimal places: for example, a typical USD/EUR quote would be 1.3500 and not 1.35. The price point at the fourth decimal place is commonly referred to as a "pip." Professional FX traders also refer to what is called the "big figure" or the "handle," which is the integer to the left side of the decimal place as well as the first two decimal places of the quote. For example, for a USD/EUR quote of 1.3568, 1.35 is the handle and there are 68 pips.

There are exceptions to this four decimal place rule. First, forward quotes—discussed later—will often be quoted out to five and sometimes six decimal places. Second, because of the relative magnitude of some currency values, some currency quotes will only be quoted out to two decimal places. For example, because it takes many Japanese yen to buy one US dollar, the typical spot quote for JPY/USD is priced out to only two decimal places (for example, 86.35 and not 86.3500).[2]

The spot exchange rate is usually for settlement on the second business day after the trade date, referred to as $T + 2$ settlement.[3] In foreign exchange markets—as in other financial markets—market participants confront a two-sided price in the form of a bid price and an offer price (also called an ask price) being quoted by potential counterparties. The **bid price** is the price, defined in terms of the price currency, at

---

[2] Many electronic dealing platforms in the FX market are moving to five decimal place pricing for spot quotes, using what are referred to as "deci-pips." In this case, for example, a USD/EUR spot quote might be shown as 1.37645. Spot quotes for JPY/USD on these systems will be given out to three decimal places.
[3] The exception among the major currencies is CAD/USD, for which standard spot settlement is $T + 1$.

which the counterparty providing a two-sided price quote is willing to buy one unit of the **base** currency. Similarly, **offer price** is the price, in terms of the price currency, at which that counterparty is willing to sell one unit of the base currency. For example, given a price request from a client, a dealer might quote a two-sided price on the spot USD/EUR exchange rate of 1.3648/1.3652. This quote means that the dealer is willing to pay USD1.3648 to buy one euro (bid) and that the dealer will sell one euro (offer) for USD1.3652. The market width, usually referred to as dealer's spread or the bid–offer spread, is the difference between the bid and the offer. When transacting on a dealer's bid-offer two-sided price quote, a client is said to either "hit the bid" (selling the base currency) or "pay the offer" (buying the base currency).

An easy check to see whether the bid or offer should be used for a specific transaction is that the party *asking* the dealer for a price should be on the more expensive side of the market. For example, if one wants to buy 1 EUR, 1.3652 is more USD per EUR than 1.3648. Hence, paying the offer involves paying more USD. Similarly, when selling 1 EUR, hitting the bid at 1.3648 means less USD received than 1.3652.

## 2.2 Forward Markets

Forward contracts are agreements to exchange one currency for another on a future date at an exchange rate agreed on today.[4] In contrast to spot rates, forward contracts are any exchange rate transactions that occur with settlement longer than the usual $T + 2$ settlement for spot delivery.

In professional FX markets, forward exchange rates are typically quoted in terms of "points." The points on a forward rate quote are simply the difference between the forward exchange rate quote and the spot exchange rate quote; that is, the forward premium or discount, with the points scaled so that they can be related to the last decimal place in the spot quote. Forward points are adjustments to the spot price of the base currency, using our standard price/base (P/B) currency notation.

This means that forward rate quotes in professional FX markets are typically shown as the bid–offer on the spot rate and the number of forward points at each maturity.[5] For illustration purposes, assume that the bid–offer for the spot and forward points for the USD/EUR exchange rate are as shown in Exhibit 3.

| Exhibit 3 | Sample Spot and Forward Quotes (Bid–Offer) |
|---|---|
| **Maturity** | **Spot Rate or Forward Points** |
| Spot (USD/EUR) | 1.3549/1.3651 |
| One month | −5.6/−5.1 |
| Three months | −15.9/−15.3 |
| Six months | −37.0/−36.3 |
| Twelve months | −94.3/−91.8 |

To convert any of these quoted forward points into a forward rate, one would divide the number of points by 10,000 (to scale down to the fourth decimal place, the last decimal place in the USD/EUR spot quote) and then add the result to the spot

---

[4] These are sometimes called outright forwards to distinguish them from FX swaps, which are discussed later.
[5] Maturity is defined in terms of the time between spot settlement, usually $T + 2$, and the settlement of the forward contract.

exchange rate quote.[6] But one must be careful about which side of the market (bid or offer) is being quoted. For example, suppose a market participant was *selling* the EUR forward against the USD. Given the USD/EUR quoting convention, the EUR is the base currency. This means the market participant must use the *bid* rates (i.e., the market participant will "hit the bid") given the USD/EUR quoting convention. Using the data in Exhibit 3, the three-month forward *bid* rate in this case would be based on the bid for both the spot and the forward points, and hence would be:

$$1.3549 + \left(\frac{-15.9}{10,000}\right) = 1.35331$$

This result means that the market participant would be selling EUR three months forward at a price of USD1.35331 per EUR. Note that the quoted points are already scaled to each maturity—they are not annualized—so there is no need to adjust them.

Although there is no cash flow on a forward contract until settlement date, it is often useful to do a mark-to-market valuation on a forward position before then to (1) judge the effectiveness of a hedge based on forward contracts (i.e., by comparing the change in the mark-to-market of the underlying asset with the change in the mark-to-market of the forward), and (2) to measure the profitability of speculative currency positions at points before contract maturity.

As with other financial instruments, the mark-to-market value of forward contracts reflects the profit (or loss) that would be realized from closing out the position at current market prices. To close out a forward position, it must be offset with an equal and opposite forward position using the spot exchange rate and forward points available in the market when the offsetting position is created. When a forward contract is initiated, the forward rate is such that no cash changes hands (i.e., the mark-to-market value of the contract at initiation is zero). From that moment onward, however, the mark-to-market value of the forward contract will change as the spot exchange rate changes as well as when interest rates change in either of the two currencies.

Consider an example. Suppose that a market participant bought GBP10,000,000 for delivery against the AUD in six months at an "all-in" forward rate of 1.6100 AUD/GBP. (The all-in forward rate is simply the sum of the spot rate and the forward points, appropriately scaled to size.) Three months later, the market participant wants to close out this forward contract. To do that would require selling GBP10,000,000 three months forward using the AUD/GBP spot exchange rate and forward points in effect at that time. Assume the bid–offer for spot and forward points three months prior to the settlement date are as follows:

| Spot rate (AUD/GBP) | 1.6210/1.6215 |
| Three-month points | 130/140 |

To sell GBP (the base currency in the AUD/GBP quote) means calculating the *bid* side of the market. Hence, the appropriate all-in three-month forward rate to use is

1.6210 + 130/10,000 = 1.6340

Thus, the market participant originally bought GBP10,000,000 at an AUD/GBP rate of 1.6100 and subsequently sold them at a rate of 1.6340. These GBP amounts will net to zero at settlement date (GBP10 million both bought and sold), but the AUD amounts will not net to zero because the forward rate has changed. The AUD cash flow at settlement date will be equal to

(1.6340 − 1.6100) × 10,000,000 = AUD240,000

---

[6] Because the JPY/USD exchange rate is only quoted to two decimal places, forward points for the dollar/yen currency pair are divided by 100.

# Review of Foreign Exchange Concepts

This amount is a cash *inflow* because the market participant was long the GBP with the original forward position and the GBP subsequently appreciated (the AUD/GBP rate increased).

This cash flow is paid at settlement day, which is still three months away. To calculate the mark-to-market value on the dealer's position, this cash flow must be discounted to the present. The present value of this amount is found by discounting the settlement day cash flow by the three-month discount rate. Because it is an AUD amount, the three-month AUD discount rate is used. If Libor is used and the three-month AUD Libor is 4.80% (annualized), the present value of this future AUD cash flow is then

$$\frac{AUD240{,}000}{1 + 0.048\left[\dfrac{90}{360}\right]} = AUD237{,}154$$

This is the mark-to-market value of the original long GBP10 million six-month forward contract when it is closed out three months prior to settlement.

To summarize, the process for marking-to-market a forward position is relatively straightforward:

1. Create an equal and offsetting forward position to the original forward position. (In the example earlier, the market participant is long GBP10 million forward, so the offsetting forward contract would be to sell GBP10 million.)
2. Determine the appropriate all-in forward rate for this new, offsetting forward position. If the base currency of the exchange rate quote is being sold (bought), then use the bid (offer) side of the market.
3. Calculate the cash flow at settlement day. This calculation will be based on the original contract size times the difference between the original forward rate and the rate calculated in Step 2. If the currency the market participant was originally long (short) subsequently appreciated (depreciated), then there will be a cash *inflow*. Otherwise, there will be a cash outflow. (In the earlier example, the market participant was long the GBP and it subsequently appreciated; this appreciation led to a cash inflow at the settlement day.)
4. Calculate the present value of this cash flow at the future settlement date. The currency of the cash flow and the discount rate must match. (In the example earlier, the cash flow at the settlement date is in AUD, so an AUD Libor rate is used to calculate the present value.)

Finally, we note that in the example, the mark-to-market value is given in AUD. It would be possible to translate this AUD amount into any other currency value using the current spot rate for the relevant currency pair. In the example above, this would be done by redenominating the mark-to-market in USD, by selling 240,000 AUD 90-days forward against the USD at the prevailing USD/AUD 90-day forward bid rate. This will produce a USD cash flow in 90 days. This USD amount can then be present-valued at the 90-day US rate to get the USD mark-to-market value of the AUD/GBP forward position. The day-count convention used here is an "actual/360" basis.

## 2.3 FX Swap Markets

An FX swap transaction consists of offsetting and simultaneous spot and forward transactions, in which the base currency is being bought (sold) spot and sold (bought) forward. These two transactions are often referred to as the "legs" of the swap. The two legs of the swap can either be of equal size (a "matched" swap) or one can be larger than the other (a "mismatched" swap). FX swaps are distinct from currency swaps. Similar to currency swaps, FX swaps involve an exchange of principal amounts in different currencies at swap initiation that is reversed at swap maturity. Unlike currency swaps, FX swaps have no interim interest payments and are nearly always of much shorter term than currency swaps.

FX swaps are important for managing currency risk because they are used to "roll" forward contracts forward as they mature. For example, consider the case of a trader who *bought* GBP1,000,000 one month forward against the CHF in order to set up a currency hedge. One month later, the forward contract will expire. To maintain this long position in the GBP against the CHF, two days prior to contract maturity, given $T + 2$ settlement, the trader must (1) sell GBP1,000,000 against the CHF spot, to settle the maturing forward contract; and (2) buy GBP1,000,000 against the CHF forward. That is, the trader is engaging in an FX swap (a matched swap in this case because the GBP currency amounts are equal).

If a trader wanted to adjust the size of the currency hedge (i.e., the size of the outstanding forward position), the forward leg of the FX swap can be of a different size than the spot transaction when the hedge is rolled. Continuing the previous example, if the trader wanted to increase the size of the long-GBP position by GBP500,000 as the outstanding forward contract expires, the transactions required would be to (1) sell GBP1,000,000 against the CHF spot, to settle the maturing forward contract; and (2) buy GBP1,500,000 against the CHF forward. This would be a mismatched swap.

The pricing of swaps will differ slightly depending on whether they are matched or mismatched swaps. If the amount of the base currency involved for the spot and forward legs of the swap are equal (a matched swap), then these are exactly offsetting transactions; one is a buy, the other a sell, and both are for the same amount. Because of this equality, a common *spot* exchange rate is typically applied to both legs of the swap transaction; it is standard practice to use the mid-market spot exchange rate for a matched swap transaction. However, the *forward* points will still be based on either the bid or offer, depending on whether the market participant is buying or selling the base currency forward. In the earlier example, the trader is *buying* the GBP (the base currency) forward and would hence pay the *offer* side of the market for forward points.

If the FX swap is mismatched, then pricing will need to reflect the difference in trade sizes between the two legs of the transaction. Continuing the example in which the trader increased the size of the long-GBP position by GBP500,000, this mismatched swap is equivalent to (1) a matched swap for a size of GBP1,000,000, and (2) an outright forward contract buying GBP500,000. Pricing for the mismatched swap must reflect this net GBP purchase amount. Because the matched swap would already price the forward points on the offer side of the market, typically this mismatched size adjustment would be reflected in the *spot* rate quoted as the base for the FX swap. Because a net amount of GBP is being *bought*, the spot quote would now be on the *offer* side of the CHF/GBP spot rate quote. (In addition, the trader would still pay the offer side of the market for the forward points.)

We will return to these topics later in the reading when discussing in more depth the use of forward contracts and FX swaps to adjust hedge ratios. (A **hedge ratio** is the ratio of the nominal value of the derivatives contract used as a hedge to the market value of the hedged asset.)

## 2.4 Currency Options

The final product type within FX markets is currency options. The market for currency options is, in many ways, similar to option markets for other asset classes, such as bonds and equities. As in other markets, the most common options in FX markets are call and put options, which are widely used for both risk management and speculative purposes. However, in addition to these vanilla options, the FX market is also characterized by active trading in exotic options. ("Exotic" options have a variety of features that make them exceptionally flexible risk management tools, compared with vanilla options.)

The risk management uses of both vanilla and exotic currency options will be examined in subsequent sections. Although daily turnover in FX options market is small in *relative* terms compared with the overall daily flow in global spot currency markets, because the overall currency market is so large, the *absolute* size of the FX options market is still very considerable.

# CURRENCY RISK AND PORTFOLIO RISK AND RETURN 3

a analyze the effects of currency movements on portfolio risk and return;

In this section, we examine the effect of currency movements on asset returns and portfolio risk. We then turn to how these effects help determine construction of a foreign asset portfolio.

## 3.1 Return Decomposition

In this section, we examine how international exposure affects a portfolio's return. A **domestic asset** is an asset that trades in the investor's **domestic currency** (or **home currency**). From a portfolio manager's perspective, the domestic currency is the one in which portfolio valuation and returns are reported. *Domestic* refers to a relation between the currency denomination of the asset and the investor; it is not an inherent property of either the asset or the currency. An example of a domestic asset is a USD-denominated bond portfolio from the perspective of a US-domiciled investor. The return on a domestic asset is not affected by exchange rate movements of the domestic currency.

**Foreign assets** are assets denominated in currencies other than the investor's home currency. An example of a foreign asset is a USD-denominated bond portfolio from the perspective of a eurozone-domiciled investor (and for whom the euro is the home currency). The return on a foreign asset will be affected by exchange rate movements in the home currency against the **foreign currency**. Continuing with our example, the return to the eurozone-domiciled investor will be affected by the USD return on the USD-denominated bond as well as movements in the exchange rate between the home currency and the foreign currency, the EUR and USD respectively.

The return of the foreign asset measured in foreign-currency terms is known as the **foreign-currency return**. Extending the example, if the value of the USD-denominated bond increased by 10%, measured in USD, that increase is the foreign-currency return to the eurozone-domiciled investor. The **domestic-currency return** on a foreign asset will reflect both the foreign-currency return on that asset as well as percentage movements in the spot exchange rate between the home and foreign currencies. The domestic-currency return is multiplicative with respect to these two factors:

$$R_{DC} = (1 + R_{FC})(1 + R_{FX}) - 1 \qquad (1)$$

where $R_{DC}$ is the domestic-currency return (in percent), $R_{FC}$ is the foreign-currency return, and $R_{FX}$ is the percentage change of the foreign currency against the domestic currency.

Returning to the example, the domestic-currency return for the eurozone-domiciled investor on the USD-denominated bond will reflect both the bond's USD-denominated return as well as movements in the exchange rate between the USD and the EUR.

Suppose that the foreign-currency return on the USD-denominated bond is 10% and the USD appreciates by 5% against the EUR. In this case, the domestic-currency return to the eurozone investor will be:

(1 + 10%)(1 + 5%) − 1 = (1.10)(1.05) − 1 = 0.155 = 15.5%

Although the concept is seemingly straightforward, the reader should be aware that Equation 1 hides a subtlety that must be recognized. The term $R_{FX}$ is defined as the percentage change in the foreign currency against the domestic currency. However, this change is *not* always the same thing as the percentage change in the spot rate using market standard P/B quotes (for example, as shown in Exhibit 2). Specifically, it is not always the case that $R_{FX} = \%\Delta S_{P/B}$, where the term on the right side of the equal sign is defined in standard FX market convention (note that %Δ is percentage change).

In other words, $R_{FX}$ is calculated as the change in the directly quoted exchange rate, where the domestic currency is defined as the investor's home currency. Because market quotes are not always in direct terms, analysts will need to convert to direct quotes before calculating percentage changes.

With this nuance in mind, what holds for the domestic-currency return of a single foreign asset also holds for the returns on a multi-currency portfolio of foreign assets, except now the portfolio weights must be considered. More generally, the domestic-currency return on a portfolio of multiple foreign assets will be equal to

$$R_{DC} = \sum_{i=1}^{n} \omega_i \left(1 + R_{FC,i}\right)\left(1 + R_{FX,i}\right) - 1 \qquad (2)$$

where $R_{FC,i}$ is the foreign-currency return on the *i*-th foreign asset, $R_{FX,i}$ is the appreciation of the *i*-th foreign currency against the domestic currency, and $\omega_i$ are the portfolio weights of the foreign-currency assets (defined as the percentage of the aggregate domestic-currency value of the portfolio) and $\sum_{i=1}^{n} \omega_i = 1$. (Note that if short selling is allowed in the portfolio, some of the $\omega_i$ can be less than zero.) Again, it is important that the exchange rate notation in this expression (used to calculate $R_{FX,i}$) must be consistently defined with the domestic currency as the price currency.

Assume the following information for a portfolio held by an investor in India. Performance is measured in terms of the Indian rupee (INR) and the weights of the two assets in the portfolio, at the beginning of the period, are 80% for the GBP-denominated asset and 20% for the EUR-denominated asset, respectively. (Note that the portfolio weights are measured in terms of a common currency, the INR, which is the investor's domestic currency in this case.)

|  | One Year Ago | Today* |
|---|---|---|
| INR/GBP spot rate | 84.12 | 85.78 |
| INR/EUR spot rate | 65.36 | 67.81 |
| GBP-denominated asset value, in GBP millions | 43.80 | 50.70 |
| EUR-denominated asset value, in EUR millions | 14.08 | 12.17 |
| GBP-denominated asset value, in INR millions | 3,684.46 | |
| EUR-denominated asset value, in INR millions | 920.27 | |
| GBP-denominated assets, portfolio weight (INR) | 80% | |
| EUR-denominated assets, portfolio weight (INR) | 20% | |

* Today's asset values are prior to rebalancing.

## Currency Risk and Portfolio Risk and Return

The domestic-currency return ($R_{DC}$) is calculated as follows:

$$R_{DC} = 0.80(1 + R_{FC,GBP})(1 + R_{FX,GBP}) + 0.20(1 + R_{FC,EUR})(1 + R_{FX,EUR}) - 1$$

Note that given the exchange rate quoting convention, the INR is the price currency in the P/B quote for both currency pairs. Adding the data from the table leads to:

$$R_{DC} = 0.80\left(\frac{50.70}{43.80}\right)\left(\frac{85.78}{84.12}\right) + 0.20\left(\frac{12.17}{14.08}\right)\left(\frac{67.81}{65.36}\right) - 1$$

This solves to 0.124 or 12.4%.

To get the *expected* future return on a foreign-currency asset portfolio, based on Equation 2, the portfolio manager would need a market opinion for the expected price movement in each of the foreign assets ($R_{A,i}$) and exchange rates ($R_{FX,i}$) in the portfolio. There are typically correlations between all of these variables—correlations between the foreign asset price movements across countries, correlations between movements among various currency pairs, and correlations between exchange rate movements and foreign-currency asset returns. The portfolio manager would need to account for these correlations when forming expectations about future asset price and exchange rate movements.

### 3.2 Volatility Decomposition

Now we will turn to examining the effect of currency movements on the volatility of domestic-currency returns. Equation 1 can be rearranged as

$$R_{DC} = (1 + R_{FC})(1 + R_{FX}) - 1 = R_{FC} + R_{FX} + R_{FC}R_{FX}$$

When $R_{FC}$ and $R_{FX}$ are small, then the cross-term ($R_{FC}R_{FX}$) is small, and as a result this equation can be approximated as

$$R_{DC} \approx R_{FC} + R_{FX} \tag{3}$$

We return to the example in which the foreign-currency return on the USD-denominated bond was 10% and the USD appreciated by 5% against the EUR. In this example, the domestic-currency return for the Eurozone investor's holding in the USD-denominated bond was approximately equal to 10% + 5% = 15% (which is close to the exact value of 15.5%). We can combine the approximation of Equation 3 with the statistical rule that:

$$\sigma^2(\omega_x X + \omega_y Y) = \omega_x^2 \sigma^2(X) + \omega_y^2 \sigma^2(Y) + 2\omega_x \omega_y \sigma(X)\sigma(Y)\rho(X,Y) \tag{4}$$

where $X$ and $Y$ are random variables, $\omega$ are weights attached to $X$ and $Y$, $\sigma^2$ is variance of a random variable, $\sigma$ is the corresponding standard deviation, and $\rho$ represents the correlation between two random variables. Applying this result to the domestic-currency return approximation of Equation 3 leads to:

$$\sigma^2(R_{DC}) \approx \sigma^2(R_{FC}) + \sigma^2(R_{FX}) + 2\sigma(R_{FC})\sigma(R_{FX})\rho(R_{FC},R_{FX}) \tag{5}$$

This equation is for the variance of the domestic-currency returns ($R_{DC}$), but risk is more typically defined in terms of standard deviation because mean and standard deviation are measured in the same units (percent, in this case). Hence, the total risk for domestic-currency returns—that is, $\sigma(R_{DC})$—is the square root of the results calculated in Equation 5.

Note as well that because Equation 5 is based on the addition of all three terms on the right side of the equal sign, exchange rate exposure will generally cause the variance of domestic-currency returns, $\sigma^2(R_{DC})$, to increase to more than that of the foreign-currency returns, $\sigma^2(R_{FC})$, considered on their own. That is, if there was no exchange rate risk, then it would be the case that $\sigma^2(R_{DC}) = \sigma^2(R_{FC})$. Using this as our base-case scenario, adding exchange rate risk exposure to the portfolio usually adds to domestic-currency return variance (the effect is indeterminate if exchange rate movements are negatively correlated with foreign asset returns).

These results on the variance of domestic-currency return can be generalized to a portfolio of foreign-currency assets. If we define the random variables $X$ and $Y$ in Equation 4 in terms of the domestic-currency return ($R_{DC}$) of two different foreign-currency investments, and the $\omega_i$ as portfolio weights that sum to one, then the result is the variance of the domestic-currency returns for the overall foreign asset portfolio:

$$\sigma^2(\omega_1 R_1 + \omega_2 R_2) \approx \omega_1^2 \sigma^2(R_1) + \omega_2^2 \sigma^2(R_2) + 2\omega_1 \omega_2 \sigma(R_1) \sigma(R_2) \rho(R_1, R_2) \qquad (6)$$

where $R_i$ is the domestic-currency return of the $i$-th foreign-currency asset. But as shown in Equation 3, the domestic-currency return of a foreign-currency asset ($R_{DC}$) is itself based on the sum of two random variables: $R_{FC}$ and $R_{FX}$. This means that we would have to embed the variance expression shown in Equation 5 in *each* of the $\sigma^2(R_i)$ shown in Equation 6 to get the complete solution for the domestic-currency return variance of the overall portfolio. (We would also have to calculate the correlations between *all* of the $R_i$.) These requirements would lead to a very cumbersome mathematical expression for even a portfolio of only two foreign-currency assets; the expression would be far more complicated for a portfolio with many foreign currencies involved.

Thus, rather than attempt to give the complete mathematical formula for the variance of domestic-currency returns for a multi-currency portfolio, we will instead focus on the key intuition behind this expression. Namely, that the domestic-currency risk exposure of the overall portfolio—that is, $\sigma(R_{DC})$—will depend not only on the variances of *each* of the foreign-currency returns ($R_{FC}$) and exchange rate movements ($R_{FX}$) but also on how each of these *interacts* with the others. Generally speaking, negative correlations among these variables will help reduce the overall portfolio's risk through diversification effects.

Note as well that the overall portfolio's risk exposure will depend on the portfolio weights ($\omega_i$) used. If short-selling is allowed in the portfolio, some of these $\omega_i$ can be negative as long as the total portfolio weights sum to one. So, for two foreign assets with a strong positive return correlation, short selling one can create considerable diversification benefits for the portfolio. (This approach is equivalent to trading movements in the price spread between these two assets.)

As before with the difference between realized and expected domestic-currency portfolio returns ($R_{DC}$), there is a difference between realized and expected domestic-currency portfolio risk, $\sigma(R_{DC})$. For Equation 6 to apply to the expected future volatility of the domestic-currency return of a multi-currency foreign asset portfolio, we would need to replace the observed, historical values of the variances and covariances in Equation 6 with their expected future values. This can be challenging, not only because it potentially involves a large number of variables but also because historical price patterns are not always a good guide to future price behavior. Variance and correlation measures are sensitive to the time period used to estimate them and can also vary over time. These variance and correlation measures can either drift randomly with time, or they can be subject to abrupt movements in times of market stress. It should also be clear that these observed, historical volatility and correlation measures need not be the same as the forward-looking *implied* volatility (and correlation) derived from option prices. Although sometimes various survey or consensus forecasts can be used, these too can be sensitive to sample size and composition and are not always available on a timely basis or with a consistent starting point. As with any forecast, they are also not necessarily an accurate guide to future developments; judgment must be used.

Hence, to calculate the expected future risk of the foreign asset portfolio, the portfolio manager would need a market opinion—however derived—on the variance of each of the foreign-currency asset returns ($R_{FC}$) over the investment horizon as

# Currency Risk and Portfolio Risk and Return

well the variance of future exchange rate movements ($R_{FX}$) for each currency pair. The portfolio manager would also need a market opinion of how each of these future variables would interact with each other (i.e., their expected correlations). Historical price patterns can serve as a guide, and with computers and large databases, this modeling problem is daunting but not intractable. But the portfolio manager must always be mindful that historical risk patterns may not repeat going forward.

## EXAMPLE 1

### Portfolio Risk and Return Calculations

The following table shows current and future expected asset prices, measured in their domestic currencies, for both eurozone and Canadian assets (these can be considered "total return" indexes). The table also has the corresponding data for the CAD/EUR spot rate.

|  | Eurozone | | Canada | |
| --- | --- | --- | --- | --- |
|  | Today | Expected | Today | Expected |
| Asset price | 100.69 | 101.50 | 101.00 | 99.80 |
| CAD/EUR | 1.2925 | 1.3100 | | |

1. What is the expected domestic-currency return for a eurozone investor holding the Canadian asset?
2. What is the expected domestic-currency return for a Canadian investor holding the eurozone asset?
3. From the perspective of the Canadian investor, assume that $\sigma(R_{FC}) = 3\%$ (the expected risk for the foreign-currency asset is 3%) and the $\sigma(R_{FX}) = 2\%$ (the expected risk of exchange rate movements is 2%). Furthermore, the expected correlation between movements in foreign-currency asset returns and movements in the CAD/EUR rate is +0.5. What is the expected risk of the domestic-currency return $[\sigma(R_{DC})]$?

### Solution to 1:

For the eurozone investor, the $R_{FC} = (99.80/101.00) - 1 = -1.19\%$. Note that, given we are considering the eurozone to be "domestic" for this investor and given the way the $R_{FX}$ expression is defined, we will need to convert the CAD/EUR exchange rate quote so that the EUR is the *price* currency. This leads to $R_{FX} = [(1/1.3100)/(1/1.2925)] - 1 = -1.34\%$. Hence, for the eurozone investor, $R_{DC} = (1 - 1.19\%)(1 - 1.34\%) - 1 = -2.51\%$.

### Solution to 2:

For the Canadian investor, the $R_{FC} = (101.50/100.69) - 1 = +0.80\%$. Given that in the CAD/EUR quote the CAD is the price currency, for this investor the $R_{FX} = (1.3100/1.2925) - 1 = +1.35\%$. Hence, for the Canadian investor the $R_{DC} = (1 + 0.80\%)(1 + 1.35\%) - 1 = 2.16\%$.

### Solution to 3:

Because this is a single foreign-currency asset we are considering (not a portfolio of such assets), we can use Equation 5:

$$\sigma^2(R_{DC}) \approx \sigma^2(R_{FC}) + \sigma^2(R_{FX}) + 2\sigma(R_{FC})\sigma(R_{FX})\rho(R_{FC},R_{FX})$$

Inserting the relevant data leads to

$$\sigma^2(R_{DC}) \approx (3\%)^2 + (2\%)^2 + 2(3\%)(2\%)(0.50) = 0.0019$$

> Taking the square root of this leads to $\sigma(R_{DC}) \approx 4.36\%$. (Note that the units in these expressions are all in percent, so in this case 3% is equivalent to 0.03 for calculation purposes.)

## 4. STRATEGIC DECISIONS IN CURRENCY MANAGEMENT: OVERVIEW

**b** discuss strategic choices in currency management;

There are a variety of approaches to currency management, ranging from trying to avoid all currency risk in a portfolio to actively seeking foreign exchange risk in order to manage it and enhance portfolio returns.

There is no firm consensus—either among academics or practitioners—about the most effective way to manage currency risk. Some investment managers try to hedge all currency risk, some leave their portfolios unhedged, and others see currency risk as a potential source of incremental return to the portfolio and will actively trade foreign exchange. These widely varying management practices reflect a variety of factors including investment objectives, investment constraints, and beliefs about currency markets.

Concerning beliefs, one camp of thought holds that in the long run currency effects cancel out to zero as exchange rates revert to historical means or their fundamental values. Moreover, an efficient currency market is a zero-sum game (currency "A" cannot appreciate against currency "B" without currency "B" depreciating against currency "A"), so there should not be any long-run gains overall to speculating in currencies, especially after netting out management and transaction costs. Therefore, both currency hedging and actively trading currencies represent a cost to a portfolio with little prospect of consistently positive active returns.

At the other extreme, another camp of thought notes that currency movements can have a dramatic impact on short-run returns and return volatility and holds that there are pricing inefficiencies in currency markets. They note that much of the flow in currency markets is related to international trade or capital flows in which FX trading is being done on a need-to-do basis and these currency trades are just a spinoff of the other transactions. Moreover, some market participants are either not in the market on a purely profit-oriented basis (e.g., central banks, government agencies) or are believed to be "uninformed traders" (primarily retail accounts). Conversely, speculative capital seeking to arbitrage inefficiencies is finite. In short, marketplace diversity is believed to present the potential for "harvesting alpha" through active currency trading.

This ongoing debate does not make foreign-currency risk in portfolios go away; it still needs to managed, or at least, recognized. Ultimately, each portfolio manager or investment oversight committee will have to reach their own decisions about how to manage risk and whether to seek return enhancement through actively trading currency exposures.

Fortunately, there are a well-developed set of financial products and portfolio management techniques that help investors manage currency risk no matter what their individual objectives, views, and constraints. Indeed, the potential combinations of trading tools and strategies are almost infinite, and can shape currency exposures to custom-fit individual circumstance and market opinion. In this section, we explore various points on a spectrum reflecting currency exposure choices (a risk spectrum) and the guidance that portfolio managers use in making strategic decisions about where to locate their portfolios on this continuum. First, however, the implication of investment objectives and constraints as set forth in the investment policy statement must be recognized.

## 4.1 The Investment Policy Statement

The Investment Policy Statement (IPS) mandates the degree of discretionary currency management that will be allowed in the portfolio, how it will be benchmarked, and the limits on the type of trading polices and tools (e.g., such as leverage) than can be used.

The starting point for organizing the investment plan for any portfolio is the IPS, which is a statement that outlines the broad objectives and constraints of the beneficial owners of the assets. Most IPS specify many of the following points:

- the general objectives of the investment portfolio;
- the risk tolerance of the portfolio and its capacity for bearing risk;
- the time horizon over which the portfolio is to be invested;
- the ongoing income/liquidity needs (if any) of the portfolio; and
- the benchmark against which the portfolio will measure overall investment returns.

The IPS sets the guiding parameters within which more specific portfolio management policies are set, including the target asset mix; whether and to what extent leverage, short positions, and derivatives can be used; and how actively the portfolio will be allowed to trade its various risk exposures.

For most portfolios, currency management can be considered a sub-set of these more specific portfolio management policies within the IPS. The currency risk management policy will usually address such issues as the

- target proportion of currency exposure to be passively hedged;
- latitude for active currency management around this target;
- frequency of hedge rebalancing;
- currency hedge performance benchmark to be used; and
- hedging tools permitted (types of forward and option contracts, etc.).

Currency management should be conducted within these IPS-mandated parameters.

## 4.2 The Portfolio Optimization Problem

Having described the IPS as the guiding framework for currency management, we now examine the strategic choices that have to be made in deciding the benchmark currency exposures for the portfolio, and the degree of discretion that will be allowed around this benchmark. This process starts with a decision on the optimal foreign-currency asset and FX exposures.

Optimization of a multi-currency portfolio of foreign assets involves selecting portfolio weights that locate the portfolio on the efficient frontier of the trade-off between risk and expected return defined in terms of the investor's domestic currency. As a simplification of this process, consider the portfolio manager examining the expected return and risk of the multi-currency portfolio of foreign assets by using different combinations of portfolio weights ($\omega_i$) that were shown in Equations 2 and 6, respectively, which are repeated here:

$$R_{DC} = \sum_{i=1}^{n} \omega_i \left(1 + R_{FC,i}\right)\left(1 + R_{FX,i}\right) - 1$$

$$\sigma^2(\omega_1 R_1 + \omega_2 R_2) \approx \omega_1^2 \sigma^2(R_1) + \omega_2^2 \sigma^2(R_2) + 2\omega_1 \sigma(R_1)\omega_2 \sigma(R_2)\rho(R_1, R_2)$$

Recall that the $R_i$ in the equation for variance are the $R_{DC}$ for each of the foreign-currency assets. Likewise, recall that the $R_{FX}$ term is defined such that the investor's "domestic" currency is the price currency in the P/B exchange rate quote. In other words, this calculation may require using the algebraic reciprocal of the standard market quote convention. These two equations together show the domestic-currency return and risk for a multi-currency portfolio of foreign assets.

When deciding on an optimal investment position, these equations would be based on the *expected* returns and risks for each of the foreign-currency assets; and hence, including the *expected* returns and risks for each of the foreign-currency exposures. As we have seen earlier, the number of market parameters for which the portfolio manager would need to have a market opinion grows geometrically with the complexity (number of foreign-currency exposures) in the portfolio. That is, to calculate the expected efficient frontier, the portfolio manager must have a market opinion for *each* of the $R_{FC,i}$, $R_{FX,i}$, $\sigma(R_{FC,i})$, $\sigma(R_{FX,i})$, and $\rho(R_{FC,i} R_{FX,i})$, as well as for each of the $\rho(R_{FC,i} R_{FC,j})$ and $\rho(R_{FX,i} R_{FX,j})$. This would be a daunting task for even the most well-informed portfolio manager.

In a perfect world with complete (and costless) information, it would likely be optimal to *jointly* optimize all of the portfolio's exposures—over all currencies and all foreign-currency assets—simultaneously. In the real world, however, this can be a much more difficult task. Confronted with these difficulties, many portfolio managers handle asset allocation with currency risk as a two-step process: (1) portfolio optimization over fully hedged returns; and (2) selection of active currency exposure, if any. Derivative strategies can allow the various risk exposures in a portfolio to be "unbundled" from each other and managed separately. The same applies for currency risks. Because the use of derivatives allows the price risk ($R_{FC,i}$) and exchange rate risk ($R_{FX,j}$) of foreign-currency assets to be unbundled and managed separately, a starting point for the selection process of portfolio weights would be to assume a complete currency hedge. That is, the portfolio manager will choose the exposures to the foreign-currency assets first, and then decide on the appropriate currency exposures afterward (i.e., decide whether to relax the full currency hedge). These decisions are made to simplify the portfolio construction process.

If the currency exposures of foreign assets could be perfectly and costlessly hedged, the hedge would completely neutralize the effect of currency movements on the portfolio's domestic-currency return ($R_{DC}$).[7] In Equation 2, this would set $R_{FX} = 0$, meaning that the domestic-currency return is then equal to the foreign-currency return ($R_{DC} = R_{FC}$). In Equation 5, this would set $\sigma^2(R_{DC}) = \sigma^2(R_{FC})$, meaning that the domestic-currency return risk is equal to the foreign-currency return risk.

Removing the currency effects leads to a simpler, two-step process for portfolio optimization. First the portfolio manager could pick the set of portfolio weights ($\omega_i$) for the foreign-currency assets that optimize the expected foreign-currency asset risk–return trade-off (assuming there is no currency risk). Then the portfolio manager could choose the desired currency exposures for the portfolio and decide whether and by how far to relax the constraint to a full currency hedge for each currency pair.

---

**7** A "costless" hedge in this sense would not only mean zero transaction costs, but also no "roll yield."

## 4.3 Choice of Currency Exposures

A natural starting point for the strategic decisions is the "currency-neutral" portfolio resulting from the two-step process described earlier. The question then becomes, How far along the risk spectrum between being fully hedged and actively trading currencies should the portfolio be positioned?

### 4.3.1 Diversification Considerations

The time horizon of the IPS is important. Many investment practitioners believe that in the long run, adding unhedged foreign-currency exposure to a portfolio does not affect expected long-run portfolio returns; hence in the long run, it would not matter if the portfolio was hedged. (Indeed, portfolio management costs would be reduced without a hedging process.) This belief is based on the view that in the long run, currencies "mean revert" to either some fair value equilibrium level or a historical average; that is, that the *expected* $\%\Delta S = 0$ for a sufficiently long time period. This view typically draws on the expectation that purchasing power parity (PPP) and the other international parity conditions that link movements in exchange rates, interest rates, and inflation rates will eventually hold over the long run.

Supporting this view, some studies argue that in the long-run currencies will in fact mean revert, and hence that currency risk is lower in the long run than in the short run (an early example is Froot 1993). Although much depends on how long run is defined, an investor (IPS) with a very long investment horizon and few immediate liquidity needs—which could potentially require the liquidation of foreign-currency assets at disadvantageous exchange rates—might choose to forgo currency hedging and its associated costs. Logically, this would require a portfolio benchmark index that is also unhedged against currency risk.

Although the international parity conditions may hold in the long run, it can be a *very* long time—possibly decades. Indeed, currencies can continue to drift away from the fair value mean reversion level for much longer than the time period used to judge portfolio performance. Such time periods are also typically longer than the patience of the portfolio manager's oversight committee when portfolio performance is lagging the benchmark. If this very long-run view perspective is not the case, then the IPS will likely impose some form of currency hedging.

Diversification considerations will also depend on the *asset composition* of the foreign-currency asset portfolio. The reason is because the foreign-currency asset returns ($R_{FC}$) of different asset classes have different correlation patterns with foreign-currency returns ($R_{FX}$). If there is a negative correlation between these two sets of returns, having at least some currency exposure may help portfolio diversification and moderate the domestic-currency return risk, $\sigma(R_{DC})$. (Refer to Equation 5 in Section 3.)

It is often asserted that the correlation between foreign-currency returns and foreign-currency asset returns tends to be greater for fixed-income portfolios than for equity portfolios. This assertion makes intuitive sense: both bonds and currencies react strongly to movements in interest rates, whereas equities respond more to expected earnings. As a result, the implication is that currency exposures provide little diversification benefit to fixed-income portfolios and that the currency risk should be hedged. In contrast, a better argument can be made for carrying currency exposures in global equity portfolios.

To some degree, various studies have corroborated this relative advantage to currency hedging for fixed income portfolios. But the evidence seems somewhat mixed and depends on which markets are involved. One study found that the hedging advantage for fixed-income portfolios is not always large or consistent (Darnell 2004). Other studies (Campbell 2010; Martini 2010) found that the optimal hedge ratio for foreign-currency equity portfolios depended critically on the investor's domestic currency. (Recall that the hedge ratio is defined as the ratio of the nominal value of the hedge to the market value of the underlying.) For some currencies, there was no risk-reduction advantage to hedging foreign equities (the optimal hedge ratio was close to 0%), whereas for other currencies, the optimal hedge ratio for foreign equities was close to 100%.

Other studies indicate that the optimal hedge ratio also seems to depend on *market conditions* and longer-term trends in currency pairs. For example, Campbell, Serfaty-de Medeiros, and Viceira (2007) found that there were no diversification benefits from currency exposures in foreign-currency bond portfolios, and hence to minimize the risk to domestic-currency returns these positions should be fully hedged. The authors also found, however, that during the time of their study (their data spanned 1975 to 2005), the US dollar seemed to be an exception in terms of its correlations with foreign-currency asset returns. Their study found that the US dollar tended to appreciate against foreign currencies when global bond prices fell (for example, in times of global financial stress there is a tendency for investors to shift investments into the perceived safety of reserve currencies). This finding would suggest that keeping some exposure to the US dollar in a global bond portfolio would be beneficial. For non-US investors, this would mean under-hedging the currency exposure to the USD (i.e., a hedge ratio less than 100%), whereas for US investors it would mean over-hedging their foreign-currency exposures back into the USD. Note that some currencies—the USD, JPY, and CHF in particular—seem to act as a safe haven and appreciate in times of market stress. Keeping some of these currency exposures in the portfolio—having hedge ratios that are not set at 100%--can help hedge losses on riskier assets, especially for foreign currency equity portfolios (which are more risk exposed than bond portfolios).

Given this diversity of opinions and empirical findings, it is not surprising to see actual hedge ratios vary widely in practice among different investors. Nonetheless, it is still more likely to see currency hedging for fixed-income portfolios rather than equity portfolios, although actual hedge ratios will often vary between individual managers.

#### 4.3.2 Cost Considerations

The costs of currency hedging also guide the strategic positioning of the portfolio. Currency hedges are not a "free good" and they come with a variety of expenses that must be borne by the overall portfolio. Optimal hedging decisions will need to balance the benefits of hedging against these costs.

Hedging costs come mainly in two forms: trading costs and opportunity costs. The most immediate costs of hedging involve trading expenses, and these come in several forms:

- Trading involves dealing on the bid–offer spread offered by banks. Their profit margin is based on these spreads, and the more the client trades and "pays away the spread," the more profit is generated by the dealer. Maintaining a 100% hedge and rebalancing frequently with every minor change in market conditions would be expensive. Although the bid–offer spreads on many FX-related products (especially the spot exchange rate) are quite narrow, "churning" the hedge portfolio would progressively add to hedging costs and detract from the hedge's benefits.

- Some hedges involve currency options; a long position in currency options requires the payment of up-front premiums. If the options expire out of the money (OTM), this cost is unrecoverable.

- Although forward contracts do not require the payment of up-front premiums, they do eventually mature and have to be "rolled" forward with an FX swap transaction to maintain the hedge. Rolling hedges will typically generate cash inflows or outflows. These cash flows will have to be monitored, and as necessary, cash will have to be raised to settle hedging transactions. In other words,

## Strategic Decisions in Currency Management: Overview

even though the currency hedge may *reduce* the volatility of the domestic mark-to-market value of the foreign-currency asset portfolio, it will typically *increase* the volatility in the organization's cash accounts. Managing these cash flow costs can accumulate to become a significant portion of the portfolio's value, and they become more expensive (for cash outflows) the higher interest rates go.

- One of the most important trading costs is the need to maintain an administrative infrastructure for trading. Front-, middle-, and back-office operations will have to be set up, staffed with trained personnel, and provided with specialized technology systems. Settlement of foreign exchange transactions in a variety of currencies means having to maintain cash accounts in these currencies to make and receive these foreign-currency payments. Together all of these various overhead costs can form a significant portion of the overall costs of currency trading.

A second form of costs associated with hedging are the opportunity cost of the hedge. To be 100% hedged is to forgo any possibility of favorable currency rate moves. If skillfully handled, accepting and managing currency risk—or any financial risk—can potentially add value to the portfolio, even net of management fees. (We discuss the methods by which this might be done in Sections 7–8.)

These opportunity costs lead to another motivation for having a strategic hedge ratio of less than 100%: regret minimization. Although it is not possible to accurately predict foreign exchange movements in advance, it is certainly possible to judge after the fact the results of the decision to hedge or not. Missing out on an advantageous currency movement because of a currency hedge can cause *ex post* regret in the portfolio manager or client; so too can having a foreign-currency loss if the foreign-currency asset position was unhedged. Confronted with this *ex ante* dilemma of whether to hedge, many portfolio managers decide simply to "split the difference" and have a 50% hedge ratio (or some other rule-of-thumb number). Both survey evidence and anecdotal evidence show that there is a wide variety of hedge ratios actually used in practice by managers, and that these variations cannot be explained by more "fundamental" factors alone. Instead, many managers appear to incorporate some degree of regret minimization into hedging decisions (for example, see Michenaud and Solnik 2008).

All of these various hedging expenses—both trading and opportunity costs—will need to be managed. Hedging is a form of insurance against risk, and in purchasing any form of insurance the buyer matches their needs and budgets with the policy selected. For example, although it may be possible to buy an insurance policy with full, unlimited coverage, a zero deductible, and no co-pay arrangements, such a policy would likely be prohibitively expensive. Most insurance buyers decide that it is not necessary to insure against every outcome, no matter how minor. Some minor risks can be accepted and "self-insured" through the deductible; some major risks may be considered so unlikely that they are not seen as worth paying the extra premium. (For example, most ordinary people would likely not consider buying insurance against being kidnapped.)

These same principles apply to currency hedging. The portfolio manager (and IPS) would likely not try to hedge every minor, daily change in exchange rates or asset values, but only the larger adverse movements that can materially affect the overall domestic-currency returns ($R_{DC}$) of the foreign-currency asset portfolio. The portfolio manager will need to balance the benefits and costs of hedging in determining both strategic positioning of the portfolio as well as any latitude for active currency management. However, around whatever strategic positioning decision taken by the IPS in terms of the benchmark level of currency exposure, hedging cost considerations alone will often dictate a *range* of permissible exposures instead of a single point. (This discretionary range is similar to the deductible in an insurance policy.)

# 5 STRATEGIC DECISIONS IN CURRENCY MANAGEMENT: SPECTRUM OF CURRENCY RISK MANAGEMENT STRATEGIES

**b** discuss strategic choices in currency management;

The strategic decisions encoded in the IPS with regard to the trade-off between the benefits and costs of hedging, as well as the potential for incremental return to the portfolio from active currency management, are the foundation for determining specific currency management strategies. These strategies are arrayed along a spectrum from very risk-averse passive hedging, to actively seeking out currency risk in order to manage it for profit. We examine each in turn.

## 5.1 Passive Hedging

In this approach, the goal is to keep the portfolio's currency exposures close, if not equal to, those of a benchmark portfolio used to evaluate performance. Note that the benchmark portfolio often has no foreign exchange exposure, particularly for fixed-income assets; the benchmark index is a "local currency" index based only on the foreign-currency asset return ($R_{FC}$). However, benchmark indexes that have some foreign exchange risk are also possible.

Passive hedging is a rules-based approach that removes almost all discretion from the portfolio manager, regardless of the manager's market opinion on future movements in exchange rates or other financial prices. In this case, the manager's job is to keep portfolio exposures as close to "neutral" as possible and to minimize tracking errors against the benchmark portfolio's performance. This approach reflects the belief that currency exposures that differ from the benchmark portfolio inject risk (return volatility) into the portfolio without any sufficiently compensatory return. Active currency management—taking positional views on future exchange rate movements—is viewed as being incapable of consistently adding incremental return to the portfolio.

But the hedge ratio has a tendency to "drift" with changes in market conditions, and even passive hedges need periodic rebalancing to realign them with investment objectives. Often the management guidance given to the portfolio manager will specify the rebalancing period—for example, monthly. There may also be allowance for intra-period rebalancing if there have been large exchange rate movements.

## 5.2 Discretionary Hedging

This approach is similar to passive hedging in that there is a "neutral" benchmark portfolio against which actual portfolio performance will be measured. However, in contrast to a strictly rules-based approach, the portfolio manager now has some limited discretion on how far to allow actual portfolio risk exposures to vary from the neutral position. Usually this discretion is defined in terms of percentage of foreign-currency market value (the portfolio's currency exposures are allowed to vary plus or minus x% from the benchmark). For example, a eurozone-domiciled investor may have a US Treasury bond portfolio with a mandate to keep the hedge ratio within 95% to 105%. Assuming no change in the foreign-currency return ($R_{FC}$), but allowing exchange rates ($R_{FX}$) to vary, this means the portfolio can tolerate exchange rate movements between the EUR and USD of up to 5% before the exchange rate exposures in the portfolio are considered excessive. The manager is allowed to manage currency exposures within these limits without being considered in violation of the IPS.

This discretion allows the portfolio manager at least some limited ability to express directional opinions about future currency movements—to accept risk in an attempt to earn reward—in order to add value to the portfolio performance. Of course, the portfolio manager's actual performance will be compared with that of the benchmark portfolio.

## 5.3 Active Currency Management

Further along the spectrum between extreme risk aversion and purely speculative trading is active currency management. In principle, this approach is really just an extension of discretionary hedging: the portfolio manager is allowed to express directional opinions on exchange rates, but is nonetheless kept within mandated risk limits. The performance of the manager—the choices of risk exposures assumed—is benchmarked against a "neutral" portfolio. But for all forms of active management (i.e., having the discretion to express directional market views), there is no allowance for unlimited speculation; there are risk management systems in place for even the most speculative investment vehicles, such as hedge funds. These controls are designed to prevent traders from taking unusually large currency exposures and risking the solvency of the firm or fund.

In many cases, the difference between discretionary hedging and active currency management is one of emphasis more than degree. The primary duty of the discretionary hedger is to protect the portfolio from currency risk. As a secondary goal, within limited bounds, there is some scope for directional opinion in an attempt to enhance overall portfolio returns. If the manager lacks any firm market conviction, the natural neutral position for the discretionary hedger is to be flat—that is, to have no meaningful currency exposures. In contrast, the active currency manager is supposed to take currency risks and manage them for profit. The primary goal is to add alpha to the portfolio through successful trading. Leaving actual portfolio exposures near zero for extended periods is typically not a viable option.

## 5.4 Currency Overlay

Active management of currency exposures can extend beyond limited managerial discretion within hedging boundaries. Sometimes accepting and managing currency risk for profit can be considered a portfolio objective. Active currency management is often associated with what are called **currency overlay programs**, although this term is used differently by different sources.

- In the most limited sense of the term, currency overlay simply means that the portfolio manager has outsourced managing currency exposures to a firm specializing in FX management. This could imply something as limited as merely having the external party implement a fully passive approach to currency hedges. If dealing with FX markets and managing currency hedges is beyond the professional competence of the investment manager, whose focus is on managing foreign equities or some other asset class, then hiring such external professional help is an option. Note that typically currency overlay programs involve external managers. However, some large, sophisticated institutional investors may have in-house currency overlay programs managed by a separate group of specialists within the firm.
- A broader view of currency overlay allows the externally hired currency overlay manager to take directional views on future currency movements (again, with the caveat that these be kept within predefined bounds). Sometimes a distinction is made between currency overlay and "foreign exchange as an asset class." In this classification, currency overlay is limited to the currency exposures

already in the foreign asset portfolio. For example, if a eurozone-domiciled investor has GBP- and CHF-denominated assets, currency overlay risks are allowed only for these currencies.

- In contrast, the concept of foreign exchange as an asset class does not restrict the currency overlay manager, who is free to take FX exposures in any currency pair where there is value-added to be harvested, regardless of the underlying portfolio. In this sense, the currency overlay manager is very similar to an FX-based hedge fund. To implement this form of active currency management, the currency overlay manager would have a *joint* opinion on a range of currencies, and have market views not only on the expected movements in the spot rates but also the likelihood of these movements (the variance of the expected future spot rate distribution) as well as the expected correlation between future spot rate movements. Basically, the entire portfolio of currencies is actively managed and optimized over all of the expected returns, risks, and correlations among all of the currencies in the portfolio.

We will focus on this latter form of currency overlay in this reading: active currency management conducted by external, FX-specialized sub-advisors to the portfolio.

It is quite possible to have the foreign-currency asset portfolio fully hedged (or allow some discretionary hedging internally) but then also to add an external currency overlay manager to the portfolio. This approach separates the hedging and alpha function mandates of the portfolio. Different organizations have different areas of expertise; it often makes sense to allocate managing the hedge (currency "beta") and managing the active FX exposures (currency "alpha") to those individuals with a comparative advantage in that function.

Adding this form of currency overlay to the portfolio (FX as an asset class) is similar in principle to adding any type of alternative asset class, such as private equity funds or farmland. In each case, the goal is the search for alpha. But to be most effective in adding value to the portfolio, the currency overlay program should add incremental returns (alpha) and/or greater diversification opportunities to improve the portfolio's risk–return profile. To do this, the currency alpha mandate should have minimum correlation with both the major asset classes and the other alpha sources in the portfolio.

Once this FX as an asset class approach is taken, it is not necessary to restrict the portfolio to a single overlay manager any more than it is necessary to restrict the portfolio to a single private equity fund. Different overlay managers follow different strategies (these are described in more detail in Sections 7–8). Within the overall portfolio allocation to "currency as an alternative asset class", it may be beneficial to diversify across a range of active management styles, either by engaging several currency overlay managers with different styles or by applying a fund-of-funds approach, in which the hiring and management of individual currency overlay managers is delegated to a specialized external investment vehicle.

Whether managed internally or externally (via a fund of funds) it will be necessary to monitor, or benchmark, the performance of the currency overlay manager: Do they generate the returns expected from their stated trading strategy? Many major investment banks as well as specialized market-information firms provide a wide range of proprietary indexes that track the performance of the investible universe of currency overlay managers; sometimes they also offer sub-indexes that focus on specific trading strategies (for example, currency positioning based on macroeconomic fundamentals). However, the methodologies used to calculate these various indexes vary between suppliers. In addition, different indexes show different aspects of active currency management. Given these differences between indexes, there is no simple answer for which index is most suitable as a benchmark; much depends on the specifics of the active currency strategy.

## EXAMPLE 2

### Currency Overlay

Windhoek Capital Management is a South Africa-based investment manager that runs the Conservative Value Fund, which has a mandate to avoid all currency risk in the portfolio. The firm is considering engaging a currency overlay manager to help with managing the foreign exchange exposures of this investment vehicle. Windhoek does not consider itself to have the in-house expertise to manage FX risk.

Brixworth & St. Ives Asset Management is a UK-based investment manager, and runs the Aggressive Growth Fund. This fund is heavily weighted toward emerging market equities, but also has a mandate to seek out inefficiencies in the global foreign exchange market and exploit these for profit. Although Brixworth & St. Ives manages the currency hedges for all of its investment funds in-house, it is also considering engaging a currency overlay manager.

1 Using a currency overlay manager for the Conservative Value Fund is *most likely* to involve:
   A  joining the alpha and hedging mandates.
   B  a more active approach to managing currency risks.
   C  using this manager to passively hedge their foreign exchange exposures.

2 Using a currency overlay manager for the Aggressive Growth Fund is *most likely* to involve:
   A  separating the alpha and hedging mandates.
   B  a less discretionary approach to managing currency hedges.
   C  an IPS that limits active management to emerging market currencies.

3 Brixworth & St. Ives is *more likely* to engage multiple currency overlay managers if:
   A  their returns are correlated with asset returns in the fund.
   B  the currency managers' returns are correlated with each other.
   C  the currency managers' use different active management strategies.

### Solution to 1:

C is correct. The Conservative Value Fund wants to avoid all currency exposures in the portfolio and Windhoek believes that it lacks the currency management expertise to do this.

### Solution to 2:

A is correct. Brixworth & St. Ives already does the FX hedging in house, so a currency overlay is more likely to be a pure alpha mandate. This should not change the way that Brixworth & St. Ives manages its hedges, and the fund's mandate to seek out inefficiencies in the global FX market is unlikely to lead to a restriction to actively manage only emerging market currencies.

### Solution to 3:

C is correct. Different active management strategies may lead to a more diversified source of alpha generation, and hence reduced portfolio risk. Choices A and B are incorrect because a higher correlation with foreign-currency assets in the portfolio or among overlay manager returns is likely to lead to less diversification.

## 6. STRATEGIC DECISIONS IN CURRENCY MANAGEMENT: FORMULATING A CURRENCY MANAGEMENT PROGRAM

c  formulate an appropriate currency management program given financial market conditions and portfolio objectives and constraints;

We now try to bring all of these previous considerations together in describing how to formulate an appropriate currency management program given client objectives and constraints, as well as overall financial market conditions. Generally speaking, the *strategic* currency positioning of the portfolio, as encoded in the IPS, should be biased toward a more-fully hedged currency management program the more

- short term the investment objectives of the portfolio;
- risk averse the beneficial owners of the portfolio are (and impervious to *ex post* regret over missed opportunities);
- immediate the income and/or liquidity needs of the portfolio;
- fixed-income assets are held in a foreign-currency portfolio;
- cheaply a hedging program can be implemented;
- volatile (i.e., risky) financial markets are;[8] and
- skeptical the beneficial owners and/or management oversight committee are of the expected benefits of active currency management.

The relaxation of any of these conditions creates latitude to allow a more proactive currency risk posture in the portfolio, either through wider tolerance bands for discretionary hedging, or by introducing foreign currencies as a separate asset class (using currency overlay programs as an alternative asset class in the overall portfolio). In the latter case, the more currency overlay is expected to generate alpha that is uncorrelated with other asset or alpha-generation programs in the portfolio, the more it is likely to be allowed in terms of strategic portfolio positioning.

> **INVESTMENT POLICY STATEMENT**
>
> Kailua Kona Advisors runs a Hawaii-based hedge fund that focuses on developed market equities located outside of North America. Its investor base consists of local high-net-worth individuals who are all considered to have a long investment horizon, a high tolerance for risk, and no immediate income needs. In its prospectus to investors, Kailua Kona indicates that it actively manages both the fund's equity and foreign-currency exposures, and that the fund uses leverage through the use of loans as well as short-selling.
>
> Exhibit 4 presents the hedge fund's currency management policy included in the IPS for this hedge fund.

---

8  As we will see, this also increases hedging costs when currency options are used.

### Exhibit 4  Hedge Fund Currency Management Policy: An Example

| | |
|---|---|
| **Overall Portfolio Benchmark:** | MSCI EAFE Index (local currency) |
| **Currency Exposure Ranges:** | Foreign-currency exposures, based on the USD market value of the equities actually held by the fund at the beginning of each month, will be hedged back into USD within the following tolerance ranges of plus or minus: <br><br> ▪ EUR: 20% <br> ▪ GBP: 15% <br> ▪ JPY: 10% <br> ▪ CHF: 10% <br> ▪ AUD: 10% <br> ▪ SEK: 10% <br><br> Other currency exposures shall be left unhedged. |
| **Rebalancing:** | The currency hedges will be rebalanced at least monthly, to reflect changes in the USD-denominated market value of portfolio equity holdings. |
| **Hedging Instruments:** | ▪ Forward contracts up to 12 months maturity; <br> ▪ European put and call options can be bought or written, for maturities up to 12 months; and <br> ▪ Exotic options of up to 12 months maturity can be bought or sold. |
| **Reporting:** | Management will present quarterly reports to the board detailing net foreign-currency exposures and speculative trading results. Speculative trading results will be benchmarked against a 100% hedged currency exposure. |

With this policy, Kailua Kona Advisors is indicating that it is willing to accept foreign-currency exposures within the portfolio but that these exposures must be kept within pre-defined limits. For example, suppose that at the beginning of the month the portfolio held EUR10 million of EUR-denominated assets. Also suppose that this EUR10 million exposure, combined with all the other foreign-currency exposures in the portfolio, matches Kailua Kona Advisors' desired portfolio weights by currency (as a US-based fund, these desired percentage portfolio allocations across all currencies will be based in USD).

The currency-hedging guidelines indicate that the hedge (for example, using a short position in a USD/EUR forward contract) should be between EUR8 million and EUR12 million, giving some discretion to the portfolio manager on the size of the net exposure to the EUR. At the beginning of the next month, the USD values of the foreign assets in the portfolio are measured again, and the process repeats. If there has been either a large move in the foreign-currency value of the EUR-denominated assets and/or a large move in the USD/EUR exchange rate, it is possible that Kailua Kona Advisors' portfolio exposure to EUR-denominated assets will be too far away from the desired

> percentage allocation.[9] Kailua Kona Advisors will then need to either buy or sell EUR-denominated assets. If movements in the EUR-denominated value of the assets or in the USD/EUR exchange rate are large enough, this asset rebalancing may have to be done before month's end. Either way, once the asset rebalancing is done, it establishes the new EUR-denominated asset value on which the currency hedge will be based (i.e., plus or minus 20% of this new EUR amount).
>
> If the portfolio is not 100% hedged—for example, continuing the Kailua Kona illustration, if the portfolio manager only hedges EUR9 million of the exposure and has a residual exposure of being long EUR1 million—the success or failure of the manager's tactical decision will be compared with a "neutral" benchmark. In this case, the comparison would be against the performance of a 100% fully hedged portfolio—that is, with a EUR10 million hedge.

## 7. ACTIVE CURRENCY MANAGEMENT: BASED ON ECONOMIC FUNDAMENTALS, TECHNICAL ANALYSIS AND THE CARRY TRADE

**d** compare active currency trading strategies based on economic fundamentals, technical analysis, carry-trade, and volatility trading;

**e** describe how changes in factors underlying active trading strategies affect tactical trading decisions;

The previous section discussed the *strategic* decisions made by the IPS on locating the currency management practices of the portfolio along a risk spectrum ranging from a very conservative approach to currency risk to very active currency management. In this section, we consider the case in which the IPS has given the portfolio manager (or currency overlay manager) at least some limited discretion for actively managing currency risk within these mandated strategic bounds. This then leads to *tactical* decisions: which FX exposures to accept and manage within these discretionary limits. In other words, tactical decisions involve active currency management.

A market view is a prerequisite to any form of active management. At the heart of the trading decision in FX (and other) markets, lies a view on future market prices and conditions. This market opinion guides all decisions with respect to currency risk exposures, including whether currency hedges should be implemented and, if so, how they should be managed.

In what follows, we will explore some of the methods used to form directional views about the FX market. However, a word of caution that cannot be emphasized enough: *There is no simple formula, model, or approach that will allow market participants to precisely forecast exchange rates (or any other financial prices) or to be able to be confident that any trading decision will be profitable.*

### 7.1 Active Currency Management Based on Economic Fundamentals

This section sets out a broad framework for developing a view about future exchange rate movements based on underlying fundamentals. In contrast to other methods for developing a market view (which are discussed in subsequent sections), at the heart

---

[9] The overall portfolio percentage allocations by currency will also depend on the price moves of all *other* foreign-currency assets and exchange rates as well, but we will simplify our example by ignoring this nuance.

of this approach is the assumption that, in a flexible exchange rate system, exchange rates are determined by logical economic relationships and that these relationships can be modeled.

The simple economic framework is based on the assumption that in the long run, the real exchange rate will converge to its "fair value," but short- to medium-term factors will shape the convergence path to this equilibrium.[10]

Recall that the real exchange rate reflects the ratio of the real purchasing power between two countries; that is, the once nominal purchasing power in each country is adjusted by its respective price level as well as the spot exchange rate between the two countries. The long-run equilibrium level for the real exchange rate is determined by purchasing power parity or some other model of an exchange rate's fair value, and serves as the anchor for longer-term movements in exchange rates.

Over shorter time frames, movements in real exchange rates will also reflect movements in the real interest rate differential between countries. Recall that the real interest rate ($r$) is the nominal interest rate adjusted by the expected inflation rate, or $r = i - \pi^e$, where $i$ is the nominal interest rate and $\pi^e$ is the expected inflation rate over the same term as the nominal and real interest rates. Movements in risk premiums will also affect exchange rate movements over shorter-term horizons. The riskier a country's assets are perceived to be by investors, the more likely they are to move their investments out of that country, thereby depressing the exchange rate. Finally, the framework recognizes that there are two currencies involved in an exchange rate quote (the price and base currencies) and hence movements in exchange rates will reflect movements in the *differentials* between these various factors.

As a result, all else equal, the base currency's real exchange rate should appreciate if there is an upward movement in

- its long-run equilibrium real exchange rate;
- either its real or nominal interest rates, which should attract foreign capital;
- expected foreign inflation, which should cause the foreign currency to depreciate; and
- the foreign risk premium, which should make foreign assets less attractive compared with the base currency nation's domestic assets.

The real exchange rate should also increase if it is currently below its long-term equilibrium value. All of this makes intuitive sense.

In summary, the exchange rate forecast is a mix of long-term, medium-term, and short-term factors. The long-run equilibrium real exchange rate is the anchor for exchange rates and the point of long-run convergence for exchange rate movements. Movements in the short- to medium-term factors (nominal interest rates, expected inflation) affect the timing and path of convergence to this long-run equilibrium. A stylized depiction of the price dynamics generated by this interaction between short-, medium-, and longer-term pricing factors is shown in Exhibit 5.

---

10 This model was derived and explained by Rosenberg and Barker (2017).

**Exhibit 5  Interaction of Long-term and Short-term Factors in Exchange Rates**

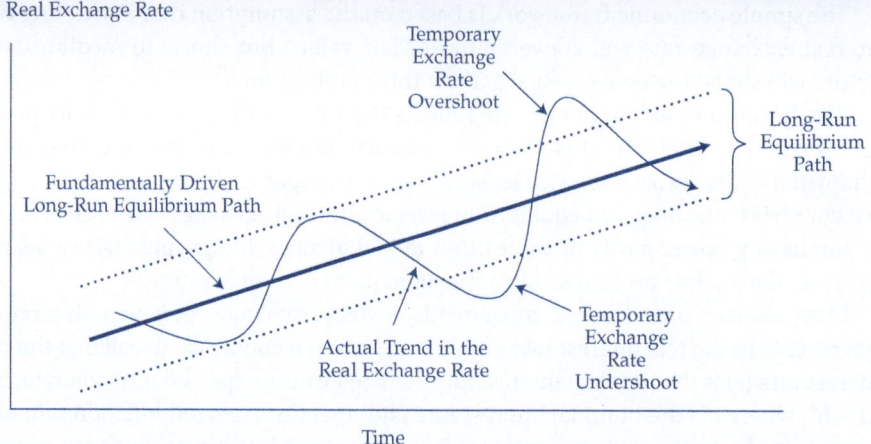

*Source:* Based on Rosenberg (2002), page 32.

It needs to be stressed that it can be very demanding to model how each of these separate effects—nominal interest rate, expected inflation, and risk premium differentials—change over time and affect exchange rates. It can also be challenging to model movements in the long-term equilibrium real exchange rate. A broad variety of factors, such as fiscal and monetary policy, will affect all of these variables in our simple economic model.[11]

## 7.2 Active Currency Management Based on Technical Analysis

Another approach to forming a market view is based on technical analysis. This approach is based on quite different assumptions compared with modeling based on economic fundamentals. Whereas classical exchange rate economics tends to view market participants as rational, markets as efficient, and exchange rates as driven by underlying economic factors, technical analysis ignores economic analysis. Instead, technical analysis is based on three broad themes.[12]

First, market technicians believe that in a liquid, freely traded market the historical price data can be helpful in projecting future price movements.[13] The reason is because many traders have already used any useful data external to the market to generate their trading positions, so this information is already reflected in current prices. Therefore, it is not necessary to look outside of the market to form an opinion on future price movements. This means it is not necessary to examine interest rates, inflation rates, or risk premium differentials (the factors in our fundamentally based model) because exchange rates already incorporate these factors.

Second, market technicians believe that historical patterns in the price data have a tendency to repeat, and that this repetition provides profitable trade opportunities. These price patterns repeat because market prices reflect human behavior and human beings have a tendency to react in similar ways to similar situations, even if this

---

11 A broader discussion of exchange rate economics can be found in Rosenberg and Barker (2017).
12 Some material in this section is based on Sine and Strong (2012).
13 In many other asset classes, technical analysis is based on trade volume data as well as price data. But there are no reliable, timely, and high-frequency trade volume data that are publicly available for over-the-counter (OTC) FX markets.

repetitive behavior is not always fully rational. For example, when confronted with an upward price trend, many market participants eventually come to believe that it will extrapolate (an attitude of "irrational exuberance" or "this time it is different"). When the trend eventually breaks, a panicked position exit can cause a sharp overshoot of fair value to the downside. Broadly speaking, technical analysis can be seen as the study of market psychology and how market participant emotions—primarily greed and fear—can be read from the price data and used to predict future price moves.

Third, technical analysis does not attempt to determine where market prices *should* trade (fair value, as in fundamental analysis) but where they *will* trade. Because these price patterns reflect trader emotions, they need not reflect—at least immediately—any cool, rational assessment of the underlying economic or fundamental situation. Although market prices may eventually converge to fair value in the long run, the long run can be a very long time indeed. In the meanwhile, there are shorter-term trading opportunities available in trading the technical patterns in the price data.

Combined, these three principles of technical analysis define a discipline dedicated to identifying patterns in the historical price data, especially as it relates to identifying market trends and market turning points. (Technical analysis is less useful in a trendless market.) Technical analysis tries to identify when markets have become **overbought** or **oversold**, meaning that they have trended too far in one direction and are vulnerable to a trend reversal, or correction. Technical analysis also tries to identify what are called **support levels** and **resistance levels**, either within ongoing price trends or at their extremities (i.e., turning points). These support and resistance levels are price points on dealers' order boards where one would except to see clustering of bids and offers, respectively. At these exchange rate levels, the price action is expected to get "sticky" because it will take more order flow to pierce the wall of either bids or offers. But once these price points are breached, the price action can be expected to accelerate as **stops** are triggered. (Stops, in this sense, refer to stop-loss orders, in which traders leave resting bids or offers away from the current market price to be filled if the market reaches those levels. A stop-loss order is triggered when the price action has gone against a trader's position, and it gets the trader out of that position to limit further losses.)

Technical analysis uses visual cues for market patterns as well as more quantitative technical indicators. There is a wide variety of technical indexes based on market prices that are used in this context. Some technical indicators are as simple as using moving averages of past price points. The 200-day moving average of daily exchange rates is often seen as an important indicator of likely support and resistance. Sometimes two moving averages are used to establish when a price trend is building momentum. For example, when the 50-day moving average crosses the 200-day moving average, this is sometimes seen as a price "break out" point.

Other technical indicators are based on more complex mathematical formulae. There is an extremely wide variety of these more mathematical indicators, some of them very esoteric and hard to connect intuitively with the behavior of real world financial market participants.

In summary, many FX active managers routinely use technical analysis—either alone or in conjunction with other approaches—to form a market opinion or to time position entry and exit points. Even though many technical indicators lack the intellectual underpinnings provided by formal economic modeling, they nonetheless remain a prominent feature of FX markets.

## 7.3 Active Currency Management Based on the Carry Trade

The **carry trade** is a trading strategy of borrowing in low-yield currencies and investing in high-yield currencies. The term "carry" is related to what is known as the cost of carry—that is, of carrying or holding an investment. This investment has either an implicit or explicit cost (borrowing cost) but may also produce income. The net cost of carry is the difference between these two return rates.

If technical analysis is based on ignoring economic fundamentals, then the carry trade is based on exploiting a well-recognized violation of one of the international parity conditions often used to describe these economic fundamentals: uncovered interest rate parity. Recall that uncovered interest rate parity asserts that, *on a longer-term average*, the return on an unhedged foreign-currency asset investment will be the same as a domestic-currency investment. Assuming that the base currency in the P/B quote is the low-yield currency, stated algebraically uncovered interest rate parity asserts that

$$\%\Delta S_{H/L} \approx i_H - i_L$$

where $\%\Delta S_{H/L}$ is the percentage change in the $S_{H/L}$ spot exchange rate (the low-yield currency is the base currency), $i_H$ is the interest rate on the high-yield currency and $i_L$ is the interest rate on the low-yield currency. If uncovered interest rate parity holds, the yield spread *advantage* for the high-yielding currency (the right side of the equation) will, on average, be matched by the *depreciation* of the high-yield currency (the left side of the equation; the low-yield currency is the base currency and hence a positive value for $\%\Delta S_{H/L}$ means a depreciation of the high-yield currency). According to the uncovered interest rate parity theorem, it is this offset between (1) the yield advantage and (2) the currency depreciation that equates, on average, the unhedged currency returns.

But in reality, the historical data show that there are persistent deviations from uncovered interest rate parity in FX markets, at least in the short to medium term. Indeed, high-yield countries often see their currencies *appreciate*, not depreciate, for extended periods of time. The positive returns from a combination of a favorable yield differential plus an appreciating currency can remain in place long enough to present attractive investment opportunities.

This persistent violation of uncovered interest rate parity described by the carry trade is often referred to as the **forward rate bias**. An implication of uncovered interest rate parity is that the forward rate should be an unbiased predictor of future spot rates. The historical data, however, show that the forward rate is not the center of the distribution for future spot rates; in fact, it is a *biased* predictor (for example, see Kritzman 1999). Hence the name "forward rate bias." With the forward rate premium or discount defined as $F_{P/B} - S_{P/B}$ the "bias" in the forward rate bias is that the premium typically overstates the amount of appreciation of the base currency, and the discount overstates the amount of depreciation. Indeed, the forward discount or premium often gets even the *direction* of future spot rate movements wrong.

The carry trade strategy (borrowing in low-yield currencies, investing in high-yield currencies) is equivalent to a strategy based on trading the forward rate bias. Trading the forward rate bias involves buying currencies selling at a forward discount, and selling currencies trading at a forward premium. This makes intuitive sense: It is desirable to buy low and sell high.

To show the equivalence of the carry trade and trading the forward rate bias, recall that covered interest rate parity (which is enforced by arbitrage) is stated as

$$\frac{F_{P/B} - S_{P/B}}{S_{P/B}} = \frac{(i_P - i_B)\left(\frac{t}{360}\right)}{1 + i_B\left(\frac{t}{360}\right)}$$

This equation shows that when the base currency has a lower interest rate than the price currency (i.e., the right side of the equality is positive) the base currency will trade at a forward premium (the left side of the equality is positive). That is, being low-yield currency and trading at a forward premium is synonymous. Similarly, being a high-yield currency means trading at a forward discount. Borrowing in the low-yield currency and investing in the high-yield currency (the carry trade) is hence equivalent to selling currencies that have a forward premium and buying currencies that have a forward discount (trading the forward rate bias). We will return to these concepts in Section 9 when we discuss the roll yield in hedging with forward contracts. Exhibit 6 summarizes several key points about the carry trade.

**Exhibit 6  The Carry Trade: A Summary**

|  | Buy/Invest | Sell/Borrow |
|---|---|---|
| Implementing the carry trade | High-yield currency | Low-yield currency |
| Trading the forward rate bias | Forward discount currency | Forward premium currency |

The gains that one can earn through the carry trade (or equivalently, through trading the forward rate bias) can be seen as the risk premiums earned for carrying an unhedged position—that is, for absorbing currency risk. (In efficient markets, there is no extra reward without extra risk.) Long periods of market stability can make these extra returns enticing to many investors, and the longer the yield differential persists between high-yield and low-yield currencies, the more carry trade positions will have a tendency to build up. But these high-yield currency advantages can be erased quickly, particularly if global financial markets are subject to sudden bouts of stress. This is especially true because the carry trade is a *leveraged* position: borrowing in the low-yielding currency and investing in the high-yielding currency. These occasional large losses mean that the return distribution for the carry trade has a pronounced negative skew.

This negative skew derives from the fact that the **funding currencies** of the carry trade (the low-yield currencies in which borrowing occurs) are typically the safe haven currencies, such as the USD, CHF, and JPY. In contrast, the **investment currencies** (the high-yielding currencies) are typically currencies perceived to be higher risk, such as several emerging market currencies. Any time global financial markets are under stress there is a flight to safety that causes rapid movements in exchange rates, and usually a panicked unwinding of carry trades. As a result, traders running carry trades often get caught in losing positions, with the leverage involved magnifying their losses. Because of the tendency for long periods of relatively small gains in the carry trade to be followed by brief periods of large losses, the carry trade is sometimes characterized as "picking up nickels in front of a steamroller." One guide to the riskiness of the carry trade is the volatility of spot rate movements for the currency pair; all else equal, lower volatility is better for a carry trade position.

We close this section by noting that although the carry trade can be based on borrowing in a single funding currency and investing in a single high-yield currency, it is more common for carry trades to use multiple funding and investment currencies. The number of funding currencies and investment currencies need not be equal: for example, there could be five of one and three of the other. Sometimes the portfolio weighting of exposures between the various funding and investment currencies are simply set equal to each other. But the weights can also be optimized to reflect the trader's market view of the expected movements in each of the exchange rates, as well as their individual risks ($\sigma[\%\Delta S]$) and the expected correlations between movements in the currency pairs. These trades can be dynamically rebalanced, with the relative weights among both funding and investment currencies shifting with market conditions.

## 8. ACTIVE CURRENCY MANAGEMENT: BASED ON VOLATILITY TRADING

d  compare active currency trading strategies based on economic fundamentals, technical analysis, carry-trade, and volatility trading;

e  describe how changes in factors underlying active trading strategies affect tactical trading decisions;

Another type of active trading style is unique to option markets and is known as volatility trading (or simply "vol trading").[14] To explain this trading style, we will start with a quick review of some option basics.

The derivatives of the option pricing model show the sensitivity of the option's premium to changes in the factors that determine option value. These derivatives are often referred to as the "Greeks" of option pricing. There is a very large number of first, second, third, and cross-derivatives that can be taken of an option pricing formula, but the two most important Greeks that we will consider here are the following:

- **Delta:** The sensitivity of the option premium to a small change in the price of the underlying[15] of the option, typically a financial asset. This sensitivity is an indication of *price* risk.

- **Vega:** The sensitivity of the option premium to a small change in implied volatility. This sensitivity is an indication of *volatility* risk.

The most important concept to grasp in terms of volatility trading is that the use of options allows the trader, through a variety of trading strategies, to *unbundle* and isolate all of the various risk factors (the Greeks) and trade them separately. Once an initial option position is taken (either long or short), the trader has exposure to *all* of the various Greeks/risk factors. The unwanted risk exposures, however, can then be hedged away, leaving *only* the desired risk exposure to express that specific directional view.

**Delta hedging** is the act of hedging away the option position's exposure to delta, the price risk of the underlying (the FX spot rate, in this case). Because delta shows the sensitivity of the option price to changes in the spot exchange rate, it thus defines the option's hedge ratio: The size of the offsetting hedge position that will set the *net* delta of the combined position (option plus delta hedge) to zero. Typically implementing

---

14 In principle, this trading style can be applied to all asset classes with options, not just FX trading. But FX options are the most liquid and widely traded options in the world, so it is in FX where most of volatility trading likely takes place in global financial markets.

15 The underlying asset of a derivative is typically referred to simply as the "underlying."

# Active Currency Management: Based on Volatility Trading

this delta hedge is done using either forward contracts or a spot transaction (spot, by definition, has a delta of one, and no exposure to any other of the Greeks; forward contracts are highly correlated with the spot rate). For example, if a trader was long a call option on USD/EUR with a nominal value of EUR1 million and a delta of +0.5, the delta hedge would involve a short forward position in USD/EUR of EUR0.5 million. That is, the size of the delta hedge is equal to the option's delta times the nominal size of the contract. This hedge size would set the net delta of the overall position (option and forward) to zero.[16] Once the delta hedge has set the net delta of the position to zero, the trader then has exposure *only* to the other Greeks, and can use various trading strategies to position in these (long or short) depending on directional views.

Although one could theoretically trade *any* of the other Greeks, the most important one traded is vega; that is, the trader is expressing a view on the future movements in implied volatility, or in other words, is engaged in volatility trading. Implied volatility is not the same as realized, or observed, historical volatility, although it is heavily influenced by it. By engaging in volatility trading, the trader is expressing a view about the future volatility of exchange rates *but not their direction* (the delta hedge set the net delta of the position to zero).

One simple option strategy that implements a volatility trade is a **straddle**, which is a combination of both an at-the-money (ATM) put and an ATM call. A long straddle buys both of these options. Because their deltas are −0.5 and +0.5, respectively, the net delta of the position is zero; that is, the long straddle is delta neutral. This position is profitable in more volatile markets, when either the put or the call go sufficiently in the money to cover the upfront cost of the two option premiums paid. Similarly, a short straddle is a bet that the spot rate will stay relatively stable. In this case, the payout on any option exercise will be less than the twin premiums the seller has collected; the rest is net profit for the option seller. A similar option structure is a **strangle** position for which a long position is buying out-of-the-money (OTM) puts and calls with the same expiry date and the same degree of being out of the money (we elaborate more on this subject later). Because OTM options are being bought, the cost of the position is cheaper—but conversely, it also does not pay off until the spot rate passes the OTM strike levels. As a result, the risk–reward for a strangle is more moderate than that for a straddle.

The interesting thing to note is that by using delta-neutral trading strategies, volatility is turned into a product that can be actively traded like any other financial product or asset class, such as equities, commodities, fixed-income products, and so on. Volatility is not constant nor are its movements completely random. Instead volatility is determined by a wide variety of underlying factors—both fundamental and technical—that the trader can express an opinion on. Movements in volatility are cyclical, and typically subject to long periods of relative stability punctuated by sharp upward spikes in volatility as markets come under periodic bouts of stress (usually the result of some dramatic event, financial or otherwise). Speculative vol traders—for example, among currency overlay managers—often want to be net-short volatility. The reason is because most options expire out of the money, and the option writer then gets to keep the option premium without delivery of the underlying currency pair. The amount of the option premium can be considered the risk premium, or payment, earned by the option writer for absorbing volatility risk. It is a steady source of income under "normal" market conditions. Ideally, these traders would want to "flip" their position and be long volatility ahead of volatility spikes, but these episodes can be notoriously difficult to time. Most hedgers typically run options positions that are net-long volatility because they are buying protection from unanticipated price

---

16 Strictly speaking, the net delta would be *approximately* equal to zero because forward contracts do not have identical price properties to those of the spot exchange rate. But it is close enough for our purposes here, and we will ignore this small difference.

volatility. (Being long the option means being exposed to the time decay of the option's time value; that is similar to paying insurance premiums for the protection against exchange rate volatility.)

We can also note that just as there are *currency overlay* programs for actively trading the portfolio's currency exposures (as discussed in Section 5) there can also be *volatility overlay* programs for actively trading the portfolio's exposures to movements in currencies' implied volatility. Just as currency overlay programs manage the portfolio's exposure to currency delta (movements in spot exchange rates), volatility overlay programs manage the portfolio's exposure to currency vega. These volatility overlay programs can be focused on earning speculative profits, but can also be used to hedge the portfolio against risk (we will return to this concept in the discussion of macro hedges in Section 11.).

Enumerating all the potential strategies for trading foreign exchange volatility is beyond the scope of this reading. Instead, the reader should be aware that this dimension of trading FX volatility (not price) exists and sees a large amount of active trading. Moreover, the best traders are able to think and trade in both dimensions simultaneously. Movements in volatility are often correlated with directional movements in the price of the underlying. For example, when there is a flight to safety as carry trades unwind, there is typically a spike in volatility (and options prices) at the same time. Although pure vol trading is based on a zero-delta position, this need not always be the case; a trader can express a market opinion on volatility (vega exposure) and still have a directional exposure to the underlying spot exchange rate as well (delta exposure). That is, the overall trading position has net vega and delta exposures that reflect the *joint* market view.

We end this section by explaining how currency options are quoted in professional FX markets. (This information will be used in Sections 9–12 when we discuss other option trading strategies.) Unlike exchanged-traded options, such as those used in equity markets, OTC options for currencies are not described in terms of specific strike levels (i.e., exchange rate levels). Instead, in the interdealer market, options are described in terms of their "delta." Deltas for puts can range from a minimum of −1 to a maximum of 0, with a delta of −0.5 being the point at which the put option is ATM; OTM puts have deltas between 0 and −0.5. For call options, delta ranges from 0 to +1, with 0.5 being the ATM point. In FX markets, these delta values are quoted both in *absolute* terms (i.e., in positive rather than negative values) and as percentages, with standard FX option quotes usually in terms of 25-delta and 10-delta options (i.e., a delta of 0.25 and 0.10, respectively; the 10-delta option is deeper OTM and hence cheaper than the 25-delta option). The FX options market is the most liquid around these standard delta quoting points (ATM, 25-delta, 10-delta), but of course, as a flexible OTC market, options of any delta/strike price can be traded. The 25-delta put option (for example) will still go in the money if the spot price dips below a *specific* exchange rate level; this *implied* strike price is *backed out* of an option pricing model once all the other pricing factors, including the current spot rate and the 25-delta of the option, are put into the option pricing model. (The specific option pricing model used is agreed on by both parties to the trade.)

These standard delta price points are often used to define option trading strategies. For example, a 25-delta strangle would be based on 25-delta put and call options. Similarly, a 10-delta strangle would be based on 10-delta options (and would cost less and have a more moderate payoff structure than a 25-delta strangle). Labeling option structures by their delta is common in FX markets.

## EXAMPLE 3

### Active Strategies

Annie McYelland works as an analyst at Scotland-based Kilmarnock Advisors, an investment firm that offers several investment vehicles for its clients. McYelland has been put in charge of formulating the firm's market views for some of the foreign currencies that these vehicles have exposures to. Her market views will be used to guide the hedging and discretionary positioning for some of the actively managed portfolios.

McYelland begins by examining yield spreads between various countries and the implied volatility extracted from the option pricing for several currency pairs. She collects the following data:

| One-Year Yield Levels | |
|---|---|
| Switzerland | −0.103% |
| United States | 0.162% |
| Poland | 4.753% |
| Mexico | 4.550% |

| One-Year Implied Volatility | |
|---|---|
| PLN/CHF | 8.4% |
| MXN/CHF | 15.6% |
| PLN/USD | 20.3% |
| MXN/USD | 16.2% |

*Note*: PLN = Polish zloty; the Swiss yields are negative because of Swiss policy actions.

McYelland is also examining various economic indicators to shape her market views. After studying the economic prospects for both Japan and New Zealand, she expects that the inflation rate for New Zealand is about to accelerate over the next few years, whereas the inflation rate for Japan should remain relatively stable. Turning her attention to the economic situation in India, McYelland believes that the Indian authorities are about to tighten monetary policy, and that this change has not been fully priced into the market. She reconsiders her short-term view for the Indian rupee (i.e., the INR/USD spot rate) after conducting this analysis.

McYelland also examines the exchange rate volatility for several currency pairs to which the investment trusts are exposed. Based on her analysis of the situation, she believes that the exchange rate between Chilean peso and the US dollar (CLP/USD) is about to become much more volatile than usual, although she has no strong views about whether the CLP will appreciate or depreciate.

One of McYelland's colleagues, Catalina Ortega, is a market technician and offers to help McYelland time her various market position entry and exit points based on chart patterns. While examining the JPY/NZD price chart, Ortega notices that the 200-day moving average is at 62.0405 and the current spot rate is 62.0315.

**1** Based on the data she collected, all else equal, McYelland's *best* option for implementing a carry trade position would be to fund in:

   **A** USD and invest in PLN.

- **B** CHF and invest in MXN.
- **C** CHF and invest in PLN.

2 Based on McYelland's inflation forecasts, all else equal, she would be *more likely* to expect a(n):
- **A** depreciation in the JPY/NZD.
- **B** increase in capital flows from Japan to New Zealand.
- **C** more accommodative monetary policy by the Reserve Bank of New Zealand.

3 Given her analysis for India, McYelland's short-term market view for the INR/USD spot rate is now *most likely* to be:
- **A** biased toward appreciation.
- **B** biased toward depreciation.
- **C** unchanged because it is only a short-run view.

4 Using CLP/USD options, what would be the *cheapest* way for McYelland to implement her market view for the CLP?
- **A** Buy a straddle
- **B** Buy a 25-delta strangle
- **C** Sell a 40-delta strangle

5 Based on Ortega's analysis, she would *most likely* expect:
- **A** support near 62.0400.
- **B** resistance near 62.0310.
- **C** resistance near 62.0400.

## Solution to 1:

C is correct. The yield spread between the funding and investment currencies is the widest and the implied volatility (risk) is the lowest. The other choices have a narrower yield spread and higher risk (implied volatility).

## Solution to 2:

A is correct. All else equal, an increase in New Zealand's inflation rate will decrease its real interest rate and lead to the real interest rate differential favoring Japan over New Zealand. This would likely result in a depreciation of the JPY/NZD rate over time. The shift in the relative real returns should lead to reduced capital flows from Japan to New Zealand (so Choice B is incorrect) and the RBNZ—New Zealand's central bank—is more likely to tighten monetary policy than loosen it as inflation picks up (so Choice C is incorrect).

## Solution to 3:

B is correct. Tighter monetary policy in India should lead to higher real interest rates (at least in the short run). This increase will cause the INR to appreciate against the USD, but because the USD is the base currency, this will be represented as depreciation in the INR/USD rate. Choice C is incorrect because a tightening of monetary policy that is not fully priced-in to market pricing is likely to move bond yields and hence the exchange rate in the short run (given the simple economic model in Section 7).

> **Solution to 4:**
>
> B is correct. Either a long straddle or a long strangle will profit from a marked increase in volatility in the spot rate, but a 25-delta strangle would be cheaper (because it is based on OTM options). Writing a strangle—particularly one that is close to being ATM, which is what a 40-delta structure is—is likely to be exercised in favor of the counterparty if McYelland's market view is correct.
>
> **Solution to 5:**
>
> C is correct. The 200-day moving average has not been crossed yet, and it is higher than the current spot rate. Hence this technical indicator suggests that resistance lies above the current spot rate level, likely in the 62.0400 area. Choice A is incorrect because the currency has not yet appreciated to 62.0400, so it cannot be considered a "support" level. Given that the currency pair has already traded through 62.0310 and is still at least 90 pips away from the 200-day moving average, it is more likely to suspect that resistance still lies above the current spot rate.

# CURRENCY MANAGEMENT TOOLS: FORWARD CONTRACTS, FX SWAPS AND CURRENCY OPTIONS

**f** describe how forward contracts and FX (foreign exchange) swaps are used to adjust hedge ratios;

In this section, we focus on how the portfolio manager uses financial derivatives to implement both the *strategic* positioning of the portfolio along the risk spectrum (i.e., the performance benchmark) as well as the *tactical* decisions made in regard to variations around this "neutral" position. The manager's market view—whether based on carry, fundamental, currency volatility, or technical considerations—leads to this active management of risk positioning around the strategic benchmark point. Implementing both strategic and tactical viewpoints requires the use of trading tools, which we discuss in this section.

The balance of this reading will assume that the portfolio's strategic foreign-currency asset exposures and the maximum amount of currency risk desired have already been determined by the portfolio's IPS. We begin at the conservative end of the risk spectrum by describing a passive hedge for a single currency (with a 100% hedge ratio). After discussing the costs and limitations of this approach, we move out further along the risk spectrum by describing strategies in which the basic "building blocks" of financial derivatives can be combined to implement the manager's tactical positioning and construct much more customized risk–return profiles. Not surprisingly, the basic trading tools themselves—forwards, options, FX swaps—are used for both strategic and tactical risk management and by both hedgers and speculators alike (although for different ends). Note that the instruments covered as tools of currency management are not nearly an exhaustive list. For example, exchange-traded funds for currencies are a vehicle that can be useful in managing currency risk.

## 9.1 Forward Contracts

In this section, we consider the most basic form of hedging: a 100% hedge ratio for a single foreign-currency exposure. Futures or forward contracts on currencies can be used to obtain full currency hedges, although most institutional investors prefer to use forward contracts for the following reasons:

1 Futures contracts are standardized in terms of settlement dates and contract sizes. These may not correspond to the portfolio's investment parameters.

2 Futures contracts may not always be available in the currency pair that the portfolio manager wants to hedge. For example, the most liquid currency futures contracts trade on the Chicago Mercantile Exchange (CME). Although there are CME futures contracts for all major exchange rates (e.g., USD/EUR, USD/GBP) and many cross rates (e.g., CAD/EUR, JPY/CHF), there are not contracts available for all possible currency pairs. Trading these cross rates would need multiple futures contracts, adding to portfolio management costs. In addition, many of the "second tier" emerging market currencies may not have liquid futures contracts available against any currency, let alone the currency pair in which the portfolio manager is interested.

3 Futures contracts require up-front margin (initial margin). They also have intra-period cash flow implications, in that the exchange will require the investor to post additional variation margin when the spot exchange rate moves against the investor's position. These initial and ongoing margin requirements tie up the investor's capital and require careful monitoring through time, adding to the portfolio management expense. Likewise, margin flows can go in the investor's favor, requiring monitoring and reinvestment.

In contrast, forward contracts do not suffer from any of these drawbacks. Major global investment dealers (such as Deutsche Bank, Royal Bank of Scotland, UBS, etc.) will quote prices on forward contracts for practically every possible currency pair, settlement date, and transaction amount. They typically do not require margin to be posted or maintained.

Moreover, the daily trade volume globally for OTC currency forward and swap contracts dwarfs that for exchange-traded currency futures contracts; that is, forward contracts are more liquid than futures for trading in large sizes. Reflecting this liquidity, forward contracts are the predominant hedging instrument in use globally. For the balance of this section, we will focus only on currency forward contracts. However, separate side boxes discuss exchange-traded currency futures contracts and currency-based exchange-traded funds (ETFs).

### 9.1.1 Hedge Ratios with Forward Contracts

In principle, setting up a full currency hedge is relatively straight forward: match the current market value of the foreign-currency exposure in the portfolio with an equal and offsetting position in a forward contract. In practice, of course, it is not that simple because the market value of the foreign-currency assets will change with market conditions. This means that the actual hedge ratio will typically *drift* away from the desired hedge ratio as market conditions change. A **static hedge** (i.e., unchanging hedge) will avoid transaction costs, but will also tend to accumulate unwanted currency exposures as the value of the foreign-currency assets change. This characteristic will cause a mismatch between the market value of the foreign-currency asset portfolio and the nominal size of the forward contract used for the currency hedge; this is pure currency risk. For this reason, the portfolio manager will typically need to implement a **dynamic hedge** by rebalancing the portfolio periodically. This hedge rebalancing will mean adjusting some combination of the size, number, and maturities of the forward currency contracts.

# Currency Management Tools: Forward Contracts, FX Swaps and Currency Options

A simple example will illustrate this rebalancing process. Suppose that an investor domiciled in Switzerland has a EUR-denominated portfolio that, at the start of the period, is worth EUR1,000,000. Assume a monthly hedge-rebalancing cycle. To hedge this portfolio, the investor would sell EUR1,000,000 one month forward against the CHF. Assume that one month later, the EUR-denominated investment portfolio is then actually worth only EUR950,000. To roll the hedge forward for the next month, the investor will engage in a mismatched FX swap. (Recall that a "matched" swap means that both the spot and forward transactions—the near and far "legs" of the swap, respectively—are of equal size). For the near leg of the swap, EUR1 million will be bought at spot to settle the expiring forward contract. (The euro amounts will then net to zero, but a Swiss franc cash flow will be generated, either a loss or a gain for the investor, depending on how the CHF/EUR rate has changed over the month). For the far leg of the swap, the investor will sell EUR950,000 forward for one month.

Another way to view this rebalancing process is to consider the case in which the original short forward contract has a three-month maturity. In this case, rebalancing after one month would mean that the manager would have to *buy* 50,000 CHF/EUR two months forward. There is no cash flow at the time this second forward contract is entered, but the *net* amount of euro for delivery at contract settlement two months into the future is now the euro hedge amount desired (i.e., EUR950,000). There will be a net cash flow (denominated in CHF) calculated over these two forward contracts on the settlement date two months hence.

Although rebalancing a dynamic hedge will keep the actual hedge ratio close to the target hedge ratio, it will also lead to increased transaction costs compared with a static hedge. The manager will have to assess the cost–benefit trade-offs of how frequently to dynamically rebalance the hedge. These will depend on a variety of idiosyncratic factors (manager risk aversion, market view, IPS guidelines, etc.), and so there is no single "correct" answer—different managers will likely make different decisions.

However, we can observe that the higher the degree of risk aversion, the more frequently the hedge is likely to be rebalanced back to the "neutral" hedge ratio. Similarly, the greater the tolerance for active trading, and the stronger the commitment to a particular market view, the more likely it is that the actual hedge ratio will be allowed to vary from a "neutral" setting, possibly through entering into new forward contracts. (For example, if the P/B spot rate was seen to be oversold and likely to rebound higher, an actively traded portfolio might buy the base currency through forward contracts to lock in this perceived low price—and thus change the actual hedge ratio accordingly.) The sidebar on executing a hedge illustrates the concepts of rolling hedges, FX swaps and their pricing (bid–offer), and adjusting hedges for market views and changes in market values.

### EXECUTING A HEDGE

Jiao Yang works at Hong Kong SAR-based Kwun Tong Investment Advisors; its reporting currency is the Hong Kong Dollar (HKD). She has been put in charge of managing the firm's foreign-currency hedges. Forward contracts for two of these hedges are coming due for settlement, and Yang will need to use FX swaps to roll these hedges forward three months.

**Hedge #1:** Kwun Tong has a short position of JPY800,000,000 coming due on a JPY/HKD forward contract. The market value of the underlying foreign-currency assets has not changed over the life of the contract, and Yang does not have a firm opinion on the expected future movement in the JPY/HKD spot rate.

**Hedge #2:** Kwun Tong has a short position of EUR8,000,000 coming due on a HKD/EUR forward contract. The market value of the EUR-denominated assets has increased (measured in EUR). Yang expects the HKD/EUR spot rate to decrease.

The following spot exchange rates and three-month forward points are in effect when Yang transacts the FX swaps necessary to roll the hedges forward:

|         | Spot Rate       | Three-Month Forward Points |
|---------|-----------------|----------------------------|
| JPY/HKD | 10.80/10.82     | −20/−14                    |
| HKD/EUR | 10.0200/10.0210 | 125/135                    |

*Note*: The JPY/HKD forward points will be scaled by 100; the HKD/EUR forward points will be scaled by 10,000

As a result, Yang undertakes the following transactions:

For **Hedge #1**, the foreign-currency value of the underlying assets has not changed, and she does not have a market view that would lead her to want to either over- or under-hedge the foreign-currency exposure. Therefore, to roll these hedges forward, she uses a matched swap. For matched swaps (see Section 2), the convention is to base pricing on the mid-market spot exchange rate. Thus, the spot leg of the swap would be to buy JPY800,000,000 at the mid-market rate of 10.81 JPY/HKD. The forward leg of the swap would require selling JPY800,000,000 forward three months. Selling JPY (the price currency in the JPY/HKD quote) is equivalent to buying HKD (the base currency). Therefore, she uses the offer-side forward points, and the all-in forward rate for the forward leg of the swap is as follows:

$$10.81 + \frac{-14}{100} = 10.67$$

For **Hedge #2**, the foreign-currency value of the underlying assets has increased; Yang recognizes that this implies that she should increase the size of the hedge greater than EUR8,000,000. She also believes that the HKD/EUR spot rate will decrease, and recognizes that this implies a hedge ratio of more than 100% (Kwun Tong Advisors has given her discretion to over- or under-hedge based on her market views). This too means that the size of the hedge should be increased more than EUR8,000,000, because Yang will want a larger short position in the EUR to take advantage of its expected depreciation. Hence, Yang uses a mismatched swap, buying EUR8,000,000 at spot rate against the HKD, to settle the maturing forward contract and then *selling* an amount *more* than EUR8,000,000 forward to increase the hedge size. Because the EUR is the base currency in the HKD/EUR quote, this means using the *bid* side for both the spot rate and the forward points when calculating the all-in forward rate:

$$10.0200 + \frac{125}{10,000} = 10.0325$$

The spot leg of the swap—buying back EUR8,000,000 to settle the outstanding forward transaction—is also based on the bid rate of 10.0200. This is because Yang is selling an amount larger than EUR8,000,000 forward, and the all-in forward rate of the swap is already using the bid side of the market (as it would for a matched swap). Hence, to pick up the net increase in forward EUR sales, the dealer Yang is transacting with would price the swap so that Yang also has to use bid side of the *spot* quote for the spot transaction used to settle the maturing forward contract.

### 9.1.2 *Roll Yield*

The roll yield (also called the roll return) on a hedge results from the fact that forward contracts are priced at the spot rate adjusted for the number of forward points at that maturity (see the example shown in Exhibit 3). This forward point adjustment can either benefit or detract from portfolio returns (positive and negative roll yield, respectively) depending on whether the forward points are at a premium or discount, and what side of the market (buying or selling) the portfolio manager is on.

# Currency Management Tools: Forward Contracts, FX Swaps and Currency Options

The concept of roll yield is illustrated with the simplified example shown in Exhibit 7.

### Exhibit 7  The Forward Curve and Roll Yield

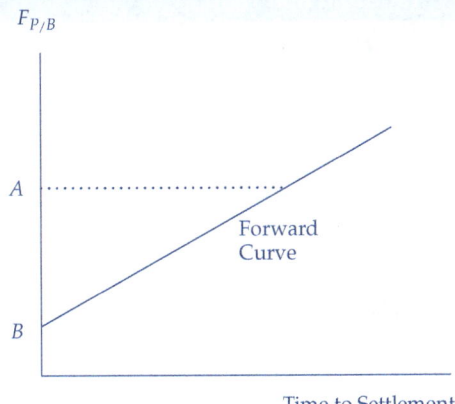

The magnitude of roll yield is given by $|(F_{P/B} - S_{P/B})/S_{P/B}|$ where "||" indicates absolute value. The sign depends on whether the investor needs to buy or to sell the base currency forward in order to maintain the hedge. A *positive* roll yield results from buying the base currency at a forward discount or selling it at a forward premium (the intuition here is that it is profitable to "buy low and sell high"). Otherwise, the roll yield is negative (i.e., a positive cost). Examining the case of negative roll yield, assume that to implement the hedge requires buying the base currency in the P/B quote, and that the base currency is trading at a forward premium (as shown in Exhibit 7). By using a long position in a forward contract to implement this hedge, it means paying the forward price of A. All else equal, as time passes the price of the forward contract will "roll down the curve" toward Price B as the forward contract's settlement date approaches. (Note that in reality the curve is not always linear.) At the settlement date of the forward contract, it is necessary to roll the hedging position forward to extend the currency hedge. This rolling forward will involve selling the base currency at the then-current spot exchange rate to settle the forward contract, and then going long another far-dated forward contract (i.e., an FX swap transaction). Note that the portfolio manager originally bought the base currency at Price A and then subsequently sold it at a lower Price B—and that buying high and selling low will be a cost to the portfolio. Or put differently, all else equal, the roll yield would be negative in this case. Note that the "all else equal" caveat refers to the fact that the all-in price of the forward contract consists of the spot rate and forward points, and both are likely to change over the life of the forward contract. It is possible that at the settlement date the spot rate would have moved higher than A, in which case the roll yield would be positive. But the larger the gap between A and B at contract initiation, the less likely this is to occur.

The concept of roll yield is very similar to the concept of forward rate bias (and the carry trade) introduced in Sections 7–8. Indeed, a negative roll yield typically indicates that the hedger was trading *against* the forward rate bias by buying a currency at a forward premium (as in Exhibit 7) or selling a currency at a forward discount. This is the exact opposite of trading the forward rate bias, which is to buy at a discount and sell at a premium. Given the equivalence between the forward rate bias and the carry trade, by trading against the forward rate bias the hedger with a negative roll yield is also essentially entering into *negative* carry trade, in effect borrowing at high rates and investing at low rates. On average, this will not be a winning strategy. Given the equivalence between implementing a carry trade, trading the forward rate bias, and earning positive roll yield, we can now complete Exhibit 6 introduced in Section 7 on the carry trade:

**Exhibit 8  The Carry Trade and Roll Yield**

|  | Buy/Invest | Sell/Borrow |  |
|---|---|---|---|
| Implementing the carry trade | High-yield currency | Low-yield currency | Earning a positive roll yield |
| Trading the forward rate bias | Forward discount currency | Forward premium currency | |

Note as well that this concept of roll yield applies to forward and futures contracts used to trade *any* asset class, not just currencies: It applies equally well to forwards and futures on equities, fixed-income securities, commodities, and indeed, any financial product. For example, consider the case of a commodity processor that hedges the costs of its production process by going long corn futures contracts. If the futures curve for corn futures contracts is in contango (upward sloping, as in Exhibit 7), then this hedging position will also face the potential for negative roll yield.

To be fair, it is also possible for the level of, and movement in, forward points to be in the portfolio manager's favor. Extending our previous example, consider the case of a portfolio manager that has to *sell* the base currency to implement the currency hedge. In this case, the manager would be selling the base currency forward at Price A in Exhibit 7 and, all else equal and through entering an FX swap at settlement date, buying the currency back at the lower Price B—essentially, short selling a financial product with a declining price. In this case, the roll yield is positive.

Because the level of and movements in forward points can either enhance or reduce currency-hedged returns, it explains an observed tendency in foreign exchange markets for the amount of currency hedging to generally vary with movements in forward points. As forward points move against the hedger, the amount of hedging activity typically declines as the cost/benefit ratio of the currency hedge deteriorates. The opposite occurs when movements in forward points reduce hedging costs. Essentially the tendency to hedge will vary depending on whether implementing the hedge happens to be trading in the same direction of the forward rate bias strategy or against it. It is easier to sell a currency forward if there is a "cushion" when it is selling at a forward premium. Likewise, it is more attractive to buy a currency when it is trading at a forward discount. This swings the forward rate bias (and carry trade advantage) in favor of the hedge.

Combined with the manager's market view of future spot rate movements, what this concept implies is that, when setting the hedge ratio, the portfolio manager must balance the effect of expected future exchange rate movements on portfolio returns against the expected effect of the roll yield (i.e., the expected cost of the hedge).

A simple example can illustrate this effect. Consider a portfolio manager that needs to sell forward the base currency of a currency pair (P/B) to implement a currency hedge. Clearly, the manager would prefer to sell this currency at as high a price as possible. Assume that given the forward points for this currency pair and the time horizon for the hedge, the expected roll yield (cost of the hedge) is −3%. Suppose the portfolio manager had a market view that the base currency would depreciate by 4%. In this case, the hedge makes sense: It is better to pay 3% for the hedge to avoid an expected 4% loss.

Now, suppose that with a movement in forward points the new forward discount on the base currency is 6% away from the current spot rate. If the manager's market view is unchanged (an expected depreciation of the base currency of 4%), then now the use of the hedge is less clear: Does it make sense to pay 6% for the hedge to avoid an expected 4% loss? A *risk-neutral* manager would not hedge under these circumstances because the net expected value of the hedge is negative. But a *risk-averse* manager might still implement the hedge regardless of the negative net expected value. The reason is because it is possible that the market forecast is wrong and that the *actual* depreciation of the base currency (and realized loss to the portfolio) may be higher than the 6% cost of the hedge. The risk-averse manager must then weigh the *certainty* of a hedge that costs 6% against the *risk* that actual unhedged currency losses might be much higher than that.

Clearly, the cost/benefit analysis has shifted against hedging in this case, but many risk-averse investors would still undertake the hedge anyway. The risk-averse manager would likely only take an unhedged currency position if the difference between the expected cost of the hedge and the expected return on an unhedged position was so great as to make the risk acceptable. Balancing these two considerations would depend on the type of market view the manager held and the degree of conviction in it, as well as the manager's degree of risk aversion. The decision taken will vary among investors, so no definitive answer can be given as to what would be the appropriate hedging choice (different portfolio managers will make different choices given the same opportunity set). But hedging costs will vary with market conditions and the higher the expected cost of the hedge (negative roll yield) the more the cost/benefit calculation moves against using a fully hedged position. Or put another way, if setting up the hedge involves selling the low-yield currency and buying the high-yield currency in the P/B pair (i.e., an implicit carry position), then the more likely the portfolio will be fully hedged or even over-hedged. The opposite is also true: Trading against the forward rate bias is likely to lead to lower hedge ratios, all else equal.

### EXAMPLE 4

### The Hedging Decision

The reporting currency of Hong Kong SAR-based Kwun Tong Investment Advisors is the Hong Kong dollar (HKD). The investment committee is examining whether it should implement a currency hedge for the firm's exposures to the GBP and the ZAR (the firm has long exposures to both of these foreign currencies). The hedge would use forward contracts. The following data relevant to assessing the expected cost of the hedge and the expected move in the spot exchange rate has been developed by the firm's market strategist.

|   | Current Spot Rate | Six-Month Forward Rate | Six-Month Forecast Spot Rate |
|---|---|---|---|
| HKD/GBP | 12.4610 | 12.6550 | 12.3000 |
| HKD/ZAR | 0.9510 | 0.9275 | 0.9300 |

1 Recommend whether to hedge the firm's long GBP exposure. Justify your recommendation.

2 Discuss the trade-offs in hedging the firm's long ZAR exposure.

> **Solution to 1:**
>
> Kwun Tong is long the GBP against the HKD, and HKD/GBP is selling at a forward premium of +1.6% compared with the current spot rate. All else equal, this is the expected roll yield—which is in the firm's favor, in this case, because to implement the hedge Kwun Tong would be *selling* GBP, the base currency in the quote, at a price *higher* than the current spot rate. Moreover, the firm's market strategist expects the GBP to *depreciate* by 1.3% against the HKD. Both of these considerations argue for hedging this exposure.
>
> **Solution to 2:**
>
> Kwun Tong is long the ZAR against the HKD, and HKD/ZAR is selling at a forward discount of –2.5% compared with the current spot rate. Implementing the hedge would require the firm to *sell* the base currency in the quote, the ZAR, at a price *lower* than the current spot rate. This would imply that, all else equal, the roll yield would go against the firm; that is, the expected cost of the hedge would be 2.5%. But the firm's strategist also forecasts that the ZAR will depreciate against the HKD by 2.2%. This makes the decision to hedge less certain. A risk-neutral investor would not hedge because the expected cost of the hedge is more than the expected depreciation of the ZAR. But this is only a point forecast and comes with a degree of uncertainty—there is a risk that the HKD/ZAR spot rate might depreciate by more than the 2.5% cost of the hedge. In this case, the decision to hedge the currency risk would depend on the trade-offs between (1) the level of risk aversion of the firm; and (2) the conviction the firm held in the currency forecast—that is, the level of certainty that the ZAR would not depreciate by more than 2.5%.

## 9.2 Currency Options

One of the costs of forward contracts is the opportunity cost. Once fully hedged, the portfolio manager forgoes any upside potential for future currency moves in the portfolio's favor. Currency options remove this opportunity cost because they provide the manager the right, but not the obligation, to buy or sell foreign exchange at a future date at a rate agreed on today. The manager will only exercise the option at the expiry date if it is favorable to do so.[17]

Consider the case of a portfolio manager who is long the base currency in the P/B quote and needs to sell this currency to implement the hedge. One approach is to simply buy an at-the-money put option on the P/B currency pair. Matching a long position in the underlying with a put option is known as a **protective put** strategy. Suppose the current spot rate is 1.3650 and the strike price on the put option bought is 1.3650. If the P/B rate subsequently goes down (P appreciates and B depreciates) by the expiry date, the manager can exercise the option, implement the hedge, and guarantee a selling price of 1.3650. But if the P/B rate increases (P depreciates and B appreciates), the manager can simply let the option expire and collect the currency gains.

Unfortunately, like forward contracts, currency options are not "free goods" and, like any form of insurance, there is always a price to be paid for it. Buying an option means paying an upfront premium. This premium is determined, first, by its **intrinsic value**, which is the difference between the spot exchange rate and the strike price of

---

[17] Almost all options in the FX market are European-style options, which only allow for exercise at the expiry date.

the option (i.e., whether the option is in the money, at the money, or out of the money, respectively). ATM options are more expensive than OTM options, and frequently these relatively expensive options expire without being exercised.

The second determinant of an option's premium is its **time value**, which in turn is heavily influenced by the volatility in exchange rates. Regardless of exchange rate volatility, however, options are always moving toward expiry. In general, the time value of the option is always declining. This is the time decay of the option's value (theta, one of the "Greeks" of option prices, describes this effect) and is similar in concept to that of negative roll yield on forward contracts described earlier. Time decay always works against the owner of an option.

As with forward contracts, a portfolio manager will have to make judgments about the cost/benefit trade-offs of options-based strategies. Although options do allow the portfolio upside potential from favorable currency movements, options can also be a very expensive form of insurance. The manager will have to balance any market view of potential currency gains against hedging costs and the degree of risk aversion. There is no "right" answer; different managers will make different decisions about the cost/benefit trade-offs when given the same opportunity set.

### EXAMPLE 5

### Hedging Problems

Brixworth & St. Ives Asset Management is a UK-based firm managing a dynamic hedging program for the currency exposures in its Aggressive Growth Fund. One of the fund's foreign-currency asset holdings is denominated in the Mexican peso (MXN), and one month ago Brixworth & St. Ives fully hedged this exposure using a two-month MXN/GBP forward contract. The following table provides the relevant information.

|  | One Month Ago | Today |
|---|---|---|
| Value of assets (in MXN) | 10,000,000 | 9,500,000 |
| MXN/GBP spot rate (bid–offer) | 20.0500/20.0580 | 19.5985/20.0065 |
| One-month forward points (bid–offer) | 625/640 | 650/665 |
| Two-month forward points (bid–offer) | 875/900 | 900/950 |

The Aggressive Growth Fund also has an unhedged foreign-currency asset exposure denominated in the South African rand (ZAR). The current mid-market spot rate in the ZAR/GBP currency pair is 5.1050.

1. One month ago, Brixworth & St. Ives *most likely* sold:
   A  MXN9,500,000 forward at an all-in forward rate of MXN/GBP 19.6635.
   B  MXN10,000,000 forward at an all-in forward rate of MXN/GBP 20.1375.
   C  MXN10,000,000 forward at an all-in forward rate of MXN/GBP 20.1480.

2. To rebalance the hedge today, the firm would *most likely* need to:
   A  buy MXN500,000 spot.
   B  buy MXN500,000 forward.
   C  sell MXN500,000 forward.

3. Given the data in the table, the roll yield on this hedge at the forward contracts' maturity date is *most likely* to be:

- **A** zero.
- **B** negative.
- **C** positive.

4 Assuming that all ZAR/GBP options considered have the same notional amount and maturity, the *most* expensive hedge that Brixworth & St. Ives could use to hedge its ZAR exposure is a long position in a(n):
- **A** ATM call.
- **B** 25-delta call.
- **C** put with a strike of 5.1050.

### Solution to 1:

C is correct. Brixworth & St. Ives is long the MXN and hence must sell the MXN forward against the GBP. Selling MXN against the GBP means buying GBP, the base currency in the MXN/GBP quote. Therefore, the offer side of the market must be used. This means the all-in rate used one month ago would have been 20.0580 + 900/10,000, which equals 20.1480. Choice A is incorrect because it uses today's asset value and the bid side of the spot and one-month forward quotes and Choice B is incorrect because it uses the wrong side of the market (the bid side).

### Solution to 2:

B is correct. The foreign investment went down in value in MXN terms. Therefore Brixworth & St. Ives must reduce the size of the hedge. Previously it had sold MXN10,000,000 forward against the GBP, and this amount must be reduced to MXN9,500,000 by buying MXN500,000 forward. Choice A is incorrect because hedging is done with forward contracts not spot deals. Choice C is incorrect because selling MXN forward would increase the size of the hedge, not decrease it.

### Solution to 3:

B is correct. To implement the hedge, Brixworth & St. Ives must sell MXN against the GBP, or equivalently, buy GBP (the base currency in the P/B quote) against the MXN. The base currency is selling forward at a premium, and—all else equal—its price would "roll down the curve" as contract maturity approached. Having to settle the forward contract means then selling the GBP spot at a lower price. Buying high and selling low will define a negative roll yield. Moreover, the GBP has depreciated against the MXN, because the MXN/GBP spot rate declined between one month ago and now, which will also add to the negative roll yield.

### Solution to 4:

A is correct. The Aggressive Growth Fund is long the ZAR through its foreign-currency assets, and to hedge this exposure it must sell the ZAR against the GBP, or equivalently, buy GBP—the base currency in the P/B quote—against the ZAR. Hedging a required purchase means a long position in a call option (not a put, which is used to hedge a required sale of the base currency in the P/B quote). An ATM call option is more expensive than a 25-delta call option.

# CURRENCY MANAGEMENT STRATEGIES

g   describe trading strategies used to reduce hedging costs and modify the risk–return characteristics of a foreign-currency portfolio;

In the previous sections, we showed that completely hedging currency risk is possible—but can also be expensive. It can be even more expensive when trying to avoid all downside risk while keeping the full upside potential for favorable currency movements (i.e., a protective put strategy with ATM options). Hedging can be seen as a form of insurance, but it is possible to overpay for insurance. Judgments have to be made to determine at what point the costs outweigh the benefits.

As with any form of insurance, there are always steps that can be taken to reduce hedging costs. For most typical insurance products, these cost-reduction measures include such things as higher deductibles, co-pay arrangements, and lower maximum payouts. The same sorts of measures exist in the FX derivatives market; we will explore these various alterative measures in this section. The key point to keep in mind is that all of these various cost-reduction measures invariably involve some combination of *less downside protection* and/or *less upside potential* for the hedge. In efficient markets, lower insurance premiums mean lower insurance.

These cost-reduction measures also start moving the portfolio away from a passively managed 100% hedge ratio toward discretionary hedging in which the manager is allowed to take directional positions. Once the possibility of accepting some downside risk, and some upside potential, is introduced into the portfolio, the manager is moving away from a rules-based approach to hedging toward a more active style of trading. The portfolio manager can then use the trading tools and strategies described in the following sections to express a market view and/or cut hedging costs.

The variety of trading strategies—involving various combinations of forwards, options, and swaps—that can be deployed to this end is almost infinite. We will not attempt to explore all of them in this reading, but rather to give a sense of the range of trading tools and strategies available for managing currency risk. We begin with Exhibit 9, which gives a high-level description of some of these various trading strategies that will then be explained in more detail in subsequent sections. Note that as this section progresses, we will be describing strategies at different points along the risk spectrum described in Sections 4–6, moving in turn from passive hedge-based approaches to strategies used in more active currency management schemes.

| Exhibit 9 | Select Currency Management Strategies | |
|---|---|---|
| Forward Contracts | Over-/under-hedging | Profit from market view |
| Option Contracts | OTM options | Cheaper than ATM |
| | Risk reversals | Write options to earn premiums |
| | Put/call spreads | Write options to earn premiums |
| | Seagull spreads | Write options to earn premiums |
| Exotic Options | Knock-in/out features | Reduced downside/upside exposure |
| | Digital options | Extreme payoff strategies |

We will make one simplifying assumption for the following sections. Currency management strategies will differ fundamentally depending on whether the base currency of the P/B price quote must be bought or sold to decrease the foreign-currency exposure. To simplify the material and impose consistency on the discussions that follow, we will assume that the portfolio manager must sell the base currency in the P/B quote to reduce currency risk. In addition, unless otherwise noted, the notional amounts and expiration dates on all forward and options contracts are the same.[18]

## 10.1 Over-/Under-Hedging Using Forward Contracts

When the IPS gives the manager discretion either to over- or under-hedge the portfolio, relative to the "neutral" benchmark, there is the possibility to add incremental value based on the manager's market view. Profits from successful tactical positioning help reduce net hedging costs. For example, if the neutral benchmark hedge ratio is 100% for the base currency being hedged, and the portfolio manager has a market opinion that the base currency is likely to depreciate, then *over*-hedging through a short position in P/B forward contracts might be implemented—that is, the manager might use a hedge ratio higher than 100%. Similarly, if the manager's market opinion is that the base currency is likely to appreciate, the currency exposure might be *under*-hedged.

A variant of this approach would be to adjust the hedge ratio based on exchange rate movements: to increase the hedge ratio if the base currency depreciated, but decrease the hedge ratio if the base currency appreciated. Essentially, this approach is a form of "delta hedging" that tries to mimic the payoff function of a put option on the base currency. That is, this form of dynamic hedging with forward contracts tries to increasingly participate in any upside moves of the base currency, but increasingly hedge any downside moves. Doing so adds "convexity" to the portfolio, meaning that the hedge's payoff function will be a convex curve when this function is graphed with profit on the vertical axis and the spot rate on the horizontal axis. (Note that this concept of convexity is identical in intent to the concept of convexity describing bonds; as convexity increases the price of a bond rises more quickly in a declining yield environment and drops more slowly in a rising yield environment. Convexity is a desirable characteristic in both the fixed-income and currency-hedging contexts.)

## 10.2 Protective Put Using OTM Options

In the previous section, we examined a dynamic hedging strategy using forward contracts that tries to mimic the payoff function of an option and put convexity into the hedge's payoff function. The payoff functions for options are naturally convex to begin with. However, this can be a costly form of convexity (relatively high option premiums), and fully hedging a currency position with a protective put strategy using an ATM option is the most expensive means of all to buy convexity.

One way to reduce the cost of using options is to accept some downside risk by using an OTM option, such as a 25- or 10-delta option. These options will be less costly, but also do not fully protect the portfolio from adverse currency movements. Conversely, it makes sense to insure against larger risks but accept some smaller day-to-day price movements in currencies. As an analogy, it may be possible to buy a home or car insurance policy with a zero deductible—but the premiums would be exorbitant. It may be more rational to have a cheaper insurance policy and accept responsibility for minor events, but insure against extreme damage.

---

[18] Examples of implementing a hedge by *buying* the base currency will be provided in some of the practice examples.

## 10.3 Risk Reversal (or Collar)

Another set of option strategies involves *selling* options (also known as writing options) to earn income that can be used to offset the cost of buying a put option, which forms the "core" of the hedge. Recall that in this section, we are using the simplifying convention that the manager is long the base currency in the P/B quote; hence puts and not calls would be used for hedging in this case.

One strategy to obtain downside protection at a lower cost than a straight protective put position is to *buy* an OTM put option and *write* an OTM call option. Essentially, the portfolio manager is selling some of the upside potential for movements in the base currency (writing a call) and using the option's premiums to help pay the cost of the long put option being purchased. This approach is similar to creating a collar in fixed-income markets. The portfolio is protected against downside movements, but its upside is limited to the strike price on the OTM call option; the exchange rate risk is confined to a corridor or "collar."

In professional FX markets, having a long position in a call option and a short position in a put option is called a **risk reversal**. For example, buying a 25-delta call and writing a 25-delta put is referred to as a *long* position in a 25-delta risk reversal. The position used to create the collar position we just described (buying a put, writing a call) would be a *short* position in a risk reversal.

The majority of currency hedging for foreign-currency asset portfolios and corporate accounts is based on the use of forward contracts and simple option strategies (protective puts/covered calls and risk reversals/collars). We now begin to transition to more active trading strategies that are designed to express market views for speculative profit.

## 10.4 Put Spread

A variation of the short risk reversal position is a **put spread**, which is also used to reduce the upfront cost of buying a protective put. The short risk reversal is structured by buying a put option and writing a call option: the premiums received by writing the call help cover the cost of the put. Similarly, the put spread position involves buying a put option and writing another put option to help cover the cost of the long put's premiums. This position is typically structured by buying an OTM put, and writing a deeper-OTM put to gain income from premiums; both options involved have the same maturity.

To continue our previous example, with the current spot rate at 1.3550, the portfolio manager might set up the following put spread: buy a put with a strike of 1.3500 and write a put with a strike of 1.3450. The payoff on the put spread position will then be as follows: there is no hedge protection between 1.3550 and 1.3500; the portfolio is hedged from 1.3500 down to 1.3450; at spot rates below 1.3450, the portfolio becomes unhedged again. The put spread reduces the cost of the hedge, but at the cost of more limited downside protection. The portfolio manager would then use this spread only for cases in which a modest decline in the spot exchange rate was expected, and this position would have to be closely monitored against adverse exchange rate movements.

Note that the put spread structure will not be zero-cost because the deeper-OTM put (1.3450) being written will be cheaper than the less-OTM put (1.3500) being bought. However, there are approaches that will make the put spread (or almost any other option spread position) cheaper or possibly zero-cost: the manager could alter: (a) the strike prices of the options; (b) the notional amounts of the options; or (c) some combination of these two measures.

Altering the strike prices of the put options would mean moving them closer together (and hence more equal in cost). However, this would reduce the downside protection on the hedge. Instead, the portfolio manager could write a larger notional amount for the deeper-OTM option; for example, the ratio for the notionals for the options written versus bought might be 1:2. (In standard FX market notation, this would be a 1 × 2 put spread—the option with exercise price closest to being ATM is given first. However, to avoid confusion it is good practice to specify explicitly in the price quote which is the long and short positions, and what their deltas/strike prices are.) Although this structure may now be (approximately) zero-cost it is not without risks: for spot rates below 1.3450 the portfolio has now seen its exposure to the base currency double-up (because of the 1:2 proportion of notionals) and at a worse spot exchange rate for the portfolio on top of it. Creating a zero-cost structure with a 1 × 2 put spread is equivalent to adding leverage to the options position, because you are selling more options than you are buying. This means that this put spread position will have to be carefully managed. For example, the portfolio manager might choose to close out the short position in the deep-OTM put (by going long/buying an equivalent put option) before the base currency depreciates to the 1.3450 strike level. This may be a costly position exit, however, as the market moves against the manager's original positioning. Because of this, this sort of 1 × 2 structure may be more appropriate for expressing directional opinions rather than as a pure hedging strategy.

## 10.5 Seagull Spread

An alternative, and somewhat safer approach, would be to combine the original put spread position (1:1 proportion of notionals) with a covered call position. This is simply an extension of the concept behind risk reversals and put spreads. The "core" of the hedge (for a manager long the base currency) is the long position in a put option. This is expensive. To reduce the cost, a short risk reversal position writes a call option while a put spread writes a deep-OTM put option. Of course, the manager can always do both: that is, be long a protective put and then write *both* a call and a deep-OTM put. This option structure is sometimes referred to as a **seagull spread**.

As with the names for other option strategies based on winged creatures, the "seagull" indicates an option structure with at least three individual options, and in which the options at the most distant strikes—the wings—are on the opposite side of the market from the middle strike(s)—the body. For example, if the current spot price is 1.3550, a seagull could be constructed by going *long* an ATM put at 1.3550 (the middle strike is the "body"), *short* an OTM put at 1.3500, and *short* an OTM call at 1.3600 (the latter two options are the "wings"). Because the options in the "wings" are being written (sold) this is called a *short* seagull position. The risk/return profile of this structure gives full downside protection from 1.3550 to 1.3500 (at which point the short put position neutralizes the hedge) and participation in the upside potential in spot rate movements to 1.3600 (the strike level for the short call option).

Note that because *two* options are now being written to gain premiums instead of one, this approach allows the strike price of the long put position to be ATM, increasing the downside protection. The various strikes and/or notional sizes of these options (and hence their premiums) can always be adjusted up or down until a zero-cost structure is obtained. However, note that this particular seagull structure gives away some upside potential (the short call position) as well as takes on some downside risk (if the short put position is triggered, it will disable the hedge coverage coming from the long put position). As always, lower structure costs come with some combination of lower downside protection and/or less upside potential.

There are many variants of these seagull strategies, each of which provides a different risk–reward profile (and net cost). For example, for the portfolio manager wishing to hedge a long position in the base currency in the P/B quote when the current spot rate is 1.3550, another seagull structure would be to write an ATM call at 1.3550 and use the proceeds to buy an OTM put option at 1.3500 and an OTM call option at 1.3600. Note that in this seagull structure, the "body" is now a *short* option position, not a long position as in the previous example, and the "wings" are the long position. Hence, it is a *long* seagull spread. This option structure provides cheap downside protection (the hedge kicks in at the put's 1.3500 strike) while providing the portfolio manager with unlimited participation in any rally in the base currency beyond the 1.3600 strike of the OTM call option. As before, the various option strikes and/or notional sizes on the options bought and written can be adjusted so that a zero-cost structure is obtained.

## 10.6 Exotic Options

In this section, we move even further away from derivatives and trading strategies used mainly for hedging, and toward the more speculative end of the risk spectrum dominated by active currency management. Exotic options are often used by more sophisticated players in the professional trading market—for example, currency overlay managers—and are less frequently used by institutional investors, investment funds, or corporations for hedging purposes. There are several reasons for this relatively light usage of "exotics" for hedging purposes, some related to the fact that many smaller entities lack familiarity with these products. Another reason involves the difficulty of getting hedge accounting treatment in many jurisdictions, which is more advantageous for financial reporting reasons. Finally, the specialized terms of such instruments make them difficult to value for regulatory and accounting purposes.

In general, the term "exotic" refers to all options that are not "vanilla." In FX, vanilla refers essentially to European-style put and call options. The full range of exotic options is both very broad and constantly evolving; many are extraordinarily complex both to price and even to understand. However, all exotics, no matter how complex, typically share one defining feature in common: They are designed to customize the risk exposures desired by the client and provide them at the lowest possible price.[19] Much like the trading strategies described previously, they usually involve some combination of lower downside protection and/or lower upside potential while providing the client with the specific risk exposures they are prepared to manage, and to do so at what is generally a lower cost than vanilla options.

The two most common type of exotic options encountered in foreign exchange markets are those with **knock-in/knock-out** features and digital options.

An option with a knock-in feature is essentially a vanilla option that is created only when the spot exchange rate touches a pre-specified level (this trigger level, called the "barrier," is not the same as the strike price). Similarly a knock-out option is a vanilla option that ceases to exist when the spot exchange rate touches some pre-specified barrier level. Because these options only exist (i.e., get knocked-in or knocked-out) under certain circumstances, they are more restrictive than vanilla options and hence are cheaper. But again, the knock-in/out features provide less upside potential and/ or downside protection.

Digital options are also called binary options, or all-or-nothing options. The expiry value of an in-the-money vanilla option varies based on the amount of difference between the expiry level and strike price. In contrast, digital options pay out a fixed amount if they are determined to be in-the-money. For example, American digital options pay a *fixed* amount if they "touch" their exercise level at any time before expiry (even if by a single pip). This characteristic of "extreme payoff" options makes them almost akin to a lottery ticket. Because of these large payoffs, digital options usually cost more than vanilla options with the same strike price. But digitals also provide highly leveraged exposure to movements in the spot rate. This makes these exotic products more appropriate as trading tools for active currency management,

---

[19] Although the price is low for the client compared with vanilla options, exotics are typically nonetheless high profit margin items for investment dealers.

rather than as hedging tools. In practice, digital options are typically used by more sophisticated speculative accounts in the FX market to express directional views on exchange rates.

A full exposition of exotic options is beyond the scope of this reading, but the reader should be aware of their existence and why they exist.

## 10.7 Section Summary

Clearly, loosening the constraint of a fully hedged portfolio begins to introduce complicated active currency management decisions. The following steps can be helpful to sort things out:

**a** First, identify the *base* currency in the P/B quote (currency pair) you are dealing with. Derivatives are typically quoted in terms of either buying or selling the *base* currency when the option is exercised. A move upward in the P/B quote is an appreciation of the base currency.

**b** Then, identify whether the base currency must be *bought* or *sold* to establish the hedge. These are the price movements you will be protecting against.

**c** If *buying* the base currency is required to implement the hedge, then the core hedge structure will be based on some combination of a long call option and/or a long forward contract. The cost of this core hedge can be reduced by buying an OTM call option or writing options to earn premiums. (But keep in mind, lower hedging costs equate to less downside protection and/or upside potential.)

**d** If *selling* the base currency is required to implement the hedge, then the core hedge structure will be based on some combination of a long put option and/or a short forward contract. The cost of this core hedge can be reduced by buying an OTM put option or writing options to earn premiums.

**e** The higher the allowed discretion for active management, the lower the risk aversion; and the firmer a particular market view is held, the more the hedge is likely to be structured to allow risk exposures in the portfolio. This approach involves positioning in derivatives that "lean the same way" as the market view. (For example, a market view that the base currency will depreciate would use some combination of short forward contracts, writing call options, buying put options, and using "bearish" exotic strategies.) This directional bias to the trading position would be superimposed on the core hedge position described in steps "c" and "d," creating an active-trading "tilt" in the portfolio.

**f** For these active strategies, varying the strike prices and notional amounts of the options involved can move the trading position toward a zero-cost structure. But as with hedges, keep in mind that lower cost implies less downside protection and/or upside potential for the portfolio.

A lot of different hedging tools and strategies have been named and covered in this section. Rather than attempting to absorb all of them by rote memorization (a put spread is "X" and a seagull is "Y"), the reader is encouraged instead to focus on the intuition behind a hedge, and how and why it is constructed. It matters less what name (if any) is given to any specific approach; what is important is understanding how all the moving parts fit together. The reader should focus on a "building blocks" approach in understanding how and why the parts of the currency hedge are assembled in a given manner.

# Currency Management Strategies

## EXAMPLE 6

### Alternative Hedging Strategies

Brixworth & St. Ives Asset Management, the UK-based investment firm, has hedged the exposure of its Aggressive Growth Fund to the MXN with a long position in a MXN/GBP forward contract. The fund's foreign-currency asset exposure to the ZAR is hedged by buying an ATM call option on the ZAR/GBP currency pair. The portfolio managers at Brixworth & St. Ives are looking at ways to modify the risk–reward trade-offs and net costs of their currency hedges.

Jasmine Khan, one of the analysts at Brixworth & St. Ives, proposes an option-based hedge structure for the long-ZAR exposure that would replace the hedge based on the ATM call option with either long or short positions in the following three options on ZAR/GBP:

a  ATM put option
b  25-delta put option
c  25-delta call option

Khan argues that these three options can be combined into a hedge structure that will have some limited downside risk, but provide complete hedge protection starting at the relevant 25-delta strike level. The structure will also have unlimited upside potential, although this will not start until the ZAR/GBP exchange rate moves to the relevant 25-delta strike level. Finally, this structure can be created at a relatively low cost because it involves option writing.

1  The *best* method for Brixworth & St. Ives to gain some upside potential for the hedge on the Aggressive Growth Fund's MXN exposure using MXN/GBP options is to replace the forward contract with a:

   A  long position in an OTM put.
   B  short position in an ATM call.
   C  long position in a 25-delta risk reversal.

2  While keeping the ATM call option in the ZAR/GBP, the method that would lead to *greatest* cost reduction on the hedge would be to:

   A  buy a 25-delta put.
   B  write a 10-delta call.
   C  write a 25-delta call.

3  Setting up Khan's proposed hedge structure would *most likely* involve being:

   A  long the 25-delta options and short the ATM option.
   B  long the 25-delta call, and short both the ATM and 25-delta put options.
   C  short the 25-delta call, and long both the ATM and 25-delta put options.

### Solution to 1:

C is correct. The Aggressive Growth Fund has a long foreign-currency exposure to the MXN in its asset portfolio, which is hedged by selling the MXN against the GBP, or equivalently, buying the GBP—the base currency in the P/B quote—against the MXN. This need to protect against an *appreciation* in the GBP is why the hedge is using a *long* position in the forward contract. To set a collar around the MXN/GBP rate, Brixworth & St. Ives would want a long call option position with a strike greater than the current spot rate (this gives upside potential to the hedge) and a short put position with a strike less than the current spot rate (this reduces net cost of the hedge). A long call and a short put defines a long position in a risk reversal.

Choice A is incorrect because, if exercised, buying a put option would increase the fund's exposure to the MXN (sell GBP, buy MXN). Similarly, Choice B is incorrect because, if exercised, the ATM call option would increase the MXN exposure (the GBP is "called" away from the fund at the strike price with MXN delivered). Moreover, although writing the ATM call option would gain some income from premiums, writing options (on their own) is never considered the "best" hedge because the premium income earned is fixed but the potential losses on adverse currency moves are potentially unlimited.

### Solution to 2:

C is correct. As before, the hedge is implemented in protecting against an *appreciation* of the base currency of the P/B quote, the GBP. The hedge is established with an ATM call option (a long position in the GBP). Writing an OTM call option (i.e., with a strike that is more than the current spot rate of 5.1050) establishes a call spread (although hedge protection is lost if ZAR/GBP expires at or above the strike level). Writing a 25-delta call earns more income from premiums than a deeper-OTM 10-delta call (although the 25-delta call has less hedge protection). Buying an option would increase the cost of the hedge, and a put option on the ZAR/GBP would increase the fund's ZAR exposure if exercised (the GBP is "put" to the counterparty at the strike price and ZAR received).

### Solution to 3:

A is correct. Once again, the hedge is based on hedging the need to sell ZAR/buy GBP, and GBP is the base currency in the ZAR/GBP quote. This means the hedge needs to protect against an *appreciation* of the GBP (an appreciation of the ZAR/GBP rate). Based on Khan's description, the hedge provides protection after a certain loss point, which would be a long 25-delta call. Unlimited upside potential after favorable (i.e., down) moves in the ZAR/GBP past a certain level means a long 25-delta put. Getting the low net cost that Khan refers to means that the cost of these two long positions is financed by selling the ATM option. (Together these three positions define a long seagull spread). Choice B is incorrect because although the first two legs of the position are right, a short position in the put does not provide any unlimited upside potential (from a down-move in ZAR/GBP). Choice C is incorrect because any option-based hedge, given the need to hedge against an up-move in the ZAR/GBP rate, is going to be based on a long call position. C does not contain any of these.

## 11 HEDGING MULTIPLE FOREIGN CURRENCIES

h   describe the use of cross-hedges, macro-hedges, and minimum-variance-hedge ratios in portfolios exposed to multiple foreign currencies;

We now expand our discussion to hedging a portfolio with multiple foreign-currency assets. The hedging tools and strategies are very similar to those discussed for hedging a single foreign-currency asset, except now the currency hedge must consider the *correlation* between the various foreign-currency risk exposures.

## Hedging Multiple Foreign Currencies

For example, consider the case of a US-domiciled investor who has exposures to foreign-currency assets in Australia and New Zealand. These two economies are roughly similar in that they are resource-based and closely tied to the regional economy of the Western Pacific, especially the large emerging markets in Asia. As a result, the movements in their currencies are often closely correlated; the USD/AUD and USD/NZD currency pairs will tend to move together. If the portfolio manager has the discretion to take short positions, the portfolio may (for example) possibly have a net long position in the Australian foreign-currency asset and a net short position in the New Zealand foreign-currency asset. In this case, there may be less need to hedge away the AUD and NZD currency exposures separately because the portfolio's long exposure to the AUD is diversified by the short position on the NZD.

### 11.1 Cross Hedges and Macro Hedges

A **cross hedge** occurs when a position in one asset (or a derivative based on the asset) is used to hedge the risk exposures of a different asset (or a derivative based on it). Normally, cross hedges are not needed because, as we mentioned earlier, forward contracts and other derivatives are widely available in almost every conceivable currency pair. However, if the portfolio already has "natural" cross hedges in the form of negatively correlated residual currency exposures—as in the long-AUD/short-NZD example in Section 11—this helps moderate portfolio risk ($\sigma[R_{DC}]$) without having to use a direct hedge on the currency exposure.

Sometimes a distinction is made between a "proxy" hedge and a "cross" hedge. When this distinction is made, a *proxy hed*ge removes the foreign currency risk by hedging it back to the investor's domestic currency—such as in the example with USD/AUD and USD/NZD discussed in the text. In contrast, a *cross hed*ge moves the currency risk from one foreign currency to another foreign currency. For example, a US-domiciled investor may have an exposure to both the Indonesian rupiah (IDR) and the Thai baht (THB), but based on a certain market view, may only want exposure to the THB. In this context, the manager might use currency derivatives as a cross hedge to convert the IDR/USD exposure to a THB/USD exposure. But not all market participants make this sharp of a distinction between proxy hedges and cross hedges, and these terms are often used interchangeably. The most common term found among practitioners in most asset classes is simply a cross hedge, as we are using the term here: hedging an exposure with a closely correlated product (i.e., a proxy hedge when this distinction is made). The cross hedge of moving currency exposures between various *foreign* currencies is more of a special-case application of this concept. In our example, a US investor wanting to shift currency exposures between the IDR and THB would only need to shift the relative size of the IDR/USD and THB/USD forward contracts *already* being used. As mentioned earlier, forwards are available on almost every currency pair, so a cross hedge from foreign currency "A" to foreign currency "B" would be a special case when derivatives on one of the currencies are not available.

### EXAMPLE 7

#### Cross Hedges

Mai Nguyen works at Cape Henlopen Advisors, which runs a US-domiciled fund that invests in foreign-currency assets of Australia and New Zealand. The fund currently has equally weighted exposure to one-year Australian and New Zealand treasury bills (i.e., both of the portfolio weights, $\omega_i = 0.5$). Because the foreign-currency return on these treasury bill assets is risk-free and known in advance, their expected $\sigma(R_{FC})$ is equal to zero.

Nguyen wants to calculate the USD-denominated returns on this portfolio as well as the cross hedging effects of these investments. She collects the following information:

| Expected Values | Australia | New Zealand |
|---|---|---|
| Foreign-currency asset return $R_{FC}$ | 4.0% | 6.0% |
| Foreign-currency return $R_{FX}$ | 5.0% | 5.0% |
| Asset risk $\sigma(R_{FC})$ | 0% | 0% |
| Currency risk $\sigma(R_{FX})$ | 8.0% | 10.0% |
| Correlation (USD/AUD; USD/NZD) | | +0.85 |

Using Equation 1, Nguyen calculates that the expected domestic-currency return for the Australian asset is

$$(1.04)(1.05) - 1 = 0.092$$

or 9.2%. Likewise, she determines that the expected domestic-currency return for the New Zealand asset is

$$(1.06)(1.05) - 1 = 0.113$$

or 11.3%. Together, the result is that the expected domestic-currency return ($R_{DC}$) on the equally weighted foreign-currency asset portfolio is the weighted average of these two individual country returns, or

$$R_{DC} = 0.5(9.2\%) + 0.5(11.3\%) = 10.3\%$$

Nguyen now turns her attention to calculating the portfolio's investment risk $[\sigma(R_{DC})]$. To calculate the expected risk for the domestic-currency return, the currency risk of $R_{FX}$ needs to be multiplied by the *known* return on the treasury bills. The portfolio's investment risk, $\sigma(R_{DC})$, is found by calculating the standard deviation of the right-hand-side of:

$$R_{DC} = (1 + R_{FC})(1 + R_{FX}) - 1$$

Although $R_{FX}$ is a random variable—it is not known in advance—the $R_{FC}$ term is in fact known in advance because the asset return is risk-free. Because of this Nguyen can make use of the statistical rules that, first, $\sigma(kX) = k\sigma(X)$, where X is a random variable and $k$ is a constant; and second, that the correlation between a random variable and a constant is zero. These results greatly simplify the calculations because, in this case, she does not need to consider the correlation between exchange rate movements and foreign-currency asset returns. Instead, Nguyen needs to calculate the risk only on the currency side. Applying these statistical rules to the above formula leads to the following results:

A  The expected risk (i.e., standard deviation) of the domestic-currency return for the Australian asset is equal to (1.04) × 8% = 8.3%.

B  The expected risk (i.e., standard deviation) of the domestic-currency return for the New Zealand asset is equal to (1.06) × 10% = 10.6%.

Adding all of these numerical values into Equation 4 leads Nguyen to calculate:

$$\sigma^2(R_{DC}) = (0.5)^2(8.3\%)^2 + (0.5)^2(10.6\%)^2 + [(2)0.5(8.3\%)0.5(10.6\%)0.85]$$
$$= 0.8\%$$

The standard deviation of this amount—that is, $\sigma(R_{DC})$—is 9.1%. Note that in the expression, all of the units are in percent, so for example, 8.3% is equivalent to 0.083 for calculation purposes. The careful reader may also note that Nguyen is able to use an exact expression for calculating the variance of the portfolio returns, rather than the approximate expressions shown in Equations 3 and 5. This is because, with risk-free foreign-currency assets, the variance of these foreign-currency returns $\sigma^2(R_{FC})$ is equal to zero.

Nguyen now considers an alternative scenario in which, instead of an equally weighted portfolio (where the $\omega_i = 0.5$), the fund has a long exposure to the New Zealand asset and a short exposure to the Australian asset (i.e., the $\omega_i$ are +1 and –1, respectively; this is similar to a highly leveraged carry trade position). Putting these weights into Equations 2 and 4 leads to

$$R_{DC} = -1.0(9.2\%) + 1.0(11.3\%) = 2.1\%$$

$$\sigma^2(R_{DC}) = (1.0)^2(8.3\%)^2 + (1.0)^2(10.6\%)^2 + [-2.0(8.3\%)(10.6\%)0.85]$$
$$= 0.3\%$$

The standard deviation—that is, $\sigma(R_{DC})$—is now 5.6%, less than either of the expected risks for foreign-currency asset returns (results A and B). Nguyen concludes that having long and short positions in positively correlated currencies can lead to much lower portfolio risk, through the benefits of cross hedging. (Nguyen goes on to calculate that if the expected correlation between USD/AUD and USD/NZD increases to 0.95, with all else equal, the expected domestic-currency return risk on the long–short portfolio drops to 3.8%.)

Some types of cross hedges are often referred to as macro hedges. The reason is because the hedge is more focused on the entire portfolio, particularly when individual asset price movements are highly correlated, rather than on individual assets or currency pairs. Another way of viewing a macro hedge is to see the portfolio not just as a collection of financial assets, but as a collection of risk exposures. These various risk exposures are typically defined in categories, such as term risk, credit risk, and liquidity risk. These risks can also be defined in terms of the potential financial scenarios the portfolio is exposed to, such as recession, financial sector stress, or inflation. Often macro hedges are defined in terms of the financial scenario they are designed to protect the portfolio from.

Putting gold in the portfolio sometimes serves this purpose by helping to provide broad portfolio protection against extreme market events. Using a volatility overlay program can also hedge the portfolio against such risks because financial stress is typically associated with a spike in exchange rates' implied volatility. Using a derivative product based on an index, rather than specific assets or currencies, can also define a macro hedge. One macro hedge specific to foreign exchange markets uses derivatives based on fixed-weight baskets of currencies (such derivatives are available in both exchange-traded and OTC form). In a multi-currency portfolio, it may not always be cost efficient to hedge each single currency separately, and in these situations a macro hedge using currency basket derivatives is an alternative approach.

## 11.2 Minimum-Variance Hedge Ratio

A mathematical approach to determining the optimal cross hedging ratio is known as the **minimum-variance hedge ratio**. Recall that regression analysis based on ordinary least squares (OLS) is used to minimize the variance of $\hat{\varepsilon}$, the residual between actual and fitted values of the regression

$$y_t = \alpha + \beta x_t + \varepsilon_t \text{ where } \hat{\varepsilon}_t = y_t - \left(\hat{\alpha} + \hat{\beta} x_t\right)$$

This same principle can be used to minimize the tracking error between the value of the hedged asset and the hedging instrument. In the regression formula, we substitute the percentage change in the value of the asset to be hedged for $y_t$, and the percentage change in value of the hedging instrument for $x_t$ (both of these values are measured in terms of the investor's domestic currency). The calculated coefficient in this regression ($\hat{\beta}$) gives the optimal hedging ratio, which means it minimizes the variance of $\hat{\varepsilon}$ and minimizes the tracking error between changes in the value of the hedge and changes in the value of the asset it is hedging. It can be shown that the formula for the minimum-variance hedge ratio—the formula for calculating the $\hat{\beta}$ coefficient in the regression—is mathematically equal to:

$$\frac{\text{covariance}(y,x)}{\text{variance}(x)} = \text{correlation}(y,x) \times \left[\frac{\text{std. dev.}(y)}{\text{std. dev.}(x)}\right]$$

where $y$ and $x$ are defined as before, the change in the domestic-currency value of the asset and the hedge, respectively.

Calculating the minimum-variance hedge ratio typically applies only for "indirect" hedges based on cross hedging or macro hedges; it is not typically applied to a "direct" hedge in which exposure to a spot rate is hedged with a forward contract in that same currency pair. This is because the correlation between movements in the spot rate and its forward contract is likely to be very close to +1. Likewise, the variance in spot price movements and movements in the price of the forward contract are also likely to be approximately equal. Therefore, calculating the minimum-variance hedge ratio by regressing changes in the spot exchange rate against changes in the forward rate will almost always result is a $\hat{\beta}$ regression estimate very close to 1, and hence a minimum-variance hedge ratio close to 100%. So, undertaking the regression analysis is superfluous.

But the minimum-variance hedge ratio can be quite different from 100% when the hedge is *jointly* optimized over *both* exchange rate movements $R_{FX}$ and changes in the foreign-currency value of the asset $R_{FC}$. A sidebar discusses this case.

There can also be cases when the optimal hedge ratio may not be 100% because of the market characteristics of a specific currency pair. For example, a currency pair may not have a (liquid) forward contract available and hence an alternative cross hedging instrument or a macro hedge must be used instead. We examine when such situations might come up in Section 13.

### 11.3 Basis Risk

The portfolio manager must be aware that any time a direct currency hedge (i.e., a spot rate hedged against its own forward contract) is replaced with an indirect hedge (cross hedge, macro hedge), **basis risk** is brought into the portfolio. This risk reflects the fact that the price movements in the exposure being hedged and the price movements in the cross hedge instrument are not perfectly correlated, and that the correlation will change with time—and sometimes both dramatically and unexpectedly. For a minimum-variance hedge ratio, this risk is expressed as instability in the $\hat{\beta}$ coefficient estimate as more data become available.

For an example of basis risk, return to the illustration earlier of the foreign-currency asset portfolio that cross hedged a long USD/AUD exposure with a short USD/NZD exposure. It is not only possible, but highly likely, that the correlation between movements in the USD/AUD and the USD/NZD spot rates will vary with time. This varying correlation would reflect movements in the NZD/AUD spot rate. Another example of basis risk would be that the correlation between a multi-currency portfolio's domestic-currency market value and the value of currency basket derivatives being used as a macro hedge will neither be perfect nor constant.

At a minimum, this means that all cross hedges and macro hedges will have to be carefully monitored and, as needed, rebalanced to account for the drift in correlations. It also means that minimum-variance hedge ratios will have to be re-estimated as more data become available. The portfolio manager should beware that sudden, unexpected spikes in basis risk can sometimes turn what was once a minimum-variance hedge or an effective cross hedge into a position that is highly correlated with the underlying assets being hedged—the opposite of a hedge.

Basis risk is also used in the context of forward and futures contracts because the price movements of these derivatives products do not always correspond exactly with those of the underlying currency. This is because the price of the forward contract also reflects the interest rate differential between the two countries in the currency pair as well as the term to contract maturity. But with futures and forwards, the derivatives price converges to the price of the underlying as maturity approaches, which is enforced by arbitrage. This convergence is not the case with cross hedges, which potentially can go disastrously wrong with sudden movements in market risk (price correlations), credit risk, or liquidity risk.

## OPTIMAL MINIMUM-VARIANCE HEDGES

For simple foreign-currency asset portfolios, it may be possible to use the single-variable OLS regression technique to do a *joint* optimization of the hedge over both the foreign-currency value of the asset $R_{FC}$ and the foreign-currency risk exposure $R_{FX}$. This approach will reduce the variance of the all-in domestic-currency return $R_{DC}$, which is the risk that matters most to the investor, not just reducing the variance of the foreign exchange risk $R_{FX}$.

Calculating the minimum-variance hedge for the foreign exchange risk $R_{FX}$ proceeds by regressing changes in the spot rate against changes in the value of the hedging instrument (i.e., the forward contract). But as indicated in the text, performing this regression is typically unnecessary; for all intents and purposes, the minimum-variance hedge for a spot exchange rate using a forward contract will be close to 100%.

But when there is only a *single* foreign-currency asset involved, one can perform a joint optimization over both of the foreign-currency risks (i.e., both $R_{FC}$ and $R_{FX}$) by regressing changes in the domestic-currency return ($R_{DC}$) against percentage changes in the value of the hedging instrument. Basing the optimal hedge ratio on the OLS estimate for β in this regression will minimize the variance of the domestic-currency return $σ^2(R_{DC})$. The result will be a better hedge ratio than just basing the regression on $R_{FX}$ alone because this joint approach will also pick up any *correlations* between $R_{FX}$ and $R_{FC}$. (Recall from Section 4 that the asset mix in the portfolio, and hence the correlations between $R_{FX}$ and $R_{FC}$, can affect the optimal hedge ratio.) This single-variable OLS approach, however, will only work if there is a single foreign-currency asset in the portfolio.

Work by Campbell (2010) has shown that the optimal hedge ratio based jointly on movements in $R_{FC}$ and $R_{FX}$ for international *bond* portfolios is almost always close to 100%. However, the optimal hedge ratio for single-country foreign *equity* portfolios varies widely between currencies, and will depend on *both* the investor's domestic currency and the currency of the foreign investment. For example, the optimal hedge ratio for a US equity portfolio will be different for UK and eurozone-based investors; and for eurozone investors, the optimal hedge ratio for a US equity portfolio can be different from that of a Canadian equity portfolio. The study found that the optimal hedge ratio for foreign equity exposures can vary widely from 100% between countries. But as the author cautions, these optimal hedge ratios are calculated on historical data that may not be representative of future price dynamics.

### Minimum-Variance Hedge Ratio Example

Annie McYelland is an analyst at Scotland-based Kilmarnock Capital. Her firm is considering an investment in an equity index fund based on the Swiss Stock Market Index (SMI). The SMI is a market-cap weighted average of the twenty largest and most liquid Swiss companies, and captures about 85% of the overall market capitalization of the Swiss equity market.

McYelland is asked to formulate a currency-hedging strategy. Because this investment involves only one currency pair and one investment (the SMI), she decides to calculate the minimum-variance hedge ratio for the entire risk exposure, not just the currency exposure. McYelland collects 10 years of monthly data on the CHF/GBP spot exchange rate and movements in the Swiss Market Index.

McYelland notes that the GBP is the base currency in the CHF/GBP quote and that the formula for domestic-currency returns ($R_{DC}$) shown in Equation 1 requires that the domestic currency be the price currency. Accordingly, she starts by inverting the CHF/GBP quote to a GBP/CHF quote ($S_{GBP/CHF}$). Then she calculates the monthly percentage changes for this adjusted currency series (%$\Delta S_{GBP/CHF}$) as well as for the SMI (%$\Delta SMI$). This allows her to calculate the monthly returns of an unhedged investment in the SMI with these unhedged returns measured in the "domestic" currency, the GBP:

$$R_{DC} = (1 + R_{FC})(1 + R_{FX}) - 1$$

where $R_{FC}$ = %$\Delta SMI$ and $R_{FX}$ = %$\Delta S_{GBP/CHF}$. Because McYelland wants to minimize the variance of these unhedged domestic-currency returns, she calculates the minimum-variance hedge ratio with the following OLS regression:

$$R_{DC} = \alpha + \beta(\%\Delta S_{GBP/CHF}) + \varepsilon$$

The calculated regression coefficients show that $\hat{\alpha}$ = –0.21 and $\hat{\beta}$ = 1.35. McYelland interprets these results to mean that the estimated $\hat{\beta}$-coefficient is the minimum-variance hedge ratio. This conclusion makes sense because $\hat{\beta}$ represents the sensitivity of the domestic-currency return on the portfolio to percentage changes in the spot rate. In this case, the return on the SMI seems very sensitive to the appreciation of the CHF. Indeed, over the 10 years of data she collected, McYelland notices that the correlation between %$\Delta SMI$ and %$\Delta S_{GBP/CHF}$ is equal to +0.6.

On the basis of these calculations, she recommends that the minimum-variance hedge ratio for Kilmarnock Capital's exposure to the SMI be set at approximately 135%. This recommendation means that a *long* CHF1,000,000 exposure to the SMI should be hedged with a *short* position in CHF against the GBP of approximately CHF1,350,000. Because forward contracts in professional FX markets are quoted in terms of CHF/GBP for this currency pair, this would mean a *long* position in the forward contract ($F_{CHF/GBP}$)—that is, *selling* the CHF means *buying* the base currency GBP.

McYelland cautions the Investment Committee at Kilmarnock Capital that this minimum-variance hedge ratio is only approximate and must be closely monitored because it is estimated over historical data that may not be representative of future price dynamics. For example, the +0.6 correlation estimated between %$\Delta SMI$ and %$\Delta S_{GBP/CHF}$ is the 10-year *average* correlation; future market conditions may not correspond to this historical average.

## 12. CURRENCY MANAGEMENT TOOLS AND STRATEGIES: A SUMMARY

f   describe how forward contracts and FX (foreign exchange) swaps are used to adjust hedge ratios;

## Currency Management Tools and Strategies: A Summary

**g** describe trading strategies used to reduce hedging costs and modify the risk–return characteristics of a foreign-currency portfolio;

**h** describe the use of cross-hedges, macro-hedges, and minimum-variance-hedge ratios in portfolios exposed to multiple foreign currencies;

This section has covered only some of the most common currency management tools and strategies used in FX markets—there are a great many other derivatives products and strategies that have not been covered. The key points are that there are *many* different hedging and active trading strategies, there are many possible *variations* within each of these strategies, and these strategies can be used in *combination* with each other. There is no need to cover all of what would be a very large number of possible permutations and combinations. Instead, we will close this section with a key thought: Each of these many approaches to either hedging or expressing a directional view on currency movements has its advantages and disadvantages, its risks, and its costs.

As a result, there is no single "correct" approach to initiating and managing currency exposures. Instead, at the strategic level, the IPS of the portfolio sets guidelines for risk exposures, permissible hedging tools, and strategies, which will vary among investors. At the tactical level, at which the portfolio manager has discretion on risk exposures, currency strategy will depend on the manager's management style, market view, and risk tolerance. It will also depend on the manager's perceptions of the relative costs and benefit of any given strategy. Market conditions will affect the cost/benefit calculations behind the hedging decision, as movements in forward points (expected roll yield) or exchange rate volatility (option premiums) affect the expected cost of the hedge; the same hedge structure can be "rich" or "cheap" depending on current market conditions.

Reflecting all of these considerations, different managers will likely make different decisions when confronted with the same opportunity set; and each manager will likely have a good reason for their individual decision. The most important point is that the portfolio manager be aware of all the benefits, costs, and risks of the chosen strategy and be comfortable that any remaining residual currency risks in the hedge are acceptable.

To summarize the key insights of Sections 9–12—and continuing our example of a portfolio manager who is long the base currency in the P/B quote and wants to hedge that price risk—the manager needs to understand the following:

**1** Because the portfolio has a *long* exposure to base currency, to neutralize this risk the hedge will attempt to build a *short* exposure out of that currency's derivatives using some combination of forward and/or option contracts.

**2** A currency hedge is not a free good, particularly a complete hedge. The hedge cost, real or implied, will consist of some combination of lost upside potential, potentially negative roll yield (forward points at a discount or time decay on long option positions), and upfront payments of option premiums.

**3** The cost of any given hedge structure will vary depending on market conditions (i.e., forward points and implied volatility).

**4** The cost of the hedge is focused on its "core." For a manager with a long exposure to a currency, the cost of this "core" hedge will be the implicit costs of a short position in a forward contract (no upside potential, possible negative roll yield) or the upfront premium on a long position in a put option. Either of these two forms of insurance can be expensive. However, there are various cost mitigation methods that can be used alone or in combination to reduce these core hedging costs:

   **a** Writing options to gain upfront premiums.

   **b** Varying the strike prices of the options written or bought.

**c** Varying the notional amounts of the derivative contracts.

**d** Using various "exotic" features, such as knock-ins or knock-outs.

**5** There is nothing inherently wrong with any of these cost mitigation approaches—but the manager *must* understand that these invariably involve some combination of reduced upside potential and/or reduced downside protection. A reduced cost (or even a zero-cost) hedge structure is perfectly acceptable, but only as long as the portfolio manager fully understands all of the residual risks in the hedge structure and is prepared to accept and manage them.

**6** There are often "natural" hedges within the portfolio, in which some residual risk exposures are uncorrelated with each other and offer portfolio diversification effects. Cross hedges and macro hedges bring basis risk into the portfolio, which will have to be monitored and managed.

**7** There is no single or "best" way to hedge currency risk. The portfolio manager will have to perform a due diligence examination of potential hedge structures and make a rational decision on a cost/benefit basis.

### EXAMPLE 8

#### Hedging Strategies

Ireland-based Old Galway Capital runs several investment trusts for its clients. Fiona Doyle has just finished rebalancing the dynamic currency hedge for Overseas Investment Trust III, which has an IPS mandate to be fully hedged using forward contracts. Shortly after the rebalancing, Old Galway receives notice that one of its largest investors in the Overseas Investment Trust III has served notice of a large withdrawal from the fund.

Padma Bhattathiri works at Malabar Coast Capital, an India-based investment company. Her mandate is to seek out any alpha opportunities in global FX markets and aggressively manage these for speculative profit. The Reserve Bank of New Zealand (RBNZ) is New Zealand's central bank, and is scheduled to announce its policy rate decision within the week. The consensus forecast among economists is that the RBNZ will leave rates unchanged, but Bhattathiri believes that the RBNZ will surprise the markets with a rate hike.

Jasmine Khan, analyst at UK-based Brixworth & St. Ives Asset Management, has been instructed by the management team to reduce hedging costs for the firm's Aggressive Growth Fund, and that more currency exposure—both downside risk and upside potential—will have to be accepted and managed. Currently, the fund's ZAR-denominated foreign-currency asset exposures are being hedged with a 25-delta risk reversal (on the ZAR/GBP cross rate). The current ZAR/GBP spot rate is 13.1350.

Bao Zhang is a market analyst at South Korea–based Kwangju Capital, an investment firm that offers several actively managed investment trusts for its clients. She notices that the exchange rate for the Philippines Peso (PHP/USD) is increasing (PHP is depreciating) toward its 200-day moving average located in the 42.2500 area (the current spot rate is 42.2475). She mentions this to Akiko Takahashi, a portfolio manager for one of the firm's investment vehicles. Takahashi's view, based on studying economic fundamentals, is that the PHP/USD rate should continue to increase, but after speaking with Zhang she is less sure. After further conversation, Zhang and Takahashi come to the view that the PHP/USD spot rate will either break through the 42.2500 level and gain upward momentum through the 42.2600 level, or stall at the 42.2500 level and then drop down through the 42.2400 level as frustrated long positions exit the market. They decide that either scenario has equal probability over the next month.

Annie McYelland is an analyst at Scotland-based Kilmarnock Capital. The firm is considering a USD10,000,000 investment in an S&P 500 Index fund. McYelland is asked to calculate the minimum-variance hedge ratio. She collects the following statistics based on 10 years of monthly data:

| $s(\%\Delta S_{GBP/USD})$ | $\sigma(R_{DC})$ | $\rho(R_{DC};\%\Delta S_{GBP/USD})$ |
|---|---|---|
| 2.7% | 4.4% | 0.2 |

*Source:* Data are from Bloomberg.

1. Given the sudden liquidity need announced, Doyle's *best* course of action with regard to the currency hedge is to:
   A  do nothing.
   B  reduce the hedge ratio.
   C  over-hedge by using currency options.

2. Given her market view, Bhattathiri would *most likely* choose which of the following long positions?
   A  5-delta put option on NZD/AUD
   B  10-delta put option on USD/NZD
   C  Put spread on JPY/NZD using 10-delta and 25-delta options

3. Among the following, replacing the current risk reversal hedge with a long position in which of the following would *best* meet Khan's instructions? (All use the ZAR/GBP.)
   A  10-delta risk reversal
   B  Put option with a 13.1300 strike
   C  Call option with a 13.1350 strike

4. Which of the following positions would *best* implement Zhang's and Takahashi's market view?
   A  Long a 42.2450 put and long a 42.2550 call
   B  Long a 42.2450 put and short a 42.2400 put
   C  Long a 42.2450 put and short a 42.2550 call

5. Which of the following positions would *best* implement Kilmarnock Capital's minimum-variance hedge?
   A  Long a USD/GBP forward contract with a notional size of USD1.2 million
   B  Long a USD/GBP forward contract with a notional size of USD3.3 million
   C  Short a USD/GBP forward contract with a notional size of USD2.0 million

## Solution to 1:

A is correct. After rebalancing, the Overseas Investment Trust III is fully hedged; currency risk is at a minimum, which is desirable if liquidity needs have increased. Choices B and C are incorrect because they increase the currency risk exposures.

## Solution to 2:

A is correct. The surprise rate hike should cause the NZD to appreciate against most currencies. This appreciation would mean a depreciation of the NZD/AUD rate, which a put option can profit from. A 5-delta option is deep-OTM, but the price reaction on the option premiums will be more extreme than a higher-delta option. That is to say, the *percentage* change in the premiums for a 5-delta option for a given percentage change in the spot exchange rate will be higher than the percentage change in premiums for a 25-delta option. In a sense, a very low delta option is like a highly leveraged lottery ticket on the event occurring. With a surprise rate hike, the odds would swing in Bhattathiri's favor. Choice B is incorrect because the price reaction in the USD/NZD spot rate after the surprise rate hike would likely cause the NZD to appreciate; so Bhattathiri would want a call option on the USD/NZD currency pair. Choice C is incorrect because an appreciation of the NZD after the surprise rate hike would best be captured by a call spread on the JPY/NZD rate, which will likely increase (the NZD is the base currency).

## Solution to 3:

A is correct. Moving to a 10-delta risk reversal will be cheaper (these options are deeper-OTM than 25-delta options) and widen the bands in the corridor being created for the ZAR/GBP rate. Choice B is incorrect because a long put provides no protection against an upside movement in the ZAR/GBP rate, which Brixworth & St. Ives is trying to hedge (recall that the fund is long ZAR in its foreign-currency asset exposure and hence needs to sell ZAR/buy GBP to hedge). Also, if Brixworth & St. Ives exercises the option, they would "put" GBP to the counterparty at the strike price and receive ZAR in return. Although this option position may be considered profitable in its own right, it nonetheless causes the firm to double-up its ZAR exposure. Choice C is incorrect because although an ATM call option on ZAR/GBP will provide complete hedge protection, it will be expensive and clearly more expensive than the current 25-delta risk reversal.

## Solution to 4:

A is correct. Zhang's and Takahashi's market view is that, over the next month, a move in PHP/USD to either 42.2400 or 42.2600 is equally likely. A strangle would express this view of heightened volatility but without a directional bias, and would require a long put and a long call positions. Choice B is incorrect because it is a put spread; it will profit by a move in PHP/USD between 42.2450 and 42.2400. If it moves below 42.2400 the short put gets exercised by the counterparty and neutralizes the long put. Although less costly than an outright long put position, this structure is not positioned to profit from a move higher in PHP/USD. Choice C is incorrect because it is a short risk reversal position. It provides relatively cheap protection for a down-move in PHP/USD but is not positioned to profit from an up-move in PHP/USD.

## Solution to 5:

B is correct. The formula for the minimum-variance hedge ratio ($h$) is:

$$h = \rho(R_{DC}; R_{FX}) \times \left[ \frac{\sigma(R_{DC})}{\sigma(R_{FX})} \right]$$

After inputting the data from the table, this equation solves to 0.33. This means that for a USD10 million investment in the S&P 500 (long position), Kilmarnock Capital would want to be *short* approximately USD3.3 million in a forward contract. Because the standard market quote for this currency pair is USD/GBP, to be short the USD means one would have to buy the GBP; that is, a

> *long* position in a USD/GBP forward contract. Choice A is incorrect because it inverts the ratio in the formula. Choice C is incorrect because it shows a short position in the USD/GBP forward, and because it only uses the correlation to set the contract size.

# CURRENCY MANAGEMENT FOR EMERGING MARKET CURRENCIES

**i.** discuss challenges for managing emerging market currency exposures.

Most of the material in this reading has focused on what might be described as the major currencies, such as the EUR, GBP, or JPY. This focus is not a coincidence: The vast majority of daily flow in global FX markets is accounted for by the top half dozen currencies. Moreover, the vast majority of investable assets globally, as measured by market capitalization, are denominated in the major currencies. Nonetheless, more investors are looking at emerging markets, as well as "frontier markets," for potential investment opportunities. And many developing economies are beginning to emerge as major forces in the global economy. In the following sections, we survey the challenges for currency management and the use of non-deliverable forwards as one tool to address them.

## 13.1 Special Considerations in Managing Emerging Market Currency Exposures

Managing emerging market currency exposure involves unique challenges. Perhaps the two most important considerations are (1) higher trading costs than the major currencies under "normal" market conditions, and (2) the increased likelihood of extreme market events and severe illiquidity under stressed market conditions.

Many emerging market currencies are thinly traded, causing higher transaction costs (bid–offer spreads). There may also be fewer derivatives products to choose from, especially exchange-traded products. Although many global investment banks will quote spot rates and OTC derivatives for almost any conceivable currency pair, many of these are often seen as "specialty" products and often come with relatively high mark-ups. This mark-up increases trading and hedging costs. (In addition, the underlying foreign-currency asset in emerging markets can be illiquid and lack the full array of derivatives products.)

These higher currency trading costs would especially be the case for "crosses" in these currency pairs. For example, there is no reason why an investor in Chile (which uses the Chilean peso, currency code CLP) could not have an investment in assets denominated in the Thai baht (THB). But the CLP/THB cross is likely to be very thinly traded; there simply are not enough trade or capital flows between these two countries. Typically, any trade between these two currencies would go through a major intermediary currency, usually the USD. Hence, the trade would be broken into two legs: a trade in the CLP/USD pair and another in the THB/USD pair. These trades might go through different traders or trading desks at the same bank; or perhaps one leg of the trade would be done at one bank and the other leg through a different bank. There may also be time zone issues affecting liquidity; one leg of the trade may be relatively liquid at the same time as the other leg of the trade may be more thinly traded. The reason is because liquidity in most emerging market currencies is typically deepest in their domestic time zones. In any event, there are two bid–offer spreads—one for each leg of the trade—to be covered. This is often the case for many of the cross-rate currency pairs among developed market currencies as well. However, the bid–offer spreads are usually tighter for major currency pairs.

The liquidity issue is especially important when trades in these less-liquid currencies get "crowded," for example, through an excessive build-up of carry trades or through a fad-like popularity among investors for investing in a particular region or trading theme. Trades can be much easier to gradually enter into than to quickly exit, particularly under stressed market conditions. For example, after a long period of slow build-up, carry trades into these currencies can occasionally be subject to panicked unwinds as market conditions suddenly turn. This situation typically causes market liquidity to evaporate and leaves traders locked into positions that continue to accumulate losses.

The investment return probability distributions for currency (and other) trades subject to such relatively frequent extreme events have fatter tails than the normal distribution as well as a pronounced negative skew. Risk measurement and control tools (such as value at risk, or VaR) that depend on normal distributions can be misleading under these circumstances and greatly understate the risks the portfolio is actually exposed to. Many investment performance measures are also based on the normal distribution. Historical investment performance measured by such indexes as the Sharpe ratio can look very attractive during times of relative tranquility; but this seeming outperformance can disappear into deep losses faster than most investors can react (investors typically do a poor job of timing crises). As mentioned in the prior section on volatility trading, price volatility in financial markets is very cyclical and implied volatility can be subject to sharp spikes. These volatility spikes can severely affect both option prices and hedging strategies based on options. Even if the initial option protection is in place, it will eventually have to be rolled as options expire—but then at much higher prices for the option buyer.

The occurrence of currency crises can also affect hedging strategies based on forward contracts. Recall that hedging a long exposure to a foreign currency typically involves selling the foreign currency forward. However, when currencies are under severe downward pressure, central banks often react by hiking the policy rate to support the domestic currency. But recall that the higher interest rates go in a country, then, all else equal, the deeper the forward discount for its currency (enforced by the arbitrage conditions of covered interest rate parity). Having to sell the currency forward at increasingly deep discounts will cause losses through negative roll yield and undermine the cost effectiveness of the hedging program.

Extreme price movements in financial markets can also undermine many hedging strategies based on presumed diversification. Crises not only affect the volatility in asset prices but also their correlations, primarily through "contagion" effects. The history of financial markets (circa 2012) has been characterized by a "risk-on, risk-off" environment dominated by swings in investor sentiment between speculative enthusiasm and pronounced flight-to-safety flows. In the process, there is often little differentiation between individual currencies, which tend to get traded together in broader baskets (such as "haven currencies"—USD, JPY, and CHF—and "commodity currencies"—AUD, NZD, and ZAR). Investors who may have believed that they had diversified their portfolio through a broad array of exposures in emerging markets may find instead in crises that they doubled-up their currency exposures. (Likewise, there can be correlated and extreme movements in the underlying assets of these foreign-currency exposures.)

Another potential factor affecting currency management in these "exotic" markets is government involvement in setting the exchange rate through such measures as foreign exchange market intervention, capital controls, and pegged (or at least tightly managed) exchange rates. These measures too can lead to occasional extreme events in markets; for example, when central banks intervene or when currency pegs change

# Currency Management for Emerging Market Currencies

or get broken. Short-term stability in these government-influenced markets can lull traders into a false sense of overconfidence and over-positioning. When currency pegs break, the break can happen quickly. Assuming that investment returns will be normally distributed according to parameters estimated on recent historical data, or that correlation factors and liquidity will not change suddenly, can be lethal.

It bears noting that currency crises and government involvement in FX markets is not limited to emerging market currencies, but often occur among the major currencies as well. The central banks of major currencies will, on occasion, intervene in their own currencies or use other polices (such as sharp movements in policy rates) to influence exchange rate levels. These too can lead to extreme events in currency markets.

## 13.2 Non-Deliverable Forwards

Currencies of many emerging market countries trade with some form of capital controls. Where capital controls exist and delivery in the controlled currency is limited by the local government, it is often possible to use what are known as **non-deliverable forwards** (NDFs). These are similar to regular forward contracts, but they are cash settled (in the non-controlled currency of the currency pair) rather than physically settled (the controlled currency is neither delivered nor received). The non-controlled currency for NDFs is usually the USD or some other major currency. A partial list of some of the most important currencies with NDFs would include the Chinese yuan (CNY), Korean won (KRW), Russian ruble (RUB), Indian rupee (INR), and Brazilian real (BRL). The NDF is essentially a cash-settled "bet" on the movement in the spot rate of these currencies.

For example, a trader could enter into a long position in a three-month NDF for the BRL/USD. Note that the BRL—the currency with capital controls—is the price currency and the base currency, the USD, is the currency that settlement of the NDF will be made in. Assume that the current all-in rate for the NDF is 2.0280 and the trader uses an NDF with a notional size of USD1,000,000. Suppose that three months later the BRL/USD spot rate is 2.0300 and the trader closes out the existing NDF contract with an equal and offsetting spot transaction at this rate. Settlement proceeds by noting that the USD amounts net to zero (USD1,000,000 both bought and sold on settlement date), so the net cash flow generated would normally be in BRL if this was an ordinary forward contract. The net cash flow to the long position in this case would be calculated as

$(2.0300 - 2.0280) \times 1,000,000 = BRL2,000$

But with an NDF, there is no delivery in the controlled currency (hence the name *non-deliverable* forward). Settlement must be in USD, so this BRL amount is converted to USD at the then-current spot rate of 2.0300. This leads to a USD cash inflow for the long position in the NDF of

$BRL2,000 \div 2.0300 \text{ BRL/USD} = USD985.22$

The credit risk of an NDF is typically lower than for the outright forward because the principal sums in the NDF do not move, unlike with an outright "vanilla" forward contract. For example, in the illustration the cash pay-off to the "bet" was the relatively small amount of USD985.22—there was no delivery of USD1,000,000 against receipt of BRL2,028,000. Conversely, as noted previously, NDFs exist because of some form of government involvement in foreign exchange markets. Sudden changes in government policy can lead to sharp movements in spot and NDF rates, often reversing any investment gains earned during long periods of seeming (but artificial) market calm. The implicit market risk of the NDF embodies an element of "tail risk."

Finally, we note that when capital controls exist, the free cross-border flow of capital that enforces the arbitrage condition underlying covered interest rate parity no longer functions consistently. Therefore, the pricing on NDFs need not be exactly in accord with the covered interest rate parity theorem. Instead, NDF pricing will reflect the individual supply and demand conditions (and risk premia) in the offshore market, which need not be the same as the onshore market of the specific emerging market country. Some of the most active participants in the NDF market are offshore hedge funds and proprietary traders making directional bets on the emerging market currency, rather than corporate or institutional portfolio managers hedging currency exposures. Volatility in the net speculative demand for emerging market exposure can affect the level of forward points. We also note that the type and strictness of capital controls can vary among emerging markets; hence, the need for knowledge of local market regulations is another factor influencing currency risk management in these markets.

## SUMMARY

In this reading, we have examined the basic principles of managing foreign exchange risk within the broader investment process. International financial markets create a wide range of opportunities for investors, but they also create the need to recognize, measure, and control exchange rate risk. The management of this risk starts with setting the overall mandate for the portfolio, encoding the investors' investment objectives and constraints into the investment policy statement and providing strategic guidance on how currency risk will be managed in the portfolio. It extends to tactical positioning when portfolio managers translate market views into specific trading strategies within the overall risk management guidelines set by the IPS. We have examined some of these trading strategies, and how a range of portfolio management tools—positions in spot, forward, option, and FX swap contracts—can be used either to hedge away currency risk, or to express a market opinion on future exchange rate movements.

What we have emphasized throughout this reading is that there is no simple or single answer for the "best" currency management strategies. Different investors will have different strategic mandates (IPS), and different portfolio managers will have different market opinions and risk tolerances. There is a near-infinite number of possible currency trading strategies, each with its own benefits, costs, and risks. Currency risk management—both at the strategic and tactical levels—means having to manage the trade-offs between all of these various considerations.

Some of the main points covered in this reading are as follows:

- In professional FX markets, currencies are identified by standard three-letter codes, and quoted in terms of a price and a base currency (P/B).

- The spot exchange rate is typically for $T + 2$ delivery, and forward rates are for delivery for later periods. Both spot and forward rates are quoted in terms of a bid–offer price. Forward rates are quoted in terms of the spot rate plus forward points.

- An FX swap is a simultaneous spot and forward transaction; one leg of the swap is buying the base currency and the other is selling it. FX swaps are used to renew outstanding forward contracts once they mature, to "roll them forward."

# Summary

- The domestic-currency return on foreign-currency assets can be broken into the foreign-currency asset return and the return on the foreign currency (the percentage appreciation or depreciation of the foreign currency against the domestic currency). These two components of the domestic-currency return are multiplicative.
- When there are several foreign-currency assets, the portfolio domestic-currency return is the weighted average of the individual domestic-currency returns (i.e., using the portfolio weights, which should sum to one)
- The risk of domestic-currency returns (its standard deviation) can be approximated by using a variance formula that recognizes the individual variances and covariances (correlations) among the foreign-currency asset returns and exchange rate movements.
- The calculation of the domestic-currency risk involves a large number of variables that must be estimated: the risks and correlations between all of the foreign-currency asset returns and their exchange rate risks.
- Guidance on where to target the portfolio along the risk spectrum is part of the IPS, which makes this a *strategic* decision based on the investment goals and constraints of the beneficial owners of the portfolio.
- If the IPS allows currency risk in the portfolio, the amount of desired currency exposure will depend on both portfolio diversification considerations and cost considerations.
  - Views on the diversifying effects of foreign-currency exposures depend on the time horizon involved, the type of foreign-currency asset, and market conditions.
  - Cost considerations also affect the hedging decision. Hedging is not free: It has both direct transactional costs as well as opportunity costs (the potential for favorable outcomes is foregone). Cost considerations make a perfect hedge difficult to maintain.
- Currency management strategies can be located along a spectrum stretching from:
  - passive, rules-based, complete hedging of currency exposures;
  - discretionary hedging, which allows the portfolio manager some latitude on managing currency exposures;
  - active currency management, which seeks out currency risk in order to manage it for profit; and to
  - currency overlay programs that aggressively manage currency "alpha."
- There are a variety of methods for forming market views.
  - The use of macroeconomic fundamentals to predict future currency movements is based on estimating the "fair value" for a currency with the expectation that spot rates will eventually converge on this equilibrium value.
  - Technical market indicators assume that, based on market psychology, historical price patterns in the data have a tendency to repeat. Technical indicators can be used to predict support and resistance levels in the market, as well as to confirm market trends and turning points.
  - The carry trade is based on violations of uncovered interest rate parity, and is also based on selling low-yield currencies in order to invest in high-yield currencies. This approach is equivalent to trading the forward rate bias, which means selling currencies trading at a forward premium and buying currencies trading at a forward discount.

- Volatility trading uses the option market to express views on the distribution of future exchange rates, not their levels.
■ Passive hedging will typically use forward contracts (rather than futures contracts) because they are more flexible. However, currency futures contracts are an option for smaller trading sizes and are frequently used in private wealth management.
■ Forward contracts have the possibility of negative roll yield (the forward points embedded in the forward price can work for or against the hedge). The portfolio manager will have to balance the advantages and costs of hedging with forward contracts.
■ Foreign-currency options can reduce opportunity costs (they allow the upside potential for favorable foreign-currency movements). However, the upfront option premiums must be paid.
■ There are a variety of means to reduce the cost of the hedging with either forward or option contracts, but these cost-reduction measures always involve some combination of less downside protection and/or less upside potential.
■ Hedging multiple foreign currencies uses the same tools and strategies used in hedging a single foreign-currency exposure; except now the correlation between residual currency exposures in the portfolio should be considered.
■ Cross hedges introduce basis risk into the portfolio, which is the risk that the correlation between exposure and its cross hedging instrument may change in unexpected ways. Forward contracts typically have very little basis risk compared with movements in the underlying spot rate.
■ The number of trading strategies that can be used, for hedging or speculative purposes, either for a single foreign currency or multiple foreign currencies, is near infinite. The manager must assess the costs, benefits, and risks of each in the context of the investment goals and constraints of the portfolio. There is no single "correct" approach.

# REFERENCES

Bank for International Settlements. 2013. "Triennial Central Bank Survey of Foreign Exchange and Derivatives Market Activity."

Campbell, John Y. 2010. "Global Currency Hedging: What Role Should Foreign Currency Play in a Diversified Investment Portfolio?" *CFA Institute Conference Proceedings Quarterly*, vol. 27, no. 4 (December):8–18.

Campbell, John Y., Karine Serfaty-de Medeiros, and Luis M. Viceira. 2007. "Global Currency Hedging," NBER Working Paper 13088 (May).

Darnell, R. Max. 2004. "Currency Strategies to Enhance Returns." In *Fixed-Income Tools for Enhancing Return and Meeting Client Objectives*. Charlottesville, VA: Association for Investment Management and Research.

Froot, Kenneth A. 1993. "Currency Hedging Over Long Horizons." NBER Working Paper 4355 (April): www.people.hbs.edu/kfroot/oldwebsite/cvpaperlinks/currency_hedging.pdf.

Hnatkovska, Viktoria, and Martin Evans. 2005. "International Capital Flows in a World of Greater Financial Integration." NBER Working Paper 11701 (October).

Kritzman, Mark P. 1999. "The Forward-Rate Bias." In *Currency Risk in Investment Portfolios*. Charlottesville, VA: Association for Investment Management and Research.

Martini, Giulio. 2010. "The Continuum from Passive to Active Currency Management." *CFA Institute Conference Proceedings Quarterly*, vol. 27, no. 1 (March):1–11.

Michenaud, Sébastien, and Bruno Solnik. 2008. "Applying Regret Theory to Investment Choices: Currency Hedging Decisions." *Journal of International Money and Finance*, vol. 27, no. 5:677–694.

Rosenberg, Michael R. 2002. *Deutsche Bank Guide to Exchange-Rate Determination*. London: Irwin Professional Publishing (May).

Rosenberg, Michael R., and William A. Barker. 2017. "Currency Exchange Rates: Understanding Equilibrium Value." CFA Program Curriculum, Level II.

Sine, Barry M., and Robert A. Strong. 2012. "Technical Analysis." CFA Program Curriculum, Level I.

US Department of the Treasury. 2007. "Semiannual Report on International Economic and Exchange Rate Policies, Appendix I." (December).

# PRACTICE PROBLEMS

## The following information relates to Questions 1–9

Kamala Gupta, a currency management consultant, is hired to evaluate the performance of two portfolios. Portfolio A and Portfolio B are managed in the United States and performance is measured in terms of the US dollar (USD). Portfolio A consists of British pound (GBP) denominated bonds and Portfolio B holds euro (EUR) denominated bonds.

Gupta calculates a 19.5% domestic-currency return for Portfolio A and 0% domestic-currency return for Portfolio B.

1. **Analyze** the movement of the USD against the foreign currency for Portfolio A. **Justify** your choice.

**Template for Question 1**

| Asset | Foreign-Currency Portfolio Return | USD Relative to Foreign-Currency (circle one) |
|---|---|---|
| Portfolio A | 15% | appreciated / depreciated |
| Justification | | |

2. **Analyze** the foreign-currency return for Portfolio B. **Justify** your choice.

**Template for Question 2**

| Asset | Percentage Movement in the Spot Exchange Rate | Foreign-Currency Portfolio Return (circle one) |
|---|---|---|
| Portfolio B | EUR appreciated 5% against the USD | positive / negative |

*(continued)*

| (Continued) |
| --- |
| Justification |

The fund manager of Portfolio B is evaluating an internally-managed 100% foreign-currency hedged strategy.

3. **Discuss** *two* forms of trading costs associated with this currency management strategy.

Gupta tells the fund manager of Portfolio B:

> "We need to seriously consider the potential costs associated with favorable currency rate movements, given that a 100% hedge-ratio strategy is being applied to this portfolio."

4. **Explain** Gupta's statement in light of the strategic choices in currency management available to the portfolio manager.

The investment policy statement (IPS) for Portfolio A provides the manager with discretionary authority to take directional views on future currency movements. The fund manager believes the foreign currency assets of the portfolio could be fully hedged internally. However, the manager also believes existing firm personnel lack the expertise to actively manage foreign-currency movements to generate currency alpha.

5. **Recommend** a solution that will provide the fund manager the opportunity to earn currency alpha through active foreign exchange management.

Gupta and the fund manager of Portfolio A discuss the differences among several active currency management methods.

6. **Evaluate** each statement independently and select the active currency approach it *best* describes. **Justify** each choice.

**Template for Question 6**

| Gupta's Statements | Active Currency Approach (circle one) | Justification |
| --- | --- | --- |
| "Many traders believe that it is not necessary to examine factors like the current account deficit, inflation, and interest rates because current exchange rates already reflect the market view on how these factors will affect future exchange rates." | carry trade<br>technical analysis<br>economic fundamental | |

# Practice Problems

### (Continued)

| Gupta's Statements | Active Currency Approach (circle one) | Justification |
|---|---|---|
| "The six-month interest rate in India is 8% compared to 1% in the United States. This presents a yield pick-up opportunity." | carry trade<br><br>technical analysis<br><br>economic fundamental | |
| "The currency overlay manager will estimate the fair value of the currencies with the expectation that observed spot rates will converge to long-run equilibrium values described by parity conditions." | carry trade<br><br>technical analysis<br><br>economic fundamental | |

## The following information is used for Question 7

Gupta interviews a currency overlay manager on behalf of Portfolio A. The foreign currency overlay manager describes volatility-based trading, compares volatility-based trading strategies and explains how the firm uses currency options to establish positions in the foreign exchange market. The overlay manager states:

Statement 1    "Given the current stability in financial markets, several traders at our firm take advantage of the fact that most options expire out-of-the money and therefore are net-short volatility."

Statement 2    "Traders that want to minimize the impact of unanticipated price volatility are net-long volatility."

7. **Compare** Statement 1 and Statement 2 and **identify** which *best* explains the view of a speculative volatility trader and which best explains the view of a hedger of volatility. **Justify** your response.

## The following information is used for Questions 8 and 9

The fund manager of Portfolio B believes that setting up a full currency hedge requires a simple matching of the *current* market value of the foreign-currency exposure in the portfolio with an equal and offsetting position in a forward contract.

8 **Explain** how the hedge, as described by the fund manager, will eventually expose the portfolio to currency risk.

9 **Recommend** an alternative hedging strategy that will keep the hedge ratio close to the target hedge ratio. **Identify** the main disadvantage of implementing such a strategy.

## The following information relates to Questions 10–15

Guten Investments GmbH, based in Germany and using the EUR as its reporting currency, is an asset management firm providing investment services for local high net worth and institutional investors seeking international exposures. The firm invests in the Swiss, UK, and US markets, after conducting fundamental research in order to select individual investments. Exhibit 1 presents recent information for exchange rates in these foreign markets.

**Exhibit 1  Exchange Rate Data**

|  | One Year Ago | Today |
|---|---|---|
| Euro-dollar (USD/EUR)* | 1.2730 | 1.2950 |
| Euro-sterling (GBP/EUR) | 0.7945 | 0.8050 |
| Euro-Swiss (CHF/EUR) | 1.2175 | 1.2080 |

* The amount of USD required to buy one EUR

In prior years, the correlation between movements in the foreign-currency asset returns for the USD-denominated assets and movements in the exchange rate was estimated to be +0.50. After analyzing global financial markets, Konstanze Ostermann, a portfolio manager at Guten Investments, now expects that this correlation will increase to +0.80, although her forecast for foreign-currency asset returns is unchanged.

Ostermann believes that currency markets are efficient and hence that long-run gains cannot be achieved from active currency management, especially after netting out management and transaction costs. She uses this philosophy to guide hedging decisions for her discretionary accounts, unless instructed otherwise by the client.

Ostermann is aware, however, that some investors hold an alternative view on the merits of active currency management. Accordingly, their portfolios have different investment guidelines. For these accounts, Guten Investments employs a currency specialist firm, Umlauf Management, to provide currency overlay programs specific to each client's investment objectives. For most hedging strategies, Umlauf Management develops a market view based on underlying fundamentals in exchange rates. However,

# Practice Problems

when directed by clients, Umlauf Management uses options and a variety of trading strategies to unbundle all of the various risk factors (the "Greeks") and trade them separately.

Ostermann conducts an annual review for three of her clients and gathers the summary information presented in Exhibit 2.

| Exhibit 2 | Select Clients at Guten Investments |
|---|---|
| **Client** | **Currency Management Objectives** |
| **Adele Kastner** – A high net worth individual with a low risk tolerance. | Keep the portfolio's currency exposures close, if not equal to, the benchmark so that the domestic-currency return is equal to the foreign-currency return. |
| **Braunt Pensionskasse** – A large private-company pension fund with a moderate risk tolerance. | Limited discretion which allows the actual portfolio currency risk exposures to vary plus-or-minus 5% from the neutral position. |
| **Franz Trading GmbH** – An exporting company with a high risk tolerance. | Discretion with respect to currency exposure is allowed in order to add alpha to the portfolio. |

10 Based on Exhibit 1, the domestic-currency return over the last year (measured in EUR terms) was *higher* than the foreign-currency return for:
   A  USD-denominated assets.
   B  GBP-denominated assets.
   C  CHF-denominated assets.

11 Based on Ostermann's correlation forecast, the expected domestic-currency return (measured in EUR terms) on USD-denominated assets will *most* likely:
   A  increase.
   B  decrease.
   C  remain unchanged.

12 Based on Ostermann's views regarding active currency management, the percentage of currency exposure in her discretionary accounts that is hedged is *most likely*:
   A  0%.
   B  50%.
   C  100%.

13 The active currency management approach that Umlauf Management is *least* likely to employ is based on:
   A  volatility trading.
   B  technical analysis.
   C  economic fundamentals.

14 Based on Exhibit 2, the currency overlay program *most* appropriate for Braunt Pensionskasse would:
   A  be fully passive.
   B  allow limited directional views.

**C** actively manage foreign exchange as an asset class.

15 Based on Exhibit 2, the client *most likely* to benefit from the introduction of an additional overlay manager is:
   **A** Adele Kastner.
   **B** Braunt Pensionskasse.
   **C** Franz Trading GmbH.

# The following information relates to Questions 16–19

Li Jiang is an international economist operating a subscription website through which she offers financial advice on currency issues to retail investors. One morning she receives four subscriber e-mails seeking guidance.

Subscriber 1  "As a French national now working in the United States, I hold US dollar-denominated assets currently valued at USD 700,000. The USD/EUR exchange rate has been quite volatile and now appears oversold based on historical price trends. With my American job ending soon, I will return to Europe. I want to protect the value of my USD holdings, measured in EUR terms, before I repatriate these funds back to France. To reduce my currency exposure I am going to use currency futures contracts. Can you explain the factors most relevant to implementing this strategy?"

Subscriber 2  "I have observed that many of the overseas markets for Korean export goods are slowing, while the United States is experiencing a rise in exports. Both trends can combine to possibly affect the value of the won (KRW) relative to the US dollar. As a result, I am considering a speculative currency trade on the KRW/USD exchange rate. I also expect the volatility in this exchange rate to increase."

Subscriber 3  "India has relatively high interest rates compared to the United States and my market view is that this situation is likely to persist. As a retail investor actively trading currencies, I am considering borrowing in USD and converting to the Indian rupee (INR). I then intend to invest these funds in INR-denominated bonds, but without using a currency hedge."

Subscriber 4  "I was wondering if trading in emerging market currencies provides the more opportunities for superior returns through active management than trading in Developed Market currencies."

16 For Subscriber 1, the *most* significant factor to consider would be:
   **A** margin requirements.
   **B** transaction costs of using futures contracts.
   **C** different quoting conventions for future contracts.

17 For Subscriber 2, and assuming all of the choices relate to the KRW/USD exchange rate, the *best* way to implement the trading strategy would be to:
   **A** write a straddle.
   **B** buy a put option.
   **C** use a long NDF position.

18 Which of the following market developments would be *most* favorable for Subscriber 3's trading plan?

A   A narrower interest rate differential.

   B   A higher forward premium for INR/USD.

   C   Higher volatility in INR/USD spot rate movements.

19 Jiang's *best* response to Subscriber 4 would be that active trading in trading in emerging market currencies:

   A   typically leads to return distributions that are positively skewed.

   B   should not lead to higher returns because FX markets are efficient.

   C   often leads to higher returns through carry trades, but comes with higher risks and trading costs.

## The following information relates to Questions 20–23

Rika Björk runs the currency overlay program at a large Scandinavian investment fund, which uses the Swedish krona (SEK) as its reporting currency. She is managing the fund's exposure to GBP-denominated assets, which are currently hedged with a GBP 100,000,000 forward contract (on the SEK/GBP cross rate, which is currently at 10.6875 spot). The maturity for the forward contract is December 1, which is still several months away. However, since the contract was initiated the value of the fund's assets has declined by GBP 7,000,000. As a result, Björk wants to rebalance the hedge immediately.

Next Björk turns her attention to the fund's Swiss franc (CHF) exposures. In order to maintain some profit potential Björk wants to hedge the exposure using a currency option, but at the same time, she wants to reduce hedging costs. She believes that there is limited upside for the SEK/CHF cross rate.

Björk then examines the fund's EUR-denominated exposures. Due to recent monetary tightening by the Riksbank (the Swedish central bank) forward points for the SEK/EUR rate have swung to a premium. The fund's EUR-denominated exposures are hedged with forward contracts.

Finally Björk turns her attention to the fund's currency exposures in several emerging markets. The fund has large positions in several Latin American bond markets, but Björk does not feel that there is sufficient liquidity in the related foreign exchange derivatives to easily hedge the fund's Latin American bond markets exposures. However, the exchange rates for these countries, measured against the SEK, are correlated with the MXN/SEK exchange rate. (The MXN is the Mexican peso, which is considered to be among the most liquid Latin American currencies). Björk considers using forward positions in the MXN to cross-hedge the fund's Latin American currency exposures.

20 To rebalance the SEK/GBP hedge, and assuming all instruments are based on SEK/GBP, Björk would buy:

   A   GBP 7,000,000 spot.

   B   GBP 7,000,000 forward to December 1.

   C   SEK 74,812,500 forward to December 1.

21 Given her investment goals and market view, and assuming all options are based on SEK/CHF, the *best* strategy for Björk to manage the fund's CHF exposure would be to buy an:

   A   ATM call option.

   B   ITM call option and write an OTM call option.

   C   OTM put option and write an OTM call option.

**22** Given the recent movement in the forward premium for the SEK/EUR rate, Björk can expect that the hedge will experience higher:

　**A** basis risk.

　**B** roll yield.

　**C** premia income.

**23** The *most* important risk to Björk's Latin American currency hedge would be changes in:

　**A** forward points.

　**B** exchange rate volatility.

　**C** cross-currency correlations.

## The following information relates to Question 24

Kalila Al-Khalili has been hired as a consultant to a Middle Eastern sovereign wealth fund. The fund's oversight committee has asked her to examine the fund's financial characteristics and recommend an appropriate currency management strategy given the fund's Investment Policy Statement. After a thorough study of the fund and its finances, Al-Khalili reaches the following conclusions:

- The fund's mandate is focused on the long-term development of the country, and the royal family (who are very influential on the fund's oversight committee) are prepared to take a long-term perspective on the fund's investments.
- The fund's strategic asset allocation is tilted towards equity rather than fixed-income assets.
- Both its fixed-income and equity portfolios have a sizeable exposure to emerging market assets.
- Currently, about 90% of exchange rate exposures are hedged although the IPS allows a range of hedge ratios.
- Liquidity needs of the fund are minimal, since the government is running a balanced budget and is unlikely to need to dip into the fund in the near term to cover fiscal deficits. Indeed, the expected lifetime of country's large oil reserves has been greatly extended by recent discoveries, and substantial oil royalties are expected to persist into the future.

**24** Based on her investigation, Al-Khalili would *most* likely recommend:

　**A** active currency management.

　**B** a hedging ratio closer to 100%.

　**C** a narrow discretionary band for currency exposures.

## The following information relates to Questions 25–27

Mason Darden is an adviser at Colgate & McIntire (C&M), managing large-cap global equity separate accounts. C&M's investment process restricts portfolio positions to companies based in the United States, Japan, and the eurozone. All C&M clients are US-domiciled, with client reporting in US dollars.

# Practice Problems

Darden manages Ravi Bhatt's account, which had a total (US dollar) return of 7.0% last year. Darden must assess the contribution of foreign currency to the account's total return. Exhibit 1 summarizes the account's geographic portfolio weights, asset returns, and currency returns for last year.

### Exhibit 1  Performance Data for Bhatt's Portfolio Last Year

| Geography | Portfolio Weight | Asset Return | Currency Return |
|---|---|---|---|
| United States | 50% | 10.0% | NA |
| Eurozone | 25% | 5.0% | 2.0% |
| Japan | 25% | −3.0% | 4.0% |
| Total | 100% | | |

**25** **Calculate** the contribution of foreign currency to the Bhatt account's total return. **Show** your calculations.

Darden meets with Bhatt and learns that Bhatt will be moving back to his home country of India next month to resume working as a commodity trader. Bhatt is concerned about a possible US recession. His investment policy statement (IPS) allows for flexibility in managing currency risk. Overall returns can be enhanced by capturing opportunities between the US dollar and the Indian rupee (INR) within a range of plus or minus 25% from the neutral position using forward contracts on the currency pair. C&M has a currency overlay team that can appropriately manage currency risk for Bhatt's portfolio.

**26** **Determine** the *most appropriate* currency management strategy for Bhatt. **Justify** your response.

**Determine** the *most appropriate* currency management strategy for Bhatt. (Circle one.)

| Passive hedging | Discretionary hedging | Active currency management |
|---|---|---|
| | | |

**Justify** your response.

Following analysis of Indian economic fundamentals, C&M's currency team expects continued stability in interest rate and inflation rate differentials between the United States and India. C&M's currency team strongly believes the US dollar will appreciate relative to the Indian rupee.

C&M would like to exploit the perceived alpha opportunity using forward contracts on the USD10,000,000 Bhatt portfolio.

**27** **Recommend** the trading strategy C&M should implement. **Justify** your response.

## The following information relates to Questions 28–29

Renita Murimi is a currency overlay manager and market technician who serves institutional investors seeking to address currency-specific risks associated with investing in international assets. Her firm also provides volatility overlay programs. She is developing a volatility-based strategy for Emil Konev, a hedge fund manager focused on option trading. Konev seeks to implement an "FX as an asset class" approach distinct to his portfolio to realize speculative gains and believes the long-term strength of the US dollar is peaking.

28  **Describe** how a volatility-based strategy for Konev would *most likely* contrast with Murimi's other institutional investors. **Justify** your response.

29  **Discuss** how Murimi can use her technical skills to devise the strategy.

---

30  Carnoustie Capital Management, Ltd. (CCM), a UK-based global investment advisory firm, is considering adding an emerging market currency product to its offerings. CCM has for the past three years managed a "model" portfolio of emerging market currencies using the same investment approach as its developed economy currency products. The risk and return measures of the "model" portfolio compare favorably with the one- and three-year emerging market benchmark performance net of CCM's customary advisory fee and estimated trading costs. Mindful of the higher volatility of emerging market currencies, CCM management is particularly pleased with the "model" portfolio's standard deviation, Sharpe ratio, and value at risk (VAR) in comparison to those of its developed economy products.

Recognizing that market conditions have been stable since the "model" portfolio's inception, CCM management is sensitive to the consequences of extreme market events for emerging market risk and return.

**Evaluate** the application of emerging market and developed market investment return probability distributions for CCM's potential new product.

---

## The following information relates to Questions 31–32

Wilson Manufacturing (Wilson) is an Australian institutional client of Ethan Lee, who manages a variety of portfolios across asset classes. Wilson prefers a neutral benchmark over a rules-based approach, with its investment policy statement (IPS) requiring a currency hedge ratio between 97% and 103% to protect against currency risk. Lee has assessed various currency management strategies for Wilson's US dollar-denominated fixed-income portfolio to optimally locate it along the currency risk spectrum. The portfolio is currently in its flat natural neutral position because of Lee's lack of market conviction.

31  **Identify** the *most likely* approach for Lee to optimally locate Wilson's portfolio on the currency risk spectrum, consistent with the IPS. **Justify** your response with *two* reasons supporting the approach.

# Practice Problems

**Identify** the *most likely* approach for Lee to optimally locate Wilson's portfolio on the currency risk spectrum, consistent with IPS. (Circle one.)

| Passive Hedging | Discretionary Hedging | Active Currency Management | Currency Overlay |
|---|---|---|---|
|  |  |  |  |

**Justify** your response with *two* reasons supporting the approach.

| 1. | 2. |
|---|---|
|  |  |

Lee and Wilson recently completed the annual portfolio review and determined the IPS is too short-term focused and excessively risk averse. Accordingly, the IPS is revised and foreign currency is introduced as a separate asset class. Lee hires an external foreign exchange sub-adviser to implement a currency overlay program, emphasizing that it is important to structure the program so that the currency overlay is allowed in terms of strategic portfolio positioning.

**32** **Discuss** a key attribute of the currency overlay that would *increase* the likelihood it would be allowed in terms of strategic portfolio positioning.

## The following information relates to Questions 33–35

Rosario Delgado is an investment manager in Spain. Delgado's client, Max Rivera, seeks assistance with his well-diversified investment portfolio denominated in US dollars.

Rivera's reporting currency is the euro, and he is concerned about his US dollar exposure. His portfolio IPS requires monthly rebalancing, at a minimum. The portfolio's market value is USD2.5 million. Given Rivera's risk aversion, Delgado is considering a monthly hedge using either a one-month forward contract or one-month futures contract.

**33** **Determine** which type of hedge instrument combination is *most* appropriate for Rivera's situation. **Justify** your selection.

**Determine** which type of hedge instrument combination is *most* appropriate for Rivera's situation. (Circle one.)

| Static Forward | Static Futures | Dynamic Forward | Dynamic Futures |
|---|---|---|---|
|  |  |  |  |

**Justify** your selection.

Assume Rivera's portfolio was perfectly hedged. It is now time to rebalance the portfolio and roll the currency hedge forward one month. The relevant data for rebalancing are provided in Exhibit 1.

### Exhibit 1  Portfolio and Relevant Market Data

| | One Month Ago | Today |
|---|---|---|
| Portfolio value of assets (USD) | 2,500,000 | 2,650,000 |
| USD/EUR spot rate (bid–offer) | 0.8913/0.8914 | 0.8875/0.8876 |
| One-month forward points (bid–offer) | 25/30 | 20/25 |

**34** **Calculate** the net cash flow (in euros) to maintain the desired hedge. **Show** your calculations.

With the US dollar currently trading at a forward premium and US interest rates lower than Spanish rates, Delgado recommends trading against the forward rate bias to earn additional return from a positive roll yield.

**35** **Identify** *two* strategies Delgado should use to earn a positive roll yield. **Describe** the specific steps needed to execute each strategy.

| **Identify** *two* strategies Delgado should use to earn a positive roll yield. | **Describe** the specific steps needed to execute *each* strategy. |
|---|---|
| 1. | |
| 2. | |

# SOLUTIONS

**1**

### Template for Question 1

| Asset | Foreign-Currency Portfolio Return | USD Relative to Foreign-Currency (circle one) |
|---|---|---|
| Portfolio A | 15% | appreciated |
|  |  | **depreciated** |

**Justification**

The 19.5% domestic-currency return for Portfolio A is higher than the 15% foreign-currency portfolio return in GBP; therefore, the USD necessarily depreciated relative to the GBP.

The domestic-currency return on a foreign portfolio will reflect both the foreign-currency return on the portfolio and the percentage movements in the spot exchange rate between the domestic and foreign currency. The domestic-currency return is multiplicative with respect to these two factors:

$$R_{DC} = (1 + R_{FC})(1 + R_{FX}) - 1$$

where $R_{DC}$ is the domestic-currency return (in percent), $R_{FC}$ is the foreign-currency return of the asset (portfolio), and $R_{FX}$ is the percentage change of the foreign currency against the domestic currency. (Note that in the $R_{FX}$ expression the domestic currency—the USD in this case—is the price currency.)

Solving for $R_{FX}$: $(1 + 15\%)(1 + R_{FX}) - 1 = 19.50\%$; $R_{FX} = 3.91\%$

Thus, the USD depreciated relative to the GBP. That is, the GBP appreciated against the USD because $R_{FX}$ is quoted in terms of USD/GBP, with the USD as the price currency and GBP as the base currency, and in this example $R_{FX}$ is a positive number (3.91%).

**2**

### Template for Question 2

| Asset | Percentage Movement in the Spot Exchange Rate | Foreign-Currency Portfolio Return (circle one) |
|---|---|---|
| Portfolio B | EUR appreciated 5% against the USD | positive |
|  |  | **negative** |

**Justification**

The domestic-currency return for Portfolio B is 0%, and the EUR appreciated 5% against the USD; therefore, the foreign-currency return for Portfolio B is necessarily negative.

The domestic-currency return on a foreign portfolio will reflect both the foreign-currency return on the portfolio and the percentage movements in the spot exchange rate between the domestic and foreign currency. The domestic-currency return is multiplicative with respect to these two factors:

$$R_{DC} = (1 + R_{FC})(1 + R_{FX}) - 1$$

where $R_{DC}$ is the domestic-currency return (in percent), $R_{FC}$ is the foreign-currency return of the asset (portfolio), and $R_{FX}$ is the percentage change of the foreign currency against the domestic currency. (Note that once again, the domestic currency—the USD—is the price currency in the USD/EUR quote for $R_{FX}$.)

Solving for $R_{FC}$: $(1 + R_{FC})(1 + 5\%) - 1 = 0\%$; $R_{FC} = -4.76\%$

3. Any *two* of the following four points is acceptable:
   - Trading requires dealing on the bid/offer spread offered by dealers. Dealer profit margin is based on these spreads. Maintaining a 100% hedge will require frequent rebalancing of minor changes in currency movements and could prove to be expensive. "Churning" the hedge portfolio would progressively add to hedging costs and reduce the hedge's benefits.
   - A long position in currency options involves an upfront payment. If the options expire out-of-the-money, this is an unrecoverable cost.
   - Forward contracts have a maturity date and need to be "rolled" forward with an FX swap transaction to maintain the hedge. Rolling hedges typically generate cash inflows and outflows, based on movements in the spot rate as well as roll yield. Cash may have to be raised to settle the hedging transactions (increases the volatility in the organization's cash accounts). The management of these cash flow costs can accumulate and become a large portion of the portfolio's value, and they become more expensive for cash outflows as interest rates increase.
   - Hedging requires maintaining the necessary administrative infrastructure for trading (personnel and technology systems). These overhead costs can become a significant portion of the overall costs of currency trading.

4. Optimal hedging decisions require balancing the benefits of hedging against the costs of hedging. Hedging costs come mainly in two forms: trading costs and opportunity costs. Gupta is referring to the opportunity cost of the 100% hedge strategy. The opportunity cost of the 100% hedge strategy for Portfolio B is the forgone opportunity of benefiting from favorable currency rate movements. Gupta is implying that accepting some currency risk has the potential to enhance portfolio return. A complete hedge eliminates this possibility.

5. A solution is to put in place a currency overlay program for active currency management. Because internal resources for active management are lacking, the fund manager would outsource currency exposure management to a sub-advisor that specializes in foreign exchange management. This approach would allow the fund manager of Portfolio A to separate the currency hedging function (currency beta), which can be done effectively internally, and the active currency management function (currency alpha) which can be managed externally by a foreign currency specialist.

# Solutions

## 6

### Template for Question 6

| Gupta's Statements | Active Currency Approach (circle one) | Justification |
|---|---|---|
| "Many traders believe that it is not necessary to examine factors like the current account deficit, inflation, and interest rates because current exchange rates already reflect the market view on how these factors will affect future exchange rates." | carry trade<br>**technical analysis**<br>economic fundamentals | Gupta is describing active currency management based on market technicals. Market technicians believe that in a liquid, freely-traded market the historical price data already incorporates all relevant information on future price movements. Technicians believe that it is not necessary to look outside the market at data like the current account deficit, inflation and interest rates because current exchange rates already reflect the market consensus view on how these factors will affect future exchange rates. |
| "The six-month interest rate in India is 8% compared to 1% in the United States. This presents a yield pick-up opportunity." | **carry trade**<br>technical analysis<br>economic fundamentals | Gupta is describing active currency management based on the carry trade. This strategy is implemented by borrowing in low-yield currencies (USD at 1%) and investing in high-yield currencies (INR at 8%). |
| "The currency overlay manager will estimate the fair value of the currencies with the expectation that observed spot rates will converge to long-run equilibrium values described by parity conditions." | carry trade<br>technical analysis<br>**economic fundamentals** | Gupta is describing active currency management based on economic fundamentals. This approach assumes that, in free markets, exchange rates are determined by logical economic relationships that can be modeled. A fundamentals-based approach estimates the "fair value" of the currency, with the expectation that observed spot rates will converge to long-run equilibrium values described by parity conditions. |

7. Statements 1 and 2 compare differences between speculative volatility traders and hedgers of volatility. Statement 1 best explains the view of a speculative volatility trader. Speculative volatility traders often want to be net-short volatility, if they believe that market conditions will remains stable. The reason for this is that most options expire out-of-the money, and the option writer can then keep the option premium as a payment earned for accepting volatility risk. (Speculative volatility traders would want to be long volatility if they thought volatility was likely to increase.) Statement 2 best describes the view of a hedger of volatility. Most hedgers are net-long volatility since they want to buy protection from unanticipated price volatility. Buying currency risk protection generally means a long option position. This can be thought of as paying an insurance premium for protection against exchange rate volatility.

8. In practice, matching the *current* market value of the foreign-currency exposure in the portfolio with an equal and offsetting position in a forward contract is likely to be ineffective over time because the market value of foreign-currency assets will change with market conditions. A static hedge (i.e., an unchanging hedge) will tend to accumulate unwanted currency exposures as the value of the foreign-currency assets change. This will result in a mismatch between the market value of the foreign-currency asset portfolio and the nominal size of the

forward contract used for the currency hedge (resulting in currency risk). For this reason, the portfolio manager will generally need to implement a dynamic hedge by rebalancing the portfolio periodically.

9 The fund manager should implement a dynamic hedging approach. Dynamic hedging requires rebalancing the portfolio periodically. The rebalancing would require adjusting some combination of the size, number, and maturities of the foreign-currency contracts.

Although rebalancing a dynamic hedge will keep the actual hedge ratio close to the target hedge ratio, it has the disadvantage of increased transaction costs compared to a static hedge.

10 C is correct. The domestic-currency return is a function of the foreign-currency return and the percentage change of the foreign currency against the domestic currency. Mathematically, the domestic-currency return is expressed as:

$$R_{DC} = (1 + R_{FC})(1 + R_{FX}) - 1$$

where $R_{DC}$ is the domestic-currency return (in percent), $R_{FC}$ is the foreign-currency return, and $R_{FX}$ is the percentage change of the foreign currency against the domestic currency. Note that this $R_{FX}$ expression is calculated using the investor's domestic currency (the EUR in this case) as the *price* currency in the P/B quote. This is different than the market-standard currency quotes in Exhibit 1, where the EUR is the *base* currency in each of these quotes. Therefore, for the foreign currency (USD, GBP, or CHF) to *appreciate* against the EUR, the market-standard quote (USD/EUR, GBP/EUR, or CHF/EUR, respectively) must *decrease*; i.e. the EUR must depreciate.

The Euro-Swiss (CHF/EUR) is the only spot rate with a negative change (from 1.2175 to 1.2080), meaning the EUR depreciated against the CHF (the CHF/EUR rate decreased). Or put differently, the CHF appreciated against the EUR, adding to the EUR-denominated return for the German investor holding CHF-denominated assets. This would result in a higher domestic-currency return ($R_{DC}$), for the German investor, relative to the foreign-currency return ($R_{FC}$) for the CHF-denominated assets. Both the Euro-dollar (USD/EUR) and Euro-sterling (GBP/EUR) experienced a positive change in the spot rate, meaning the EUR appreciated against these two currencies (the USD/EUR rate and the GBP/EUR rate both increased). This would result in a lower domestic-currency return ($R_{DC}$) for the German investor relative to the foreign-currency return ($R_{FC}$) for the USD- and GBP-denominated assets.

A is incorrect because the Euro-dollar (USD/EUR) experienced a positive change in the spot rate, meaning the EUR appreciated against the USD (the USD/EUR rate increased). This would result in a lower domestic-currency (i.e. EUR-denominated) return relative to the foreign-currency return for the USD-denominated assets, since the USD has depreciated against the EUR.

B is incorrect because the Euro-sterling (GBP/EUR) experienced a positive change in the spot rate, meaning the EUR appreciated against the GPB (the GBP/EUR rate increased). This would result in a lower domestic-currency (i.e. EUR-denominated) return relative to the foreign-currency return for the GBP-denominated assets, since the GBP has depreciated against the EUR.

11 C is correct. An increase in the expected correlation between movements in the foreign-currency asset returns and movements in the spot exchange rates from 0.50 to 0.80 would increase the domestic-currency return *risk* but would not change the *level* of expected domestic-currency return. The domestic-currency

return risk is a function of the foreign-currency return risk [$\sigma(R_{FC})$] the exchange rate risk [$\sigma(R_{FX})$] and the correlation between the foreign-currency returns and exchange rate movements. Mathematically, this is expressed as:

$$\sigma^2(R_{DC}) \approx \sigma^2(R_{FC}) + \sigma^2(R_{FX}) + 2\sigma(R_{FC})\sigma(R_{FX})\rho(R_{FC}R_{FX})$$

If the correlation increases from +0.50 to +0.80, then the *variance* of the expected domestic-currency return will increase—but this will not affect the *level* of the expected domestic-currency return ($R_{DC}$). Refer to the equation shown for the answer in Question 1 and note that Ostermann's expected $R_{FC}$ has not changed. (Once again, note as well that $R_{FX}$ is defined with the domestic currency as the price currency.)

A and B are incorrect. An increase in the expected correlation between movements in the foreign-currency asset returns and movements in the spot rates from 0.50 to 0.80 would increase the domestic-currency return risk but would not impact the expected domestic-currency return.

12  A is correct. Guten believes that, due to efficient currency markets, there should not be any long-run gains for speculating (or active management) in currencies, especially after netting out management and transaction costs. Therefore, both currency hedging and actively trading currencies represent a cost to the portfolio with little prospect of consistently positive active returns. Given a long investment horizon and few immediate liquidity needs, Guten is most likely to choose to forgo currency hedging and its associated costs.

B and C are incorrect because given a long investment horizon and little immediate liquidity needs, Guten is most likely to choose to forgo currency hedging and its associated costs. Guten believes that due to efficient currency markets there should not be any long-run gains when speculating in currencies, especially after netting out management and transaction costs.

13  B is correct. Umlauf develops a market view based on underlying fundamentals in exchange rates (an economic fundamental approach). When directed by clients, Umlauf uses options and a variety of trading strategies to *unbundle* all of the various risk factors and trades them separately (a volatility trading approach). A market technical approach would entail forming a market view based on technical analysis (i.e., a belief that historical prices incorporate all relevant information on future price movements and that such movements have a tendency to repeat).

A is incorrect because, in using options and a variety of trading strategies to *unbundle* all of the various risk factors and trade them separately, Umlauf is likely to periodically employ volatility trading-based currency strategies.

C is incorrect because, in developing a market view based on underlying fundamentals in exchange rates, Umlauf does utilize an economic fundamentals approach.

14  B is correct. Braunt Pensionskasse provides the manager with limited discretion in managing the portfolio's currency risk exposures. This would be most consistent with allowing the currency overlay manager to take directional views on future currency movements (within predefined bounds) where the currency overlay is limited to the currency exposures already in the foreign asset portfolio. It would not be appropriate to use a fully-passive hedging approach since it would eliminate any alpha from currency movements. Further, a currency overlay program, which considers "foreign exchange as an asset class", would likely expose Braunt's portfolio to more currency risk than desired given the given primary performance objectives.

A is incorrect because a directional view currency overlay program is most appropriate given the limited discretion Braunt Pensionskasse has given the manager. A fully passive currency overlay program is more likely to be used when a client seeks to hedge all the currency risk.

C is incorrect because a directional view currency overlay program is most appropriate given the limited discretion Braunt Pensionskasse has given the manager. In contrast, the concept of "foreign exchange as an asset class" allows the currency overlay manager to take currency exposure positions in any currency pair where there is value-added to be harvested.

15  C is correct. The primary performance objective of Franz Trading GmbH is to add alpha to the portfolio, and thus has given the manager discretion in trading currencies. This is essentially a "foreign exchange as an asset class" approach. Braunt Pensionskasse and Kastner have more conservative currency strategies, and thus are less likely to benefit from the different strategies that a new overlay manager might employ.

A is incorrect because Franz Trading GmbH is more likely to benefit from the introduction of an additional overlay manager. Kastner is more likely to have a fully passive currency overlay program.

B is incorrect because Franz Trading GmbH is more likely to benefit from the introduction of an additional overlay manager. Braunt is more likely to have a currency overlay program where the manager takes a directional view on future currency movements.

16  A is correct. Exchange-traded futures contract not only have initial margin requirements, they also have daily mark-to-market and, as a result, can be subject to daily margin calls. Market participants must have sufficient liquidity to meet margin calls, or have their positions involuntarily liquidated by their brokers. Note that the risk of daily margin calls is not a feature of most forwards contracts; nor is initial margin. (However, this is changing among the largest institutional players in FX markets as many forward contracts now come with what are known as Collateral Support Annexes—CSAs—in which margin can be posted. Posting additional margin would typically not be a daily event, however, except in the case of extreme market moves.)

B is incorrect because futures contracts have low transactions costs. C is incorrect because whether the EUR is the price or the base currency in the quote will not affect the hedging process. In fact, on the CME the quote would be the market-standard USD/EUR quote, with the EUR as the base currency.

17  C is correct. Based on predicted export trends, Subscriber 2 most likely expects the KRW/USD rate to increase (i.e., the won—the price currency—to depreciate relative to the USD). This would require a long forward position in a forward contract, but as a country with capital controls, a NDF would be used instead. (Note: While forward contracts offered by banks are generally an institutional product, not retail, the retail version of a non-deliverable forward contract is known as a "contract for differences" (CFD) and is available at several retail FX brokers.)

A is incorrect because Subscriber 2 expects the KRW/USD rate to increase. A short straddle position would be used when the direction of exchange rate movement is unknown and volatility is expected to remain low.

B is incorrect because a put option would profit from a decrease of the KRW/USD rate, not an increase (as expected). Higher volatility would also make buying a put option more expensive.

**18** B is correct. Subscriber 3's carry trade strategy is equivalent to trading the forward rate bias, based on the historical evidence that the forward rate is not the center of the distribution for the spot rate. Applying this bias involves buying currencies selling at a forward discount and selling currencies trading at a forward premium. So a higher forward premium on the lower yielding currency—the USD, the base currency in the INR/USD quote—would effectively reflect a more profitable trading opportunity. That is, a higher premium for buying or selling the USD forward is associated with a lower US interest rate compared to India. This would mean a wider interest rate differential in favor of Indian instruments, and hence potentially more carry trade profits.

A is incorrect because Subscriber 3's carry trade strategy depends on a wide interest rate differential between the high-yield country (India) and the low-yield country (the United States). The differential should be wide enough to compensate for the unhedged currency risk exposure.

C is incorrect because a guide to the carry trade's riskiness is the volatility of spot rates on the involved currencies, with rapid movements in exchange rates often associated with a panicked unwinding of carry trades. All things being equal, higher volatility is worse for carry trades.

**19** C is correct. Emerging market currencies are often the investment currencies in the carry trade. This reflects the higher yields often available in their money markets compared to Developed Market economies (funding currencies are typically low-yield currencies such as the JPY). This can lead to higher holding returns, but these higher returns can also come with higher risks: carry trades are occasionally subject to panicked unwinds in stressed market conditions. When this occurs, position exit can be made more difficult by market illiquidity and higher trading costs (wider bid/offer spreads). The leverage involved in the carry trade can magnify trading losses under these circumstances.

A is incorrect because return distributions are often *negatively* skewed, reflecting the higher event risk (panicked carry trade unwinds, currency pegs being re-set, etc.) associated with the carry trade.

B is incorrect because although FX markets are typically efficient (or very close thereto) this does not mean that higher returns are not available. The key question is whether these are abnormally high *risk-adjusted* returns. Higher return in an efficient market comes with higher risk. The higher (short-term) return in the carry trade reflects the risk premia for holding unhedged currency risk, in the context of a favorable interest rate differential.

**20** B is correct. The GBP value of the assets has declined, and hence the hedge needs to be *reduced* by GBP 7,000,000. This would require buying the GBP forward to net the outstanding (short) forward contract to an amount less than GBP 100,000,000.

A is incorrect because to rebalance the hedge (reduce the net size of the short forward position) the GBP must be bought *forward*, not with a spot transaction.

C is incorrect because the GBP must be bought, not sold. Buying SEK against the GBP is equivalent to selling GBP. Moreover, the amount of SEK that would be sold forward (to buy GBP 7,000,000 forward) would be determined by the *forward* rate, not the spot rate (7,000,000 × 10.6875 = 74,812,500).

**21** C is correct. The fund holds CHF-denominated assets and hence Björk wants to protect against a depreciation of the CHF against the SEK, which would be a down-move in the SEK/CHF cross rate. An OTM put option provides some downside protection against such a move, while writing an OTM call option helps reduce the cost of this option structure. Note that Björk does not expect that the SEK/CHF rate will increase, so this option (in her view) will likely expire OTM and allow her to keep the premia. This hedging structure is known as a short risk reversal (or a collar) and is a popular hedging strategy.

A is incorrect because the ATM call option will not protect against a decrease in the SEK/CHF rate. An ATM option is also expensive (compared to an OTM option). Note that Björk does not expect the SEK/CHF rate to increase, so would not want a long call option position for this rate.

B is incorrect because this structure is expensive (via the long ITM call option) and does not protect against a decrease in the SEK/CHF rate.

22. B is correct. To hedge the EUR-denominated assets Björk will be selling forward contracts on the SEK/EUR cross rate. A higher forward premium will result in higher roll return as Björk is selling the EUR forward at a higher all-in forward rate, and closing out the contract at a lower rate (all else equal), given that the forward curve is in contango.

A is incorrect because Björk is hedging EUR-denominated assets with a EUR-denominated forward contract. While it is true that the gap between spot and forward rates will be higher the higher the interest rate differential between countries, this gap (basis) converges to zero near maturity date, when the forward contracts would be rolled.

C is incorrect because forward contracts do not generate premia income; writing options does.

23. C is correct. A cross hedge exposes the fund to basis risk; that is, the risk that the hedge fails to protect against adverse currency movements because the correlations between the value of the assets being hedged and the hedging instrument change.

A is incorrect because movements in forward points (and hence roll yield) would be of secondary importance compared to the basis risk of a cross hedge.

B is incorrect because exchange rate volatility would not necessarily affect a hedge based on forward contracts, as long as the correlations between the underlying assets and the hedge remained stable. Although relevant, volatility in itself is not the "most" important risk to consider for a cross-hedge. (However, movements in volatility would affect hedges based on currency options.)

24. A is correct. The fund has a long-term perspective, few immediate liquidity needs, and a lower weight in fixed income that in equities (bond portfolios are typically associated with hedge ratios closer to 100% than equity portfolios). The emerging market exposure would also support active management, given these countries' typically higher yields (carry trade) and often volatile exchange rates.

B is incorrect because the characteristics of the fund and the beneficial investor (in this case, the royal family) do not argue for a conservative currency strategy.

C is incorrect because a more active currency management strategy would be more suitable for this fund.

25. Currency movements contributed 1.5% to the account's 7.0% total (US dollar) return, calculated as follows:

The domestic-currency return ($R_{DC}$) on a portfolio of multiple foreign assets is

$$R_{DC} = \sum_{i=1}^{n} \acute{E}_i (1 + R_{FC,i})(1 + R_{FX,i}) - 1$$

## Solutions

Where $R_{FC,i}$ is the foreign-currency return on the $i$th foreign asset, $R_{FX,i}$ is the appreciation of the $i$th foreign currency against the domestic currency, and $\acute{E}_i$ is the weight of the asset as a percentage of the aggregate domestic-currency value of the portfolio. This equation can be rearranged as

$$R_{DC} = \sum_{i=1}^{n} \acute{E}_i [R_{FC,i} + R_{FX,i} + (R_{FC,i} \times R_{FX,i})]$$

Therefore, the domestic-currency return is equal to the sum of the weighted asset return, the weighted currency return, and the weighted cross-product of the asset return and the currency return. The latter two terms explain the effects of foreign-currency movements on the Bhatt account's total (US dollar) return of 7.0%.

The weighted asset return is equal to 5.5%, calculated as follows:

(0.50 × 10.0%) + (0.25 × 5.0%) + [0.25 × (−3.0%)] = 5.5%.

The weighted currency return is equal to 1.5% calculated as follows:

(0.50 × 0.0%) + (0.25 × 2.0%) + (0.25 × 4.0%) = 1.5%.

The weighted cross-product is equal to −0.005%, calculated as follows:

[0.50 × (10.0% × 0.0%)] + [0.25 × (5.0% × 2.0%)] + [0.25 × (−3.0% × 4.0%)] = −0.005%.

Therefore, the contribution of foreign currency equals 1.5%, calculated as the 7.0% total (US dollar) return less the 5.5% weighted asset return. Alternatively, the contribution of foreign currency to the total return can be calculated as the sum of the weighted currency return of 1.5% and the weighted cross-product of −0.005%:

1.5% + (−0.005%) = 1.495%, which rounds to 1.5%.

## 26

**Determine** the *most appropriate* currency management strategy for Bhatt. (Circle one.)

| Passive hedging | Discretionary hedging | Active currency management |
|---|---|---|
| | | |

**Justify** your response.

Active currency management is the most appropriate currency management strategy because with this approach, the portfolio manager is supposed to take currency risks and manage them for profit with the primary goal of adding alpha to the portfolio through successful trading. This primary goal differs from the discretionary hedging approach in which the manager's primary duty is to protect the portfolio from currency risk and secondarily seek alpha within limited bounds. While the difference between active currency management and discretionary hedging is one of emphasis more than degree, the bounded discretion that Bhatt has granted Darden (plus or minus 25% from the neutral position) strongly suggests that Darden is expected to take currency risk and seek alpha with priority over portfolio protection from currency risk.

Passive hedging is not appropriate because with this approach, the goal is to keep the portfolio's currency exposures close, if not equal to, those of a benchmark portfolio used to evaluate performance. Passive hedging is a rules-based approach that removes all discretion from the portfolio manager, regardless of the manager's market opinion on future movements in exchange rates. In this case, Bhatt has granted Darden the discretion to manage currency exposures within a range of plus or minus 25% from the neutral benchmark position.

A discretionary hedging approach is not appropriate because Bhatt has granted Darden more than limited discretion (plus or minus 25% from the neutral position), indicative of an active currency management approach. The discretion granted suggests that Darden's primary goal is to take currency risks and manage them for profit with a secondary goal of protecting the portfolio from currency risk. The primary goal of a discretionary hedging approach is to protect the portfolio from currency risk while secondarily seeking alpha within limited bounds.

27 Given C&M's research conclusion and the IPS constraints, the currency team should under-hedge Bhatt's portfolio by selling the US dollar forward against the Indian rupee in a forward contract (or contracts) at no less than a 75% hedge ratio of the portfolio's USD10,000,000 market value. By under-hedging the portfolio relative to the "neutral" (100% hedge ratio) benchmark, the team seeks to add incremental value on the basis of its view that the US dollar will appreciate against the Indian rupee while maintaining compliance with the IPS.

Since the Indian rupee is assumed to depreciate against the US dollar, a 100% hedge ratio would largely eliminate any alpha opportunity. However, a hedge ratio greater than 75% but less than 100% (as dictated by the plus or minus 25% versus neutral IPS constraint) provides the opportunity to capture currency return in the expected US dollar appreciation against the Indian rupee.

28 In currency markets, volatility is not constant, nor are its movements completely random. Instead, volatility is determined by a wide variety of underlying factors, both fundamental and technical, for which a trader can express an opinion. Movements in volatility are cyclical and typically subject to long periods of relative stability punctuated by sharp upward spikes in volatility as markets come under stress. Speculative volatility traders among overlay managers often want to be net short volatility because most options expire out of the money and the option writer then gets to keep the premium without delivery of the underlying currency pair. Ideally these traders would want to flip their position and be long volatility ahead of the volatility spikes, but these episodes can be notoriously difficult to time. Most hedgers, in contrast, typically run option positions that are net long volatility because they are buying protection from the unanticipated price volatility.

In this case, Konev would most likely be interested in speculative gains on US dollar weakness, while the other institutional clients would be hedgers seeking to minimize trading risks. The concept of foreign exchange as an asset class for Konev will most likely permit Murimi to take foreign exchange exposure in any currency pair where there is additional value to capture. A volatility-based strategy for Konev would typically be net short, as opposed to net long, volatility to earn the related risk premium for absorbing volatility risk. In contrast, the institutional investors, as hedgers in managing net long volatility positions, would be exposed to the time decay of an option's time value.

29 In forming a market view on such turning points in future exchange rate movements (e.g., peaking in the US dollar) or timing-related position entry and exit points, market technicians follow three principles: (1) Historical price data can be helpful in projecting future movements, (2) historical price patterns have a tendency to repeat and identify profitable trade opportunities, and (3) technical analysis attempts to determine not where market prices *should* trade but where they *will* trade.

# Solutions

Thus, when devising a volatility strategy, Murimi can use her technical skills to time entry and exit points of positions. She can identify patterns in the historical price data on the US dollar, such as when it was overbought or oversold, meaning it has trended too far in one direction and is vulnerable to a trend reversal. She would appropriately position US dollar trades to maximize potential returns from volatility shifts that could be associated with US dollar exchange rate movements.

**30** Emerging market currency trades are subject to relatively frequent extreme events and market stresses. Thus, return probability distributions for emerging market investments exhibit fatter tails than the normal distributions that are customarily used to evaluate developed market investment performance. Additionally, emerging market return probability distributions also have a pronounced negative skew when compared with developed market (normal) distributions.

Given these differences, risk management and control tools (such as VAR) that depend on normal distributions can be misleading under extreme market conditions and greatly understate the risks to which the portfolio is exposed. Likewise, many investment performance measures used to evaluate performance are also based on the normal distribution. As a result, historical performance evaluated by such measures as the Sharpe ratio can look very attractive when market conditions are stable, but this apparent outperformance can disappear into deep losses faster than most investors can react.

Short-term stability in emerging markets can give investors a false sense of overconfidence and thereby encourage over-positioning based on the illusion of normally distributed returns. Thus, CCM should not assume a normal distribution for its "model" emerging market portfolio. CCM should assume a fatter-tailed, negatively skewed return probability distribution better reflecting the risk exposure to extreme events.

**31**

**Identify** the *most likely* approach for Lee to optimally locate Wilson's portfolio on the currency risk spectrum, consistent with IPS.
(Circle one.)

| Passive Hedging | Discretionary Hedging | Active Currency Management | Currency Overlay |
|---|---|---|---|
| | | | |

**Justify** your response with *two* reasons supporting the approach.

| 1. The portfolio is said to be in its flat natural neutral position because Lee does not have market conviction, which is consistent with a discretionary hedging approach. | 2. The currency hedge ratio requirement reflects some discretion with actual portfolio currency risk exposures allowed to vary from the neutral position within a 3% band. |
|---|---|

Passive hedging is not likely because the IPS allows the 3% band around the neutral position. In addition, passive hedging is a rules-based approach, which is contrary to Wilson's preference.

Active currency management is not likely because the 3% band around the neutral position is too limited for that approach. In many cases, the difference between discretionary hedging and active currency management is more of emphasis than degree. The primary duty of the discretionary hedger is to protect the portfolio from currency risk. Active currency management is supposed to take currency risks and manage them for profit. Leaving actual portfolio exposures near zero for extended periods is typically not a viable option.

Currency overlay is not likely because the 3% band is too small to indicate active currency management in a currency overlay program. In addition, currency overlay programs are often conducted by external, FX-specialized sub-advisers to a portfolio, whereas Lee is a generalist managing a variety of portfolios across asset classes. Finally, currency overlay allows for taking directional views on future currency movements, and a lack of market conviction is noted here.

32  The IPS revision allows for a more proactive currency risk approach in the portfolio because it was determined Wilson was too short-term focused and risk averse. Lee should structure the currency overlay so that it is as uncorrelated as possible with other asset or alpha-generation programs in the portfolio. By introducing foreign currencies as a separate asset class, the more currency overlay is expected to generate alpha that is uncorrelated with the other programs in the portfolio, the more likely it is to be allowed in terms of strategic portfolio positioning.

33

**Determine** which type of hedge instrument combination is *most* appropriate for Rivera's situation. (Circle one.)

| Static Forward | Static Futures | Dynamic Forward | Dynamic Futures |
| --- | --- | --- | --- |

**Justify** your selection.

Static vs. Dynamic Justifications:
1. Both Rivera and Delgado are risk averse.
2. The portfolio's IPS requires monthly rebalancing.

Forward vs. Futures Justifications:
1. A forward contract is less expensive.
2. A forward contract has greater liquidity.

The hedge instrument combination most appropriate for Rivera's portfolio is a dynamic forward hedge for the reasons noted below.

First, a dynamic hedge is most appropriate here. A static hedge (i.e., unchanging hedge) will avoid transaction costs but will also tend to accumulate unwanted currency exposures as the value of the foreign-currency assets change. This characteristic will cause a mismatch between the market value of the foreign-currency asset portfolio and the nominal size of the forward contract used for the currency hedge; this is pure currency risk. Given this potential mismatch and because both Rivera and Delgado are risk averse, Delgado should implement a dynamic hedge by rebalancing the portfolio at least on a monthly basis.

Delgado must assess the cost–benefit trade-offs of how frequently to dynamically rebalance the hedge. This depends on a variety of factors (manager risk aversion, market view, IPS guidelines). The higher the degree of risk aversion, the more frequently the hedge is likely to be rebalanced back to the "neutral" hedge ratio.

A forward contract is more suitable because in comparison to a futures contract, a forward contract is more flexible in terms of currency pair, settlement date, and transaction amount. Forward contracts are also simpler than futures contracts from an administrative standpoint owing to the absence of margin requirements, reducing portfolio management expense. Finally, forward contracts are more liquid than futures for trading in large sizes because the daily trade volume for OTC currency forward contracts dwarfs those for exchange-traded futures contracts.

**34** When hedging one month ago, Delgado would have sold USD2,500,000 one month forward against the euro. Now, with the US dollar-denominated portfolio increasing in value to USD2,650,000, a mismatched FX swap is needed to settle the initial expiring forward contract and establish a new hedge given the higher market value of the US dollar-denominated portfolio.

To calculate the net cash flow (in euros) to maintain the desired hedge, the following steps are necessary:

1 Buy USD2,500,000 at the spot rate. Buying US dollars against the euro means selling euros, which is the base currency in the USD/EUR spot rate. Therefore, the bid side of the market must be used to calculate the outflow in euros.

USD2,500,000 × 0.8875 = EUR2,218,750.

2 Sell USD2,650,000 at the spot rate adjusted for the one-month forward points (all-in forward rate). Selling the US dollar against the euro means buying euros, which is the base currency in the USD/EUR spot rate. Therefore, the offer side of the market must be used to calculate the inflow in euros.

All-in forward rate = 0.8876 + (25/10,000) = 0.8901.

USD2,650,000 × 0.8901 = EUR2,358,765.

3 Therefore, the net cash flow is equal to EUR2,358,765 − EUR2,218,750, which is equal to EUR140,015.

**35**

| **Identify** two strategies Delgado should use to earn a positive roll yield. | **Describe** the specific steps needed to execute *each* strategy. |
|---|---|
| 1. Implement the carry trade. | Buy (invest in) the high-yield currency and sell (borrow) the low-yield currency. |
| 2. Trade the forward rate bias. | Buy (invest in) the forward discount currency and sell (borrow) the forward premium currency. |

Given that the base currency (the US dollar) is trading at a forward premium, the hedge requires the sale of US dollar forward, resulting in a positive roll yield. The concept of roll yield is very similar to forward rate bias and the carry trade. Here, Delgado is suggesting a strategy to pursue when there is a negative roll yield, because a hedger trading against the forward bias would be buying US dollars at a forward premium instead of selling them. The carry trade strategy of borrowing in low-yield currencies and investing in high-yield currencies is equivalent to trading the forward rate bias, not against it.

# PORTFOLIO MANAGEMENT
## STUDY SESSION

# 5

# Fixed-Income Portfolio Management (1)

Fixed-income securities represent a significant portion of all available financial assets and are included in most investor portfolios.

This study session begins by explaining the role played by fixed-income securities in portfolios and then introduces the two primary types of fixed-income mandates (liability-based and total return). A model for decomposing expected bond returns, which identifies the driving forces behind expected returns, is presented. Fixed-income portfolio risk measures such as duration and convexity are addressed, and the effects of liquidity, leverage, and taxes on fixed-income portfolios are discussed. The session reviews alternatives to direct bond investments such as mutual funds and exchange-traded funds as well as fixed-income derivatives and their role in a portfolio. Next, liability-driven and index-based strategies are examined in greater detail. Coverage includes approaches, risks, and challenges associated with both immunization of single and multiple liabilities and the indexation and laddering of a fixed-income portfolio. Primary risk factors associated with an index, enhanced indexing and benchmark selection are also covered in this session.

## READING ASSIGNMENTS

| | |
|---|---|
| Reading 11 | Overview of Fixed-Income Portfolio Management<br>by Bernd Hanke, PhD, CFA, and Brian J. Henderson, PhD, CFA |
| Reading 12 | Liability-Driven and Index-Based Strategies<br>by James F. Adams, PhD, CFA, and Donald J. Smith, PhD |

© 2021 CFA Institute. All rights reserved.

# READING
# 11

# Overview of Fixed-Income Portfolio Management

by Bernd Hanke, PhD, CFA, and Brian J. Henderson, PhD, CFA

*Bernd Hanke, PhD, CFA, is at Global Systematic Investors LLP (United Kingdom). Brian J. Henderson, PhD, CFA, is at the George Washington University (USA).*

| LEARNING OUTCOMES | |
|---|---|
| Mastery | The candidate should be able to: |
| ☐ | a. discuss roles of fixed-income securities in portfolios and how fixed-income mandates may be classified; |
| ☐ | b. describe fixed-income portfolio measures of risk and return as well as correlation characteristics; |
| ☐ | c. describe bond market liquidity, including the differences among market sub-sectors, and discuss the effect of liquidity on fixed-income portfolio management; |
| ☐ | d. describe and interpret a model for fixed-income returns; |
| ☐ | e. discuss the use of leverage, alternative methods for leveraging, and risks that leverage creates in fixed-income portfolios; |
| ☐ | f. discuss differences in managing fixed-income portfolios for taxable and tax-exempt investors. |

## INTRODUCTION 1

Investors often seek regular income from their investments as well as a predetermined date when their capital will be returned. Fixed-income investments offer both.

Fixed-income instruments include a broad range of publicly traded securities (such as commercial paper, notes, and bonds traded through exchanges as well as OTC) and non-publicly traded instruments (such as loans and private placements). Individual loans or fixed-income obligations may be bundled into a pool of assets supporting such instruments as asset-backed securities and covered bonds. Fixed-income portfolio managers combine these diverse instruments across issuers, maturities, and jurisdictions to meet the various needs of investors. We discuss the different roles of fixed-income securities in portfolios and explain the two main types of fixed-income mandates—liability-based mandates and total return mandates—as well as bond

© 2021 CFA Institute. All rights reserved.

market liquidity. We also provide an overview of portfolio measures, instruments, and vehicles used in fixed-income portfolio management and introduce a model of how a bond position's total expected return can be decomposed.

## 2. ROLES OF FIXED-INCOME SECURITIES IN PORTFOLIOS

a discuss roles of fixed-income securities in portfolios and how fixed-income mandates may be classified

Fixed-income securities serve important roles in investment portfolios, including diversification, regular cash flows, and possible inflation hedging. We will briefly review the roles in turn.

### 2.1 Diversification Benefits

Fixed-income investments can provide diversification benefits when combined with other asset classes in a portfolio. Recall that a major reason portfolios can effectively reduce risk is that combining securities whose returns are not perfectly correlated (i.e., a correlation coefficient of less than +1.0) provides risk diversification. Lower correlations are associated with higher diversification benefits and lower risk. The challenge in diversifying risk is to find assets with correlations much lower than +1.0.

Correlations of fixed-income and equity securities vary, but adding fixed-income exposure to portfolios that include equity securities is usually an effective way to obtain diversification benefits. Fixed-income investments may also provide risk reduction because of their low correlations with other asset classes, such as real estate and commodities. Exhibit 1 shows the correlation between the S&P 500 Index and various fixed-income categories based on total returns (monthly) over a 20-year period ending in December 2019.

**Exhibit 1   Total Return Correlations between US Fixed Income and Equities**

| | Fixed-Income Indexes | | | | | | |
|---|---|---|---|---|---|---|---|
| | US Aggregate | 10Y US Treasury | US Corporate Bonds | Global Aggregate | US TIPS | US High Yield | Emerging Market (USD) |
| S&P 500 | −0.09 | −0.30 | 0.20 | 0.15 | 0.02 | 0.63 | 0.51 |

*Note:* Bloomberg Barclays Indices are shown.
*Source:* Bloomberg.

Exhibit 2 shows the divergent performance of US equities and bonds from the end of 2019 to the end of March 2020. For example, bonds outperformed equities amid the fears over the global COVID-19 pandemic in Q1 2020.

**Exhibit 2: Returns of S&P 500 vs. 10-Year Treasuries, 12 December 2019–31 March 2020**

*Note:* Daily data; constant-maturity 10-year Treasuries used.

Within the fixed-income asset class, the correlation between fixed-income indexes will be driven largely by the interest rate component (i.e., duration) and by geography. Rate changes can explain a significant amount of movement in fixed-income securities prices. The credit component or credit spread will likely result in diversification given differences in sectors, credit quality, and geography. For example, investment-grade securities may exhibit less correlation with below-investment-grade securities and with emerging market securities and equities. The rate component of the return can be isolated by calculating correlations using excess returns (this is more meaningful when evaluating returns across fixed-income sectors). Exhibit 3 shows correlations on an excess return basis between various fixed-income indexes.

**Exhibit 3: Excess Return Correlations of Barclays Bloomberg Indexes over a 20-Year Period**

|  | US Aggregate | US Corporate | Global Aggregate | US High Yield | Emerging Market (USD) |
|---|---|---|---|---|---|
| US Aggregate | 1.00 | | | | |
| US Corporate | 0.93 | 1.00 | | | |
| Global Aggregate | 0.88 | 0.86 | 1.00 | | |
| US High Yield | 0.86 | 0.84 | 0.76 | 1.00 | |
| Emerging Market (USD) | 0.79 | 0.76 | 0.74 | 0.80 | 1.00 |

*Notes:* Bloomberg Barclays Indices shown. Based on monthly data over 20 years ending December 2019.
*Source:* Bloomberg.

Importantly, correlations are not constant over time. During a long historical period, the average correlation of returns between two asset classes may be low, but in any particular period, the correlation can differ from the average correlation. During periods of market stress, investors may exhibit a "flight to quality" by buying safer assets, such as government bonds (increasing their prices), and selling riskier assets, such as equity securities and high-yield bonds (lowering their prices). These actions may decrease the correlation between government bonds and equity securities, as well as between government bonds and high-yield bonds. At the same time, the correlation between riskier assets, such as equity securities and high-yield bonds, may increase.

Note that similar to correlations, volatility (standard deviation) of asset class returns may also vary over time. If interest rate volatility increases, bonds, particularly those with long maturities, can exhibit higher near-term volatility relative to the average volatility over a long historical period. The standard deviation of returns for lower-credit-quality (high-yield) bonds can rise significantly during times of financial stress, because as credit quality declines and the probability of default increases, investors often view these bonds as being more similar to equities.

Exhibit 4 shows the annual returns of the S&P 500 versus the Bloomberg Barclays US Corporate High Yield Index over a 20-year period ending in December 2019. It illustrates how the fixed-income sector and equities can behave in a similar way. Recall that both asset classes are strongly linked to the issuer's business performance and fundamentals. Over the 20-year period, the average return was 7.96% and 6.26% for the high-yield index and the S&P 500, respectively, and the standard deviation was 15.54% and 17.02%, respectively. The correlation was 0.69.

**Exhibit 4  Relationship between S&P 500 and High-Yield Returns**

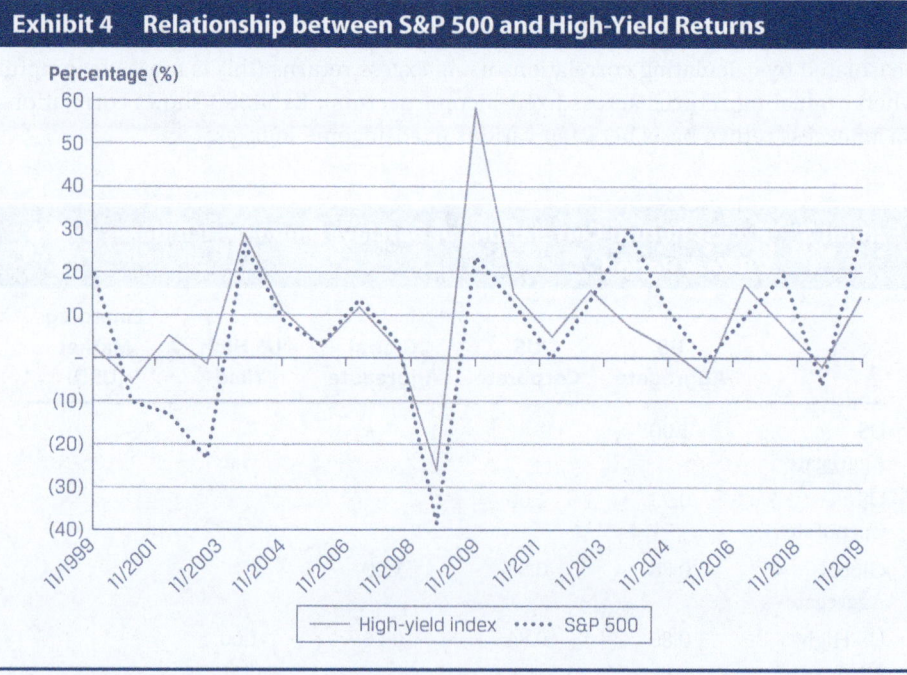

## 2.2 Benefits of Regular Cash Flows

Fixed-income investments typically produce regular cash flows for a portfolio. Regular cash flows allow investors—both individual and institutional—to meet known future obligations, such as tuition payments, pension obligations, and payouts on life insurance policies. In these cases, future liabilities can be estimated with some reasonable certainty. Fixed-income securities are often acquired and "dedicated" to funding those future liabilities. In dedicated portfolios, fixed-income securities are selected with cash flows matching the timing and magnitude of projected future liabilities.

It is important to note that reliance on regular cash flows assumes that no credit event (such as an issuer missing a scheduled interest or principal payment) or other market event (such as a decrease in interest rates that causes an increase in prepayments of mortgages underlying mortgage-backed securities) will occur. These events may cause actual cash flows of fixed-income securities to differ from expected cash flows. If any credit or market event occurs or is forecasted to occur, a portfolio manager may need to adjust the portfolio.

## 2.3 Inflation-Hedging Potential

Some fixed-income securities can provide a hedge for inflation. Bonds with floating-rate coupons can protect interest income from inflation because the market reference rate should adjust for inflation over time. The principal payment at maturity is unadjusted for inflation. Inflation-linked bonds provide investors with valuable inflation-hedging benefits by paying a return that is directly linked to an index of consumer prices and adjusting the principal for inflation. The return on inflation-linked bonds, therefore, includes a real return plus an additional component that is tied directly to the inflation rate. All else equal, inflation-linked bonds typically exhibit lower return volatility than conventional bonds and equities do because the volatility of the returns on inflation-linked bonds depends on the volatility of *real*, rather than *nominal*, interest rates. The volatility of real interest rates is typically lower than the volatility of nominal interest rates that drive the returns of conventional bonds and equities.

Many governments in developed countries and some in developing countries have issued inflation-linked bonds, as have financial and non-financial corporate issuers. For investors with long investment horizons, especially institutions facing long-term liabilities (for example, defined benefit pension plans and life insurance companies), inflation-linked bonds are particularly useful.

Adding inflation-indexed bonds to diversified portfolios of bonds and equities typically results in superior risk-adjusted real portfolio returns. This improvement occurs because inflation-linked bonds can effectively represent a separate asset class, since they offer returns that differ from those of other asset classes and add to market completeness. Introducing inflation-linked bonds to an asset allocation strategy can result in a superior mean–variance-efficient frontier.

### EXAMPLE 1

### Adding Fixed-Income Securities to a Portfolio

Mary is anxious about the level of risk in her portfolio because of a recent period of increased equity market volatility. Most of her wealth is invested in a diversified global equity portfolio.

She contacts two wealth management firms (Firm A and Firm B) for advice. In her conversations with each adviser, she expresses her desire to reduce her portfolio's risk and to have a portfolio that generates a cash flow stream with consistent purchasing power over her 15-year investment horizon.

The correlation coefficient of Mary's diversified global equity portfolio with a diversified fixed-coupon bond portfolio is −0.10 and with a diversified inflation-linked bond portfolio is 0.10. The correlation coefficient between a diversified fixed-coupon bond portfolio and a diversified inflation-linked bond portfolio is 0.65.

> The adviser from Firm A suggests diversifying half of her investment assets into nominal fixed-coupon bonds. The adviser from Firm B also suggests diversification but recommends that Mary invest 25% of her investment assets in fixed-coupon bonds and 25% in inflation-linked bonds.
>
> Evaluate the advice given to Mary by each adviser on the basis of her stated desires regarding portfolio risk reduction and cash flow stream. Recommend which advice Mary should follow, making sure to discuss the following concepts in your answer:
>
> a Diversification benefits
> b Cash flow benefits
> c Inflation-hedging benefits
>
> ### Solution:
>
> *Advice from Firm A:*
>
> Diversifying into fixed-coupon bonds would offer substantial diversification benefits in lowering overall portfolio volatility (risk) given the negative correlation of −0.10. The portfolio's volatility, measured by standard deviation, would be lower than the weighted sum of standard deviations of the diversified global equity portfolio and the diversified fixed-coupon bond portfolio. The portfolio will generate regular cash flows because it includes fixed-coupon bonds. This advice, however, does not address Mary's desire to have the cash flows maintain purchasing power over time and thus serve as an inflation hedge.
>
> *Advice from Firm B:*
>
> Diversifying into both fixed-coupon bonds and inflation-linked bonds offers additional diversification benefits beyond that offered by fixed-coupon bonds only. The correlation between diversified global equities and inflation-linked bonds is only 0.10. The correlation between nominal fixed-coupon bonds and inflation-linked bonds is 0.65, which is also less than 1.0. The portfolio will generate regular cash flows because of the inclusion of fixed-coupon and inflation-linked bonds. Adding the inflation-linked bonds helps at least partially address Mary's desire for consistent purchasing power over her investment horizon.
>
> *Which Advice to Choose:*
>
> On the basis of her stated desires and the analysis given, Mary should follow the advice provided by Firm B.

## 3. CLASSIFYING FIXED-INCOME MANDATES

The previous section covered the roles of fixed-income securities in portfolios and the benefits these securities provide. When investment mandates include an allocation to fixed income, investors need to decide how to add fixed-income securities to portfolios. Fixed-income mandates can be broadly classified into liability-based mandates and total return mandates. Exhibit 5 provides a broad overview of the different types of mandates, splitting the universe into two broad categories—liability-based mandates and total return mandates.

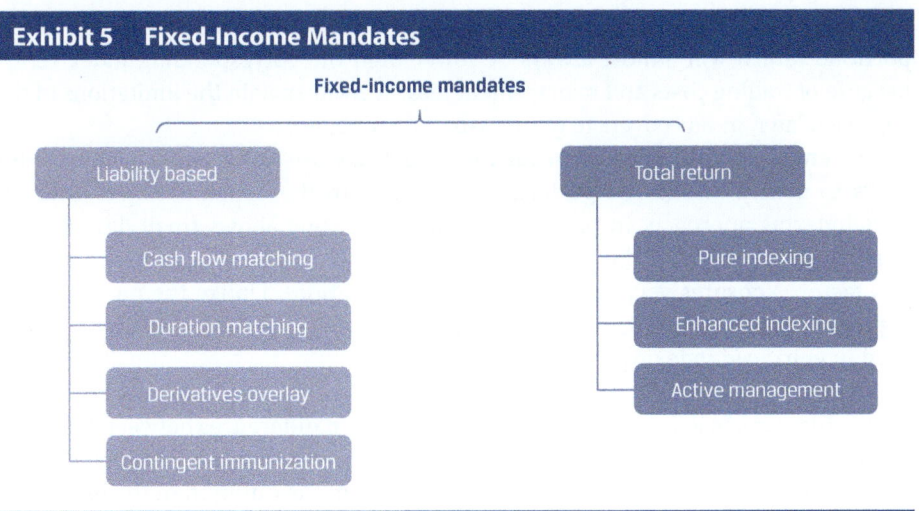

**Exhibit 5  Fixed-Income Mandates**

## 3.1 Liability-Based Mandates

**Liability-based mandates** are investments that take an investor's future obligations into consideration. Liability-based mandates are managed to match or cover expected liability payments (future cash outflows) with future projected cash inflows. As such, they are also referred to as asset/liability management (ALM) or mandates that use liability-driven investments (LDIs). These types of mandates are structured in a way to ensure that a liability or a stream of liabilities (e.g., a company's pension liabilities or those projected by insurance companies) can be covered and that any risk of shortfalls or deficient cash inflows is minimized. **Cash flow matching** is an immunization approach that attempts to ensure that all future liability payouts are matched precisely by cash flows from bonds or fixed-income derivatives. **Duration matching** is an immunization approach that is based on the duration of assets and liabilities. Ideally, the liabilities being matched (the liability portfolio) and the portfolio of assets (the bond portfolio) should be affected similarly by a change in interest rates. The mandates may use futures contracts (such as in a derivatives overlay) and, as in the case of **contingent immunization**—a hybrid approach that combines immunization with an active management approach when assets exceed the present value of liabilities—may allow for active bond portfolio management. Such liability-based mandates, which will be covered in detail later, are important because of their extensive use by such entities as pension plans and insurance companies.

## 3.2 Total Return Mandates

Total return mandates are generally managed to either track or outperform a market-weighted fixed-income benchmark, such as the Bloomberg Barclays Global Aggregate Bond Index. They are used by many types of investors, including individuals, foundations, endowments, sovereign wealth funds, and defined contribution retirement plans. Liability-based and total return mandates exhibit common features, such as the goal to achieve the highest risk-adjusted returns (or perhaps highest yields to maturity) given a set of constraints. The two types of mandates, however, have fundamentally different objectives. A common total return approach is **pure indexing**. It attempts to replicate a bond index as closely as possible and is sometimes referred to as "full replication." Under this approach, the targeted **active return** (portfolio return minus benchmark return, also known as "tracking difference") and **active risk** (annualized standard deviation of active returns, also known as the benchmark **tracking risk** or

**tracking error**) are both zero. In practice, even if the active risk is zero, the realized portfolio return will almost always be lower than the corresponding index return because of trading costs and management fees. We will explain the limitations of this approach later, in our coverage of index-based strategies.

An **enhanced indexing approach** maintains a close link to the benchmark but seeks to generate some outperformance relative to the benchmark. As with the pure indexing approach, in practice, enhanced indexing allows small deviations in portfolio holdings from the benchmark index but tracks the benchmark's primary risk factor exposures very closely (particularly duration). Unlike the pure indexing approach, however, minor risk factor mismatches (e.g., sector or quality bets) are used in enhanced indexing.

**Active management** allows larger risk factor mismatches relative to a benchmark index. These mismatches may cause significant return differences between the active portfolio and the underlying benchmark. Most notably, portfolio managers may take views on portfolio duration that differ markedly from the duration of the underlying benchmark. To take advantage of potential opportunities in changing market environments, active managers may incur significant portfolio turnover—often considerably higher than the underlying benchmark's turnover. Active portfolio managers normally charge higher management fees than pure or enhanced indexing managers charge.

Exhibit 6 summarizes the key features of the total return approaches.

**Exhibit 6   Total Return Approaches: Key Features**

|  | Pure Indexing | Enhanced Indexing | Active Management |
|---|---|---|---|
| Objective | Match benchmark return and risk as closely as possible | Modest outperformance (generally 20–30 bps) of benchmark while active risk is kept low (typically around 50 bps or lower) | Higher outperformance (generally around 50 bps or more) of benchmark and higher active risk levels |
| Portfolio weights | Ideally the same as benchmark or only slight mismatches | Small deviations from underlying benchmark | Significant deviations from underlying benchmark |
| Target risk factor profile | Aims to match risk factors exactly | Most primary risk factors are closely matched (in particular, duration) | Large risk factor deviations from benchmark (in particular, duration; note that some active strategies do not take large risk factor deviations and focus on high idiosyncratic risk) |
| Turnover | Similar to underlying benchmark | Slightly higher than underlying benchmark | Considerably higher than underlying benchmark |

## 3.3 Fixed-Income Mandates with ESG Considerations

Some fixed-income mandates include a requirement that environmental, social, and governance (ESG) factors be considered during the investment process. When considering these factors, an analyst or portfolio manager may look for evidence of whether the portfolio contains companies whose operations are favorable or unfavorable in the context of ESG and whether such companies' actions and resource management practices reflect a sustainable business model. For example, the analyst or portfolio manager may consider whether a company's activities involved significant environmental damage, instances of unfair labor practices, or lapses in corporate governance integrity. For companies that do not fare favorably in an ESG analysis, investors may assume that these companies are more likely to encounter future ESG-related incidents

# Classifying Fixed-Income Mandates

that could cause serious reputational and financial damage to the company. Such incidents could impair a company's credit quality and result in a decline in both the price of the company's bonds and the performance of a portfolio containing those bonds.

### EXAMPLE 2

## The Characteristics of Different Total Return Approaches

A consultant for a large corporate pension plan is looking at three funds (Funds X, Y, and Z) as part of the pension plan's global fixed-income allocation. All three funds use the Bloomberg Barclays Global Aggregate Bond Index as a benchmark. Exhibit 7 provides characteristics of each fund and the index. Identify the approach (pure indexing, enhanced indexing, or active management) that is *most likely* used by each fund and support your choices by referencing the information in Exhibit 7.

**Exhibit 7  Characteristics of Funds X, Y, and Z and the Bloomberg Barclays Global Aggregate Bond Index**

| Risk and Return Characteristics | Fund X | Fund Y | Fund Z | Bloomberg Barclays Global Aggregate Bond Index |
|---|---|---|---|---|
| Average maturity (years) | 8.61 | 8.35 | 9.45 | 8.34 |
| Modified duration (years) | 6.37 | 6.35 | 7.37 | 6.34 |
| Average yield to maturity (%) | 1.49 | 1.42 | 1.55 | 1.43 |
| Convexity | 0.65 | 0.60 | 0.72 | 0.60 |
| **Quality** | | | | |
| AAA | 41.10 | 41.20 | 40.11 | 41.24 |
| AA | 15.32 | 15.13 | 14.15 | 15.05 |
| A | 28.01 | 28.51 | 29.32 | 28.78 |
| BBB | 14.53 | 14.51 | 15.23 | 14.55 |
| BB | 0.59 | 0.55 | 1.02 | 0.35 |
| Not rated | 0.45 | 0.10 | 0.17 | 0.05 |
| **Maturity Exposure** | | | | |
| 0–3 years | 21.43 | 21.67 | 19.20 | 21.80 |
| 3–5 years | 23.01 | 24.17 | 22.21 | 24.23 |
| 5–10 years | 32.23 | 31.55 | 35.21 | 31.67 |
| 10+ years | 23.33 | 22.61 | 23.38 | 22.30 |
| **Country Exposure** | | | | |
| United States | 42.55 | 39.44 | 35.11 | 39.56 |
| Japan | 11.43 | 18.33 | 13.33 | 18.36 |
| France | 7.10 | 6.11 | 6.01 | 6.08 |
| United Kingdom | 3.44 | 5.87 | 4.33 | 5.99 |
| Germany | 6.70 | 5.23 | 4.50 | 5.30 |
| Italy | 4.80 | 4.01 | 4.43 | 4.07 |

*(continued)*

**Exhibit 7** (Continued)

| Risk and Return Characteristics | Fund X | Fund Y | Fund Z | Bloomberg Barclays Global Aggregate Bond Index |
|---|---|---|---|---|
| Canada | 4.44 | 3.12 | 5.32 | 3.15 |
| Other | 19.54 | 17.89 | 26.97 | 17.49 |

*Notes:* Quality, maturity exposure, and country exposure are shown as a percentage of the total for each fund and the index. Weights do not always sum to 100 because of rounding. Historical data used as of February 2016.
*Source:* Barclays Research.

**Solution:**

Fund X most likely uses an enhanced indexing approach. Fund X's modified duration and convexity are very close to those of the benchmark but still differ slightly. The average maturity of Fund X is slightly longer than that of the benchmark, whereas Fund X's average yield to maturity is slightly higher than that of the benchmark. Fund X also has deviations in quality, maturity exposure, and country exposures from the benchmark, providing further evidence of an enhanced indexing approach. Some of these deviations are meaningful; for example, Fund X has a relatively strong underweighting in Japan.

Fund Y most likely uses a pure indexing approach because it provides the closest match to the Bloomberg Barclays Global Aggregate Bond Index. The risk and return characteristics are almost identical for Fund Y and the benchmark. Furthermore, quality, maturity exposure, and country exposure deviations from the benchmark are very minor.

Fund Z most likely uses an active management approach because risk and return characteristics, quality, maturity exposure, and country exposure differ markedly from the index. The difference can be seen most notably with the mismatch in modified duration (7.37 for Fund Z versus 6.34 for the benchmark). Other differences between Fund Z and the index exist, but a sizable duration mismatch provides the strongest evidence of an active management approach.

## 4. FIXED-INCOME PORTFOLIO MEASURES

**b** describe fixed-income portfolio measures of risk and return as well as correlation characteristics

We first provide a brief review of fixed-income risk and return measures introduced in earlier lessons (Exhibit 8).

# Fixed-Income Portfolio Measures

## Exhibit 8   Bond Risk and Return Measures

| | |
|---|---|
| **Macaulay duration (MacDur)** | Macaulay duration is a weighted average of the time to receipt of the bond's promised payments, where the weights are the shares of the full price that correspond to each of the bond's promised future payments. |
| **Modified duration (ModDur)** | The Macaulay duration statistic divided by one plus the yield per period, which estimates the percentage price change (including accrued interest) for a bond given a change in its yield to maturity. |
| **Effective duration (EffDur)** | The sensitivity of the bond's price to a change in a benchmark yield curve (i.e., using a parallel shift in the benchmark yield curve (ΔCurve). Effective duration is essential to the measurement of the interest rate risk of a complex bond where future cash flows are uncertain. |
| **Key rate duration (KeyRatDur, also called *partial duration*)** | A measure of a bond's sensitivity to a change in the benchmark yield curve at a specific maturity point or segment. Key rate durations help identify "shaping risk" for a bond or a portfolio—that is, its sensitivity to changes in the shape of the benchmark yield curve (e.g., the yield curve becoming steeper or flatter or showing more or less curvature). |
| **Empirical duration** | A measure of interest rate sensitivity that is determined from market data—that is, run a regression of bond price returns on changes in a benchmark interest rate (for example, the price returns of a 10-year euro-denominated corporate bond could be regressed on changes in the 10-year German bund or the 10-year Euribor swap rate). |
| **Money duration** | A measure of the price change in units of the currency in which the bond is denominated. Money duration can be stated per 100 of par value or in terms of the bond's actual position size in the portfolio. Commonly called "dollar duration" in the United States. |
| **Price value of a basis point (PVBP)** | An estimate of the change in a bond's price given a 1 bp change in yield to maturity. PVBP "scales" money duration so that it can be interpreted as money gained or lost for each basis point change in the reference interest rate. |
| | Also referred to in North America as the "dollar value of an 0.01" (pronounced *oh-one*) and abbreviated as DV01. It is calibrated to a bond's par value of 100; for example, a DV01 of $0.08 is equivalent to 8 cents per 100 points. (The terms PVBP and DV01 are used interchangeably; we will generally use PVBP, but DV01 has the same meaning). |
| | A related statistic to PVBP, sometimes called "basis point value" (or BPV), is the money duration times 0.0001 (1 bp). |

*(continued)*

| | |
|---|---|
| **Exhibit 8** | **(Continued)** |
| Convexity | A second-order effect that describes a bond's price behavior for larger yield movements. It captures the extent to which the yield/price relationship deviates from a linear relationship. |
| | If a bond has positive convexity, the expected return of the bond will be higher than the return of an identical-duration, lower-convexity bond if interest rates change. |
| | This price behavior is valuable to investors, and therefore, a bond with higher convexity might be expected to have a lower yield to maturity than a similar-duration bond with less convexity. |
| | Nominal convexity calculations assume that the cash flows do not change when yields to maturity change. |
| Effective convexity (EffCon) | A curve convexity statistic that measures the secondary effect of a change in a benchmark yield curve. A pricing model is used to determine the new prices when the benchmark curve is shifted upward (PV+) and downward (PV−) by the same amount (ΔCurve), holding other factors constant. |

Exhibit 8 provides a reminder of convexity and why it is valuable. It is likely to be even more valuable when interest rate volatility is expected to increase. This dynamic tends to drive changes in the shape of the yield curve: As convexity becomes more valuable, investors will bid up prices on the longer-maturity bonds (which have more convexity), and the long end of the curve may decline or even invert (or invert further), increasing the curvature of the yield curve. A helpful heuristic for understanding convexity is that for zero-coupon (option free) bonds, the following are true:

- Macaulay durations increase linearly with maturity: A 30-year zero-coupon bond has three times the duration of a 10-year zero-coupon bond. Convexity is approximately proportional to duration squared; therefore, a 30-year zero-coupon bond has about nine times the convexity of a 10-year zero-coupon bond.

- Coupon-paying bonds have more convexity than zero-coupon bonds of the same duration: A 30-year coupon-paying bond with a duration of approximately 18 years has more convexity than an 18-year zero-coupon bond. The more widely dispersed a bond's cash flows are around the duration point, the more convexity it will exhibit. For this reason, a zero-coupon bond has the lowest convexity of all bonds of a given duration.

### SCALING CONVENTIONS

Convexity statistics must always be interpreted carefully because there is no convention for how they should be presented. When calculating the impact of convexity in approximating returns, the proper accounting for the scaling of convexity is important. Note that some data vendors report the convexity statistic divided by 100, whereas other applications may use the "raw" number.

# Fixed-Income Portfolio Measures

## 4.1 Portfolio Measures of Risk and Return

Building on the measures of risk and return that apply to individual fixed-income securities, we now provide an overview of measures of risk and return applicable to portfolios of fixed-income securities. We will then illustrate their use in fixed income in a portfolio management scenario and refer to them in the subsequent coverage of liability-driven investing and total return strategies.

*Bond portfolio duration* is the sensitivity of a portfolio of bonds to small changes in interest rates. Recall that it can be calculated as the weighted average of time to receipt of the aggregate cash flows or, more commonly, as the weighted average of the individual bond durations of the portfolio.

*Modified duration of a bond portfolio* indicates the percentage change in the market value given a change in yield to maturity. If the modified duration of a portfolio is 15, then for a 100 bp increase or decrease in yield to maturity, the market value of the portfolio is expected to decrease or increase by about 15%. Modified duration of a portfolio comprising $j$ fixed-income securities can be estimated as

$$\text{AvgModDur} = \sum_{j=1}^{J} \text{ModDur}_j \left( \frac{\text{MV}_j}{\text{MV}} \right), \tag{1}$$

where MV stands for market value of the portfolio and $\text{MV}_j$ is the market value of a specific bond.

*Convexity of a bond portfolio* can be a valuable tool when positioning a portfolio. Importantly, it is a second-order effect; it operates behind duration in importance and can largely be ignored for small yield changes. When convexity is added with the use of derivatives, however, it can be extremely important to returns. This effect will be demonstrated later. Negative convexity may also be an important factor in a bond's or a portfolio's returns. For bonds with short option positions embedded in their structures (such as mortgage-backed securities or callable bonds) or portfolios with short option positions, the convexity effect may be large. For a portfolio comprising $j$ fixed-income securities, it can be estimated as

$$\text{AvgConvexity} = \sum_{j=1}^{J} \text{Convexity}_j \left( \frac{\text{MV}_j}{\text{MV}} \right). \tag{2}$$

Adding convexity to a portfolio is not costless. Portfolios with higher convexity are most often characterized by lower yields to maturity. Investors will be willing to pay for increased convexity when they expect yields to change by more than enough to cover the amount given up in yield to maturity. Convexity is more valuable when yields to maturity are more volatile. A portfolio's convexity can be altered by shifting the maturity/duration distribution of bonds in the portfolio, by adding individual bonds with the desired convexity properties, or by using derivatives.

*Effective duration and convexity of a portfolio* are the relevant summary statistics when future cash flows of bonds in a portfolio are contingent on interest rate changes.

$$\text{Effective duration}(\text{EffDur}) = \frac{(PV_-) - (PV_+)}{2(\Delta \text{Curve})(PV_0)}. \tag{3}$$

$$\text{Effective convexity}(\text{EffCon}) = \frac{(PV_-) + (PV_+) - 2(PV_0)}{(\Delta \text{Curve})^2 (PV_0)}. \tag{4}$$

**Spread duration** is a useful measure for determining a portfolio's sensitivity to changes in credit spreads. Duration indicates the percentage price effect of an interest rate change on a bond, and spread duration measures the effect of a change in yield spread on a bond's price. Spread duration provides the approximate percentage increase (decrease) in bond price expected for a 1% decrease (increase) in credit spread.

**Duration times spread** (DTS) is a modification of the spread duration definition to incorporate the empirical observation that spread changes across the credit spectrum tend to occur on a *proportional percentage* basis rather than being based on *absolute* basis point changes. This measure, reviewed in detail in a later lesson, weights the spread duration by a factor equal to the current credit spread, increasing the magnitude of expected price changes for a given change in spread.

*Portfolio dispersion* captures the variance of the times to receipt of cash flows with respect to the duration. It is used in measuring interest rate immunization for liabilities. Whereas Macaulay duration is the weighted *average* of the times to receipt of cash flows, dispersion is the weighted *variance*. It measures the extent to which the payments are spread out around the duration. Convexity is affected by the dispersion of cash flows. Higher cash flow dispersion leads to an increase in convexity.

## 4.2 Correlations between Fixed-Income Sectors

Correlation characteristics refer to the interplay between benchmark rates, spreads, and such factors as currencies. Correlations between fixed-income sectors within a market are likely to be higher than those across markets given country-specific factors, such as central bank policy, economic growth, and inflation. In developed economies, investment-grade securities with a low probability of default are highly correlated with interest rate changes in the sovereign yield curve. Below-investment-grade securities are affected more by changes in spread than by changes in general interest rates and often exhibit stronger correlations with equity markets. Recall that correlations between interest rates and spreads can often be negative. As the economy worsens, interest rates fall and spreads widen, and the reverse occurs when the economy improves. Correlations for global government bonds will be partly driven by changes in interest rates but also by changes in local currency exchange rates.

## 4.3 Use of Measures of Risk and Return in Portfolio Management

We now provide an overview of how portfolio measures may be used by fund managers to reflect their views.

### 4.3.1 *Portfolio Duration in Total Return Mandates*

Total return mandates that are actively managed often use a top-down approach to establish the large risk factors in a portfolio combined with a bottom-up approach of individual security selection. The analytics discussed earlier can be used to measure and manage the macroeconomic risk factors in the portfolio. Portfolio managers develop or use a forecast of the direction of the economy and an assessment of the current business, political, and regulatory environment to develop themes that can be reflected in the portfolio. On the basis of expectations for changes in interest rates and the shape of the yield curve, portfolio managers can adjust the duration of a portfolio to reflect their view. For example, if the portfolio manager expects interest rates to rise and the yield curve to steepen, she would reduce the exposure of the portfolio to longer-dated bonds relative to the benchmark, which would reduce portfolio duration. If her view materialized as expected, all else equal, the fund would outperform the benchmark, resulting in active excess returns.

### 4.3.2 *Managing Credit Exposure Using Spread Duration*

Portfolio managers often use the spread duration measures introduced earlier to gauge the portfolio's sensitivity to changes in credit spreads. A portfolio manager expecting credit spreads to narrow may wish to increase the spread duration in an

# Fixed-Income Portfolio Measures

actively managed portfolio. The manager may face constraints, such as a target duration, rating-based restrictions, or limits to derivatives use, as part of the investment mandate. A second way to increase the portfolio credit exposure is to reduce the average credit rating of the portfolio; for example, reduce A rated names and increase BBB rated credits. In this case, the duration times spread measure may be a more appropriate measure of portfolio value changes. These active portfolio management tools are addressed in more detail in a later lesson on credit strategies.

The single bond risk and return measures discussed previously at an aggregate level will determine the large risk factors for the portfolio. The portfolio manager will select securities as part of the portfolio construction process to achieve a targeted level of tracking error or active risk relative to a benchmark. The contribution to duration, convexity, spread duration, and DTS of a single bond to the portfolio is weighted by the market value of the position relative to the total market value of the portfolio. The portfolio manager will select a diversified universe of holdings to construct the portfolio in the manner he believes will optimize expected return and risk.

### 4.3.3 Relative Value Concept

**Relative value** is a key concept in the active management of fixed-income portfolios that describes the selection of the most attractive individual securities to populate the portfolio with, using ranking and comparing. Portfolio managers analyze and rank securities on the basis of such considerations as valuation, issuer fundamentals, and market technical conditions (supply and demand). This analysis is carried out across sectors, issuers, and individual securities to select securities with the most attractive risk and return profiles. The portfolio manager will establish a time horizon over which the relative value analysis is applied. The single bond characteristics can be used to express an active position relative to the benchmark. For example, each bond has a distinct key rate duration (KeyRateDur) profile. If the portfolio manager wants to establish a bullet or barbell position as part of the active risk decision, bonds with a specific KeyRateDur profile will be selected. Similarly, the portfolio manager can select securities that in aggregate have more/less DTS than the benchmark if she is bullish/bearish on corporate bond spreads. The selection of the most attractive individual securities to populate the portfolio will apply relative value analysis to compare and rank securities. In the context of the efficient frontier, those securities that offer the most expected return for a given level of risk would offer the best relative value.

The positioning of the portfolio reflects the portfolio manager's total return expectations for the market and relative returns versus the benchmark, given his views with regard to both the direction of interest rates and credit spread changes. Diversification considerations ensure that idiosyncratic risks are within acceptable risk parameters.

> **EXAMPLE 3**
>
> 1. Which of the following best describes a measure of sensitivity to changes in yields to maturity for a portfolio of bonds with cash flows contingent on interest rate changes?
>    - **A** Portfolio dispersion
>    - **B** Modified duration
>    - **C** Effective duration
> 2. Which of the following is a true statement about portfolio dispersion?
>    - **A** It can be described as the variance of time to the receipt of cash flows.
>    - **B** The higher the dispersion, the lower the convexity of the portfolio.
>    - **C** It determines the portfolio's sensitivity to changes in credit spreads.

> **Solutions:**
>
> 1 C is correct. Effective duration is particularly relevant in scenarios where the cash flows from the bonds held in a portfolio are contingent on changes in interest rates.
>
> 2 A is correct. Dispersion measures the variance of the time to receive cash flows from the fixed-income securities held.

## 5. BOND MARKET LIQUIDITY

c describe bond market liquidity, including the differences among market sub-sectors, and discuss the effect of liquidity on fixed-income portfolio management

A liquid security is one that may be transacted quickly with little effect on the security's price. Fixed-income securities vary greatly in their liquidity.

Compared with equities, fixed-income markets are generally less liquid. The global fixed-income universe contains many individual bonds with varying features. Many issuers have multiple bonds outstanding with their own unique maturity dates, coupon rates, early redemption features, and other specific features.

An important structural feature affecting liquidity is that fixed-income markets are typically over-the-counter dealer markets. Search costs (the costs of finding a willing counterparty) exist in bond markets because investors may have to locate desired bonds. In addition, when either buying or selling, investors may have to obtain quotes from various dealers to obtain the most advantageous pricing. With limited, although improving, sources for transaction prices and quotes, bond markets are ordinarily less transparent than equity markets. Liquidity, search costs, and price transparency are closely related to the type of issuer and its credit quality. An investor is likely to find that bonds of a highly creditworthy government issuer are more liquid, have greater price transparency, and have lower search costs than bonds of, for example, a corporate issuer with lower credit quality.

Bond liquidity is typically highest immediately after issuance. For example, an on-the-run bond issue (the most recently issued bonds) of a highly creditworthy sovereign entity is typically more liquid than a bond with similar features—including maturity—that was issued previously (an off-the-run bond). On-the-run bonds also trade at narrow bid–ask spreads. This difference in liquidity is typically present even if the off-the-run bond was issued only one or two months earlier. One reason for this phenomenon is that soon after bonds are issued, dealers normally have a supply of the bonds in inventory, but as time goes by and bonds are traded, many are purchased by buy-and-hold investors. Once in the possession of such investors, those bonds are no longer available for trading.

Recall that liquidity typically affects bond yields to maturity. Bond investors require higher yields for investing in illiquid securities relative to otherwise identical securities that are more liquid. The higher yield to maturity compensates investors for the costs they may encounter if they try to sell illiquid bonds prior to maturity. These costs include the opportunity costs associated with the delays in finding trading counterparties, as well as the bid–ask spread (which is a direct loss of wealth). The incremental yield to maturity investors require for holding illiquid bonds instead of liquid bonds is referred to as a *liquidity premium.* The magnitude of the liquidity premium normally varies depending on such factors as the issuer, the issue size, and time to maturity. For example, when a 10-year US Treasury bond shifts from on-the-run to off-the-run status, it typically trades at a yield to maturity several basis points above that of the new on-the-run bond.

## 5.1 Liquidity among Bond Market Sub-Sectors

Bond market liquidity varies across sub-sectors. These sub-sectors can be categorized by such key features as issuer type, credit quality, issue size, and maturity. The global bond market includes sovereign government bonds, non-sovereign government bonds, government-related bonds, corporate bonds, and securitized bonds (such as asset-backed securities and commercial mortgage-backed securities). Sovereign government bonds are typically more liquid than corporate and non-sovereign government bonds. Their superior liquidity relates to their large issuance size, use as benchmark bonds, acceptance as collateral in the repo market, and well-recognized issuers. Sovereign government bonds of countries with high credit quality and large issuance are typically more liquid than bonds of lower-credit-quality countries.

Corporate bonds are issued by many different companies and represent a wide spectrum of credit quality. For corporate bonds with low credit quality, it can be difficult to find a counterparty dealer with the securities in inventory or willing to take them into inventory. Bonds of infrequent issuers are often less liquid than the bonds of issuers with many outstanding issues because market participants are less familiar with companies that seldom issue debt. In addition, smaller issues are generally less liquid than larger issues because small bond issues are typically excluded from major bond indexes with minimum issue size requirements.

## 5.2 The Effects of Liquidity on Fixed-Income Portfolio Management

Liquidity concerns influence fixed-income portfolio management in multiple ways, including pricing, portfolio construction, and consideration of alternatives to bonds (such as derivatives).

### 5.2.1 *Pricing*

Sources for pricing of recent bond transactions—notably corporate bonds—are not always readily available. Note that price transparency is improving in some bond markets. In the United States, the Financial Industry Regulatory Authority's Trade Reporting and Compliance Engine (TRACE) and the Municipal Securities Rulemaking Board's Electronic Municipal Market Access (EMMA) are electronic systems that help increase transparency in corporate and municipal bond markets, and similar initiatives play a similar role elsewhere for corporate bonds traded on market exchanges, increasing pricing transparency. In most bond markets, however, the lack of transparency in corporate bond trading presents a challenge.

Because many bonds do not trade or trade infrequently, using recent transaction prices to represent current value is not practical. Reliance on last traded prices, which may be out of date and may not incorporate current market conditions, could result in costly trading decisions. The determinants of corporate bond value, including interest rates, credit spreads, and liquidity premiums, change frequently. One solution to the pricing problem is to use matrix pricing that makes use of observable liquid benchmark yields of similar maturity and duration as well as benchmark spreads of bonds with comparable times to maturity, credit quality, and sector or security type to estimate the current market yield and price.

### 5.2.2 Portfolio Construction

Investors' liquidity preferences directly influence portfolio construction. In constructing a portfolio, investors must consider the important trade-off between yield to maturity and liquidity. As mentioned previously, illiquid bonds typically have higher yields to maturity; a buy-and-hold investor seeking higher returns will often prefer less liquid bonds with higher yields to maturity. In contrast, investors who prefer greater liquidity will likely sacrifice returns and choose more liquid bonds with lower yields to maturity. Some investors may restrict their portfolio holdings to bonds within a certain maturity range. This restriction reduces the need to sell bonds to generate needed cash inflows. In such cases, the investors that anticipate their liquidity needs may give up the higher yield to maturity typically available to longer-term bonds. In addition to avoiding longer-term bonds, investors with liquidity concerns may also avoid small issues and private placements of corporate bonds.

A challenge in bond portfolio construction relates to the dealer market. Bond dealers often carry an inventory of bonds because buy and sell orders do not arrive simultaneously. A dealer is not certain how long bonds will remain in its inventory. Less liquid bonds are likely to remain in inventory longer than liquid bonds. A dealer provides bid–ask quotes (prices at which it will buy and sell) on bonds of its choice. Some illiquid bonds will not have quotes, particularly bid quotes, from any dealer. A number of different factors determine the bid–ask spread. Riskier bonds often have higher bid–ask spreads because of dealers' aversion to hold those bonds in inventory. Because bond dealers must finance their inventories, the dealers incur costs in both obtaining funding and holding those bonds. Dealers seek to cover their costs and make a profit through the bid–ask spread, and therefore, the spread will be higher for illiquid bonds that are likely to remain in inventory longer.

A bond's bid–ask spread is also a function of the bond's complexity and how easily market participants can analyze the issuer's creditworthiness. Bid–ask spreads in government bonds are generally lower than spreads in corporate bonds or structured financial instruments, such as asset-backed securities. Conventional (plain vanilla) corporate bonds normally have lower spreads than corporate bonds with non-standard or complex features, such as embedded options. Bonds of large, high-credit-quality corporations that have many outstanding bond issues are the most liquid among corporate bonds, and thus they have relatively low bid–ask spreads compared with smaller, less creditworthy companies.

Illiquidity directly increases bid–ask spreads of bonds, which increases the cost of trading. Higher transaction costs reduce the benefits of active portfolio decisions and may decrease portfolio managers' willingness to adjust their portfolios to take advantage of opportunities that present themselves. As an example to quantify trading costs, if a corporate bond with a 15-year duration is being quoted by dealers with a 10 bp bid–ask spread, the cost impact to the portfolio is approximately 1.50% (0.0010 × 15 × 100 = 1.50%). The portfolio manager would buy the bond at $100, and when the portfolio is priced (typically at bid or the midpoint between the bid and the ask), the bond would have a value of $98.50, reducing total portfolio return. This is the price that would be realized if the bond were sold, holding other factors constant. To mitigate trading costs, investors can participate in the primary or new issue market where bonds are typically issued at a discount to the price at which a similar issue trades in the secondary market.

**KNOWLEDGE CHECK**

Rank the following instruments from the usually most liquid to the least liquid:

- Low-credit-quality corporate bond

- Recently issued on-the-run sovereign bond issued by a high-credit-quality government
- High-credit-quality corporate bond
- Sovereign bond issued a year ago by a high-credit-quality government

**Solution:**

- Recently issued on-the-run sovereign bond issued by a high-credit-quality government
- Sovereign bond issued a year ago by a high-credit-quality government
- High-credit-quality corporate bond
- Low-credit-quality corporate bond

### 5.2.3 Alternatives to Direct Investment in Bonds

Because transacting in fixed-income securities may present challenges resulting from low liquidity in many segments of the fixed-income market, fund managers may use alternative methods to establish bond market exposures. The methods we outline are applicable across different fixed-income mandates. We will take a more in-depth look at the ones particularly relevant to passive and liability-driven mandates later as part of our coverage dedicated to such mandates. Next, we provide an overview of the most common methods—specifically, mutual funds, exchange-traded funds (ETFs), exchange-traded derivatives, and OTC derivatives. In considering direct versus indirect investments, the asset manager must weigh the ongoing fees associated with such instruments as mutual funds and ETFs against the bid–offer cost of direct investment in the underlying securities.

*ETFs and mutual funds.* These products provide an alternative to transacting in individual bonds. They are more liquid than the underlying securities. Mutual funds are pooled investment vehicles whose shares or units represent a proportional share in the ownership of the assets in an underlying portfolio. In the case of open-end mutual funds, new shares may be redeemed or issued at the fund's net asset value (NAV) established at the end of each trading day based on the fund's valuation of all existing assets minus liabilities, divided by the total number of shares outstanding. Bond mutual fund investors enjoy the advantage of being able to redeem holdings at the fund's NAV rather than needing to sell illiquid positions. The benefit from economies of scale is usually the overriding factor for smaller investors in their choice of a bond mutual fund over direct investment. Because bonds often trade at a minimum lot size of USD1 million or higher per bond, successful replication of a broad index or construction of a diversified actively managed portfolio could easily require hundreds of millions of dollars in investments. Therefore, the greater diversification across fixed-income markets achievable by a larger fund may be well worth the additional cost in terms of an upfront load in some instances and an annual management fee.

Although investors benefit from increased diversification, the fund must outline its stated investment objectives and periodic fees, but actual security holdings are available only on a retroactive basis. Unlike the underlying securities, bond mutual funds have no maturity date; the fund manager continuously purchases and sells bonds to track index performance, and monthly interest payments fluctuate on the basis of fund holdings.

Exchange-traded funds share some mutual fund characteristics but have more tradability features. Investors benefit from greater bond ETF liquidity versus mutual funds given their availability to be purchased or sold throughout the trading day.

*Exchange traded derivatives.* Futures and options on futures provide exposure to underlying bonds. Being exchange traded, they involve financial instruments with standardized terms, documentation, and pricing traded on an organized exchange. Exchange-traded products also include interest rate products and options for interest rate–related ETFs.

*OTC derivatives.* Interest rate swaps are the most widely used OTC derivative worldwide and entail customized arrangements between two counterparties that reference an underlying market price or index. Some interest rate swaps are liquid, with multiple swap dealers posting competitive two-way quotes. In addition to interest rate swaps, fixed-income portfolio managers use inflation swaps, total return swaps, and credit swaps to alter their portfolio exposure. Because they trade over the counter, swaps may be tailored to an investor's specific needs.

A total return swap (TRS), a common over-the-counter portfolio derivative strategy, combines elements of interest rate swaps and credit derivatives. Similar to an interest rate swap, a total return swap involves the periodic exchange of cash flows between two parties for the life of the contract. Unlike an interest rate swap, in which counterparties exchange a stream of fixed cash flows versus a floating-rate benchmark such as the MRR (the market reference rate) to transform fixed assets or liabilities to a variable exposure, a TRS has a periodic exchange based on a reference obligation that is an underlying equity, commodity, or bond index. Exhibit 9 outlines the most basic TRS structure. The **total return receiver** receives both the cash flows from the underlying index and any appreciation in the index over the period in exchange for paying the MRR plus a predetermined spread. The **total return payer** is responsible for paying the reference obligation cash flows and return to the receiver but will also be compensated by the receiver for any depreciation in the index or default losses incurred by the portfolio.

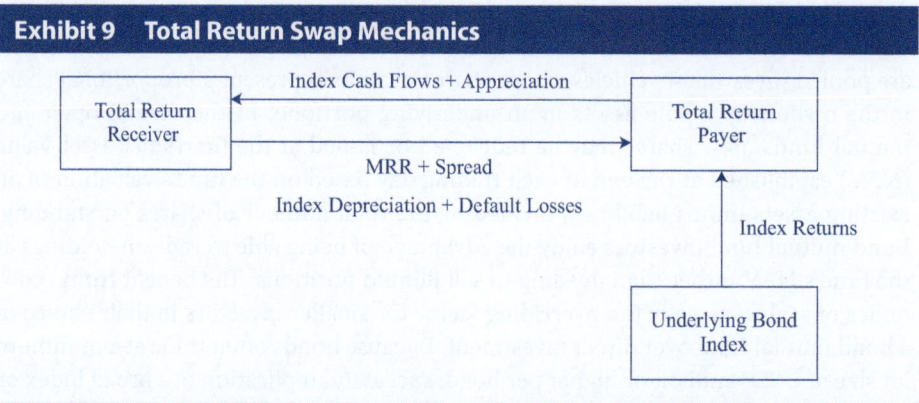

**Exhibit 9  Total Return Swap Mechanics**

The TRS transaction is an over-the-counter derivative contract based on an ISDA (International Swaps and Derivatives Association) master agreement. This contract specifies a notional amount, periodic cash flows, and final maturity, as well as the credit and other legal provisions related to the transaction. The historical attractiveness of using TRS stemmed from the efficient risk transfer on the reference obligation from one counterparty to another on a confidential basis without requiring the full cash outlay associated with the mutual fund or ETF purchase. In fact, another way to think of the TRS is as a synthetic secured financing transaction in which the investor (the total return receiver) benefits from more-advantageous funding terms faced by a dealer (typically the total return payer) offering to facilitate the transaction.

The potential for both a smaller initial cash outlay and lower swap bid–offer costs compared with the transaction costs of direct purchase or use of a mutual fund or ETF are the most compelling reasons to consider a TRS to add fixed-income exposure. That said, several considerations may offset these benefits in a number of instances:

- The investor does not legally own the underlying assets but, rather, has a combined synthetic long position in both the market and the credit risk of the index that is contingent on the performance of the total return payer. The total return receiver must both perform the necessary credit due diligence on its counterparty and face the rollover risk at maturity of having the ability to renew the contract with reasonable pricing and business terms in the future.

- Structural changes to the market and greater regulatory oversight, particularly capital rules affecting dealers, have raised the cost and increased the operational burden of these transactions because of the need to collateralize mark-to-market positions frequently and within shorter timeframe.

- As a funding cost arbitrage transaction, the TRS can allow investors to gain particular access to subsets of the fixed-income markets, such as bank loans or high-yield instruments for which cash markets are relatively illiquid or the cost and administrative complexity of maintaining a portfolio of these instruments is prohibitive for the investor.

# A MODEL FOR FIXED-INCOME RETURNS

d   describe and interpret a model for fixed-income returns

Investors often have views on future changes in the yield curve and structure or restructure their portfolios accordingly. Investment strategies should be evaluated in terms of expected returns rather than just yields to maturity. A bond's yield to maturity provides an incomplete measure of its expected return. Instead, expected fixed-income returns consist of a number of different components in addition to yield to maturity. Examining these components leads to a better understanding of the driving forces behind expected returns—on individual bonds and fixed-income portfolios. The focus is on *expected* as opposed to *realized* returns, which may be decomposed in a similar manner.

## 6.1 Decomposing Expected Returns

Decomposing expected fixed-income returns allows an investor to differentiate among several important return components. At the most general level, expected returns, denoted as E(R), can be decomposed (approximately) in the following manner:

$E(R) \approx$ Coupon income

+/– Rolldown return

+/– E($\Delta$Price due to investor's view of benchmark yield)

+/– E($\Delta$Price due to investor's view of yield spreads)

+/– E($\Delta$Price due to investor's view of currency value changes),

where E(...) represents effects on expected returns based on expectations of the item in parentheses and $\Delta$ represents "change." The decomposition holds only approximately and ignores taxes (note that some of the material on decomposing expected returns has been adapted from Hanke and Seals [2010]).

### 6.1.1 Coupon Income

Coupon income is the income that an investor receives from coupon payments relative to the bond's price and interest on reinvestment income. Assuming there is no reinvestment income, coupon income equals a bond's annual current yield.

Coupon income (or Current yield) = Annual coupon payment/Current bond price.

### 6.1.2 Rolldown Return

The rolldown return, sometimes referred to as "rolldown and carry return," results from the bond "rolling down" the yield curve as the time to maturity decreases (see Exhibit 10), assuming zero interest rate volatility. Bond prices change as time passes even if the market discount rate remains the same. As time passes, a bond's price typically moves closer to par. This price movement is illustrated by the constant-yield price trajectory, which shows the "pull to par" effect on the price of a bond trading at a premium or a discount to par value. If the issuer does not default, the price of a bond approaches par value as its time to maturity approaches zero.

**Exhibit 10  Rolling down the Yield Curve Effect**

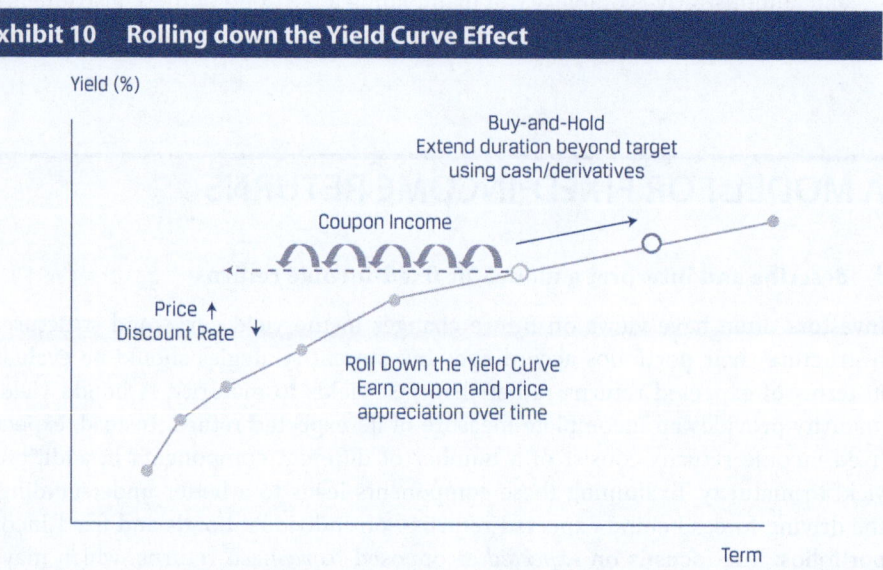

The rolldown return equals the bond's percentage price change assuming an unchanged yield curve over the strategy horizon. Bonds trading at a premium to their par value will experience capital losses during their remaining life, and bonds trading at a discount relative to their par value will experience capital gains during their remaining life.

To compute the rolldown return, the bond has to be revalued at the end of the strategy horizon assuming an unchanged yield curve. Then the rolldown return is as follows:

$$\text{Rolldown return} = \frac{\left(\text{Bond price}_{End\text{-}of\text{-}horizon\ period} - \text{Bond price}_{Beginning\text{-}of\text{-}horizon\ period}\right)}{\text{Bond price}_{Beginning\text{-}of\text{-}horizon\ period}}. \quad (5)$$

The sum of the coupon income and the rolldown return may be referred to as the bond's *rolling yield*.

### 6.1.3 Views of Benchmark Yields

The expected change in price based on investor's views of benchmark yields to maturity and the term structure of yield volatility reflects an investor's expectation of changes in yields to maturity and yield volatility over the investment horizon. This expected change is zero if the investor expects yield curves and yield volatility to remain unchanged. Assuming the investor does expect a change in the yield curve, this expected return component is computed as follows:

E(Change in price based on investor's views of yields and yield volatility)
$$= (-\text{ModDur} \times \Delta\text{Yield}) + [½ \times \text{Convexity} \times (\Delta\text{Yield})^2], \quad (6)$$

where ModDur is the modified duration of a bond, ΔYield is the expected change in yield to maturity, and Convexity reflects the second-order effect of the price–yield relationship. Note that for bonds with embedded options, the duration and convexity measures used should be effective duration and effective convexity. Also, in contrast to fixed-coupon bonds, floating-rate notes have a modified duration that is largely due to spread changes, as described in detail later.

### 6.1.4 Views of Yield Spreads

The expected change in price based on investor's views of yield spreads reflects an investor's expectation of changes in market credit spreads over the investment horizon. When economic or credit conditions are improving, spreads are typically said to tighten, thereby reducing the required yield to maturity on the bond. Deteriorating conditions would conversely result in higher required yields to maturity. This component of expected return reflects general market conditions rather than any spread changes due to issuer-specific (or idiosyncratic) risk and is computed as follows:

E(ΔPrice based on investor's views of yield spreads)
$$= (-\text{ModDur} \times \Delta\text{Yield}) + [½ \times \text{Convexity} \times (\Delta\text{Yield})^2]. \quad (7)$$

Yield spreads can also fluctuate on the basis of idiosyncratic risk. Credit migration refers to credit quality changes that may result in an issuer downgrade or upgrade. This can result in either lower spreads for higher ratings or higher spreads for lower ratings affecting the expected return on bonds. Higher-quality credits tend to have low probabilities of default but can experience changes in bond prices due to an anticipated or actual migration. The price impact is calculated in the same way as noted previously for market changes in yield to maturity. Note that investors face price declines on non-defaulted bonds if spreads widen. Yearly default rates can vary significantly and are more severe for speculative-grade (high-yield) issues.

### 6.1.5 Views of Currency Value Changes

If an investor holds bonds denominated in a currency other than her home currency, she also needs to factor in any expected fluctuations in the currency exchange rate or expected currency gains or losses over the investment horizon. The magnitude and direction of the change in the exchange rate can be based on a variety of factors, including the manager's own view, results from surveys, or a quantitative model output. It can also be based on the exchange rate that can be locked in over the investment horizon using currency forwards.

Return measured in functional currency terms (domestic currency returns of foreign currency assets) can be shown as $R_{DC} = (1 + R_{FC})(1 + R_{FX}) - 1$ for a single asset or

$$R_{DC} = \sum_{i=1}^{n} \omega_i \left(1 + R_{FC,i}\right)\left(1 + R_{FX,i}\right) - 1 \qquad (8)$$

for a portfolio, where $R_{DC}$ and $R_{FC}$ are the domestic and foreign currency returns expressed as a percentage, $R_{FX}$ is the percentage change of the domestic currency versus the foreign currency, and $\omega_i$ is the respective portfolio weight of each foreign currency asset (in domestic currency terms), with the sum of $\omega_i$ equal to 1. In the context of the return decomposition framework, $R_{DC}$ simply combines the third factor, E(ΔPrice due to investor's view of benchmark yield), and the fifth factor, (+/− E(ΔFunctional currency value), in the expected fixed-income return model.

## EXAMPLE 4

### Decomposing Expected Returns

Ann Smith works for a US investment firm in its London office. She manages the firm's British pound–denominated corporate bond portfolio. Her department head in New York City has asked Smith to make a presentation on next year's total expected return of her portfolio in US dollars and the components of this return. Exhibit 11 shows information on the portfolio and Smith's expectations for the next year. Expected return (for the bond portfolio) and its components are on an annualized basis, and any potential coupons are assumed to be paid annually. Calculate the total expected return of Smith's bond portfolio, assuming no reinvestment income.

| Exhibit 11  Portfolio Characteristics and Expectations | |
|---|---|
| Notional principal of portfolio (in millions) | £100 |
| Average bond coupon payment (per £100 par value) | £2.75 |
| Coupon frequency | Annual |
| Investment horizon | 1 year |
| Current average bond price | £97.12 |
| Expected average bond price in one year (assuming an unchanged yield curve) | £97.27 |
| Average bond convexity in one year | 18 |
| Average bond modified duration in one year | 3.70 |
| Expected average benchmark yield-to-maturity change | 0.26% |
| Expected change in spread (spread expected to narrow in this scenario) | -0.10% |
| Expected currency losses (£ depreciation versus US$) | 0.50% |

### Solution:

The portfolio's coupon income is 2.83%. The portfolio has an average coupon of £2.75 on a £100 notional principal and currently trades at £97.11. The coupon income over a one-year horizon is 2.83% = £2.75/£97.11.

In one year's time, assuming an unchanged yield curve and zero interest rate volatility, the rolldown return is 0.17% = (£97.27 − £97.11)/£97.11.

# A Model for Fixed-Income Returns

The rolling yield, which is the sum of the coupon income and the rolldown return, is 3.00% = 2.83% + 0.17%.

The expected change in price based on Smith's views of benchmark yields to maturity is –0.96%, calculated as follows: The bond portfolio has a modified duration of 3.70 and a convexity statistic of 18. Smith expects an average benchmark yield-to-maturity change of 0.26%. Smith expects to incur a decrease in prices and a reduction in return based on her rate view. The expected change in price based on Smith's views of yields to maturity and yield spreads is thus $-0.0096 = (-3.70 \times 0.0026) + [½ \times 18 \times (0.0026)^2]$. So the expected reduction in return based on Smith's rate view is 0.96%.

Smith expects an impact from the 0.1% change (narrowing in this scenario) in spread in her well-diversified investment-grade bond portfolio. The impact on the expected return is, therefore, $0.37\% = [-3.70 \times (-0.0010)] + [1/2 \times 18 \times (-0.0010)^2]$.

Smith expects the British pound, the foreign currency in which her bond position is denominated, to depreciate by an annualized 50 bps (or 0.5%) over the investment horizon against the US dollar, the home country currency. The expected currency loss to the portfolio is thus 0.50%.

The total expected return on Smith's bond position is 1.91%, as summarized in Exhibit 12.

**Exhibit 12  Return Component Calculations**

| Return Component | Formula | Calculation |
|---|---|---|
| Coupon income | Annual coupon payment/Current bond price | £2.75/£97.11 = 2.83% |
| + Rolldown return | $\dfrac{\text{Bond price}_{End\text{-}of\text{-}horizon\ period} - \text{Bond price}_{Beginning\text{-}of\text{-}horizon\ period}}{\text{Bond price}_{Beginning\text{-}of\text{-}horizon\ period}}$ | (£97.27 – £97.11)/£97.11 = 0.17% |
| = Rolling yield | Coupon income + Rolldown return | 2.83% + 0.17% = 3.00% |
| +/– E(ΔPrice* based on Smith's benchmark yield view) | $(-\text{ModDur} \times \Delta\text{Yield}) + [½ \times \text{Convexity} \times (\Delta\text{Yield})^2]$ | $(-3.70 \times 0.0026) + [½ \times 18 \times (0.0026)^2]$ = –0.96% |
| +/– E(ΔPrice due to investor's view of credit spreads) | $(-\text{ModDur} \times \Delta\text{Spread}) + [½ \times \text{Convexity} \times (\Delta\text{Spread})^2]$ | $(-3.70 \times -0.0010) + [1/2 \times 18 \times (-0.0010)^2]$ = 0.37 |
| +/– E(Currency gains or losses) | Given | –0.50% |
| = Total expected return |  | 1.91% |

*Note that the change in price in the context of this example refers to the change in portfolio value.

## 6.2 Estimation of the Inputs

In the model for fixed-income returns discussed earlier, some of the individual expected return components can be more easily estimated than others. The easiest component to estimate is the coupon income. The return model's most uncertain individual components are the investor's views of changes in benchmark yields and yield spreads and expected currency movements. These components are normally based on purely qualitative (subjective) criteria, a quantitative model (including surveys), or a mixture of the two. Although a quantitative approach may seem more objective, there are a number of quantitative models that can be used, each with different methodologies associated with the underlying calculations.

## 6.3 Limitations of the Expected Return Decomposition

The return decomposition just described is an approximation; only duration and convexity are used to summarize the price–yield relationship. In addition, the model implicitly assumes that all intermediate cash flows of the bond are reinvested at the yield to maturity, which results in different coupon reinvestment rates for different bonds.

The model also ignores other factors, such as local richness/cheapness effects and potential financing advantages. Local richness/cheapness effects are deviations of individual maturity segments from the fitted yield curve, which was obtained using a curve estimation technique. Yield curve estimation techniques produce relatively smooth curves, and there are likely slight deviations from the curve in practice. There may be financing advantages to certain maturity segments in the repo market. The repo market provides a form of short-term borrowing for dealers in government securities who sell government bonds to other market participants overnight and buy them back, typically on the following day. In most cases, local richness/cheapness effects and financing advantages tend to be relatively small and are thus not included in the expected return decomposition model.

---

**EXAMPLE 5**

### Components of Expected Return

Kevin Tucker manages a global bond portfolio. At a recent investment committee meeting, Tucker discussed his portfolio's domestic (very high-credit-quality) government bond allocation with another committee member. The other committee member argued that if the yield curve is expected to remain unchanged, the only determinants of a domestic government bond's expected return are its coupon payment and its price.

Explain why the other committee member is incorrect, including a description of the additional expected return components that need to be included.

**Solution:**

A bond's coupon payment and its price allow only its coupon income to be computed. Coupon income is an incomplete measure of a bond's expected return. For domestic government bonds, in addition to coupon income, the rolldown return needs to be considered. The rolldown return results from the fact that bonds are pulled to par as the time to maturity decreases, even if the yield curve is expected to remain unchanged over the investment horizon. Currency gains and losses would also need to be considered in a global portfolio. Because the portfolio consists of government bonds with very high credit quality, the view on yield spreads is less relevant for Tucker's analysis. For government and corporate bonds with lower credit quality, however, yield spreads would also need to be considered as additional return components.

---

# LEVERAGE

**e** discuss the use of leverage, alternative methods for leveraging, and risks that leverage creates in fixed-income portfolios

Leverage is the use of borrowed capital to increase the magnitude of portfolio positions, and it is an important tool for fixed-income portfolio managers. By using leverage, fixed-income portfolio managers may be able to increase portfolio returns relative to what they can achieve in unleveraged portfolios.

Managers often have mandates that place limits on the types of securities they may hold. Simultaneously, managers may have return objectives that are difficult to achieve, especially during low–interest rate environments. Through the use of leverage, a manager can increase his investment exposure and may be able to increase the returns to fixed-income asset classes that typically have low returns. The increased return potential, however, comes at the cost of increased risk: If losses occur, these would be higher than in unleveraged positions.

## 7.1 Using Leverage

Leverage increases portfolio returns if the securities in the portfolio have returns higher than the cost of borrowing. In an unleveraged portfolio, the return on the portfolio ($r_p$) equals the return on invested funds ($r_I$). When the manager uses leverage, however, the invested funds exceed the portfolio's equity by the amount that is borrowed.

The leveraged portfolio return, $r_p$, can be expressed as the total investment gains per unit of invested capital:

$$r_P = \frac{\text{Portfolio return}}{\text{Portfolio equity}} = \frac{r_I \times (V_E + V_B) - (V_B \times r_B)}{V_E}, \quad (9)$$

where

$V_E$ = Value of the portfolio's equity
$V_B$ = Borrowed funds
$r_B$ = Borrowing rate (cost of borrowing)
$r_I$ = Return on the invested funds (investment returns)
$r_p$ = Return on the levered portfolio

The numerator represents the total return on the portfolio assets, $r_I \times (V_E + V_B)$, minus the cost of borrowing, $V_B \times r_B$, divided by the portfolio's equity.

The leveraged portfolio return can be decomposed further to better identify the effect of leverage on returns:

$$r_P = \frac{r_I \times (V_E + V_B) - (V_B \times r_B)}{V_E}$$

$$= \frac{(r_I \times V_E) + [V_B \times (r_I - r_B)]}{V_E}$$

$$= r_I + \frac{V_B}{V_E}(r_I - r_B).$$

This expression decomposes the leveraged portfolio return into the return on invested funds and a portion that accounts for the effect of leverage. If $r_I > r_B$, then the second term is positive because the rate of return on invested funds exceeds the borrowing rate; in this case, leverage increases the portfolio's return. If $r_I < r_B$, then the second term is negative because the rate of return on invested funds is less than the borrowing rate; in this case, the use of leverage decreases the portfolio's return.

The degree to which the leverage increases or decreases portfolio returns is proportional to the use of leverage (amount borrowed), $V_B/V_E$, and the amount by which investment return differs from the cost of borrowing, $r_I - r_B$.

## 7.2 Methods for Leveraging Fixed-Income Portfolios

Fixed-income portfolio managers have a variety of tools available to create leveraged portfolio exposures—notably, the use of financial derivatives and borrowing via collateralized money markets. Derivatives and borrowing are explicit forms of leverage. Other forms of leverage, such as the use of structured financial instruments, are more implicit. We provide a description of the most common ones.

### 7.2.1 Futures Contracts

Futures contracts embed significant leverage because they permit the counterparties to gain exposure to a large quantity of the underlying asset without having to actually transact in the underlying. Futures contracts can be obtained for a modest investment that comes in the form of a margin deposit. A futures contract's notional value equals the current value of the underlying asset multiplied by the multiplier, or the quantity of the underlying asset controlled by the contract.

The futures leverage is the ratio of the futures exposure (in excess of the margin deposit) normalized by the amount of margin required to control the notional amount. We can calculate the futures leverage using the following equation:

$$\text{Leverage}_{Futures} = \frac{\text{Notional value} - \text{Margin}}{\text{Margin}}. \tag{10}$$

### 7.2.2 Swap Agreements

An interest rate swap can be viewed as a portfolio of bonds. In an interest rate swap, the fixed-rate payer is effectively short a fixed-rate bond and long a floating-rate bond. When interest rates increase, the value of the swap to the fixed-rate payer increases because the present value of the fixed-rate liability decreases and the floating-rate payments received increase. The fixed-rate receiver in the interest rate swap agreement effectively has a long position in a fixed-rate bond and a short position in a floating-rate bond. If interest rates decline, the value of the swap to the fixed-rate receiver increases because the present value of the fixed-rate asset increases and the floating-rate payments made decrease.

Because interest rate swaps are economically equivalent to a long–short bond portfolio, they provide leveraged exposure to bonds; the only capital required to enter into swap agreements is collateral required by the counterparties. Collateral for interest rate swap agreements has historically occurred between the two (or more) counterparties in the transaction. Increasingly, collateral for interest rate and other swaps occurs through central clearinghouses.

### 7.2.3 Repurchase Agreements

**Repurchase agreements** (repos) are an important source of short-term financing for fixed-income security dealers and other financial institutions, as evidenced by the trillions of dollars of repo transactions that take place annually. In a repurchase agreement, a security owner agrees to sell a security for a specific cash amount while simultaneously agreeing to repurchase the security at a specified future date (typically one day later) and price. Repos are thus effectively collateralized loans. When discussing a repo, the transaction normally refers to the borrower's standpoint; from the standpoint of the lender (such as a money market fund), these agreements are referred to as **reverse repos**. Exhibit 13 illustrates the transaction.

# Leverage

The interest rate on a repurchase agreement, called the **repo rate**, is the difference between the security's selling price and its repurchase price. For example, consider a dealer wishing to finance a EUR15 million bond position with a repurchase agreement. The dealer enters into an overnight repo at a repo rate of 5%. We can compute the price at which she agrees to repurchase this bond after one day as the EUR15 million value today plus one day of interest. The interest amount is computed as follows:

Dollar interest = Principal amount × Repo rate × (Term of repo in days/360)

Continuing with the example, the dollar interest is EUR2,083.33 = EUR15 million × 5% × (1/360). Thus, the dealer will repurchase the bond the next day for EUR15,002,083.33.

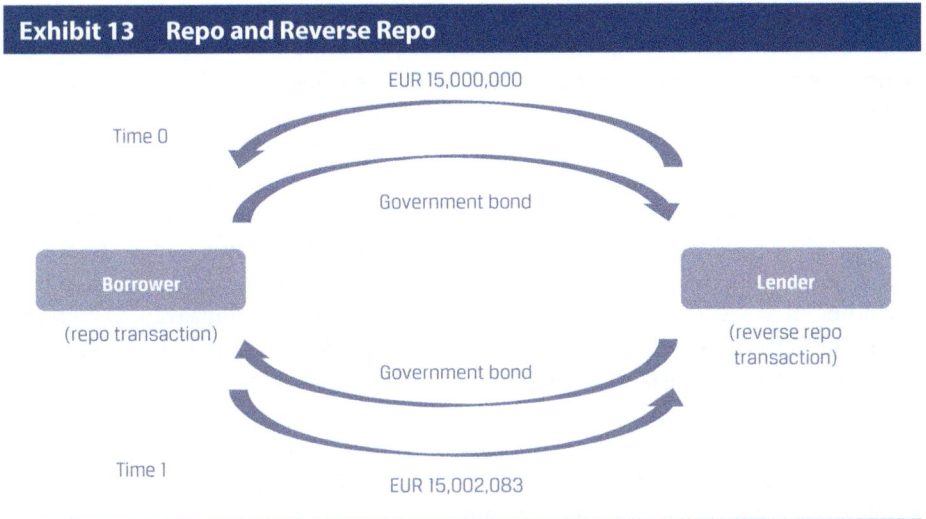

Exhibit 13  Repo and Reverse Repo

The term, or length, of a repurchase agreement is measured in days. Overnight repos are common, although they are often rolled over to create longer-term funding. A repo agreement may be cash driven or security driven. Cash-driven transactions feature one party that owns bonds and wants to borrow cash, as in the foregoing example. Cash-driven transactions usually feature "general collateral"—securities commonly accepted by investors and dealers, such as Treasury bonds. In a security-driven transaction, the lender typically seeks a particular security. The motives may be for hedging, arbitrage, or speculation.

Credit risk is a concern in a repo agreement, in particular for the counterparty that lends capital. Protection against a default by the borrower is provided by the underlying collateral bonds. Additional credit protection comes from the "haircut," the amount by which the collateral's value exceeds the repo principal amount. For example, haircuts for high-quality government bonds typically range from 1% to 3% and are higher for other types of bonds. The size of the haircut serves to not only protect the lender against a potential default by the borrower but also to limit the borrower's net leverage capacity. Generally, the size of the haircut increases as the price volatility of the underlying collateral increases.

Repos are categorized as bilateral repos or tri-party repos, depending on the way they are settled. Bilateral repos are conducted directly between two institutions, and settlement is typically conducted as "delivery versus payment," meaning that the exchanges of cash and collateral occur simultaneously through a central custodian (for example, the Depository Trust Company in the United States). Bilateral repos are usually used for security-driven transactions. Tri-party repo transactions involve a third party that provides settlement and collateral management services. Most cash-motivated repo transactions against general collateral are conducted as tri-party repo transactions.

#### 7.2.4 Security Lending

Security lending is another form of collateralized lending and is closely linked to the repo market. The primary motive of security lending transactions is to facilitate short sales, which involve the sale of securities the seller does not own. A short seller must borrow the securities he has sold short in order to deliver them upon trade settlement. Another motive for security lending transactions is financing, or collateralized borrowing. In a financing-motivated security loan, a bond owner lends the bond to another investor in exchange for cash.

Security lending transactions are collateralized by cash or high-credit-quality bonds. In the United States, most transactions feature cash collateral, although in many other countries, highly rated bonds are used as collateral. Typically, security lenders require collateral valued in excess of the value of the borrowed securities when bonds are used as collateral. For example, if high-quality government bonds are used as collateral, the lender may require bonds valued at 102% of the value of the borrowed securities. The extra 2% functions in the same way as the haircut in the repo market, providing extra protection against borrower default. The collateral required will increase if lower-quality bonds are used as collateral.

In security lending transactions with cash collateral, the security borrower typically pays the security lender, typically a long-only investment fund, a fee equal to a percentage of the value of the securities loaned. For securities that are readily available for lending, that fee is small. The security lender earns an additional return by reinvesting the cash collateral. In cases where the security loan is initiated for financing purposes, the lending fee is typically negative, indicating that the security lender pays the security borrower a fee in exchange for its use of the cash.

When bonds are posted as collateral, the income earned on the collateral usually exceeds the security lending rate; the security lender (who is in possession of the bonds as collateral) usually repays the security borrower a portion of the interest earned on the bond collateral. The term **rebate rate** refers to the portion of the collateral earnings rate that is repaid to the security borrower by the security lender. This relationship can be expressed as follows:

Rebate rate = Collateral earnings rate − Security lending rate.

When securities are difficult to borrow, typically because there is high demand to short those securities, the rebate rate may be negative, which means the fee for borrowing the securities is greater than the return earned on the collateral. In this case, the security borrower pays a fee to the security lender in addition to forgoing the interest earned on the collateral.

There are important differences between repurchase agreements and security lending transactions. Unlike repurchase agreements, security lending transactions are typically open-ended. The security lender may recall the securities at any time, forcing the borrower to deliver the bonds by buying them back or borrowing from another lender. Similarly, the borrower may deliver the borrowed securities back to the lender at any time, forcing the lender, or its agent, to return the collateral (cash or bonds) and search for another borrower.

### 7.3 Risks of Leverage

Leverage alters the risk–return properties of an investment portfolio. A heavily leveraged portfolio may incur significant losses even when portfolio assets suffer only moderate valuation declines.

Leverage can lead to forced liquidations. If the value of the portfolio decreases, the portfolio's equity relative to borrowing levels is reduced and the portfolio's leverage increases. Portfolio assets may be sold in order to pay off borrowing and reduce leverage. If portfolio assets are not liquidated, then the overall leverage increases, corresponding to higher levels of risk. Decreases in portfolio value can lead to forced liquidations even if market conditions are unfavorable for selling—for example, during crisis periods. The term "fire sale" refers to forced liquidations at prices that are below fair value as a result of the seller's need for immediate liquidation. Reducing leverage, declining asset values, and forced sales have the potential to create spiraling effects that can result in severe declines in values and reduction in market liquidity.

Additionally, reassessments of counterparty risk typically occur during extreme market conditions, such as during the 2008–09 financial crisis. During periods of financial crisis, counterparties to short-term financing arrangements, such as credit lines, repurchase agreements, and security lending agreements, may withdraw their financing. These withdrawals undermine the ability of leveraged market participants to maintain their investment exposures. Thus, leveraged investors may be forced to reduce their investment exposure at exactly the worst time—that is, when prices are depressed.

> **EXAMPLE 6**
>
> ### Using Leverage in a Fixed-Income Portfolio
>
> Arturo manages a mutual fund that is benchmarked to the Global Aggregate Bond Index. He currently has a bullish view of the global economy and believes corporate bond spreads are attractive. He is bearish on US Treasury interest rates given his economic growth forecast and expects rates to increase. The fund's US corporate bond holdings have a duration of seven years. He believes the best opportunities are in emerging market securities, and in particular, he is bullish on Brazilian rates, expecting them to decrease. The fund has experienced strong inflows recently and is fully invested. Arturo is evaluating tools to potentially increase the fund's total return by creating leveraged fixed-income exposures.
>
> Given Arturo's plan to leverage exposures in his fund, discuss how he would achieve his objectives and identify the strategy risks.
>
> **Solution:**
>
> The mutual fund is fully invested and, therefore, Arturo needs to use leverage to potentially increase his returns. His bearish view on US Treasury interest rates would require that he reduce the fund's seven-year duration contributed by the US corporate bond holdings. He can sell the number of futures contracts on US Treasuries whose notional value and associated duration would offset the duration of the corporate bonds to his new target duration. Doing so would allow him to retain exposure (spread duration) to the corporate bonds whose spreads may contract as the economy grows while shedding the interest rate exposure, since he believes rates will rise, adversely affecting bond prices.
>
> Arturo's bullish view on Brazilian rates can be expressed by entering into a receive fixed-rate, pay floating-rate swap on Brazilian rates. The fund will effectively have the equivalent of a fixed-rate bond that will appreciate in price if his view materializes and Brazilian interest rates fall.
>
> Both the short US Treasury futures and long Brazilian interest rate swap positions are leveraged since the only capital used is the collateral required by the counterparties. The risk to the leveraged strategy is that if Arturo's view on either position turns out to be incorrect, losses are magnified. This may also require positions to be closed and assets sold to cover the losses, which may occur at an inopportune time if the markets have sold off.

## 8  FIXED-INCOME PORTFOLIO TAXATION

**f** discuss differences in managing fixed-income portfolios for taxable and tax-exempt investors

A tax-exempt investor's objective is to achieve the highest possible risk-adjusted returns net of fees and transaction costs. A prudent taxable investor needs to also consider the effects of taxes on both expected and realized net investment returns.

The investment management industry has traditionally made investment decisions based on pretax returns as though investors are tax exempt (such as pension funds in many countries; see Rogers [2006]). The majority of the world's investable assets, however, are owned by taxable investors, who are concerned with after-tax, rather than pretax, returns.

Taxes may differ among investor types, among countries, and on the basis of income source, such as interest or capital gains. In many countries, pension funds are exempt from taxes but corporations generally have to pay tax on their investments. Many countries make some allowance for tax-sheltered investments that individuals can use (up to certain limits). These types of tax shelters generally offer either an exemption from tax on investment income or a deferral of taxes until an investor draws money from the shelter (usually after retirement). Such shelters allow returns to accrue on a pretax basis until retirement, which can provide substantial benefits. In a fixed-income context for taxable investors, coupon payments (interest income) are typically taxed at the investor's normal income tax rate. Capital gains, however, may be taxed at a lower effective rate than an investor's normal income tax rate. In some countries, income from special types of fixed-income securities, such as bonds issued by a sovereign government, a non-sovereign government, or various government agencies, may be taxed at a lower effective rate or even not taxed.

Specific tax rules vary among jurisdictions. Any discussion of the effect of taxes on investor returns—and, therefore, on how portfolios should optimally be managed for taxable investors—is especially challenging if it needs to apply on a global level. Although accounting standards have become more harmonized globally, any kind of tax harmonization among countries is not likely to occur anytime soon. An investor should consider how taxes affect investment income in the country where the income is earned and how the investment income is treated when it is repatriated to the investor's home country. Treaties between countries may affect tax treatment of investment income. Taxes are complicated and can make investment decisions difficult. Portfolio managers who manage assets for taxable individual investors, as opposed to tax-exempt investors, need to consider a number of issues.

### 8.1  Principles of Fixed-Income Taxation

Although tax codes differ among jurisdictions, there are certain principles that most tax codes have in common with regard to taxation of fixed-income investments:

- The two primary sources of investment income that affect taxes for fixed-income securities are coupon payments (interest income) and capital gains or losses.

- In general, tax is payable only on capital gains and interest income that have actually been received. In some countries, an exception to this rule applies to zero-coupon bonds. Imputed interest that is taxed throughout a zero-coupon bond's life may be calculated. This method of taxation ensures that tax is paid over the bond's life and that the return on a zero-coupon bond is not taxed entirely as a capital gain.

- Capital gains are frequently taxed at a lower effective tax rate than interest income.
- Capital losses generally cannot be used to reduce sources of income other than capital gains. Capital losses reduce capital gains in the tax year in which they occur. If capital losses exceed capital gains in the year, they can often be "carried forward" and applied to gains in future years; in some countries, losses may also be "carried back" to reduce capital gains taxes paid in prior years. Limits on the number of years that capital losses can be carried forward or back typically exist.
- In some countries, short-term capital gains are taxed at a different (usually higher) rate than long-term capital gains.

An investor or portfolio manager generally has no control over the timing of when coupon income is received and the related income tax must be paid. However, he or she can generally decide the timing of the sale of investments and, therefore, has some control over the timing of realized capital gains and losses. This control can be valuable for a taxable investor because it may be optimal to delay realizing gains and related tax payments and to realize losses as early as possible. This type of tax-driven strategic behavior is referred to as tax-loss harvesting.

Key points for managing taxable fixed-income portfolios include the following:

- Selectively offset capital gains and losses for tax purposes.
- If short-term capital gains tax rates are higher than long-term capital gains tax rates, then be judicious when realizing short-term gains.
- Realize losses taking into account tax consequences. They may be used to offset current or future capital gains for tax purposes.
- Control turnover in the fund. In general, the lower the turnover, the longer capital gains tax payments can be deferred.
- Consider the trade-off between capital gains and income for tax purposes.

## 8.2 Investment Vehicles and Taxes

The choice of investment vehicle often affects how investments are taxed at the final investor level. In a pooled investment vehicle (sometimes referred to as a *collective investment scheme*), such as a mutual fund, interest income is generally taxed at the final investor level when it occurs—regardless of whether the fund reinvests interest income or pays it out to investors. In other words, for tax purposes the fund is considered to have distributed interest income for tax purposes in the year it is received even if it does not actually pay it out to investors. Taxation of capital gains arising from the individual investments within a fund is often treated differently in different countries.

Some countries, such as the United States, use what is known as *pass-through treatment* of capital gains in mutual funds. Realized net capital gains in the underlying securities of a fund are treated as if distributed to investors in the year that they arise, and investors need to include the gains on their tax returns. Other countries, such as the United Kingdom, do not use pass-through treatment. Realized capital gains arising within a fund increase the net asset value of the fund shares that investors hold. Investors pay taxes on the net capital gain when they sell their fund shares. This tax treatment leads to a deferral in capital gains tax payments. A UK portfolio manager's decisions on when to realize capital gains or losses do not affect the timing of tax payments on capital gains by investors.

In a separately managed account, an investor typically pays tax on realized gains in the underlying securities at the time they occur. The investor holds the securities directly rather than through shares in a fund. For separately managed accounts, the portfolio manager needs to consider tax consequences for the investor when making investment decisions.

Tax-loss harvesting, which we defined earlier as deferring the realization of gains and realizing capital losses early, allows investors to accumulate gains on a pretax basis. The deferral of taxes increases the present value of investments for the investor.

### EXAMPLE 7

### Managing Taxable and Tax-Exempt Portfolios

A bond portfolio manager needs to raise €10,000,000 in cash to cover outflows in the portfolio she manages. To satisfy her cash demands, she considers one of two corporate bond positions for potential liquidation: Position A and Position B. For tax purposes, capital gains receive pass-through treatment; realized net capital gains in the underlying securities of a fund are treated as if distributed to investors in the year that they arise. Assume that the capital gains tax rate is 28% and the income tax rate for interest is 45%. Exhibit 14 provides relevant data for the two bond positions.

**Exhibit 14  Selected Data for Two Bonds**

|  | Position A | Position B |
|---|---|---|
| Current market value | €10,000,000 | €10,000,000 |
| Capital gain/loss | €1,000,000 | –€1,000,000 |
| Coupon rate | 5.00% | 5.00% |
| Remaining maturity | 10 years | 10 years |
| Income tax rate | 45% | |
| Capital gains tax rate | 28% | |

The portfolio manager considers Position A to be slightly overvalued and Position B to be slightly undervalued. Assume that the two bond positions are identical with regard to all other relevant characteristics. How should the portfolio manager optimally liquidate bond positions if she manages the portfolio for:

1  tax-exempt investors?
2  taxable investors?

### Solution to 1:

The taxation of capital gains and capital losses has minimal consequences for tax-exempt investors. Consistent with the portfolio manager's investment views, the portfolio manager would likely liquidate Position A, which she considers slightly overvalued, rather than liquidating Position B, which she considers slightly undervalued.

### Solution to 2:

All else equal, portfolio managers for taxable investors should have an incentive to defer capital gains taxes and realize capital losses early (tax-loss harvesting) so that losses can be used to offset current or future capital gains. Despite the

> slight undervaluation of the position, the portfolio manager might want to liquidate Position B because of its embedded capital loss, which will result in a lower realized net capital gain being distributed to investors. This decision is based on the assumption that there are no other capital losses in the portfolio that can be used to offset other capital gains. Despite the slight overvaluation of Position A, its liquidation would be less desirable for a taxable investor because of the required capital gains tax.

## SUMMARY

- Fixed-income investments provide diversification benefits in a portfolio context. These benefits arise from the generally low correlations of fixed-income investments with other major asset classes, such as equities.
- Floating-rate and inflation-linked bonds can be used to hedge inflation risk.
- Fixed-income investments have regular cash flows, which is beneficial for the purposes of funding future liabilities.
- For liability-based fixed-income mandates, portfolio construction follows two main approaches—cash flow matching and duration matching—to match fixed-income assets with future liabilities.
- Total return mandates are generally structured to either track or outperform a benchmark.
- Total return mandates can be classified into various approaches according to their target active return and active risk levels. Approaches range from pure indexing to enhanced indexing to active management.
- Bond Portfolio Duration is the sensitivity of a portfolio of bonds to small changes in interest rates. It can be calculated as the weighted average of time to receipt of the aggregate cash flows or, more commonly, as the weighted average of the individual bond durations that comprise the portfolio.
- Modified Duration of a Bond Portfolio indicates the percentage change in the market value given a change in yield-to-maturity. Modified duration of a portfolio comprising $j$ fixed income securities can be estimated as

$$\text{AvgModDur} = \sum_{j=1}^{J} \text{ModDur}_j \left( \frac{\text{MV}_j}{\text{MV}} \right)$$

  where MV stands for market value of the portfolio and $\text{MV}_j$ is the market value of a specific bond.
- Convexity of a bond portfolio is a second-order effect; it operates behind duration in importance and can largely be ignored for small yield changes. When convexity is added with the use of derivatives, however, it can be extremely important to returns.
- Effective duration and convexity of a portfolio are the relevant summary statistics when future cash flows of bonds in a portfolio are contingent on interest rate changes.
- Spread duration is a useful measure for determining a portfolio's sensitivity to changes in credit spreads. It provides the approximate percentage increase (decrease) in bond price expected for a 1% decrease (increase) in credit spread.

- Duration times spread is a modification of the spread duration definition to incorporate the empirical observation that spread changes across the credit spectrum tend to occur on a *proportional percentage* basis rather than being based on *absolute* basis point changes.
- Portfolio dispersion captures the variance of the times to receipt of cash flows around the duration. It is used in measuring interest rate immunization for liabilities.
- Duration management is the primary tool used by fixed-income portfolio managers.
- Convexity supplements duration as a measure of a bond's price sensitivity for larger movements in interest rates. Adjusting convexity can be an important portfolio management tool.
- For two portfolios with the same duration, the portfolio with higher convexity has higher sensitivity to large declines in yields to maturity and lower sensitivity to large increases in yields to maturity.
- Interest rate derivatives can be used effectively to increase or decrease duration and convexity in a bond portfolio.
- Liquidity is an important consideration in fixed-income portfolio management. Bonds are generally less liquid than equities, and liquidity varies greatly across sectors.
- Liquidity affects pricing in fixed-income markets because many bonds either do not trade or trade infrequently.
- Liquidity affects portfolio construction because there is a trade-off between liquidity and yield to maturity. Less liquid bonds have higher yields to maturity, all else being equal, and may be more desirable for buy-and-hold investors. Investors anticipating liquidity needs may forgo higher yields to maturity for more liquid bonds.
- Investors can obtain exposure to the bond market using mutual funds and ETFs that track a bond index. Shares in mutual funds are redeemable at the net asset value with a one-day time lag. ETF shares have the advantage of trading on an exchange.
- A total return swap, an over-the-counter derivative, allows an institutional investor to transform an asset or liability from one asset category to another—for instance, from variable-rate cash flows referencing the market reference rate to the total return on a particular bond index.
- A total return swap can have some advantages over a direct investment in a bond mutual fund or ETF. As a derivative, it requires less initial cash outlay than direct investment in the bond portfolio for similar performance but carries counterparty risk.
- As a customized over-the-counter product, a TRS can offer exposure to assets that are difficult to access directly, such as some high-yield and commercial loan investments.
- When evaluating fixed-income investment strategies, it is important to consider expected returns and to understand the various components of expected returns.
- Decomposing expected fixed-income returns allows investors to understand the different sources of returns given expected changes in bond market conditions.

- A model for expected fixed-income returns can decompose them into the following components: coupon income, rolldown return, expected change in price based on investor's views of yields to maturity and yield spreads, and expected currency gains or losses.
- Leverage is the use of borrowed capital to increase the magnitude of portfolio positions. By using leverage, fixed-income portfolio managers may be able to increase portfolio returns relative to what they can achieve in unleveraged portfolios. The potential for increased returns, however, comes with increased risk.
- Methods for leveraging fixed-income portfolios include the use of futures contracts, swap agreements, repurchase agreements, structured financial instruments, and security lending.
- Taxes can complicate investment decisions in fixed-income portfolio management. Complications result from the differences in taxation among investor types, countries, and income sources.
- The two primary sources of investment income that affect taxes for fixed-income securities are coupon payments (interest income) and capital gains or losses. Tax is usually payable only on capital gains and interest income that have actually been received.
- Capital gains are frequently taxed at a lower effective tax rate than interest income. If capital losses exceed capital gains in the year, they can often be "carried forward" and applied to gains in future years.

# REFERENCES

Hanke, B., and G. Seals. 2010. "Fixed-Income Analysis: Yield Curve Construction, Trading Strategies, and Risk Analysis." CFA Institute online course.

Rogers, D. 2006. Tax-Aware Investment Management: The Essential Guide. New York: Bloomberg Press.

# PRACTICE PROBLEMS

## The following information relates to Questions 1–6

Cécile is a junior analyst for an international wealth management firm. Her supervisor, Margit, asks Cécile to evaluate three fixed-income funds as part of the firm's global fixed-income offerings. Selected financial data for the funds Aschel, Permot, and Rosaiso are presented in Exhibit 1. In Cécile's initial review, she assumes that there is no reinvestment income and that the yield curve remains unchanged.

| Exhibit 1 Selected Data on Fixed-Income Funds | | | |
|---|---|---|---|
| | Aschel | Permot | Rosaiso |
| Current average bond price | $117.00 | $91.50 | $94.60 |
| Expected average bond price in one year (end of Year 1) | $114.00 | $96.00 | $97.00 |
| Average modified duration | 7.07 | 7.38 | 6.99 |
| Average annual coupon payment | $3.63 | $6.07 | $6.36 |
| Present value of portfolio's assets (millions) | $136.33 | $68.50 | $74.38 |
| Bond type* | | | |
|    Fixed-coupon bonds | 95% | 38% | 62% |
|    Floating-coupon bonds | 2% | 34% | 17% |
|    Inflation-linked bonds | 3% | 28% | 21% |
| Quality* | | | |
|    AAA | 65% | 15% | 20% |
|    BBB | 35% | 65% | 50% |
|    B | 0% | 20% | 20% |
|    Not rated | 0% | 0% | 10% |
| Value of portfolio's equity (millions) | $94.33 | | |
| Value of borrowed funds (millions) | $42.00 | | |
| Borrowing rate | 2.80% | | |
| Return on invested funds | 6.20% | | |

*Bond type and quality are shown as a percentage of total for each fund.

After further review of the composition of each of the funds, Cécile makes the following notes:

Note 1   Aschel is the only fund of the three that uses leverage.

Note 2   Rosaiso is the only fund of the three that holds a significant number of bonds with embedded options.

## Practice Problems

Margit asks Cécile to analyze liability-based mandates for a meeting with Villash Foundation. Villash Foundation is a tax-exempt client. Prior to the meeting, Cécile identifies what she considers to be two key features of a liability-based mandate.

| | |
|---|---|
| Feature 1 | It can minimize the risk of deficient cash inflows for a company. |
| Feature 2 | It matches expected liability payments with future projected cash inflows. |

Two years later, Margit learns that Villash Foundation needs $5 million in cash to meet liabilities. She asks Cécile to analyze two bonds for possible liquidation. Selected data on the two bonds are presented in Exhibit 2.

### Exhibit 2   Selected Data for Bonds 1 and 2

| | Bond 1 | Bond 2 |
|---|---|---|
| Current market value | $5,000,000 | $5,000,000 |
| Capital gain/loss | $400,000 | –$400,000 |
| Coupon rate | 2.05% | 2.05% |
| Remaining maturity | 8 years | 8 years |
| Investment view | Overvalued | Undervalued |
| Income tax rate | 39% | |
| Capital gains tax rate | 30% | |

1. Based on Exhibit 1, which fund provides the highest level of protection against inflation for coupon payments?
   - **A** Aschel
   - **B** Permot
   - **C** Rosaiso

2. Based on Exhibit 1, the rolling yield of Aschel over a one-year investment horizon is *closest* to:
   - **A** −2.56%.
   - **B** 0.54%.
   - **C** 5.66%.

3. The leveraged portfolio return for Aschel is *closest* to:
   - **A** 7.25%.
   - **B** 7.71%.
   - **C** 8.96%.

4. Based on Note 2, Rosaiso is the only fund for which the expected change in price based on the investor's views of yields to maturity and yield spreads should be calculated using:
   - **A** convexity.
   - **B** modified duration.
   - **C** effective duration.

5. Is Cécile correct with respect to key features of liability-based mandates?
   - **A** Yes
   - **B** No, only Feature 1 is correct.

**C** No, only Feature 2 is correct.

6 Based on Exhibit 2, the optimal strategy to meet Villash Foundation's cash needs is the sale of:
   **A** 100% of Bond 1.
   **B** 100% of Bond 2.
   **C** 50% of Bond 1 and 50% of Bond 2.

## The following information relates to Questions 7–12

Celia is chief investment officer for the Topanga Investors Fund, which invests in equities and fixed income. The clients in the fund are all taxable investors. The fixed-income allocation includes a domestic (US) bond portfolio and an externally managed global bond portfolio.

The domestic bond portfolio has a total return mandate, which specifies a long-term return objective of 25 basis points (bps) over the benchmark index. Relative to the benchmark, small deviations in sector weightings are permitted, such risk factors as duration must closely match, and tracking error is expected to be less than 50 bps per year.

The objectives for the domestic bond portfolio include the ability to fund future liabilities, protect interest income from short-term inflation, and minimize the correlation with the fund's equity portfolio. The correlation between the fund's domestic bond portfolio and equity portfolio is currently 0.14. Celia plans to reduce the fund's equity allocation and increase the allocation to the domestic bond portfolio. She reviews two possible investment strategies.

   Strategy 1    Purchase AAA rated fixed-coupon corporate bonds with a modified duration of two years and a correlation coefficient with the equity portfolio of –0.15.

   Strategy 2    Purchase US government agency floating-coupon bonds with a modified duration of one month and a correlation coefficient with the equity portfolio of –0.10.

Celia realizes that the fund's return may decrease if the equity allocation of the fund is reduced. Celia decides to liquidate $20 million of US Treasuries that are currently owned and to invest the proceeds in the US corporate bond sector. To fulfill this strategy, Celia asks Dan, a newly hired analyst for the fund, to recommend specific Treasuries to sell and corporate bonds to purchase.

Dan recommends Treasuries from the existing portfolio that he believes are overvalued and will generate capital gains. Celia asks Dan why he chose only overvalued bonds with capital gains and did not include any bonds with capital losses. Dan responds with two statements.

   Statement 1    Taxable investors should prioritize selling overvalued bonds and always sell them before selling bonds that are viewed as fairly valued or undervalued.

   Statement 2    Taxable investors should never intentionally realize capital losses.

Regarding the purchase of corporate bonds, Dan collects relevant data, which are presented in Exhibit 1.

# Practice Problems

### Exhibit 1  Selected Data on Three US Corporate Bonds

| Bond Characteristics | Bond 1 | Bond 2 | Bond 3 |
|---|---|---|---|
| Credit quality | AA | AA | A |
| Issue size ($ millions) | 100 | 75 | 75 |
| Maturity (years) | 5 | 7 | 7 |
| Total issuance outstanding ($ millions) | 1,000 | 1,500 | 1,000 |
| Months since issuance | New issue | 3 | 6 |

Celia and Dan review the total expected 12-month return (assuming no reinvestment income) for the global bond portfolio. Selected financial data are presented in Exhibit 2.

### Exhibit 2  Selected Data on Global Bond Portfolio

| | |
|---|---|
| Notional principal of portfolio (in millions) | €200 |
| Average bond coupon payment (per €100 par value) | €2.25 |
| Coupon frequency | Annual |
| Investment horizon | 1 year |
| Current average bond price | €98.45 |
| Expected average bond price in one year (assuming an unchanged yield curve) | €98.62 |
| Average bond convexity | 22 |
| Average bond modified duration | 5.19 |
| Expected average benchmark yield-to-maturity change | 0.15% |
| Expected change in credit spread (widening) | 0.13% |
| Expected currency gains (€ appreciation vs. $) | 0.65% |

Celia contemplates adding a new manager to the global bond portfolio. She reviews three proposals and determines that each manager uses the same index as its benchmark but pursues a different total return approach, as presented in Exhibit 3.

### Exhibit 3  New Manager Proposals: Fixed-Income Portfolio Characteristics

| Sector Weights (%) | Manager A | Manager B | Manager C | Index |
|---|---|---|---|---|
| Government | 53.5 | 52.5 | 47.8 | 54.1 |
| Agency/quasi-agency | 16.2 | 16.4 | 13.4 | 16.0 |

*(continued)*

### Exhibit 3   (Continued)

| Sector Weights (%) | Manager A | Manager B | Manager C | Index |
|---|---|---|---|---|
| Corporate | 20.0 | 22.2 | 25.1 | 19.8 |
| MBS | 10.3 | 8.9 | 13.7 | 10.1 |

| Risk and Return Characteristics | Manager A | Manager B | Manager C | Index |
|---|---|---|---|---|
| Average maturity (years) | 7.63 | 7.84 | 8.55 | 7.56 |
| Modified duration (years) | 5.23 | 5.25 | 6.16 | 5.22 |
| Average yield to maturity (%) | 1.98 | 2.08 | 2.12 | 1.99 |
| Turnover (%) | 207 | 220 | 290 | 205 |

7  Which approach to its total return mandate is the fund's domestic bond portfolio *most likely* to use?

   A  Pure indexing

   B  Enhanced indexing

   C  Active management

8  Strategy 2 is *most likely* preferred to Strategy 1 for meeting the objective of:

   A  protecting against inflation.

   B  funding future liabilities.

   C  minimizing the correlation of the fund's domestic bond portfolio and equity portfolio.

9  Are Dan's statements to Celia that support Dan's choice of bonds to sell correct?

   A  Only Statement 1 is correct.

   B  Only Statement 2 is correct.

   C  Neither Statement 1 nor Statement 2 is correct.

10  Based on Exhibit 1, which bond *most likely* has the highest liquidity premium?

   A  Bond 1

   B  Bond 2

   C  Bond 3

11  Based on Exhibit 2, the total expected return of the fund's global bond portfolio is *closest* to:

   A  0.90%.

   B  1.66%.

   C  3.76%.

12  Based on Exhibit 3, which manager is *most likely* to have an active management total return mandate?

   A  Manager A

   B  Manager B

   C  Manager C

# SOLUTIONS

1. **B is correct.** Permot has the highest percentage of floating-coupon bonds and inflation-linked bonds. Bonds with floating coupons protect interest income from inflation because the reference rate should adjust for inflation. Inflation-linked bonds protect against inflation by paying a return that is directly linked to an index of consumer prices and adjusting the principal for inflation. Inflation-linked bonds protect both coupon and principal payments against inflation.

    The level of inflation protection for coupons equals the percentage of the portfolio in floating-coupon bonds plus the percentage of the portfolio in inflation-linked bonds:

    Aschel = 2% + 3% = 5%.

    Permot = 34% + 28% = 62%.

    Rosaiso = 17% + 21% = 38%.

    Thus, Permot has the highest level of inflation protection, with 62% of its portfolio in floating-coupon and inflation-linked bonds.

2. **B is correct.** The rolling yield is the sum of the coupon income and the rolldown return. Coupon income is the sum of the bond's annual current yield and interest on reinvestment income. Cécile assumes that there is no reinvestment income for any of the three funds, and the yield income for Aschel will be calculated as follows:

    Coupon income = Annual average coupon payment/Current bond price
    = $3.63/$117.00
    = 0.0310, or 3.10%.

    The rolldown return is equal to the bond's percentage price change assuming an unchanged yield curve over the horizon period. The rolldown return will be calculated as follows:

    $$\text{Rolldown return} = \frac{\left(\text{Bond price}_{End\text{-}of\text{-}horizon\ period} - \text{Bond price}_{Beginning\text{-}of\text{-}horizon\ period}\right)}{\text{Bond price}_{Beginning\text{-}of\text{-}horizon\ period}}$$

    $$= \frac{(\$114.00 - \$117.00)}{\$117.00}$$

    $$= -0.0256, \text{ or } -2.56\%.$$

    Rolling yield = Coupon income + Rolldown return = 3.10% − 2.56% = 0.54%.

3. **B is correct.** The return for Aschel is 7.71%, calculated as follows:

    $$r_P = \frac{r_I \times (V_E + V_B) - V_B \times r_B}{V_E}$$

    $$= r_I + \frac{V_B}{V_E}(r_I - r_B)$$

    $$= 6.20\% + \frac{\$42.00 \text{ million}}{\$94.33 \text{ million}}(6.20\% - 2.80\%)$$

= 7.71%.

**4** C is correct. Rosaiso is the only fund that holds bonds with embedded options. Effective duration should be used for bonds with embedded options. For bonds with embedded options, the duration and convexity measures used to calculate the expected change in price based on the investor's views of yields to maturity and yield spreads are effective duration and effective convexity. For bonds without embedded options, convexity and modified duration are used in this calculation.

**5** A is correct. Liability-based mandates are investments that take an investor's future obligations into consideration. Liability-based mandates are managed to match expected liability payments with future projected cash inflows. These types of mandates are structured in a way to ensure that a liability or a stream of liabilities can be covered and that any risk of shortfalls or deficient cash inflows for a company is minimized.

**6** A is correct. The optimal strategy for Villash is the sale of 100% of Bond 1, which Cécile considers to be overvalued. Because Villash is a tax-exempt foundation, tax considerations are not relevant and Cécile's investment views drive her trading recommendations.

**7** B is correct. The domestic bond portfolio's return objective is to modestly outperform the benchmark. Its risk factors, such as duration, are to closely match the benchmark. Small deviations in sector weights are allowed, and tracking error should be less than 50 bps year. These features are typical of enhanced indexing.

**8** A is correct. Floating-coupon bonds provide inflation protection for the interest income because the reference rate should adjust for inflation. The purchase of fixed-coupon bonds as outlined in Strategy 1 provides no protection against inflation for either interest or principal. Strategy 1 would instead be superior to Strategy 2 in funding future liabilities (better predictability as to the amount of cash flows) and reducing the correlation between the fund's domestic bond portfolio and equity portfolio (better diversification).

**9** C is correct. Since the fund's clients are taxable investors, there is value in harvesting tax losses. These losses can be used to offset capital gains within the fund that will otherwise be distributed to the clients and result in higher tax payments, which decreases the total value of the investment to clients. The fund has to consider the overall value of the investment to its clients, including taxes, which may result in the sale of bonds that are not viewed as overvalued. Tax-exempt investors' decisions are driven by their investment views without regard to offsetting gains and losses for tax purposes.

**10** C is correct. Bond 3 is most likely to be the least liquid of the three bonds presented in Exhibit 1 and will thus most likely require the highest liquidity premium. Low credit ratings, longer time since issuance, smaller issuance size, smaller issuance outstanding, and longer time to maturity typically are associated with lower liquidity (and thus a higher liquidity premium). Bond 3 has the lowest credit quality and the longest time since issuance of the three bonds. Bond 3 also has a smaller issue size and a longer time to maturity than Bond 1. The total issuance outstanding for Bond 3 is smaller than that of Bond 2 and equal to that of Bond 1.

**11** B is correct. The total expected return is calculated as follows:

Total expected return =

Rolling yield

# Solutions

+/− E(Change in price based on investor's benchmark yield view)

+/− E(Change in price due to investor's view of credit spread)

+/− E(Currency gains or losses),

where Rolling yield = Coupon income + Rolldown return.

| Return Component | Formula | Calculation |
|---|---|---|
| Coupon income | Annual coupon payment/Current bond price | €2.25/€98.45 = 2.29% |
| + Rolldown return | $\dfrac{\text{Bond price}_{End\text{-}of\text{-}horizon\ period} - \text{Bond price}_{Beginning\text{-}of\text{-}horizon\ period}}{\text{Bond price}_{Beginning\text{-}of\text{-}horizon\ period}}$ | (€98.62 − €98.45)/€98.45 = 0.17% |
| = Rolling yield | Coupon income + Rolldown return | 2.29% + 0.17% = 2.46% |
| +/− E(Change in price based on investor's benchmark yield view) | $(-MD \times \Delta Yield) + [½ \times Convexity \times (\Delta Yield)^2]$ | $(-5.19 \times 0.0015) + [½ \times 22 \times (0.0015)^2] = -0.78\%$ |
| +/− E(Change in price due to investor's view of credit spread) | $(-MD \times \Delta Spread) + [½ \times Convexity \times (\Delta Spread)^2]$ | $(-5.19 \times 0.0013) + [½ \times 22 \times (0.0013)^2] = -0.67\%$ |
| +/− E(Currency gains or losses) | Given | 0.65% |
| = Total expected return | | 1.66% |

12  C is correct. The sector weights, risk and return characteristics, and turnover for Manager C differ significantly from those of the index, which is typical of an active management mandate. In particular, Manager C's modified duration of 6.16 represents a much larger deviation from the benchmark index modified duration of 5.22 than that of the other managers, which is a characteristic unique to an active management mandate.

# READING
# 12

# Liability-Driven and Index-Based Strategies

by James F. Adams, PhD, CFA, and Donald J. Smith, PhD

*James F. Adams, PhD, CFA, is at New York University (USA). Donald J. Smith, PhD, is at Boston University Questrom School of Business (USA).*

| LEARNING OUTCOMES | |
|---|---|
| Mastery | The candidate should be able to: |
| ☐ | a. describe liability-driven investing; |
| ☐ | b. evaluate strategies for managing a single liability; |
| ☐ | c. compare strategies for a single liability and for multiple liabilities, including alternative means of implementation; |
| ☐ | d. describe construction, benefits, limitations, and risk–return characteristics of a laddered bond portfolio; |
| ☐ | e. evaluate liability-based strategies under various interest rate scenarios and select a strategy to achieve a portfolio's objectives; |
| ☐ | f. explain risks associated with managing a portfolio against a liability structure; |
| ☐ | g. discuss bond indexes and the challenges of managing a fixed-income portfolio to mimic the characteristics of a bond index; |
| ☐ | h. compare alternative methods for establishing bond market exposure passively; |
| ☐ | i. discuss criteria for selecting a benchmark and justify the selection of a benchmark. |

## INTRODUCTION 1

Fixed-income instruments make up nearly three-quarters of all global financial assets available to investors. It is thus not surprising that bonds are a critical component of most investment portfolios. In our coverage of structured and passive total return fixed-income investment strategies, we explain that "passive" does not simply mean "buy and hold." The primary strategies discussed—immunization and indexation—can entail frequent rebalancing of the bond portfolio. We also note that "passive" stands in contrast to "active" fixed-income strategies that are based on the asset manager's particular view on interest rate and credit market conditions.

We explain liability-driven investing by demonstrating how to best structure a fixed-income portfolio when considering both the asset and liability sides of the investor's balance sheet. It is first important to have a thorough understanding of both the timing and relative certainty of future financial obligations. Because it is rare to find a bond investment whose characteristics perfectly match one's obligations, we introduce the idea of structuring a bond portfolio to match the future cash flows of one or more liabilities that have bond-like characteristics. Asset–liability management (ALM) strategies are based on the concept that investors incorporate both rate-sensitive assets and liabilities into the portfolio decision-making process. When the liabilities are given and assets are managed, liability-driven investing (LDI), a common type of ALM strategy, may be used to ensure adequate funding for an insurance portfolio, a pension plan, or an individual's budget after retirement. The techniques and risks associated with LDI are introduced using a single liability and then are expanded to cover both cash flow and duration-matching techniques and multiple liabilities. This strategy, known as immunization, may be viewed simply as a special case of interest rate hedging.

We then turn our attention to index-based investment strategies, through which investors gain a broader exposure to fixed-income markets, rather than tailoring investments to match a specific liability profile. We explain the advantages of index-based investing, such as diversification, but we also note that the depth and breadth of bond markets make both creating and tracking an index more challenging than in the equity markets. We also explore a variety of alternatives in matching a bond index, from full replication to enhanced indexing using primary risk factors. Finally, we explain that it is critical to select a benchmark that is most relevant to a specific investor based on factors such as the targeted duration profile and risk appetite.

## 2  LIABILITY-DRIVEN INVESTING

a   describe liability-driven investing

Let us start with the example of a 45-year-old investor who plans to retire at age 65 and who would like to secure a stable stream of income thereafter. It is quite probable that he currently has a diversified portfolio that includes bonds, equities, and possibly other asset classes. Our focus here is on the fixed-income portion of his overall portfolio. We will assume that the investor builds the bond portfolio (immediately) and will add to it each year. Upon retirement, he plans to sell the bonds and buy an annuity that will pay a fixed benefit for his remaining lifetime. This investor's initial 20-year time horizon is critical to identifying and measuring the impact on retirement income arising from future interest rate volatility, and it forms the initial frame of reference for understanding and dealing with interest rate risk.

More generally, the frame of reference is in the form of a balance sheet of rate-sensitive assets and liabilities. In the example of the 45-year-old investor, the asset is the growing bond portfolio and the liability is the present value of the annuity that the investor requires to satisfy the fixed lifetime benefit.

## 2.1 Liability-Driven Investing vs. Asset-Driven Liabilities

Liability-driven investing (LDI) and asset-driven liabilities (ADL) are special cases of ALM. The key difference is that with ADL, the assets are given and the liabilities are structured to manage interest rate risk; whereas with LDI, which is much more common, the liabilities are given and the assets are managed. As an example of LDI, a life insurance company acquires a liability portfolio based on the insurance policies underwritten by its sales force. Another example involves the future employee benefits promised by a defined benefit pension plan, which create a portfolio of rate-sensitive liabilities. In each circumstance, the liabilities are defined and result from routine business and financial management decisions. The present value of those liabilities depends on current interest rates (as well as other factors). A life insurance or pension manager will use the estimated interest rate sensitivity of plan liabilities as a starting point when making investment portfolio decisions. This process often requires building a model for the liabilities.

With ADL, the asset side of the balance sheet results from a company's underlying businesses, and the debt manager seeks a liability structure to reduce interest rate risk. One example might be a leasing company with short-term contracts that chooses to finance itself with short-term debt. The company is aiming to match the maturities of its assets and liabilities to minimize risk. Alternatively, a manufacturing company might identify that its operating revenues are highly correlated with the business cycle. Monetary policy is typically managed so there is positive correlation between interest rates and the business cycle. Central banks lower policy rates when the economy is weak and raise them when it is strong. Therefore, this company has a natural preference for variable-rate liabilities so that operating revenue and interest expense rise and fall together.

## 2.2 Types of Liabilities

An LDI strategy starts with analyzing the size and timing of the entity's liabilities. Exhibit 1 shows a classification scheme for this analysis.

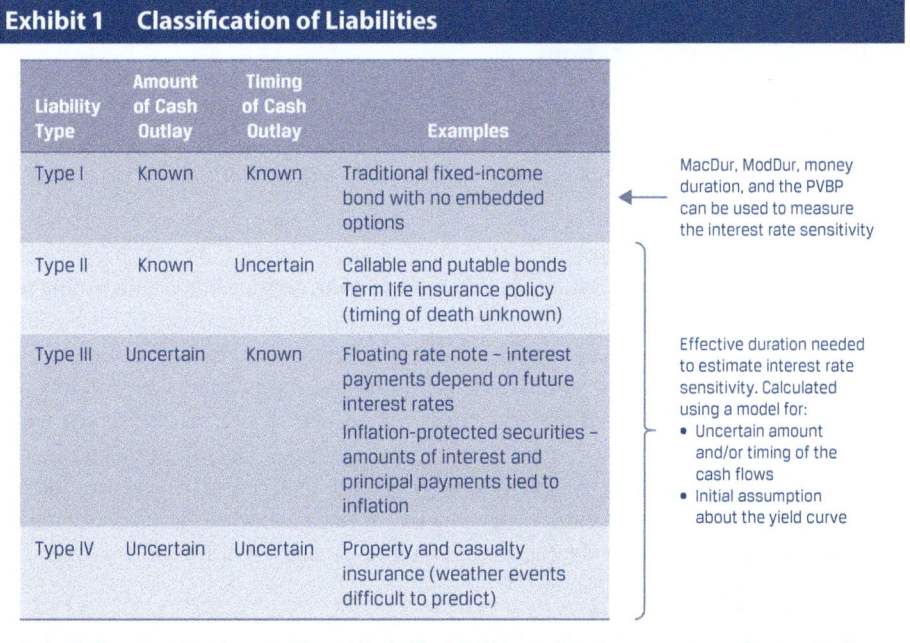

Exhibit 1  Classification of Liabilities

| Liability Type | Amount of Cash Outlay | Timing of Cash Outlay | Examples | |
|---|---|---|---|---|
| Type I | Known | Known | Traditional fixed-income bond with no embedded options | MacDur, ModDur, money duration, and the PVBP can be used to measure the interest rate sensitivity |
| Type II | Known | Uncertain | Callable and putable bonds  Term life insurance policy (timing of death unknown) | |
| Type III | Uncertain | Known | Floating rate note – interest payments depend on future interest rates  Inflation-protected securities – amounts of interest and principal payments tied to inflation | Effective duration needed to estimate interest rate sensitivity. Calculated using a model for:  • Uncertain amount and/or timing of the cash flows  • Initial assumption about the yield curve |
| Type IV | Uncertain | Uncertain | Property and casualty insurance (weather events difficult to predict) | |

Note that effective duration is needed with Types II, III, and IV liabilities, based on initial assumptions about the yield curve. Then, the yield curve is shifted up and down to obtain new estimates for the present value of the liabilities. We demonstrate this process later for the sponsor of a defined benefit pension plan, which is another example of an entity with Type IV liabilities.

> **EXAMPLE 1**
>
> Modern Mortgage, a savings bank, decides to establish an ALCO (asset–liability committee) to improve risk management and coordination of its loan and deposit rate-setting processes. Modern's primary assets are long-term, fixed-rate, monthly payment, fully amortizing residential mortgage loans. The mortgage loans are prime quality and have loan-to-value ratios that average 80%. The loans are pre-payable at par value by the homeowners at no fee. Modern also holds a portfolio of non-callable, fixed-income government bonds (considered free of default risk) of varying maturities to manage its liquidity needs. The primary liabilities are demand and time deposits that are fully guaranteed by a government deposit insurance fund. The demand deposits are redeemable by check or debit card. The time deposits have fixed rates and maturities ranging from 90 days to three years and are redeemable before maturity at a small fee. The banking-sector regulator in the country in which Modern operates has introduced a new capital requirement for savings banks. In accordance with the requirement, contingent convertible long-term bonds are issued by the savings bank and sold to institutional investors. The key feature is that if defaults on the mortgage loans reach a certain level or the savings bank's capital ratio drops below a certain level, as determined by the regulator, the bonds convert to equity at a specified price per share.
>
> As a first step, the ALCO needs to identify the types of assets and liabilities that comprise its balance sheet using the classification scheme in Exhibit 1. Type I has certain amounts and dates for its cash flows; Type II has known amounts but uncertain dates; Type III has specified dates but unknown amounts; and Type IV has uncertain amounts and dates.
>
> Specify and explain the classification scheme for the following:
>
> 1  Residential mortgage loans
> 2  Government bonds
> 3  Demand and time deposits
> 4  Contingent convertible bonds
>
> **Solution to 1:**
>
> Residential mortgage loans are Type IV assets to the savings bank. The timing of interest and principal cash flows is uncertain because of the prepayment option held by the homeowner. This type of call option is complex. Homeowners might elect to prepay for many reasons, including sale of the property as well as the opportunity to refinance if interest rates come down. Therefore, a prepayment model is needed to project the timing of future cash flows. Default risk also affects the projected amount of the cash flow for each date. Even if the *average* loan-to-value ratio is 80%, indicating high-quality mortgages, some loans could have higher ratios and be more subject to default, especially if home prices decline.
>
> **Solution to 2:**
>
> Fixed-rate government bonds are Type I assets because the coupon and principal payment dates and amounts are determined at issuance.

### Solution to 3:

Demand and time deposits are Type II liabilities from the savings bank's perspective. The deposit amounts are known, but the depositor can redeem the deposits prior to maturity, creating uncertainty about timing.

### Solution to 4:

The contingent convertible bonds are Type IV liabilities. The presence of the conversion option makes both the amount and timing of cash flows uncertain.

## 3. INTEREST RATE IMMUNIZATION: MANAGING THE INTEREST RATE RISK OF A SINGLE LIABILITY

**b** evaluate strategies for managing a single liability

Liability-driven investing in most circumstances is used to manage the interest rate risk on multiple liabilities. In this section, we focus on only a single liability to demonstrate the techniques and risks of the classic investment strategy known as interest rate **immunization**. Immunization is the process of structuring and managing a fixed-income bond portfolio to minimize the variance in the realized rate of return over a known time horizon. This variance arises from the volatility of future interest rates. Default risk is neglected at this point because the portfolio bonds are assumed to have default probabilities that approach zero.

The most obvious way to immunize the interest rate risk on a single liability is to buy a zero-coupon bond that matures on the obligation's due date. The bond's face value matches the liability amount. There is no cash flow reinvestment risk because there are no coupon payments to reinvest, and there is no price risk because the bond is held to maturity. Any interest rate volatility over the bond's lifetime is irrelevant in terms of the asset's ability to pay off the liability. The problem is that in many financial markets, zero-coupon bonds are not available. Nevertheless, the perfect immunization provided by a zero-coupon bond sets a standard to measure the performance of immunizing strategies using coupon-bearing bonds.

Exhibit 2 and Exhibit 3 illustrate the connection between immunization and the duration of a traditional coupon-bearing fixed-income bond.

**Exhibit 2   Immunization with a Single Bond: Rate Rise Scenario**

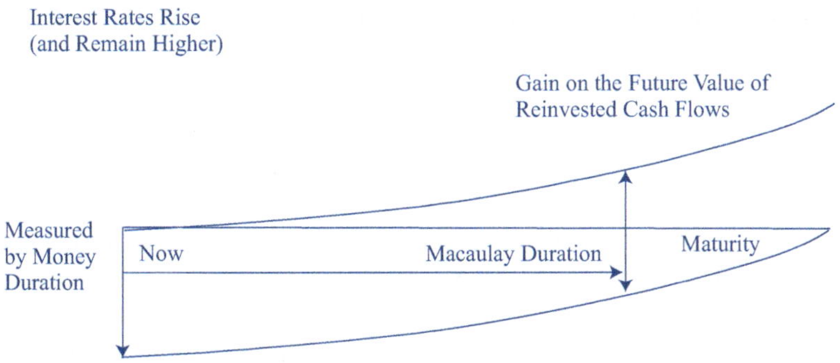

Assume that the bond is currently priced at par value. Then, an instantaneous, one-time, upward (parallel) shift occurs in the yield curve. The bond's value falls. That drop in value is estimated by the money duration of the bond. Recall that the money duration is the bond's modified duration statistic multiplied by the price. Subsequently, the bond price will be "pulled to par" as the maturity date nears (assuming no default, of course). But another factor is at work. Assuming interest rates remain higher, the future value of reinvested coupon payments goes up. It is shown by the rising line as more and more payments are received and reinvested at the higher interest rates.

The key detail to note in Exhibit 2 is that at some point in time, the two effects—the price effect and the coupon reinvestment effect—cancel each other out. The remarkable result is that this point in time turns out to be the bond's Macaulay duration (for a zero-coupon bond, its Macaulay duration is its maturity). Therefore, an investor having an investment horizon equal to the bond's Macaulay duration is effectively protected, or immunized, from interest rate risk in that price, and coupon reinvestment effects offset for either higher or lower rates. Exhibit 3 shows the same effect for an immediate downward shift in interest rates.

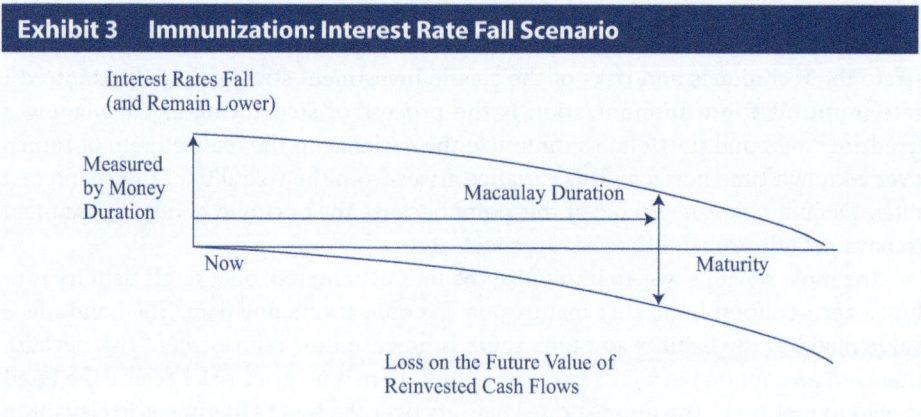

**Exhibit 3  Immunization: Interest Rate Fall Scenario**

## 3.1 A Numerical Example of Immunization

We now show that the strategy of matching the Macaulay duration to the investment horizon works for a bond portfolio as well as for an individual security. Suppose that some entity has a single liability of EUR 250 million due 15 February 2027. Further assume that the current date is 15 February 2021, so the investment horizon is six years. The asset manager for the entity seeks to build a three-bond portfolio to earn a rate of return sufficient to pay off the obligation.

### 3.1.1 Portfolio Features

Exhibit 4 reports the prices, yields, risk statistics (Macaulay duration and convexity), and par values for the chosen portfolio. The portfolio's current market value is EUR 200,052,250 (= EUR 47,117,500 + EUR 97,056,750 + EUR 55,878,000). The semi-annual coupon payments on the bonds occur on 15 February and 15 August of each year (note that we have chosen to use bonds that pay coupons semi-annually, which is not always the case). The price is per 100 of par value, and the yield to maturity is on a street-convention semi-annual bond basis (meaning an annual percentage rate having a periodicity of two). Both the Macaulay duration and the convexity are annualized. (Note that in practice, some bond data vendors report the convexity statistic divided by 100.)

# Interest Rate Immunization: Managing the Interest Rate Risk of a Single Liability

### Exhibit 4: The Bond Portfolio to Immunize the Single Liability

|  | 2.5-Year Bond | 7-Year Bond | 10-Year Bond |
|---|---|---|---|
| Coupon rate | 1.50% | 3.25% | 5.00% |
| Maturity date | 15 August 2023 | 15 February 2028 | 15 February 2031 |
| Price | 100.25 | 99.75 | 100.50 |
| Yield to maturity | 1.3979% | 3.2903% | 4.9360% |
| Par value | 47,000,000 | 97,300,000 | 55,600,000 |
| Market value | 47,117,500 | 97,056,750 | 55,878,000 |
| Macaulay duration | 2.463 | 6.316 | 7.995 |
| Convexity | 7.253 | 44.257 | 73.747 |
| Allocation | 23.55% | 48.52% | 27.93% |

Exhibit 5 shows the cash flows and calculations used to obtain the relevant portfolio statistics. The third column aggregates the coupon and principal payments received for each date from the three bonds.

### Exhibit 5: Portfolio Statistics

| Time | Date | Cash Flow | PV of Cash Flow | Weight | Time × Weight | Dispersion | Convexity |
|---|---|---|---|---|---|---|---|
| 0 | 15-Feb-21 | −200,052,250 | | | | | |
| 1 | 15-Aug-21 | 3,323,625 | 3,262,282 | 0.0163 | 0.0163 | 1.9735 | 0.0326 |
| 2 | 15-Feb-22 | 3,323,625 | 3,202,071 | 0.0160 | 0.0320 | 1.6009 | 0.0960 |
| 3 | 15-Aug-22 | 3,323,625 | 3,142,971 | 0.0157 | 0.0471 | 1.2728 | 0.1885 |
| 4 | 15-Feb-23 | 3,323,625 | 3,084,962 | 0.0154 | 0.0617 | 0.9871 | 0.3084 |
| 5 | 15-Aug-23 | 50,323,625 | 45,847,871 | 0.2292 | 1.1459 | 11.2324 | 6.8754 |
| 6 | 15-Feb-24 | 2,971,125 | 2,656,915 | 0.0133 | 0.0797 | 0.4782 | 0.5578 |
| 7 | 15-Aug-24 | 2,971,125 | 2,607,877 | 0.0130 | 0.0913 | 0.3260 | 0.7300 |
| 8 | 15-Feb-25 | 2,971,125 | 2,559,744 | 0.0128 | 0.1024 | 0.2048 | 0.9213 |
| 9 | 15-Aug-25 | 2,971,125 | 2,512,500 | 0.0126 | 0.1130 | 0.1131 | 1.1303 |
| 10 | 15-Feb-26 | 2,971,125 | 2,466,127 | 0.0123 | 0.1233 | 0.0493 | 1.3560 |
| 11 | 15-Aug-26 | 2,971,125 | 2,420,610 | 0.0121 | 0.1331 | 0.0121 | 1.5972 |
| 12 | 15-Feb-27 | 2,971,125 | 2,375,934 | 0.0119 | 0.1425 | 0.0000 | 1.8527 |
| 13 | 15-Aug-27 | 2,971,125 | 2,332,082 | 0.0117 | 0.1515 | 0.0116 | 2.1216 |
| 14 | 15-Feb-28 | 100,271,125 | 77,251,729 | 0.3862 | 5.4062 | 1.5434 | 81.0931 |
| 15 | 15-Aug-28 | 1,390,000 | 1,051,130 | 0.0053 | 0.0788 | 0.0473 | 1.2610 |
| 16 | 15-Feb-29 | 1,390,000 | 1,031,730 | 0.0052 | 0.0825 | 0.0825 | 1.4028 |
| 17 | 15-Aug-29 | 1,390,000 | 1,012,688 | 0.0051 | 0.0861 | 0.1265 | 1.5490 |
| 18 | 15-Feb-30 | 1,390,000 | 993,997 | 0.0050 | 0.0894 | 0.1788 | 1.6993 |
| 19 | 15-Aug-30 | 1,390,000 | 975,651 | 0.0049 | 0.0927 | 0.2389 | 1.8533 |
| 20 | 15-Feb-31 | 56,990,000 | 39,263,380 | 0.1963 | 3.9253 | 12.5585 | 82.4316 |
|  |  |  | 200,052,250 | 1.0000 | 12.0008 | 33.0378 | 189.0580 |

For instance, EUR 3,323,625 is the sum of the coupon payments for the first four dates:

(1.50% × 0.5 × EUR 47,000,000) + (3.25% × 0.5 × EUR 97,300,000) + (5.00% × 0.5 × EUR 55,600,000) = EUR 352,500 + EUR 1,581,125 + EUR 1,390,000 = EUR 3,323,625

On 15 August 2023, the principal of EUR 47,000,000 is redeemed so that the total cash flow is EUR 50,323,625. The next eight cash flows represent the coupon payments on the second and third bonds, and so forth.

The internal rate of return on the cash flows in column 3 for the 20 semi-annual periods, including the portfolio's initial market value on 15 February 2021, is 1.8804%. Annualized on a semi-annual bond basis, the portfolio's cash flow yield is 3.7608% (= 2 × 1.8804%). This yield is significantly higher than the market value-weighted average of the individual bond yields-to-maturity presented in Exhibit 4, which equals 3.3043%.

(1.3979% × 0.2355) + (3.2903% × 0.4852) + (4.9360% × 0.2793) = 3.3043%.

This difference arises because of the steepness in the yield curve. The key point is that the goal of the immunization strategy is to achieve a rate of return close to 3.76%, not 3.30%.

The fourth column in Exhibit 5 shows the present values for each of the aggregate cash flows, calculated using the internal rate of return per period (1.8804%) as the discount rate. For example, the combined payment of EUR100,271,125 due on 15 February 2028 has a present value of EUR77,251,729. [*Note: Calculations are carried out on a spreadsheet that preserves precision. For readability and to avoid clutter, the exhibits and text report rounded results. For example, the following calculation gives 77,251,498 with the numbers shown on the left hand-side, but it gives 77,251,729, the amount shown on the right hand-side, when the precise semi-annual cash flow yield, 1.0188037819%, is used.*]

$$\frac{100,271,125}{(1.018804)^{14}} = 77,251,729$$

The sum of the present values in column 4 of Exhibit 5 is EUR200,052,250, the current market value for the bond portfolio.

### 3.1.2 Portfolio Duration

The sixth column of Exhibit 5 is used to obtain the portfolio's Macaulay duration. This duration statistic is the weighted average of the times to the receipt of cash flow, whereby the share of total market value for each date is the weight. Column 5 shows the weights, which are the PV of each cash flow divided by the total PV of EUR200,052,250. The times to receipt of cash flow (the times from column 1) are multiplied by the weights and then summed. For example, the contribution to total portfolio duration for the second cash flow on 15 February 2022 is 0.0320 (= 2 × 0.0160). The sum of column 6 is 12.0008. That is the Macaulay duration for the portfolio in terms of semi-annual periods. Annualized, it is 6.0004 (= 12.0008/2). It is now clear why the asset manager for the entity chose this portfolio: The portfolio Macaulay duration matches the investment horizon of six years.

In practice, it is common to estimate the portfolio duration using the market value-weighted average of the individual durations for each bond. Exhibit 4 shows those individual durations and the allocation percentages for each bond. The average Macaulay duration is (2.463 × 0.2355) + (6.316 × 0.4852) + (7.995 × 0.2793) = 5.8776.

The difference, as with the cash flow yield and the market value-weighted average yield, arises because the yield curve is not flat. When the yield curve is upwardly sloped, average duration (5.8776) is less than the portfolio duration (6.0004). This difference in duration statistics is important because using the average duration in building the immunizing portfolio instead of the portfolio duration would introduce model risk to the strategy, as we will see later.

### 3.1.3 Portfolio Dispersion

The sum of the seventh column in Exhibit 5 is the portfolio dispersion statistic. Recall that whereas Macaulay duration is the weighted *average* of the times to receipt of cash flow, dispersion is the weighted *variance*. It measures the extent to which the payments are spread out around the duration. For example, the contribution to total portfolio dispersion for the fifth cash flow on 15 August 2023 is 11.2324: $(5 - 12.0008)^2 \times 0.2292 = 11.2324$.

This portfolio's dispersion is 33.0378 in terms of semi-annual periods. Annualized, it is 8.2594 (= 33.0378/4). The Macaulay duration statistic is annualized by dividing by the periodicity of the bonds (two payments per year); dispersion (and convexity, which follows) is annualized by dividing by the periodicity squared (i.e., 2^2 = 4 for semi-annual payment bonds).

### 3.1.4 Portfolio Convexity

The portfolio convexity is calculated with the eighth column. It is the sum of the times to the receipt of cash flow, multiplied by those times plus one, multiplied by the shares of market value for each date (weight), and all divided by one plus the cash flow yield squared. For example, the contribution to the sum for the 14th payment on 15 February 2028 is 81.0931 (= 14 × 15 × 0.3862). The sum of the column is 189.0580. The convexity in semi-annual periods is 182.1437:

$$\frac{189.0580}{(1.018804)^2} = 182.1437$$

The annualized convexity for the portfolio is 45.5359 (= 182.1437/4). This result is slightly higher than the market value-weighted average of the individual convexity statistics (for each bond) reported in Exhibit 4:

$(7.253 \times 0.2355) + (44.257 \times 0.4852) + (73.747 \times 0.2793) = 43.7786$.

As with the average yield and duration, this difference results from the slope of the yield curve. The convexity statistic can be used to improve the estimate for the change in portfolio market value following a change in interest rates than is provided by duration alone. That is, convexity is the second-order effect, whereas duration is the first-order effect.

There is an interesting connection among the portfolio convexity, Macaulay duration, dispersion, and cash flow yield in immunized portfolio convexity, also known as the "portfolio convexity statistic":

$$\text{Immunized Portfolio Convexity} = \frac{\text{MacDur}^2 + \text{MacDur} + \text{Dispersion}}{(1 + \text{Cash flow yield})^2} \quad (1)$$

In terms of semi-annual periods, the Macaulay duration for this portfolio is 12.0008, the dispersion is 33.0378, and the cash flow yield is 1.8804%.

$$\text{Immunized Portfolio Convexity} = \frac{12.0008^2 + 12.0008 + 33.0378}{(1.018804)^2} = 182.1437.$$

The portfolio dispersion and convexity statistics are used to assess the structural risk to the interest rate immunization strategy. Structural risk arises from the potential for shifts and twists to the yield curve. This risk is discussed later.

### 3.1.5 Investment Horizon and Immunization

We now demonstrate how matching the Macaulay duration for the portfolio to the investment horizon leads to interest rate immunization. The first three columns of Exhibit 6 are identical to the ones in Exhibit 5.

The fourth column shows the values of the cash flows as of the horizon date of 15 February 2027, assuming that the cash flow yield remains unchanged at 3.7608%. For instance, the future value of the EUR3,323,625 in coupon payments received on 15 August 2021 is EUR4,079,520:

$$3{,}323{,}625 \times \left(1 + \frac{0.037608}{2}\right)^{11} = 4{,}079{,}520$$

The value of the last cash flow for EUR56,990,000 on 15 February 2031 is EUR49,099,099 as of the horizon date of 15 February 2027:

$$\frac{56{,}990{,}000}{\left(1 + \frac{0.037608}{2}\right)^{8}} = 49{,}099{,}099$$

We assume that all of the payments received before the horizon date are reinvested at the cash flow yield. All of the payments received after the horizon date are sold at their discounted values. The sum of the fourth column in Exhibit 6 is EUR250,167,000, which is more than enough to pay off the EUR250 million liability. The six-year holding period rate of return (ROR), also called the horizon yield, is 3.7608%. It is based on the original market value and the total return and is the solution for ROR:

$$200{,}052{,}250 = \frac{250{,}167{,}000}{\left(1 + \frac{ROR}{2}\right)^{12}}, \quad ROR = 0.037608.$$

The holding period rate of return equals the cash flow yield for the portfolio. This equivalence is the multi-bond version of the well-known result for a single bond: The realized rate of return matches the yield to maturity only if coupon payments are reinvested at that same yield and if the bond is held to maturity or sold at a point on the constant-yield price trajectory.

### Exhibit 6  Interest Rate Immunization

| Time | Date | Cash Flow | Total Return at 3.7608% | Total Return at 2.7608% | Total Return at 4.7608% |
|---|---|---|---|---|---|
| 0 | 15-Feb-21 | −200,052,250 | | | |
| 1 | 15-Aug-21 | 3,323,625 | 4,079,520 | 3,864,613 | 4,305,237 |
| 2 | 15-Feb-22 | 3,323,625 | 4,004,225 | 3,811,992 | 4,205,138 |
| 3 | 15-Aug-22 | 3,323,625 | 3,930,319 | 3,760,088 | 4,107,366 |
| 4 | 15-Feb-23 | 3,323,625 | 3,857,777 | 3,708,891 | 4,011,868 |
| 5 | 15-Aug-23 | 50,323,625 | 57,333,230 | 55,392,367 | 59,332,093 |
| 6 | 15-Feb-24 | 2,971,125 | 3,322,498 | 3,225,856 | 3,421,542 |
| 7 | 15-Aug-24 | 2,971,125 | 3,261,175 | 3,181,932 | 3,341,989 |
| 8 | 15-Feb-25 | 2,971,125 | 3,200,984 | 3,138,607 | 3,264,286 |
| 9 | 15-Aug-25 | 2,971,125 | 3,141,904 | 3,095,871 | 3,188,390 |
| 10 | 15-Feb-26 | 2,971,125 | 3,083,914 | 3,053,718 | 3,114,258 |
| 11 | 15-Aug-26 | 2,971,125 | 3,026,994 | 3,012,138 | 3,041,850 |
| 12 | 15-Feb-27 | 2,971,125 | 2,971,125 | 2,971,125 | 2,971,125 |

# Interest Rate Immunization: Managing the Interest Rate Risk of a Single Liability

**Exhibit 6 (Continued)**

| Time | Date | Cash Flow | Total Return at 3.7608% | Total Return at 2.7608% | Total Return at 4.7608% |
|---|---|---|---|---|---|
| 13 | 15-Aug-27 | 2,971,125 | 2,916,287 | 2,930,670 | 2,902,045 |
| 14 | 15-Feb-28 | 100,271,125 | 96,603,888 | 97,559,123 | 95,662,614 |
| 15 | 15-Aug-28 | 1,390,000 | 1,314,446 | 1,333,991 | 1,295,282 |
| 16 | 15-Feb-29 | 1,390,000 | 1,290,186 | 1,315,827 | 1,265,166 |
| 17 | 15-Aug-29 | 1,390,000 | 1,266,373 | 1,297,911 | 1,235,750 |
| 18 | 15-Feb-30 | 1,390,000 | 1,242,999 | 1,280,238 | 1,207,018 |
| 19 | 15-Aug-30 | 1,390,000 | 1,220,058 | 1,262,806 | 1,178,955 |
| 20 | 15-Feb-31 | 56,990,000 | 49,099,099 | 51,070,094 | 47,213,270 |
|   |   |   | 250,167,000 | 250,267,858 | 250,265,241 |

### 3.1.6 A Drop in the Cash Flow Yield Scenario

The fifth column in Exhibit 6 repeats the calculations for the assumption of an instantaneous, one-time, 100 bp drop in the cash flow yield on 15 February 2021. The future values of all cash flows received are now lower because they are reinvested at 2.7608% instead of 3.7608%. For example, the payment of EUR50,323,625 on 15 August 2023, which contains the principal redemption on the 2.5-year bond, grows to only EUR55,392,367:

$$50{,}323{,}625 \times \left(1 + \frac{0.027608}{2}\right)^7 = 55{,}392{,}367$$

The value of the last cash flow is now higher because it is discounted at the lower cash flow yield:

$$\frac{56{,}990{,}000}{\left(1 + \frac{0.027608}{2}\right)^8} = 51{,}070{,}094$$

The important result is that the total return as of the horizon date is EUR250,267,858, demonstrating that the cash flow reinvestment effect is balanced by the price effect, as illustrated for a single bond in Exhibit 2. The holding-period rate of return is 3.7676%:

$$200{,}052{,}250 = \frac{250{,}267{,}858}{\left(1 + \frac{ROR}{2}\right)^{12}}, \quad ROR = 0.037676.$$

### 3.1.7 An Increase in the Cash Flow Yield Scenario

To complete the example, the sixth column in Exhibit 6 reports the results for an instantaneous, one-time, 100 bp jump in the cash flow yield, up to 4.7608% from 3.7608%. In this case, the future values of the reinvested cash flows are higher and the discounted values of cash flows due after the horizon date are lower. Nevertheless, the total return of EUR250,265,241 for the six-year investment horizon is enough to pay off the liability. The horizon yield is 3.7674%:

$$200{,}052{,}250 = \frac{250{,}265{,}241}{\left(1 + \frac{ROR}{2}\right)^{12}}, \quad ROR = 0.037674.$$

This numerical exercise demonstrates interest rate immunization using a portfolio of fixed-income bonds. The total returns and holding period rates of return are virtually the same—in fact, slightly higher because of convexity—whether the cash flow yield goes up or down.

### 3.1.8 Immunization and Rebalancing

Exhibit 5 is somewhat misleading, however, because it suggests that immunization is a buy-and-hold passive investment strategy. It suggests that the entity will (a) hold on the horizon date of 15 February 2027 the same positions in what then will be one-year, 3.25% and four-year, 5% bonds and (b) sell the bonds on that date. This suggestion is misleading because the portfolio must be frequently rebalanced to stay on its target duration. As time passes, the portfolio's Macaulay duration changes but not in line with the change in the remainder of the investment horizon. For example, after five years, the investment horizon as of 15 February 2026 is just one remaining year. The portfolio Macaulay duration at that time needs to be 1.000. The asset manager will have had to execute some trades by then, substantially reducing the holdings in what is then the five-year, 5% bond.

Exhibit 7 offers another way to illustrate interest rate immunization. An immunization strategy is essentially "zero replication." We know that the perfect bond to lock in the six-year holding period rate of return is a six-year zero-coupon bond having a face value that matches the EUR250 million liability. The idea is to originally structure and then manage over time a portfolio of coupon-bearing bonds that replicates the period-to-period performance of the zero-coupon bond. Therefore, immunization is essentially just an interest rate hedging strategy. As the yield on the zero-coupon bond rises and falls, there will be unrealized losses and gains. In Exhibit 7, this is illustrated by the zero-coupon bond's value moving below and above the constant-yield price trajectory. Two paths for the zero-coupon yield are presented: Path A for generally lower rates (and higher values) and Path B for higher rates (and lower values). Regardless, the market value of the zero-coupon bond will be "pulled to par" as maturity nears.

**Exhibit 7  Interest Rate Immunization as Zero Replication**

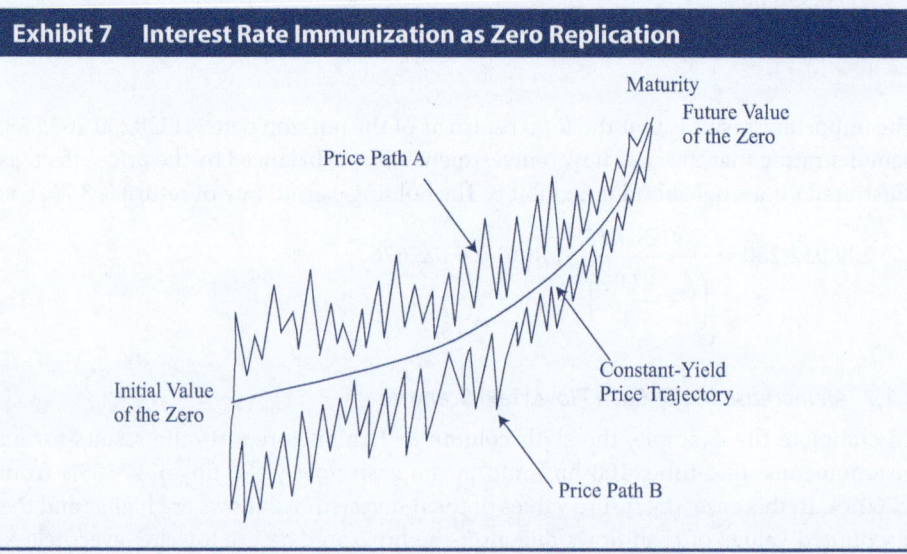

Immunizing with coupon-bearing bonds entails continuously matching the portfolio Macaulay duration with the Macaulay duration of the zero-coupon bond over time and as the yield curve shifts, even though the zero-coupon bond could be hypothetical and not exist in reality. Also, in order to fully match the liability, the bond portfolio's initial market value has to match or exceed the present value of the zero-coupon bond. The Macaulay duration of that, perhaps hypothetical, zero-coupon bond always matches

# Interest Rate Immunization: Managing the Interest Rate Risk of a Single Liability

the investment horizon. Immunization will be achieved if any ensuing change in the cash flow yield on the bond portfolio is equal to the change in the yield to maturity on the zero-coupon bond. That equivalence will ensure that the change in the bond portfolio's market value is close to the change in the market value of the zero-coupon bond. Therefore, at the end of the six-year investment horizon, the bond portfolio's market value should meet or exceed the face value of the zero-coupon bond, regardless of the path for interest rates over the six years.

### 3.1.9 Immunization and Shifts in the Yield Curve

The key assumption to achieve immunization is the statement that "any ensuing change in the cash flow yield on the bond portfolio is equal to the change in the yield to maturity on the zero-coupon bond." A *sufficient*, but not *necessary*, condition for that statement is a parallel (or shape-preserving) shift to the yield curve whereby all yields change by the same amount. *Sufficient* means that if the yield curve shift is parallel, the change in the bond portfolio's cash flow yield will equal the change in yield to maturity of the zero-coupon bond, which is enough to ensure immunization. To achieve immunization, however, it is not *necessary* that the yield curve shifts in a parallel manner. That is, in some cases, the immunization property can prevail even with non-parallel yield curve movements, such as an upward and steepening shift (sometimes called a "bear steepener"), an upward and flattening shift (a "bear flattener"), a downward and steepening shift (a "bull steepener"), or a downward and flattening shift (a "bull flattener").

Exhibits 8 and 9 demonstrate this observation. Exhibit 8 presents three different upward yield curve shifts. The first is a parallel shift of 102.08 bps for each of the three bond yields. The second is a steepening shift of 72.19 bps for the 2.5-year bond, 94.96 bps for the 7-year bond, and 120.82 bps for the 10-year bond. The third is a flattening shift, whereby the yields on the three bonds increase by 145.81 bps, 109.48 bps, and 79.59 bps, respectively. The key point is that each of these yield curve shifts results in the same 100 bp increase in the cash flow yield from 3.7608% to 4.7608%. Moreover, each shift in the yield curve produces virtually the same reduction in the portfolio's market value.

### Exhibit 8   Some Upward Yield Curve Shifts That Achieve Interest Rate Immunization

|  | Change in 2.5-Year Yield | Change in 7-Year Yield | Change in 10-Year Yield | Change in Cash Flow Yield | Change in Market Value |
|---|---|---|---|---|---|
| Upward and parallel | +102.08 bps | +102.08 bps | +102.08 bps | +100 bps | −11,340,537 |
| Upward and steepening | +72.19 bps | +94.96 bps | +120.82 bps | +100 bps | −11,340,195 |
| Upward and flattening | +145.81 bps | +109.48 bps | +79.59 bps | +100 bps | −11,340,183 |

Exhibit 9 shows the results for three downward shifts in the yield curve. The first is a parallel shift of 102.06 bps. The second and third are downward and steepening (−129.00 bps, −104.52 bps, and −92.00 bps for the 2.5-year, 7-year, and 10-year bonds) and downward and flattening (−55.76 bps, −86.32 bps, and −134.08 bps). Each shift results in the same 100 bp decrease in the cash flow yield from 3.7608% to 2.7608% and virtually the same increase in the market value of the portfolio.

**Exhibit 9  Some Downward Yield Curve Shifts That Achieve Interest Rate Immunization**

|  | Change in 2.5-Year Yield | Change in 7-Year Yield | Change in 10-Year Yield | Change in Cash Flow Yield | Change in Market Value |
|---|---|---|---|---|---|
| Downward and parallel | −102.06 bps | −102.06 bps | −102.06 bps | −100 bps | 12,251,212 |
| Downward and steepening | −129.00 bps | −104.52 bps | −92.00 bps | −100 bps | 12,251,333 |
| Downward and flattening | −55.76 bps | −86.32 bps | −134.08 bps | −100 bps | 12,251,484 |

Notice that the interest rate immunization property shown in Exhibit 6 rests only on the change in the cash flow yield going up or down by 100 bps. It is not necessary to assume that the change in the value of the immunizing portfolio arises only from a parallel shift in the yield curve. In the same manner, the immunization property illustrated in Exhibit 7 requires only that the change in the value of the immunizing portfolio, one that has a Macaulay duration matching the investment horizon, is close to the change in the value of the zero-coupon bond that provides perfect immunization. Exhibits 8 and 9 demonstrate that some non-parallel as well as parallel shifts can satisfy those conditions. Of course, there are many other non-parallel shifts for which those conditions are not met.

In general, the interest rate risk to an immunization strategy is that the change in the cash flow yield on the portfolio is not the same as on the ideal zero-coupon bond. This difference can occur with twists to the shape of the yield curve, in addition to some non-parallel shifts.

Exhibits 10 and 11 portray two such twists. To exaggerate the risk, assume that the immunizing portfolio has a "barbell" structure in that it is composed of half short-term bonds and half long-term bonds. The portfolio Macaulay duration for the barbell is six years. The zero-coupon bond that provides perfect immunization has a maturity (and Macaulay duration) also of six years.

Exhibit 10 shows a steepening twist to the yield curve. The twist is assumed to occur at the six-year point to indicate that the value of the zero-coupon bond does not change. Short-term yields go down and long-term yields go up by approximately the same amount. The value of the barbell portfolio goes down because the losses on the long-term positions exceed the gains on the short-term holdings as a result of the difference in duration between the holdings and the equivalence in the assumed changes in yield. Therefore, this portfolio does not track the value of the zero-coupon bond for such a scenario.

**Exhibit 10    Immunization Risk and Steepening Twist**

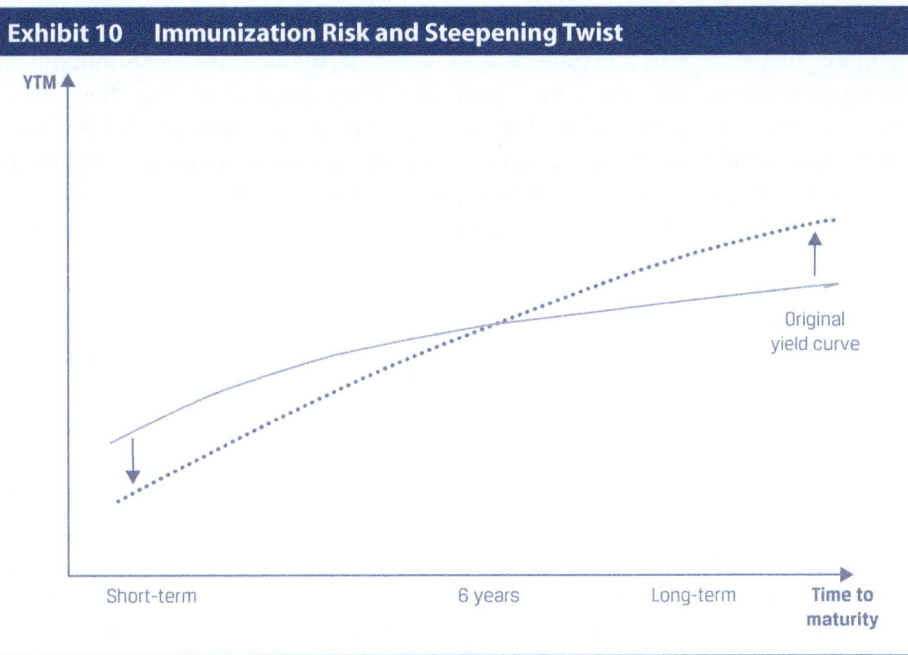

Exhibit 11 illustrates a dramatic twist in the shape of the yield curve. Short-term and long-term yields go up while the six-year yields go down. This type of twist is a butterfly movement, in this case a "positive butterfly." (In a "negative butterfly" twist, short-term and long-term yields go down and intermediate-term yields go up.) The immunizing portfolio decreases in value as its yields go up and the zero-coupon bond goes up in value. Again, for this particular scenario, the portfolio does not track the change in the value of the bond that provides perfect immunization. Fortunately for those entities that pursue interest rate immunization, these types of twists are rare. Most yield curve shifts are generally parallel, with some steepening and flattening, especially for maturities beyond a few years.

**Exhibit 11    Immunization Risk and a Butterfly Yield Curve Movement**

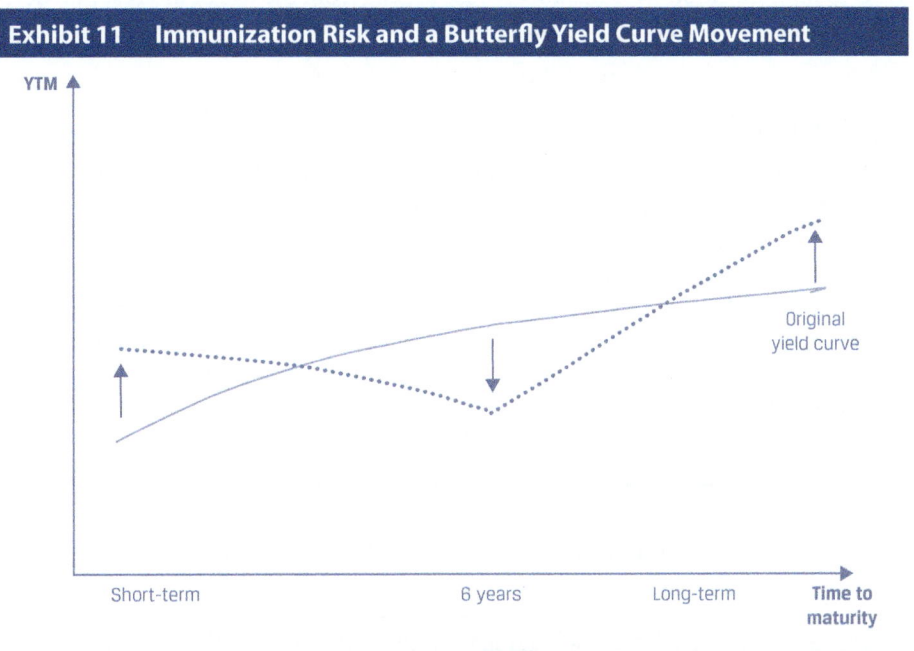

### 3.1.10 Structural Risk in Immunization Strategy

Exhibits 10 and 11 also illustrate how to reduce **structural risk** to an immunizing strategy. Structural risk arises from portfolio design, particularly the choice of the portfolio allocations. The risk is that yield curve twists and non-parallel shifts lead to changes in the cash flow yield that do not match the yield to maturity of the zero-coupon bond that provides for perfect immunization. Structural risk is reduced by minimizing the dispersion of the bond positions, going from a barbell design to more of a bullet portfolio that concentrates the component bonds' durations around the investment horizon. At the limit, a zero-coupon bond that matches the date of the single obligation has, by design, no structural risk.

Equation 1 (immunized portfolio convexity) indicates that minimizing portfolio dispersion is the same as minimizing the portfolio convexity for a given Macaulay duration and cash flow yield. An advantage to using convexity to measure the extent of structural risk is that the portfolio statistic can be approximated by the market value-weighted average of the individual bonds' convexities. A problem with estimating portfolio dispersion using the weighted average of dispersion statistics for individual bonds is that it can be misleading. Consider a portfolio of all zero-coupon bonds of varying maturities. Each individual bond has zero dispersion (because it has only one payment), so the market value-weighted average is also zero. Clearly, the portfolio overall can have significant (non-zero) dispersion.

In summary, the characteristics of a bond portfolio structured to immunize a single liability are that it:

- has an initial market value that equals or exceeds the present value of the liability;
- has a portfolio Macaulay duration that matches the liability's due date;
- minimizes the portfolio convexity statistic.

This portfolio must be regularly rebalanced over the horizon to maintain the target duration, because the portfolio Macaulay duration changes as time passes and as yields change. The portfolio manager needs to weigh the trade-off between incurring transaction costs from rebalancing and allowing some duration gap. This and other risks to immunization—for instance, those arising from the use of interest rate derivatives to match the duration of assets to the investment horizon—are covered later.

---

**EXAMPLE 2**

An institutional client asks a fixed-income investment adviser to recommend a portfolio to immunize a single 10-year liability. It is understood that the chosen portfolio will need to be rebalanced over time to maintain its target duration. The adviser proposes two portfolios of coupon-bearing government bonds because zero-coupon bonds are not available. The portfolios have the same market value. The institutional client's objective is to minimize the variance in the realized rate of return over the 10-year horizon. The two portfolios have the following risk and return statistics:

|  | Portfolio A | Portfolio B |
|---|---|---|
| Cash flow yield | 7.64% | 7.65% |
| Macaulay duration | 9.98 | 10.01 |
| Convexity | 107.88 | 129.43 |

These statistics are based on aggregating the interest and principal cash flows for the bonds that constitute the portfolios; they are not market value-weighted averages of the yields, durations, and convexities of the individual bonds. The cash flow yield is stated on a semi-annual bond basis, meaning an annual percentage rate having a periodicity of two; the Macaulay durations and convexities are annualized.

Indicate the portfolio that the investment adviser should recommend, and explain the reasoning.

**Solution:**

The adviser should recommend Portfolio A. First, notice that the cash flow yields of both portfolios are virtually the same and that both portfolios have Macaulay durations very close to 10, the horizon for the liability. It would be wrong and misleading to recommend Portfolio B because it has a "higher yield" and a "duration closer to the investment horizon of 10 years." In practical terms, a difference of 1 bp in yield is not likely to be significant, nor is the difference of 0.03 in annual duration.

Given the fact that the portfolio yields and durations are essentially the same, the choice depends on the difference in convexity. The difference between 129.43 and 107.88, however, is meaningful. In general, convexity is a desirable property of fixed-income bonds. All else being equal (meaning the same yield and duration), a more convex bond gains more if the yield goes down and loses less if the yield goes up than a less convex bond.

The client's objective, however, is to minimize the variance in the realized rate of return over the 10-year horizon. That objective indicates a conservative immunization strategy achieved by building the duration-matching portfolio and minimizing the portfolio convexity. Such an approach minimizes the dispersion of cash flows around the Macaulay duration and makes the portfolio closer to the zero-coupon bond that would provide perfect immunization; see Equation 1.

The structural risk to the immunization strategy is the potential for non-parallel shifts and twists to the yield curve, which lead to changes in the cash flow yield that do not track the change in the yield on the zero-coupon bond. This risk is minimized by selecting the portfolio with the lower convexity (and dispersion of cash flows).

Note that default risk is neglected in this discussion because the portfolio consists of government bonds that presumably have default probabilities approaching zero.

# INTEREST RATE IMMUNIZATION: MANAGING THE INTEREST RATE RISK OF MULTIPLE LIABILITIES

c   compare strategies for a single liability and for multiple liabilities, including alternative means of implementation

d   describe construction, benefits, limitations, and risk–return characteristics of a laddered bond portfolio

The principle of interest rate immunization applies to multiple liabilities in addition to a single liability. For now, we continue to assume that these are Type I cash flows in that the scheduled amounts and payment dates are known to the asset manager. In particular, we assume that the same three bonds from Exhibits 4 and 5, which were assets in the single-liability immunization, are now themselves liabilities to be immunized. This assumption allows us to use the same portfolio statistics as in the previous section. The entity in the examples that follow seeks to immunize the cash flows in column 3 (the cash flow column) of Exhibit 5 from Dates 1 through 20, and so it needs to build a portfolio of assets that will allow it to pay those cash flows. The present value of the (now) corporate debt liabilities is EUR200,052,250. The cash flow yield is 3.76%; the Macaulay duration is 6.00; and the convexity is 45.54. We use the portfolio statistics rather than the market value-weighted averages because they better summarize Type I liabilities.

In this section, we discuss several approaches to manage these liabilities:

- *Cash flow matching*, which entails building a dedicated portfolio of zero-coupon or fixed-income bonds to ensure that there are sufficient cash inflows to pay the scheduled cash outflows (a related concept, the so-called "laddered portfolio," also falls into the cash flow matching category of approaches);
- *Duration matching*, which extends the ideas of the previous section to a portfolio of debt liabilities;
- *Derivatives overlay*, in particular using futures contracts on government bonds in the immunization strategy; and
- *Contingent immunization*, which allows for active bond portfolio management as long as the surplus is above a designated threshold.

## 4.1 Cash Flow Matching

A classic strategy to eliminate the interest rate risk arising from multiple liabilities is to build a dedicated asset portfolio of high-quality fixed-income bonds that, as closely as possible, matches the amount and timing of the scheduled cash outflows. "Dedicated" means that the bonds are placed in a held-to-maturity portfolio. A natural question is, if the entity has enough cash to build the dedicated bond portfolio, why not just use that cash to buy back and retire the liabilities? The answer is that the buyback strategy is difficult and costly to implement if the bonds are widely held by buy-and-hold institutional and retail investors. Most corporate bonds are rather illiquid, so buying them back on the open market is likely to drive up the purchase price. Cash flow matching can be a better use of the available cash assets.

A corporate finance motivation for cash flow matching is to improve the company's credit rating. The entity has sufficient cash assets to retire the debt liabilities, and dedicating the bonds effectively accomplishes that objective. Under some circumstances, a corporation might even be able to remove both the dedicated asset portfolio and the debt liabilities from its balance sheet through the process of **accounting defeasance**. Also called in-substance defeasance, accounting defeasance is a way of extinguishing a debt obligation by setting aside sufficient high-quality securities, such as US Treasury notes, to repay the liability.

Panel A in Exhibit 12 illustrates the dedicated cash flow matching asset portfolio. These assets could be zero-coupon bonds or traditional fixed-income securities. Panel B represents the amount and timing of the debt liabilities. The amounts come from the third column in Exhibit 5 and are the sum of the coupon and principal payments on the three debt securities.

# Interest Rate Immunization: Managing the Interest Rate Risk of Multiple Liabilities

## Exhibit 12   Cash Flow Matching

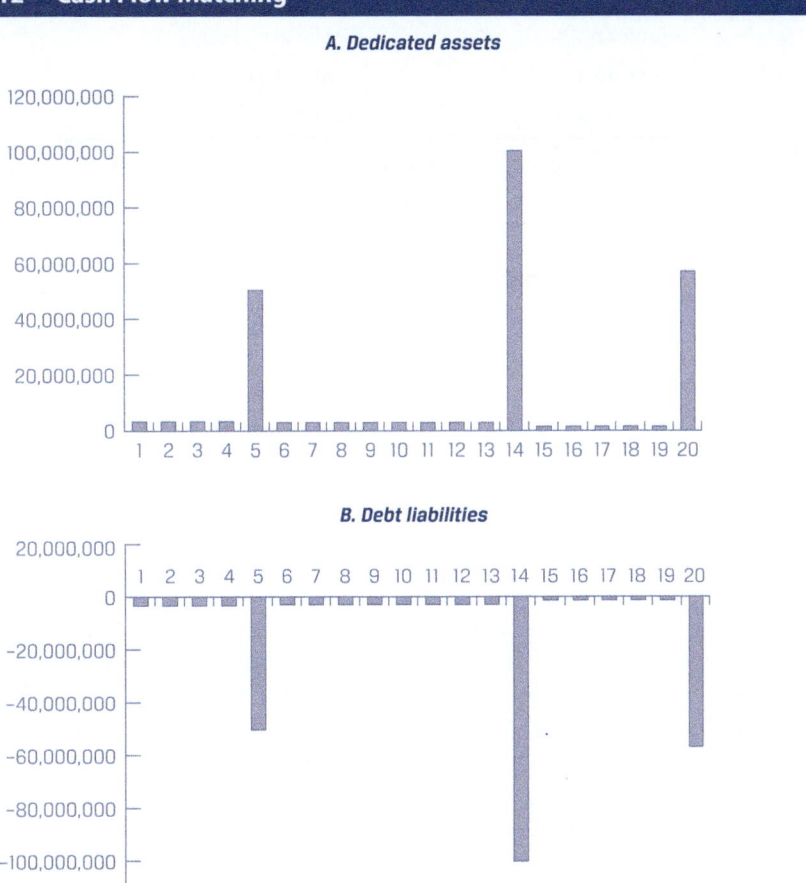

A concern when implementing this strategy is the *cash-in-advance constraint*. That means securities are not sold to meet obligations; instead, sufficient funds must be available on or before each liability payment date to meet the obligation. The design of traditional bonds—a fixed coupon rate and principal redemption at maturity—is a problem if the liability stream, unlike in Exhibit 12, is a level payment annuity. That scenario could lead to large cash holdings between payment dates and, therefore, cash flow reinvestment risk, especially if yields on high-quality, short-term investments are low (or worse, negative).

### EXAMPLE 3

Alfred Simonsson is assistant treasurer at a Swedish lumber company. The company has sold a large tract of land and now has sufficient cash holdings to retire some of its debt liabilities. The company's accounting department assures Alfred that its external auditors will approve of a defeasement strategy if Swedish government bonds are purchased to match the interest and principal payments on the liabilities. Following is the schedule of payments due on the debt as of June Year 1 that the company plans to defease:

| | |
|---|---|
| June Year 2 | SEK 3,710,000 |
| June Year 3 | SEK 6,620,000 |
| June Year 4 | SEK 4,410,000 |
| June Year 5 | SEK 5,250,000 |

The following Swedish government bonds are available. Interest on the bonds is paid annually in May of each year.

| Coupon Rate | Maturity Date |
|---|---|
| 2.75% | May Year 2 |
| 3.50% | May Year 3 |
| 4.75% | May Year 4 |
| 5.50% | May Year 5 |

How much in par value for each government bond will Alfred need to buy to defease the debt liabilities, assuming that the minimum denomination in each security is SEK 10,000?

**Solution:**

The cash flow matching portfolio is built by starting with the last liability of SEK 5,250,000 in June Year 5. If there were no minimum denomination, that liability could be funded with the 5.50% bonds due May Year 5 having a par value of SEK 4,976,303 (= SEK 5,250,000/1.0550). To deal with the constraint, however, Alfred buys SEK 4,980,000 in par value. That bond pays SEK 5,253,900 (= SEK 4,980,000 × 1.0550) at maturity. This holding also pays SEK 273,900 (= SEK 4,980,000 × 0.0550) in coupon interest in May Year 2, 3, and 4.

Then move to the June Year 4 obligation, which is SEK 4,136,100 after subtracting the SEK 273,900 received on the 5.50% bond: SEK 4,410,000 − SEK 273,900 = SEK 4,136,100. Alfred buys SEK 3,950,000 in par value of the 4.75% bond due May Year 4. That bond pays SEK 4,137,625 (= SEK 3,950,000 × 1.0475) at maturity and SEK 187,625 in interest in May Year 2 and Year 3.

The net obligation in June Year 3 is SEK 6,158,475 (= SEK 6,620,000 − SEK 273,900 − SEK 187,625) after subtracting the interest received on the longer-maturity bonds. The company can buy SEK 5,950,000 in par value of the 3.50% bond due May Year 3. At maturity, this bond pays SEK 6,158,250 (= SEK 5,950,000 × 1.0350). The small shortfall of SEK 225 (= SEK 6,158,475 − SEK 6,158,250) can be made up because the funds received in May are reinvested until June. This bond also pays SEK 208,250 in interest in May Year 2.

Finally, Alfred needs to buy SEK 2,960,000 in par value of the 2.75% bond due May Year 2. This bond pays SEK 3,041,400 (= SEK 2,960,000 × 1.0275) in May Year 2. The final coupon and principal, plus the interest on the 5.50%, 4.75%, and 3.50% bonds, total SEK 3,711,175 (= SEK 3,041,400 + SEK 273,900 + SEK 187,625 + SEK 208,250). That amount is used to pay off the June Year 2 obligation of SEK 3,710,000. Note that the excess could be kept in a bank account to cover the Year 3 shortfall.

In sum, Alfred buys the following portfolio:

| Bond | Par Value |
|---|---|
| 2.75% due May Year 2 | SEK 2,960,000 |
| 3.50% due May Year 3 | SEK 5,950,000 |
| 4.75% due May Year 4 | SEK 3,950,000 |
| 5.50% due May year 5 | SEK 4,980,000 |

The following chart illustrates the cash flow matching bond portfolio: Each bar represents the par amount of a bond maturing in that year plus coupon payments from bonds maturing in later years.

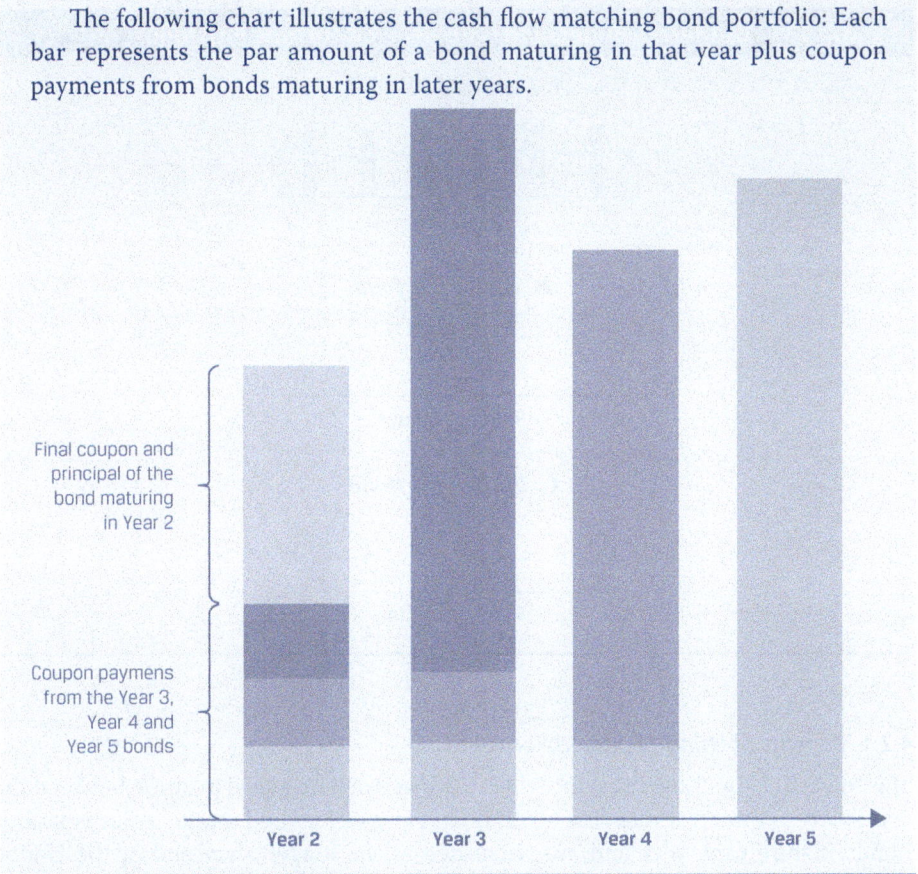

## 4.2 Laddered Portfolios

A popular fixed-income investment strategy in the wealth management industry is to build a "laddered" portfolio for clients. Exhibit 13 illustrates this approach, along with two other maturity-based strategies—a "bullet" portfolio and a "barbell" portfolio. The laddered portfolio spreads the bonds' maturities and par values more or less evenly along the yield curve. The bullet portfolio concentrates the bonds at a particular point on the yield curve, whereas the barbell portfolio places the bonds at the short-term and long-term ends of the curve. In principle, each can have the same portfolio duration statistic and approximately the same change in value for a parallel shift in the yield curve. A non-parallel shift or a twist in the curve, however, leads to very different outcomes for the bullet and barbell structures. An obvious advantage to the laddered portfolio is protection from shifts and twists—the cash flows are essentially "diversified" across the time spectrum.

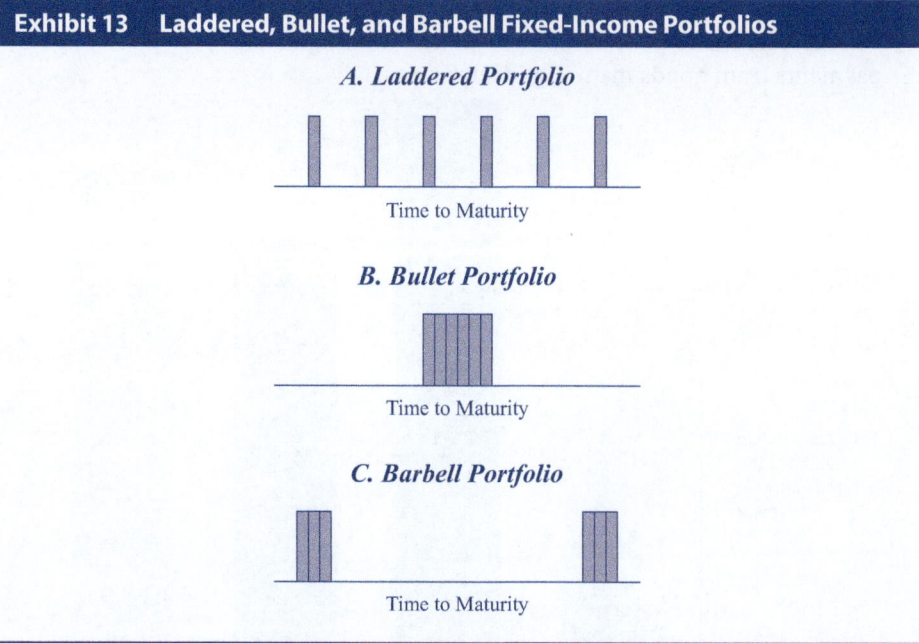

**Exhibit 13  Laddered, Bullet, and Barbell Fixed-Income Portfolios**

### 4.2.1 Benefits of Using Laddered Portfolios

This "diversification" over time provides the investor a balanced position between the two sources of interest rate risk—cash flow reinvestment and market price volatility. Bonds mature each year and are reinvested at the longer-term end of the ladder, typically at higher rates than short-term securities. Over time, the laddered portfolio likely includes bonds that were purchased at high interest rates as well as low interest rates. Investors familiar with "dollar cost averaging" will see the similarity. In addition, reinvesting funds as bonds mature maintains the duration of the overall portfolio.

Another attractive feature to the laddered portfolio apparent in Exhibit 13 is in convexity. Convexity, technically, is the second-order effect on the value of an asset or liability given a change in the yield to maturity. Importantly, it is affected by the dispersion of cash flows, as indicated in Equation 1, repeated here:

$$\text{Immunized Portfolio Convexity} = \frac{\text{MacDur}^2 + \text{MacDur} + \text{Dispersion}}{(1 + \text{Cash flow yield})^2}$$

If the three portfolios have the same duration (and cash flow yield), then the barbell clearly has the highest convexity and the bullet the lowest. The laddered portfolio will tend to have relatively high convexity because its cash flows by design are spread over the time line. Compared with the barbell, the laddered portfolio has much less cash flow reinvestment risk.

In practice, perhaps the most desirable aspect of the laddered portfolio is in liquidity management. This aspect is particularly relevant if the bonds are not actively traded, as is the case for many corporate securities. As time passes, there is always a bond that is close to redemption. Its duration will be low so that its price is fairly stable even in a time of interest rate volatility. If the client needs immediate cash, the soon-to-mature bond makes for high-quality collateral on a personal loan or, for an institution, a repo contract. As the bonds mature, the final coupon and principal can be deployed for consumption or reinvested in a long-term bond at the back of the ladder.

### 4.2.2 Using ETFs to Build Laddered Portfolios

Another way for a wealth manager to build a laddered portfolio for a client is to use fixed-maturity corporate bond exchange-traded funds (ETFs). These ETFs have a designated year of maturity and credit risk profile—for instance, 2024 investment-grade corporate bonds. The passively managed, low-cost ETF seeks to replicate the performance of an index of, for instance, 50 held-to-maturity investment-grade corporate bonds that mature in 2021. As discussed in previous sections, the ETF manager can use a stratified sampling approach to track the index.

Suppose that in 2021, the wealth manager buys for the client roughly equal positions in the 2022 through 2029 fixed-maturity corporate bond ETFs. These purchases create a laddered portfolio that should provide the same benefits as holding the bonds directly—price stability in the soonest-to-mature ETF and greater convexity than holding more of a bullet portfolio. Moreover, the ETFs should be more liquid than positions in the actual bonds.

But laddered portfolios are not without limitations. For many investors, the decision to build a laddered bond portfolio should be weighed against buying shares in a fixed-income mutual fund, especially if the portfolio consists of a limited number of corporate bonds. Clearly, the mutual fund provides greater diversification of default risk. Moreover, actual bonds can entail a much higher cost of acquisition. If the entire investment needs to be liquidated, the mutual fund shares can be redeemed more quickly than the bonds can be sold, and likely at a better price.

> **EXAMPLE 4**
>
> Mr. Zheng is a Shanghai-based wealth adviser. A major client of his, the Wang family, holds most of its assets in residential property and equity investments and relies on regular cash flows from those holdings. Zheng recommends that the Wang family also have a laddered portfolio of Chinese government bonds. He suggests the following portfolio, priced for settlement on 1 January 2021:
>
> | Coupon Rate | Payment Frequency | Maturity | Flat Price | Yield (s.a.) | Par Value (CNY) | Market Value (CNY) |
> |---|---|---|---|---|---|---|
> | 3.22% | Annual | 26-Mar-22 | 101.7493 | 1.758% | 10 Million | 10,422,826 |
> | 3.14% | Annual | 8-Sept-24 | 102.1336 | 2.508% | 10 Million | 10,312,292 |
> | 3.05% | Annual | 22-Oct-26 | 101.4045 | 2.764% | 10 Million | 10,199,779 |
> | 2.99% | Semi-annual | 15-Oct-29 | 101.4454 | 2.803% | 10 Million | 10,208,611 |
> | | | | | | 40 Million | 41,143,508 |
>
> The yields to maturity on the first three bonds have been converted from a periodicity of one to two in order to report them on a consistent semi-annual bond basis, as indicated by "(s.a.)." The total market value of the portfolio is CNY 41,143,508. The cash flow yield for the portfolio is 2.661%, whereas the market value-weighted average yield is 2.455%.
>
> Most important for his presentation to the senior members of the Wang family is the schedule for the 30 cash flows:
>
> | | | | | | | |
> |---|---|---|---|---|---|---|
> | 1 | 26-Mar-21 | 322,000 | 16 | 8-Sep-24 | 10,314,000 |
> | 2 | 15-Apr-21 | 149,500 | 17 | 15-Oct-24 | 149,500 |
> | 3 | 8-Sep-21 | 314,000 | 18 | 22-Oct-24 | 305,000 |
> | 4 | 15-Oct-21 | 149,500 | 19 | 15-Apr-25 | 149,500 |
> | 5 | 22-Oct-21 | 305,000 | 20 | 15-Oct-25 | 149,500 |
> | 6 | 26-Mar-22 | 10,322,000 | 21 | 22-Oct-25 | 305,000 |
>
> *(continued)*

| | | | | | |
|---|---|---|---|---|---|
| 7 | 15-Apr-22 | 149,500 | 22 | 15-Apr-26 | 149,500 |
| 8 | 8-Sep-22 | 314,000 | 23 | 15-Oct-26 | 149,500 |
| 9 | 15-Oct-22 | 149,500 | 24 | 22-Oct-26 | 10,305,000 |
| 10 | 22-Oct-22 | 305,000 | 25 | 15-Apr-27 | 149,500 |
| 11 | 15-Apr-23 | 149,500 | 26 | 15-Oct-27 | 149,500 |
| 12 | 8-Sep-23 | 314,000 | 27 | 15-Apr-28 | 149,500 |
| 13 | 15-Oct-23 | 149,500 | 28 | 15-Oct-28 | 149,500 |
| 14 | 22-Oct-23 | 305,000 | 29 | 15-Apr-29 | 149,500 |
| 15 | 15-Apr-24 | 149,500 | 30 | 15-Oct-29 | 10,149,500 |

Indicate the main points that Zheng should emphasize in this presentation about the laddered portfolio to senior members of the Wang family.

**Solution:**

Zheng should emphasize three features of the portfolio:

1 **High credit quality.** Given that the family already has substantial holdings in residential property and equity, which are subject to price volatility and risk, investments in government bonds provide the Wang family with holdings in a very low-risk asset class.

2 **Liquidity.** The schedule of payments shows that coupon payments are received each year. These funds can be used for any cash need, including household expenses. The large principal payments can be reinvested in longer-term government bonds at the back of the ladder.

3 **Yield curve diversification.** The bond investments are spread out along four segments of the government bond yield curve. If they were concentrated at a single point, the portfolio would have the risk of higher yields at that point. By spreading out the maturities in the ladder formation, the portfolio has the benefit of diversification.

## 4.3 Duration Matching

e evaluate liability-based strategies under various interest rate scenarios and select a strategy to achieve a portfolio's objectives

Duration matching to immunize multiple liabilities is based on similar principles to those covered earlier in relation to a single liability. A portfolio of fixed-income bonds is structured and managed to track the performance of the zero-coupon bonds that would perfectly lock in the rates of return needed to pay off the corporate debt liabilities identified in Exhibit 5. Recall that in the case of a single liability, the immunization strategy is to match the portfolio Macaulay duration with the investment horizon. Also, the initial investment needs to match (or exceed) the present value of the liability. These two conditions can be combined to prescribe that the money duration of the immunizing portfolio matches the money duration of the debt liabilities. Money duration, or "dollar duration," is the portfolio modified duration multiplied by the market value (recall that modified duration is the portfolio Macaulay duration divided by one plus the cash flow yield per period). With multiple liabilities, matching money durations is useful because the market values and cash flow yields of the assets and liabilities are not necessarily equal.

The money duration for the debt liabilities is EUR 1,178,237,935:

$$\left[\frac{\text{Portfolio MacDur}}{\left(1 + \frac{\text{Annualized CF Yield}}{2}\right)}\right] \times \text{PV of Debt liabilities}$$

$$= \left[\frac{6.0004}{\left(1 + \frac{0.037608}{2}\right)}\right] \times 200{,}052{,}250 = 1{,}178{,}237{,}935.$$

The term in brackets is the annualized modified duration for the bond portfolio. To keep the numbers manageable, we use the basis point value (BPV) measure for money duration. This measure is the money duration multiplied by 1 bp. The BPV is EUR 117,824 (= EUR 1,178,237,935 × 0.0001). For each 1 bp change in the cash flow yield, the market value changes by approximately EUR 117,824. It is an approximation because convexity is not included. A closely related risk measure is the present value of a basis point (PVBP), also called the PV01 (present value of an "01," meaning 1 bp) and, in North America, the DV01 (dollar value of an "01").

Exhibit 14 shows the three bonds purchased by the asset manager on 15 February 2021. The total cash outlay on that date is EUR 202,224,094 (= EUR 41,772,719 + EUR 99,750,000 + EUR 60,701,375 = the market values of the three bonds). Exhibit 15 presents the table used to calculate the cash flow yield and the risk statistics. The annualized cash flow yield is 3.5822%. It is the internal rate of return on the cash flows in the second column of Exhibit 15, multiplied by two. The annualized Macaulay duration for the portfolio is 5.9308 (= 11.8615/2), and the modified duration is 5.8264 (= 5.9308/[1 + 0.035822/2]). The annualized dispersion and convexity statistics are 12.3048 (= 49.2194/4) and 48.6846 (= {201.7767/[1 + 0.035822/2]$^2$}/4), respectively. Notice that the first few cash flows for the assets in Exhibit 15 are less than the liability payments in Exhibit 5. That disparity indicates that some of the bonds held in the asset portfolio will need to be sold to meet the obligations.

**Exhibit 14   The Bond Portfolio to Immunize the Multiple Liabilities**

|  | 1.5-Year Bond | 6-Year Bond | 11.5-Year Bond |
|---|---|---|---|
| Coupon rate | 1.00% | 2.875% | 4.50% |
| Maturity date | 15 August 2022 | 15 February 2027 | 15 August 2032 |
| Price | 99.875 | 99.75 | 100.25 |
| Yield to maturity | 1.0842% | 2.9207% | 4.4720% |
| Par value | 41,825,000 | 100,000,000 | 60,550,000 |
| Market value | 41,772,719 | 99,750,000 | 60,701,375 |
| Macaulay duration | 1.493 | 5.553 | 9.105 |
| Convexity | 2.950 | 34.149 | 96.056 |
| Allocation | 20.657% | 49.326% | 30.017% |

### Exhibit 15  Portfolio Statistics

| Time | Date | Cash Flow | PV of Cash Flow | Weight | Time × Weight | Dispersion | Convexity |
|---|---|---|---|---|---|---|---|
| 0 | 15-Feb-21 | −202,224,094 | | | | | |
| 1 | 15-Aug-21 | 3,009,000 | 2,956,054 | 0.0146 | 0.0146 | 1.7245 | 0.0292 |
| 2 | 15-Feb-22 | 3,009,000 | 2,904,040 | 0.0144 | 0.0287 | 1.3966 | 0.0862 |
| 3 | 15-Aug-22 | 44,834,000 | 42,508,728 | 0.2102 | 0.6306 | 16.5068 | 2.5225 |
| 4 | 15-Feb-23 | 2,799,875 | 2,607,951 | 0.0129 | 0.0516 | 0.7970 | 0.2579 |
| 5 | 15-Aug-23 | 2,799,875 | 2,562,062 | 0.0127 | 0.0633 | 0.5965 | 0.3801 |
| 6 | 15-Feb-24 | 2,799,875 | 2,516,981 | 0.0124 | 0.0747 | 0.4276 | 0.5228 |
| 7 | 15-Aug-24 | 2,799,875 | 2,472,692 | 0.0122 | 0.0856 | 0.2890 | 0.6847 |
| 8 | 15-Feb-25 | 2,799,875 | 2,429,183 | 0.0120 | 0.0961 | 0.1791 | 0.8649 |
| 9 | 15-Aug-25 | 2,799,875 | 2,386,440 | 0.0118 | 0.1062 | 0.0966 | 1.0621 |
| 10 | 15-Feb-26 | 2,799,875 | 2,344,449 | 0.0116 | 0.1159 | 0.0402 | 1.2753 |
| 11 | 15-Aug-26 | 2,799,875 | 2,303,196 | 0.0114 | 0.1253 | 0.0085 | 1.5034 |
| 12 | 15-Feb-27 | 102,799,875 | 83,075,901 | 0.4108 | 4.9297 | 0.0079 | 64.0865 |
| 13 | 15-Aug-27 | 1,362,375 | 1,081,607 | 0.0053 | 0.0695 | 0.0069 | 0.9734 |
| 14 | 15-Feb-28 | 1,362,375 | 1,062,575 | 0.0053 | 0.0736 | 0.0240 | 1.1034 |
| 15 | 15-Aug-28 | 1,362,375 | 1,043,878 | 0.0052 | 0.0774 | 0.0508 | 1.2389 |
| 16 | 15-Feb-29 | 1,362,375 | 1,025,510 | 0.0051 | 0.0811 | 0.0869 | 1.3794 |
| 17 | 15-Aug29 | 1,362,375 | 1,007,465 | 0.0050 | 0.0847 | 0.1315 | 1.5245 |
| 18 | 15-Feb-30 | 1,362,375 | 989,738 | 0.0049 | 0.0881 | 0.1844 | 1.6738 |
| 19 | 15-Aug-30 | 1,362,375 | 972,323 | 0.0048 | 0.0914 | 0.2450 | 1.8271 |
| 20 | 15-Feb-31 | 1,362,375 | 955,214 | 0.0047 | 0.0945 | 0.3129 | 1.9839 |
| 21 | 15-Aug-31 | 1,362,375 | 938,406 | 0.0046 | 0.0974 | 0.3875 | 2.1439 |
| 22 | 15-Feb-32 | 1,362,375 | 921,894 | 0.0046 | 0.1003 | 0.4686 | 2.3067 |
| 23 | 15-Aug-32 | 61,912,375 | 41,157,805 | 0.2035 | 4.6811 | 25.2505 | 112.3462 |
| | | | 202,224,094 | 1.0000 | 11.8615 | 49.2194 | 201.7767 |

The market value of the immunizing fixed-income bonds is EUR 202,224,094. That amount is higher than the value of the liabilities, which is EUR 200,052,250. The reason for the difference in market values as of 15 February 2021 is the difference in the cash flow yields. The high-quality assets needed to immunize the corporate liabilities have a cash flow yield of 3.5822%, which is lower than the cash flow yield of 3.7608% on the debt obligations. The assets grow at a lower rate and, therefore, need to start at a higher level. If we discount the debt liabilities scheduled in the third column of Exhibit 5 at 3.5822%, the present value is EUR 202,170,671, indicating that initially, the immunizing portfolio is slightly overfunded. Importantly, the asset portfolio BPV is EUR 117,824 (= 202,224,094 × 5.8264 × 0.0001), matching the BPV for the debt liabilities.

There is another meaningful difference in the structure of the asset and liability portfolios. Although the money durations are the same, the dispersion and convexity statistics for the assets are greater than for the liabilities—12.30 compared with 8.26 for dispersion, and 48.68 compared with 45.54 for convexity. This difference is required to achieve immunization for multiple liabilities. (Mathematically, in the optimization problem, to minimize the difference in the change in the values of assets and liabilities, the first derivative leads to matching money duration [or BPV] and the second derivative to having higher dispersion.) Intuitively, this condition follows from the general result that, for equal durations, a more convex portfolio generally outperforms a less convex portfolio (higher gains if yields fall, lower losses if yields rise). But, as in the case of immunizing a single liability, the dispersion of the assets should be as low as possible subject to being greater than or equal to the dispersion of the liabilities to mitigate the effect of non-parallel shifts in the yield curve. Note that from Equation 1, higher dispersion implies higher convexity when the Macaulay durations and cash flow yields are equal.

### 4.3.1 Duration Matching—Parallel Shift Example

Some numerical examples are useful to illustrate that immunization of multiple liabilities is essentially an interest rate risk hedging strategy. The idea is that changes in the market value of the asset portfolio closely match changes in the debt liabilities whether interest rates rise or fall. Exhibits 16 through 19 demonstrate this dynamic.

First, we allow the yield curve to shift upward in a parallel manner. The yields on the bonds in Exhibit 14 go up instantaneously by 25 bps on 15 February 2021, immediately after the asset portfolio is purchased. That increase results in a drop in market value of EUR 2,842,408. The yields on the debt liabilities in Exhibit 5 also go up by 25 bps, dropping the market value by EUR 2,858,681. The difference is EUR 16,273, a small amount given that the size of portfolios exceeds EUR 200 million. This scenario implicitly assumes no change in the corporate entity's credit risk.

**Exhibit 16   Immunizing Multiple Liabilities: Upward Parallel Shift**

|  | Immunizing Assets | Debt Liabilities | Difference |
|---|---|---|---|
| ΔMarket value | −2,842,408 | −2,858,681 | 16,273 |
| ΔCash flow yield | 0.2437% | 0.2449% | −0.0012% |
| ΔPortfolio BPV | −2,370 | −2,207 | −163 |

Next, we shift the yield curve downward by 25 bps. Both the asset and liability portfolios gain market value by almost the same amount. The difference is only EUR 12,504.

**Exhibit 17   Immunizing Multiple Liabilities: Downward Parallel Shift**

| Downward Parallel Shift | Immunizing Assets | Debt Liabilities | Difference |
|---|---|---|---|
| ΔMarket value | 2,900,910 | 2,913,414 | −12,504 |
| ΔCash flow yield | −0.2437% | −0.2449% | 0.0012% |
| ΔPortfolio BPV | 2,429 | 2,256 | 173 |

The driving factor behind the success of the strategy given these upward and downward shifts is that the portfolio durations are matched and changes in the cash flow yields are very close: 24.37 bps for the assets and 24.49 bps for the liabilities. In Exhibit 17, the asset portfolio rises slightly less than the liabilities when the yield curve shifts down in a parallel manner by 25 bps. Hence, the loss is EUR 12,504 despite the greater convexity of the assets. That disparity is explained by the slightly higher decrease in the cash flow yield on the liabilities. As explained in the previous section, a parallel shift is a sufficient but not necessary condition for immunization. Although not shown in the exhibits, an upward non-parallel shift of 15.9 bps in the 1.5-year bond, 23.6 bps in the 6-year bond, and 27.5 bps in the 11.5-year bond leads to virtually the same change in market value (EUR 2,842,308) as the 25 bp parallel shift. Those particular changes are chosen because they result in the same change in the cash flow yield of 24.37 bps.

#### 4.3.2 Duration Matching—Yield Curve Twist Scenario

The structural risk to the immunization strategy is apparent in Exhibit 18. This scenario is the steepening twist in which short-term yields on high-quality bonds go down while long-term yields go up. The 1.5-year yield is assumed to drop by 25 bps. The 6-year yield remains the same, and the 11.5-year yield goes up by 25 bps. These changes lead to a loss of EUR 1,178,071 in the asset portfolio as the cash flow yield increases by 10.04 bps. The maturities of the debt liabilities differ from those of the assets. For simplicity, we assume that those yields change in proportion to the differences in maturity around the six-year pivot point for the twist. The 2.5-year yield drops by 19.44 bps (= 25 bps × 3.5/4.5), the 7-year yield goes up by 4.55 bps (= 25 bps × 1/5.5), and the 10-year goes up by 18.18 bps (= 25 bps × 4/5.5). The market value of the liabilities drops by only EUR 835,156 because the cash flow yield increases by only 7.11 bps. The value of the assets goes down by more than the liabilities—the difference is EUR 342,915. The steepening twist to the shape of the yield curve is the source of the loss.

**Exhibit 18    Immunizing Multiple Liabilities: Steepening Twist**

|  | Immunizing Assets | Debt Liabilities | Difference |
|---|---|---|---|
| ΔMarket value | −1,178,071 | −835,156 | −342,915 |
| ΔCash flow yield | 0.1004% | 0.0711% | 0.0293% |
| ΔPortfolio BPV | −984 | −645 | −339 |

The results of the fourth scenario show that a flattening twist can lead to a comparable gain if long-term high-quality yields fall while short-term yields rise (Exhibit 19). We make the same assumptions about proportionate changes in the yields. In this case, the cash flow yield of the assets goes down more and the market value rises higher than the debt liabilities. Clearly, an entity that pursues immunization of multiple liabilities hopes that steepening twists are balanced out by flattening twists and that most yield curve shifts are more or less parallel.

**Exhibit 19    Immunizing Multiple Liabilities: Flattening Twist**

|  | Immunizing Assets | Debt Liabilities | Difference |
|---|---|---|---|
| ΔMarket value | 1,215,285 | 850,957 | 364,328 |
| ΔCash flow yield | −0.1027% | −0.0720% | −0.0307% |
| ΔPortfolio BPV | 1,016 | 658 | 358 |

The above illustrations (in Exhibits 16-19) also report the changes in the portfolio BPVs for the assets and liabilities. Before the yield curve shifts and twists, the BPVs are matched at EUR 117,824. Afterward, there is a small money duration mismatch. In theory, the asset manager needs to rebalance the portfolio immediately. In practice, the manager likely waits until the mismatch is large enough to justify the transaction costs in selling some bonds and buying others. Another method to rebalance the portfolio is to use interest rate derivatives.

### EXAMPLE 5

A Japanese corporation recently sold one of its lines of business and would like to use the cash to retire the debt liabilities that financed those assets. Summary statistics for the multiple debt liabilities, which range in maturity from three to seven years, are market value, JPY 110.4 billion; portfolio modified duration, 5.84; portfolio convexity, 46.08; and BPV, JPY 64.47 million.

An investment bank working with the corporation offers three alternatives to accomplish the objective:

1 **Bond tender offer.** The corporation would buy back the debt liabilities on the open market, paying a premium above the market price. The corporation currently has a single-A rating and hopes for an upgrade once its balance sheet is improved by retiring the debt. The investment bank anticipates that the tender offer would have to be at a price commensurate with a triple-A rating to entice the bondholders to sell. The bonds are widely held by domestic and international institutional investors.

2 **Cash flow matching.** The corporation buys a portfolio of government bonds that matches, as closely as possible, the coupon interest and principal redemptions on the debt liabilities. The investment bank is highly confident that the corporation's external auditors will agree to accounting defeasement because the purchased bonds are government securities. That agreement will allow the corporation to remove both the defeasing asset portfolio and the liabilities from the balance sheet.

3 **Duration matching.** The corporation buys a portfolio of high-quality corporate bonds that matches the duration of the debt liabilities. Interest rate derivatives contracts will be used to keep the duration on its target as time passes and yields change. The investment bank thinks it is very unlikely that the external auditors will allow this strategy to qualify for accounting defeasement. The corporation can explain to investors and the rating agencies in the management section of its annual report, however, that it is aiming to "effectively defease" the debt. To carry out this strategy, the investment bank suggests three different portfolios of investment-grade corporate bonds that range in maturity from 2 years to 10 years. Each portfolio has a market value of about JPY 115 billion, which is considered sufficient to pay off the liabilities.

|  | Portfolio A | Portfolio B | Portfolio C |
| --- | --- | --- | --- |
| Modified duration | 5.60 | 5.61 | 5.85 |
| Convexity | 42.89 | 50.11 | 46.09 |
| BPV (in millions) | JPY 64.50 | JPY 64.51 | JPY 67.28 |

> After some deliberation and discussion with the investment bankers and external auditors, the corporation's CFO chooses Strategy 3, duration matching.
>
> 1 Indicate the likely trade-offs that led the corporate CFO to choose the duration-matching strategy over the tender offer and cash flow matching.
> 2 Indicate the portfolio that the corporation should choose to carry out the duration-matching strategy.
>
> **Solution to 1:**
>
> The likely trade-offs are between removing the debt liabilities from the balance sheet, either by directly buying the bonds from investors or by accounting defeasance via cash flow matching, and the cost of the strategy. The tender offer entails buying the bonds at a triple-A price, which would likely be considerably higher than at a single-A price. Cash flow matching entails buying even more expensive government bonds. The duration-matching strategy can be implemented at a lower cost because the asset portfolio consists of less expensive investment-grade bonds. The CFO has chosen the lowest-cost strategy, even though the debt liabilities will remain on the balance sheet.
>
> **Solution to 2:**
>
> The corporation should recommend Portfolio B. Portfolio C closely matches the modified duration (as well as the convexity) of the liabilities. Duration matching when the market values of the assets and liabilities differ, however, entails matching the money durations, in particular the BPVs. The choice then comes down to Portfolios A and B. Although both have BPVs close to the liabilities, it is incorrect to choose A based on its BPV being "closer."
>
> The important difference between Portfolios A and B lies in the convexities. To immunize multiple liabilities, the convexity (and dispersion of cash flows) of the assets needs to be greater than the liabilities. Therefore, Portfolio A does not meet that condition.
>
> Recall that in Example 2, the correct immunizing portfolio is the one with the lower convexity, which minimizes the structural risk to the strategy. But, that bond portfolio still has a convexity greater than the zero-coupon bond that would provide perfect immunization. This greater convexity of the immunizing portfolio is because the dispersion of the zero-coupon bond is zero and the durations are the same. As seen in Equation 1, that dispersion implies a lower convexity statistic.

## 4.4 Derivatives Overlay

Interest rate derivatives can be a cost-effective method to rebalance the immunizing portfolio to keep it on its target duration as the yield curve shifts and twists and as time passes. Suppose that in the duration-matching example shown earlier, there is a much larger instantaneous upward shift in the yield curve on 15 February 2021. In particular, all yields shift up by 100 bps. Because yields and duration are inversely related, the portfolio duration statistics go down, as does the market value. The BPV of the immunizing asset portfolio decreases from EUR 117,824 to EUR 108,679, a drop of EUR 9,145. The BPV for the debt liabilities goes down to EUR 109,278, a drop of EUR 8,546. There is now a money duration gap of −EUR 599 (= EUR 108,679 − EUR 109,278). The asset manager could sell some of the 1%, 1.5-year bonds and buy some more of the 4.50%, 11-year bonds to close the money duration gap. A more efficient and lower-cost rebalancing strategy, however, is likely to buy, or go long, a few interest rate futures contracts to rebalance the portfolio.

To address the question of the required number of contracts to close, or reduce, a duration gap, we change the example from euros to US dollars. Doing so allows us to illustrate the calculations for the required number of futures contracts using the actively traded 10-year US Treasury note futures contract offered at the CME Group. The present value of corporate debt liabilities shown in Exhibits 4 and 5 now is assumed to be USD 200,052,250. Risk and return statistics are invariant to currency denomination, so the portfolio Macaulay duration is still 6.0004 and the BPV is USD 117,824.

In the previous example for duration matching of multiple liabilities, the asset manager purchased three bonds with maturities of 1, 6, and 11 years. In this next scenario, we assume that the asset manager buys a portfolio of high-quality, short-term bonds. This portfolio has a market value of USD 222,750,000, Macaulay duration of 0.8532, and cash flow yield of 1.9804%. Discounting the debt liabilities in the third column of Exhibit 5 at 1.9804% gives a present value of USD 222,552,788. This value indicates that the immunizing portfolio is overfunded on 15 February 2021. The BPV for the asset portfolio is USD 18,819:

$$\left[\frac{0.8532}{\left(1+\frac{0.019804}{2}\right)}\right] \times 222{,}750{,}000 \times 0.0001 = 18{,}819$$

The asset manager might elect to hold a portfolio of short-term bonds rather than intermediate-term and long-term securities for a number of reasons, including greater liquidity, perception of finer pricing in the short-term market, or that the entity faces liquidity constraints and needs to hold these short-term bonds to meet regulatory requirements. A derivatives overlay strategy is then used to close the duration gap while keeping the underlying portfolio unchanged. In general, a derivatives overlay transforms some aspect of the underlying portfolio—the currency could be changed with foreign exchange derivatives or the credit risk profile with credit default swap contracts. Here, interest rate derivatives are used to change the interest rate risk profile, increasing the portfolio BPV from USD 18,819 to USD 117,824.

Details of interest rate futures contracts are covered elsewhere. Here we note some specific features of the 10-year US Treasury note contract traded at the CME Group relevant for this example. Each contract is for USD 100,000 in par value and has delivery dates in March, June, September, and December.

Conversion factors that are used to make the qualifying T-notes roughly equivalent for delivery by the contract seller, or short position, are based on an arbitrary yield to maturity of 6.00%. If the eligible T-note has a coupon rate below (above) 6.00%, the conversion factor is less (more) than 1.0000. The invoice price paid by the buyer of the contract, the long position, at the expiration of the contract is the futures price multiplied by the conversion factor, plus accrued interest. The logic of this design is that if the contract seller chooses to deliver a qualifying T-note having a lower (higher) coupon rate than 6.00%, the buyer pays a lower (higher) price.

The key point is that, although the eligible T-notes are roughly equivalent, one will be identified as the cheapest-to-deliver (CTD) security. Importantly, the duration of the 10-year T-note futures contract is assumed to be the duration of the CTD T-note. A factor in determining the CTD T-note is that the conversion factors for each qualifying security are based on the arbitrary assumption of a 6.00% yield to maturity. In practice, when yields are below 6.00% the CTD security typically is the qualifying T-note having the lowest duration. Therefore, the 10-year T-note futures contract essentially has been acting as a 6.5-year contract. (That explains the motivation for introducing the Ultra 10-year contract—to provide a hedging instrument more closely tied to the 10-year T-note traded in the cash market.)

To illustrate the importance of using the risk statistics for the CTD T-note, Exhibit 20 reports two hypothetical qualifying securities for the March 2021 10-year futures contract. One is designated the 6.5-year T-note. It has a coupon rate of 2.75% and matures on 15 November 2027. As of 15 February 2021, it is assumed to be priced to yield 3.8088%. Its BPV per USD 100,000 in par value is USD 56.8727, and its conversion factor is 0.8226. The other is the on-the-run 10-year T-note. Its coupon rate is 4.00%, and it matures on 15 February 2031. Its BPV is USD 81.6607, and its conversion factor is 0.8516.

**Exhibit 20  Two Qualifying T-Notes for the March 2021 10-Year T-Note Futures Contract as of 15 February 2021 (hypothetical example)**

|  | 6.5-Year T-Note | 10-Year T-Note |
|---|---|---|
| Coupon rate | 2.75% | 4.00% |
| Maturity date | 15 November 2027 | 15 February 2031 |
| Full price per 100,000 in par value | USD 94,449 | USD 99,900 |
| Yield to maturity | 3.8088% | 4.0122% |
| Modified duration | 6.0215 | 8.1742 |
| BPV per 100,000 in par value | 56.8727 | 81.6607 |
| Conversion factor | 0.8226 | 0.8516 |

The calculation of the required number of futures contract, denoted $N_f$, comes from this relationship:

$$\text{Asset portfolio BPV} + (N_f \times \text{Futures BPV}) = \text{Liability portfolio BPV}. \quad (2)$$

Inherent in this expression is the important idea that although futures contracts have a market value of zero as a result of daily mark-to-market valuation and settlement, they can add to or subtract from the asset portfolio BPV. This equation can be rearranged to isolate $N_f$:

$$N_f = \frac{\text{Liability portfolio BPV} - \text{Asset portfolio BPV}}{\text{Futures BPV}}. \quad (3)$$

If $N_f$ is a positive number, the asset manager buys, or goes long, the required number of futures contracts. Doing so raises the money duration of the assets to match that of the liabilities. If $N_f$ is a negative number, the asset manager sells, or goes short, futures contracts to reduce the money duration. In our problem, the asset portfolio BPV is USD 18,819 and the liability portfolio BPV is USD 117,824. Therefore, $N_f$ is a large positive number and depends on the BPV for the futures contract. The exact formulation for the Futures BPV is complicated, however, and goes beyond the scope of our coverage. It involves such details as the number of days until the expiration of the contract, the interest rate for that period, and the accrued interest on the deliverable bond. To simplify, we use an approximation formula that is common in practice:

$$\text{Futures BPV} \approx \frac{\text{BPV}_{CTD}}{\text{CF}_{CTD}}, \quad (4)$$

where $\text{CF}_{CTD}$ is the conversion factor for the CTD security.

# Interest Rate Immunization: Managing the Interest Rate Risk of Multiple Liabilities

If the CTD security is the 6.5-year T-note shown in Exhibit 20, the Futures BPV is estimated to be USD 69.1377 (= 56.8727/0.8226). Then, the required number of contracts is approximately 1,432:

$$\frac{117{,}824 - 18{,}819}{69.1377} = 1{,}432$$

But, if the CTD security is the 10-year T-note, the Futures BPV is USD 95.8909 (= 81.6607/0.8516). To close the money duration gap, the required number of contracts is only 1,032:

$$\frac{117{,}824 - 18{,}819}{95.8909} = 1{,}032$$

Clearly, the asset manager must know the CTD T-note to use in the derivatives overlay strategy. The difference of 400 futures contracts is significant.

The asset manager has established a synthetic "barbell" strategy: having positions in the short-term and longer-term segments of the yield curve. The term "synthetic" means "created with derivatives." The underlying asset portfolio is concentrated in the short-term market. The derivatives portfolio is either at the 6.5-year or 10-year segment of the yield curve. CME Group also has actively traded two-year and five-year Treasury futures contracts. Therefore, the asset manager could choose to spread out the futures contracts across other segments of the yield curve. That diversification reduces the structural risk to the immunization strategy arising from non-parallel shifts and twists to the curve.

### EXAMPLE 6

A Frankfurt-based asset manager uses the Long Bund contract traded at the Intercontinental Exchange (ICE) futures exchange to manage the gaps that arise from "duration drift" in a portfolio of German government bonds that are used to immunize a portfolio of corporate debt liabilities. This futures contract has a notional principal of EUR 100,000 and is based on a 6% coupon rate. The German government bonds that are eligible for delivery have maturities between 8.5 years and 10.5 years.

Currently, the corporate debt liabilities have a market value of EUR 330,224,185, a modified duration of 7.23, and a BPV of EUR 238,752. The asset portfolio has a market value of EUR 332,216,004, a modified duration of 7.42, and a BPV of EUR 246,504. The duration drift has arisen because of a widening spread between corporate and government bond yields as interest rates in general have come down. The lower yields on government bonds have increased the modified durations relative to corporates.

Based on the deliverable bond, the asset manager estimates that the BPV for each futures contract is EUR 65.11.

1. Does the asset manager go long (buy) or go short (sell) the futures contract?
2. How many contracts does the manager buy or sell to close the duration gap?

### Solution to 1:

The asset manager needs to go short (or sell) Long Bund futures contracts. The money duration of the assets, as measured by the BPV, is greater than the money duration of debt liabilities. This relationship is true of the modified duration statistics as well, but the money duration is a better measure of the gap because the market values differ.

> **Solution to 2:**
>
> Use Equation 3 to get the requisite number of futures contracts to sell.
>
> $$N_f = \frac{\text{Liability portfolio BPV} - \text{Asset portfolio BPV}}{\text{Futures BPV}}$$
>
> where Liability portfolio BPV = 238,752, Asset portfolio BPV = 246,504, and Futures BPV = 65.11.
>
> $$N_f = \frac{238,752 - 246,504}{65.11} = -119.06$$
>
> The minus sign indicates the need to go short (or sell) 119 contracts to close the duration gap.

### 4.5 Contingent Immunization

We have seen that the initial market value for the immunizing asset portfolio can vary according to the strategy chosen by the asset manager. Earlier, in the duration-matching example, the initial market value of the asset portfolio was EUR 202,224,094, while the liabilities were EUR 200,052,250. The derivatives overlay example is to hold a portfolio of short-term bonds having a market value of USD 222,750,000 and 1,432 10-year futures contracts (assuming that the CTD eligible security is the 6.5-year T-note) to immunize the liability of USD 200,052,250.

The difference between the market values of the assets and liabilities is the **surplus**. The initial surplus in the duration-matching example is EUR 2,171,844 (= EUR 202,224,094 − EUR 200,052,250); the surplus in the derivatives overlay example is USD 22,697,750 (= EUR 222,750,000 −EUR 200,052,250). The presence of a significant surplus allows the asset manager to consider a hybrid passive–active strategy known as **contingent immunization**. The idea behind contingent immunization is that the asset manager can pursue active investment strategies, as if operating under a total return mandate, as long as the surplus is above a designated threshold. If the actively managed assets perform poorly, however, and the surplus evaporates, the mandate reverts to the purely passive strategy of building a duration-matching portfolio and then managing it to remain on duration target.

In principle, when the surplus is above a sufficient threshold, the manager may increase portfolio risk in any asset category, including equity, fixed income, and alternative investments. The manager could also buy out-of-the-money commodity options contracts or credit default swaps. The objective is to attain portfolio gains in order to reduce the cost of retiring the debt obligations without falling below the minimum funding threshold. Obviously, liquidity is an important criterion in selecting the investments because the positions would need to be unwound if losses cause the surplus to near the threshold.

A natural setting for contingent immunization is in the fixed-income derivatives overlay strategy. Instead of buying, or going long, 1,432 10-year T-note futures contracts, the asset manager could intentionally over-hedge or under-hedge, depending on the held view on rate volatility at the 6.5-year segment of the Treasury yield curve. That segment matters because the 10-year T-note futures contract price responds to changes in the yield of the CTD security. The asset manager could buy more (less) than 1,432 contracts if she expects the 6.5-year Treasury yield to go down (up) and the futures price to go up (down).

Suppose that on 15 February 2021, the price of the March 10-year T-note futures contract is quoted to be 121-03. The price is 121 and 3/32 percent of USD 100,000, which is the contract size. Therefore, the delivery price in March would be USD 121,093.75 multiplied by the conversion factor, plus the accrued interest. What matters

# Interest Rate Immunization: Managing the Interest Rate Risk of Multiple Liabilities

to the asset manager is the change in the settlement futures price from day to day. For each futures contract, the gain or loss is USD 31.25 for each 1/32nd change in the futures price, calculated as 1/32 percent of USD 100,000.

Now suppose that the asset manager anticipates an upward shift in the yield curve. Such a shift would cause bond prices to drop in both the Treasury cash and futures markets. Suppose that the quoted March futures price drops from 121-03 to 119-22. That is a 45/32nd change in the price and causes a loss of USD 1,406.25 (= 45 × USD 31.25) per contract. If the asset manager holds 1,432 long contracts, the loss that day is USD 2,013,750 (= USD 1,406.25 × 1,432). But if the asset manager is allowed to under-hedge, he could have dramatically reduced the number of long futures contracts and maybe even gone short in anticipation of the upward shift. The presence of the surplus allows the manager the opportunity to take a view on interest rates and save some of the cost of the strategy to retire the debt liabilities. The objective is to be over-hedged when yields are expected to fall and under-hedged when they are expected to rise.

### EXAMPLE 7

An asset manager is asked to build and manage a portfolio of fixed-income bonds to retire multiple corporate debt liabilities. The debt liabilities have a market value of GBP 50,652,108, a modified duration of 7.15, and a BPV of GBP 36,216.

The asset manager buys a portfolio of British government bonds having a market value of GBP 64,271,055, a modified duration of 3.75, and a BPV of GBP 24,102. The initial surplus of GBP 13,618,947 and the negative duration gap of GBP 12,114 are intentional. The surplus allows the manager to pursue a contingent immunization strategy to retire the debt at, hopefully, a lower cost than a more conservative duration-matching approach. The duration gap requires the manager to buy, or go long, interest rate futures contracts to close the gap. The manager can choose to over-hedge or under-hedge, however, depending on market circumstances.

The futures contract that the manager buys is based on 10-year gilts having a par value of GBP 100,000. It is estimated to have a BPV of GBP 98.2533 per contract. Currently, the asset manager has purchased, or gone long, 160 contracts.

Which statement *best* describes the asset manager's hedging strategy and the held view on future 10-year gilt interest rates? The asset manager is:

A  over-hedging because the rate view is that 10-year yields will be rising.

B  over-hedging because the rate view is that 10-year yields will be falling.

C  under-hedging because the rate view is that 10-year yields will be rising.

D  under-hedging because the rate view is that 10-year yields will be falling.

### Solution:

B is correct. The asset manager is over-hedging because the rate view is that 10-year yields will be falling. First calculate the number of contracts ($N_f$) needed to fully hedge (or immunize) the debt liabilities. The general relationship is Equation 2: Asset portfolio BPV + ($N_f$ × Futures BPV) = Liability portfolio BPV.

Asset portfolio BPV is GBP 24,102; Futures BPV is 98.2533; and Liability portfolio BPV is 36,216.

$$24{,}102 + (N_f \times 98.2533) = 36{,}216$$
$$N_f = 123.3.$$

> The asset manager is over-hedging because a position in 160 long futures contracts is more than what is needed to close the duration gap. Long, or purchased, positions in interest rate futures contracts gain when futures prices rise and rates go down. The anticipated gains from the strategic decision to over-hedge in this case further increase the surplus and reduce the cost of retiring the debt liabilities.

## 5. LIABILITY-DRIVEN INVESTING: AN EXAMPLE OF A DEFINED BENEFIT PENSION PLAN

Earlier we introduced four types of liabilities: Types I, II, III, and IV. Defined benefit (DB) pension plan obligations are a good example of Type IV liabilities for which both the aggregate amounts and dates are uncertain. An LDI strategy for this entity starts with a model for these liabilities. We first explain the model assumptions and then calculate future liabilities.

### 5.1 Model Assumptions

We reveal some of the assumptions that go into this complex financial modeling problem by assuming the work history and retirement profile for a representative employee covered by the pension plan. We assume that this employee has worked for $G$ years, a sufficient length of time to ensure that the retirement benefits are vested. The employee is expected to work for another $T$ years and then to retire and live for $Z$ years. Exhibit 21 illustrates this time line.

**Exhibit 21  Timeline Assumptions for the Representative Employee**

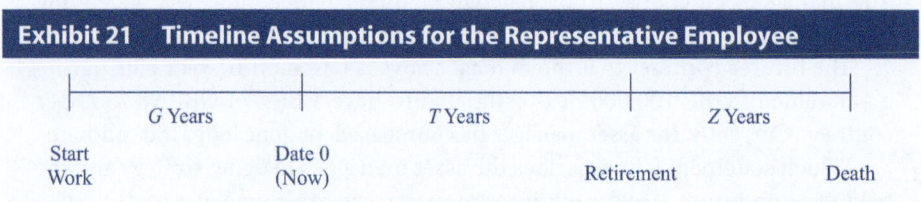

In this final pay DB example, the retired employee receives a fixed lifetime annuity based on her wage at the time of retirement, denoted $W_T$. Some pension plans index the annual retirement benefit to inflation. Our example assumes an annuity fixed in nominal terms, calculated as the final wage, $W_T$, multiplied by a multiplier, $m$, multiplied by the total number of years worked, $G + T$.

There are two general measures of the retirement obligations as of Time 0—the accumulated benefit obligation (ABO) and the projected benefit obligation (PBO). The ABO calculates the liability based on the $G$ years worked and the current annual wage, denoted $W_0$, even though the annuity paid in retirement is based on $W_T$ (final wage) and $G + T$ years. The use of the current annual wage and the number of years worked is because the ABO represents the *legal liability* today of the plan sponsor if the plan were to be closed or converted to another type of plan, such as a defined contribution (DC) plan. The ABO is the present value of the projected annuity, discounted at an annual rate $r$ on high-quality corporate bonds (government regulators and the accounting authorities allow high-quality corporate bonds to be used to discount the future liabilities), which for simplicity we assume applies for all periods (a flat yield curve).

$$\text{ABO} = \frac{1}{(1+r)^T} \times \left[ \frac{m \times G \times W_0}{1+r} + \frac{m \times G \times W_0}{(1+r)^2} + \cdots + \frac{m \times G \times W_0}{(1+r)^Z} \right]$$

The term in brackets is the value of the $Z$-year annuity as of year $T$, and that sum is discounted back over $T$ years to Time 0.

The PBO liability measure uses the projected wage for year $T$ instead of the current wage in the $Z$-year annuity.

$$\text{PBO} = \frac{1}{(1+r)^T} \times \left[ \frac{m \times G \times W_T}{1+r} + \frac{m \times G \times W_T}{(1+r)^2} + \cdots + \frac{m \times G \times W_T}{(1+r)^Z} \right]$$

Although the ABO is the legal obligation to the plan sponsor, the PBO is the liability reported in financial statements and used to assess the plan's funding status. The plan is over-funded (under-funded) if the current fair value of assets is more (less) than the present value of the promised retirement benefits.

The next step is to consider how wages evolve between dates 0 and $T$. We denote $w$ to be the average annual wage growth rate for the employee's remaining work life of $T$ years. Therefore, the relationship between $W_0$ and $W_T$ is $W_T = W_0 \times (1 + w)^T$.

After some algebraic manipulation and substitution, the two liability measures can be written more compactly as follows:

$$\text{ABO} = \frac{m \times G \times W_0}{(1+r)^T} \times \left[ \frac{1}{r} - \frac{1}{r \times (1+r)^Z} \right] \text{ and}$$

$$\text{PBO} = \frac{m \times G \times W_0 \times (1+w)^T}{(1+r)^T} \times \left[ \frac{1}{r} - \frac{1}{r \times (1+r)^Z} \right].$$

Note that the PBO always will be larger than the ABO by the factor of $(1 + w)^T$, assuming positive wage growth in nominal terms.

We see in this simple model several of the important assumptions that go into using an LDI strategy to manage these Type IV liabilities. The assumed post-retirement lifetime ($Z$ years) is critical. A higher value for $Z$ increases both the ABO and PBO measures of liability. The pension plan faces *longevity risk*, which is the risk that employees live longer in their retirement years than assumed in the models. Some plans have become under-funded and have had to increase assets because regulators required that they recognize longer life expectancies. Another important assumption is the time until retirement ($T$ years). In the ABO measure, increases in $T$ reduce the liability. That result also holds for the PBO as long as wage growth ($w$) is lower than the discount rate ($r$). Assuming $w$ is less than $r$ is reasonable if it can be assumed that employees over time generally are compensated for price inflation and some part of real economic growth, as well as for seniority and productivity improvements, but overall the labor income growth rate does not quite keep pace with the nominal return on high-quality financial assets.

## 5.2 Model Inputs

We now use a numerical example to show how the effective durations of ABO and PBO liability measures are calculated. Assume that $m = 0.02$, $G = 25$, $T = 10$, $Z = 17$, $W_0 = \text{USD } 50{,}000$ and $r = 0.05$. We also assume that the wage growth rate $w$ is an arbitrarily chosen constant fraction of the yield on high-quality corporate bonds $r$—in particular, that $w = 0.9 \times r$ so that $w = 0.045$ ($= 0.9 \times 0.05$). Based on these assumptions, the ABO and PBO for the representative employee are USD 173,032 and USD 268,714, respectively.

$$\text{ABO} = \frac{m \times G \times W_0}{(1+r)^T} \times \left[\frac{1}{r} - \frac{1}{r \times (1+r)^Z}\right]$$

$$= \frac{0.02 \times 25 \times 50{,}000}{(1.05)^{10}} \times \left[\frac{1}{0.05} - \frac{1}{0.05 \times (1.05)^{17}}\right] = 173{,}032.$$

$$\text{PBO} = \frac{m \times G \times W_0 \times (1+w)^T}{(1+r)^T} \times \left[\frac{1}{r} - \frac{1}{r \times (1+r)^Z}\right]$$

$$= \frac{0.02 \times 25 \times 50{,}000 \times (1.045)^{10}}{(1.05)^{10}} \times \left[\frac{1}{0.05} - \frac{1}{0.05 \times (1.05)^{17}}\right] = 268{,}714.$$

If the plan covers 10,000 similar employees, the total liability is approximately USD 1.730 billion ABO and USD 2.687 billion PBO. Assuming that the pension plan has assets with a market value of USD 2.700 billion, the plan currently is overfunded by both measures of liability.

## 5.3 Calculating Durations

Recall that in general, the effective durations for assets or liabilities are obtained by raising and lowering the assumed yield curve in the valuation model and recalculating the present values.

$$\text{Effective duration} = \frac{(PV_-) - (PV_+)}{2 \times \Delta\text{Curve} \times (PV_0)} \tag{5}$$

$PV_0$ is the initial value, $PV_-$ is the new value after the yield curve is lowered by $\Delta$Curve, and $PV_+$ is the value after the yield curve is raised. In this simple model with a flat yield curve, we raise $r$ from 0.05 to 0.06 (and $w$ from 0.045 to 0.054) and lower $r$ from 0.05 to 0.04 (and $w$ from 0.045 to 0.036); therefore, $\Delta$Curve = 0.01.

Given our assumptions, $\text{ABO}_0$ is USD 173,032. Redoing the calculations for the higher and lower values for $r$ and $w$ gives USD 146,261 for $\text{ABO}_+$ and USD 205,467 for $\text{ABO}_-$. The ABO effective duration is 17.1.

$$\text{ABO duration} = \frac{(PV_-) - (PV_+)}{2 \times \Delta\text{Curve} \times (PV_0)} = \frac{205{,}467 - 146{,}261}{2 \times 0.01 \times 173{,}032} = 17.1.$$

Repeating the calculations for the PBO liability measure gives USD 247,477 for $\text{PBO}_+$ and USD 292,644 for $\text{PBO}_-$. Given that $\text{PBO}_0$ is 268,714, the PBO duration is 8.4.

$$\text{PBO} = \frac{292{,}644 - 247{,}477}{2 \times 0.01 \times 268{,}714} = \frac{(PV_-) - (PV_+)}{2 \times \Delta\text{Curve} \times (PV_0)} = 8.4.$$

These calculations indicate the challenge facing the fund manager. There is a significant difference between having liabilities of USD 1.730 billion and an effective duration of 17.1, as measured by the ABO, and liabilities of USD 2.687 billion and an effective duration of 8.4, as measured by the PBO. The ABO BPV is USD 2,958,300 (= USD 1.730 billion × 17.1 × 0.0001), and the PBO BPV is USD 2,257,080 (= USD 2.687 billion × 8.4 × 0.0001). The plan sponsor must decide which liability measure to use for risk management and asset allocation. For example, if the corporation anticipates that it might be a target for an acquisition and that the acquirer likely would want to convert the retirement plan from defined benefit to defined contribution, the ABO measure matters more than the PBO.

We assume that the corporate sponsor sees itself as an ongoing independent institution that preserves the pension plan's current design. Therefore, PBO is the appropriate measure for pension plan liabilities. The plan is fully funded in that the market value of assets, assumed to be USD 2.700 billion, exceeds the PBO of USD 2.687 billion, giving a surplus of only USD 13 million. That surplus disappears quickly if yields on high-quality corporate bonds that are used to discount the projected benefits drop by about 5 bps to 6 bps. Note that the surplus divided by the PBO BPV is 5.76 (= 13,000,000/2,257,080). Interest rate risk is a major concern to the plan sponsor because changes in the funding status flow through the income statement, thereby affecting reported earnings per share.

Lower yields also raise the market value of assets depending on how those assets are allocated. We assume that the current asset allocation is 50% equity, 40% fixed income, and 10% alternatives. The fixed-income portfolio is managed to track an index of well-diversified corporate bonds—such indexes are covered later. Relevant at this point is that the chosen bond index reports a modified duration of 5.5.

The problem is to assign a duration for the equity and alternative investments. To be conservative, we assume that there is no stable and predictable relationship between valuations on those asset classes and market interest rates. Therefore, equity duration and alternatives duration are assumed to be zero. Assuming zero duration does not imply that equity and alternatives have no interest rate risk. Effective duration estimates the percentage change in value arising from a change in nominal interest rates. The effect on equity and alternatives depends on *why* the nominal rate changes, especially if that rate change is not widely anticipated in the market. Higher or lower interest rates can arise from a change in expected inflation, a change in monetary policy, or a change in macroeconomic conditions. Only fixed-income securities have a well-defined connection between market values and the yield curve. Nevertheless, assumptions are a source of model risk, as discussed in the next section.

Given these assumptions, we conclude that the asset BPV is USD 594,000 = USD 2.700 billion × [(0.50 × 0) + (0.40 × 5.5) + (0.10 × 0)] × 0.0001. The term in brackets is the estimated effective duration for the asset portfolio, calculated using the shares of market value as the weights. Clearly, the pension plan is running a significant duration gap—the asset BPV of USD 594,000 is much lower than the liability BPV of USD 2,257,080, using the PBO measure. If all yields go down by 10 bps, the market value of assets goes up by approximately USD 5.940 million and the present value of liabilities goes up by USD 22.571 million. The pension plan would have a deficit and be deemed under-funded.

## 5.4 Addressing the Duration Gap

The pension fund manager can choose to reduce, or even eliminate, the duration gap using derivatives. We consider several scenarios, starting with futures. We then consider the use of swaps and options to enter an interest rate swap.

### 5.4.1 Using Futures to Reduce the Duration Gap

For example, suppose the Ultra 10-year Treasury futures contract at the Chicago Mercantile Exchange (CME) has a BPV of USD 95.8909 because the on-the-run T-note is the CTD security. Using Equation 3, the pension plan would need to buy, or go long, 17,343 contracts to fully hedge the interest rate risk created by the duration gap:

$$N_f = \frac{\text{Liability portfolio BPV} - \text{Asset portfolio BPV}}{\text{Futures BPV}}$$

$$= \frac{2{,}257{,}080 - 594{,}000}{95.8909} = 17{,}343.$$

One concern with hedging with futures is the need for daily oversight of the positions. That need arises because futures contracts are marked to market and settled at the end of each trading day into the margin account. Suppose that the fund did buy 17,343 futures contracts and 10-year Treasury yields go up by 5 bps. Given that the Futures BPV is USD 95.8909 per contract, the *realized* loss that day is more than USD 8.315 million: USD 95.8909 × 5 × 17,343 = 8,315,179. That amount is offset by the *unrealized* reduction in the present value of liabilities. Such a large position in futures contracts would lead to significant daily cash inflows and outflows. For that reason, such hedging problems as the one facing the pension fund often are addressed with over-the-counter interest rate swaps rather than exchange-traded futures contracts.

### 5.4.2 Using Interest Rate Swaps to Reduce Duration Gap

Suppose that the pension fund manager can enter a 30-year, receive-fixed, interest rate swap against the three-month Market Reference Rate (MRR). The fixed rate on the swap is 4.16%. Assume its effective duration is +16.73, and its BPV is +0.1673 per USD 100 of notional principal. Exhibit 22 illustrates this swap.

**Exhibit 22  Interest Rate Swap**

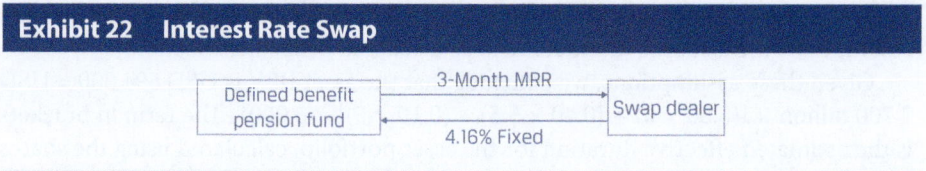

The risk statistics for an interest rate swap can be obtained from interpreting the contract as a combination of bonds. From the pension fund's perspective, the swap is viewed as buying a 30-year, 4.16% fixed-rate bond from the swap dealer and financing that purchase by issuing a 30-year floating-rate note (FRN) that pays the three-month MRR.

> Swaps are typically quoted as a fixed rate against the MRR flat, meaning no spread. The spread over the MRR is put into the fixed rate. For instance, a swap of 4.00% against the MRR flat is the same as a swap of 4.25% against MRR + 0.25%. The swap's money duration is taken to be the (high) duration of the fixed-rate bond minus the (low) duration of the FRN. That explains why a receive-fixed swap has positive duration. From the swap dealer's perspective, the contract is viewed as purchasing a (low duration) FRN that is financed by issuing a (high duration) fixed-rate bond. Hence, the swap has negative duration to the dealer.

# Liability-Driven Investing: An Example of a Defined Benefit Pension Plan

The notional principal (NP) on the interest rate swap needed to close the duration gap to zero can be calculated with this expression:

$$\text{Asset BPV} + \left[ \text{NP} \times \frac{\text{Swap BPV}}{100} \right] = \text{Liability BPV} \qquad (6)$$

This is similar to Equation 2 for futures contracts. Given that the Asset BPV is USD 594,000 and the Liability BPV is USD 2,257,080 using the PBO measure, the required notional principal for the receive-fixed swap having a BPV of 0.1673 is about USD 994 million.

$$594{,}000 + \left[ \text{NP} \times \frac{0.1673}{100} \right] = 2{,}257{,}080, \text{ NP} = 994{,}070{,}532.$$

Exhibit 23 shows the simplified payoff from entering into the receive-fixed swap.

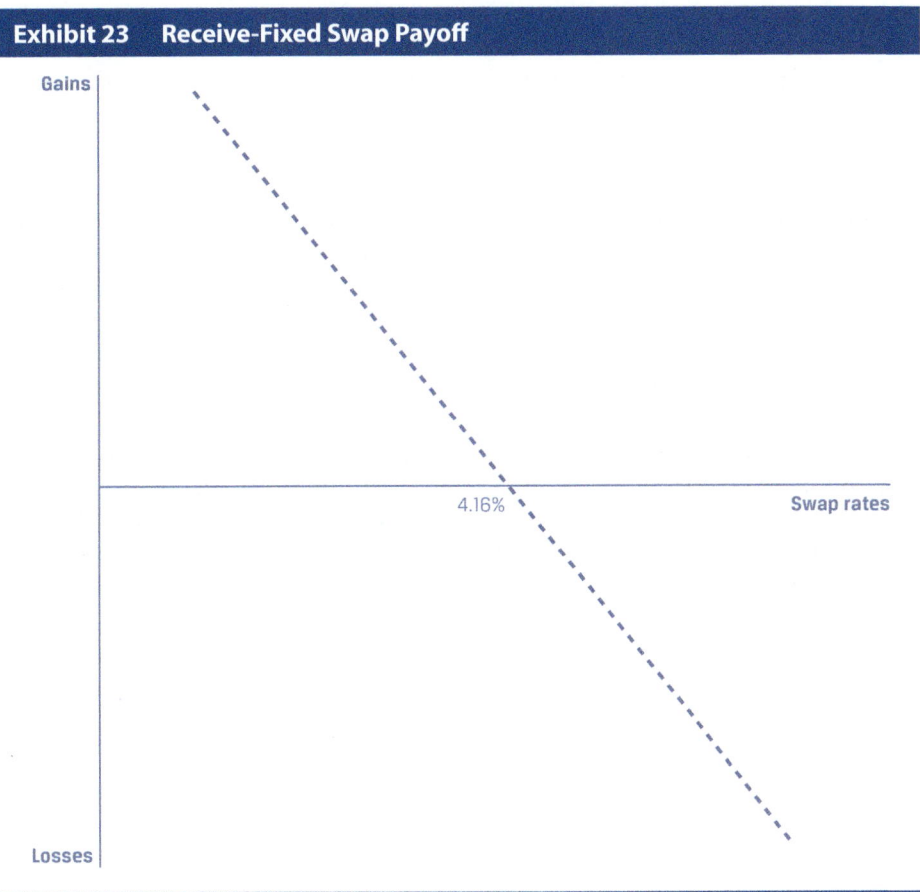

**Exhibit 23  Receive-Fixed Swap Payoff**

We use the term "hedging ratio" (or "interest rate hedging ratio," since the focus is on reducing interest rate risk) to indicate the extent of interest rate risk management. A hedging ratio of 0% indicates no hedging at all. The pension plan retains the significant negative duration gap and the risk of lower corporate bond yields if it does not hedge. A hedging ratio of 100% indicates an attempt to fully balance, or to immunize, the assets and liabilities. In this case, the plan manager enters the receive-fixed swap for a notional principal of USD 994 million. In practice, partial hedges are common—the manager's task is to select the hedging ratio between 0% and 100%. The initial use of derivatives entails moving up a substantial learning curve. It is important that all stakeholders to the retirement plan understand the hedging strategy. These stakeholders include the plan sponsor, the regulatory authorities, the auditors, the employees covered by the plan, and perhaps even the employees' union representatives. Interest rate swaps typically have a value of zero at initiation. If swap rates rise, the value of the receive-fixed swap becomes negative and stakeholders will need an explanation of those losses. If the contract is collateralized, the pension fund will have to post cash or marketable securities with the swap dealer. We discuss collateralization further in the next section. The key point is that in all likelihood, the prudent course of action for the plan manager is to use a partial hedge rather than attempt to reduce the duration gap to zero.

One possibility is that the plan sponsor allows the manager some flexibility (called "strategic hedging") in selecting the hedging ratio. For example, the mandate could be to stay within a range of 25% to 75%. When the manager anticipates lower market rates and gains on receive-fixed interest rate swaps, the manager prefers to be at the top of an allowable range. On the other hand, if market (swap) rates are expected to go up, the manager could reduce the hedging ratio to the lower end of the range. The performance of the strategic hedging decisions can be measured against a strategy of maintaining a preset hedging ratio, for instance, 50%. That strategy means entering the receive-fixed swap for a notional principal of USD 497 million, which is about half of the notional principal needed to attempt to immunize the plan from interest rate risk.

### 5.4.3 Using Options to Reduce Duration Gap

Another consideration for the plan manager is whether to use an option-based derivatives overlay strategy. Instead of entering a 30-year, receive-fixed interest rate swap against the three-month MRR, the pension fund could purchase an option to enter a similar receive-fixed swap. This contract is called a receiver swaption. The cost is a known amount paid upfront. Suppose that the strike rate on the swaption is 3.50%. Given that the current 30-year swap fixed rate is assumed to be 4.16%, this receiver swaption is out of the money. The swap rate would have to fall by 66 bps (= 4.16% − 3.50%) for the swap contract to have intrinsic value. Suppose that the swaption premium is 100 bps, an amount based on the assumed level of interest rate volatility and the time to expiration (the next date that liabilities are measured and reported). Given a notional principal of USD 497 million, the pension plan pays USD 4.97 million (= USD 497 million × 0.0100) up front to buy the swaption. (This example neglects that the 3.50% swap has a somewhat higher effective duration and BPV than the 4.16% swap.) Exhibit 24 shows the payoff profile of the receiver swaption.

## Exhibit 24  Received Swaption Payoff Profile

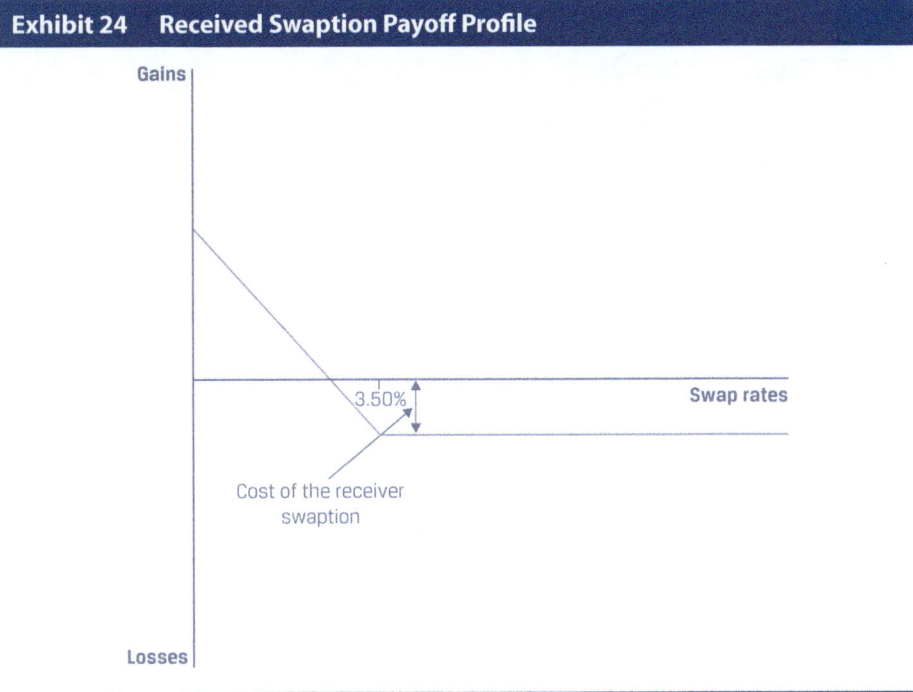

When the expiration date arrives, the plan exercises the swaption if 30-year swap rates are below 3.50%. The plan could "take delivery" of the swap and receive what has become an above-market fixed rate for payment of the three-month MRR. Or, the plan could close out the swap with the counterparty to capture the present value of the annuity based on the difference between the contractual fixed rate of 3.50% and the fixed rate in the swap market, multiplied by the notional principal. This gain partially offsets the loss incurred on the higher value for the pension plan liabilities. If 30-year swap rates are equal to or above 3.50% at expiration, the plan lets the swaption expire.

### 5.4.4 Using a Swaption Collar

Another derivatives overlay is a swaption collar. The plan buys the same receiver swaption, but instead of paying the premium of USD 4.97 million in cash, the plan writes a payer swaption. Suppose that a strike rate of 5.00% on the payer swaption generates an upfront premium of 100 bps. Therefore, the combination is a "zero-cost" collar, at least in terms of the initial expense. If 30-year swap rates are below 3.50% at expiration, the purchased receiver swaption is in the money and the option is exercised. If the swap rate is between 3.50% and 5.00%, both swaptions are out of the money. But if the swap rate exceeds 5.00%, the payer swaption is in the money to the counterparty. As the writer of the contract, the pension plan is obligated to receive a fixed rate of only 5.00% when the going market rate is higher. The plan could continue with the swap but, in practice, would more likely seek to close it out by making a payment to the counterparty for the fair value of the contract. Note that potential losses on the receive-fixed swap and swaption collar are *time-deferred* and *rate-contingent* and therefore are uncertain. Exhibit 25 illustrates the payoff profile of the swaption collar.

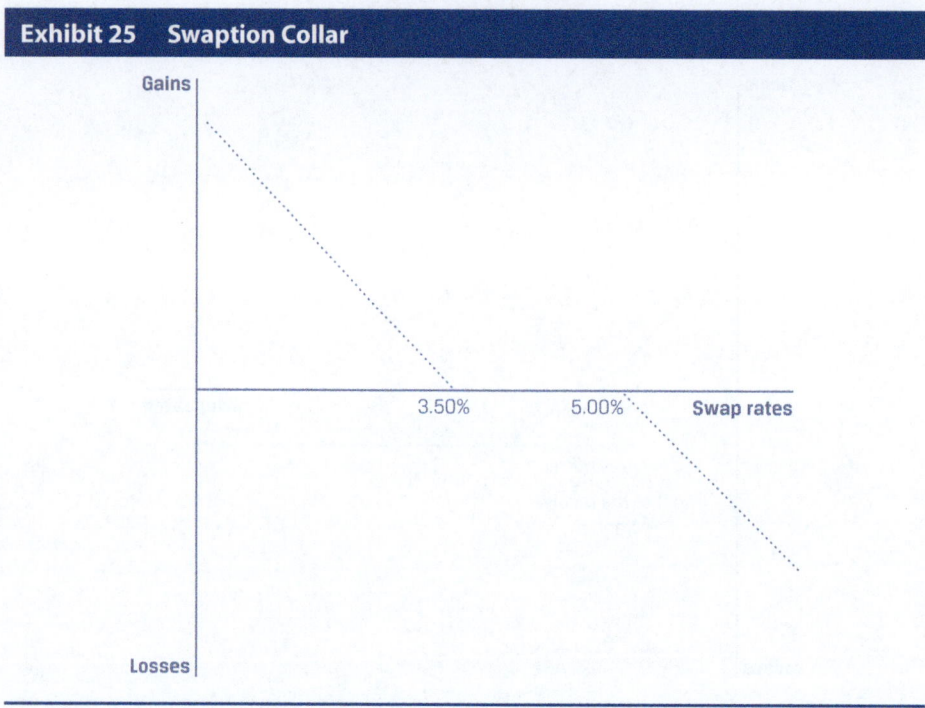

Exhibit 25  Swaption Collar

### 5.4.5 Selecting a Suitable Hedging Strategy

Hedging decisions involve a number of factors, including accounting and tax treatment for the derivatives used in the overlay strategy. An important consideration is the various stakeholders' sensitivity to losses on the derivatives. Obviously, the plan manager is a "hero" if yields suddenly go down and if any of the three strategies—enter the receive-fixed swap, buy the receiver swaption, or enter the swaption collar—are undertaken. Note that swap rates do not need to go below 3.50% for the receiver swaption to generate an immediate gain. Its market value would go up if market rates fall (an increase in the value of the option), and it could be sold for more than the purchase price. The problem for the manager, however, occurs if yields suddenly and unexpectedly go up, leading to a significant loss on the hedge. Will being hedged be deemed a managerial mistake by some of the stakeholders?

A factor in the choice of derivatives overlay is the plan manager's view on future interest rates, particularly on high-quality corporate bond yields at the time of the next reporting for liabilities. An irony to interest rate risk management is that the view on rates is part of decision making even when uncertainty about future rates is the motive for hedging. Exhibit 26 brings together the payoffs on the three derivatives and the breakeven rates that facilitate the choice of contract.

# Liability-Driven Investing: An Example of a Defined Benefit Pension Plan

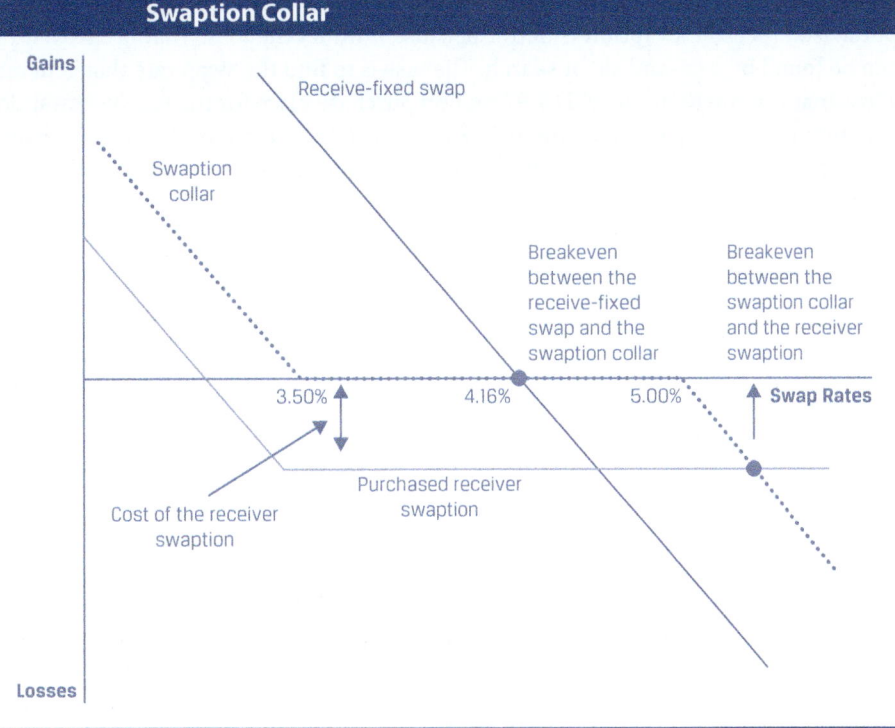

**Exhibit 26  Payoffs on Received-Fixed Swap, Receiver Swaption, and Swaption Collar**

Consider first the receive-fixed swap payoff. We assume it has a notional principal of USD 497 million (a 50% hedging ratio). There are gains (losses) if rates on otherwise comparable 30-year swaps are below (above) 4.16%. In reality, the payoff line is not linear as shown in the exhibit. Suppose the swap rate moves down to 4.10%. The gain is the present value of the 30-year annuity of USD 149,100 (= [0.0416 − 0.0410] × 0.5 × USD 497,000,000) per period, assuming semi-annual payments. Assuming that 4.10% is the correct rate for discounting, the gain is about USD 5.12 million:

$$\frac{149{,}100}{\left(1+\frac{0.0410}{2}\right)^1} + \frac{149{,}100}{\left(1+\frac{0.0410}{2}\right)^2} + \cdots + \frac{149{,}100}{\left(1+\frac{0.0410}{2}\right)^{60}} = 5{,}120{,}670$$

If the swap rate moves up to 4.22%, the annuity is still USD 149,100. But the loss is about USD 5.05 million using 4.22% to discount the cash flows.

$$\frac{149{,}100}{\left(1+\frac{0.0422}{2}\right)^1} + \frac{149{,}100}{\left(1+\frac{0.0422}{2}\right)^2} + \cdots + \frac{149{,}100}{\left(1+\frac{0.0422}{2}\right)^{60}} = 5{,}047{,}526$$

The payoffs, including the initial cost, for the purchased 3.50% receiver swaption are shown as the thin line in Exhibit 26. The premium paid at purchase is USD 4.97 million, assuming that the quoted price is 100 bps and the notional principal is USD 497 million. The dotted line shows the payoffs on the swaption collar. It is composed of the long position in the 3.50% receiver swaption and the short position in the 5.00% payer swaption. There is a gain if the swap rate is below 3.50% and a loss if the rate is above 5.00%.

Decision making is facilitated by breakeven numbers. It is easier to ask "do we expect the rate to be above or below a certain number" than to state a well-articulated probability distribution for the future rate. Exhibit 26 shows two breakeven rates. If the plan manager expects the swap rate to be at or below 4.16%, the receive-fixed swap is preferred. Its gains are higher than the other two derivatives overlays. If the manager expects the swap rate to be above 4.16%, however, the swaption collar is attractive because the swap would be incurring a loss. At some point above 5.00%, the purchased receiver swaption is better because it limits the loss. That breakeven rate can be found by trial-and-error search. The task is to find the swap rate that generates a loss that is more than the USD 4.97 million purchase price for the receiver swaption.

Suppose the swap rate goes up to 5.07% on the date that the liabilities are measured and reported. The fair value of the written 5.00% payer swaption starts with the 30-year annuity of USD 173,950 [= (0.0507 − 0.0500) × 0.5 × USD 497,000,000]. The loss of about USD 5.33 million is the present value of that annuity, discounted at 5.07%.

$$\frac{173{,}950}{\left(1+\frac{0.0507}{2}\right)^1} + \frac{173{,}950}{\left(1+\frac{0.0507}{2}\right)^2} + \cdots + \frac{173{,}950}{\left(1+\frac{0.0507}{2}\right)^{60}} = 5{,}333{,}951$$

Therefore, if the plan manager expects the swap rate to be above 5.07%, the purchased receiver swaption is preferred.

In summary, many decisions go into the LDI strategy for defined benefit pension plans. Given the assumptions that lie behind the calculations of the asset BPV and the liability BPV, including the important choice between the ABO and PBO measure of liabilities, the plan manager faces a significant duration gap. The hedging ratio—the percentage of the duration gap to close—is a key decision that might depend on the held view on future interest rates—in particular, on high-quality corporate bond yields that are used to measure the liabilities. Then, given the determined hedging ratio, the choice of derivatives overlay is made. That decision once again depends on many factors, including the view on future rates.

### EXAMPLE 8

A corporation is concerned about the defined benefit pension plan that it sponsors for its unionized employees. Because of recent declines in corporate bond yields and weak performance in its equity investments, the plan finds itself to be only about 80% funded based on the PBO measure. That fact is raising concerns with its employees as well as with the rating agencies. Currently, the present value of the corporation's retirement obligations is estimated by the plan's actuarial advisers to be about USD 1.321 billion using the PBO measure of liabilities. The corporation has no plans to close the defined benefit plan but is concerned about having to report the funding status in its financial statements. The market value of its asset portfolio is USD 1.032 billion—the plan is underfunded by USD 289 million.

The pension fund's asset allocation is rather aggressive: 70% equity, 10% alternative assets, and 20% fixed income. The fund manager hopes that a recovering equity market will reverse the deficit and ultimately return the plan to a fully funded position. Still, the manager is concerned about tightening corporate spreads as the economy improves. That scenario could lead to lower discount rates that are used to calculate the present value of the liabilities and offset any gains in the stock market. The actuarial advisers to the plan estimate that the effective duration of the liabilities is 9.2, so the BPV is USD 1.215 million. The corporate sponsor requires that the manager assume an effective duration of zero on equity and alternative assets. The fixed-income portfolio consists mostly of long-term bonds, including significant holdings of zero-coupon government securities. Its effective duration is estimated to be 25.6. Taken together, the asset BPV is USD 528,384. The negative money duration gap is substantial.

# Liability-Driven Investing: An Example of a Defined Benefit Pension Plan

The pension plan has hired a qualified professional asset manager (QPAM) to offer advice on derivatives overlay strategies and to execute the contracts with a commercial bank. The QPAM suggests that the pension plan consider the use of interest rate derivatives to partially close the duration gap between its assets and liabilities.

The QPAM has identified three interest rate derivatives strategies that can be executed with the commercial bank. The first is a 30-year, 3.80% receive-fixed swap referencing the three-month MRR. The swap's effective duration is +17.51, and its BPV is 0.1751 per USD 100 of notional principal. The second is a receiver swaption having a strike rate of 3.60%. The plan pays a premium of 145 bps upfront to buy the right to enter a 30-year swap as the fixed-rate receiver. The expiration date is set to match the date when the pension plan next reports its funding status. The third is a swaption collar, the combination of buying the 3.60% receiver swaption and writing a 4.25% payer swaption. The premiums on the two swaptions offset, so this is a "zero-cost" collar.

After some discussions with the rates desk at the commercial bank and a conversation with the bank's strategy group, the plan manager instructs the QPAM to select the 3.80% receive-fixed interest rate swap. Moreover, the manager chooses a hedging ratio of 75%.

1. Calculate the notional principal on the interest rate swap to achieve the 75% hedging ratio.
2. Indicate the plan manager's likely view on future 30-year swap fixed rates given the decision to choose the swap rather than the purchased receiver swaption or the swaption collar.

## Solution to 1:

First calculate the notional principal needed to close the duration gap between assets and liabilities to zero using Equation 6.

$$\text{Asset BPV} + \left(\text{NP} \times \frac{\text{Swap BPV}}{100}\right) = \text{Liability BPV}$$

Asset BPV is USD 528,384; Swap BPV is 0.1751 per 100 of notional principal; and Liability BPV is USD 1.215 million.

$$528{,}384 + \left(\text{NP} \times \frac{0.1751}{100}\right) = 1{,}215{,}000; \text{NP} = 392{,}127{,}927.$$

A 100% hedging ratio requires a receive-fixed interest rate swap having a notional principal of about USD 392 million. For a hedging ratio of 75%, the notional principal needs to be about USD 294 million (= 392 × 0.75).

## Solution to 2:

The plan manager's likely view is that the 30-year swap rate will be less than 3.80%. Then the gains on the receive-fixed interest rate swap exceed those on the swaption collar (i.e., not profitable until the swap rate falls below 3.60%) and on the purchased receiver swaption (i.e., not profitable until the swap rate falls sufficiently below 3.60% to recover the premium paid), as illustrated in Exhibit 26. Note that if the 30-year swap rate exceeds 3.80%, then the receive-fixed interest rate swap will begin losing immediately. Losses on the swaption collar will not begin until the rate rises above 4.25%, while losses on the purchased receiver swaption (at any swap rate above 3.60%) are limited to the premium paid.

Notice that this rate view is also consistent with the concern about lower corporate bond yields and the relatively high hedging ratio.

# 6 RISKS IN LIABILITY-DRIVEN INVESTING

**f** explain risks associated with managing a portfolio against a liability structure

We have mentioned in previous sections some of the risks to LDI strategies for single and multiple liabilities. In this section, we review those risks and introduce some new ones. The essential relationship for full interest rate hedging is summarized in this expression:

$$\text{Asset BPV} \times \Delta\text{Asset yields} + \text{Hedge BPV} \times \Delta\text{Hedge yields} \approx \text{Liability BPV} \times \Delta\text{Liability yields} \tag{7}$$

$\Delta$Asset yields, $\Delta$Hedge yields, and $\Delta$Liability yields are measured in basis points. This equation describes an immunization strategy (a hedging ratio of 100%) whereby the intent is to match the changes in market value on each side of the balance sheet when yields change. Doing so entails matching the money duration of assets and liabilities. We know, however, that entities also choose to partially hedge interest rate risk by selecting a hedging ratio less than 100%. In any case, Equation 7 serves to indicate the source of the risks to LDI. The "approximately equals" sign ($\approx$) in the equation results from ignoring higher-order terms, such as convexity.

## 6.1 Model Risk in Liability-Driven Investing

We encounter model risk in financial modeling whenever assumptions are made about future events and approximations are used to measure key parameters. The risk is that those assumptions turn out to be wrong and the approximations are inaccurate. For example, in our earlier defined benefit pension plan example, we assumed that the effective durations for investments in equity and alternative assets are zero. That assumption introduces the risk that Asset BPV is mis-measured if, in fact, those market values change as the yield curve shifts. The modeling problem is that the effect on those asset classes is not predictable or stable because it depends on the reason for the change in nominal interest rates. Unlike fixed-income bonds, an increase in expected inflation can have a very different effect on equity and alternative asset valuations than an increase in the real rate.

Measurement error for Asset BPV can even arise in the classic immunization strategy for Type I cash flows, which have set amounts and dates. In practice, it is common to approximate the asset portfolio duration using the weighted average of the individual durations for the component bonds. A better approach to achieve immunization, however, uses the cash flow yield to discount the future coupon and principal payments. This error is minimized when the underlying yield curve is flat or when future cash flows are concentrated in the flattest segment of the curve.

A similar problem arises in measuring Hedge BPV. When we illustrated the use of derivatives overlays to immunize, we used a common approximation for the Futures BPV. Equation 4 estimates it to be the BPV for the qualifying CTD security divided by its conversion factor. A more developed calculation involving short-term rates and accrued interest, however, could change the number of contracts needed to hedge the interest rate risk. Although the error introduced by using an approximation might not be large, it still can be a source of underperformance in the hedging strategy.

Model risk in obtaining a measure of Liability BPV is evident in the earlier defined benefit pension plan example. Measuring a defined benefit pension plan's liability is clearly a difficult financial modeling problem. Even the simple models for the two liability measures (the ABO and PBO) necessarily require many assumptions about the future, including the dates when employees retire and their wage levels at those times. The difficulty in projecting life spans of retirees covered by the pension plan leads to longevity risk. The risk is the sponsor has not provided sufficient assets to make the longer-than-expected payout stream. More, and harder-to-make, assumptions are needed to deal with Type IV liabilities and lead to greater uncertainty regarding the models' outputs.

Implicit in Equation 7 is the assumption that all yields change by the same number of basis points—that is, ΔAsset Yields, ΔHedge Yields, and ΔLiability Yields are equal. That is a strong assumption—and a source of risk—if the particular fixed-income assets, the derivatives, and the liabilities are positioned at varying points along the benchmark bond yield curve and at varying spreads to that curve. In Section 3 on immunizing the interest rate risk on a single liability by structuring and managing a portfolio of fixed-income bonds, we point out that a parallel yield curve shift is a sufficient, but not necessary, condition to achieve the desired outcome. Non-parallel shifts as well as twists to the yield curve can result in changes to the cash flow yield on the immunizing portfolio that do not match the change in the yield on the zero-coupon bond that provides perfect immunization. Minimizing dispersion of the cash flows in the asset portfolio mitigates this risk.

Generally, the framework for thinking about interest rate risk rests on changes in the benchmark bond yield curve, which usually is the yield curve for government bonds. In practice, however, ΔAsset Yields and ΔLiability Yields often refer to various classes of corporate bonds. In the pension fund example, the fund holds a portfolio of fixed-income bonds that tracks a well-diversified index of corporate bonds that may include non-investment-grade securities. The present value of retirement benefits, however, depends on yields on high-quality corporate bonds. Therefore, a risk is that the respective spreads on the broad index and the high-quality sector do not move in unison with a shift in the government bond yield curve. A similar spread risk is present in the earlier example of immunizing multiple Type I liabilities. The difference is that the assets in that example are of higher quality than the liabilities.

## 6.2 Spread Risk in Liability-Driven Investing

Spread risk also is apparent in the derivatives overlay LDI strategies. We illustrated how futures contracts can be used to hedge the interest rate risk of the multiple liabilities, either passively or contingently. In particular, the futures contracts are on 10-year US Treasury notes, whereas the liabilities are corporate obligations. Movements in the corporate–Treasury yield spread introduce risk to the hedging strategy. Usually, yields on high-quality corporate bonds are less volatile than on more-liquid Treasuries. Government bonds are used in a wide variety of hedging as well as speculative trading strategies by institutional investors. Also, inflows of international funds typically are placed in government bonds, at least until they are allocated to other asset classes. Those factors lead to greater volatility in Treasury yields than comparable-maturity corporate bonds.

Another source of spread risk is the use of interest rate swap overlays. We showed how receive-fixed swaps, purchased receiver swaptions, and swaption collars can reduce the duration gap between pension plan assets and liabilities. In that example, ΔHedge Yields refers to fixed rates on interest rate swaps referencing the three-month MRR. The spread risk is between high-quality corporate bond yields and swap rates. Typically, there is less volatility in the corporate/swap spread than in the corporate/Treasury spread because both the MRR and corporate bond yields contain credit risk vis-à-vis Treasuries. Therefore, one of the usual advantages to hedging corporate bond risk with interest rate swaps is that those derivatives pose less spread risk than Treasury futures contracts.

## 6.3 Counterparty Credit Risk

Counterparty credit risk is a concern if the interest rate swap overlays are uncollateralized, as was common before the 2008–2009 global financial crisis. Suppose that the interest rate swap portrayed in Exhibit 22 does not have a collateral agreement, or Credit Support Annex (CSA), to the standard International Swaps and Derivatives Association (ISDA) contract. The credit risk facing the pension plan is that the swap dealer defaults at a time when the replacement swap fixed rate is below 4.16%. In the same manner, the credit risk facing the dealer is that the pension plan defaults at the time when the market rate on a comparable swap is above 4.16%. Therefore, credit risk entails the joint probability of default by the counterparty and movement in market rates that results in the swap being valued as an asset.

Since the 2008–2009 global financial crisis, over-the-counter derivatives increasingly include a CSA to the ISDA contract to mitigate counterparty credit risk. Collateral provisions vary. A typical CSA calls for a zero threshold, meaning that only the counterparty for which the swap has negative market value posts collateral, which usually is cash but can be highly marketable securities. The CSA can be one way (only the "weaker" counterparty needs to post collateral when the swap has negative market value from its perspective) or two way (either counterparty is obligated to post collateral when the swap has negative market value). The threshold could be positive, meaning that the swap has to have a certain negative value before collateral needs to be exchanged. Another possibility is that one or both counterparties are required to post a certain amount of collateral, called an independent amount, even if the swap has zero or positive value. This provision makes the CSA similar to the use of margin accounts with exchange-traded futures contracts.

Collateralization on derivatives used in an LDI strategy introduces a new risk factor—the risk that available collateral becomes exhausted. That risk is particularly important for the pension plan example, in which the plan would need to enter a sizable derivatives overlay to even use a 50% hedging ratio, let alone to fully hedge the interest rate risk. That is because the duration gap between assets and liabilities is often large, especially for plans having a significant equity allocation. Therefore, the probability of exhausting collateral is a factor in determining the hedging ratio and the permissible range in the ratio if strategic hedging is allowed.

The same concern about cash management and collateral availability arises with the use of exchange-traded futures contracts. These contracts entail daily mark-to-market valuation and settlement into a margin account. This process requires daily oversight because cash moves into or out of the margin account at the close of each trading day. In contrast, the CSA on a collateralized swap agreement typically allows the party a few days to post additional cash or marketable securities. Also, there usually is a *minimum transfer amount* to mitigate the transaction costs for small inconsequential payments.

## 6.4 Asset Liquidity Risk

Asset liquidity becomes a risk factor in strategies that combine active investing to the otherwise passive fixed-income portfolios. This risk is particularly important with contingent immunization. In the presence of a surplus above a sufficient threshold, the manager may increase portfolio risk by using active management. But if losses reduce the surplus to some minimum amount, the positions need to be adjusted to revert to a passive duration-matching fixed-income portfolio of high- quality bonds. Distressed assets that become hard to value, such as tranches of subprime mortgage-backed securities, also become illiquid during financial crises.

# Risks in Liability-Driven Investing

In summary, an LDI manager has a fundamental choice between managing interest rate risk with asset allocation and with derivatives overlays. As with all financial management decisions, the choice depends on a thorough evaluation of risk and return trade-offs. In some circumstances, derivatives might be deemed too expensive or risky, particularly with regard to available collateral and cash holdings. Then the manager might choose to increase holdings of long-term, high-quality bonds that have high duration statistics. The growth of government zero-coupon bonds, such as US Treasury STRIPS (Separate Trading of Registered Interest and Principal of Securities), facilitates that asset reallocation process.

### EXAMPLE 9

A derivatives consultant, a former head of interest rate swaps trading at a major London bank, is asked by a Spanish corporation to devise an overlay strategy to "effectively defease" a large debt liability. That means that there are dedicated assets to retire the debt even if both assets and the liability remain on the balance sheet. The corporation currently has enough euro-denominated cash assets to retire the bonds, but its bank advises that acquiring the securities via a tender offer at this time will be prohibitively expensive.

The 10-year fixed-rate bonds are callable at par value in three years. This is a one-time call option. If the issuer does not exercise the option, the bonds are then non-callable for the remaining time to maturity. The corporation's CFO anticipates higher benchmark interest rates in the coming years. Therefore, the strategy of investing the available funds for three years and then calling the debt is questionable because the embedded call option might be "out of the money" when the call date arrives. Moreover, it is likely that the cost to buy the bonds on the open market at that time will still be prohibitive.

The corporation has considered a cash flow matching approach by buying a corporate bond having the same credit rating and a call structure (call date and call price) close to the corporation's own debt liability. However, the bank working with the CFO has been unable to identify an acceptable bond. Instead, the bank suggests that the corporation buy a 10-year non-callable, fixed-rate corporate bond and use a swaption to mimic the characteristics of the embedded call option. The idea is to transform the callable bond (the liability) into a non-callable security synthetically using the swaption. Then the newly purchased non-callable bond "effectively" defeases the transformed "non-callable" debt liability.

To confirm the bank's recommendation for the derivatives overlay, the CFO turns to the derivatives consultant, asking if the corporation should (1) buy a payer swaption, (2) buy a receiver swaption, (3) write a payer swaption, or (4) write a receiver swaption. The time frames for the swaptions correspond to the embedded call option. They are "3y7y" contracts, an option to enter a seven-year interest rate swap in three years. The CFO also asks the consultant about the risks to the recommended swaption position.

**1** Indicate the swaption position that the derivatives consultant should recommend to the corporation.

**2** Indicate the risks in using the derivatives overlay.

### Solution to 1:

The derivatives consultant should recommend that the corporation choose the fourth option and write a receiver swaption—that is, an option that gives the swaption buyer the right to enter into a swap to receive fixed and pay floating. When the corporation issued the callable bond, it effectively bought the call option, giving the corporation the flexibility to refinance at a lower cost of borrowed funds if benchmark rates and/or the corporation's credit spread narrows. Writing the receiver swaption "sells" that call option, and the corporation captures the value of the embedded call option by means of the premium received. Suppose that market rates in three years are higher than the strike rate on the swaption and the yield on the debt security. Then both options—the embedded call option in the bond liability, as well as the swaption—expire out of the money. The asset and liability both have seven years until maturity and are non-callable. Suppose instead that market rates fall and bond prices go up. Both options are now in the money. The corporation sells the seven-year bonds (the assets) and uses the proceeds to call the debt liabilities at par value. The gain on that transaction offsets the loss on closing out the swaption with the counterparty.

**Solution to 2:**

Potential risks to using swaptions include (1) credit risk if the swaption is not collateralized, (2) "collateral exhaustion risk" if it is collateralized, and (3) spread risk between swap fixed rates and the corporation's cost of funds. First, suppose the receiver swaption is not collateralized. In general, the credit risk on an option is unilateral, meaning that the buyer bears the credit risk of the writer. That unilateral risk assumes the premium is paid in full upon entering the contract; in other words, the buyer has met their entire obligation. Therefore, the corporation as the swaption writer would have no additional credit exposure to the buyer. Second, assume that the swaption is collateralized. As the writer of the option, the corporation would need to regularly post cash collateral or marketable securities with either the counterparty or a third-party clearinghouse. The risk is that the corporation exhausts its available cash or holdings of marketable securities and cannot maintain the hedge. Spread risk arises because the value of the embedded call option in three years depends on the corporation's cost of funds at that time, including its credit risk. The value of the swaption depends only on seven-year swap fixed rates at that time. In particular, the risk is that the corporate/swap spread widens when benchmark rates are low and both options can be exercised. If the corporate spread over the benchmark rate goes up, the gain in the embedded call option is reduced. If the swap spread over the same benchmark rate goes down, the loss on the swaption increases. Fortunately, corporate and swap spreads over benchmark rates are usually positively correlated, but still the risk of an unexpected change in the spread should be identified.

## 7. BOND INDEXES AND THE CHALLENGES OF MATCHING A FIXED-INCOME PORTFOLIO TO AN INDEX

g   discuss bond indexes and the challenges of managing a fixed-income portfolio to mimic the characteristics of a bond index

Though the need to offset liabilities through immunization requires a specific bond portfolio, many investors seek a broader exposure to the fixed-income universe. These investors may be attracted to the risk versus return characteristics available in bond markets, or they may seek to allocate a portion of their investable assets to fixed income as part of a well-diversified multi-asset portfolio. In either case, an investment strategy based on a bond market index offers an investor the ability to gain broad exposure

# Bond Indexes and the Challenges of Matching a Fixed-Income Portfolio to an Index

to the fixed-income universe. Index-based investments generally offer investors the possibility of greater diversification and lower fees as well as avoiding the downside risk from seeking positive excess returns over time from active management.

An investor seeking to offset a specific liability through immunization gauges the success of his strategy based on how closely the chosen bonds offset the future liability or liabilities under different interest rate scenarios. In contrast, an investor seeking to match the returns of a bond market index will gauge an investment strategy's success in terms of how closely the chosen market portfolio mirrors the return of the underlying bond market index. Deviation of returns on the selected portfolio from bond market index returns are referred to as **tracking risk** or **tracking error**. Investors use several methods to match an underlying market index (Volpert 2012). The first of these is **pure indexing**, in which the investor aims to replicate an existing market index by purchasing all of the constituent securities in the index to minimize tracking risk. The purchase of all securities within an index is known as the **full replication approach**. In **enhanced indexing strategy**, the investor purchases fewer securities than the full set of index constituents but matches primary risk factors (discussed later) reflected in the index. This strategy aims to replicate the index performance under different market scenarios more efficiently than the full replication of a pure indexing approach. **Active management** involves taking positions in primary risk factors that deviate from those of the index in order to generate excess return.

Casual financial market observers usually refer to an equity market index to gauge overall financial market sentiment. Examples often consist of a small set of underlying securities, such as the Dow Jones Industrial Average of 30 US stocks, the CAC 40 traded on Euronext in Paris, or the 50 constituent companies in the Hang Seng Index, which represent more than half the market capitalization of the Hong Kong stock market. When bond markets are mentioned at all, the price and yield of the most recently issued benchmark government bond is typically referenced rather than a bond market index. This contrast reflects the unwieldy nature of bond markets for both the average investor and financial professionals alike.

Although rarely highlighted in the financial press, investments based on bond market indexes form a very substantial proportion of financial assets held by investors. Fixed-income markets have unique characteristics that make them difficult to track, and investors therefore face significant challenges in replicating a bond market index. These challenges include:

- the size and breadth of bond markets,
- the wide array of fixed-income security characteristics,
- unique issuance and trading patterns of bonds versus other securities, and
- the effect of these patterns on index composition and construction, pricing, and valuation.

We will tackle each of these issues and their implications for fixed-income investors.

## 7.1 Size and Breadth of the Fixed-Income Universe

Fixed-income markets are much larger and broader than equity markets, and the number of fixed-income securities outstanding is vastly larger as reflected in broad market indexes. For instance, the MSCI World Index, capturing equities in 23 developed market countries and 85% of the available market capitalization in each market, consists of about 1,600 securities, whereas the Bloomberg Barclays Global Aggregate Index, covering global investment-grade debt from 24 local currency markets, consists of more than 16,000 securities. Those fixed-income issuers represent a much wider range of borrowers than the relatively narrow universe of companies issuing equity securities. For example, the oldest and most widely recognized US bond market index, the Bloomberg Barclays US Aggregate Index (one of four regional aggregate benchmarks that constitute the Bloomberg Barclays Global Aggregate Index), includes US Treasuries, government agency securities, corporate bonds, mortgage-backed securities, asset-backed securities, and commercial mortgage-backed securities. Although the large number of index constituents provides a means of risk diversification, in practice it is neither feasible nor cost-effective for investors to pursue a full replication approach with a broad fixed-income market index.

## 7.2 Array of Characteristics

Different maturities, ratings, call/put features, and varying levels of security and subordination give rise to a much wider array of public and private bonds available to investors. Exhibit 27 illustrates the number of publicly traded fixed-income and equity securities outstanding for a select group of major global issuers.

**Exhibit 27  Debt and Equity Securities Outstanding for Select Issuers**

| Issuer | Fixed-Income Securities | Common Equity Securities | Preferred Equity Securities |
|---|---|---|---|
| Royal Dutch Shell PLC | 57 | 1 | 0 |
| BHP Billiton Limited | 22 | 1 | 0 |
| Johnson & Johnson | 37 | 1 | 0 |
| Ford Motor Company | 104 | 2 | 2 |

*Source:* Bloomberg as of 14 October 2020. Bonds with more than $50 million outstanding included.

As of October 2020, Royal Dutch Shell had 57 bonds outstanding across four currencies, some of which were both fixed and floating rate, with a range of maturities from under a year to bonds maturing in 2052. The existence of many debt securities for a particular issuer suggests that many near substitutes may exist for an investor seeking to pursue an enhanced index strategy. That said, the relative liquidity and performance characteristics of those bonds may differ greatly depending on how recently the bond was issued and how close its coupon is to the yield currently required to price the bond at par.

## 7.3 Unique Issuance and Trading Patterns

Unlike equity securities, which trade primarily over an exchange, fixed-income markets are largely over-the-counter markets that rely on broker/dealers as principals to trade in these securities using a quote-based execution process rather than the order-based trading systems common in equity markets. The rising cost of maintaining risk-weighted assets on dealer balance sheets as a result of Basel III capital requirements has had an adverse effect on fixed-income trading and liquidity. Broker/dealers have reduced bond inventories because of higher capital costs. With lower trading inventories, dealers have both a limited appetite to facilitate trading at narrow bid–offer spreads and are less willing to support larger "block" trades, preferring execution in smaller trade sizes. Finally, a significant decline in proprietary trading among dealers has had a greater pricing effect on less liquid or "off-the-run" bonds. Although many see these structural changes in fixed-income trading acting as a catalyst for more electronic trading, this trend will likely be most significant for the most liquid fixed-income securities in developed markets, with a more gradual effect on less frequently traded fixed-income securities worldwide. Fixed-income trading in many markets is difficult to track. In some markets, regulators developed systems that facilitate mandatory reporting of over-the-counter transactions in eligible fixed-income securities, such as the US Trade Reporting and Compliance Engine (TRACE) system. All broker/dealers that are Financial Industry Regulatory Authority (FINRA) member firms must report corporate bond transactions within 15 minutes of occurrence. It is important to note the distinct nature of fixed-income trading versus equities. The vast majority of fixed-income securities either do not trade at all or trade only a few times during the year. Only a small fraction trade every business day, according to MarketAxess, a leading electronic trading provider. It is also important to note that the average trade size in dollar terms in the US investment-grade bond market is roughly 70 times the size of the average stock trade.

The illiquid nature of most fixed-income instruments gives rise to pricing and valuation challenges for asset managers. For fixed-income instruments that are not actively traded and therefore do not have an observable price, it is common to use an estimation process known as **matrix pricing** or **evaluated pricing**. Matrix pricing makes use of observable liquid benchmark yields, such as Treasuries of similar maturity and duration, as well as the benchmark spreads of bonds with comparable times to maturity, credit quality, and sector or security type in order to estimate the current market yield and price. In practice, asset managers will typically outsource this function to a global custodian or external vendor. This estimation analysis is another potential source of variation between index performance and portfolio returns.

The complexity of trading and valuing individual fixed-income securities further underscores the challenges associated with managing an index-based bond portfolio. Fixed-income indexes change frequently as a result of both new debt issuance and the maturity of outstanding bonds. Bond index eligibility is also affected by changes in ratings and bond callability. As a result, rebalancing of bond market indexes usually occurs monthly rather than semi-annually or annually as it does for equity indexes. Fixed-income investors pursuing a pure indexing strategy therefore must also incur greater transaction costs associated with maintaining a bond portfolio consistent with the index.

## 7.4 Primary Risk Factors

Given the significant hurdles involved in bond index matching, asset managers typically seek to target the primary risk factors present in a fixed-income index through a diversified portfolio. Volpert (2012) summarized these primary indexing risk factors as follows:

- **Portfolio modified adjusted duration.** Effective duration, or the sensitivity of a bond's price to a change in a benchmark yield curve, is an important primary factor as a first approximation of an index's exposure to interest rate changes. It is important to factor in option-adjusted duration so that the analysis reflects securities with embedded call risk. Larger rate moves should incorporate the second-order convexity adjustment to increase accuracy.

- **Key rate duration.** Although effective duration may be a sufficient measure for small rate changes and parallel yield curve shifts, the **key rate duration** takes into account rate changes in a specific maturity along the yield curve while holding the remaining rates constant. This measure of duration gauges the index's sensitivity to non-parallel yield curve shifts. By effectively matching the key rate durations between the portfolio and the underlying index, a manager can significantly reduce the portfolio's exposure to changes in the yield curve.

- **Percent in sector and quality.** Index yield is most effectively matched by targeting the same percentage weights across fixed-income sectors and credit quality, assuming that maturity parameters have also been met.

- **Sector and quality spread duration contribution.** The portfolio manager can minimize deviations from the benchmark by matching the amounts of index duration associated with the respective issuer sectors and quality categories. The former refers to the issuer type and/or industry segment of the bond issuer. In the case of the latter, the risk that a bond's price will change in response to an idiosyncratic rate move rather than an overall market yield change is known as spread risk. For non-government fixed-income securities, we separate the yield to maturity into a benchmark yield (typically the most recently issued or on-the-run government bond with the closest time to maturity) and a spread reflecting the difference between the benchmark yield and the security-specific yield. **Spread duration** refers to the change in a non-Treasury security's price given a widening or narrowing of the spread compared with the benchmark. Matching the relative quality between the portfolio and the fixed-income index will minimize this risk.

- **Sector/coupon/maturity call weights.** Asset managers face a number of challenges in matching price/yield sensitivity beyond the use of effective duration. Although convexity is a useful second-order condition that should be used to improve this approximation, the negative convexity of callable bonds may distort the call exposure of an index and lead to costly rebalancing when rates shift. As a result, managers should seek to match the sector, coupon, and maturity weights of callable bonds by sector. Doing so is particularly important in the mortgage sector because of the refinancing of high-coupon securities with lower-coupon bonds.

- **Issuer exposure.** Concentration of issuers within a portfolio exposes the asset manager to issuer-specific event risk. The manager should therefore seek to match the portfolio duration effect from holdings in each issuer.

Another method used to address a portfolio's sensitivity to rate changes along the yield curve is referred to as the **present value of distribution of cash flows methodology**. This approach seeks to approximate and match the yield curve risk of an index over discrete time periods referred to as cash flow vertices, and it involves several steps, as follows:

1. The manager divides the cash flows for each non-callable security in the index into discrete semi-annual periods, aggregates them, and then adds the cash flows for callable securities in the index based on the probability of call for each given period.

2. The present value of aggregated cash flows for each semi-annual period is computed, with the total present value of all such aggregated cash flows equal to the index's present value. The percentage of the present value of each cash flow vertex is calculated.

3. The time period is then multiplied by the vertex's proportionate share of the index. (The first cash flow at 6 months is equal to 1; the second cash flow at 12 months is equal to 2; the third cash flow at 18 months is equal to 3, etc.) Because each cash flow represents an effective zero-coupon payment in the

corresponding period, the time period reflects the duration of the cash flow. For example, if the third vertex represents 3% of all cash flows, the third period's contribution to duration might be 1.5 years × 3.0%, or 0.045."

4  Finally, each period's contribution to duration is added to arrive at a total representing the bond index's duration. The portfolio being managed will be largely protected from deviations from the benchmark associated with yield curve changes by matching the percentage of the portfolio's present value that comes due at specific points in time with that of the index.

The goal of matching these primary indexing risk factors is to minimize tracking error, the standard deviation of a portfolio's active return for a given period, whereby active return is defined as follows:

Active return = Portfolio return – Benchmark index return.

If we assume that returns are normally distributed around the mean, then from a statistical perspective, 68% of those returns will lie within one standard deviation of the mean. Therefore, if a fund's tracking error is 50 bps, then for approximately two-thirds of the time period observations, we would expect the fund's return to be less than 50 bps above or below the index's return.

### EXAMPLE 10

Cindy Cheng, a Hong Kong-based portfolio manager, has established the All Asia Dragon Fund, a fixed-income fund designed to outperform the Markit iBoxx Asian Local Bond Index (ALBI). The ALBI tracks the total return performance of liquid bonds denominated in local currencies in the following markets: Chinese mainland, Hong Kong SAR, India, Indonesia, Korea, Malaysia, the Philippines, Singapore, Taiwan region, and Thailand. The index includes both government and non-government bond issues, with constituent selection criteria by government as well as weights designed to balance the desire for liquidity and stability ("Markit iBoxx ALBI Index Guide," January 2016, Markit Ltd).

Individual bond weightings in the index are based on market capitalization, and market weights, reviewed annually, are designed to reflect the investability of developing Asian local currency bonds available to international investors. These weights are driven by local market size and market capitalization, secondary bond market liquidity, accessibility to foreign investors, and development of infrastructure that supports fixed-income investment and trading, such as credit ratings, yield curves, and derivatives products.

Given the large number of bonds in the index, Cheng uses a representative sample of the bonds to construct the fund. She chooses bonds so that the fund's duration, market weights, and sector/quality percentage weights closely match the ALBI. Given the complexity of managing bond investments in these local markets, Cheng is targeting a 1.25% tracking error for the fund.

1  Interpret Cheng's tracking error target for the All Asia Dragon Fund.
2  One of Cheng's largest institutional investors has encouraged her to reduce tracking error. Suggest steps Cheng could take to minimize this risk in the fund.

### Solution to 1:

The target tracking error of 1.25% means that assuming normally distributed returns, in 68% or two-thirds of time periods, the All Asia Dragon Fund should have a return that is within 1.25% of the ALBI.

> **Solution to 2:**
>
> Cheng could further reduce tracking error beyond her choice of duration, market, and sector/quality weightings to mirror the index by using the present value of distribution of cash flows methodology outlined earlier. By doing so, she can better align the contribution to portfolio duration that comes from each market, sector, and issuer type based on credit quality.
>
> Cheng should consider matching the amount of index duration that comes from each sector, as well as matching the amount of index duration that comes from various quality categories across government and non-government bonds, to minimize tracking error.
>
> Finally, Cheng should evaluate the portfolio duration coming from each issuer to minimize event risk. Again, this evaluation should occur on a duration basis rather than as a percentage of market value to quantify the exposure more accurately versus the benchmark ALBI.

## 8. ALTERNATIVE METHODS FOR ESTABLISHING PASSIVE BOND MARKET EXPOSURE

h   compare alternative methods for establishing bond market exposure passively

Why is passive bond market exposure attractive for investors? A **passive investment** in the fixed-income market may be defined as one that seeks to mimic the prevailing characteristics of the overall investments available in terms of credit quality, type of borrower, maturity, and duration rather than express a specific market view. This approach is consistent with the efficient markets hypothesis in that the portfolio manager seeks to simply replicate broader fixed-income market performance rather than outperform the market. Stated differently, establishing passive bond market exposure does not require the in-depth economic, market, or security analysis necessary to achieve an above-market return, nor does it require the high trading frequency of active management, which should lead to lower costs for managing and servicing a portfolio. Finally, the stated goal of matching the performance of a broad-based bond index is consistent with the highest degree of portfolio diversification.

Several methods exist for establishing a passive bond market exposure. In what follows, we will explore both full index replication as well as an enhanced indexing strategy and compare the risks, costs, and relative liquidity of these strategies when applied to the bond market.

### 8.1 Full Replication

Bond market index replication is the most straightforward strategy that a manager can use to mimic index performance. Use of full replication reflects the belief or expectation that i) an active manager cannot consistently outperform the index on a risk-adjusted basis; ii) the investor cannot identify a skilled manager in advance; or iii) the investor is not prepared to go through periods of underperformance. Initial index replication does not require manager analysis but rather involves sourcing a wide range of securities in exact proportion to the index, many of which may be thinly traded. The manager's ongoing task under full replication is to purchase or sell bonds when there are changes to the index in addition to managing inflows and outflows for a specific fund. For example, the manager may have to sell when a security no longer meets the index criteria, such as when a security either matures or is downgraded. For the Bloomberg Barclays US Aggregate Bond Index, a fixed-income security becomes ineligible when it either has a maturity of less than one year or is downgraded below an average minimum investment-grade rating. On the other hand, managers must purchase newly issued securities that meet index criteria to maintain full replication, which, depending on the index, may occur quite frequently. Rolling bond maturities, as well as frequent new issuance eligible for inclusion in the index, drive a monthly rebalancing for most fixed-income indexes. The number of purchases and sales required to maintain an exact proportional allocation would be very significant for most bond indexes. As a result, although the large number of index constituents may well provide the best means of risk diversification, in practice it is neither feasible nor cost-effective for investors to pursue full replication for broad-based fixed-income indexes. It is impractical for all but the most narrow indexes. Investors that wish to have exposure to an index would in practice rely on one of many ETFs that exist in this space.

## 8.2 Enhanced Indexing

Many limitations of the full replication approach are addressed by an enhanced indexing strategy. This approach's goal is to mirror the most important index characteristics and still closely track index performance over time while purchasing fewer securities. This general approach is referred to as a **stratified sampling** or **cell approach** to indexing. First, each cell or significant index portfolio characteristic is identified and mapped to the current index. Second, the fixed-income portfolio manager identifies a subset of bonds or bond-linked exposures, such as derivatives, with characteristics that correspond to the index. Finally, the positions in each cell are adjusted over time given changes to the underlying index versus existing portfolio positions. For example, say a fixed-income index contains 1,000 fixed-income securities, 10% of which are AAA rated. The portfolio manager might choose five to ten AAA rated securities within a cell in order to mimic the performance of the AAA rated bonds within the index.

Enhanced indexing is also of critical importance to investors who consider environmental, social, or other factors when selecting a fixed-income portfolio. These comprise several categories, including ESG or socially responsible investing (SRI), which refer to the explicit inclusion of ethical, environmental, or social criteria when selecting a portfolio. Additional categories include sustainability, which includes companies addressing their ESG risks, and green bonds, which fund projects with direct environmental benefits. There are two main components to incorporating ESG factors in an index. First, a business involvement screen excludes issuers involved in business lines or such activities as alcohol, gambling, tobacco, adult entertainment, nuclear power, and firearms. Second, an ESG rating, provided by one of numerous third-party companies, is applied. MSCI, one such company, provides ratings on an 'AAA to CCC' scale using a rules-based methodology according to the companies' exposure to ESG risks and how well they are managed relative to peers. When building a sustainable index, for example, Bloomberg will apply such rules as those previously described and then further filter the constituents for business involvement and an MSCI minimum rating requirement of BBB. Given the proliferation of ESG data providers, there are differences across methodologies and ratings. Consider also that the pillar of ESG that may be most important to an investor may not have the same emphasis in the rating criteria used by the index provider.

#### 8.2.1 *Enhancement Strategies*

Volpert (2012) outlines a number of enhancement strategies available to portfolio managers seeking to reduce the component of tracking error associated with the expenses and transaction costs of portfolio management as follows:

- **Lower cost enhancements.** The most obvious enhancement is in the area of cost reduction, whether this involves minimizing fund expenses or introducing a more competitive trading process to reduce the bid–offer cost of trading.
- **Issue selection enhancements.** The use of bond valuation models to identify specific issues that are undervalued or "cheap" to their implied value provides another opportunity to enhance return.
- **Yield curve enhancements.** The use of analytical models to gauge and calculate relative value across the term structure of interest rates allows managers to develop strategies to both overweight maturities that are considered undervalued and underweight those that appear to be richly priced.
- **Sector/quality enhancements.** This strategy involves overweighting specific bond and credit sectors across the business cycle to enhance returns. Other sectors are underweighted as a result. This approach may tilt exposure toward corporates given a greater yield spread per unit of duration exposure or shorter maturities, or it may over- or underweight specific sectors or qualities based on analysis of the business cycle.

For example, a manager may increase her allocation to Treasuries over corporates when significant spread widening is anticipated, or reverse this allocation if spread narrowing is deemed more likely.

- **Call exposure enhancements.** Because effective duration is a sufficient risk measure only for relatively small rate changes, anticipated larger yield changes may affect bond performance significantly, especially when a bond shifts from trading to maturity to trading to an earlier call date. Large expected yield changes increase the value of call protection, and any significant differences from index exposure should incorporate potentially large tracking risk implications, as well as the implicit market view that this difference implies. For example, an anticipated drop in yields might cause a callable bond to shift from being priced on a yield-to-maturity basis to a yield-to-call basis. Callable fixed-income securities (priced on a yield-to-call basis) trading above par tend to be less price sensitive for a given effective duration than those priced on a yield-to-maturity basis, suggesting a manager should use metrics other than effective duration in this case when changing exposure.

The stratified sampling approach provides an asset manager the ability to optimize portfolio performance across these characteristics with fewer securities than would be required through full index replication. By matching portfolio performance as closely as possible, investment managers also seek to minimize tracking error, limit the need to purchase or sell thinly traded securities, and/or frequently rebalance the portfolio as would be required when precisely matching the index.

> **EXAMPLE 11**
>
> Adelaide Super, a superannuation fund, offers a range of fixed interest (or fixed-income) investment choices to its members. Superannuation funds are Australian government-supported arrangements for Australian workers to save for retirement, which combine a government-mandated minimum percentage

of wages contributed by employers with a voluntary employee contribution that offers tax benefits. Superannuation plans are similar to defined contribution plans common in the United States, Europe, and Asia.

Three of the bond fund choices Adelaide Super offers are as follows:

- **Dundee Australian Fixed-Income Fund.** The investment objective is to outperform the Bloomberg AusBond Composite Index in the medium to long term. The index includes investment-grade fixed-interest bonds with a minimum of one month to maturity issued in the Australian debt market under Australian law, including the government, semi-government, credit, and supranational/sovereign sectors. The index includes AUD-denominated bonds only. The investment strategy is to match index duration but add value through fundamental and model-driven return strategies.

- **Newcastleton Australian Bond Fund.** The fund aims to outperform the Bloomberg AusBond Composite Index over any three-year rolling period, before fees, expenses, and taxes, and uses multiple strategies, such as duration, curve positioning, and credit and sector rotation rather than one strategy, allowing the fund to take advantage of opportunities across fixed-income markets under all market conditions.

- **Paisley Fixed-Interest Fund.** The fund aims to provide investment returns after fees in excess of the fund's benchmark, which is the Bloomberg AusBond Bank Bill Index and the Bloomberg AusBond Composite Index (equally weighted) by investing in a diversified portfolio of Australian income-producing assets. Paisley seeks to minimize transaction costs via a buy-and-hold strategy, as opposed to active management. The AusBond Bank Bill Index is based on the bank bill market, which is the short-term market (90 days or less) in which Australian banks borrow from and lend to one another via bank bills.

Rank the three fixed-income funds in order of risk profile, and suggest a typical employee for whom this might be a suitable investment.

## Solution:

The Paisley Fixed-Interest Fund represents the lowest risk of the three fund choices, given both its choice of underlying bond index (half of which is in short-term securities) and lack of active management strategies. The Paisley Fund could be a suitable choice for an investor near retirement who is seeking income with a minimum risk profile.

The Dundee Fund represents a medium risk profile given the choice of the composite benchmark and suggests an enhanced approach to indexing. This fund may be the best choice for a middle-aged worker seeking to add a fixed-income component with moderate risk to his portfolio.

The Newcastleton Fund has the highest risk of the three choices and is an example of an actively managed fund that has a mandate to take positions in primary risk factors, such as duration and credit, that deviate from those of the index in order to generate excess return. This fund could be an appropriate choice for a younger worker who is seeking exposure to fixed income but willing to accommodate higher risk.

## 8.3 Alternatives to Investing Directly in Fixed-Income Securities

Recall that a number of alternatives to direct investing into bonds are available to investment managers. We have shown earlier that index-based exposure can be obtained through the following traded products, such as ETFs that offer greater liquidity than the underlying securities or other alternatives, such as mutual funds (i.e., pooled investment vehicles whose shares or units represent a proportional share in the ownership of the assets in an underlying portfolio). Investors benefit from greater bond ETF liquidity versus mutual funds given their availability to be purchased or sold throughout the trading day. Recall that ETFs authorized participants—who enter into an agreement with the distributor of the fund, purchasing shares from or selling ETF shares to the fund creation units—would be encouraged to engage in arbitrage to profit from any significant divergence between the market price of the underlying fixed-income securities portfolio and an ETF's net asset value (NAV). That said, the fact that many fixed-income securities are either thinly traded or not traded at all might allow such a divergence to persist to a much greater degree for a bond ETF than might be the case in the equity market.

Another alternative to direct investing in fixed-income securities are index-based total return swaps, common over-the-counter instruments. Recall that similar to an interest rate swap, a **total return swap** involves the periodic exchange of cash flows between two parties for the life of the contract. Unlike an interest rate swap—in which counterparties exchange a stream of fixed cash flows versus a floating-rate benchmark, such as the MRR, to transform fixed assets or liabilities to a variable exposure—a total return swap (TRS) has a periodic exchange based on a reference obligation that is an underlying equity, commodity, or bond index. The total return receiver receives both the cash flows from the underlying index as well as any appreciation in the index over the period in exchange for paying the MRR plus a pre-determined spread. The total return payer is responsible for paying the reference obligation cash flows and return to the receiver but will also be compensated by the receiver for any depreciation in the index or default losses incurred on the portfolio.

A TRS can have some advantages over a direct investment in a bond mutual fund or ETF. As a derivative, it requires less initial cash outlay than direct investment in the bond portfolio for similar performance. A TRS also carries counterparty credit risk, however. As a customized over-the-counter product, a TRS can offer exposure to assets that are difficult to access directly, such as some high-yield and commercial loan investments.

## 9  BENCHMARK SELECTION

i. discuss criteria for selecting a benchmark and justify the selection of a benchmark

The choice of a benchmark is perhaps an investment manager's most important decision beyond the passive versus active decision or the form that the investment takes, as described earlier. Benchmark selection is one of the final steps in the broader asset allocation process.

The asset allocation process starts with a clear delineation of the portfolio manager's investment goals and objectives. Examples of such goals might include the protection of funds (especially against inflation), broad market replication, predictable returns within acceptable risk parameters, or maximum absolute returns through opportunistic means. The manager must agree on an investment policy with the asset owners,

## Benchmark Selection

beneficiaries, and other constituents outlining return objectives, risk tolerance, and constraints to narrow choices available in the broader capital markets to meet these objectives. Recall that a strategic asset allocation targeting specific weightings for each permissible asset class is the result of this process, while a tactical asset allocation range often provides the investment manager some short-term flexibility to deviate from these weightings in response to anticipated market changes.

Bonds figure prominently in most asset allocations given that they represent the largest fraction of global capital markets, capture a wide range of issuers, and, as borrowed funds, represent claims that should involve lower risk than common equity. Choosing a fixed-income benchmark is unique, however, in that the investor usually has some degree of fixed-income exposure embedded within its asset/liability portfolio, as outlined in the foregoing immunization and liability-driven investing examples. The investment manager must therefore consider these implicit or explicit duration preferences when choosing a fixed-income benchmark.

Benchmark selection must factor in the broad range of issuers and characteristics available in the fixed-income markets. In general, the use of an index as a widely accepted benchmark requires clear, transparent rules for security inclusion and weighting, investability, daily valuation and availability of past returns, and turnover. Unlike in equity indexes, fixed-income market dynamics can drive deviation from a stable benchmark sought by investors for a number of reasons:

- The finite maturity of bonds in a static portfolio implies that duration will drift downward over time.
- Market dynamics and issuer preferences tend to dictate both issuer composition for broad-based indexes as well as maturity selection for narrower indexes. For example, as shown in Exhibit 28, the composition of the Bloomberg Barclays US Aggregate Bond Index changed significantly during the years prior to and after the 2008 global financial crisis, with a large increase in securitized debt pre-crisis and a significant rise in government debt thereafter:

**Exhibit 28  Bloomberg Barclays US Aggregate Bond Index Sector Allocation, Selected Years**

| Year | Government | Corporate | Securitized |
|---|---|---|---|
| 1993 | 53.0% | 17.0% | 30.0% |
| 1998 | 46.0% | 22.0% | 32.0% |
| 2000 | 38.0% | 24.0% | 39.0% |
| 2005 | 40.2% | 19.5% | 40.2% |
| 2008 | 38.6% | 17.7% | 43.7% |
| 2010 | 45.8% | 18.8% | 35.5% |
| 2015 | 44.8% | 24.2% | 31.0% |
| 2020 | 43.4% | 27.3% | 29.3% |

*Sources:* Lehman Brothers; Barclays.

Separately, a corporate debt index investor might find her benchmark choice no longer desirable if issuers refinance maturing bonds for longer maturities and extend overall debt duration.

The dynamics of fixed-income markets require investors to more actively understand and define their underlying duration preferences as well as a desired risk and return profile within their fixed-income allocation when conducting benchmark selection. Expressed differently, the desired duration profile may be considered the portfolio "beta," with the targeted duration equal to an investor's preferred duration exposure. Once these parameters are clear, investors may wish to combine several well-defined sub-benchmark categories into an overall benchmark. Examples of sub-benchmark categories might include Treasuries (or domestic sovereign bonds), US agencies or other asset-backed securities, corporate bonds, high-yield bonds, bank loans, developed markets global debt, or emerging markets debt.

For fixed-income investors seeking to reduce the cost of active management, an alternative known as **smart beta** has emerged. Smart beta involves the use of simple, transparent, rules-based strategies as a basis for investment decisions. The starting point for smart beta investors is an analysis of the well-established, static strategies that tend to drive excess portfolio returns. In theory, asset managers who are able to isolate and pursue such strategies can capture a significant proportion of these excess returns without the significantly higher fees associated with active management. Although the use of smart beta strategies is more established among equity managers, fixed-income managers are increasing their use of these techniques as well (see Staal, Corsi, Shores, and Woida 2015).

> **EXAMPLE 12**
>
> Given the significant rise in regional bond issuance following the 2008 global financial crisis, Next Europe Asset Management Limited aims to grow its assets under management by attracting a variety of new local Eurozone investors to the broader set of alternatives available in the current fixed-income market. Several of the indexes that Next Europe offers as a basis for investment are as follows:
>
> - **S&P Eurozone Sovereign Bond Index.** This index consists of fixed-rate, sovereign debt publicly issued by Eurozone national governments for their domestic markets with various maturities including 1 to 3 years, 3 to 5 years, 5 to 7 years, 7 to 10 years, and 10+ years. For example, the 1- to 3-year index had a weighted average maturity of 1.91 years and a modified duration of 1.87 as of 31 July 2020 (www.spglobal.com).
>
> - **Bloomberg EUR Investment Grade European Corporate Bond Index (BERC).** The BERC index consists of local, EUR-based corporate debt issuance in Eurozone countries and had an effective duration of 5.28 as of September 2020.
>
> - **Bloomberg EUR High Yield Corporate Bond Index (BEUH).** This index consists of sub-investment-grade, EUR-denominated bonds issued by Eurozone-based corporations. It had an effective duration of 3.68 as of September 2020 (www.bloombergindexes.com).
>
> - **FTSE Pfandbrief Index.** The Pfandbrief, which represents the largest segment of the German private debt market, is a bond issued by German mortgage banks, collateralized by long-term assets, such as real estate or public sector loans. These securities are also referred to as covered bonds and are being used as a model for similar issuance in other European countries.
>
> The FTSE Pfandbrief indexes include jumbo Pfandbriefs from German issuers as well as those of comparable structure and quality from other Eurozone countries. The sub-indexes offer a range of maturities, including 1 to 3 years, 3 to 5 years, 5 to 7 years, 7 to 10 years, and 10+ years (www.ftse.com/products/indices).

Which of the above indexes would be suitable for the following investor portfolios?

1. A highly risk-averse investor who is sensitive to fluctuations in portfolio value.
2. A new German private university that has established an endowment with a very long-term investment horizon.
3. A Danish life insurer relying on the fixed-income portfolio managed by Next Europe to meet both short-term claims as well as offset long-term obligations.

### Solution to 1:

Given this investor's high degree of risk aversion, an index with short or intermediate duration with limited credit risk would be most appropriate to limit market value risk. Of the alternatives listed, the S&P Eurozone Sovereign Bond 1–3 Years Index or the FTSE 1–3 Years Pfandbrief Index (given the high credit quality of covered bonds) would be appropriate choices.

### Solution to 2:

This investor's very long investment horizon suggests that the BERC is an appropriate index, because it has the longest duration of the indexes given. In addition, the long-term S&P Eurozone Sovereign Bond or FTSE Pfandbrief indexes (10+ years) could be appropriate choices as well. Next Europe should consider the trade-off between duration and risk in its discussion with the endowment.

### Solution to 3:

The Danish life insurer faces two types of future obligation, namely a short-term outlay for expected claims and a long-term horizon for future obligations. For the short-term exposure, stability of market value is a primary consideration, and the insurer would seek an index with low market risk. Of the above alternatives, the 1–3 Years S&P Sovereign Bond or the FTSE Pfandbrief 1–3 Years would be the best choices. The longer-term alternatives in the Solution to 2 would be most appropriate for the long-term future obligations.

## SUMMARY

- Structured fixed-income investing requires a frame of reference, such as a balance sheet, to structure the bond portfolio. This frame of reference can be as simple as the time to retirement for an individual or as complex as a balance sheet of rate-sensitive assets and liabilities for a company.
- Assets and liabilities can be categorized by the degree of certainty surrounding the amount and timing of cash flows. Type I assets and liabilities, such as traditional fixed-rate bonds with no embedded options, have known amounts and payment dates. For Type I assets and liabilities, such yield duration statistics as Macaulay, modified, and money duration apply.

- Type II, III, and IV assets and liabilities have uncertain amounts and/or uncertain timing of payment. For Type II, III, and IV assets and liabilities, curve duration statistics, such as effective duration, are needed. A model is used to obtain the estimated values when the yield curve shifts up and down by the same amount.
- Immunization is the process of structuring and managing a fixed-income portfolio to minimize the variance in the realized rate of return over a known investment horizon.
- In the case of a single liability, immunization is achieved by matching the Macaulay duration of the bond portfolio to the horizon date. As time passes and bond yields change, the duration of the bonds changes and the portfolio needs to be rebalanced. This rebalancing can be accomplished by buying and selling bonds or using interest rate derivatives, such as futures contracts and interest rate swaps.
- An immunization strategy aims to lock in the cash flow yield on the portfolio, which is the internal rate of return on the cash flows. It is not the weighted average of the yields to maturity on the bonds that constitute the portfolio.
- The risk to immunization is that as the yield curve shifts and twists, the cash flow yield on the bond portfolio does not match the change in the yield on the zero-coupon bond that would provide for perfect immunization.
- A sufficient, but not necessary, condition for immunization is a parallel (or shape-preserving) shift whereby all yields change by the same amount in the same direction. If the change in the cash flow yield is the same as that on the zero-coupon bond being replicated, immunization can be achieved even with a non-parallel shift to the yield curve.
- Structural risk to immunization arises from some non-parallel shifts and twists to the yield curve. This risk is reduced by minimizing the dispersion of cash flows in the portfolio, which can be accomplished by minimizing the convexity statistic for the portfolio. Concentrating the cash flows around the horizon date makes the immunizing portfolio closely track the zero-coupon bond that provides for perfect immunization.
- For multiple liabilities, one method of immunization is cash flow matching. A portfolio of high-quality zero-coupon or fixed-income bonds is purchased to match as closely as possible the amount and timing of the liabilities.
- A motive for cash flow matching can be accounting defeasance, whereby both the assets and liabilities are removed from the balance sheet.
- A laddered bond portfolio is a common investment strategy in the wealth management industry. The laddered portfolio offers "diversification" over the yield curve compared with "bullet" or "barbell" portfolios. This structure is especially attractive in stable, upwardly sloped yield curve environments as maturing short-term debt is replaced with higher-yielding long-term debt at the back of the ladder.
- A laddered portfolio offers an increase in convexity because the cash flows have greater dispersions than a more concentrated (bullet) portfolio.
- A laddered portfolio provides liquidity in that it always contains a soon-to-mature bond that could provide high-quality, low-duration collateral on a repo contract if needed.
- Immunization of multiple liabilities can be achieved by structuring and managing a portfolio of fixed-income bonds. Because the market values of the assets and liabilities differ, the strategy is to match the money durations. The

# Summary

money duration is the modified duration multiplied by the market value. The basis point value is a measure of money duration calculated by multiplying the money duration by 0.0001.

- The conditions to immunize multiple liabilities are that (1) the market value of assets is greater than or equal to the market value of the liabilities, (2) the asset basis point value (BPV) equals the liability BPV, and (3) the dispersion of cash flows and the convexity of assets are greater than those of the liabilities.

- A derivatives overlay—for example, interest rate futures contracts—can be used to immunize single or multiple liabilities.

- The number of futures contracts needed to immunize is the liability BPV minus the asset BPV, divided by the futures BPV. If the result is a positive number, the entity buys, or goes long, futures contracts. If the result is a negative number, the entity sells, or goes short, futures contracts. The futures BPV can be approximated by the BPV for the cheapest-to-deliver security divided by the conversion factor for the cheapest-to-deliver security.

- Contingent immunization adds active management of the surplus, which is the difference between the asset and liability market values, with the intent to reduce the overall cost of retiring the liabilities. In principle, any asset classes can be used for the active investment. The entity can choose to over-hedge or under-hedge the number of futures contracts needed for passive immunization.

- Liability-driven investing (LDI) often is used for complex rate-sensitive liabilities, such as those for a defined benefit pension plan. The retirement benefits for covered employees depend on many variables, such as years of employment, age at retirement, wage level at retirement, and expected lifetime. There are different measures for the liabilities: for instance, the accumulated benefit obligation (ABO) that is based on current wages and the projected benefit obligation (PBO) that is based on expected future wages. For each liability measure (ABO or PBO), a model is used to extract the effective duration and BPV.

- Interest rate swap overlays can be used to reduce the duration gap as measured by the asset and liability BPVs. There often is a large gap because pension funds hold sizable asset positions in equities that have low or zero effective durations and their liability durations are high.

- The hedging ratio is the percentage of the duration gap that is closed with the derivatives. A hedging ratio of zero implies no hedging. A hedging ratio of 100% implies immunization—that is, complete removal of interest rate risk.

- Strategic hedging is the active management of the hedging ratio. Because asset BPVs are less than liability BPVs in typical pension funds, the derivatives overlay requires the use of receive-fixed interest rate swaps. Because receive-fixed swaps gain value as current swap market rates fall, the fund manager could choose to raise the hedging ratio when lower rates are anticipated. If rates are expected to go up, the manager could strategically reduce the hedging ratio.

- An alternative to the receive-fixed interest rate swap is a purchased receiver swaption. This swaption confers to the buyer the right to enter the swap as the fixed-rate receiver. Because of its negative duration gap (asset BPV is less than liability BPV), the typical pension plan suffers when interest rates fall and could become underfunded. The gain on the receiver swaption as rates decline offsets the losses on the balance sheet.

- Another alternative is a swaption collar, the combination of buying the receiver swaption and writing a payer swaption. The premium received on the payer swaption that is written offsets the premium needed to buy the receiver swaption.

- The choice among hedging with the receive-fixed swap, the purchased receiver swaption, and the swaption collar depends in part on the pension fund manager's view on future interest rates. If rates are expected to be low, the receive-fixed swap typically is the preferred derivative. If rates are expected to go up, the swaption collar can become attractive. And if rates are projected to reach a certain threshold that depends on the option costs and the strike rates, the purchased receiver swaption can become the favored choice.

- Model risks arise in LDI strategies because of the many assumptions in the models and approximations used to measure key parameters. For example, the liability BPV for the defined benefit pension plan depends on the choice of measure (ABO or PBO) and the assumptions that go into the model regarding future events (e.g., wage levels, time of retirement, and time of death).

- Spread risk in LDI strategies arises because it is common to assume equal changes in asset, liability, and hedging instrument yields when calculating the number of futures contracts, or the notional principal on an interest rate swap, to attain a particular hedging ratio. The assets and liabilities are often on corporate securities, however, and their spreads to benchmark yields can vary over time.

- Investing in a fund that tracks a bond market index offers the benefits of both diversification and low administrative costs. Tracking risk arises when the fund manager chooses to buy only a subset of the index, a strategy called enhanced indexing, because fully replicating the index can be impractical as a result of the large number of bonds in the fixed-income universe.

- Corporate bonds are often illiquid. Matrix pricing uses available data on comparable securities to estimate the fair value of the illiquid bonds.

- The primary risk factors encountered by an investor tracking a bond index include decisions regarding duration (option-adjusted duration for callable bonds, convexity for possible large yield shifts, and key rate durations for non-parallel shifts) and portfolio weights (assigned by sector, credit quality, maturity, coupon rate, and issuer).

- Index replication is one method to establish a passive exposure to the bond market. The manager buys or sells bonds only when there are changes to the index. Full replication can be expensive, however, as well as infeasible for broad-based fixed-income indexes that include many illiquid bonds.

- Several enhancement strategies can reduce the costs to track a bond index: lowering trading costs, using models to identify undervalued bonds and to gauge relative value at varying points along the yield curve, over/under weighting specific credit sectors over the business cycle, and evaluating specific call features to identify value given large yield changes.

- Investors can obtain passive exposure to the bond market using ETFs or mutual funds. Exchange-traded fund (ETF) shares have the advantage of trading on an exchange throughout the day.

- A total return swap, an over-the-counter derivative, allows an institutional investor to transform an asset or liability from one asset category to another—for instance, from variable-rate cash flows referencing the MRR to the total return on a particular bond index.

- A total return swap (TRS) can have some advantages over a direct investment in a bond mutual fund or ETF. As a derivative, it requires less initial cash outlay than direct investment in the bond portfolio for similar performance. A

TRS also carries counterparty credit risk, however. As a customized over-the-counter product, a TRS can offer exposure to assets that are difficult to access directly, such as some high-yield and commercial loan investments.

- Selecting a particular bond index is a major decision for a fixed-income investment manager. Selection is guided by the specified goals and objectives for the investment. The decision should recognize several features of bond indexes: (1) Given that bonds have finite maturities, the duration of the index drifts down over time; (2) the composition of the index changes over time with the business cycle and maturity preferences of issuers.

## REFERENCES

Staal, Arne, Marco Corsi, Sara Shores, and Chris Woida. 2015. "A Factor Approach to Smart Beta Development in Fixed Income." *Journal of Index Investing*, vol. 6, no. 1: 98–110.

Volpert, Kenneth E. 2012. "Introduction to Bond Portfolio Management." In *Handbook of Fixed-Income Securities*, 8th ed. Edited by Frank J. Fabozzi. New York: McGraw Hill: 1123–1150.

# PRACTICE PROBLEMS

## The following information relates to Questions 1–8

Serena is a risk management specialist with Liability Protection Advisors. Trey, CFO of Kiest Manufacturing, enlists Serena's help with three projects. The first project is to defease some of Kiest's existing fixed-rate bonds that are maturing in each of the next three years. The bonds have no call or put provisions and pay interest annually. Exhibit 1 presents the payment schedule for the bonds.

**Exhibit 1  Kiest Manufacturing Bond Payment Schedule (as of beginning of Year 1)**

| Maturity Date | Payment Amount |
|---|---|
| End of Year 1 | $9,572,000 |
| End of Year 2 | $8,392,000 |
| End of Year 3 | $8,200,000 |

The second project for Serena is to help Trey immunize a $20 million portfolio of liabilities. The liabilities range from 3.00 years to 8.50 years with a Macaulay duration of 5.34 years, cash flow yield of 3.25%, portfolio convexity of 33.05, and basis point value (BPV) of $10,505. Serena suggested employing a duration-matching strategy using one of the three AAA rated bond portfolios presented in Exhibit 2.

**Exhibit 2  Possible AAA Rated Duration-Matching Portfolios**

|  | Portfolio A | Portfolio B | Portfolio C |
|---|---|---|---|
| Bonds (term, coupon) | 4.5 years, 2.63%<br>7.0 years, 3.50% | 3.0 years, 2.00%<br>6.0 years, 3.25%<br>8.5 years, 3.88% | 1.5 years, 1.25%<br>11.5 years, 4.38% |
| Macaulay duration | 5.35 | 5.34 | 5.36 |
| Cash flow yield | 3.16% | 3.33% | 3.88% |
| Convexity | 31.98 | 34.51 | 50.21 |
| BPV | $10,524 | $10,506 | $10,516 |

Serena explains to Trey that the underlying duration-matching strategy is based on the following three assumptions.

1. Yield curve shifts in the future will be parallel.
2. Bond types and quality will closely match those of the liabilities.
3. The portfolio will be rebalanced by buying or selling bonds rather than using derivatives.

© 2021 CFA Institute. All rights reserved.

# Practice Problems

The third project for Serena is to make a significant direct investment in broadly diversified global bonds for Kiest's pension plan. Kiest has a young workforce, and thus, the plan has a long-term investment horizon. Trey needs Serena's help to select a benchmark index that is appropriate for Kiest's young workforce. Serena discusses three benchmark candidates, presented in Exhibit 3.

**Exhibit 3  Global Bond Index Benchmark Candidates**

| Index Name | Effective Duration | Index Characteristics |
| --- | --- | --- |
| Global Aggregate | 7.73 | Market cap weighted; Treasuries, corporates, agency, securitized debt |
| Global Aggregate GDP Weighted | 7.71 | Same as Global Aggregate, except GDP weighted |
| Global High Yield | 4.18 | GDP weighted; sovereign, agency, corporate debt |

With the benchmark selected, Trey provides guidelines to Serena directing her to (1) use the most cost-effective method to track the benchmark and (2) provide low tracking error.

After providing Trey with advice on direct investment, Serena offered him additional information on alternative indirect investment strategies using (1) bond mutual funds, (2) exchange-traded funds (ETFs), and (3) total return swaps. Trey expresses interest in using bond mutual funds rather than the other strategies for the following reasons.

- Reason 1  Total return swaps have much higher transaction costs and initial cash outlay than bond mutual funds.
- Reason 2  Unlike bond mutual funds, bond ETFs can trade at discounts to their underlying indexes, and those discounts can persist.
- Reason 3  Bond mutual funds can be traded throughout the day at the net asset value of the underlying bonds.

1  Based on Exhibit 1, Kiest's liabilities would be classified as:
   A  Type I.
   B  Type II.
   C  Type III.

2  Based on Exhibit 2, the portfolio with the greatest structural risk is:
   A  Portfolio A.
   B  Portfolio B.
   C  Portfolio C.

3  Which portfolio in Exhibit 2 fails to meet the requirements to achieve immunization for multiple liabilities?
   A  Portfolio A
   B  Portfolio B
   C  Portfolio C

4  Based on Exhibit 2, relative to Portfolio C, Portfolio B:
   A  has higher cash flow reinvestment risk.
   B  is a more desirable portfolio for liquidity management.

**C** provides less protection from yield curve shifts and twists.

5 Serena's three assumptions regarding the duration-matching strategy indicate the presence of:
   **A** model risk.
   **B** spread risk.
   **C** counterparty credit risk.

6 The global bond benchmark in Exhibit 3 that is *least* appropriate for Kiest to use is the:
   **A** Global Aggregate Index.
   **B** Global High Yield Index.
   **C** Global Aggregate GDP Weighted Index.

7 To meet both of Trey's guidelines for the pension's bond fund investment, Serena should recommend:
   **A** pure indexing.
   **B** enhanced indexing.
   **C** active management.

8 Which of Trey's reasons for choosing bond mutual funds as an investment vehicle is correct?
   **A** Reason 1
   **B** Reason 2
   **C** Reason 3

## The following information relates to questions 9–16

SD&R Capital (SD&R), a global asset management company, specializes in fixed-income investments. Molly, chief investment officer, is meeting with a prospective client, Leah of DePuy Financial Company (DFC).

Leah informs Molly that DFC's previous fixed-income manager focused on the interest rate sensitivities of assets and liabilities when making asset allocation decisions. Molly explains that, in contrast, SD&R's investment process first analyzes the size and timing of client liabilities, and then it builds an asset portfolio based on the interest rate sensitivity of those liabilities.

Molly notes that SD&R generally uses actively managed portfolios designed to earn a return in excess of the benchmark portfolio. For clients interested in passive exposure to fixed-income instruments, SD&R offers two additional approaches.

   Approach 1   Seeks to fully replicate a small range of benchmarks consisting of government bonds.

   Approach 2   Follows an enhanced indexing process for a subset of the bonds included in the Bloomberg Barclays US Aggregate Bond Index. Approach 2 may also be customized to reflect client preferences.

To illustrate SD&R's immunization approach for controlling portfolio interest rate risk, Molly discusses a hypothetical portfolio composed of two non-callable, investment-grade bonds. The portfolio has a weighted average yield-to-maturity of 9.55%, a weighted average coupon rate of 10.25%, and a cash flow yield of 9.85%.

## Practice Problems

Leah informs Molly that DFC has a single $500 million liability due in nine years, and she wants SD&R to construct a bond portfolio that earns a rate of return sufficient to pay off the obligation. Leah expresses concern about the risks associated with an immunization strategy for this obligation. In response, Molly makes the following statements about liability-driven investing:

Statement 1  Although the amount and date of SD&R's liability is known with certainty, measurement errors associated with key parameters relative to interest rate changes may adversely affect the bond portfolios.

Statement 2  A cash flow matching strategy will mitigate the risk from non-parallel shifts in the yield curve.

Molly provides the four US dollar–denominated bond portfolios in Exhibit 1 for consideration. Molly explains that the portfolios consist of non-callable, investment-grade corporate and government bonds of various maturities because zero-coupon bonds are unavailable.

### Exhibit 1  Proposed Bond Portfolios to Immunize SD&R Single Liability

|  | Portfolio 1 | Portfolio 2 | Portfolio 3 | Portfolio 4 |
|---|---|---|---|---|
| Cash flow yield | 7.48% | 7.50% | 7.53% | 7.51% |
| Average time to maturity | 11.2 years | 9.8 years | 9.0 years | 10.1 years |
| Macaulay duration | 9.8 | 8.9 | 8.0 | 9.1 |
| Market value-weighted duration | 9.1 | 8.5 | 7.8 | 8.6 |
| Convexity | 154.11 | 131.75 | 130.00 | 109.32 |

The discussion turns to benchmark selection. DFC's previous fixed-income manager used a custom benchmark with the following characteristics:

Characteristic 1  The benchmark portfolio invests only in investment-grade bonds of US corporations with a minimum issuance size of $250 million.

Characteristic 2  Valuation occurs on a weekly basis, because many of the bonds in the index are valued weekly.

Characteristic 3  Historical prices and portfolio turnover are available for review.

Molly explains that, in order to evaluate the asset allocation process, fixed-income portfolios should have an appropriate benchmark. Leah asks for benchmark advice regarding DFC's portfolio of short-term and intermediate-term bonds, all denominated in US dollars. Molly presents three possible benchmarks in Exhibit 2.

## Exhibit 2   Proposed Benchmark Portfolios

| Benchmark | Index | Composition | Duration |
|---|---|---|---|
| 1 | Bloomberg Barclays US Bond Index | 80% US government bonds<br>20% US corporate bonds | 8.7 |
| 2<br>Index Blend | 50% Bloomberg Barclays US Corporate Bond Index | 100% US corporate bonds | 7.5 |
|  | 50% Bloomberg Barclays Short-Term Treasury Index | 100% short-term US government debt | 0.5 |
| 3 | Bloomberg Barclays Global Aggregate Bond Index | 60% EUR-denominated corporate bonds<br>40% US-denominated corporate debt | 12.3 |

9. The investment process followed by DFC's previous fixed-income manager is *best* described as:
   A  asset-driven liabilities.
   B  liability-driven investing.
   C  asset–liability management.

10. Relative to Approach 1 of gaining passive exposure, an advantage of Approach 2 is that it:
    A  minimizes tracking error.
    B  requires less risk analysis.
    C  is more appropriate for socially responsible investors.

11. The two-bond hypothetical portfolio's immunization goal is to lock in a rate of return equal to:
    A  9.55%.
    B  9.85%.
    C  10.25%.

12. Which of Molly's statements about liability-driven investing is (are) correct?
    A  Statement 1 only.
    B  Statement 2 only.
    C  Both Statement 1 and Statement 2.

13. Based on Exhibit 1, which of the portfolios will *best* immunize SD&R's single liability?
    A  Portfolio 1
    B  Portfolio 2
    C  Portfolio 3

14. Which of the portfolios in Exhibit 1 *best* minimizes the structural risk to a single-liability immunization strategy?
    A  Portfolio 1
    B  Portfolio 3
    C  Portfolio 4

**Practice Problems**

15 Which of the custom benchmark's characteristics violates the requirements for an appropriate benchmark portfolio?
   A Characteristic 1
   B Characteristic 2
   C Characteristic 3

16 Based on DFC's bond holdings and Exhibit 2, Molly should recommend:
   A Benchmark 1.
   B Benchmark 2.
   C Benchmark 3.

---

## The following information relates to Questions 17–22

Doug, the newly hired chief financial officer for the City of Radford, asks the deputy financial manager, Hui, to prepare an analysis of the current investment portfolio and the city's current and future obligations. The city has multiple liabilities of different amounts and maturities relating to the pension fund, infrastructure repairs, and various other obligations.

Hui observes that the current fixed-income portfolio is structured to match the duration of each liability. Previously, this structure caused the city to access a line of credit for temporary mismatches resulting from changes in the term structure of interest rates.

Doug asks Hui for different strategies to manage the interest rate risk of the city's fixed-income investment portfolio against one-time shifts in the yield curve. Hui considers two different strategies:

Strategy 1: Immunization of the single liabilities using zero-coupon bonds held to maturity.

Strategy 2: Immunization of the single liabilities using coupon-bearing bonds while continuously matching duration.

The city also manages a separate, smaller bond portfolio for the Radford School District. During the next five years, the school district has obligations for school expansions and renovations. The funds needed for those obligations are invested in the Bloomberg Barclays US Aggregate Index. Doug asks Hui which portfolio management strategy would be most efficient in mimicking this index.

A Radford School Board member has stated that she prefers a bond portfolio structure that provides diversification over time, as well as liquidity. In addressing the board member's inquiry, Hui examines a bullet portfolio, a barbell portfolio, and a laddered portfolio.

17 A disadvantage of Strategy 1 is that:
   A price risk still exists.
   B interest rate volatility introduces risk to effective matching.
   C there may not be enough bonds available to match all liabilities.

18 Which duration measure should be matched when implementing Strategy 2?
   A Key rate
   B Modified

    **C** Macaulay

**19** An upward shift in the yield curve on Strategy 2 will *most likely* result in the:
    **A** price effect cancelling the coupon reinvestment effect.
    **B** price effect being greater than the coupon reinvestment effect.
    **C** coupon reinvestment effect being greater than the price effect.

**20** The effects of a non-parallel shift in the yield curve on Strategy 2 can be reduced by:
    **A** minimizing the convexity of the bond portfolio.
    **B** maximizing the cash flow yield of the bond portfolio.
    **C** minimizing the difference between liability duration and bond-portfolio duration.

**21** Hui's response to Doug's question about the most efficient portfolio management strategy should be:
    **A** full replication.
    **B** active management.
    **C** an enhanced indexing strategy.

**22** Which portfolio structure should Hui recommend that would satisfy the school board member's preference?
    **A** Bullet portfolio
    **B** Barbell portfolio
    **C** Laddered portfolio

## The following information relates to Questions 23–25

Chaopraya is an investment advisor for high-net-worth individuals. One of her clients, Schuylkill, plans to fund her grandson's college education and considers two options:

    Option 1    Contribute a lump sum of $300,000 in 10 years.
    Option 2    Contribute four level annual payments of $76,500 starting in 10 years.

The grandson will start college in 10 years. Schuylkill seeks to immunize the contribution today.

For Option 1, Chaopraya calculates the present value of the $300,000 as $234,535. To immunize the future single outflow, Chaopraya considers three bond portfolios given that no zero-coupon government bonds are available. The three portfolios consist of non-callable, fixed-rate, coupon-bearing government bonds considered free of default risk. Chaopraya prepares a comparative analysis of the three portfolios, presented in Exhibit 1.

## Practice Problems

**Exhibit 1: Results of Comparative Analysis of Potential Portfolios**

|  | Portfolio A | Portfolio B | Portfolio C |
|---|---|---|---|
| Market value | $235,727 | $233,428 | $235,306 |
| Cash flow yield | 2.504% | 2.506% | 2.502% |
| Macaulay duration | 9.998 | 10.002 | 9.503 |
| Convexity | 119.055 | 121.498 | 108.091 |

Chaopraya evaluates the three bond portfolios and selects one to recommend to Schuylkill.

**23** Recommend the portfolio in Exhibit 1 that would *best* achieve the immunization. Justify your response.

**Template for Question 23**

| Recommend the portfolio in Exhibit 1 that would *best* achieve the immunization. (circle one) | Justify your response. |
|---|---|
| Portfolio A <br> Portfolio B <br> Portfolio C |  |

Schuylkill and Chaopraya now discuss Option 2.

Chaopraya estimates the present value of the four future cash flows as $230,372, with a money duration of $2,609,700 and convexity of 135.142. She considers three possible portfolios to immunize the future payments, as presented in Exhibit 2.

**Exhibit 2: Data for Bond Portfolios to Immunize Four Annual Contributions**

|  | Portfolio 1 | Portfolio 2 | Portfolio 3 |
|---|---|---|---|
| Market value | $245,178 | $248,230 | $251,337 |
| Cash flow yield | 2.521% | 2.520% | 2.516% |
| Money duration | 2,609,981 | 2,609,442 | 2,609,707 |
| Convexity | 147.640 | 139.851 | 132.865 |

**24** Determine the *most appropriate* immunization portfolio in Exhibit 2. Justify your decision.

**Template for Question 24**

| Determine the *most appropriate* immunization portfolio in Exhibit 2. (circle one) | Justify your decision. |
|---|---|
| Portfolio 1 | |
| Portfolio 2 | |
| Portfolio 3 | |

After selecting a portfolio to immunize Schuylkill's multiple future outflows, Chaopraya prepares a report on how this immunization strategy would respond to various interest rate scenarios. The scenario analysis is presented in Exhibit 3.

**Exhibit 3  Projected Portfolio Response to Interest Rate Scenarios**

| | Immunizing Portfolio | Outflow Portfolio | Difference |
|---|---|---|---|
| *Upward parallel shift* | | | |
| Δ Market value | −6,410 | −6,427 | 18 |
| Δ Cash flow yield | 0.250% | 0.250% | 0.000% |
| Δ Portfolio BPV | −9 | −8 | −1 |
| *Downward parallel shift* | | | |
| Δ Market value | 6,626 | 6,622 | 4 |
| Δ Cash flow yield | −0.250% | −0.250% | 0.000% |
| Δ Portfolio BPV | 9 | 8 | 1 |
| *Steepening twist* | | | |
| Δ Market value | −1,912 | 347 | −2,259 |
| Δ Cash flow yield | 0.074% | −0.013% | 0.087% |
| Δ Portfolio BPV | −3 | 0 | −3 |
| *Flattening twist* | | | |
| Δ Market value | 1,966 | −343 | 2,309 |
| Δ Cash flow yield | −0.075% | 0.013% | −0.088% |
| Δ Portfolio BPV | 3 | 0 | 3 |

25 Discuss the effectiveness of Chaopraya's immunization strategy in terms of duration gaps.

# SOLUTIONS

1. A is correct. Type I liabilities have cash outlays with known amounts and timing. The dates and amounts of Kiest's liabilities are known; therefore, they would be classified as Type I liabilities.

2. C is correct. Structural risk arises from the design of the duration-matching portfolio. It is reduced by minimizing the dispersion of the bond positions, going from a barbell structure to more of a bullet portfolio that concentrates the component bonds' durations around the investment horizon. With bond maturities of 1.5 and 11.5 years, Portfolio C has a definite barbell structure compared with those of Portfolios A and B, and it is thus subject to a greater degree of risk from yield curve twists and non-parallel shifts. In addition, Portfolio C has the highest level of convexity, which increases a portfolio's structural risk.

3. A is correct. The two requirements to achieve immunization for multiple liabilities are for the money duration (or BPV) of the asset and liability to match and for the asset convexity to exceed the convexity of the liability. Although all three portfolios have similar BPVs, Portfolio A is the only portfolio to have a lower convexity than that of the liability portfolio (31.98, versus 33.05 for the $20 million liability portfolio), and thus, it fails to meet one of the two requirements needed for immunization.

4. B is correct. Portfolio B is a laddered portfolio with maturities spread more or less evenly over the yield curve. A desirable aspect of a laddered portfolio is liquidity management. Because there is always a bond close to redemption, the soon-to-mature bond can provide emergency liquidity needs. Barbell portfolios, such as Portfolio C, have maturities only at the short-term and long-term ends and thus are much less desirable for liquidity management.

5. A is correct. Serena believes that any shift in the yield curve will be parallel. Model risk arises whenever assumptions are made about future events and approximations are used to measure key parameters. The risk is that those assumptions turn out to be wrong and the approximations are inaccurate. A non-parallel yield curve shift could occur, resulting in a mismatch of the duration of the immunizing portfolio versus the liability.

6. B is correct. Kiest has a young workforce and thus a long-term investment horizon. The Global Aggregate and Global Aggregate GDP Weighted Indexes have the highest durations (7.73 and 7.71, respectively) and would be appropriate for this group. Global High Yield is the least appropriate due to its relatively shorter duration.

7. B is correct. Low tracking error requires an indexing approach. A pure indexing approach for a broadly diversified bond index would be extremely costly because it requires purchasing all the constituent securities in the index. A more efficient and cost-effective way to track the index is an enhanced indexing strategy, whereby Serena would purchase fewer securities than the index but would match primary risk factors reflected in the index. Closely matching these risk factors could provide low tracking error.

8. B is correct. Although a significant spread between the market price of the underlying fixed-income securities portfolio and an ETF's NAV should drive an authorized participant to engage in arbitrage, many fixed-income securities are either thinly traded or not traded at all. This situation might allow such a divergence to persist.

**9** C is correct. Asset–liability management strategies consider both assets and liabilities in the portfolio decision-making process. Leah notes that DFC's previous fixed-income manager attempted to control for interest rate risk by focusing on both the asset and the liability side of the company's balance sheet. The previous manager thus followed an asset–liability management strategy.

**10** C is correct. Enhanced indexing is especially useful for investors who consider environmental, social, or other factors when selecting a fixed-income portfolio. Environmental, social, and corporate governance (ESG) investing, also called socially responsible investing, refers to the explicit inclusion or exclusion of some sectors, which is more appropriate for an enhanced index strategy relative to a full index replication strategy. In particular, Approach 2 may be customized to reflect client preferences.

**11** B is correct. Immunization is the process of structuring and managing a fixed-income portfolio to minimize the variance in the realized rate of return and to lock in the cash flow yield (internal rate of return) on the portfolio, which in this case is 9.85%.

**12** C is correct. Molly is correct that measurement error can arise even in immunization strategies for Type 1 cash flows, which have set amounts and set dates. Also, a parallel shift in yield curves is a sufficient but not a necessary condition to achieve the desired outcome. Non-parallel shifts as well as twists in the yield curve can change the cash flow yield on the immunizing portfolio; however, minimizing the dispersion of cash flows in the asset portfolio mitigates this risk. As a result, both statements are correct.

**13** B is correct. In the case of a single liability, immunization is achieved by matching the bond portfolio's Macaulay duration with the horizon date. DFC has a single liability of $500 million due in nine years. Portfolio 2 has a Macaulay duration of 8.9, which is closer to 9 than that of either Portfolio 1 or 3. Therefore, Portfolio 2 will best immunize the portfolio against the liability.

**14** C is correct. Structural risk to immunization arises from twists and non-parallel shifts in the yield curve. Structural risk is reduced by minimizing the dispersion of cash flows in the portfolio, which can be accomplished by minimizing the convexity for a given cash flow duration level. Because Portfolio 4 has the lowest convexity compared with the other two portfolios and also has a Macaulay duration close to the liability maturity of nine years, it minimizes structural risk.

**15** B is correct. The use of an index as a widely accepted benchmark requires clear, transparent rules for security inclusion and weighting, investability, daily valuation, availability of past returns, and turnover. Because the custom benchmark is valued weekly rather than daily, this characteristic would be inconsistent with an appropriate benchmark.

**16** B is correct. DFC has two types of assets, short term and intermediate term. For the short-term assets, a benchmark with a short duration is appropriate. For the intermediate-term assets, a benchmark with a longer duration is appropriate. In this situation, DFC may wish to combine several well-defined sub-benchmark categories into an overall blended benchmark (Benchmark 2). The Bloomberg Barclays Short-Term Treasury Index is an appropriate benchmark for the short-term assets, and SD&R uses a 50% weight for this component. The longer-duration Bloomberg Barclays US Corporate Bond Index is an appropriate benchmark for the intermediate-term assets, and SD&R uses a 50% weight for this component. As a result, Molly should recommend proposed Benchmark 2.

**Solutions**

17 C is correct. It may be impossible to acquire zero-coupon bonds to precisely match liabilities because the city's liabilities have varying maturities and amounts. In many financial markets, zero-coupon bonds are unavailable.

18 C is correct. An investor having an investment horizon equal to the bond's Macaulay duration is effectively protected, or immunized, from the first change in interest rates, because price and coupon reinvestment effects offset for either higher or lower rates.

19 A is correct. An upward shift in the yield curve reduces the bond's value but increases the reinvestment rate, with these two effects offsetting one another. The price effect and the coupon reinvestment effect cancel each other out in the case of an upward shift in the yield curve for an immunized liability.

20 A is correct. Minimizing the convexity of the bond portfolio minimizes the dispersion of the bond portfolio. A non-parallel shift in the yield curve may result in changes in the bond portfolio's cash flow yield. In summary, the characteristics of a bond portfolio structured to immunize a single liability are that it (1) has an initial market value that equals or exceeds the present value of the liability, (2) has a portfolio Macaulay duration that matches the liability's due date, and (3) minimizes the portfolio convexity statistic.

21 C is correct. Under an enhanced indexing strategy, the index is replicated with fewer than the full set of index constituents but still matches the original index's primary risk factors. This strategy replicates the index performance under different market scenarios more efficiently than the full replication of a pure indexing approach.

22 C is correct. The laddered approach provides both diversification over time and liquidity. Diversification over time offers the investor a balanced position between two sources of interest rate risk: cash flow reinvestment and market price volatility. In practice, perhaps the most desirable aspect of a laddered portfolio is liquidity management, because as time passes, the portfolio will always contain a bond close to maturity.

23

**Template for Question 23**

Recommend the portfolio in Exhibit 1 that would *best* achieve the immunization.
(circle one)

| |
|---|
| Portfolio A |
| Portfolio B |
| Portfolio C |

**Justification:**

Portfolio A is the most appropriate portfolio because it is the only one that satisfies the three criteria for immunizing a single future outflow (liability), given that the cash flow yields are sufficiently close in value:

1 Market Value: Portfolio A's initial market value of $235,727 exceeds the outflow's present value of $234,535. Portfolio B is not appropriate because its market value of $233,428 is less than the present value of the future outflow

of $234,535. A bond portfolio structured to immunize a single liability must have an initial market value that equals or exceeds the present value of the liability.

2 Macaulay Duration: Portfolio A's Macaulay duration of 9.998 closely matches the 10-year horizon of the outflow. Portfolio C is not appropriate because its Macaulay duration of 9.503 is furthest away from the investment horizon of 10 years.

3 Convexity: Although Portfolio C has the lowest convexity at 108.091, its Macaulay duration does not closely match the outflow amount. Of the remaining two portfolios, Portfolio A has the lower convexity at 119.055; this lower convexity will minimize structural risk.

Default risk (credit risk) is not considered because the portfolios consist of government bonds that presumably have default probabilities approaching zero.

24

**Template for Question 24**

Determine the *most appropriate* immunization portfolio in Exhibit 2.
(circle one)

| |
|---|
| Portfolio 1 |
| Portfolio 2 |
| Portfolio 3 |

**Justification:**

Portfolio 2 is the most appropriate immunization portfolio because it is the only one that satisfies the following two criteria for immunizing a portfolio of multiple future outflows:

1 Money Duration: Money durations of all three possible immunizing portfolios match or closely match the money duration of the outflow portfolio. Matching money durations is useful because the market values and cash flow yields of the immunizing portfolio and the outflow portfolio are not necessarily equal.

2 Convexity: Given that the money duration requirement is met by all three possible immunizing portfolios, the portfolio with the lowest convexity that is above the outflow portfolio's convexity of 135.142 should be selected. The dispersion, as measured by convexity, of the immunizing portfolio should be as low as possible subject to being greater than or equal to the dispersion of the outflow portfolio. This will minimize the effect of non-parallel shifts in the yield curve. Portfolio 3's convexity of 132.865 is less than the outflow portfolio's convexity, so Portfolio 3 is not appropriate. Both Portfolio 1 and Portfolio 2 have convexities that exceed the convexity of the outflow portfolio, but Portfolio 2's convexity of 139.851 is lower than Portfolio 1's convexity of 147.640. Therefore, Portfolio 2 is the most appropriate immunizing portfolio.

The immunizing portfolio needs to be greater than the convexity (and dispersion) of the outflow portfolio. But, the convexity of the immunizing portfolio should be minimized in order to minimize dispersion and reduce structural risk.

**25** Chaopraya's strategy immunizes well for parallel shifts, with little deviation between the outflow portfolio and the immunizing portfolio in market value and BPV. Because the money durations are closely matched, the differences between the outflow portfolio and the immunizing portfolio in market value are small and the duration gaps (as shown by the difference in Δ Portfolio BPVs) between the outflow portfolio and the immunizing portfolio are small for both the upward and downward parallel shifts.

Chaopraya's strategy does not immunize well for the non-parallel steepening and flattening twists (i.e., structural risks) shown in Exhibit 3. In those cases, the outflow portfolio and the immunizing portfolio market values deviate substantially and the duration gaps between the outflow portfolio and the immunizing portfolio are large.

# Glossary

**Absolute return benchmark**   A minimum target return that an investment manager is expected to beat.

**Accounting defeasance**   Also called in-substance defeasance, accounting defeasance is a way of extinguishing a debt obligation by setting aside sufficient high-quality securities to repay the liability.

**Accumulation phase**   Phase where the government predominantly contributes to a sovereign wealth pension reserve fund.

**Active management**   A portfolio management approach that allows risk factor mismatches relative to a benchmark index causing potentially significant return differences between the active portfolio and the underlying benchmark.

**Active return**   Portfolio return minus benchmark return.

**Active risk**   The annualized standard deviation of active returns, also referred to as *tracking error* (also sometimes called *tracking risk*).

**Active risk budgeting**   Risk budgeting that concerns active risk (risk relative to a portfolio's benchmark).

**Active share**   A measure of how similar a portfolio is to its benchmark. A manager who precisely replicates the benchmark will have an Active Share of zero; a manager with no holdings in common with the benchmark will have an Active Share of one.

**Activist short selling**   A hedge fund strategy in which the manager takes a short position in a given security and then publicly presents his/her research backing the short thesis.

**After-tax excess return**   Calculated as the after-tax return of the portfolio minus the after-tax return of the associated benchmark portfolio.

**Agency trade**   A trade in which the broker is engaged to find the other side of the trade, acting as an agent. In doing so, the broker does not assume any risk for the trade.

**Alpha decay**   In a trading context, alpha decay is the erosion or deterioration in short term alpha after the investment decision has been made.

**Alternative trading systems**   (ATS) Non-exchange trading venues that bring together buyers and sellers to find transaction counterparties. Also called *multilateral trading facilities (MTF)*.

**Anchoring and adjustment**   An information-processing bias in which the use of a psychological heuristic influences the way people estimate probabilities.

**Anchoring and adjustment bias**   An information-processing bias in which the use of a psychological heuristic influences the way people estimate probabilities.

**Anomalies**   Apparent deviations from market efficiency.

**Arithmetic attribution**   An attribution approach which explains the arithmetic difference between the portfolio return and its benchmark return. The single-period attribution effects sum to the excess return, however, when combining multiple periods, the sub-period attribution effects will not sum to the excess return.

**Arrival price**   In a trading context, the arrival price is the security price at the time the order was released to the market for execution.

**Asset location**   The type of account an asset is held within, e.g., taxable or tax deferred.

**Asset-only**   With respect to asset allocation, an approach that focuses directly on the characteristics of the assets without explicitly modeling the liabilities.

**Asset swap spread (ASW)**   The spread over MRR on an interest rate swap for the remaining life of the bond that is equivalent to the bond's fixed coupon.

**Asset swaps**   Convert a bond's fixed coupon to MRR plus (or minus) a spread.

**Authorized participants**   Institutional investors who create and redeem ETF shares using an OTC primary market with an ETF sponsor.

**Availability bias**   An information-processing bias in which people take a heuristic approach to estimating the probability of an outcome based on how easily the outcome comes to mind.

**Back-fill bias**   The distortion in index or peer group data which results when returns are reported to a database only after they are known to be good returns.

**Barbell**   A fixed-income investment strategy combining short- and long-term bond positions.

**Base**   With respect to a foreign exchange quotation of the price of one unit of a currency, the currency referred to in "one unit of a currency."

**Base-rate neglect**   A type of representativeness bias in which the base rate or probability of the categorization is not adequately considered.

**Basis risk**   The risk resulting from using a hedging instrument that is imperfectly matched to the investment being hedged; in general, the risk that the basis will change in an unpredictable way.

**Bear flattening**   A decrease in the yield spread between long- and short-term maturities across the yield curve, which is largely driven by a rise in short-term bond yields-to-maturity.

**Bear spread**   An option strategy that becomes more valuable when the price of the underlying asset declines, so requires buying one option and writing another with a *lower* exercise price. A put bear spread involves buying a put with a higher exercise price and selling a put with a lower exercise price. A bear spread can also be executed with calls.

**Bear steepening**   An increase in the yield spread between long- and short-term maturities across the yield curve, which is largely driven by a rise in long-term bond yields-to-maturity.

**Behavioral finance macro**   A focus on market level behavior that considers market anomalies that distinguish markets from the efficient markets of traditional finance.

**Behavioral finance micro**   A focus on individual level behavior that examines the behavioral biases that distinguish individual investors from the rational decision makers of traditional finance.

**Bequest**   The transferring, or bequeathing, of assets in some other way upon a person's death. Also referred to as a testamentary bequest or testamentary gratuitous transfer.

**Best-in-class**  An ESG implementation approach that seeks to identify the most favorable companies and sectors based on ESG considerations. Also called *positive screening*.

**Bid price**  In a price quotation, the price at which the party making the quotation is willing to buy a specified quantity of an asset or security.

**Breadth**  The number of truly independent decisions made each year.

**Buffering**  Establishing ranges around breakpoints that define whether a stock belongs in one index or another.

**Bull flattening**  A decrease in the yield spread between long- and short-term maturities across the yield curve, which is largely driven by a decline in long-term bond yields-to-maturity.

**Bull spread**  An option strategy that becomes more valuable when the price of the underlying asset rises, so requires buying one option and writing another with a *higher* exercise price. A call bull spread involves buying a call with a lower exercise price and selling a call with a higher exercise price. A bull spread can also be executed with puts.

**Bull steepening**  An increase in the yield spread between long- and short-term maturities across the yield curve, which is largely driven by a decline in short-term bond yields-to-maturity.

**Bullet**  A fixed-income investment strategy that focuses on the intermediate term (or "belly") of the yield curve.

**Business cycle**  Fluctuations in GDP in relation to long-term trend growth, usually lasting 9-11 years.

**Butterfly spread**  A measure of yield curve shape or curvature equal to double the intermediate yield-to-maturity less the sum of short- and long-term yields-to-maturity.

**Butterfly strategy**  A common yield curve shape strategy that combines a long or short bullet position with a barbell portfolio in the opposite direction to capitalize on expected yield curve shape changes.

**Calendar rebalancing**  Rebalancing a portfolio to target weights on a periodic basis; for example, monthly, quarterly, semiannually, or annually.

**Calendar spread**  A strategy in which one sells an option and buys the same type of option but with different expiration dates, on the same underlying asset and with the same strike. When the investor buys the more distant (near-term) call and sells the near-term (more distant) call, it is a long (short) calendar spread.

**Canada model**  Characterized by a high allocation to alternatives. Unlike the endowment model, however, the Canada model relies more on internally managed assets. The innovative features of the Canada model are the: a) reference portfolio, b) total portfolio approach, and c) active management.

**Capital gain or loss**  For tax purposes equals the selling price (net of commissions and other trading costs) of the asset less its tax basis.

**Capital market expectations**  (CME) Expectations concerning the risk and return prospects of asset classes.

**Capital needs analysis**  See *capital sufficiency analysis*.

**Capital sufficiency analysis**  The process by which a wealth manager determines whether a client has, or is likely to accumulate, sufficient financial resources to meet his or her objectives; also known as *capital needs analysis*.

**Capture ratio**  A measure of the manager's gain or loss relative to the gain or loss of the benchmark.

**Carhart model**  A four factor model used in performance attribution. The four factors are: market (RMRF), size (SMB), value (HML), and momentum (WML).

**Carry trade**  A trading strategy that involves buying a security and financing it at a rate that is lower than the yield on that security.

**Carry trade across currencies**  A strategy seeking to benefit from a positive interest rate differential across currencies by combining a short position (or borrowing) in a low-yielding currency and a long position (or lending) in a high-yielding currency.

**Cash drag**  Tracking error caused by temporarily uninvested cash.

**Cash flow matching**  Immunization approach that attempts to ensure that all future liability payouts are matched precisely by cash flows from bonds or fixed-income derivatives.

**Cash-secured put**  An option strategy involving the writing of a put option and simultaneously depositing an amount of money equal to the exercise price into a designated account (this strategy is also called a fiduciary put).

**CDS curve**  Plot of CDS spreads across maturities for a single reference entity or group of reference entities in an index.

**Cell approach**  See *stratified sampling*.

**Charitable gratuitous transfers**  Asset transfers to not-for-profit or charitable organizations. In most jurisdictions charitable donations are not subject to a gift tax and most jurisdictions permit income tax deductions for charitable donations.

**Charitable remainder trust**  A trust setup to provide income for the life of named-beneficiaries. When the last named-beneficiary dies any remaining assets in this trust are distributed to the charity named in the trust, hence the term *charitable remainder* trust.

**Closet indexer**  A fund that advertises itself as being actively managed but is substantially similar to an index fund in its exposures.

**Cognitive cost**  The effort involved in processing new information and updating beliefs.

**Cognitive dissonance**  The mental discomfort that occurs when new information conflicts with previously held beliefs or cognitions.

**Cognitive errors**  Behavioral biases resulting from faulty reasoning; cognitive errors stem from basic statistical, information processing, or memory errors.

**Collar**  An option position in which the investor is long shares of stock and then buys a put with an exercise price below the current stock price and writes a call with an exercise price above the current stock price. Collars allow a shareholder to acquire downside protection through a protective put but reduce the cash outlay by writing a covered call.

**Completion overlay**  A type of overlay that addresses an indexed portfolio that has diverged from its proper exposure.

**Completion portfolio**  Is an index-based portfolio that when added to a given concentrated asset position creates an overall portfolio with exposures similar to the investor's benchmark.

**Conditional value at risk**  (CVaR) Also known as expected loss The average portfolio loss over a specific time period conditional on that loss exceeding the value at risk (VaR) threshold.

**Confirmation bias**  A belief perseverance bias in which people tend to look for and notice what confirms their beliefs, to ignore or undervalue what contradicts their beliefs, and to misinterpret information as support for their beliefs.

**Conjunction fallacy**  An inappropriate combining of probabilities of independent events to support a belief. In fact, the probability of two independent events occurring in conjunction is never greater than the probability of either event occurring alone; the probability of two independent events occurring together is equal to the multiplication of the probabilities of the independent events.

**Conservatism bias**  A belief perseverance bias in which people maintain their prior views or forecasts by inadequately incorporating new information.

**Contingent immunization**  Hybrid approach that combines immunization with an active management approach when the asset portfolio's value exceeds the present value of the liability portfolio.

**Controlled foreign corporation (CFC)**  A company located outside a taxpayer's home country in which the taxpayer has a controlling interest as defined under the home country law.

**Covered call**  An option strategy in which a long position in an asset is combined with a short position in a call on that asset.

**Covered interest rate parity**  The relationship among the spot exchange rate, the forward exchange rate, and the interest rate in two currencies that ensures that the return on a hedged (i.e., covered) foreign risk-free investment is the same as the return on a domestic risk-free investment. Also called *interest rate parity*.

**Credit cycle**  The expansion and contraction of credit over the business cycle, which translates into asset price changes based on default and recovery expectations across maturities and rating categories.

**Credit default swap (CDS) basis**  Yield spread on a bond, as compared to CDS spread of same tenor.

**Credit loss rate**  The realized percentage of par value lost to default for a group of bonds equal to the bonds' default rate multiplied by the loss severity.

**Credit migration**  The change in a bond's credit rating over a certain period.

**Credit valuation adjustment (CVA)**  The present value of credit risk for a loan, bond, or derivative obligation.

**Cross-currency basis swap**  An interest rate swap involving the periodic exchange of floating payments in one currency for another based upon respective market reference rates with an initial and final exchange of notional principal.

**Cross hedge**  A hedge involving a hedging instrument that is imperfectly correlated with the asset being hedged; an example is hedging a bond investment with futures on a non-identical bond.

**Cross-sectional consistency**  A feature of expectations setting which means that estimates for all classes reflect the same underlying assumptions and are generated with methodologies that reflect or preserve important relationships among the asset classes, such as strong correlations. It is the internal consistency across asset classes.

**Cross-sectional momentum**  A managed futures trend following strategy implemented with a cross-section of assets (within an asset class) by going long those that are rising in price the most and by shorting those that are falling the most. This approach generally results in holding a net zero (market-neutral) position and works well when a market's out- or underperformance is a reliable predictor of its future performance.

**Currency overlay**  A type of overlay that helps hedge the returns of securities held in foreign currency back to the home country's currency.

**Currency overlay programs**  A currency overlay program is a program to manage a portfolio's currency exposures for the case in which those exposures are managed separately from the management of the portfolio itself.

**Custom security-based benchmark**  Benchmark that is custom built to accurately reflect the investment discipline of a particular investment manager. Also called a *strategy benchmark* because it reflects a manager's particular strategy.

**Decision price**  In a trading context, the decision price is the security price at the time the investment decision was made.

**Decision-reversal risk**  The risk of reversing a chosen course of action at the point of maximum loss.

**Decumulation phase**  Phase where the government predominantly withdraws from a sovereign wealth pension reserve fund.

**Dedicated short-selling**  A hedge fund strategy in which the manager takes short-only positions in equities deemed to be expensively priced versus their deteriorating fundamental situations. Short exposures may vary only in terms of portfolio sizing by, at times, holding higher levels of cash.

**Default intensity**  POD over a specified time period in a reduced form credit model.

**Default risk**  Likelihood that a borrower will default or fail to meet its obligation to make full and timely payments of principal and interest according to the terms of a debt obligation.

**Deferred annuity**  An annuity that enables an individual to purchase an income stream that will begin at a later date.

**Defined benefit**  A retirement plan in which a plan sponsor commits to paying a specified retirement benefit.

**Defined contribution**  A retirement plan in which contributions are defined but the ultimate retirement benefit is not specified or guaranteed by the plan sponsor.

**Delay cost**  The (trading related) cost associated with not submitting the order to the market in a timely manner.

**Delta**  The change in an option's price in response to a change in price of the underlying, all else equal.

**Delta hedging**  Hedging that involves matching the price response of the position being hedged over a narrow range of prices.

**Demand deposits**  Accounts that can be drawn upon regularly and without notice. This category includes checking accounts and certain savings accounts that are often accessible through online banks or automated teller machines (ATMs).

**Diffusion index**  An index that measures how many indicators are pointing up and how many are pointing down.

**Direct market access**  (DMA) Access in which market participants can transact orders directly with the order book of an exchange using a broker's exchange connectivity.

**Disability income insurance**  A type of insurance designed to mitigate earnings risk as a result of a disability in which an individual becomes less than fully employed.

**Discount margin**  The discount (or required) margin is the yield spread versus the MRR such that the FRN is priced at par on a rate reset date.

**Discretionary portfolio management**   An arrangement in which a wealth manager has a client's pre-approval to execute investment decisions.

**Discretionary trust**   A trust that enables the trustee to determine whether and how much to distribute based on a beneficiary's general welfare.

**Disposition effect**   As a result of loss aversion, an emotional bias whereby investors are reluctant to dispose of losers. This results in an inefficient and gradual adjustment to deterioration in fundamental value.

**Dividend capture**   A trading strategy whereby an equity portfolio manager purchases stocks just before their ex-dividend dates, holds these stocks through the ex-dividend date to earn the right to receive the dividend, and subsequently sells the shares.

**Domestic asset**   An asset that trades in the investor's domestic currency (or home currency).

**Domestic currency**   The currency of the investor, i.e., the currency in which he or she typically makes consumption purchases, e.g., the Swiss franc for an investor domiciled in Switzerland.

**Domestic-currency return**   A rate of return stated in domestic currency terms from the perspective of the investor; reflects both the foreign-currency return on an asset as well as percentage movement in the spot exchange rate between the domestic and foreign currencies.

**Double taxation**   A term used to describe situations in which income is taxed twice. For example, when corporate earnings are taxed at the company level and then that portion of earnings paid as dividends is taxed again at the investor level.

**Drawdown**   A decline in value (represented by a series of negative returns only) following a peak fund valuation.

**Drawdown duration**   The total time from the start of the drawdown until the cumulative drawdown recovers to zero.

**Due diligence**   Investigation and analysis in support of an investment action, decision, or recommendation.

**Duration matching**   Immunization approach based on the duration of assets and liabilities. Ideally, the liabilities being matched (the liability portfolio) and the portfolio of assets (the bond portfolio) should be affected similarly by a change in interest rates.

**Duration times spread**   Weighting of spread duration by credit spread in order to incorporate the empirical observation that spread changes for lower-rated bonds tend to be consistent on a percentage, rather than absolute, basis.

**Duration Times Spread (DTS)**   Weighting of spread duration by credit spread to incorporate the empirical observation that spread changes for lower-rated bonds tend to be consistent on a percentage rather than absolute basis.

**Dynamic asset allocation**   A strategy incorporating deviations from the strategic asset allocation that are motivated by longer-term valuation signals or economic views than usually associated with tactical asset allocation.

**Dynamic hedge**   A hedge requiring adjustment as the price of the hedged asset changes.

**Earnings risk**   The risk associated with the earning potential of an individual.

**Econometrics**   The application of quantitative modeling and analysis grounded in economic theory to the analysis of economic data.

**Economic balance sheet**   A balance sheet that provides an individual's total wealth portfolio, supplementing traditional balance sheet assets with human capital and pension wealth, and expanding liabilities to include consumption and bequest goals. Also known as *holistic balance sheet*.

**Economic indicators**   Economic statistics provided by government and established private organizations that contain information on an economy's recent past activity or its current or future position in the business cycle.

**Economic net worth**   The difference between an individual's assets and liabilities; extends traditional financial assets and liabilities to include human capital and future consumption needs.

**Effective federal funds (FFE) rate**   The fed funds rate actually transacted between depository institutions, not the Fed's target federal funds rate.

**Emotional biases**   Behavioral biases resulting from reasoning influenced by feelings; emotional biases stem from impulse or intuition.

**Empirical duration**   Estimation of the price-yield relationship using historical bond market data in statistical models.

**Endowment bias**   An emotional bias in which people value an asset more when they hold rights to it than when they do not.

**Endowment model**   Characterized by a high allocation to alternative investments (private investments and hedge funds), significant active management, and externally managed assets.

**Enhanced indexing approach**   Maintains a close link to the benchmark but attempts to generate a modest amount of outperformance relative to the benchmark.

**Enhanced indexing strategy**   Method investors use to match an underlying market index in which the investor purchases fewer securities than the full set of index constituents but matches primary risk factors reflected in the index.

**Equity monetization**   A group of strategies that allow investors to receive cash for their concentrated stock positions without an outright sale. These transactions are structured to avoid triggering the capital gains tax.

**Estate**   Consists of all of the property a person owns or controls, which may consist of financial assets (e.g., bank accounts, stocks, bonds, business interests), tangible personal assets (e.g., artwork, collectibles, vehicles), immovable property (e.g., residential real estate, timber rights), and intellectual property (e.g., royalties).

**Estate planning**   The process of preparing for the disposition of one's estate upon death and during one's lifetime.

**Estate tax**   Levied on the total value of a deceased person's assets and paid out of the estate before any distributions to beneficiaries.

**Evaluated pricing**   See *matrix pricing*.

**Excess return**   Used in various senses appropriate to context: 1) The difference between the portfolio return and the benchmark return; 2) The return in excess of the risk-free rate.

**Excess spread**   Credit spread return measure that incorporates both changes in spread and expected credit losses for a given period.

**Exchange fund**   A partnership in which each of the partners have each contributed low cost-basis stock to the fund. Used in the United Sates as a mechanism to achieve a tax-free exchange of a concentrated asset position.

**Execution cost**   The difference between the (trading related) cost of the real portfolio and the paper portfolio, based on shares and prices transacted.

**Exhaustive** An index construction strategy that selects every constituent of a universe.

**Expected shortfall** The average loss conditional on exceeding the VaR cutoff; sometimes referred to as *conditional VaR* or *expected tail loss*.

**Expected tail loss** See *expected shortfall*.

**Extended portfolio assets and liabilities** Assets and liabilities beyond those shown on a conventional balance sheet that are relevant in making asset allocation decisions; an example of an extended asset is human capital.

**Factor-model-based benchmarks** Benchmarks constructed by examining a portfolio's sensitivity to a set of factors, such as the return for a broad market index, company earnings growth, industry, or financial leverage.

**Family constitution** Typically a non-binding document that sets forth an agreed-upon set of rights, values, and responsibilities of the family members and other stakeholders. Used by many wealth- and business-owning families as the starting point of conflict resolution procedures.

**Family governance** The process for a family's collective communication and decision making designed to serve current and future generations based on the common values of the family.

**Financial capital** The tangible and intangible assets (excluding human capital) owned by an individual or household.

**Fixed trust** Distributions to beneficiaries of a fixed trust are specified in the trust document to occur at certain times or in certain amounts.

**Forced heirship** Is the requirement that a certain proportion of assets must pass to specified family members, such as a spouse and children.

**Foreign assets** Assets denominated in currencies other than the investor's home currency.

**Foreign currency** Currency that is not the currency in which an investor makes consumption purchases, e.g., the US dollar from the perspective of a Swiss investor.

**Foreign-currency return** The return of the foreign asset measured in foreign-currency terms.

**Forward rate bias** An empirically observed divergence from interest rate parity conditions that active investors seek to benefit from by borrowing in a lower-yield currency and investing in a higher-yield currency.

**Foundation** A legal entity available in certain jurisdictions. Foundations are typically set up to hold assets for a specific charitable purpose, such as to promote education or for philanthropy. When set up and funded by an individual or family and managed by its own directors, it is called a *private foundation*. The term *family foundation* usually refers to a private foundation where donors or members of the donors' family are actively involved.

**Framing** An information-processing bias in which a person answers a question differently based on the way in which it is asked (framed).

**Framing bias** An information-processing bias in which a person answers a question differently based on the way in which it is asked (framed).

**Fulcrum securities** Partially-in-the-money claims (not expected to be repaid in full) whose holders end up owning the reorganized company in a corporate reorganization situation.

**Full replication approach** When every issue in an index is represented in the portfolio, and each portfolio position has approximately the same weight in the fund as in the index.

**Fund-of-funds** A fund of hedge funds in which the fund-of-funds manager allocates capital to separate, underlying hedge funds (e.g., single manager and/or multi-manager funds) that themselves run a range of different strategies.

**Funding currencies** The low-yield currencies in which borrowing occurs in a carry trade.

**G-spread** Yield spread for a fixed-rate bond over a government benchmark.

**Gamblers' fallacy** A misunderstanding of probabilities in which people wrongly project reversal to a long-term mean.

**Gamma** The change in an option's delta for a change in price of the underlying, all else equal.

**General account** Account holding assets to fund future liabilities from traditional life insurance and fixed annuities, the products in which the insurer bears all the risks—particularly mortality risk and longevity risk.

**Generation-skipping tax** Taxes levied in some jurisdictions on asset transfers (gifts) that skip one generation such as when a grandparent transfers assets to their grandchildren. (see related Gift Tax).

**Gift tax** Depending on the tax laws of the country, assets gifted by one person to another during the giftor's lifetime may be subject to a gift tax.

**Goals-based** With respect to asset allocation or investing, an approach that focuses on achieving an investor's goals (for example, related to supporting lifestyle needs or aspirations) based typically on constructing sub-portfolios aligned with those goals.

**Goals-based investing** An investment industry term for approaches to investing for individuals and families focused on aligning investments with goals (parallel to liability-driven investing for institutional investors).

**Green bonds** Fixed-income instruments issued by private or public sector borrowers that directly fund ESG initiatives.

**Grinold–Kroner model** An expression for the expected return on a share as the sum of an expected income return, an expected nominal earnings growth return, and an expected repricing return.

**Halo effect** An emotional bias that extends a favorable evaluation of some characteristics to other characteristics.

**Hard-catalyst event-driven approach** An event-driven approach in which investments are made in reaction to an already announced corporate event (mergers and acquisitions, bankruptcies, share issuances, buybacks, capital restructurings, re-organizations, accounting changes) in which security prices related to the event have yet to fully converge.

**Hazard rate** The conditional POD, or the likelihood that default will occur given that it has not already occurred in a prior period.

**Health insurance** A type of insurance used to cover health care and medical costs.

**Health risk** The risk associated with illness or injury.

**Hedge ratio** The relationship of the quantity of an asset being hedged to the quantity of the derivative used for hedging.

**Herding** When a group of investors trade on the same side of the market in the same securities, or when investors ignore their own private information and act as other investors do.

**High-water mark** A specified net asset value level that a fund must exceed before performance fees are paid to the hedge fund manager.

**Hindsight bias** A bias with selective perception and retention aspects in which people may see past events as having been predictable and reasonable to expect.

**Holdings-based attribution** A "buy and hold" attribution approach which calculates the return of portfolio and benchmark components based upon the price and foreign exchange rate changes applied to daily snapshots of portfolio holdings.

**Holdings-based style analysis** A bottom-up style analysis that estimates the risk exposures from the actual securities held in the portfolio at a point in time.

**Holistic balance sheet** See *economic balance sheet*.

**Home bias** A preference for securities listed on the exchanges of one's home country.

**Home-country bias** The favoring of domestic over non-domestic investments relative to global market value weights.

**Home currency** See *domestic currency*.

**Human capital** An implied asset; the net present value of an investor's future expected labor income weighted by the probability of surviving to each future age. Also called *net employment capital*.

**I-spread (interpolated spread)** Yield spread measure using swaps or constant maturity Treasury YTMs as a benchmark.

**Illusion of control** A bias in which people tend to believe that they can control or influence outcomes when, in fact, they cannot. Illusion of knowledge and self-attribution biases contribute to the overconfidence bias.

**Illusion of control bias** A bias in which people tend to believe that they can control or influence outcomes when, in fact, they cannot. Illusion of knowledge and self-attribution biases contribute to the overconfidence bias.

**Immediate annuity** An annuity that provides a guarantee of specified future monthly payments over a specified period of time.

**Immunization** An asset/liability management approach that structures investments in bonds to match (offset) liabilities' weighted-average duration; a type of dedication strategy.

**Impact investing** Investment approach that seeks to achieve targeted social or environmental objectives along with measurable financial returns through engagement with a company or by direct investment in projects or companies.

**Implementation shortfall** (IS) The difference between the return for a notional or paper portfolio, where all transactions are assumed to take place at the manager's decision price, and the portfolio's actual return, which reflects realized transactions, including all fees and costs.

**Implied volatility** The outlook for the future volatility of the underlying asset's price. It is the value (i.e., standard deviation of underlying's returns) that equates the model (e.g., Black–Scholes–Merton model) price of an option to its market price.

**Implied volatility surface** A three-dimensional plot, for put and call options on the same underlying asset, of days to expiration ($x$-axis), option strike prices ($y$-axis), and implied volatilities ($z$-axis). It simultaneously shows the volatility skew (or smile) and the term structure of implied volatility.

**Incremental VaR (or partial VaR)** The change in the minimum portfolio loss expected to occur over a given time period at a specific confidence level resulting from increasing or decreasing a portfolio position.

**Information coefficient** Formally defined as the correlation between forecast return and actual return. In essence, it measures the effectiveness of investment insight.

**Inheritance tax** Paid by each individual beneficiary of a deceased person's estate on the value of the benefit the individual received from the estate.

**Input uncertainty** Uncertainty concerning whether the inputs are correct.

**Interaction effect** The attribution effect resulting from the interaction of the allocation and selection decisions.

**Intertemporal consistency** A feature of expectations setting which means that estimates for an asset class over different horizons reflect the same assumptions with respect to the potential paths of returns over time. It is the internal consistency over various time horizons.

**Intestate** A person who dies without a valid will or with a will that does not dispose of their property are considered to have died intestate.

**Intrinsic value** The difference between the spot exchange rate and the strike price of a currency option.

**Investment currencies** The high-yielding currencies in a carry trade.

**Investment policy statement** A written planning document that describes a client's investment objectives and risk tolerance over a relevant time horizon, along with the constraints that apply to the client's portfolio.

**Investment style** A natural grouping of investment disciplines that has some predictive power in explaining the future dispersion of returns across portfolios.

**Irrevocable trust** The person whose assets are used to create the trust gives up the right to rescind the trust relationship and regain title to the trust assets.

**Key person risk** The risk that results from over-reliance on an individual or individuals whose departure would negatively affect an investment manager.

**Key rate duration** A method of measuring interest rate sensitivities of a fixed-income instrument or portfolio to shifts in key points along the yield curve.

**Knock-in/knock-out** Features of a vanilla option that is created (or ceases to exist) when the spot exchange rate touches a pre-specified level.

**Leading economic indicators** A set of economic variables whose values vary with the business cycle but at a fairly consistent time interval before a turn in the business cycle.

**Liability-based mandates** Mandates managed to match or cover expected liability payments (future cash outflows) with future projected cash inflows.

**Liability-driven investing** An investment industry term that generally encompasses asset allocation that is focused on funding an investor's liabilities in institutional contexts.

**Liability driven investing (LDI) model** In the LDI model, the primary investment objective is to generate returns sufficient to cover liabilities, with a focus on maximizing expected surplus return (excess return of assets over liabilities) and managing surplus volatility.

**Liability glide path** A specification of desired proportions of liability-hedging assets and return-seeking assets and the duration of the liability hedge as funded status changes and contributions are made.

**Liability insurance** A type of insurance used to manage liability risk.

**Liability-relative** With respect to asset allocation, an approach that focuses directly only on funding liabilities as an investment objective.

**Liability risk** The possibility that an individual or household may be held legally liable for the financial costs associated with property damage or physical injury.

**Life-cycle finance** A concept in finance that recognizes as an investor ages, the fundamental nature of wealth and risk evolves.

**Life insurance** A type of insurance that protects against the loss of human capital for those who depend on an individual's future earnings.

**Life settlement** The sale of a life insurance contract to a third party. The valuation of a life settlement typically requires detailed biometric analysis of the individual policyholder and an understanding of actuarial analysis.

**Limited-life foundations** A type of foundation where founders seek to maintain control of spending while they (or their immediate heirs) are still alive.

**Liquidity budget** The portfolio allocations (or weightings) considered acceptable for the liquidity categories in the liquidity classification schedule (or time-to-cash table).

**Liquidity classification schedule** A liquidity management classification (or table) that defines portfolio liquidity "buckets" or categories based on the estimated time it would take to convert assets in that particular category into cash.

**Longevity risk** The risk of outliving one's financial resources.

**Loss-aversion bias** A bias in which people tend to strongly prefer avoiding losses as opposed to achieving gains.

**Loss severity** Also known as loss given default (LGD). The amount of loss if a default occurs, usually expressed as a percentage in annual terms.

**Macro attribution** Attribution at the sponsor level.

**Manager peer group** See *manager universe*.

**Manager universe** A broad group of managers with similar investment disciplines. Also called *manager peer group*.

**Matrix pricing** An approach for estimating the prices of thinly traded securities based on the prices of securities with similar attributions, such as similar credit rating, maturity, or economic sector. Also called *evaluated pricing*.

**Matrix pricing (or evaluated pricing)** Methodology for pricing infrequently traded bonds using bonds from similar issuers and actively traded government benchmarks to establish a bond's fair value.

**Mental accounting bias** An information-processing bias in which people treat one sum of money differently from another equal-sized sum based on which mental account the money is assigned to.

**Micro attribution** Attribution at the portfolio manager level.

**Minimum-variance hedge ratio** A mathematical approach to determining the optimal cross hedging ratio.

**Mission-related investing** Aims to direct a significant portion of assets in excess of annual grants into projects promoting a foundation's mission.

**Model uncertainty** Uncertainty as to whether a selected model is correct.

**Mortality table** A table that indicates individual life expectancies at specified ages.

**Multi-class trading** An equity market-neutral strategy that capitalizes on misalignment in prices and involves buying and selling different classes of shares of the same company, such as voting and non-voting shares.

**Multi-manager fund** Can be of two types—one is a multi-strategy fund in which teams of portfolio managers trade and invest in multiple different strategies within the same fund; the second type is a fund of hedge funds (or fund-of-funds) in which the manager allocates capital to separate, underlying hedge funds that themselves run a range of different strategies.

**Multi-strategy fund** A fund in which teams of portfolio managers trade and invest in multiple different strategies within the same fund.

**Multilateral trading facilities** (MTF) See *Alternative trading systems (ATS)*.

**Negative butterfly** An increase in the butterfly spread due to lower short- and long-term yields-to-maturity and a higher intermediate yield-to-maturity.

**Negative screening** An ESG implementation approach that excludes certain sectors or companies that deviate from an investor's accepted standards.

**Non-deliverable forwards** Forward contracts that are cash settled (in the non-controlled currency of the currency pair) rather than physically settled (the controlled currency is neither delivered nor received).

**Nonstationarity** A characteristic of series of data whose properties, such as mean and variance, are not constant through time. When analyzing historical data it means that different parts of a data series reflect different underlying statistical properties.

**Norway model** Characterized by an almost exclusive reliance on public equities and fixed income (the traditional 60/40 equity/bond model falls under the Norway model), with largely passively managed assets and with very little to no allocation to alternative investments.

**OAS duration** The change in bond price for a given change in OAS.

**Offer price** The price at which a counterparty is willing to sell one unit of the base currency.

**Opportunity cost** The (trading related) cost associated with not being able to transact the entire order at the decision price.

**Option-adjusted spread (OAS)** A generalization of the Z-spread yield spread calculation that incorporates bond option pricing based on assumed interest rate volatility.

**Optional stock dividends** A type of dividend in which shareholders may elect to receive either cash or new shares.

**Options on bond futures contracts** Instruments that involve the right, but not the obligation, to enter into a bond futures contract at a pre-determined strike (bond price) on a future date in exchange for an up-front premium.

**Overbought** When a market has trended too far in one direction and is vulnerable to a trend reversal, or correction.

**Overconfidence bias** A bias in which people demonstrate unwarranted faith in their own intuitive reasoning, judgments, and/or cognitive abilities.

**Overlay** A derivative position (or positions) used to adjust a pre-existing portfolio closer to its objectives.

**Oversold** The opposite of overbought; see *overbought*.

**Packeting** Splitting stock positions into multiple parts.

**Pairs trading** An equity market-neutral strategy that capitalizes on the misalignment in prices of pairs of similar under- and overvalued equities. The expectation is the differential valuations or trading relationships will revert to their long-term mean values or their fundamentally-correct trading relationships, with the long position rising and the short position declining in value.

**Parameter uncertainty** Uncertainty arising because a quantitative model's parameters are estimated with error.

**Participant/cohort option** Pools the DC plan member with a cohort that has a similar target retirement date.

**Participant-switching life-cycle options** Automatically switch DC plan members into a more conservative asset mix as their age increases. There may be several automatic de-risking switches at different age targets.

**Passive investment** In the fixed-income context, it is investment that seeks to mimic the prevailing characteristics of the overall investments available in terms of credit quality, type of borrower, maturity, and duration rather than express a specific market view.

**Passive management** A buy-and-hold approach to investing in which an investor does not make portfolio changes based upon short-term expectations of changing market or security performance.

**Percent-range rebalancing** An approach to rebalancing that involves setting rebalancing thresholds or trigger points, stated as a percentage of the portfolio's value, around target values.

**Performance attribution** Attribution, including return attribution and risk attribution; often used as a synonym for return attribution.

**Permanent life insurance** A type of life insurance that provides lifetime coverage.

**Portfolio overlay** An array of derivative positions managed separately from the securities portfolio to achieve overall intended portfolio characteristics.

**Position delta** The overall or portfolio delta. For example, the position delta of a covered call, consisting of long 100 shares and short one at-the-money call, is +50 (= +100 for the shares and -50 for the short ATM call).

**Positive butterfly** A decrease in the butterfly spread due to higher short- and long-term yields-to-maturity and a lower intermediate yield-to-maturity.

**Positive screening** An ESG implementation approach that seeks to identify the most favorable companies and sectors based on ESG considerations. Also called *best-in-class*.

**Post-liquidation return** Calculates the return assuming that all portfolio holdings are sold as of the end date of the analysis and that the resulting capital gains tax that would be due is deducted from the ending portfolio value.

**Potential capital gain exposure (PCGE)** Is an estimate of the percentage of a fund's assets that represents gains and measures how much the fund's assets have appreciated. It can be an indicator of possible future capital gain distributions.

**Premature death risk** The risk of an individual dying earlier than anticipated; sometimes referred to as *mortality risk*.

**Present value of distribution of cash flows methodology** Method used to address a portfolio's sensitivity to rate changes along the yield curve. This approach seeks to approximate and match the yield curve risk of an index over discrete time periods.

**Principal trade** A trade in which the market maker or dealer becomes a disclosed counterparty and assumes risk for the trade by transacting the security for their own account. Also called *broker risk trades*.

**Probability of default** The likelihood that a borrower defaults or fails to meet its obligation to make full and timely payments of principal and interest.

**Probate** The legal process to confirm the validity of the will so that executors, heirs, and other interested parties can rely on its authenticity.

**Program trading** A strategy of buying or selling many stocks simultaneously.

**Progressive tax rate schedule** A tax regime in which the tax rate increases as the amount of income or wealth being taxed increases.

**Property insurance** A type of insurance used by individuals to manage property risk.

**Property risk** The possibility that a person's property may be damaged, destroyed, stolen, or lost.

**Protective put** An option strategy in which a long position in an asset is combined with a long position in a put on that asset.

**Pure indexing** Attempts to replicate a bond index as closely as possible, targeting zero active return and zero active risk.

**Put spread** A strategy used to reduce the upfront cost of buying a protective put, it involves buying a put option and writing another put option.

**Qualified dividends** Generally dividends from shares in domestic corporations and certain qualified foreign corporations which have been held for at least a specified minimum period of time.

**Quantitative market-neutral** An approach to building market-neutral portfolios in which large numbers of securities are traded and positions are adjusted on a daily or even an hourly basis using algorithm-based models.

**Quoted margin** The yield spread over the MRR established upon issuance of an FRN to compensate investors for assuming an issuer's credit risk.

**Re-base** With reference to index construction, to change the time period used as the base of the index.

**Realized volatility** Historical volatility, the square root of the realized variance of returns, which is a measure of the range of past price outcomes for the underlying asset.

**Rebalancing** In the context of asset allocation, a discipline for adjusting the portfolio to align with the strategic asset allocation.

**Rebalancing overlay** A type of overlay that addresses a portfolio's need to sell certain constituent securities and buy others.

**Rebalancing range** A range of values for asset class weights defined by trigger points above and below target weights, such that if the portfolio value passes through a trigger point, rebalancing occurs. Also known as a corridor.

**Rebate rate** The portion of the collateral earnings rate that is repaid to the security borrower by the security lender.

**Reduced form credit models** Credit models that solve for default probability over a specific time period using observable company-specific variables such as financial ratios and macroeconomic variables.

**Reduced-form models** Models that use economic theory and other factors such as prior research output to describe hypothesized relationships. Can be described as more compact representations of underlying structural models. Evaluate endogenous variables in terms of observable exogenous variables.

**Regime** The governing set of relationships (between variables) that stem from technological, political, legal, and regulatory environments. Changes in such environments or policy stances can be described as changes in regime.

**Regret** The feeling that an opportunity has been missed; typically an expression of *hindsight bias*.

**Regret-aversion bias** An emotional bias in which people tend to avoid making decisions that will result in action out of fear that the decision will turn out poorly.

**Relative value** A concept that describes the selection of the most attractive individual securities to populate the portfolio with, using ranking and comparing.

**Relative value volatility arbitrage** A volatility trading strategy that aims to source and buy cheap volatility and sell more expensive volatility while netting out the time decay aspects normally associated with options portfolios.

## Glossary

**Relative VaR** The minimum portfolio loss expected to occur over a given time period at a specific confidence level based on a portfolio containing active positions minus benchmark holdings.

**Repo rate** The interest rate on a repurchase agreement.

**Representativeness bias** A belief perseverance bias in which people tend to classify new information based on past experiences and classifications.

**Repurchase agreements** In repurchase agreements, or *repos*, a security owner agrees to sell a security for a specific cash amount while simultaneously agreeing to repurchase the security at a specified future date (typically one day later) and price.

**Request for quote** (RFQ) A non-binding quote provided by a market maker or dealer to a potential buyer or seller upon request. Commonly used in fixed income markets these quotes are only valid at the time they are provided.

**Reserve portfolio** The component of an insurer's general account that is subject to specific regulatory requirements and is intended to ensure the company's ability to meet its policy liabilities. The assets in the reserve portfolio are managed conservatively and must be highly liquid and low risk.

**Resistance levels** Price points on dealers' order boards where one would expect to see a clustering of offers.

**Return attribution** A set of techniques used to identify the sources of the excess return of a portfolio against its benchmark.

**Returns-based attribution** An attribution approach that uses only the total portfolio returns over a period to identify the components of the investment process that have generated the returns. The Brinson–Hood–Beebower approach is a returns-based attribution approach.

**Returns-based benchmarks** Benchmarks constructed by examining a portfolio's sensitivity to a set of factors, such as the returns for various style indexes (e.g., small-cap value, small-cap growth, large-cap value, and large-cap growth).

**Returns-based style analysis** A top-down style analysis that involves estimating the sensitivities of a portfolio to security market indexes.

**Reverse repos** Repurchase agreements from the standpoint of the lender.

**Revocable trust** The person whose assets are used to create the trust retains the right to rescind the trust relationship and regain title to the trust assets.

**Risk attribution** The analysis of the sources of risk.

**Risk aversion** The degree of an investor's unwillingness to take risk; the inverse of risk tolerance.

**Risk budgeting** The establishment of objectives for individuals, groups, or divisions of an organization that takes into account the allocation of an acceptable level of risk.

**Risk capacity** The ability to accept financial risk.

**Risk perception** The subjective assessment of the risk involved in the outcome of an investment decision.

**Risk premium** An extra return expected by investors for bearing some specified risk.

**Risk reversal** A strategy used to profit from the existence of an implied volatility skew and from changes in its shape over time. A combination of long (short) calls and short (long) puts on the same underlying with the same expiration is a long (short) risk reversal.

**Risk tolerance** The capacity to accept risk; the level of risk an investor (or organization) is willing and able to bear.

**Sample-size neglect** A type of representativeness bias in which financial market participants incorrectly assume that small sample sizes are representative of populations (or "real" data).

**Scenario analysis** What-if analysis that involves changing multiple assumptions at the same time in order to evaluate the change in an investment's value.

**Seagull spread** An extension of the risk reversal foreign exchange option strategy that limits downside risk.

**Securities lending** A form of collateralized lending that may be used to generate income for portfolios.

**Selective** An index construction methodology that targets only those securities with certain characteristics.

**Self-attribution bias** A bias in which people take personal credit for successes and attribute failures to external factors outside the individual's control.

**Self-control bias** A bias in which people fail to act in pursuit of their long-term, overarching goals because of a lack of self-discipline.

**Separate accounts** Accounts holding assets to fund future liabilities from variable life insurance and variable annuities, the products in which customers make investment decisions from a menu of options and themselves bear investment risk.

**Sharpe ratio** The average return in excess of the risk-free rate divided by the standard deviation of return; a measure of the average excess return earned per unit of standard deviation of return. Also known as the *reward-to-variability ratio*.

**Short-biased** A hedge fund strategy in which the manager uses a less extreme version of dedicated short-selling. It involves searching for opportunities to sell expensively priced equities, but short exposure may be balanced with some modest value-oriented, or index-oriented, long exposure.

**Shortfall probability** The probability of failing to meet a specific liability or goal.

**Shrinkage estimation** Estimation that involves taking a weighted average of a historical estimate of a parameter and some other parameter estimate, where the weights reflect the analyst's relative belief in the estimates.

**Single-manager fund** A fund in which one portfolio manager or team of portfolio managers invests in one strategy or style.

**Smart beta** Involves the use of transparent, rules-based strategies as a basis for investment decisions.

**Smart order routers** (SOR) Smart systems used to electronically route small orders to the best markets for execution based on order type and prevailing market conditions.

**Social proof** A bias in which individuals tend to follow the beliefs of a group.

**Soft-catalyst event-driven approach** An event-driven approach in which investments are made proactively in anticipation of a corporate event (mergers and acquisitions, bankruptcies, share issuances, buybacks, capital restructurings, re-organizations, accounting changes) that has yet to occur.

**Special dividends** A dividend paid by a company that does not pay dividends on a regular schedule, or a dividend that supplements regular cash dividends with an extra payment.

**Spread duration** The change in bond price for a given change in yield spread. Also referred to as *OAS duration* when the option-adjusted spread (OAS) is the yield measure used.

**Staged diversification strategy** The simplest approach to managing the risk of a concentrated position involves selling the concentrated position over some period of time, paying associated tax, and reinvesting the proceeds in a diversified portfolio.

**Static hedge** A hedge that is not sensitive to changes in the price of the asset hedged.

**Status quo bias** An emotional bias in which people do nothing (i.e., maintain the "status quo") instead of making a change.

**Stock lending** Securities lending involving the transfer of equities.

**Stop-losses** A trading order that sets a selling price below the current market price with a goal of protecting profits or preventing further losses.

**Stops** Stop-loss orders involve leaving bids or offers away from the current market price to be filled if the market reaches those levels.

**Straddle** An option combination in which one buys *both* puts and calls, with the same exercise price and same expiration date, on the same underlying asset. In contrast to this long straddle, if someone *writes* both options, it is a short straddle.

**Strangle** A variation on a straddle in which the put and call have different exercise prices; if the put and call are held long, it is a long strangle; if they are held short, it is a short strangle.

**Stratified sampling** A sampling method that guarantees that subpopulations of interest are represented in the sample. Also called *representative sampling* or *cell approach*.

**Structural credit models** Credit models that apply market-based variables to estimate the value of an issuer's assets and the volatility of asset value.

**Structural models** Models that specify functional relationships among variables based on economic theory. The functional form and parameters of these models are derived from the underlying theory. They may include unobservable parameters.

**Structural risk** Risk that arises from portfolio design, particularly the choice of the portfolio allocations.

**Stub trading** An equity market-neutral strategy that capitalizes on misalignment in prices and entails buying and selling stock of a parent company and its subsidiaries, typically weighted by the percentage ownership of the parent company in the subsidiaries.

**Support levels** Price points on dealers' order boards where one would expect to see a clustering of bids.

**Surplus** The difference between the value of assets and the present value of liabilities. With respect to an insurance company, the net difference between the total assets and total liabilities (equivalent to policyholders' surplus for a mutual insurance company and stockholders' equity for a stock company).

**Surplus portfolio** The component of an insurer's general account that is intended to realize higher expected returns than the reserve portfolio and so can assume some liquidity risk. Surplus portfolio assets are often managed aggressively with exposure to alternative assets.

**Survivorship bias** Bias that arises in a data series when managers with poor track records exit the business and are dropped from the database whereas managers with good records remain; when a data series of a given date reflects only entitites that have survived to that date.

**Swaption** This instrument grants a party the right, but not the obligation, to enter into an interest rate swap at a pre-determined strike (fixed swap rate) on a future date in exchange for an up-front premium.

**Synthetic long forward position** The combination of a long call and a short put with identical strike price and expiration, traded at the same time on the same underlying.

**Synthetic short forward position** The combination of a short call and a long put at the same strike price and maturity (traded at the same time on the same underlying).

**Tactical asset allocation** Asset allocation that involves making short-term adjustments to asset class weights based on short-term predictions of relative performance among asset classes.

**Tax alpha** Calculated by subtracting the pre-tax excess return from the after-tax excess return, the tax alpha isolates the benefit of tax management of the portfolio.

**Tax avoidance** The legal activity of understanding the tax laws and finding approaches that avoid or minimize taxation.

**Tax basis** In many cases, the tax basis is the amount that was paid to acquire an asset, or its 'cost' basis, and serves as the foundation for calculating a capital gain or loss.

**Tax-deferred account** An account where investments and contributions may be made on a pre-tax basis and investment returns accumulate on a tax-deferred basis until funds are withdrawn, at which time they are taxed at ordinary income tax rates.

**Tax-efficiency ratio (TER)** Is calculated as the after-tax return divided by the pre-tax return. It is used to understand if a fund is appropriate for the taxable account of a client.

**Tax-efficient decumulation strategy** Is the process of taking into account the tax considerations involved in deploying retirement assets to support spending needs over a client's remaining lifetime during retirement.

**Tax-efficient strategy** An investment strategy that is designed to give up very little of its return to taxes.

**Tax evasion** The illegal concealment and non-payment of taxes that are otherwise due.

**Tax-exempt account** An account on which no taxes are assessed during the investment, contribution, or withdrawal phase, nor are they assessed on investment returns.

**Tax haven** A country or independent area with no or very low tax rates for foreign investors.

**Tax loss harvesting** Selling securities at a loss to offset a realized capital gain or other income. The rules for what can be done vary by jurisdiction.

**Tax lot accounting** Important in tax loss harvesting strategies to identify the cost of securities sold from a portfolio that has been built up over time with purchases and sales over time. Tax lot accounting keeps track of how much was paid for an investment and when it was purchased for the portfolio. Not allowed in all jurisdictions.

**Taxable account** An account on which the normal tax rules of the jurisdiction apply to investments and contributions.

**Taylor rule** A rule linking a central bank's target short-term interest rate to the rate of growth of the economy and inflation.

**Temporary life insurance** A type of life insurance that covers a certain period of time, specified at purchase. Commonly referred to as "term" life insurance.

**Term deposits** Interest-bearing accounts that have a specified maturity date. This category includes savings accounts and certificates of deposit (CDs).

**Term structure of volatility**  The plot of implied volatility (y-axis) against option maturity (x-axis) for options with the same strike price on the same underlying. Typically, implied volatility is not constant across different maturities – rather, it is often in contango, meaning that the implied volatilities for longer-term options are higher than for near-term ones.

**Territorial tax systems**  Jurisdictions operate where only locally-sourced income is taxed.

**Testamentary bequest**  See *Bequest*.

**Testamentary gratuitous transfer**  See *Bequest*.

**Testator**  The person who authored the will and whose property is disposed of according to the will.

**Thematic investing**  An investment approach that focuses on companies within a specific sector or following a specific theme, such as energy efficiency or climate change.

**Theta**  The daily change in an option's price, all else equal. Theta measures the sensitivity of the option's price to the passage of time, known as time decay.

**Time deposits**  Interest-bearing accounts that have a specified maturity date. This category includes savings accounts and certificates of deposit (CDs).

**Time-series estimation**  Estimators that are based on lagged values of the variable being forecast; often consist of lagged values of other selected variables.

**Time-series momentum**  A managed futures trend following strategy in which managers go long assets that are rising in price and go short assets that are falling in price. The manager trades on an absolute basis, so be net long or net short depending on the current price trend of an asset. This approach works best when an asset's own past returns are a good predictor of its future returns.

**Time-to-cash table**  See *liquidity classification schedule*.

**Time value**  The difference between the market price of an option and its intrinsic value, determined by the uncertainty of the underlying over the remaining life of the option.

**Total factor productivity**  A variable which accounts for that part of $Y$ not directly accounted for by the levels of the production factors ($K$ and $L$).

**Total return payer**  Party responsible for paying the reference obligation cash flows and return to the receiver but that is also compensated by the receiver for any depreciation in the index or default losses incurred by the portfolio.

**Total return receiver**  Receives both the cash flows from the underlying index and any appreciation in the index over the period in exchange for paying the MRR plus a predetermined spread.

**Total return swap**  A swap in which one party agrees to pay the total return on a security. Often used as a credit derivative, in which the underlying is a bond.

**Tracking error**  The standard deviation of the differences between a portfolio's returns and its benchmark's returns; a synonym of active risk. Also called *tracking risk*.

**Tracking risk**  The standard deviation of the differences between a portfolio's returns and its benchmark's returns; a synonym of active risk. Also called *tracking error*.

**Trade urgency**  A reference to how quickly or slowly an order is executed over the trading time horizon.

**Transactions-based attribution**  An attribution approach that captures the impact of intra-day trades and exogenous events such as a significant class action settlement.

**Transfer coefficient**  The ability to translate portfolio insights into investment decisions without constraint.

**Trigger points**  In the context of portfolio rebalancing, the endpoints of a rebalancing range (corridor).

**Trust**  A legal is a vehicle through which an individual (called a settlor) entrusts certain assets to a trustee (or trustees) who manages the assets for the benefit of assigned beneficiaries. A trust may be either a testamentary trust—a trust created through the testator's will—or a living or inter-vivos trust—a trust created during the settlor's lifetime.

**Uncovered interest rate parity**  The proposition that the expected return on an uncovered (i.e., unhedged) foreign currency (risk-free) investment should equal the return on a comparable domestic currency investment.

**Unsmoothing**  An adjustment to the reported return series if serial correlation is detected. Various approaches are available to unsmooth a return series.

**Value at risk (VaR)**  A measure of the minimum portfolio loss expected to occur over a given time period at a specific confidence level.

**Variance notional**  The notional amount of a variance swap; it equals vega notional divided by two times the volatility strike price [i.e., (vega notional)/(2 × volatility strike)].

**Vega**  The change in an option's price for a change in volatility of the underlying, all else equal.

**Vega notional**  The trade size for a variance swap, which represents the average profit and loss of the variance swap for a 1% change in volatility from the strike.

**Vesting**  A term indicating that employees only become eligible to receive a pension after meeting certain criteria, typically a minimum number of years of service.

**Volatility clustering**  The tendency for large (small) swings in prices to be followed by large (small) swings of random direction.

**Volatility skew**  The skewed plot (of implied volatility (y-axis) against strike price (x-axis) for options on the same underlying with the same expiration) that occurs when the implied volatility increases for OTM puts and decreases for OTM calls, as the strike price moves away from the current price.

**Volatility smile**  The U-shaped plot (of implied volatility (y-axis) against strike price (x-axis) for options on the same underlying with the same expiration) that occurs when the implied volatilities priced into both OTM puts and calls trade at a premium to implied volatilities of ATM options.

**Will (or Testament)**  A document that outlines the rights others will have over one's property after death.

**Withholding taxes**  Taxes imposed on income in the country in which an investment is made without regard for offsetting investment expenses or losses that may be available from the taxpayer's other investment activities.

**Worldwide tax system**  Jurisdictions that tax all income regardless of its source.

**Yield spread**  The simple difference between a bond's YTM and the YTM of an on-the-run government bond of similar maturity.

**Z-score**  Credit risk model that uses financial ratios and market-based information weighted by coefficients to create a composite score used to classify firms based on the likelihood of financial distress.

**Zero-discount margin (Z-DM)**  A yield spread calculation for FRNs that incorporates forward MRR.

**Zero-volatility spread (Z-spread)**  Constant yield spread over a government (or interest rate swap) spot curve.